Und Business Marketing and Purchasing

Books by IMP Group Members and Co-Workers

Håkansson, H. (ed.), *International Marketing and Purchasing of Industrial Goods*, Chichester, John Wiley (1982).

Turnbull, P. and Cunningham, M. T., *International Marketing and Purchasing*, London, Macmillan (1981).

Turnbull, P. and Valla, J.-P. (eds), *Strategies for International Industrial Marketing*, London, Croom Helm (1986).

Turnbull, P. and Paliwoda, S. (eds), *Research Developments in International Marketing*, London, Croom Helm (1986).

Håkansson, H. and Gadde, L.-E., *Professional Purchasing*, London, Routledge (1992).

Håkansson, H. (ed.), *Industrial Technological Development: A Network Approach*, London, Croom Helm (1987).

Håkansson, H., *Corporate Technological Behaviour: Co-operation and Networks*, London, Routledge (1989).

Håkansson, H. and Snehota, I. (eds), *Developing Relationships in Business Networks*, London, Routledge, (1995).

Wilson, D. and Möller, K., *Business Marketing: An Interaction and Network Perspective*, Boston, Kluwer Academic Publishers (1995).

Sharma, D. D., *Advances in International Marketing*, Greenwich, Connecticut, JAI Press inc (1993).

Axelsson, B. and Easton, G. (eds), *Industrial Networks: A New View of Reality*, London, Routledge (1992).

Gross, A. C., Banting, P. M., Meredith, L. N. and Ford, D., *Business Marketing*, Boston, Houghton Mifflin (1993).

Ford, D. and Saren, M., *Technology Strategy for Business*, London, International Thomson Business Press (1996).

Forsgren, M. and Johanson, J. (eds), *Managing Networks in International Business*, Philadelphia, Gordon and Breach (1992).

Ford, D., Gadde, L. G., Håkansson, H., Lundgren, A., Snehota, I., Turnbull, P. W. and Wilson, D. *Managing Business Relationships*, Chichester, John Wiley, 1998.

Naude, P. and Turnbull, P.W. (eds), *Network Dynamics in International Marketing*, Pergamon (1998).

Gemunden, H. G., Ritter, T. and Walter, A., *Relationships and Networks in International Markets*, Pergamon (1999).

Ghauri, P., *Advances in International Marketing*, Volume 9, International Purchasing and Marketing, Stamford, Connecticut, (1999).

Ford, D. and Saren, M., *Managing and Marketing Technology*, London, Thomson Learning (2001).

Understanding Business Marketing and Purchasing

An interaction approach

Third edition

**Edited by David Ford
on behalf of the IMP Group**

THOMSON

Australia • Canada • Mexico • Singapore • Spain • United Kingdom • United States

THOMSON

Understanding Business Marketing and Purchasing – 3rd Edition

Copyright © Thomson Learning 2002

The Thomson logo is a registered trademark used herein under licence.

For more information, contact Thomson Learning, High Holborn House; 50-51 Bedford Row, London WC1R 4LR or visit us on the World Wide Web at:
http://www.thomsonlearning.co.uk

British Library Cataloguing-in-Publication Data
A catalogue record for this book is available from the British Library

ISBN 1-86152-769-1

Second edition publishing 1997 by The Dryton Press
This edition published by Thomson Learning 2002
Reprinted by Thomson Learning 2003

Typeset by Photoprint, Torquay, Devon
Printed by TJ International Ltd, Padstow, Cornwall

Contents

Introduction

The first edition of this book, published in 1990, was intended to introduce academics and students to the ideas of the IMP (Industrial Marketing and Purchasing) Group on how to understand and operate effectively in business markets. The book became a popular choice for recommendation by many professors and was bought by lots of students. The second edition of the book, published in 1997 added new ideas on how to understand what happens in the complicated *networks* of companies, in which managers have to operate.

This third edition has been radically revised and includes more recently published articles by the IMP Group and some of our co-workers. In selecting the items for the book I have tried to include those works that will be most *interesting* for students, academics and managers and which explain the *reality* of business markets. This has meant leaving out a number that either develop concepts much further than would interest the average reader or which contain a mass of detailed data analysis. In addition to new articles, I have also included some from the early days of the group that are still highly influential. The book also includes work by a number of people who are not part of the original IMP group, but who we have met over the years and from whom we have learned a great deal. There are also pieces in here from some second or even third generation researchers within what has become known as the "*Interaction Approach*". These people have developed some basic ideas much further than the "old men". As always, there are many readings that could well have been included, but aren't, and perhaps a few that are there, but shouldn't be. Overall, we hope that the book presents a comprehensive and up-to-date coverage of the IMP Group's work and of the Interaction Approach to understanding and managing in complex business networks.

THE INTERACTION APPROACH

It's perhaps a good idea to start the book by outlining the development of the interaction approach and why it seems to be useful for students who are trying to understand business markets and for managers who must try to make profits in them. This introduction may also help readers to relate some of the ideas in the book to what is found in more general marketing texts. It will also provide a background to show how the readings that follow are related to each other and are part of a continuing attempt to understand business markets. Most of us started as marketing people and it is with ideas on marketing that we can start our explanation.

The traditional approach to marketing

The traditional approach both to understanding and to managing a company's marketing activities had its roots in consumer marketing, particularly in the marketing of fast-moving, non-durable goods, such as personal care products. This approach was built around a core of the marketing mix, or the relatively small set of variables considered to be available for the marketer to manipulate – The "4Ps"; the product itself; the price charged for it; the way it was promoted and the distribution methods used (or "place" in which it was sold). Marketing within companies was organised around the management of individual brands and the creative task for each brand manager was to manipulate the mix for that brand, to achieve growth in market share and profitability. At the same time, academic debate continued about whether there were really only four "Ps" that marketers could manipulate, or whether other "Ps" such as the "People" involved in the process should be added to the list. Meanwhile, marketing research centred on two aims. The first was to gain a greater understanding of the effectiveness of different approaches within each mix variable, such as the ways in which companies determined their prices, or the promotional techniques that would bring the best response from the market. The second area of research was to understand consumers better and in particular, the processes by which they responded to the mix and eventually came to choose a particular brand and make a purchase. Researchers were also interested in the differences between the behaviour and choice criteria of different groups of consumers within the market.

We can summarise this approach to marketing as follows:

> The seller is the only active party in the process of marketing and its task is to assemble the mix – to *do* the marketing. The role of the customer is passive and limited to choosing whether to respond or not to the mix which the manufacturer launches at the market as a whole. Each customer is considered to be individually insignificant and part of a relatively homogeneous market, or segment within that market. The approach also infers that marketing is mainly carried out by manufacturers and it implies that retailers simply provide shelf-space after they have been selected by the manufacturer to be part of its mix. A side-effect of this is that the marketing literature still tends to downplay the importance of marketing by retailers, despite the fact that many of them are major brands in their own right and who often develop innovative products.

Business markets

Now the story gets slightly more complicated because this same approach was also followed when marketing researchers turned their attention to the way in which companies marketed to other companies in business or industrial markets. Most marketing textbooks had chapters on business marketing, which was regarded as some sort of special-case of "normal" marketing. Academics also tried to map the purchase process that companies went through which seemed to be even more complicated than that of consumers. The researchers categorised the different types of purchases, different types of customers and who was influential in taking purchase decisions. They also tried to find out what were the most effective mixes that a seller could use to get the desired response from the market. These mixes for the business marketer also seemed to be more complicated. Instead of an emphasis on advertising, the promotional element was more likely to favour personal sales effort and somewhere in the 4 "Ps" it was necessary to find room for things like the importance of after-sales service etc.

This way of looking at and doing business marketing had three problems:

- It was based on the *separate* analysis of the marketing and purchasing process.
- It concentrated on the purchase process for a single purchase.
- It carried over from the consumer-marketing literature of the time the implicit view that buyers were individually insignificant, passive and part of a relatively homogeneous market.

Of course, this way of seeing business markets didn't just exist in the academic literature. This was the way in which it was taught to those who were to become business marketers, although paradoxically, it did not closely coincide with what experienced practitioners were actually *doing* in the real world.

Interaction

The development of the interaction approach to understanding business markets started because of a realisation that the prevailing literature didn't seem to relate closely to what really happened in business markets. In particular:

- Business markets don't consist of a large number of individually insignificant customers – customers vary widely in size and requirements. Some of them are bigger than their suppliers and marketers often talk about their customers individually and have clear ideas of how and for what they are important.
- Business markets don't consist simply of active sellers and passive customers. Often, a customer, faced with a particular requirement has to seek out suitable suppliers, assess them and even sometimes persuade them to meet those requirements. This task is difficult if the customer's requirements are hard to satisfy, or the potential purchases are small. More generally, what is supplied and bought is not a fixed, standard product determined by the seller. The product is often modified or even designed specially at the customer's request. It may also be manufactured in a particular way, perhaps even in a purpose-designed plant. It may be delivered on a mutually agreed schedule and at a price that is individually negotiated. Lots of people from different functional areas in both companies are likely to be involved in the process; not just marketing, sales and purchasing staff, but also people from engineering, production and finance etc. This means that the process is not one of action and reaction; it is one of *interaction*.
- Sales and buying people in business markets don't usually just meet, do a deal and then never see each other again. Sometimes, there may be a long period before the first purchase, involving lots of interaction – months of initial meetings, product and production development and negotiation. More importantly, this first purchase may be the forerunner of others. At one extreme, deliveries are likely to be continuous in the case of production components, perhaps over many years. For capital equipment each customer may only make a purchase infrequently, but each time it will remember its previous purchases and what the pattern of interaction with the successful and unsuccessful suppliers before, during and after the purchase was like. Some other purchases will be less important to either of the parties involved and the interaction between them may be limited to a phone call each time a product is required. Even here, each purchase will be influenced by what has happened before and each in turn will influence what happens the next time a similar purchase takes place.

All of this means that each business purchase is just a single *episode* among many in a *relationship* between the two companies, and each purchase can only be fully understood within the context of that relationship. Each episode, whether it is the exchange of product, service, finance or even a social interaction is affected by the relationship of which it forms part and each interaction, in turn, affects the relationship itself. These business relationships have a life of their own, which is separate from the companies which are part of it. To understand business marketing and purchasing we must understand business relationships and many of the papers in this book look at ways to do that.

Many, perhaps most, of the relationships in business markets are close, complex and long-term, like that for a middle-aged, married couple. But, just as with a married couple, it doesn't mean that the parties know everything about each other, or indeed that they always act in each others' best interests. Other relationships centre on a single transaction; like that for the purchase of a major piece of capital equipment that could take months or years to complete. Some business relationships are characterised by domination by one or other of the partners, or by conflict and deceit. Some relationships between companies simply lose their reason for existence and become inert or end in divorce. Others are short-term, such as when one of the parties seeks to take advantage of the other. Perhaps a customer will seek to exploit the technical resources of a supplier with the implied promise of a long-term relationship that it has no intention of fulfilling. Here again there is a close analogy with the relationships that can exist between people. Yet other relationships are more distant and the only contact between the two companies is impersonal, by advertising or mail. In this way they approximate to the situation in many consumer markets.

Relationships

Early work by the IMP Group took the *relationship* as its unit of analysis, instead of an individual purchase or a single company. This approach was not just an academic device: It was based on the belief that the critical task for the business marketer and purchaser is the development and management of its relationships with its customers or suppliers. This, in turn led to two further elements of the group's approach.

Firstly, the task of managing a buyer–seller relationship is essentially similar for both of the companies involved. Both customers and suppliers enter a relationship for their own ends and seek to achieve them through that relationship, sometimes at the expense of the other party and sometimes in cooperation with it. Both companies bring resources to their relationship and will use these to design, manufacture and transfer products between themselves and onwards to other companies. Both companies will have to take decisions about how much to adapt their products, processes or administrative procedures to suit the requirements of the other company. This view of the similarity of the task of customer and supplier influenced our research process, because we believed that it is only possible to make sense of what happens in business markets by simultaneously studying *both* sides of a relationship. Also, we were struck by the fact that the value of a company's purchases often accounts for 60–80% of its cost-of-goods sold. This means that purchasing has a major contribution to cost-reduction and profit enhancement. Perhaps even more importantly, purchasing is the function that is concerned with using the skills and resources of supplier companies to achieve positive competitive advantage. Despite this, purchasing continues to be viewed as a relatively low-status, routine, non-strategic and efficiency-oriented function in many companies. It is still under-researched, under-funded and misunderstood. For this reason, studies within by the Group have taken a strong interest in purchasing management itself.

Secondly, the relationship management task is not confined to a single relationship. Instead, each company has a *portfolio* of purchase and sales relationships in which it is enmeshed and it must manage that portfolio. These relationship portfolios have some of the characteristics of an investment portfolio. For example, a marketing company will see some of its customers as sources of future profits and will be likely to commit considerable resources to meet their requirements. Other customers may have particularly demanding technical requirements and so provide the supplier with the opportunity to develop its technology and then apply it elsewhere in its relationship portfolio. Similarly, a customer may identify those companies it sees as the source of its next generation of requirements and share information and joint development resources with them. It may characterise others solely as suppliers of standardised offerings who can be easily replaced. Close relationships are not always a good idea. It may well be in a company's best interests to keep its distance when dealing with some counterparts, perhaps because it doesn't trust them or perhaps because there are simply no advantages in getting close. Similarly, co-operating with another counterpart may not be in the company's best interests and it may be better to seek advantage at the expense of the other side, even to the extent of exploiting it for short-term gain – it's a hard world out there!

Networks

The early work of the Group concentrated on sales and purchases in the context of a single relationship or in a company's portfolio of relationships. But this level of analysis doesn't give a realistic picture of what happens in business markets. Each business company is enmeshed in a complex *network* of relationships. This network consists of the direct relationships that it has with its suppliers and customers, as well as with other organisations such as financial institutions and development partners. Also in the network are the relationships of these counterparts with other suppliers or customers. For example, a major supplier to a particular company will probably also have relationships with other customers. What the supplier does in these relationships will also affect what happens in its relationships with the first company. This can be because of what it learns in those relationships and the way it uses its resources in them, or how it regards its relationship with the focal company when compared to them. The network also consists of the relationships between companies with which the focal company has no contact, but which can affect its way of doing business. An example would be the relationship between two companies which also supply one of the focal company's customers. What happens in this distant relationship could well affect this customer's requirements from the focal company or its attitude towards it. Similarly, a technology or way of working that is developed between companies elsewhere in the network could lead to a change in the thinking of the focal company's suppliers.

Networks of relationships have their own dynamic and each company and its relationships are part of the pattern of influence and change that flows through them. Sometimes, a company will seek to influence many of the companies around it and try to alter its position in the network. For example, a powerful retailer may seek to affect the operations of its product suppliers and also of their suppliers. More commonly, the state of a network and the direction of its evolution is the result of the actions and motivations of many different companies, some acting alone and some together. In the same way that a company cannot unilaterally design or control its relationships with others, it is even less likely to be able to design or control the wider network that surrounds it.

In order to understand what goes on inside a business company we need to try to understand its relationships. In order to understand what goes on inside a company's relationships we need to try to understand the network of which they form part. It is for this reason that the later research within the interaction approach has moved from the study of business relationships to a wider, network perspective.

Relationship marketing and CRM

Ideas on *Relationship Marketing* have come to prominence, particularly in the consumer marketing literature and it is worthwhile to distinguish these from the work within the interaction approach. Relationship marketing has two main origins. The first is a realisation that consumer marketing, just like business marketing, is about repeat purchases – there really is very little profit to be had in getting someone to buy a particular brand of coffee on just one occasion. The second origin is in the direct-marketing literature. For a long time direct-marketing practitioners have emphasised the difference between customers who buy once and clients who buy frequently. Improved customer information means that consumer marketers now know much more about the attitudes, purchase habits and overall life-styles of potential customers. This has led practitioners to change their emphasis from constructing a good offering and a suitable message, to maximising their return on their client base *over time* by "relationship marketing". However, relationship marketing is still a largely one-sided process with an active seller and a passive buyer. The major difference between it and conventional consumer marketing is that its emphasis is on repeat purchases by an identifiable customer. Relationship marketing may be perfectly appropriate in consumer markets, but in business markets we are concerned with two active parties, suppliers and customers, both of which are involved in *relationship management* for their own and for their mutual benefit.

"Customer Relationship Management" or CRM is a more recent vogue in the management literature and is often advertised by major software houses, one of which currently offers "Global CRM in 90 days"! What is being sold by these companies is the software to record and analyse account information, including such things as contact-management and customer sales records. Although CRM may be an important part of Relationship Management, it is frequently tactical in approach and can only be a part of a wider approach to selecting, developing and managing customer relationships. CRM also shares with Relationship Marketing the implication that what happens in business markets is a one-sided activity by marketers and indeed that customers are happy to be "managed" by their suppliers!

STRUCTURE OF THE BOOK

This edition of the book has a revised structure in five parts. The first part starts with three readings that together present the basic structure of the IMP approach, its process of development and the ideas that we have about business networks. Two of these readings are included for the first time. The second part consists of six readings which attempt to provide a thorough introduction to the nature of business relationships and the patterns of interaction within them. This part includes for the first time an important article by Keith Blois which explains how and why companies can have a variety of approaches to their business relationships. The third part tries to provide a full analysis of the issues in networks of relationships. Of particular note here is the new article by Aino Halinen, Asta Salmi and Virpi Havilla on the dynamics of networks. There are then two parts which look at the problems of managing in complex networks from the perspectives of marketing and purchasing respectively. One of these parts will be of obvious importance to those whose area of work or interest is either marketing or purchasing. But we would argue that it is vitally important for practitioners and researchers to understand interaction, relationships and networks from the perspective of marketing and purchasing. So *both* of these parts should be important all those involved in business networks. These sections include a small number of readings from previous editions, but the majority are new to this edition.

We hope that the book as a whole brings an up-to-date approach to understanding business marketing and purchasing that builds on our earlier concepts.

On behalf of the IMP Group
David Ford

University of Bath School of Management
May 2001

Part 1
The IMP Approach to Understanding Business Marketing and Purchasing

The first part of the book explains some bases of the IMP approach to understanding business marketing and purchasing. The first reading, "Interaction, Relationships and Networks" by Peter Turnbull, David Ford and Malcolm Cunningham (all founder members of the IMP Group) provides a review of the development of the approach of the IMP Group and introduces ideas on investment in relationships, on the bonds between the individuals who are involved and on the management of portfolios of relationships. Each of these will be discussed further in later readings in the book.

The second reading is taken from the initial book by the IMP Group, edited by Håkan Håkansson in 1982. It presents a general model of buyer–seller interaction and contrasts this approach with earlier literature and other approaches. The reading uses a number of the basic ideas which are developed further in other readings in this book and that we have referred to in the introduction. Industrial marketers and purchasers are both seen as active participants who take part in an often complex series of "episodes" in exchanging product or service, information, money and sociability. These episodes are part of a relationship between the two companies and this relationship provides the "atmosphere" within which interaction takes place. The final paper in this section is also by two founder-members of the IMP Group, Håkan Håkansson and Ivan Snehota. This paper distinguishes between the economic, technical and social content of inter-company interaction and presents four "cornerstones" of the IMP Approach.

CONTENTS

1.1 Interaction, relationships and networks in business markets: an evolving perspective

Peter Turnbull, David Ford and Malcolm Cunningham

INTRODUCTION

The basis of this paper is the series of studies which have been carried out over the past 20 years into the nature of buyer–seller relationships by the International Marketing and Purchasing (IMP) Group and a number of other contributors to the growing theoretical and empirical research base in business-to-business marketing. The themes of interaction, relationships and networks encapsulate the major research thrusts of this group and underlie much of the contemporary academic research in Europe. This paper addresses these themes, which represent the major phases of challenging conceptual and empirical research with which the IMP Group has been concerned since its inception in 1976. The aim of this paper is to show the development process of the IMP research and to integrate some of its various themes and findings.

By 1974, early fragmented research into industrial markets in the USA and Europe had established that purchasing was a multi-person activity, that customers were often reluctant to change their sources of supply and that there was a surprising degree of stability and durability in their dealings with many of their suppliers. Risk reduction and satisfying behavior were evident and even large, powerful customers frequently sought cooperation with suppliers rather than brutally and unilaterally exercising their purchasing power in the market. Such cooperative behavior developed through relationships often entailed modification of systems and adaptations of products and service by both seller and buyer.

In Europe, during the 1970s, various explanations for these phenomena were offered, drawing on research conducted in Sweden, Britain and France (Håkansson and Wootz, 1979). It was apparent that increasing market concentration resulting in a few powerful players gave a more restricted choice of partners, and the large increment of change of partner became of increasing importance. Risk perception and risk reducing strategies were clearly possible explanations. High costs of change (switching costs) and strong source loyalty and inertia were observed in studies of organizational buying behavior (Cunningham, 1986; Håkansson and Wootz, 1979). It also became clear that buyers take an active role in seeking out suppliers and influencing the interaction.

By 1975 these studies had led to a recognition that supplier–customer relationships were complex phenomena and that independent studies of buying behavior or marketing activities should give way to research focused directly on the patterns of interaction between the two partners to a relationship (Johanson and Wootz, 1977, Håkansson, 1982).

The IMP Group was formed in 1976 to develop and carry out cooperative research into the nature of the relationships between companies in these complex markets. Rather than following the previous research tradition of studying discrete purchasing decisions, it was agreed that it was important to understand the pattern of dependencies between companies, the evolution of their dealings over time, the adaptations that each made to meet the requirements of the other party, and the inter-organizational person contact that took place. As a result of a number of in-depth case studies carried out in France, Germany, Italy, Sweden and the UK a revised framework was proposed by the IMP Group to guide the development of research in business-to-business markets. This became known as the Interaction Approach (see Håkansson, 1982; Turnbull and Cunningham, 1981).

THE INTERACTION APPROACH

The paradigm which has become known as the Interaction Approach marked a reaction against the previous research tradition in business markets which had sought to analyze the different categories of single industrial purchases and the processes by which these individual purchase decisions are taken (Håkansson, 1982). Briefly stated, our observation at that time led us to a continuing research approach based on several ideas. First, the great majority of business purchases do not exist as individual events and hence cannot be fully understood if each one is examined in isolation. Nor did we believe that business purchases could be characterised as a process of action by the seller and reaction (or not) by the buyer. Instead we saw business markets as arenas within which buying and selling companies interacted with each other. This interaction takes place within the context of a relationship between the companies. The previous experience of individuals and their companies in that relationship and in others are important influences on attitude and behavior in both purchasing and selling. These relationships vary widely in nature; they can be distant and largely impersonal, so that they have similarities to those which might exist between consumers and the marketers of nondurable goods. However, we observed that for a majority of companies in business markets, a small number of suppliers and/or customers were individually responsible for large volumes of their purchases or sales, and that in these circumstances the relationships between companies and these important customers and suppliers tend to be close, complex and long term, with extensive contact patterns between many individuals from each company and significant mutual adaptation by both parties. This view contrasted with previous studies which tended to see markets as atomistic and consisting of large numbers of more or less anonymous customers with which marketers dealt at a distance.

Whatever its closeness or distance, the relationship between companies is the receptacle for the combined experience of the participants. The relationship consists of learned rules and norms of behavior. It provides the atmosphere within which individual episodes take place. These episodes include negotiations, payments, deliveries and social contacts etc. Each episode in turn is affected by and affects the overall relationship. Furthermore, relationships evolve over time and can be considered to traverse a series of stages characterised by increasing mutual adaptation, reduced "distance" and increasing commitment (Ford, 1982).

Relationship is not a dichotomous variable and the question for researchers is not whether a relationship exists in any particular situation. Similarly for business people it is not a question of whether a company should establish a relationship in a particular case. Relationships do exist in a wide variety of forms and the agenda for researchers is to understand the nature of the relationships. Inter-company relationships are complex. It is simplistic to suggest that they can or should develop along a single continuum between "distant" and "close", "good" and "bad." All inter-company relationships simultaneously exhibit conflict and cooperation, with guile and self-seeking.

The Interaction Approach takes the relationship as its unit of analysis rather than the individual transaction. It involves simultaneous analysis of the attitudes and actions of both parties and emphasizes the essential similarity between the purchasing and marketing tasks in relationships. It sees relationships both as important in themselves and as predictors of individual transaction behavior and is reviewed in detail in Håkansson (1982). Among the individual research tasks which have been addressed has been to find the variables which can best be used to describe relationships;

how these relationships evolve over time; the variation in the nature of relationships in different circumstances; the atmosphere within which interaction takes place; the contact patterns between the two parties and the bonding which occurs between the companies.

The research has highlighted the importance of separating the short-term management of individual relationships from the longer-term development of a strategy for the company's portfolio of supplier and customer relationships (Turnbull and Valla, 1986). The research has also shown the inter-relationship between the resources possessed by companies and how these are used in and affected by their relationship activities. A review of this work is found in Ford (1990). This research has lead to the view that it is the co-ordination and mobilization of the company's portfolio of relationships and the use and enhancement of the resources of both companies through interaction in those relationships that is the basis for enhancing a company's network position and hence its competitive advantage (Ford *et al.*, 1996). This conceptual link between networks and competitiveness leads us to consider several contemporary research thrusts in the area of market competitiveness.

AN INTERACTION APPROACH VIEW OF COMPETITIVENESS

Research studies in the field of competitiveness and competitive performance have assumed increasing importance in recent years and were originally stimulated by the contribution of Porter (1981) and Peters and Waterman (1982). Obviously achieving a competitive position in a market depends on many inter-related factors. Gains in productivity, market share dominance, high R&D investment, achieving economies of scale and concentration on knowledge-intensive, high value-added products have been the subject of study (for a brief summary see Cunningham, 1986).

Several researchers have linked competitiveness with a company's ability to develop and manage its array of network relationships. For example, Easton and Araujo (1985) and Araujo and Easton (1986) categorize the competition between suppliers in terms of the indirect and direct relationships which occur in selected industrial markets. Competition is viewed as being based on either conflict, competitive advantage, co-existence, cooperation or collusion. They use three theoretical frameworks for their analysis, first the traditional marketing strategy paradigms; second, the interaction approach and, third, the network approach. Their methodology is based on mapping, comparing and contrasting the perceptions and behavior of suppliers and customers in terms of identifying and characterizing competitors, examining competitive strategies and analysing inter-competitor communications through technical and marketing networks. This leads to a view of competitiveness as a dynamic process over time. Active rivalry between firms within a product market occurs simultaneously with competition coming from other product markets. This "competitive field" transcends the narrowly defined industry or product market. Hence, the industrial economist's paradigm of the market structure-conduct-performance relationship is clearly an inadequate representation of the competitive forces and real determinants of competitiveness.

INTERACTION AND RELATIONSHIP STRATEGY

The importance of inter-company relationships as a way of exploiting and enhancing resources requires that a strategic approach is made to their analysis and management. But it is important to base ideas on the development of relationship strategy on an understanding of those wider factors which strategy must bear in mind and seek to change. Without a wider network view, any approach to relationship strategy runs the risk of degenerating into short-termism. It can also mean that the company may be unaware of the potential effects on itself and its relationships arising from the actions of other companies elsewhere in the network or of the opportunities for improving its overall position in the wider network which can be achieved through its interaction in its relationships. This means that development of relationship strategy depends on analysis of the company, its individual relationships and its overall relationship portfolio and network position.

The starting point for the development of relationship strategy is the interdependence of companies. This interdependence takes many forms. Perhaps the most obvious is the need to generate revenue from other companies for the continuing existence and development of the company. Interdependence is also based on the need to use the knowledge and abilities of others, delivered in the form of products or services. Perhaps even more importantly, a company may also need to acquire some of the knowledge of other companies for itself, or wish to develop its own knowledge through interaction with the other company.

The basis for the interdependence of companies in business relationships is the resources which they possess. Companies interact with each other and develop relationships in order to exploit and develop their resources (Turnbull and Wilson, 1989). In order to do this they seek those companies which have matching resources. Resources can be discussed in at least three categories:

The first is financial resources; these obviously affect the company's ability to acquire new resources, or to use the resources of others. The second category of resource is a company's network position. Network position consists of the company's relationships and the rights and obligations which go with them. For example, one aspect of a company's position which is a valuable resource is its access to a major consumer market as would be the case with a retail store chain, another would be its brand as a measure of reputation in the network. This reputation may be important as it can make a company an important reference customer and its "seal of approval" can lead to the company being able to develop further relationships elsewhere in the network. On the other hand, preservation of this relationship may inhibit a company from taking short-term advantage of a situation. For example, it may feel inhibited in raising its prices to make short-term profits in a situation of a product shortage. Many aspects of a company's network position are a function of the development of its resources through its interaction with others in its network relationships. In this way, network position is a dynamic and evolving characteristic.

The third category of resources are the skills which companies possess and these skills can be understood as a set of technologies. For our purposes, technologies can be separated into three areas:

(1) product technology, which consists of the ability to design products or services;
(2) process technologies which comprise the ability to manufacture or produce these products or services;
(3) marketing technologies which consist of the abilities to analyze the requirements of others and to assemble the means to influence these others and deliver them to a recipient – this includes relationship competence; skills in managing relationships themselves.

A number of points need to be made about these technologies. First, they are all learned abilities which can be applied in a variety of ways. They can be used to provide an offering of a product or service, or they can be transferred "whole" to others for their use. Technologies are the basis of all companies' existence, but, in themselves, the technologies have no value. They exist only as potential and are only valuable if they are worth something to another company. This value to others is transmitted through the process of interaction between the companies.

A company's pattern of interaction with others, based on the technologies of all parties, effectively defines the nature of the company and its position in the network. Interaction in business markets involves the technologies of both companies. For example, company A may buy components from B. The components may be to A's design (based on its product technology) but manufactured by B (based on its process technologies). In turn, A may use the components in its production (based on its process skills) and use its marketing technology to sell them to a number of resellers who will, in turn, use their marketing skills to reach a wider market. In the case of conventional product or service exchange, interaction between companies can take place on the basis of one or, more usually, a number of technologies of the supplier. For that technology to be effective it will have to be combined with one or more technologies of the buyer to transfer and/or transform an offering for a buyer elsewhere in the network.

Any one company in a network will have a variety of relationships each with different characteristics. These characteristics will depend on the respective motivations of the two parties but also the technologies which are involved. For example, a relationship which is based on the purchase of a component to the buyer's design – "make to order" is likely to be different to that for a component based on a supplier's proprietary technology. Similarly, the relationship between a franchisee and a franchiser (where product, process and marketing technologies are provided by the franchiser) is likely to be different to that between a major retailer and a manufacturer which supplies garments to its specification. It will also be different to that between joint-venture partners in a new technology development relationship. A company's relationship with its main bank is likely to be different to that which it has with a financial or other professional advisor. Finally, of course, relationships with large suppliers or customers will differ from those with small ones.

Relationship strategy comprises the tasks of managing each of these relationships both individually and as part of an interrelated portfolio, each element of which has a different function for both of the parties involved (Turnbull and Valla, 1986). It involves the process of exploiting the company's technologies in its relationships so as to maximize the return on the company's technological investment. It involves the task of acquiring technology directly, such as through a licensing relationship. It also involves acquiring technology indirectly through interaction. Examples of this include developing a product for a specific customer, which may then be sold to others; when a customer learns to "reverse engineer" a product from a supplier so that it can then make it for itself. Finally, relationship strategy can also be used to maintain or alter the company's network position. For example, by extending its access to the resources of other companies, a company may be able to use these resources elsewhere in the network.

RELATIONSHIP DEVELOPMENT AND INVESTMENT

Ford (1980) suggests that supplier–customer relationships in business-to-business markets evolve over time, and considering the process of relationship development, careful management can obtain the best possible value from these relationships. Consequently, Ford analyses the process of establishment and development of supplier–customer relationships over time according to the variables of experience, uncertainty, distance (including aspects of social, geographical, cultural, technical and time distance), commitment and adaptation. By considering the extent to which each of these variables is present in a supplier–customer relationship, it is suggested that such relationships follow a five-stage evolution process – pre-relationship, early, development, long term and final stage. Thus the development of supplier–customer relationships can be seen as an evolutionary process in terms of:

- the increasing experience of both partners;
- the reduction in their uncertainty and all kinds of distance in the relationship;
- the growth of both actual and perceived commitment;
- the formal and informal adaptations, and investment and savings involved in both sides' organizations (Ford, 1980).

In order that supplier–customer relationships develop over time, it is necessary for both suppliers and customers to make some degree of investment in relationships. Consequently, business-to-business marketing can be seen as:

> A process of investments in market positions at the micro- and macro level (Turnbull and Wilson, 1989).

Investment is of particular interest as investments in the relationship can be made by both the buyer and the seller. Johanson and Mattson (1985, p. 187) suggest that marketing expenditures can be viewed as investments in market networks. They point out that most of the literature on investment in marketing deals with methods of calculating investments and not with the conceptualisation

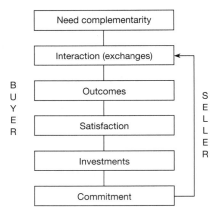

Source: Wilson and Mummalaneni

Figure 1 A framework of relationship development.

of investments within marketing theory, although they quote two Swedish studies on the topic. Hammarkvist *et al.* (1982) positions marketing problems as investments, organization and cooperation with other firms. Hagg and Johanson (1982) classify marketing investments as general, market-specific and relationship-specific.

Although there have been a number of studies focusing on investments in relationships, (Hagg and Johanson, 1982; Hammarkvist *et al.*, 1982; Johanson and Mattson, 1985), it is worthwhile to consider one of these studies, the framework developed by Wilson and Mummalaneni (1986), in more detail (Figure 1).

The framework begins with the assumption of need complementarily leading to exchanges through interactions, as does the Johanson and Mattson (1985) model. It suggests that "relationships develop through incremental investments of resources", which have to be made by both supplier and customer organizations. Such investments tend to be made only if the outcomes of these interactions within the relationship are perceived to be satisfactory, either now or potentially in the future. These investments may take the form of adaptations to the areas of product, process and organization (Håkansson, 1982). However, such investments are made not only to intensify the relationship and to demonstrate the interest that the partner has in developing a strong relationship, but also with the faith that the other partner will reciprocate (Turnbull and Wilson, 1989).

In addition to furthering the development of supplier–customer relationships, according to Hammarkvist *et al.* (1982), these investment and adaptation activities may create social and structural (economic) bonds. These lead to mutual commitment as a measure of true source loyalty (Jarvis and Wilcox, 1977) and thus to long-term strong and profitable relationships which are cemented with social and structural bonds and which become difficult to break (Wilson and Mummalaneni, 1986).

It follows then that most cost factors and marketing expenses involved in supplier–customer relationships can be regarded as investments in relationship development (Johanson and Mattson, 1985). Such investments are classified as "general", "market-specific" and "relationship-specific" by Hagg and Johanson (1982). These investments "made by one party in a relationship with another party have an important impact on the costs of that party's current or future transactions with the other" (Williamson, 1979, 1981).

It might be expected then that supplier–customer relationships will be very costly, perhaps making a negative contribution to supplier profitability, in their early stages. However, the costs of managing supplier–customer relationships might also be expected to decrease over time as a result of decreasing levels of investment and other marketing expenses in the following stages of the relationship (Fiocca, 1982; Turnbull and Wilson, 1989). Thus, the analysis of customer profitability is a key tool of strategic marketing management.

CUSTOMER PORTFOLIOS

Throughout this paper it has been explicitly recognized that the successful management of supplier–customer relationships depends on the company's relationship management skills, the investments in initiating, developing and maintaining relationships and the allocation of resources between different relationships according to their likely return (Ford, 1980). To achieve this both sides of a dyadic relationship need to analyze the current and projected benefits resulting from the relationship. Ultimately, and specifically taking the supply side perspective, current and projected profits of customers (existing and potential) need to be analyzed and forecast, ideally on an individual basis but at least at market segment level. Such analysis, if combined with an identification of the stage of each customer relationship allows a better understanding of the potential of the customer base and helps in the strategic and tactical planning and allocation of resources between customers of all types.

In the development of customer relationship strategy, portfolio theory applied to the customer base can help maximize long-term profitability. As Turnbull points out, portfolio types of analysis can be:

> A useful management tool for enforcing a discipline in the allocation of suppliers' limited resources to an optimal combination of customers (Turnbull, 1990).

Portfolio analysis has its theoretical origins in financial theory but has been applied extensively in business strategy, product planning and supply chain management (Cunningham, 1986; Turnbull, 1990). The application of portfolio theory to customer relationships is more recent. Two of the earlier and influential attempts have been those of Fiocca (1982) and Campbell and Cunningham (1984a). In both papers, the analysis is derived from the theoretical view of business-to-business marketing embedded in the interaction approach and are intended to provide guidelines for marketing strategy formulation and resource allocation. These ideas were further developed by Yorke (1986).

Shapiro *et al.* (1987) also developed the concept when investigating customer behavior and produced a matrix to classify customer types on "cost to serve and net price dimensions". They identify four types of customers – passive, carriage trade, bargain basement and aggressive – and argue that profitability will vary between the groups. They further suggest managerial actions to manage this profit dispersion.

Krapfel *et al.* (1991) have further developed the strategic approach to managing buyer/seller relationships. They suggest a model in which relationship types and relationship management modes are mapped together to assess the optimal relationship portfolio. This mapping takes into account the transaction costs involved. As part of the relationship management process they also recognize the importance of matching the relationships and signalling intentions to partners. They see signalling as an important aspect in the adaptation process. The relationship types they identify (partner, friend, acquaintance and rival) are determined by two factors: relationship value and interest commonality (commonality of a firm's economic goals with its perception of its potential partner's economic goals). While the relationship management modes, again identified two-dimensionally by perceived power position and interest commonality, suggested are collaboration, negotiation, administration, domination, accommodation and submission).

Turnbull and Zolkiewski (1995) test both the Shapiro *et al.* and Krapfel *et al.* portfolio models through an empirical analysis of a large UK computer supplier. While they found the Shapiro *et al.* customer classification the most appropriate for the researched company, they suggest a three-dimensional grid, with cost to serve, net price and relationship value as more generally valuable as a marketing analysis and planning tool.

Despite these rather normative outputs regarding customer-base management, our research indicates that resource allocation decisions are often taken without full assessment of the potential of and threats to each relationship. There are at least two reasons for this.

First, relationship analysis at either the individual or group level is an essential preliminary to investment and management decisions. For those companies with a few major relationships then individual analysis is likely to be both achievable and worthwhile. For companies with large numbers of relationships then such an individual analysis is unlikely to be feasible. Because of this it is important, although rare, for companies to develop a system of categorization of relationship types as an aid to analysis.

Second, relationship portfolio management inevitably involves choice. It is this choice which is perhaps the most difficult aspect for managers to handle. An interesting example of this issue is found in relationships between UK grocery manufacturers and the major retail store groups. These manufacturers are very concerned to develop their relationship with individual stores and in many cases have extended the relationship as the unit of analysis from the sales area into their marketing decision making. However, the development of a closer relationship with one store group, perhaps involving product modification, exclusivity, joint advertising etc., will, beyond a certain point, inevitably involve a level of commitment which will mean that the company has to accept a more distant relationship with others. The extent of this commitment and its associated costs in other relationships is difficult for some managers to accept. Their reluctance may be based on a realistic appraisal of the potential benefits of further commitment.

However, if the supplier is unwilling to incur the costs of a closer relationship with one customer (partially expressed in terms of a more distance relationship with others) then the limitations of that relationship in terms of customer commitment to stock levels, information, etc. must be accepted by the supplier. If it is not accepted then the managers involved are also likely to be subject to two common self delusions. The first is that their relationships are actually "closer" than they are in reality. The second delusion is the equally common view of relationship management as simply "being nice to customers". This view is false for at least three reasons. First, "niceness" involves resources and companies are unlikely to have sufficient resources to be "nice" to everyone. Second, the level of niceness given to each customer is unlikely to be significant if applied to all. Third, relationships are unlikely to be successful in the long term if based solely on one party's subservience to the other – as any marriage guidance counsel will relate!

ORGANIZATIONAL EVOLUTION AND BONDING

The notion that industrial marketing is essentially an organization problem (Håkansson and Ostberg, 1975) has precipitated many research studies. The internationalization process of Swedish firms (Johanson and Vahlne, 1977; Johanson and Wiedersheim-Paul, 1975) postulated an approach to organization development linked to the sequential entry into countries according to the perceived psychic distance. The various levels of organizational commitment and resources allocation in companies was modelled with progressive evolution from direct selling to the ultimate establishment of subsidiaries in foreign countries. This work has been extended by Turnbull and Ellwood (1984) in their studies of UK companies involved in the IT industry as they penetrate French, German and Spanish markets. Turnbull (1986) also investigated organizations and interactions involving sales subsidiaries.

The massive data bank of the IMP group of researchers has led to a description and classification of the organization structures adopted by French companies (Valla, 1985), by German companies (Johanson and Wootz, 1986), by Swedish companies (Håkansson, 1986b) and by British companies (Cunningham, 1986) in their respective approaches to Europe.

Hallen (1986) argues that organization structures can be analyzed at two levels. First, the global market level, in which the use of agents, subsidiaries etc., in foreign markets can be observed and studied over time. Second, the transaction or customer level which is the level of involvement in the interaction process and with handling the relationship. Valla (1985) observes that at global market level the choice of organization may be determined by obligation (conforming to company norms), by opportunity or chance and finally, by deliberate design and strategy. It is significant that these structures change over time and between markets, are not uni-directional towards greater investments, nor are they followed in a sequential step process. Cunningham (1986) undertook inter-industry comparisons of organizational structures and pointed to the important influence on structures adopted of market factors (market structure, competition), market potential, situation factors (product complexity and the purchasing process) and supplier strategy factors (objectives and types of customer relationships to be managed).

Hallen (1986) draws attention to the formal organization structure (which indicates a commitment of resources and a choice among options) and to the informal organization as is portrayed by the inter-company personal contacts and in the experience and language skills of executives which influences how these contacts are implemented.

Clearly organizational development and contact not only has favorable consequences in terms of developing commitment and loyalty bonds over time but there are also significant cost consequences. Turnbull (1974) demonstrated from research in the steel industry how large investments in personal selling and service were required and how they dominated other expenditure in a supplier's communications mix to customers in industrial markets. Following their classification of the roles of personal contacts, Cunningham and Turnbull (1982) proposed a series of measures of the resources involved, such as the numbers of people involved, the diversity of functions and the hierarchical levels in an organization who interacted with their counterparts in the other customer or supplier company. Extensive research in the German packaging industry (Campbell and Cunningham, 1984b), and the UK automotive component and chemical industry (Cunningham and Homse, 1986) in the Swedish metallurgical industries (Hamfelt and Lindberg, 1987), has led to new means of evaluating the resources involved. It has shed light on how the behavior of marketers and purchasers can lead to the manipulation of the interactions and to the mobilisation of the technical know-how network through interpersonal contacts throughout the industry.

Thus, industrial marketing is increasingly being recognized as a process of investment in market positions at the micro- and macro-level. However, little research has been aimed at analyzing the actual costs of establishing and maintaining either a given supplier–customer relationship or a particular market position.

Wilson and Mummalaneni (1986) see relationship development as a process of bonding which leads to mutual commitment to the relationship. The Wilson and Mummalaneni framework draws on the work of Turner (1970) and McCall (1970) on bonding and on Rusbult's (1980) work on investments in relationships. As with the Johanson and Mattson (1985) model it begins with the assumption of need complementarily leading to exchange through interactions.

When the outcomes of these interactions yield satisfaction to both parties, bonds emerge that link the parties. These bonds might be structural or social in nature. Both parties have to make "investments" in relationships in order to develop them and thus relationships develop through incremental investments of resources. Such investments are usually made in satisfactory relationships and might take the form of several adaptations in the product and process areas (Håkansson, 1982). Investments and adaptations in the technical area may lead to shared technical and social bonds (Hammarkvist et al., 1982).

Investments by any party serve to intensify the relationship for they demonstrate not only the interest that the party has in building a strong relationship, but its faith that the other party will reciprocate. Commitment results from satisfaction and investment and is the measure of true source loyalty as its involves the bond of attachment to the source of supply (Jarvis and Wilcox, 1977). Investments are key elements in the development, or structural bonds. Structural bonds have four components: investments, termination procedures, social pressures and available alternatives. A detailed description of the model and its operationalization is contained in Wilson and Mummalaneni (1987).

Termination procedures are the steps that must be taken to end a relationship. The ease or difficulty of ending a relationship is a measure of the strength of a termination procedure bond. For example, if a legal contract exists that has large penalty clauses for early termination there is a significant cost to ending a supplier relationship. On the other hand, if the buyer can easily place an order for the equivalent product with another supplier the costs of switching sources of supply are low. Social pressure is exerted by other individuals or groups in the organization opposed to terminating a relationship. This could be due to both the personal interest of a superior in the organization or to another department that has a vested interest in maintaining the relationship.

The ability or the desirability for one party to terminate a relationship will depend on the attractiveness of available alternatives to the current relationship. It may be noted that to the extent that one party to the relationship has more alternatives to the current relationship than the other, the relationship is asymmetrical and the former has more power over the latter.

NETWORKS AND NETWORK MANAGEMENT

We have already noted that both from an analytical and a managerial perspective it is not feasible to examine any inter-company relationship in isolation. Relationships are influenced by other organizations that also interact and influence the parties to a dyadic interaction. The early IMP research largely focused on dyadic relationships and, indeed, the greater part of the theory and empirical research cases presented in Håkansson (1982) related to relationships with only two parties. This was the result of the methodology used and the explicit decision to focus initially on the dyad while recognizing that relationships are often, if not always, more complexly connected. Turnbull and Ellwood (1984) developed the approach by examining tri-partite interaction involving international sales subsidiaries and agents.

Concurrently, both theoretical and empirical research was developing in the understanding that individual relationships could not be fully understood in isolation from the other relationships in which each party was involved and from the effects of relationships which surrounded them in the wider network of relationships (Campbell, 1984; Håkansson, 1986a; Smith and Easton, 1986). This has led to the development of theory on network structure and dynamics. Unfortunately, the pace of conceptual development in the network area has not always been matched by empirical study. This means that the network literature does not always provide clarity of description of network phenomena, let alone guidelines for managerial decision making. However, the network view does provide a useful framework for analysis of business situations. It highlights the range of influences on individual companies and relationships as well as the nature and implications of different actions by relationship participants. But, it does add another level of complexity to description of business market behavior and understanding of buyer–seller relationships. A useful overview of the literature is provided in Axelsson and Easton (1993) and in Henders (1992).

Analysis of network position

A full discussion of the concept of network position is provided by Henders (1992). We have previously discussed the idea of network position as a description of a company's portfolio of relationships and the rights and obligations that go with it. Network position is both an outcome of past relationship strategy and a resource for future strategy. Relationships, rights and obligations are the result of the resources which the company initially brought to the network, the experience it has gained and the investments it has made in its relationships. This means that in addition to analysis of the company's relationship portfolio, an understanding of network position involves a listing of those additional resources which have been built through interaction. These could be analyzed using a conventional view of the bases of power which companies may possess. However, we suggest a threefold categorization in somewhat more managerial terms as follows.

(1) *Access* – to the resources of other network members. The resources include their financial and spending power as well as the ability to transform or transfer product or service. A company may also have access to the knowledge resources of other network members in the product, process or marketing areas.

(2) *Reputation* – This is a function of other network members' experience and relates to such things as the belief that new offerings from a particular network member will be of a certain "quality" etc. Reputation also refers to the ability which a company may have to exercise leadership, or to influence the decision making of other network members, based on their supposed expertise.

(3) *Expectations* – These can both facilitate and restrict the freedom of action of a company. For example, network members could have the expectation that a particular company will effectively set prices for a number of other companies. On the other hand, a company may be expected not to take advantage of product shortages by raising prices or to conform to "conventional" competition or to set higher ethical standards than others.

AN INTERACTION AND NETWORK APPROACH TO COMPETITIVENESS: AN INTEGRATION

In this paper we have portrayed some of the major themes and research thrusts that have emerged from the work of the IMP Group. The early study of supplier–customer relationships and the evolution of the Interaction Approach has led to several linked research projects in Interaction strategies, portfolios of customers, organization evolution, personal contact patterns and finally to networks, technological developments and competitiveness. A retrospective logic can be imposed upon these sequential and, often parallel, studies – especially as they relate to competitiveness.

Competitiveness and interaction with customers

A fundamental pre-requisite to achieve and sustain competitiveness in markets is to meet the customers' needs and the expectations which they have of suppliers. This view recognizes that customers' attitudes to different suppliers is not conditioned simply by narrowly defined product or service attributes or by customer assessment of the technical or commercial competence of a supplier, but also through the pattern and characteristics of the interaction with those suppliers. The achievement of a capability to compete on the basis of these interaction skills is a crucial ingredient of competitiveness. This is assessed by customers within their relationships with suppliers through the processes of interaction (Ford, 1984).

Competitiveness and interaction strategies

The strategic approach to markets and the type of customer interaction strategies pursued by a supplier is another ingredient of competitiveness. A set of five strategic options used by British firms to enter markets has been identified (Cunningham, 1986). These are:

(1) technical innovativeness;
(2) availability and supply security;
(3) low price competitiveness;
(4) product adaptation;
(5) total conformity as a second supplier.

Competitiveness through organization evolution

The ways in which companies structure their internal activities and their external organizations to serve domestic and foreign markets is of vital importance in presenting to customers a co-ordinated and cohesive presence and competitive ability. We have argued that industrial marketing is an organizational problem. The organization structures which companies evolve, either by obligation, opportunity or by deliberate design are manifest in the way in which they operate and are perceived to be effective by customers in a competitive environment. The formal and the informal structures within supplier companies are of vital significance to customers in their assessment of the reputation, and all-round performance of different suppliers.

Competitiveness through improvements in customer portfolios

A supplier's portfolio of customers represents not only an opportunity for change and improvement towards an optimum mix of customers but long-standing relationships with current customers in the portfolio act as a constraint on the optimum allocation of scarce technical and human resources among customers of varying strategic importance. The application of the portfolio concept allows for selectivity and focus on strategically important customers and segments and is a vital aspect of the competitive process.

Competitiveness through inter-organizational personal contacts

The importance of personal contacts in the establishment and maintenance of customer relationships has also been discussed. Personal contacts occur between various individuals, groups and hierarchical levels in organizational structures. Information is exchanged, adaptations are agreed, negotiations are performed, crises are overcome and social bonding occurs. Competitiveness is likely to be a function of how this interface with customers is managed and how the human resources involved are distributed and coordinated among different types of customers and among different members of their purchasing decision-making unit.

Competitiveness through mobilizing the network

The research studies discussed in the previous section testify to the power of network approach to technological competitiveness through the processes of knowledge development, resource mobilisation and resource co-ordination. Network relationships with a wide array of partners are important, as are the direct interactive relationships with customers. Findings (Håkansson, 1986a) suggest that:

- Success is associated with the firm's ability to use the resources of the surrounding network.
- Existing nearby network resources need to be supplemented by new, distant ones.
- Cooperation in product development creates problems of confidentiality and protection of knowledge. Participation in several co-operative projects with different partners in the network helps to overcome this.
- The relationships with different partners in a network have to be handled in quite different ways.
- There are substantial differences between companies in their ability to handle the network. Some companies become highly talented, others remain amateurs.

CONCLUSION

It is not easy to write a conclusion to a report of the historical evolution of a very wide-ranging research process; the work continues! However, there are a number of issues which we shall revisit here to emphasize their importance to further research and to marketing management in practice.

The first thing to be said is that there are no nice neat stages in the ways in which relationships evolve and develop, so we must say "sorry! " to those who like to take a structured view of the world. Second, and at the widest level of generality, we have seen that relationships are built on the capabilities of both parties. This means that it is possible to view a network as a pattern of technologies and capabilities. These capabilities are unevenly distributed and the network is not perfect in ensuring their transfer of value from those which have the technologies to those which seek to use them. Nevertheless, in increasingly high technology networks a successful company is one which has a very clear idea of its technology portfolio, how this is broken down into basic, distinctive and external technologies and how these technologies relate to the requirements of others. However, to successfully audit one's own technologies is extremely difficult, as research suggests (Clarke *et al.*, 1995). Also, a manager should not be so concerned with technology that he holds the belief that only the possessor of distinctive technologies can succeed in relationships and networks. Instead, we should emphasize that the ability to put together a package of basic product and process technologies and tailor that package to the particular requirements of others is a key element of competitive strategy.

Second, we must reiterate the importance of viewing relationships as a portfolio. This is not expressed simply in terms of the sales potential or current sales or purchases embodied in a relationship, but as a portfolio in technological terms. Thus, the seller is selling to an organization which may add its product process and marketing technologies to the further refinement of an offering. A buyer is acquiring product as a vehicle for acquiring technology and this is an alternative to acquiring that technology via licence, joint venture or any other means. A portfolio of relationships is a way of managing a portfolio of technologies.

Perhaps the major difficulty in accommodating this view is that we tend to look at the world in terms of products and markets and it is extremely difficult for us to look at the technologies on which those products and markets are based. Similarly, we have emphasized here the extent to which a structure of meanings surrounds the actions of participants in relationships and networks and how these meanings are not just a function of the individual's experience but are socially determined through the relationship itself and the "normal" ways of doing things. This means that an industrial marketing or buying company must examine continually the ways in which it interacts with its relationship partners to determine whether that interaction reflects both the other parties requirements, as well as just its expectations and whether that interaction pattern relates to the company's own objectives. In detail, this means analysis and planning the width, depth and closeness of relationships.

Our current research into the network of relationships surrounding a company shows little consistency between companies' interactions in their various relationships. There is no necessary reason for there being such consistency and strong arguments for the contrary. However, so far the clearly developing impression is that this inconsistency is unconscious rather than conscious.

Finally, an understanding of buyer–seller relationships for any participant in those relationships depends on being able to understand the definition of the situation and the expectations of the other party in a relationship and parties in a network. We believe that there is a strong tendency in the academic literature to look at networks as entities in themselves. This reified network restricts our abilities to explain the actions of any individual within that network in terms of its definition of the situation and its view of its own defined network. For the practising manager, this is a reaffirmation of the nature of marketing – that the good marketer is a person who can stand outside his own company and see that company in the eyes of those customers and competitors which surround it. It is also a reaffirmation of the ideas of the symbolic interactionists in trying to understand society. They reacted against those who had taken a structural-functionalist view of individual action and society as a whole. They emphasized the importance of looking at individual meanings and individual definitions of situations. There is a strong parallel between that criticism and the approach of some recent network ideas.

Our continuing work is to try to understand the patterns of meanings and the beliefs which guide managers in their interactions with others in the increasingly complex networks in which they operate.

REFERENCES

Araujo, L. and Easton, G. (1986), "Competition in industrial markets: perceptions and frameworks", *3rd International IMP Research Seminar on International Marketing*, IRE, September.

Axelsson, B. and Easton, G. (Eds) (1993), *Industrial Networks: A New View of Reality*, Routledge, London.

Campbell, N. C. G. (1984), "The structure and stability of industrial market networks: developing a research methodology", *First IMP Conference on Research Developments in International Marketing*, UMIST, Manchester, September.

Campbell, N. C. G. and Cunningham, M. T. (1984a), "Customer analysis for strategy development in industrial markets", *Strategic Management Journal*, Vol. 4, pp. 369–80.

Campbell, N. C. G. and Cunningham, M. T. (1984b), "Managing customer relationships: the challenge of deploying scarce managerial resources", *Research Seminar on Industrial Marketing*, Stockholm School of Economics, September.

Clark, K., Ford, D., Saren, M. and Thomas, R. (1995), "Technology Strategy in UK firms", *Technology Analysis & Strategic Management*, Vol. 7 No. 2, pp. 169–90.

Cunningham, M. T. (1986), "The British approach to Europe", in Turnbull, P. W. and Valla J. P. (Eds), *Strategies for International Industrial Marketing*, Croom Helm, London, pp. 165–203.

Cunningham, M. T. and Homse, E. (1986), "Controlling the marketing-purchasing interface: resource deployment and organizational issues", *Industrial Marketing and Purchasing*, Vol. 1 No. 2, pp. 3–25.

Cunningham, M. T. and Turnbull, P. W. (1982), "Inter-organizational personal contact patterns", in Håkansson, H. (Ed.), *International Marketing and Purchasing of Industrial Goods : An Interaction Approach*, John Wiley, New York, NY, pp. 304–15.

Easton, G. and Araujo, L. (1985), "The network approach: an articulation", *2nd Open IMP International Research Seminar*, University of Uppsala, September.

Fiocca, R. (1982), "Account portfolio analysis for strategy development", *Industrial Marketing Management*, April.

Ford, I. D. (1980), "The development of buyer–seller relationships in industrial markets", *European Journal of Marketing*, Vol. 14 Nos 5/6, pp. 339–54.

Ford, I. D. (1982), "The development of buyer–seller relationships in industrial marketings", in Håkansson, H. (Ed.), *International Marketing and Purchasing of Industrial Goods: An Interaction Approach*, John Wiley, New York, NY, pp. 288–304.

Ford, I. D. (1984), "Buyer/seller relationships in international industrial markets", *Industrial Marketing Management*, Vol. 13 No. 2, pp 101–13.

Ford, I. D. (Ed.) (1990), *Understanding Business Markets*, Academic Press, London.

Ford, D., McDowell, R. and Tomkins, C. (1996), "Relationship strategy, investments and decision making" in Iacobucci, D. (Ed.), *Networks in Marketing*, Sage, New York, NY.

Gilbert, X. and Strebel, P. (1988), "Developing competitive advantage", in Quinn, J. B., Mintzberg, H. and James, R. (Eds), *The Strategy process: Concepts, Contexts and Cases*, Prentice-Hall, Englewood Cliffs, NJ.

Hagg, I. and Johanson, J. (Eds) (1982), *Foretag i natverk*, SNS, Stockholm, Sweden.

Håkansson, H. (Ed.) (1982), *International Marketing and Purchasing of Industrial Goods: An Interaction Approach*, John Wiley, Chichester.

Håkansson, H. (1986a), "Relationships marketing strategies and competitive strength", in Turnbull, P. W. and Valla, J. P. (Eds), *Strategies for International Industrial Marketing*, Croom Helm, London.

Håkansson H. (1986b), "The Swedish approach to Europe", in Turnbull, P. and Valla, J. P. (Eds), *Strategies for International Industrial Marketing*, Croom Helm, London, pp. 149–157.

Håkansson, H. (1986c), "The export markets and Swedish companies", in Turnbull, P. and Valla, J. P. (Eds), *Strategies for International Industrial Marketing*, Croom Helm, London.

Håkansson, H. and Ostberg, C. (1975). "Industrial marketing: an organizational problem?", *Industrial Marketing Management*. Vol. 4, pp. 113–23.

Håkansson, H. and Wootz, B. (1979), "A framework of industrial buying and selling", *Industrial Marketing Management*, Vol. 8, pp 28–39.

Håkansson, H., Johanson, J. and Wootz, B. (1977), "Influence tactics in buyer–seller relationships", *Industrial Marketing Management*, Vol. 5, pp. 319–32.

Hallen, L. (1986), "Marketing organizations: a comparison of strategic marketing approaches", in Turnbull, P. W. and Valla, J. P. (Eds), *Strategy for Informational Industrial Marketing*, Croom Helm, London.

Hamfelt, C. and Lindberg, A. K. (1987), "Technological development and the individual's contact network", in Håkansson, H. (Ed.), *Industrial Technical Development: A Network Approach*, Croom Helm, London, pp. 177–200.

Hammarkvist, K. O., Håkansson, H. and Mattson L. G. (1982), *Marknadsforing for konkurrenskraft*, Liber, Malmo.

Henders, B. (1992), "Positions in industrial networks: marketing newsprint in the UK", unpublished PhD thesis, University of Uppsala.

Jarvis, L. P. and Wilcox, J. B. (1977), "True vendor loyalty or simply repeat purchase behavior?", *Industrial Marketing Management*, Vol. 6, pp. 9–16.

Johanson, J. and Mattson, L. G. (1985), "Marketing investments and market investments in industrial networks", *International Journal of Research in Marketing*, Vol. 2, pp. 185–95.

Johanson, J. and Vahlne, J. E. (1977), "The internationalisation process of the firm – a model of knowledge development and increasing foreign market commitments", *Journal of International Business*, Vol. 8 No. 1, pp. 23–32.

Johanson, J. and Wiedersheim-Paul, F. (1975), "The internationalisation of the firm – four Swedish case studies", *Journal of Management Studies*, Vol. 2 No. 3, pp. 305–22.

Johanson, J. and Wootz, B. (1984), "A framework for the study of marketing investment processes", in Turnbull, P. W. and Palinoda, S. (Eds), *Proceedings of the IMP Conference: Research Developments in International Marketing*, UMIST, Manchester, pp. 301–17.

Johanson, J. and Wootz, B. (1986), "The German approach to Europe", in Turnbull, P. W. and Valla, J. P. (Eds), *Strategies for International Industrial Marketing*, Croom Helm, London.

Kaplan, R. S. and Cooper, R. (1991), "Profit priorities from activity-based costing", *Harvard Business Review*, May-June, pp. 130–6.

Krapfel, R. E., Salmond, D. and Spekman, R. (1991), "A strategic approach to managing buyer–seller relationships", *European Journal of Marketing*, Vol. 25 No. 9, pp. 22–37.

McCall, G. J. (1970), "The social organization of relationships", in McCall, G. J. *et al.* (Eds), *Social Relationships*, Aldine Publishing Company, Chicago, pp. 3–14.

Mintzberg, H. (1988), "Opening up the definition of strategy", in Quinn, J. B., Mintzberg, H. and James, R. M. (Eds), *The Strategy Process, Concepts, Contexts and Cases*, Prentice-Hall, Englewood Cliffs, NJ.

Peters, T. J. and Waterman, R. H. (1982), *In Search of Excellence: Lessons from America's Best Run Companies*, Harper & Row, New York, NY.

Porter, M. E. (1981), *Competitive Strategy: Techniques for Analysing Industries and Competitors*, Macmillan, The Free Press, New York, NY.

Rusbult, C. E. (1980), "Commitment and satisfaction in romantic associations: a test of the investment model", *Journal of Experimental Social Psychology*, Vol. 16, pp. 172–86.

Shapiro, B. P., Rangan, V. K., Moriarty, R. T. and Ross, E. B. (1987), "Manage customers for profits", *Harvard Business Review*, September-October, pp. 101–08.

Smith, P. and Easton, G. (1986), "Network relationships: a longitudinal study", *3rd International IMP Research Seminar on International Marketing*. IRE, Lyon, September.

Turnbull, P. W. (1974), "The allocation of resources to marketing communications in industrial markets", *Industrial Marketing Management*, Vol. 3 No. 5, pp. 2975–318.

Turnbull, P. W. (1986), "Tri-partite interaction: the role of sales subsidiaries in international marketing", in Turnbull, P. W. and Paliwoda, S. J. (Eds), *Research in International Marketing*, Croom Helm, London, pp. 162–92.

Turnbull, P. W. (1990), "A review of portfolio planning models for industrial marketing and purchasing management", *European Journal of Marketing*, Vol. 24 No. 3, pp. 7–22.

Turnbull, P. W. and Cunningham, M. T. (1981), "The quality of relationships", in Turnbull, P. W. and Cunningham, M. T. (Eds), *International Marketing and Purchasing: A Survey among Marketing and Purchasing Executives in Five European Countries*, Macmillan, New York, NY, pp. 42–50 and pp. 81–9.

Turnbull, P. W. and Ellwood, S. (1984), "Internationalisation in the information technology industry", *Proceedings of International Research Seminar in Industrial Marketing*, Stockholm School of Economics, August.

Turnbull, P. W. and Holding, A. (1992), "Psychic distance in international markets", in Salle, R., Spencer, R. and Valla, J. P. (Eds), *Proceedings of the 8th IMP Conference*, Lyon.

Turnbull, P. W. and Valla, J. P. (1986), (Eds), *Strategies for International Industrial Marketing*, Croom Helm, London.

Turnbull, P. W. and Wilson, D. (1989), "Developing and protecting profitable customer relationships", *Industrial Marketing Management*, Vol. 18 No. 1, pp. 1–6.

Turnbull, P. W. and Zolkiewski, J. (1995), "Customer portfolios: sales costs and profitability", presented to the *11th IMP International Conference*, UMIST, Manchester.

Turner, R. H. (1970), *Family Interaction*. John Wiley, New York, NY.

Valla, J. P. (1985), "The development of marketing networks and the internationalisation process", 2nd International IMP Research Seminar, University of Uppsala, September.

Valla, J. P. (1986), "Industrial marketing strategies: looking for new ways", in Turnbull, P. W. and Valla, J. P. (Eds), *Strategies for International Industrial Marketing*, Croom Helm, London.

Valla, J. P. and Turnbull, P. W. (1986), "The dimensions of industrial marketing strategy", in Turnbull. P. W. and Valla, J. P. (Eds), *Strategies for International Industrial Marketing*, Croom Helm, London.

Williamson, O. E. (1979), "Transaction-cost economics: the governance of contractual relations", *Journal of Law and Economics*, Vol. 22 No. 2, pp. 233–61.

Williamson, O. E. (1981), "The economics of organization: the transaction cost approach", *Journal of Sociology*, Vol. 87, pp. 548–77.

Wilson, D. T. and Mummalaneni, V. (1986), "Bonding and commitment in buyer–seller relationships: a preliminary conceptualisation", *Journal of Industrial Marketing and Purchasing*, Vol. 1 No. 3, pp. 44–58.

Yorke, D. A. (1986), "Customer perceptions as a basis for the development of an international supplier's portfolio of market segments", *Industrial Marketing and Purchasing*, Vol. 1 No. 2, pp. 27–47.

1.2 An interaction approach

IMP Group

INTRODUCTION

In a joint research project with several researchers with different backgrounds there are always problems in developing a common theoretical framework. This was further complicated in this project by differences in language, approach and emphasis between the researchers. We were however fortunate in having similar *basic* approaches to the analysis of Industrial Marketing and Purchasing.[1] Extensive discussion within the project group led to the discovery of important concepts and assumptions which were shared by all. It is on this theoretical basis that the design and the methodology are built. These concepts and basic assumptions are now presented in this chapter.

RELATIONS TO PREVIOUS RESEARCH

Our theoretical framework can be traced back to two major theoretical models from outside the marketing literature. These are Inter-organizational Theory and the New Institutional Economic Theory. At the same time it is possible to relate our approach to earlier thinking in marketing and purchasing as well as some emerging trends in the marketing and purchasing literature.

Inter-organizational theory and marketing literature

Much of the work in inter-organizational theory involves attempts to apply theory and concepts from intra-organizational studies to problems where several organizational units are involved. Here the focus of attention is on relationships between those organizations rather than within each individual organization. Works in this area can be classified into three groups, based upon differences in the relation between the organization and its environment as proposed by Van de Ven *et al.* (1975). It is also possible to classify marketing literature along similar lines, again depending on the perspective of researchers when dealing with organization–environmental relationships. Such a categorization of the marketing literature has been presented by Sweeney (1972). We will consider the categorization of the inter-organizational literature and the marketing literature in parallel:

(a) Organization based studies. The environment is seen as an external limitation for the organization in this group of studies. Inter-organizational studies which can be included in this group are those which examine the internal organization based on an open systems approach. Here, the organization is seen as being dependent on its environment, for example in obtaining access to certain inputs. At the same time the organization seeks to manipulate or control parts of its environment. Because of this, the characteristics of the environment will influence the shape of the internal organization structure. This organization–environment connection is central and is analysed in many studies.[2]

The predominant current viewpoint in marketing shares this perspective. It is characterized by Sweeney as the "organizational system perspective", and is exemplified in the so-called "managerial approach" to the study of marketing. In this, marketing researchers are concerned with techniques for the development and management of product, price, distribution, and promotional strategies to optimize desired market response. The boundaries of marketing are defined as those "publics" which have a "... potential impact on the resource converting efficiency of the organization" (Kotler and Levy, 1969). It is implicit in this approach that buyers are passive and only react to the stimuli of the seller by buying or not buying. The selling firm is the active partner in the buyer–seller relationship. Further, this relationship is largely seen to be between the seller, and some generic "market", rather than with individual customers.[3]

It is worth noting at this stage that a side effect of this approach to the study of marketing has been that the study of buyers has developed along somewhat separate lines from the study of sellers. Here, researchers have analysed the factors which affect both the individual and company buying processes, e.g. previous purchase experience, the importance of "task" and "non-task" variables, the effect of different organizational forms and the degree of formality in hypothesized decision-making processes. These analyses have concentrated on the stages in a *discrete* purchase. Thus, there has been an emphasis in the industrial buyer behaviour literature on single rather than continuing purchases from a particular supplier. Additionally, the study of the buying process has taken place with relatively scant regard to the influence of the selling firm in that process.[4]

Thus, the first group of studies includes two distinct and *separate* approaches to the study of what occurs in industrial markets. On the one hand, there is an analysis of the manipulation of marketing variables by the seller to achieve a desired market response. On the other hand, there is the separate analysis of a single buying process and the factors which affect that process, from which lessons can be drawn for marketing.

(b) Studies based on several organizations. In this second group of inter-organization studies, the organization is seen as part of a group of interacting units. Studies within this category are often based on the dependence between the particular organization and its environment as defined by studies from category (a). In order to obtain necessary resources, the organization is seen to develop relations with a number of other organizational units and thus it enters into a network of relationships.

Two aspects of this network have mainly been studied. Firstly, the characteristics of the different organizations have been investigated as they relate to the other organizations within the same network. Secondly, the links between the units have been analysed in terms of, for example, formalization, intensity, and standardization.[5]

The parallel to these studies in the marketing area are those from a "distribution system perspective". In this, the field is viewed as a system of interconnected institutions performing the economic functions required to bring about exchange of goods or services. This perspective is, of course, broader than the organizational system perspective. The boundaries of marketing at this level of aggregation include those institutions involved in the distribution of goods within the society. The focus is on the nature of the functions being performed by the system and on the structure, performance and inter-relationships of the institutions which comprise the system. Aspects of these areas which have received study are the division of roles and responsibilities between different members of a manufacturing–distribution channel, the conflicts between different levels and within levels in the channel as well as the patterns of power and communication which exist between them.[6] During recent years, a number of works on more general aspects of marketing and purchasing have appeared which fit within this group.[7]

(c) Studies of the organization in a societal context. In this third category, the organization is seen as an integrated part in a larger social system. In order to describe and understand how a certain organization functions it is necessary, according to this approach, to see the organization in relation

to the larger system. The organization is part of what some authors call "inter-organization collectives" and these groups influence to a large extent the actions of the organization.[8] The view of marketing from a "social system perspective" sees it as a social process which evolves to facilitate the society's needs for efficient and effective exchange of values. There is a clear distinction between this approach and its emphasis on analysis of the exchange process, and the organizational system approach which is concerned with the technology employed to execute that exchange process.

The view of marketing from a social system perspective is little developed. The majority of the marketing literature can be classified into group (a) above, while our approach belongs to group (b). There are also some minor attempts in our study to go in the direction of the works in group (c). However, the major focus of our attention is on the units (the buying and selling firms) and the link between them (the process of interaction).

The new institutionalists

The second theoretical area outside the marketing literature that we have built upon has been characterized by Williamson (1975) as "the New institutionalists". This line of thought within micro-economic theory is based on a criticism of certain aspects of traditional economic theory. Williamson discerns two alternative ways in which the exchange (transaction) may be handled between technologically separable units in a production or transformation process. Firstly, the transaction can take place within a market setting. On the other hand it can be internalized in one organizational unit (a hierarchy), i.e. two successive stages in the production process are vertically integrated in a hierarchically built organization. There are certain deficiencies in markets that favour the internalization of transactions. Similarly, there are also deficiencies in the way organizations function that operate in favour of keeping the transactions in the market, i.e. keeping the successive production stages under separate control and reaching agreements on buying and selling, through, for example, negotiated contracts.

Williamson argues that many transactions which are internalized in one organization could be carried out by separate organizations, from the point of view of technological separability. However, the co-ordination of these units by means of market relations involves disadvantages. Markets may be considered to operate inefficiently in certain instances, due to human and environmental factors. When the environment is characterized by complexity and uncertainty, then the bounded rationality of man makes it very costly to design and negotiate viable contracts. An example would be between two subsequent stages in a steel mill. Furthermore, the parties to such transactions may become very dependent on each other. This evolves into a small-numbers bargaining relation. Although the parties in a formal sense retain the option of selecting partners in the market, this is not a viable alternative due to transaction costs. Thus it will be very costly to design and negotiate contracts with new partners. This is because it is often difficult for one party to achieve information parity with the other party, which is necessary for a "fair" deal. Man is not just characterized by bounded rationality but also by opportunism ("self-seeking interest with guile"), and this makes markets operate inefficiently when there is an imbalanced dependence between the parties.

The high transaction costs that would be associated with operations in markets of the atomistic kind provide incentives for the internalization of such expensive transactions in vertically integrated units. Conflicts are considered to be settled in a more efficient and less costly way within an organization (by fiat rather than by haggling), and sequential, adaptive decision-making is facilitated. Opportunism is checked by control and audit.

However, there are also conditions counteracting the internalization of transactions. Firstly markets often do not operate as rigidly, and organizations do not operate as smoothly as depicted in the idealized extreme models (internal control is made more difficult as organizations grow in size), and thus transaction costs increase. Also there are checks on the opportunism in markets, e.g.

courtesy, the interest in establishing conditions for future business and the effects of the firm's reputation on business deals with others. Imbalances are not always exploited in the short term in a way that increases transaction costs. Secondly, transactions do not take place in an attitudinally neutral setting. The establishment of satisfying exchange relations (an "atmosphere") modifies and is modified by the transactions.

Thus there are several factors that influence transaction costs and there are also intermediary settings for the exchange relations. Many industrial markets can be seen as such intermediary forms. Here we find such market characteristics as established small-numbers bargaining relations and lack of information parity. There are also organizational characteristics such as checks on opportunism due to established social relationships. Often a specific atmosphere has evolved that is characterized both by environmental and human factors.

Our theoretical framework is closely related to both "inter-organizational theory" and the "new institutionalists". At the same time it is directly related to evolutions in the literature of marketing, and particularly to the emphasis on inter-company relationships. This has emerged from those studies having a distribution system perspective and more recently from those empirically based studies which have emphasized the importance of inter-company relations.

OUTLINE OF THE MODEL

Our approach to industrial markets – *The Interaction Approach* – is based on the theoretical idea described earlier. It is also built on a number of factors which our earlier empirical studies indicate are important in industrial markets and which appear to have been largely neglected in previous research:

Firstly, that both buyer and seller are active participants in the market. Each may engage in search to find a suitable buyer or seller, to prepare specifications of requirements or offerings and to manipulate or attempt to control the transaction process.

Secondly, the relationship between buyer and seller is frequently long term, close and involving a complex pattern of interaction between and within each company. The marketers' and buyers' task in this case may have more to do with maintaining these relationships than with making a straightforward sale or purchase.

Thirdly, the links between buyer and seller often become institutionalized into a set of roles that each party expects the other to perform, for example the division of product development responsibility, or the decision as to who should carry out inventory and test products. These processes may require significant adaptations in organization or operation by either or both companies. Clearly, these relationships can involve both conflict as well as co-operation.

Fourthly, close relationships are often considered in the context of continuous raw material or component supply. However, we would emphasize the importance of previous purchases, mutual evaluation and the associated relationship between the companies in the case of infrequently purchased products. Further, we are concerned in this research with the nature of the relationship between a buying and selling company which may be built up during the course of a single major transaction.

Our focus is generally on a two party relationship, but the approach can be applied also to a several party relationship. This, indeed, may be necessary to accommodate the study of the simultaneous interactions between several buying and selling companies in a particular industry. The main components of our approach are illustrated in Figure 1.

In the figure we identify four groups of variables that describe and influence the interaction between buying and selling companies:

1. Variables describing the *parties* involved, both as organizations and as individuals.
2. Variables describing the *elements and process of interaction*.

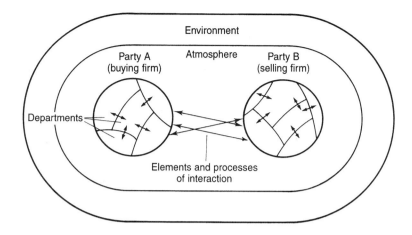

Figure 1 Main elements of the interaction model.

3. Variables describing the *environment* within which the interaction takes place.
4. Variables describing the *atmosphere* affecting and affected by the interaction.

The approach does not only involve an analysis of these groups of variables but it also includes the relations between them.

THE INTERACTION MODEL

The marketing and purchasing of industrial goods is seen as an interaction process between two parties within a certain environment. Our way of analysing industrial marketing and purchasing has four basic elements which in turn are sub-divided. These are:

1. The interaction process.
2. The participants in the interaction process.
3. The environment within which interaction takes place.
4. The atmosphere affecting and affected by the interaction.

In this section we will describe each of these four basic elements more extensively. The major focus here is on *description* of buyer–seller relationships and interactions. Only secondary emphasis is placed here on the interplay between the separate elements which we discuss.

The interaction process

We have already noted that the relationships between buying and selling companies in industrial markets are frequently long term. Thus, it is important in our analysis to distinguish between the individual "Episodes" in a relationship, e.g. the placing or delivering of a particular order, and the longer-term aspects of that relationship which both affects and may be affected by each episode. We shall consider these individual episodes first:

(a) Episodes

The episodes which occur in an industrial market relationship involve exchange between two parties. There are four elements which are exchanged:

(i)   Product or service exchange;
(ii)   Information exchange;
(iii)   Financial exchange;
(iv)   Social exchange.

(i) Product or service exchange. The exchange of product or service is often the core of the exchange. As a result, the characteristics of the product or service involved are likely to have a significant effect on the relationship as a whole. For example, one major aspect of the product or service which seems important is the uncertainty with which they are associated. The exchange process will be quite different depending on whether or not the product is able to fulfil a buyer need that is easy to identify, and for which the characteristics of an appropriate product are easy to specify. It will also be important whether either buyer or seller is uncertain as to the requirements or resources of their opposite number.[9]

(ii) Information exchange. Several aspects of information exchange are of interest. The content of information is, of course, important. This can, for example, be characterized by the degree to which technical, economic, or organizational questions dominate the exchange. Furthermore, the width and depth of the information for each of these groups of questions should also be of importance. Information can be transferred between the parties by either personal or impersonal means. Impersonal communication is often used to transfer basic technical and/or commercial data. Personal channels are more likely to be used for the transfer of "soft data" concerning, for example, the use of a product, the conditions of an agreement between the parties, or supportive or general information about either party. Finally, the formality of the information exchange is important. The degree of formality may depend on wider organizational characteristics which can affect the nature of the interaction process and the relationship between the companies as a whole.

(iii) Financial exchange. Money is the third element. The quantity of money exchange is an indicator of the economic importance of the relationship. Another important aspect is connected with the need to exchange money from one currency to another and the uncertainties in these exchanges over time.

(iv) Social exchange. Social exchange has an important function in reducing uncertainties between the two parties (Håkansson and Östberg, 1975). This is particularly significant when there exists spatial or cultural distance between the two parties or where the experience of the two parties is limited. Social exchange episodes may be important in themselves in avoiding short term difficulties between the two parties and in maintaining a relationship in the periods between transactions. However, perhaps the most important function of social exchange is in the long term process by which successive social exchange episodes gradually interlock the two firms with each other. Many aspects of the agreements between the buying and selling firms are not fully formalized nor based on legal criteria. Instead the relationship is based on mutual trust.[10] Building up this trust is a social process which takes time and must be based on personal experience, and on the successful execution of the three other elements of exchange. Furthermore, the need for mutual trust and the requirement of social exchange varies with differences in the elements exchanged in different relationships. Examples are variations in the amount of money exchanged, in the need for large amounts of informational exchange or in the complexity of the product exchanged. However, the development of trust is also dependent upon experience in exchange of the other three elements.

(b) Relationships

Social exchange episodes are, as has been described above, critical in the build up of long-term relationships. Exchanges of product and service (which can be in both directions) and of the other elements of money and information can also lead to the build up of long-term relations. The routinization of these exchange episodes over a period of time leads to clear expectations in both parties of the roles or responsibilities of their opposite numbers. Eventually these expectations become *institutionalized* to such an extent that they may not be questioned by either party and may have more in common with the traditions of an industry or a market than rational decision-making by either of the parties (Ford, 1978).

The communication or exchange of information in the episodes successively builds up inter-organizational contact patterns and role relationships. These *contact patterns* can consist of individuals and groups of people filling different roles, operating in different functional departments and transmitting different messages of a technical, commercial, or reputational nature. These patterns can interlock the two parties to a greater or lesser extent and they are therefore an important variable to consider in analysing buyer–seller relationships. It is important to note that information and social exchange between parties can continue for a considerable time without there being an exchange of product or money. Thus, literature, specification development, and visits between companies can occur before the first order is placed or between widely spaced individual orders.

Another important aspect of the relationship is the *adaptations* which one or other party may make in either the elements exchanged or the process of exchange. Examples of this are adaptations in product, in financial arrangements, in information routines or social relations. These adaptations can occur during the process of a single, major transaction or over the time of a relationship involving many individual transactions. The benefits of these adaptations can be in cost reduction, increased revenue, or differential control over the exchange. Adaptations in specific episodes may also be made in order to modify the overall relationship. Thus one party may make a decision not to offer special products to a customer out of a wish to be more distantly involved with that customer, rather than being closely involved and/or heavily dependent on it.

The manipulation of different aspects of adaptation is of course a critical marketing and purchasing issue. Although adaptations by either party can occur in an unconscious manner as a relationship develops, it is important to emphasize the conscious strategy which is involved in many of these adaptations. Thus, modifications to product, delivery, pricing, information routines and even the organization itself are part of the seller's marketing strategy. Similarly, the buying organization will consider adaptations in its own product requirements, its production methods, the price it is prepared to accept, its information needs and the modification of its own delivery or stocking policies in order to accommodate the selling organization.

The interacting parties

The process of interaction and the relationship between the organizations will depend not only on the elements of the interaction but also on the characteristics of the parties involved. This includes both the characteristics of the two organizations and the individuals who represent them. The organization factors include the companies' position in the market as manufacturer, wholesaler, etc. It also includes the products which the selling company offers, the production and application technologies of the two parties and their relative expertise in these areas. Below, we will discuss some of the major factors in more detail:

(a) Technology. Technical issues are often critical in buyer–seller interaction in industrial markets. The aims of the interaction process can be interpreted as tying the production technology of the seller to the application technology of the buyer. Thus the characteristics of the two technological systems and the differences between them give the basic conditions for the interaction. These basic conditions influence all the dimensions of the interaction processes: for example, the requirements for adaptations, mutual trust and contact patterns. Similarly, if the two organizations are separated by a wide gulf of technical expertise then the relationship between them

can be expected to be quite different from a situation where the two companies are close in their level of expertise.

(b) Organizational size, structure, and strategy. The size and the power of the parties give them basic positions from which to interact. In general, a large firm with considerable resources has a greater possibility of dominating its customers or suppliers than has a small firm. The structure of each organization and the extent of centralization, specialization and formalization influence the interaction process in several ways: this influence is seen in the number and categories of persons who are involved. It also affects the procedure of the exchange, the communications media used, the formalization of the interaction and the substance of what is exchanged – the nature of product or service and the finance which is involved. In the short term, organizational structures can be considered as the frameworks within which interaction takes place. In the longer term, it is possible that these organizational structures may be modified *by* the emerging interaction process or indeed by individual episodes.

The strategies of the parties are, of course, important influencing variables on the relationships. Later on we will describe how strategies can be formulated and analysed in relation to our theoretical approach.

(c) Organizational experience. A further factor is the company's experience not only in the relationship but also its experience and activities outside it. This experience may be the result of many other similar relationships and will equip the company with knowledge about the management of these kinds of relationships. It may also affect the level of importance attached to any one relationship, and hence the company's commitment to that relationship.

The variables which we will discuss in the next section under the title of The Interaction Environment will be mediated by the experience of specific individuals in a company as well as by the more generalized "experience" of a company. Thus the company's experience in particular markets will enable it to be more or less fitted for dealing in that market. Similarly, its experience of international operations will affect its willingness and ability to establish international relationships.

(d) Individuals. At least two individuals, one from each organization, are involved in a relationship. These are usually a buyer and a salesman. More commonly, several individuals from different functional areas, at different levels in the hierarchy and fulfilling different roles, become involved in inter-company personal interactions. They exchange information, develop relationships and build up strong social bonds which influence the decisions of each company in the business relationship.

The varied personalities, experience, and motivations of each company's representatives will mean that they will take part in the social exchange differently. Their reactions in individual episodes could condition the ways in which the overall relationship builds up. Further, the role, level, and function of central persons in the interaction affect the chances of future development occurring in the relationship.

Individual experience may result in preconceptions concerning certain suppliers or customers, for example those in a certain country. These will affect attitudes and behaviour towards those buyers or suppliers. The process of learning from experience on both an individual and corporate level is communicated to and affects detailed "Episodes" in interaction. Additionally, the experience gained in individual episodes aggregates to a total experience. Indeed, the experience of a single episode can radically change attitudes which may then be held over a long period of time.

The interaction environment

The interaction between a buying and selling firm cannot be analysed in isolation, but must be considered in a wider context. This wider context has several aspects:

(a) Market structure. Firstly, a relationship must be considered as one of a number of similar relationships existing either nationally or internationally within the same market. The structure of this market depends in part on the concentration of both buyers and sellers and the stability or rate of change of the market and its constituent members. It also consists of the extent to which the market can be viewed as strictly national or needs to be thought of in wider international terms. The extent of buyer or seller concentration determines the number of alternatives available to any firm. This has a clear bearing on the pressure to interact with a certain counterpart within the market.

(b) Dynamism. The degree of dynamism within a relationship and in the wider market affects the relationship in two ways that are opposite to each other. Firstly, a close relationship increases the knowledge of one party of the likely actions of the other party and hence its ability to make forecasts based on this inside information. Secondly, and conversely, in a dynamic environment the opportunity cost of reliance on a single or small number of relationships can be very high when expressed in terms of the developments of other market members.

(c) Internationalization. The internationalization of the buying or selling market is of interest as it affects either firm's motivations in developing international relationships. This in turn may affect the company's organization, in needing sales subsidiaries or overseas buying units, the special knowledge it may require, e.g. in languages and international trade and its more general attitudes.

(d) Position in the manufacturing channel. A further aspect of the environment which must be brought into consideration is the position of an individual relationship in an extended "channel" stretching from primary producer to final consumer. Thus, for example, manufacturer A may sell electric components to manufacturer B, who then incorporates these components into actuators that are sold to manufacturer C, who adds them to valves. These valves, with many other products, may form the stock of distributor D and so on. The marketing strategy of A may thus be influenced by and directed at several markets at different stages in the channel. Clearly his relationship with buying company B will be affected by both A's and B's relationship with C and other subsequent organizations.

(e) The social system. As well as the effects of both horizontal market and vertical channel influences on a relationship, we must also consider the characteristics of the wider environment surrounding a particular relationship – the social system. This is particularly relevant in the international context where attitudes and perceptions on a generalized level can be important obstacles when trying to establish an exchange process with a certain counterpart. An example of this is nationalistic buying practices or generalized attitudes to the reliability of buyers or customers from a particular country. Other aspects of these general influences concern regulations and constraints on business, for example exchange rates and trade regulations. There are other, more narrow social system variables which will surround a particular industry or market. For example, a supplier who has not previously delivered to a certain type of customer, e.g. in the automobile industry, has to learn both the "language" and the rules before it will be accepted in that industry.

The atmosphere

The relationships between buying and selling firms are dynamic in being affected by the individual episodes which take place within them. At the same time they have the stability which derives from the length of the relationship, its routinization and the clear expectations which become held by both parties. The relationship is influenced by the characteristics of the parties involved and the nature of the interaction itself. This in turn is a function of the technology involved and the environment within which the interaction takes place. Organizational strategy can also affect both the short-term episodes and the long-term relationships between the parties. One of the main aspects of the relationship which may be affected by conscious planning is the overall atmosphere of the relationship. This atmosphere can be described in terms of the power–dependence relationship which exists between the companies, the state of conflict or co-operation and overall closeness or distance of the relationship as well as by the companies' mutual expectations. These variables are not measured in a direct way in this study. Instead the atmosphere is considered as a group of intervening variables, defined by various combinations of environmental, company specific, and interaction process characteristics. The atmosphere is a product of the relationship, and it also mediates the influence of the groups of variables. There are reasons for the buying and selling firm to both develop a high degree of closeness with their counterpart as well as to avoid such closeness. There are both advantages and disadvantages connected with different atmospheres. We can analyse the reasons involved with regard to an economic (cost–benefit) dimension and a control dimension.

(a) The economic dimension. There are several types of cost that can be reduced for a firm by a closer interaction with a buying or selling firm. One of these costs is that which Williamson (1975) describes as the transaction cost. A closer connection means that it may be possible to handle distribution, negotiations, and administration more efficiently. Another type of cost which may be reduced is the production cost. A close relationship gives opportunities to find a more optimal division of the production process between the supplier and the customer. The supplier and buyer may reallocate some production processes between each other or co-operate in the design so as to make the product easier to produce or for the customer to develop further. There are also increased revenues which can be gained by a closer interaction. Both sides may achieve positive gains by better use of the other's competence, facilities, and other resources. New products can be developed together or old products may be redesigned. Furthermore, the parties can also often give each other valuable technical and commercial information.

(b) The control dimension. Another important reason for closer connection with a counterpart can be to reduce the uncertainty associated with that input or output by increasing its control over the other company. Such an increase in control improves the firm's chances of forecasting and determining that part of its environment. The ability to control a relationship is related to the *perceived* power of the two parties. Perceptions of power are likely to be unclear in the early stages of a relationship and one of the key functions of initial exchange episodes will be to enable each party to come to an understanding of each other's power. Even so, perceptions of power may change over the life of a relationship. They will, in turn, be related to the resources perceived to be possessed by each party as well as to their relative dependence on this individual relationship. Inter-organizational power will depend on the ability of either party to reward or coerce each other through exchange, or their relative expertise and access to information, as well as on their referent power, i.e. the value which one party places on association with another because of its wish to learn from and act similarly to the other.

The power of organization A over B is directly related to the dependence of B on A. The dependence on any one relationship by an organization is a major element in the wish to restrict interaction. Investment of time and resources in one relationship has an opportunity cost related to the value of those investments in another relationship. Also, the level of dependence on one relationship affects the vulnerability of an organization to the exercise of power by its opposite number. In everyday terms this is exemplified by a selling company which has a large proportion of its sales to one single buying company. It is the management of the closeness of the relationship, with its associated power and dependence, which is perhaps a crucial aspect of many industrial marketing and purchasing strategies.

Summing up this discussion of the reasons for a close interaction, we can conclude that relationships are established and used in order to gain economic benefits, lower costs, higher profits, and/or improving the organization's control of some part of its environment. A critical aspect of the management of these relationships is the extent to which the firm can balance its inter-dependence with others. The firm must seek to balance the advantages of a close relationship, perhaps in terms of cost reduction and ease and speed of interaction against the opportunity costs of that single relationship and the dependence which it involves.

SUMMARY

In Figure 2 we have tried to illustrate the different variables which have been presented here. The model shows the short-term and long-term aspects of the "Interaction Process" between buying and selling companies A and B. The short-term "Exchange Episodes" involve product–service, financial, information, and social exchange. These are separated from the longer term processes of "Adaptations" and "Institutionalization".

Both the short- and long-term aspects of the interaction are considered as being influenced by the characteristics of the organizations and individuals involved (circles A and B). Additionally, we see the interaction taking place within an "Environment" consisting of the vertical and horizontal market structure and general social influences.

Finally, we include "Atmosphere". As the company's relationship develops so the parties' views of their relative power may change. Previous research has shown quite clearly that the interaction between buying and selling companies is conditioned by a clear and commonly held view of the relative power of the parties to the interaction and the areas to which this power extends. At the same time we have noted that conflict can characterize these relationships as well as co-operation. Thus it is quite possible for a company to have one relationship with a particular buyer–seller which is characterized by co-operation. It is also possible for the company to have a relationship with another company which is characterized by co-operation on the *minimum* level, in order for transactions to take place but thereafter is marked by frequent conflict over means and allocations of resources. Thus the detailed interaction process is subject to the perceptions of both parties of the overall state of relations between them – power–dependence and conflict-co-operation.

The Figure shows that it is possible to identify and study connections between the variables on different levels. Firstly, at the most general level, one variable group can be related to another, for example it is possible to relate the parties in the exchange process to the interaction environment. Secondly, it is possible to investigate the linkage between variables in one variable group, for

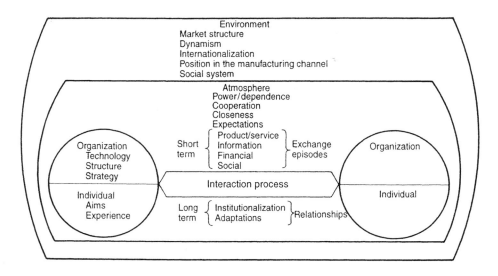

Figure 2   An illustration of the interaction model.

example between the elements of exchange and the process of exchange. Thirdly, it can be valuable to explore the relation between the variables within a sub-group. An example of this is the connection between the characteristics of the product and the characteristics of the information which is exchanged. Some of the relationships between the variables mentioned above are more obvious and are documented in other studies. Others are more hypothetical and have never been studied systematically. Furthermore, the whole picture has never been studied as a totality. Our approach is to select combinations of variables from the environment, company, and interaction categories. This provides a number of "interaction atmospheres", within which different linkages are studied as well as systematic comparisons made.

IMPLICATIONS FOR MANAGEMENT

Before starting to discuss how our theoretical model has been used in this project we would like to briefly indicate the kind of help this model can give practitioners. The practical use of a theoretical model is, of course, that it helps to structure the "world" and thereby the problems. A new model can as a consequence give new opportunities because problems which were neglected earlier may be identified and solved. We shall now give some examples of problems that can be identified for managers of marketing or purchasing departments in firms working in certain industrial markets. We shall start with the marketing side.

Marketing management

The key problems in marketing according to the marketing mix model are (1) allocation of resources and (2) design of individual competitive means.[11] In the same way we can use the interactive model and identify two groups of important problems. These groups have been named (1) limitation and (2) handling problems.[12]

Two different kinds of limitation problems can be specified. The first problem concerns the marketing firm's overall limitation of its activities in certain types of relationships. This must be achieved because the demands on its technology, organization and knowledge, etc., are closely related to the type of relationships. For example, it is very difficult for a seller to have customers with very high demands on the quality and performance of the product *and* customers which just want a standard quality as cheaply as possible. The marketing firm, thus, has to limit itself to be an efficient counterpart in a certain type of relationship and to design its technology, organization, and knowledge in accordance with this.

The second type of limitation problems for the marketing firm are concerned with its individual counterparts. The question is, should customers be treated in a uniform way, or should some customers get special treatment? Normally there is a very clear difference between how those "special" customers – often those who buy most – get special services, extra attention and so on. The customers are in other words often dealt with quite differently and it is therefore necessary for the marketing firm to develop a policy on these questions.

The handling problem concerns both the long-term aspects of the relationships as well as the short-term exchanges of different elements. The long-term problems concern handling the power–dependence and the co-operation–conflict aspects of the relationships. The aim is to have a controlled development of the relationships. This can sometimes mean closer co-operation and sometimes the opposite. The short-term problems are primarily related to attaining an efficient way of handling the elements (the different exchange processes) with individuals as well as groups of customers. One problem area, is, for example, to design one's own adaptations and to influence the counterpart's adaptations in order to make exchange processes easier. The way of solving the short-term handling problems affect, of course, the long-term problems. Adaptation is an example of one aspect of the power–dependence relationship. This means that the long- and short-term problems in a relationship cannot be divided; they can better be seen as short- and long-term effects of all of the activities which constitute the relationship.

Purchasing management

The key problem in purchasing that can be identified using the interaction model are (1) to develop an appropriate structure of suppliers and (2) to handle each relationship in an efficient way. The second group of problems are the same as the handling problems for the marketing side and we, therefore, can leave them aside and concentrate on the first group.

A supplier can be seen as an external resource by the buying firm. The buyer's aim in relationships is to use these external resources in an efficient way. But in order to be attractive as a counterpart, the purchasing firm has to have some internal resources. One strategic purchasing question, therefore, is to find and maintain a balance between the external and the internal resources. The problem in the short term can be formulated as using these external resources as much as possible given the internal resources of the buying firm.

Another problem is that suppliers can be used in different ways. In some situations the purchasing firm may want to use a supplier's ability to develop and design a special product, while in other situations it may just want to use the supplier's ability to produce a standardized product at low cost. The counterparts are used in different ways and a problem is then to find the right combination of suppliers, i.e. to develop an appropriate external resources structure.

NOTES

1. The background of the research teams can be seen in the following references: Cunningham and White (1974), Cunningham and White (1973/6), Cunningham and Kettlewood (1976), Cunningham and Roberts (1974), Ford (1976), (1978), Håkansson and Wootz (1975a), (1975b), (1975c), (1975d), (1979), Håkansson, Johanson, and Wootz (1977), Håkansson et al. (1979), Håkansson and Östberg (1975), Johanson and Vahlne (1977), Johanson and Wiedersheim-Paul (1975), Kutschker (1975), Kutschker and Roth (1975), Kirsch, Lutschewitz, Kutschker (1977), Lutschewitz and Kutschker (1977), Kirsch and Kutchker (1978), Kutschker and Kirsch (1978), and Valla (1978a), (1978b), (1978c), (1978d), and (1978e).
2. Important works within this category: Dill (1958), Burns and Stalker (1961), Thompson (1967), Emery and Trist (1968), Aiken and Hage (1968), and Hall (1972).
3. Important works within this area are textbooks such as Kotler (1976) and McCarthy (1978). These deal mainly with consumer marketing but these and similar works have formed a basis for the development of literature in the industrial marketing field. Examples within industrial marketing which share this approach are Corey (1976), Hill et al. (1975), Hill (1972), and Wilson (1972) and (1973).
4. Important works regarding purchasing using this approach are textbooks such as England (1970), Lee and Dobler (1971) and Westing, Fine, and Zenz (1976) and research oriented books like Buckner (1966), Robinson and Faris (1967), and Webster and Wind (1972a). The two most well-known models of purchasing are Webster and Wind (1972b) and Sheth (1973).
5. Important works within this category: Levine and White (1961), Litwak and Hylton (1962), Evan (1966), Warren (1967), Marrett (1971), and Aldrich (1972).
6. See for example Rosenberg and Stern (1970), Little (1970), Heskett, Stern, and Beier (1970), El-Ansary and Stern (1972), Hunt and Nevin (1974), Angelmar (1976), and Reve and Stern (1979).
7. Examples are Blois (1975), Guillet de Monthoux (1975), Mattsson (1975), Jarvis and Wilcox (1977), Melin (1977), Webster (1979), and Arndt (1979).
8. Important works are: Levine and White (1972), Warren (1973), Van de Ven et al. (1975), Zeitz (1975), and Aldrich (1979).
9. Need uncertainty has for example been used as a variable by Håkansson, Johanson, and Wootz (1977) in order to describe this aspect.
10. See for example Macaulay (1963).
11. See IMP Group (1982).
12. This section builds on Håkansson, Johanson, and Wootz (1977), and Håkansson and Wootz (1979).

REFERENCES

Aiken, M. and Hage, J. Organizational interdependence and intra-organizational structure. *American Sociological Review*, **33:6**, 912–30 (1968).

Aldrich, H. E. Cooperation and conflict between organizations in the manpower training system: an organization–environment perspective. In Negandhi, A. R. (ed) *Conflict and Power in Complex Organizations: An Inter-Institutional Perspective*. Kent State University Press, Kent, Ohio (1972).

Aldrich, H. E. *Organizations and Environments*. Prentice-Hall, Englewood Cliffs, New Jersey (1979).

Angelmar, R. Structure and determinants of bargaining behaviour in a distribution channel simulation: A content analytic approach. *Unpublished Ph.D. Dissertation*. Northwestern University, New York (1976).

Arndt, J. Toward a concept of domesticated markets. *Journal of Marketing*, **43**, (4), 69–76, (1979).

Blois, K. J. Supply contracts in the Galbraithian planning system. *Journal of Industrial Economics*, **24**, (1), 29–39 (1975).

Buckner, H. *How British Industry Buys*. Hutchinson, London (1966).

Burns, T. and Stalker, G. M. *The Management of Innovation*. Tavistock Publications, London (1961).

Corey, E. R. *Industrial Marketing: Cases and Concepts*, 2nd ed., Prentice-Hall, Englewood Cliffs, New Jersey (1976).

Cunningham, M. T. and Kettlewood, K. Source loyalty in freight transport buying. *European Journal of Marketing*, **10**, (1), 60–79 (1976).

Cunningham, M. T. and Roberts, D. A. The role of customer service in industrial marketing. *European Journal of Marketing*, **8**, (1), 15–28 (1974).

Cunningham, M. T. and White, J. G. The determinants of choice of supplier. *European Journal of Marketing*, **7**, (3), 189–202 (1973).

Cunningham, M. T. and White, J. G. The behaviour of industrial buyers in their search for suppliers of machine tools. *Journal of Management Studies*, **11**, (2), 115–128 (1974).

Dill, W. R. Environment as an influence on managerial autonomy. *Administrative Science Quarterly*, **2**, (4), 409–443 (1958).

El-Ansary, A. I. and Stern, L. W. Power measurement in the distribution channel. *Journal of Marketing Research*, **9**, 47–52 (1972).

Emery, F. G. and Twist, E. L. The causal texture of organizational environments. *17th International Congress of Psychology*, Washington, DC (1968).

England, W. *Modern Procurement Management: Principles and Cases*. 5th ed., Irwin, Homewood, Illinois (1970).

Evan, W. M. The organization-set: toward a theory of interorganizational relation, in Thompson, J. (ed) *Approaches to Organizational Design*. University of Pittsburgh Press. Pittsburgh, Philadelphia (1966).

Ford, D. I. An analysis of some aspects of the relationships between companies in channels of distribution. *Unpublished Ph.D. thesis*. University of Manchester, Manchester (1976).

Ford, D. I. Stability factors in industrial marketing channels. *Industrial Marketing Management*, **7**, 410–422 (1978).

Guillet de Monthoux, P. Organizational mating and industrial marketing conservation – some reasons why industrial marketing managers resist marketing theory. *Industrial Marketing Management*, **4**, (1), 25–36 (1975).

Håkansson, H., Johanson, J. and Wootz, B. Influence tactics in buyer–seller processes. *Industrial Marketing Management*, **5**, 319–332 (1977).

Håkansson, H. and Wootz, B. Supplier selection in an international environment – an experimental study. *Journal of Marketing Research*, **12** (February), 46–51 (1975a).

Håkansson, H. and Wootz, B. *Företags inköpsbeteende* (Buying Behaviour of the Firm). Studentlitteratur, Lund (1975b).

Håkansson, H. and Wootz, B. Risk reduction and the industrial purchaser. *European Journal of Marketing*, **9**, (1), 35–51 (1975c).

Håkansson, H. and Wootz, B. *Changes in the Propensity to Import – An Interaction Model on the Firm Level*. Department of Business Studies, University of Uppsala (1975d).

Håkansson, H. and Wootz, B. A framework of industrial buying and selling. *Industrial Marketing Management*, **8**, 28–39 (1979).

Håkansson, H., Wootz, B., Andersson, O. and Hangård, P. Industrial marketing as an organizational problem. A case study. *European Journal of Marketing*, **13**, 81–93 (1979).

Håkansson, H. and Östberg, C. Industrial marketing – An organizational problem? *Industrial Marketing Management*, **4**, 113–123 (1975).

Hall, R. H. *Organization, Structure, and Process*. Prentice-Hall, Englewood Cliffs, New Jersey (1972).

Heskett, J. L., Stern, L. W. and Beijer, F. J. Bases and uses of power in interorganizational relations. In Bucklin, L. P. (ed) *Vertical Marketing Systems*. Scott, Foresman, and Company, London (1970).

Hill, R. M., Alexander, R. S. and Cross, J. S. *Industrial Marketing*. 4th ed., Homewood. Irwin, Illinois (1975).

Hill, R. W. *Marketing Technological Products to Industry*, Oxford, UK (1972).

Hunt, S. D. and Nevin, J. R. Power in a channel of distribution: sources and consequences. *Journal of Marketing Research*, **11**, 186–193 (1974).

Jarvis, L. P. and Wilcox, J. P. True vendor loyalty or simply repeat purchase behavior? *Industrial Marketing Management*, **6**, 9–14 (1977).

Johanson, J., and Vahlne, J.-E. The internationalization process of the firm – a model of knowledge development and increasing foreign market commitments. *Journal of International Business*, **8**, (1), 23–32 (1977).

Johanson, J. and Wiedersheim-Paul, F. The internationalization of the firm – four Swedish case studies. *Journal of Management Studies*, **2**, (3), 305–322 (1975).

Kirsch, W. and Kutschker, M. *Das Marketing von Investitionsgütern – Theoretische und empirische Perspektiven eines Interaktionsansatzes*. Verlag Gablers, Wiesbaden (1978).

Kirsch, W., Lutschewitz, H. and Kutschker, M. *Ansätze und Entwicklungstendenzen im Investitionsgütermarketing – Auf dem Wege zu einem Interaktionsansatz*. C. E. Poeschel Verlag, Stuttgart (1977).

Kotler, P. *Marketing Management, Analysis, Planning, and Control*. 3rd ed. Prentice-Hall, Englewood Cliffs, New Jersey (1976).

Kutschker, M. *Rationalität und Entscheidungskriterien komplexer Investitionsentscheidungen – ein empirischer Bericht*. Aus dem Sonderforschungsbereich 24 Der Universität Mannheim, Mannheim (1975).

Kutschker, M. and Kirsch. W. *Verhandlungen auf dem Markt für Investitionsgüter*. Plannungs – und Organisationswissenschaffliche Schriften, München (1978).

Kutschker, M. and Roth, K. Das Informationsverhalten vor industriellen Beschaffungsentscheidungen. *Veröffentlichung aus dem SFB 24 der Universität Mannheim*. (1975).

Lasswell, H. D. and Kaplan, A. *Power and Society*, Routledge, London (1952).

Lee, Jr. L. and Dobler, D. W. *Purchasing and Materials Management: Text and Cases*. 2nd ed. McGraw-Hill, New York (1971).

Levine, S. and White, P. Exchange as a conceptual framework for the study of interorganizational relationships. *Administrative Science Quarterly*, **5**, (4), 583–601 (1961).

Levine, S. and White, P. The community of health organizations. In Freeman, H. E., Levine, S. and Reader, L. (eds) *Handbook of Medical Sociology*, Prentice-Hall, Englewood Cliffs, New Jersey (1972).

Little, R. W. The marketing channel; who should lead this extra-corporate organization. *Journal of Marketing*, **34**, 31–38 (1970).

Litwak, E. and Hylton, L. F. Interorganizational analysis: A hypothesis on coordinating agencies. *Administrative Science Quarterly*, **6**, (4), 395–420 (1962).

Lutschewitz, H. and Kutschker, M. *Die Diffusion innovativer Investitionsgüter – Theoretische Konzeption und empirische Befunde*. Verlag Kurt Desch, München (1977).

Macaulay, S. Non-contractual relations in business: a preliminary study. *American Sociological Review*, **28**, (1), 55–67 (1963).

Marrett, C. B. On the specification of interorganization dimensions. *Sociology and Social Research*, **61**, 83–99 (1971).

Mattsson, L.-G. System interdependencies – A key concept in industrial marketing? *Proceedings from the Second Research Seminar in Marketing as Senanque*. Fondation Nationale pour l'Enseignement de la Gestion des Entreprises (1975).

McCarthy, E. J. *Basic Marketing* 6th ed. Irwin, Homewood (1978).

Melin, L. *Strategisk inköpsverksamhet – organisation och interaktion*. (Strategic Purchasing Actions – Organization and Interaction) (with summary in English). University of Linköping, Linköping (1977).

Reve, T. and Stern, L. W. Interorganizational relations in marketing channels. *Academy of Management Review*, **4**, (3), 405–416 (1979).

Robinson, P. J. and Faris, C. W. *Industrial Buying and Creative Marketing*. Allyn and Bacon Inc. and the Harbeling Science Institute, Boston, Massachusetts (1967).

Rosenberg, L. J. and Stern, L. W. Toward the analysis of conflict in distribution channels; a descriptive model. *Journal of Marketing*, **34**, 40–46 (1970).

Sheth, J. N. A model of industrial buyer behavior. *Journal of Marketing*, **37**, 50–56 (1973).

Thompson, J. *Organizations in Action*. McGraw-Hill, New York (1967).

Valla, J.-P. Basic concepts in industrial marketing: Specificities and implications. *Institut de Recherche de l'Entreprise*. Editions Verve, Lyon (1978a).

Valla, J.-P. Strategies in Industrial Marketing. *Institut de Recherche de l'Entreprise*. Editions Verve, Lyon (1978b).

Valla, J.-P. Organization and Structure in Industrial Marketing. *Institut de Recherche de l'Entreprise*. Editions Verve, Lyon (1978c).

Valla, J.-P. Information and Communication Systems in Industrial Marketing. *Institut de Recherche de l'Entreprise*. Editions Verve, Lyon (1978d).

Valla, J.-P. Implementing the marketing concept in the industrial firm: problems and possible solutions. *Institut de Recherche de l'Entreprise*. Editions Verve, Lyon (1978e).

Van de Ven, A. H., Emmit, D. C. and Koenig, R. Frameworks for interorganizational analysis. In Negandhi, A. R. (ed) *Interorganizational Theory*. Kent State University Press, Kent, Ohio (1975).

Warren, R. The interorganizational field as a focus for investigation. *Administrative Science Quarterly*, **12**, 396–419 (1967).

Warren, R. The interactions of community decision organizations: some conceptual considerations and empirical findings. In Negandhi, A. R. (ed.) *Modern Organization Theory*. Kent State University Press, Kent, Ohio (1973).

Webster, Jr., F. E. *Industrial Marketing Strategy*. John Wiley and Sons, New York (1979).

Webster, Jr., F. E. and Wind, Y. *Organizational Buying Behavior*, Prentice-Hall, Englewood Cliffs (1972a).

Webster, Jr., F. E. and Wind, Y. A general model for understanding organizational buyer behavior. *Journal of Marketing*, **36**, 12–19 (1972b).

Westing, J. H., Fine, I. V. and Zenz, G. J. *Purchasing Management: Materials in Motion*. John Wiley and Sons, New York (1976).

Wilson, A. *The Marketing of Professional Services*, Publications Service, New York (1972).

Wilson, A. *The Assessment of Industrial Markets*. International Publications Service. New York (1973).

Zeitz, G. Interorganizational relationships and social structure: A critique of some aspects of the literature. In Negandhi, A. R. (ed.) *Interorganization Theory*. Kent State University Press, Kent, Ohio (1975).

1.3 The IMP perspective: assets and liabilities of business relationships

Håkan Håkansson and Ivan J. Snehota

A keynote speaker addressing some 200 participants from more than 15 countries at the 12th annual conference of the Industrial Marketing and Purchasing (IMP) Group at the University of Karlsruhe in Germany in the fall of 1996 declared the IMP to be "a well-known trademark that has been around for 20 years and yet [it is] impossible to define what it stands for." Indeed, looking back at the fertile stream of IMP research, we can see that it consists of many different strands, with findings reported in numerous publications over a long period of time. However, what an outsider such as the speaker quoted above may consider a weakness of this research tradition is probably one of its main strengths. The IMP is a prime example of what it is also studying – a flexible network organization with floating boundaries but built around some strong relationships that connect and permit cross-fertilization of various streams of ideas and research. The IMP research program has been productive not because of a clearly defined core but because it has brought together quite different kinds of knowledge in new ways. It springs from some shared basic empirical findings and ontological assumptions, but it is spinning in numerous different directions, as do its implications.

The variety of projects that are part of IMP research may make it difficult for some to grasp the main findings and propositions of this research and to assess its implications for management and for further studies. Having taken part in it for two decades, we will in this chapter offer our picture of the essence of the IMP. We will attempt to outline briefly the history of the IMP, to review its conceptual cornerstones, and to discuss the main implications of the IMP findings both for management and for the future directions of research. Although the picture we offer is probably shared by most of our IMP colleagues, we know for sure that some of them would emphasize other aspects. The IMP has various facets and shows different ones depending on the angle from which it is approached. Indeed, although its origins and its center of gravity are in the marketing discipline, it has facets that touch on organization theory, theory of international business, and studies of technical development, to mention a few.

THE IMP STORY

One way to describe what the IMP stands for is to explain how it has evolved. The IMP began in the mid-1970s and later developed along many different trails. In hindsight, we can see that it consists of three intertwined parts that have evolved over about two decades. Two of these parts are large international research projects (IMP1 and IMP2), and the third, running in parallel with the first two, is the formation of a research network connecting researchers scattered in several countries. The history of the IMP is about bringing together, confronting, and cross-fertilizing various pieces of research and conceptual development.

IMP1

The first project of the IMP is the International/Industrial Marketing and Purchasing Project (later called IMP1), initiated in 1976 and carried out until about 1982. The key notion of this project is relationship interaction. The antecedents of IMP1 were studies conducted in Swedish export industries (Johanson, 1966), distribution systems in the United Kingdom (Ford, 1976), industrial purchasing (Håkansson and Wootz, 1975), and marketing in Sweden, the United Kingdom, and Germany (Cunningham and White, 1974; Håkansson and Östberg, 1975; Kutchker, 1975). The researchers who conducted these and other studies at that time observed the existence of lasting buyer–seller relationships in business markets and pointed out severe shortcomings of the marketing theory at hand to capture and explain this phenomenon (e.g., Arndt, 1979; Twedt, 1964).

Shared interest in industrial markets and dissatisfaction with the available marketing concepts led a group of junior researchers in several European countries to establish contacts that resulted in the design of IMP1. The research backgrounds and interests of those joining the project involved issues ranging from purchasing and industrial marketing to internationalization. However, all were focused on the role of buyer–seller relationships between companies. Relationships and interaction thus became the research object on which they converged.

Despite their heterogeneous backgrounds, the members of the group that gathered around the project had two traits in common: empirical research orientation and familiarity with emerging organization theory at that time. Their empirical orientation made the joining researchers aware of the difficulties in using mainstream analytic concepts in marketing for interpretation of the phenomena encountered in industrial markets. Certain strands of organization theory (in particular the works of Cyert and March, 1963; March and Simon, 1958; Thompson, 1967) and the emergent interorganizational theory (e.g., Aiken and Hage, 1968; Blau, 1964) provided an intellectually stimulating theoretical source. The researchers found it fruitful to borrow some of the concepts of these theories to develop interpretative schemes regarding some of the phenomena they observed in business relationships.

The initial purpose of IMP1 was empirical. The researchers were to collect descriptive data about buyer–seller relationships in industrial markets in five European countries, with the aim of creating a large database. The hypothesis underlying the project, based on previous research, was that the content of supplier–customer relationships is broader than simple economic exchanges. The project was designed, in particular, to capture elements of social exchange, interaction in customer–supplier relationships, and the variation in the content and duration of relationships for different types of companies.

The data were collected and elaborated jointly by cooperating research groups in five European countries. Data were gathered on more than 1,000 customer–supplier relationships through structured interviews, about half of which were conducted with buyers and half with sellers. Some 80% of the relationships studied were cross-border – that is, international relationships. More than 20 researchers from France, Germany, Italy, Sweden, and the United Kingdom took part in the project. The initial empirical thrust and international scope of IMP1 have come to characterize much of the subsequent IMP research.

The outcomes of IMP1 were both empirical and theoretical. A broad and rather rich empirical descriptive database was produced regarding the features of buyer–seller relationships in industrial markets. Along with the aggregated structured database, a number of in-depth cases describing relationship processes were elaborated. The main empirical findings were reported in several publications (Cunningham, 1980; Håkansson, 1982; Hallén, 1980; Kutchker and Kirsch, 1978; Perrin, 1979; Turnbull and Cunningham, 1980; Turnbull and Valla, 1985).

The theoretical outcome of IMP1 came from an intense effort to develop interpretative schemes and conceptual frames to capture the features and processes at work in buyer–seller relationships in industrial markets. These efforts resulted in elaboration of "the interaction model of buyer–seller relationships" (Håkansson, 1982). The interaction model then became a base for further elaboration of conceptual frameworks and propositions with regard to international purchasing (Hallén, 1980), marketing communication, and international industrial marketing strategies (Hallén, Johanson, and Seyed-Mohamed, 1989; Turnbull and Valla, 1985).

IMP2

IMP2, the IMP project started in 1986, represents the second part of the IMP. It originated in the empirical findings and conceptual achievements of IMP1, but it brought in other researchers, interests, and strands of research. The key notion of this part was the network form. It was inspired by indications of interdependencies in and between buyer–seller relationships and the resulting concept of the network form of business markets (Hägg and Johanson, 1982; Hammarkvist, Håkansson, and Mattsson, 1982). Building on the evidence of the existence of strong buyer–seller relationships in industrial markets, the focus of IMP2 was on interdependencies in and between the relationships and the effects of interdependencies on the companies involved. Networks of relationships thus became of main empirical and conceptual interest for IMP2.

Methodologically similar to the first project, IMP2 involved structured interviews with both buyers and sellers, having as objects both specific customer–supplier relationships and company case studies. Researchers from Australia (Wilkinson and Young, 1994), Japan (Teramoto, 1990), and the United States (Anderson and Narus, 1990; Wilson and Mummalaneni, 1986) joined IMP2, along with most of the researchers from IMP1, and brought in some new interests, evidence, and ideas. Standardized data about buyer–seller relationships have been collected and combined with a number of in-depth company cases.

The main outcomes of IMP2 are again both empirical and conceptual. The project has led to further elaboration of the concept of business networks and refinement of the conceptual frame of business relationships (Anderson, Håkansson, and Johanson, 1994; Axelsson and Easton, 1992; Håkansson and Snehota, 1995). More extensive empirical descriptions and interpretative schemes of the interaction processes in buyer–seller relationships have been produced and reported in several publications (Blankenburg and Johanson, 1990; Blankenburg Holm, 1996; Havila, 1996). Empirical studies of business networks have addressed the issue of connectedness in business relationships and the effects of interdependencies.

The research community

The third part of the IMP has been the organization of a research network that connects various streams of research with different topics (purchasing, marketing, technical development, internationalization) and different methodologies (qualitative as well as quantitative). A forum has emerged where a successively broadening research community, sharing concerns with business relationships and networks, can meet and confront community members' findings and propositions.

A visible manifestation of this forum took the form of the first annual IMP conference, held at University of Manchester in 1984; an IMP conference has been held every year since that time. From 50 to 100 working papers are produced and presented each year; these appear in the conference proceedings but also in a steady stream of other publications (e.g., Cavusgil and Sharma, 1993; Ford, 1990, 1997; Gemunden, Ritter, and Walter, 1998; Hallén and Johanson, 1989; Turnbull and Paliwoda, 1986; Wilson and Möller, 1995).

This part of the IMP, which is still going on, reflects the increasing differentiation and heterogeneity of the various strands of research spurred by the previous findings. It meets the researchers' need to explore further the impacts of buyer–seller relationships on various aspects of business management and on the functioning of business markets. It coincides with the broadening of the scope of the IMP research and with continuing conceptual development. The empirical base underlying the IMP conferences is extensive. It is a blend of case studies and quantitative analyses of firms, networks, and business relationships.

The empirical thrust of the IMP has gone hand in hand with efforts to interpret observed phenomena and to develop adequate analytic concepts. The efforts toward conceptual development have been inspired by impulses from various disciplines of management. Although rooted in marketing, the scope of the conceptual development is broader than marketing management – it involves the market process and its overall impact on business organizations. It has thus been inspired, as recurrent references indicate, by the more institutional marketing theory (e.g., Alderson, 1957, 1965; Arndt, 1979; Reve and Stern, 1979; Sheth, Gardner, and Garrett, 1988), which deals with the working of the market system rather than only with marketing management, and some developments within industrial marketing area in the United States (Sheth, 1978; Sheth and Parvatiyar, 1992; Spekman, 1988; Webster, 1992). Other sources of inspiration often referred to are certain strands of sociology (e.g., Burt, 1982, 1992; Cook and Emerson, 1978, 1984; Granovetter, 1985; Nohria and Eccles, 1992), organization theory (Aldrich, 1979; Ebers, 1997; Grabher, 1993; Weick, 1969), industrial organization (Bain, 1968; Scherer, 1970), transaction cost theory (Reve, 1990; Williamson, 1975, 1985), business strategy (Lorenzoni and Ornati, 1988; Porter, 1980, 1985), and evolutionary economics (Dosi, Freeman, Nelson, Silverberg, and Soete, 1988; Nelson and Winter, 1982).

CONCEPTUAL CORNERSTONES OF THE IMP

Although the IMP research has evolved organically, with hindsight it is possible to identify some of its important cornerstones. As these have emerged gradually, the relative importance of each has shifted over time and for individual researchers. We discuss four such cornerstones below. The first two come from major empirical findings, and they are therefore concepts shared by most of the researchers; the other two are hypotheses regarding general explanations of these findings, and thus are more questionable and personal.

The first cornerstone is the discovery and empirical findings regarding relationships between buyers and sellers in business markets:

1. *Between buyers and sellers exist relationships.* These are built from interaction processes in which technical, social, and economic issues are dealt with. Relationships are organized patterns of inter-action and interdependence with their own substance. They are an important phenomenon in the business landscape and have to be recognized and handled by management both as problems in themselves and as marketing or purchasing means. They are as often problems as they are solutions.

The importance of business relationships is both an empirical finding and a discovery. We were looking for decisions regarding single market exchange episodes when we first noticed these relationships. We could not find the discrete decisions, and when we found them, they seemed not to be related to important or interesting issues. Instead, we found that companies were dealing with each other in ways that could be characterized as relationships – that is, they were acting and reacting based on each others' acts over time and with specific considerations for their counterparts. There were interaction processes in which reactions were as important as actions, listening was as important as talking, and mutuality seemed to be a necessary condition for both parties to reach their goals. Thus the existence of relationships and their substance is an empirical finding. Clearly, some companies also tried to use relationships as marketing or purchasing means, but this seemed not to be without problems. The relationships seemed to be so heavy that they were not easily redirected in specific ways.

In the studies, three different types of issues often came into focus in the relationships: technical, social, and economic issues. This signaled the existence of three types of problems in relationships, but also indicated that the relationships could have functions in those three dimensions.

Technical content

In many cases, interactions between buyers and sellers have a technical content – at least in industrial markets. The relationship is a way of building together the technical resources of one company with the technical resources of the counterpart. Again and again, the relationship between customer and supplier turns out to be one of the most important ways a company can develop its products and production processes. At the same time, the relationship also creates technical problems within the companies involved.

The technical content in the relationship becomes manifest in a number of ways. One is that technicians often play an important role in the contacts between companies. Even if sales representatives and purchasing people have the most frequent contacts, technicians have a key role. That role can be as in one Swedish company, where the marketing manager did not like the results of market research showing that the R&D manager was perceived by key customers as the most important individual in the interaction. Technicians have a direct role as they solve the technical problems appearing over time, but they also gain knowledge about how products and production processes are combined. The existence of these contacts can be used as a means to develop the relationship, but it can also make the relationship more difficult to control.

A second way that technical content is apparent in the interaction is through the products or services. Their technical content must be in accordance with the technical parameters of the user and, at the same time, with the seller's technical features, if they are to be produced and sold in an economical way. Sometimes two parties are lucky and find a perfect fit just by chance, but in most situations the two companies have to go through a more or less continuous learning process in order to find and keep a structural fit from a technical point of view. The relationship must be fitted into two different technical systems, both of which are always changing; thus there is need for a continuous technical adaptation process. Again, this can be used in a positive way by one or both of the counterparts, but it also will be a source of difficulties and irritations.

A third way the technical content becomes apparent is through special projects performed by either of the two parties. Interaction with external parties can be an important ingredient in specific development projects, and interaction in these cases becomes part of "larger" constellations or projects. This can cause problems with integration and confrontation in technical terms. Both can be valuable, but the problems must certainly be taken care of.

Social content

The interaction between customer and supplier almost always has a social content. It is performed by individuals who, through the interaction, get the opportunity to develop social relationships. Social content is an important ingredient in several respects. One is related to trust, another to commitment, and a third to influence/power. Each of these can be used in a positive way but also will create problems.

Uncertainty is a prevailing condition in typical exchange situations, and therefore the parties have to trust each other. The uncertainty exists in different dimensions; on the buying side, for example, it is possible to distinguish between need, market, and transaction uncertainty (Håkansson, Johanson, and Wootz, 1976). Uncertainty cannot be reduced simply through increased information, as it has to do with future events; instead, the parties have to learn to trust each other. Trust is built up over time in a social exchange process whereby the parties learn, step by step, to trust each other.

Commitment is related to trust but has a specific content. A high degree of trust can exist between parties without there being much feeling of commitment. Commitment has to do with priorities and can be built up between two parties over time if they have demonstrated that they give each other a certain level of priority. Positive interactions give the parties a feeling of being related, of belonging to a high-priority group. Consequently, there can be certain feelings of responsibility for or commitment to each other. The logic behind this is that everyone has to act in relation to individual counterparts – the environment will develop a social structure that always includes some differentiation in importance. As soon as there is a structure, there are preferences. Again, commitment can have both positive and negative effects. The term *commitment* connotes the positive aspects, whereas *obligation* indicates some of the negative. In certain situations an actor has to comply; the actor cannot comply only when he or she wants to. In all relationships, there is this question of what we can demand of our counterparts and what we have to do for them.

The third aspect of social content relates to power/influence. In a group of social actors who give each other different priorities – that is, where there is a certain structure – there will always be a certain "power of influence" related to different positions. Relationships entail such positions and thus also become means for gaining and exercising influence over others.

Economic content

Interactions in business relationships have economic consequences and are subject to an economic logic. A relationship is costly to develop and involves a flow of activities/resources with substantial economic consequences. Three different and distinct economic aspects can be identified. The first is that single relationships are quite important in terms of cost and revenue volume. The 10 most important relationships with customers or suppliers often account for a large share of a company's turnover. The economic consequences of breaking one of these relationships can be very severe and might also affect other relationships for each of the two counterparts.

The second economic aspect has to do with the costs of developing and handling relationships. A relationship can be costly, as it might involve a number of persons putting in a lot of time in order to handle the technical, economic, and social aspects described above. It can entail a lot of traveling as well as many technical contacts and projects, as there might be technical adaptations and other changes. The time and cost involved in changing from one counterpart to another can thus be substantial. Some consultancies claim that the cost ratio between keeping a customer and getting a new one is 1 to 10. A consequence is that there are reasons to rationalize the handling of relationships – that is, to find ways to reduce unnecessary costs.

A relationship can be seen as an asset and a market investment. This is the third economic aspect of relationships. Looking at relationships as investments is the classical economic way of trying to evaluate substances (i.e., resources that have certain life spans). For established companies, some of their largest resources are their existing relationships. Capturing this substance is probably a common motive when companies buy into other companies in approaching new markets. One consequence of viewing relationships as market investments is the realization that they have to be in balance and coordinated with investments in other internal assets of the company.

The existence of business relationships and their technical, social, and economic content make them important economic phenomena. They are important marketing means for companies, but they are also one of the largest sources of both strategic and tactical problems.

The second cornerstone of the IMP, another empirical finding, can be summarized in the following way:

2. *Business relationships are connected.* That makes them elements of a wider economic organization that takes a network form. Companies are embedded in multidimensional ways into their counterparts – into their counterparts' contexts. This embeddedness affects companies' discretion in contradictory ways. First, it provides serious limitations; any company can only pursue things that are accepted by a number of its counterparts. However, it also offers a company the opportunity to influence its counterparts, and that can be done in a number of dimensions both directly and indirectly.

Through empirical observation, we know that single relationships are difficult to understand on their own merits, without any context. Company representatives often refer to other relationships when explaining their behavior: Acquiring new customers can reduce costs for other customers, getting new customers depends on existing relationships, and so on. The IMP researchers found that relationships were connected to each other in a number of ways, and these connections gave them a very distinct feature. They were related and therefore also relative. They were all parts of something larger and therefore all interactions were in some ways mirrors of the context. The interaction could be understood only when it was put into this context. One critical consequence is that it becomes impossible to evaluate or understand a relationship/interaction disconnected from others. Every relationship has to be seen and judged in relation to the connected relationships that either of the two counterparts has with others and, in some situations, in relation to relationships between third parties.

Whereas the first findings lead to the conclusion that relationships have their own substance, these findings indicate that every relationship is also a part of something larger; it is an integrator of surrounding relationships. This has two obvious consequences: First, the value and content of a relationship can be changed without any action within that relationship, through changes in some related relationships; second, when a change is made within a relationship, some other relationships will be influenced. Every relationship is not only a bridge between two actors but also a reflector or a projection of other relationships. It includes history and environment, still very specific and unique. This is probably the reason so many authors have spent so many pages analyzing how single relationships are influenced by the development of others.

These connections are important in all of the three dimensions – technical, social, and economical. The technical content in the interaction has to mirror all the interdependencies existing among products, production processes, and use of resources. Technological systems cut across the networks of companies in different ways, and the corresponding technical connections have to be addressed within the relationships. In the same way, individuals within companies are members of social structures with special social roles and functions, such as professional associations, school alumni groups, boards in other companies or organizations, and social clubs. Again, companies cut across these structures and the interactions between companies are also part of these structures, benefiting or being hurt by existing structures. Finally, every element – whether technical items such as products or social elements such as trust, commitment, and power – of the single business relationship is a piece of an economic puzzle for which the final outcome depends on how these pieces are related to each other. Networking, as a concept, has in this context a much deeper meaning.

The existence of business relationships and their connectedness are empirical phenomena that ought to be important also from a more general economic viewpoint. The IMP research has come up with different suggestions, hypotheses, and theory fragments that we will summarize in two propositions, which are our third and fourth cornerstones. The first of these can be summarized as follows:

3. *A relationship is a combination.* It affects productivity and efficiency in firms and can therefore be used to exploit complementarities between activities performed by different companies and their resources. At the same time, it is subject to interdependencies. Through relationships, economic benefits can be captured by technical, administrative, or temporal connections.

Traditionally, the economic organization of production activities is described in economics in terms of a dichotomy between market and hierarchy. From such a perspective buyer–seller relationships appear as market imperfections – a way to create monopolistic market situations. Transaction cost theory has shown that relationships are important in situations when the market fails to provide efficient coordination. The IMP research has moved one step further, claiming that relationships are a unique third type of coordination that includes elements of both market and hierarchy but also has its own specific features. Interaction relationships appear as an efficient coordination mechanism when there are multiplex and changing interdependencies. Thus relationships can be used to link activities to each other, combining individual adaptations and scale-effective production.

There are opportunities to take advantage of interdependencies among activities performed within the company and its customers, its customers' customers, its customers' suppliers, its own suppliers, its suppliers' suppliers, its suppliers' customers, and so on, depending upon how business relationships are designed (Dubois, 1998). Connections to suppliers and customers can be differentiated, and operations can still take advantage of important scale effects. There are also negative effects, as relationships will lock the company into a given structure, which will lead to rigidity in certain dimensions and thus to vulnerability to external changes.

The indications from IMP research are that in many industrial settings business relationships are a key mechanism of efficiency. Such relationships are important for the single company and for its counterparts. This gives relationships a hard core of economics; relationships can be a way to reach a higher level of efficiency in the combination of production and transactions. These ideas are consistent with various findings on positive economic effects of quasi-integration arrangements described by concepts such as just-in-time inventory management, time-based management, and total quality control.

It is important to note that we have used here the word *can*. Relationships can be used to link activities and tie resources, but all relationships do not automatically lead to that. Relationships create a context in which this potential exists, but very few companies work in a systematic way to capture these benefits. There are certainly also some problems with relationships, as all links between customer and supplier activities make it more difficult for both parties to establish alternative links and ties as the companies become embedded into specific others.

The discussion of relationships as ways of combining activities, resources, and individual actors has some similarities and can be seen as complementary to corresponding analysis made by economists such as Williamson (1975, 1985), Richardson (1972), and Chandler (1990).

The fourth cornerstone of IMP is the second proposition regarding the economic effects of relationships and their implications for the utilization of resources:

4. *Relationships are confrontation.* They are a way to create a confrontation of the two parties' knowledge, which affects resource development and thus innovativeness. Knowledge is often developed in the border zone between different knowledge areas. In more general terms, relationships can be means for tying resources to each other in such a way that some of their heterogeneity is utilized – that is, different dimensions of the resources are partly unknown, and through "interaction" these dimensions are identified and utilized.

Industrial companies generally have substantial resources in the forms of technical facilities, raw materials, people, knowledge, and established positions in relation to different counterparts. The importance of these for the single company's competitiveness and development is generally recognized. A relationship can be used by the two parties to activate, develop, and direct resources toward each other. This directing can include learning that will give both parties opportunities to find new and better ways to tie the resources together. Technical development within and through relationships becomes an interesting opportunity.

There are two main reasons for using relationships in this way. One has to do with the opportunity to confront and use knowledge from quite different sources in order to find new solutions. The other has to do with the interactive effect. Knowledge is often developed in the border zone between established knowledge areas. If two actors with different knowledge try to combine and confront each other's resources, there is a possibility that they will develop new knowledge.

Technical development therefore mostly takes place in the interface between companies as they represent different resources or knowledge areas. Relationships can be a crucial means to increase a company's ability to innovate and to take part in technological development. Again we use the word *can*. Relationships create a context where it is possible to develop this kind of process, but there is no simple mechanism that triggers it. Many relationships are used the other way around –

to block changes. This can be an efficient strategy for a single company, but it will certainly decrease the company's speed of development.

The analysis of the developmental effects of business relationships has driven IMP research in the direction of work by researchers such as von Hippel (1988), Hughes (1983, pp. 404–460), Teece (1980), Nelson and Winter (1982), Rosenberg (1982), Dosi et al. (1988), and Storper and Walker (1989).

PERTINENCE FOR MANAGEMENT ACTION

Because dissatisfaction with marketing theory at the time gave birth to IMP research, the issue of normative implications is important for the IMP. The dissatisfaction was focused on the positive foundations of the normative recommendations, which, in particular in the field of industrial marketing, were based on a very limited understanding of how industrial markets work. Such recommendations are not only meaningless, they are outright bad for practice. The IMP reflects the conviction that if we are to improve the practice of marketing we need first of all a better understanding of the marketing process in industrial markets. In light of our findings, that still remains a valid point. Researchers and companies still have the need for better understanding – that is, a better positive theory. All positive theories are also normative. Because we feel that the IMP Group has advanced our understanding of the marketing process, we are convinced that its findings and resulting propositions offer fruitful ground for normative recommendations for management practice.

However, there are some problems in formulating clear normative implications. One is that the main findings of the IMP research point to and confirm the complexity of relationship consequences and the risks of acting on oversimplified assumptions. The uniqueness of relationships, an empirical fact, makes the mechanical transfer of successful practices among different companies dubious at best. Another problem is that the normative implications of the findings are broad and far-reaching. They can hardly be confined to changes in techniques or methods, nor can they be limited to the domain of marketing management. They are "managerial" in a broad sense. They shed new light on some traditional problems of business management but also suggest some new problems to be considered.

Although the main empirical findings and hypotheses regarding the substance of the business relationships and the network form of business markets deserve to be tested further, once we accept them their implications are numerous and profound. Those that have been outlined and explored within the IMP regard such different areas of management as purchasing (e.g., Gadde and Håkansson, 1992; Pedersen, 1996; Torvatn, 1996), strategy development (e.g., Gadde and Mattsson, 1987; Håkansson and Snehota, 1989, 1995; Henders, 1992; Johanson and Mattsson, 1994; Kock, 1991), internationalization of the firm (e.g., Forsgren and Johanson, 1992; Halinen, 1997; Hallén et al., 1989; Herz, 1993; Pardo and Salle, 1994; Salmi, 1995; Turnbull and Valla, 1985), technological strategy in business (e.g., Biemans, 1992; Ford, 1988; Håkansson, 1987, 1989; Laage-Hellman, 1997; Lundgren, 1995; Raesfeld Meijer, 1997; Waluszewski, 1990), and organization (Havilia, 1996; Tunisini, 1997). Aside from these, there have been publications covering more general aspects of marketing management, such as the work of Easton (1996), Ford (1990, 1997), Iacobucci (1996), and Wilson and Möller (1995).

The implications of the IMP findings and propositions for marketing management contrast with those of the more traditional marketing management theory. The relationship phenomenon and interaction as a core process change the nature of the marketing problem. The existence of relationships points to the importance of specific mutual interdependencies. In a relationship the outcome of a course of action by one party will reflect the acts and counteracts of the counterpart rather than the course of action as such. This means that outcomes and consequences of behaviors depend on a series of interactions too complex to be planned or even thought through beforehand. The three traditional areas of marketing management – market analysis, market strategy options, and implementation – will all get new faces. They will also get another sequence. It becomes natural to start with the ongoing processes – that is, in the implementation.

Implementation

From an interaction perspective, we have to start with the existing processes, at what is generally seen as the "end" – the implementation. The interaction process in relationships makes the very notion of implementation questionable, sometimes even unsuitable and misleading. Customer–supplier relationship interaction consists of a series of acts and counteracts through which the situations to be acted upon continuously evolve. The requests of the customer or supplier regarding various arrangements are met in different ways, which produce new situations that have to be handled. The goals and the alternative means of the involved companies become as much results of the interaction as preconditions. In a true interaction, the involved parties have to accept that they are being transformed.

An important consequence is that extensive interaction processes are difficult to monitor and impossible to predict or plan. Both the content of the relationship (products and services rendered) and the interaction pattern of the individuals involved tend to evolve organically. In this process, choices are being made – implemented – often without having been previously conceived and considered as choice situations. In customer relationships things are being undertaken because circumstances call for solutions that are being offered by either of the two parties. The outcomes of a company's behavior in such a market reflect the interaction more than any formal plan.

The strength of a relationship and its consequences change as mutual activity coordination is tightened up or loosened, as reciprocal adaptations in resources are made, and as individuals engage in interpersonal interaction. This process is vital given the consequences, not the least economic, of activity links, resource ties, and actor bonds for the companies involved. Choices in fact are made in interaction with others, and are at best dependent on how the emerging situations are framed and made sense of.

High-involvement relationships with some strong links, ties, or bonds can be valuable assets for a company, but they always also are a heavy liability. Balance is often perceived as needed but can generally be achieved only temporarily and for a certain area. Companies have to live with imbalances and demanding relationships; they have to accept the burdens. The problem becomes how to activate and motivate the counterparts on a continuous basis – how to take part in development processes without any final state. The scope for planning of market activities becomes very limited – often reduced to a ritual whose importance is primarily symbolic.

In light of the IMP findings, the very notion of implementation becomes irrelevant because it assumes planned action. As mutual conforming is the essence of relationship, implementation has meaning only as "mediated" action. Unilaterally controlled relationships are pathological; they are not the typical case. Business markets are in that sense conceivable as "life game" situations.

The main consequence is that instead of implementing preplanned marketing activities, the company has to be an intelligent interaction partner. Key attributes become sensitivity, flexibility, and reflection. The company has to learn from what is going on, learn about the counterparts but also about itself, to learn about when and how their own company performs as an efficient interaction partner. Experimentation is important for companies that want to develop efficient ways to interact.

Market strategy options

Two features of customer–supplier relationships and networks become strategically relevant. Relationship interaction is costly, and, especially when new relationships are established, the returns lag. At the same time, the interaction mechanism and the difficulties of monitoring an adaptation's coordination and contacts tend to produce another phenomenon: Interacting with others tends to pull the company in different directions, often mirroring the development of the single counterparts.

The centrifugal force of relationship interaction leads to the need to reconsider the issue of "differentiation." Differentiation of the offering is in the network context a fact, and limiting the extent of differentiation is the issue. Strategy options emerge as interactive choices aggregate to patterns that can be given meaning. Options are tried out and interpreted rather than conceived a priori.

The economy cycle in customer relationships – or what we may call their *investment logic* – also has important consequences. Balancing efforts between the existing and new customer relationships and prioritizing customer relationships that compete for limited managerial attention and capacity constitute another strategic issue. A focus on the existing set of relationships as a platform for possible development is unavoidable.

Both features converge on the need for account management logic – that is, differentiation of the roles of the different customer relationships. Not every relationship needs to be economically profitable in the short or long run. Account management (i.e., dealing with each relationship as a distinct entity) reflects the need to keep in consideration the complementary and combinatory effects of relationships. Most important is that whereas relationships are a given, the type of relationship, in terms of high and low involvement, is a variable. Some relationships over time offer new possibilities, whereas inevitably others become a burden. There is nothing intrinsically positive about high-involvement relationships; they are assets to the extent that use can be made of them and liabilities at the same time if their usefulness is not perceived. The two are different sides of the same coin.

Market analysis

The purpose of market analysis is to gain understanding of the context of the marketing action. The question raised by the IMP findings is, What is an appropriate scope of analysis to gain that understanding? The IMP findings imply that we cannot limit market analysis to an abstract product demand analysis if we are to achieve understanding. Mapping the existing customer relationships of the company and of possible interdependencies (i.e., of the relevant network) becomes a necessary first step. The network of buyer–seller relationships rather than the product market becomes the relevant unit of analysis. The difference becomes particularly significant when we deal with companies that are not one-product firms.

Mapping the relevant business network amounts to answering questions such as the following: How large a portion of our overall business do major customers account for? How is that changing? What is the product breakdown? What are the reasons for the changes? What relationships do the customers have to their customers, suppliers, and third parties? It means anchoring the market analysis strictly in the relevant customer context.

Understanding the market context requires focusing the analysis on the customer/buyer (the one who pays for performance) rather than simply on the customer/end user (who often is the customer of the customer). Although understanding the latter remains important, understanding the former is crucial. The definition of *customer* may be tricky and deserves attention.

Mapping the network is but a first step in gaining understanding. Next is understanding the individual account (customer). Understanding the customer–buyer requires assessment not only of its buying behavior but also of the impact of supplier relationships on its operations and on its business. In practice, this amounts to assessment of the share of the customer needs and of the development and outlook of its business, and not only of its purchasing behavior. It entails assessment of the individual customer's share of the company's business and how it has developed and can develop. Knowing the principles of customer operations and their business outlook is critical to understanding their interaction behavior.

It is impossible to forecast how a network will develop, as it is always the result of unique interactions. Rather than attempting to foresee, a company needs to direct its efforts toward understanding the forces that form the network and shape its development. That cannot be accomplished without an understanding of the cliques in the network that correspond to shared interests.

DOMAINS TO EXPLORE

Reviewing the IMP research to date, we find that it stands out clearly as more basic than applied research. We believe that this is not likely to change anytime soon, as, in our opinion, the mainstream theory development in marketing is close to a paradigm shift, and we are only at the beginning of it. Future research directions are difficult to predict, as they will flow from stepwise discovery and achievements. If we were to suggest some future research directions, they would stem from three considerations.

First, there is an obvious need to increase further the empirical understanding of business relationships and networks. In particular, we believe that the variety in relationship substance has to be examined in more depth. Other areas that need further empirical investigation are the links that join relationship interaction to company performance and the dynamics of the evolution of business networks. Current classification schemes with respect to the substance of relationships offer a starting point for assessing the impacts on both network and company development, but these can be elaborated more extensively.

Second, conceptual development is in no way yet accomplished. We still need more precision in concepts – more effective language – to gauge the processes and in particular the effects and consequences. Concepts such as activity links, resource ties, and actor bonds need more precision as well as clarification of how they relate to each other and how they produce economic consequences (e.g., Håkansson and Snehota, 1995). There is a need to gain insight into the dynamics of business networks and thus deepen the understanding of the forces shaping the context of business. Concepts such as network position, internationalization, change in distribution networks, and network organization are about to be developed more fully, but the remaining path is uphill. The current state is more one of a conceptual frame than of a consistent theory.

Third, the conceptual development resulting from the IMP research is but part of a broader development of thought about the economic organization that springs from numerous sources. It is thus related to developments in economics, economic sociology, and economic history, and the link becomes interesting. The IMP findings so far point also to some more fundamental issues, such as the autonomy of action and the meaning of economic and social rationality.

REFERENCES

Aiken, M., and Hage, J. (1968). Organizational interdependence and intra-organizational structure. *American Sociological Review, 33*, 912–930.

Alderson, W. (1957). *Marketing behavior and executive action: A functionalist approach to marketing theory.* Homewood, IL: Richard D. Irwin.

Alderson, W. (1965). *Dynamic marketing behavior: A functionalist theory of marketing.* Homewood, IL: Richard D. Irwin.

Aldrich, H. E. (1979). *Organizations and environments.* Englewood Cliffs, NJ: Prentice Hall.

Anderson, J. C., Håkansson, H., and Johanson, J. (1994). Dyadic business relationships within a business network context. *Journal of Marketing, 58* (4), 1–15.

Anderson, J. C., and Narus, J. A. (1990). A model of distributor firm and manufacturer firm working partnerships. *Journal of Marketing, 54*(1), 42–58.

Arndt, J. (1979). Toward a concept of domesticated markets. *Journal of Marketing, 43*(4), 69–75.

Axelson, B., and Easton, G. (1992). *Industrial networks: A new view of reality.* London: Routledge.

Bain, J. S. (1968). *Industrial organization* (2nd ed.). New York: John Wiley.

Biemans, W. G. (1992). *Managing innovation within networks.* London: Routledge.

Blankenburg, D., and Johanson, J. (1990). Managing network connections in international business. *Scandinavian International Business Review, 1*(1), 5–19.

Blankenburg Holm, D. (1996). *Business networks connections and international business relationships.* Unpublished doctoral dissertation, Uppsala University.

Blau, P. M. (1964). *Exchange and power in social life.* New York: John Wiley.

Burt, R. S. (1982). *Toward a structural theory of action: Network models of social structure, perception and action.* New York: Academic Press.

Burt, R. S. (1992). *Structural holes: The social structure of competition.* Cambridge, MA: Harvard University Press.

Cavusgil, S., and Sharma, D. (1993). *Advances in international marketing: Vol. 5. Industrial networks.* London: JAI.

Chandler, A. D., Jr. (with Hikino, T.). (1990). *Scale and scope: The dynamics of industrial capitalism.* Cambridge, MA: Belknap.

Cook, K. S., and Emerson, R. M. (1978). Power, equity and commitment in exchange networks. *American Sociological Review, 43*, 721–739.

Cook, K. S., and Emerson, R. M. (1984). Exchange networks and the analysis of complex organizations. In S. B. Bacharach and E. J. Lawler (Eds), *Research in the sociology of organizations* (Vol. 3, pp. 1–30). Greenwich, CT: JAI.

Cunningham, M. (1980). International marketing and purchasing: Features of a European research project. *European Journal of Marketing, 14*(5–6), 5–21.

Cunningham, M., and White, J. G. (1974). The behavior of industrial buyers in their search for suppliers of machine tools. *Journal of Management Studies, 11*(2), 115–128.

Cyert, R. M., and March, J. G. (1963). *A behavioral theory of the firm.* Englewood Cliffs, NJ: Prentice Hall.

Dosi, G., Freeman, C., Nelson, R., Silverberg, G., and Soete, L. (Eds). (1988). *Technical change and economic theory.* London: Pinters.

Dubois, A. (1998). *Organizing industrial activities across firm boundaries.* London: Routledge.

Easton, G. (Ed.). (1996). Markets as networks [Special issue]. *Journal of Research in Marketing, 13*(5).

Ebers, M. (1997). *The formation of inter-organizational networks.* Oxford: Oxford University Press.

Ford, D. (1976). *An analysis of some aspects of the relationships between companies in channels of distribution.* Unpublished doctoral dissertation, University of Manchester.

Ford, D. I. (1988). Develop your technology strategy. *Long Range Planning, 21* (5), 85–95.

Ford, D. I. (Ed.). (1990). *Understanding business markets.* San Diego, CA: Academic Press.

Ford, D. I. (Ed.). (1997). *Understanding business markets* (2nd ed.). London: Dryden.

Forsgren, M., and Johanson, J. (Eds). (1992). *Managing networks in international business.* Philadelphia: Gordon and Breach.

Gadde, L.-E., and Håkansson, H. (1992). *Professional purchasing.* London: Routledge.

Gadde, L.-E., and Mattsson, L.-G. (1987). Stability and change in network relationships. *International Journal of Research in Marketing, 4*, 29–41.

Gemunden, H. G., Ritter, T., and Walter, A. (Eds). (1998). *Relationships and networks in international markets.* London: Elsevier.

Grabher, G. (Ed.). (1993). *The embedded firm: On the socioeconomics of industrial networks.* London: Routledge.

Granovetter, M. (1985). Economic action and social structure: The problem of embeddedness. *American Journal of Sociology, 91*, 481–510.

Hägg, I., and Johanson, J. (1982). *Foretag i natwork. Ny syn pa konkurrenskraft* [Enterprise in networks: New perspective on competitiveness]. Stockholm: SNS.

Håkansson, H. (Ed.). (1982). *International marketing and purchasing of industrial goods: An interaction approach.* New York: John Wiley.

Håkansson, H. (Ed.). (1987). *Industrial technological development: A network approach.* London: Croom Helm.

Håkansson, H. (1989). *Corporate technological behavior: Cooperation and networks.* London: Routledge.

Håkansson, H., Johanson, J., and Wootz, B. (1976). Influence tactics in buyer–seller processes. *Industrial Marketing Management, 5*, 319–332.

Håkansson, H., and Ostberg, K. (1975). Industrial marketing: An organizational problem? *Industrial Marketing Management, 4*, 113–123.

Håkansson, H., and Snehota, I. (1989). No business is an island. *Scandinavian Journal of Management, 5*(3), 187–200.

Håkansson, H., and Snehota, I. (1995). *Developing relationships in business networks*. London: Routledge.

Håkansson, H., and Wootz, B. (1975). Supplier selection in an international environment: An experimental study. *Journal of Marketing Research, 12*, 46–51.

Halinen, A. (1997). *Relationship marketing in professional services: A study of agency-client dynamics in the advertising sector*. London: Routledge.

Hallén, L. (1980). *Sverige på Europamarknaden. Åsikter om inköp och marknadsföring* [Sweden on the European Market: Opinions about purchasing and marketing]. Lund: Studentlitteratur.

Hallén, L., and Johanson, J. (Eds). (1989). *Networks of relationships in international industrial marketing*. Greenwich, CT: JAI.

Hallén, L., Johanson, J., and Seyed-Mohamed, N. (1989). Relationships and exchange in international and domestic business. In L. Hallén and J. Johanson (Eds), *Networks of relationships in international industrial marketing* (pp. 7–25). Greenwich, CT: JAI.

Hammarkvist, O., Håkansson, H., and Mattsson, L.-G. (1982). *Marknadsföring för konkurrenskraft* [Marketing for competitive strength]. Lund: Liber.

Havila, V. (1996). *International business-relationships triads: A study of the changing role of the intermediating actor*. Unpublished doctoral dissertation, Uppsala University.

Henders, B. (1992). *Position in industrial networks: Marketing newsprint in the UK*. Unpublished doctoral dissertation, Uppsala University.

Herz, S. (1993). *The internationalization process of freight transport companies*. Unpublished doctoral dissertation, Stockholm School of Economics.

Hughes, T. P. (1983). *Networks of power: Electrification in Western society, 1880–1930*. Baltimore: Johns Hopkins University Press.

Iacobucci, D. (Ed.). (1996). *Networks in marketing*. Thousand Oaks, CA: Sage.

Johanson, J. (1966). *Svenskt specialstål på utländska marknader* [Swedish special steel on foreign markets]. Unpublished doctoral dissertation, Uppsala University, Sweden.

Johanson, J., and Mattsson, L.-G. (1994). The market-as-networks traditions in Sweden. In G. Laurent, G. Lilien, and B. Pras (Eds), *Research traditions in marketing*. Boston: Kluwer Academic.

Kock, S. (1991). *A strategic process for gaining external resources through long-lasting relationships*. Unpublished doctoral dissertation, Swedish School of Economics and Business Administration, Helsinki, Finland.

Kutchker, M. (1975). *Rationalität und Entschedungskriterien komplexer Investitionsentscheidungen – ein empirischer Bericht* [Rationality and decision parameters in complicated investment decisions]. Unpublished doctoral dissertation, University of Mannheim.

Kutchker, M., and Kirsch, W. (1978). *Verhandlungen auf dem Markt fur Investitionsguter* [Bargaining in the market for investment goods] (Research Rep.). Munich.

Laage-Hellman, J. (1997). *Business networks in Japan: Supplier–customer interaction in product development*. London: Routledge.

Lorenzoni, G., and Ornati, J. P. (1988). Constellations of firms and new ventures. *Journal of Business Venturing, 3*(1), 41–57.

Lundgren, A. (1995). *Technical innovation and industrial evolution*. London: Routledge.

March, J. G., and Simon, H. A. (1958). *Organizations*. New York: John Wiley.

Nelson, R. R., and Winter, S. G. (1982). *An evolutionary theory of economic change*. Cambridge, MA: Belknap.

Nohria, H., and Eccles, R. G. (Eds). (1992). *Networks and organizations: Structure, form and action*. Boston, MA: Harvard Business School Press.

Pardo, C., and Salle, R. (1994). Strategic interplays of an actor in a relationship with a distributor. *Industrial Marketing Management, 23*, 403–418.

Pedersen, A.-C. (1996). *Utvikling av leverandorrelasjoner i industriella netverk* [Development of supplier relationships in industrial networks: A study of connections between relationships]. Unpublished doctoral dissertation, Norwegian School of Technology, Trondheim.

Perrin, M. (1979). *Les entreprises francaises de biens industriels face à la concurrence sur cinq marche's européens*. Paris: Centre Francais du Commerce Extérieur.

Porter, M. E. (1980). *Competitive strategy: Techniques for analyzing industries and competitors*. New York: Free Press.

Porter, M. E. (1985). *Competitive advantage: Creating and sustaining superior performance*. New York: Free Press.

Raesfeld Meijer, A. von. (1997). *Technological cooperation in networks: A socio-cognitive approach*. Unpublished doctoral dissertation, Twnte University.

Reve, T. (1990). The firm as a nexus of internal and external contracts. In M. Aoki, B. Gustafsson, and O. E. Williamson (Eds), *The firm as a nexus of treaties* (pp. 133–161). London: Sage.

Reve, T., and Stern, L. W. (1979). Interorganizational relationships in marketing channels. *Academy of Management Review*, *4*, 405–416.

Richardson, G. B. (1972). The organization of industry. *Economic Journal*, *82*, 883–896.

Rosenberg, N. (Ed.). (1982). *Inside the black box: Technology and economics*. Cambridge: Cambridge University Press.

Salmi, A. (1995). *Institutionally changing business networks*. Unpublished doctoral dissertation, Swedish School of Economics and Business Administration, Helsinki, Finland.

Scherer, F. M. (1970). *Industrial market structure and economic performance*. Chicago: Rand McNally.

Sheth, J. N. (1978). Recent developments in organizational buying behavior. *P.U. Management Review*, *1*(1), 65–91.

Sheth, J. N., Gardner, D. M., and Garrett, D. E. (1988). *Marketing theory: Evolution and evaluation*. New York: John Wiley.

Sheth, J. N., and Parvatiyar, A. (1992). Towards a theory of business alliance formation. *Scandinavian International Business Review*, *1*(3), 71–87.

Spekman, R. E. (1988, July-August). Strategic supplier selection: Understanding long-term buyer relationships. *Business Horizons*, pp. 75–81.

Storper, M., and Walker, R. (1989). *The capitalist imperative*. New York: Basil Blackwell.

Teece, D. J. (1980). Economies of scope and the scope of enterprise. *Journal of Economic Behavior and Organisations*, *1*(1), 233–247.

Teramoto, Y. (1990). *Network power*. Tokyo: NTT.

Thompson, J. D. (1967). *Organizations in action: Social science bases of administrative theory*. New York: McGraw-Hill.

Torvatn, T. (1996). *Productivity in industrial networks: A case study of the purchasing function*. Unpublished doctoral dissertation, Norwegian School of Technology, Trondheim.

Tunisini, A. (1997). *The dissolution of channels and hierarchies: An inquiry into the changing customer relationships and organization of the computer companies*. Unpublished doctoral dissertation, Uppsala University.

Turnbull, P. W., and Cunningham, M. (1980). *International marketing and purchasing: A survey among marketing and purchasing executives in five European countries*. London: Macmillan.

Turnbull, P. W., and Paliwoda, S. J. (Eds). (1986). *Research in international marketing*. London: Croom Helm.

Turnbull, P. W., and Valla, J.-P. (Eds). (1985). *Strategies for international industrial marketing*. London: Croom Helm.

Twedt, D. (1964). How stable are advertiser-advertising agency relationships? *Journal of Marketing*, *28*(3), 83–84.

von Hippel, E. A. (1988). *The sources of innovation*. New York: Oxford University Press.

Waluszewski, A. (1990). Framväxten av en ny massateknik-en utvecklingshistoria [The development of a new pulp process technology]. *Acta Universitatis Upsaliensis, Studia Oeconomia Negotiorum*, *21*.

Webster, F. E., Jr. (1992). The changing role of marketing in the corporation. *Journal of Marketing*, *56*(4), 1–17.

Weick, K. (1969). *The social psychology of organizing*. Reading, MA: Addison-Wesley.

Wilkinson, I. F., and Young, L. (1994). Business dancing: An alternative paradigm for relationship marketing. *Asia-Australia Marketing Journal*, *2*(1), 67–80.

Williamson, O. E. (1975). *Markets and hierarchies: Analysis and antitrust implications*. New York: Free Press.

Williamson, O. E. (1985). *The economic institutions of capitalism: Firms, markets, and relational contracting*. New York: Free Press.

Wilson, D. T., and Möller, K. (Eds). (1995). *Business marketing: An interaction and network perspective*. Boston: Kluwer Academic.

Wilson, D. T., and Mummalaneni, V. (1986). Bonding and commitment in supplier relationships: A preliminary conceptualization. *Industrial Marketing and Purchasing*, 1(3), 44–58.

Part 2
Understanding Interaction and Relationships

The second part of the book concentrates on *relationships*. These are at the core of business marketing and purchasing and the interaction approach to understanding them. The first paper in this part is the earliest one in the book and it outlines ideas that were among the precursors of the interaction approach. It illustrates the reality facing many companies in business markets with a limited number of important customers and suppliers that have to deal with each other individually. The reading illustrates one of the fundamental requirements for any company operating in a business market, whether as buyer or seller, which is to get "inside the head" of their counterpart. In this case, the reading describes the uncertainties faced by customers in business markets and how these uncertainties can be influenced by a supplier company to its advantage.

The second reading by David Ford introduces ideas on what happens in the relationships between customer and supplier companies and how those relationships develop. It points to some of the managerial tasks involved in these relationships. The third reading, "How do companies interact?" looks at the interaction between companies in more detail. It uses the concepts of "mutuality", "particularity" and "inconsistency" to highlight the choices open to business marketers in their relationships with customers. The reading is interesting, not just because of its usefulness to managers, but also because it illustrates the development of some of the earlier concepts within the interaction approach.

The fourth reading in this section, by Håkan Håkansson and Ivan Snehota also shows a development of earlier ideas on inter-company interaction. In particular, it is relevant to managers because it highlights that close relationships with customers and suppliers can not only produce benefits for both parties, but also involve costs and problems. The next paper by Keith Blois builds on this warning and uses case studies to show the diversity of possible approaches to relationships and when these might be appropriate.

The final paper by Ian Wilkinson and Louise Young appeared fifteen years after reading number 2 on the development of buyer–seller relationships and it shows how ideas have developed during that time. In particular, it emphasises the nature of both co-operation and conflict in buyer–seller relationships. The reading also uses the metaphor of different types of dances to describe what goes on between companies in their relationships. It contrasts this view with the more conventional idea of buyer–seller relationships as being rather like marriages.

CONTENTS

2.1 Influence tactics in buyer–seller processes*

Håkan Håkansson, Jan Johanson and Bjorn Wootz

INTRODUCTION

The industrial goods producer, like the consumer goods producer, uses various means of competition in his marketing activities. The standard literature offers chapters on advertising, sales promotion, personal selling, technical service, delivery, quality and price.[1]

When marketing a product or a service it is assumed that the firm combines these means of competition in a marketing mix. Much of the literature is devoted to decisions concerning the optimal combination and the contents of these competitive means. This approach seems appropriate in situations where the firm has many customers who can be treated in a standardized way. These situations also imply that the customers in relation to each competitive mean can be described by an average response curve. In many producer markets, however, the selling firm has a limited number of big customers who are in consequence very important and must be handled individually. The relations to these customers are often complex, involving several departments and decision-makers on both sides in order to solve technical, commercial and delivery problems. In these situations it is altogether meaningless to base the planning of marketing activities on average response curves and therefore there is a need for another approach. The aim of this chapter is to discuss such an approach and illustrate its usefulness for practical decision-making.

In this chapter the relation between the buying and the selling firm is seen as an interaction process between two active components.[2] In the first two sections we discuss this interaction process from the buying and the selling firm's point of view respectively. Our purpose is to find descriptive variables appropriate to increase our understanding of industrial markets.

In the third section attention is focused on some specific activities of the selling firm. These concern the selling firm's way of influencing the buyer – its influencing tactics. Three examples of influencing tactics used in reality are described in the last section in order to illustrate our theoretical model.

THE INTERACTION PROCESS FROM THE BUYING FIRM'S POINT OF VIEW

In the interaction processes with suppliers the buying firm strives efficiently to secure the supply of needed products and services. In some situations this is a very simple task – when there is no doubt about the firm's needs and there are several reliable suppliers on the market. Then the buyer can choose the supplier offering the lowest price among those which fulfil all the functional requirements. Other situations may be more troublesome. The need may be difficult to determine and specify for example when it is impossible to measure its characteristics. Another situation raising problems is when the market is heterogeneous and/or dynamic. A third type of situation which is difficult for the buyer to handle is when he does not completely trust the seller's reliability, or when there are problems of coordinating the actual transaction with own production or with other transactions. These three types of situation can in general terms be described as having different degrees of uncertainty in the need, the market and the transaction respectively.

In order to characterize the interaction process from the buyer's point of view, we can use these three uncertainty variables. To a certain extent the uncertainty emanates from the actual situation, but it can also be dependent on the interaction process itself. It is important to understand how the uncertainty in these three dimensions increases or decreases during different interaction processes. The three variables are presented in more detail below.

Need uncertainty

There are often difficulties in interpreting the exact nature of the needs for materials, machines, tools, services, etc., in the firm. The buyer's perceived need uncertainty is a function of these difficulties in combination with the importance of the actual need. If for example production will be stopped due to an unsuitable product the need uncertainty will be perceived as considerably higher than if it only affects a minor aspect of production.

It is important to realize that the need uncertainty can be both increased and decreased during an interaction process with a supplier. He may, for instance, have knowledge of factors not previously considered by the buying firm which will increase the need uncertainty. On the other hand the seller may know some way of interpreting the need more exactly and this will probably decrease the buyer's need uncertainty.

The need uncertainty is not directly related to the technical complexity of the product. The exact nature of the raw materials required in some production processes, as for example pulp used for producing high quality paper, may be very difficult to interpret and the buying situation for these products can consequently be characterized as having high need uncertainty. Other products with high technical complexity are standardized in terms of output and can therefore be said to have a low need uncertainty. These examples illustrate that there is no direct or clear-cut relation between the degree of need uncertainty and the technical complexity.

Market uncertainty

Market uncertainty is related to suppliers perceived by the buying firm as source alternatives. The degree of market uncertainty depends on the degree of difference between the suppliers (heterogeneity) and how these differences change over time (dynamism). The problem from the buying firm's point of view is that by working up a relation with one supplier they will lose the chances of exploiting the differences and changes. In other words, there is an opportunity cost depending on whether the degree of heterogeneity and dynamism is large or small. When the heterogeneity and dynamism are both large the opportunity cost is large and there are in consequence reasons for caution in developing extensive relations.

Transaction uncertainty

The transaction uncertainty has to do with problems of getting the product (physically, legally, on time, etc.) from the seller to the buyer. There are for example differences in the degree to which the delivery of the needed product must be coordinated in time with other events (production schedules, delivery of other products, etc.). Another important aspect of the transaction uncertainty is related to the "difference" between the buyer and the seller. When there are differences in language, culture, technology, etc., there are further obstacles to the two parties' understanding of each other. The initial difference between the two may, however, be reduced during the interaction process, which in other words can be seen as a learning process.

A third factor influencing the transaction uncertainty is the degree to which trading procedures of a certain product are standardized. The less standardized these procedures are, the greater the complexity of the discussions and negotiations will be and the greater the transaction uncertainty.

The buying firm's behaviour in response to the three uncertainty dimensions

The organizational buying model presented here was developed and tested by the authors of this chapter. In order to exemplify the theoretical discussions above we summarize some of the main results. These were presented earlier in: Håkansson and Wootz (1975a), Håkansson and Wootz (1975b), Håkansson and Wootz (1975d), Håkansson (1975) and Wootz (1975).

In situations characterized by high need uncertainty decision-makers in the buying firm:

- Are relatively more concerned with functionality and quality than price aspects;
- Prefer to interact with suppliers in countries with a small cultural distance;
- Choose to interact with suppliers which have been used earlier (high source loyalty);
- Form a more complex internal communication structure which often involves different kinds of specialists in the decision-making unit;
- Form a more complex external communication structure which often involves different kinds of specialists in direct contact with the supplier;
- Have relatively more contacts with the supplier which also means a more time consuming decision process.

High market uncertainty means that decision-makers in the buying firm:

- Have contacts with a relatively greater number of suppliers;
- Are specialized in relation to these high uncertainty markets.

High transaction uncertainty means that decision-makers in the buying firm:

- More often strive to find parallel suppliers;
- Are more concerned with delivery questions;
- Have relatively more contacts with the supplier before making the final decision.

THE INTERACTION PROCESS FROM THE SELLING FIRM's POINT OF VIEW

In the long run the seller's goal in the interaction process is to make profits by selling his product or service at a price which exceeds his costs. In order to make the buyer pay this price the seller must be able to solve some of the problems of the buying firm. Primarily the ability concerns the degree to which the seller can satisfy important aspects of a certain need, and secondly, the degree to which the seller can transfer the solution to the buyer. We label the first problem the seller's need solving ability and the second the seller's transfer ability. The need solving ability includes both the ability which is built into the product (function, quality, etc.) and the services which are given in combination with the product. It covers for example the seller's ability to understand and interpret the buyer's need and find suitable solutions.

The transfer ability concerns the capacity and reliability of the deliveries and also the extent to which problems related to the negotiations can be solved.

The selling firm's resources in terms of equipment, technical and economic knowledge, organization, etc., determine the total "stock" of both need solving and transfer abilities. The seller's total stock, i.e. its ability profile, can therefore only be increased through changes in these strategic means. Thus the ability profile cannot usually be changed by for example an advertising campaign. The ability must be demonstrated in practice before the customer's perception of the profile really can be assumed to have changed.

Of the means mentioned above only the organization is not a traditional means in marketing. Our way of analysing industrial marketing problems implies that the organizational design is of critical importance in the interaction process, where the seller is assumed to demonstrate his need solving and transfer abilities. If, for example, a firm wants to demonstrate a high need solving ability, it must be so organized as to make contact with customers easy in both depth and breadth. The authors' practical experience suggests that the strategic importance of the organization as a means in industrial marketing is underestimated. This probably means that a great number of firms have an inadequate balance between investments in equipment, knowledge and organization.[3]

The higher the ability the firm wants to attain, as regards both need solving and transfer abilities, the more resources must be invested in knowledge, equipment and organization. As a consequence the firm will finally arrive at a higher cost level. On the other hand the buyer values these abilities positively and will be prepared to pay a higher price for them only in situations where he perceives uncertainty to a particular degree. It is assumed that the higher the uncertainty, the more the buyer values the corresponding ability. Therefore it is important for the selling firm to adapt its abilities to the perceived uncertainty of the buying firm.

From a marketing point of view the above description of the seller raises two very important questions.

The first question pertains to how much of the total ability of the firm should be "offered" to each buying firm (the limitation problem). Selling firms normally do not distribute their efforts to all customers in a uniform way. Some customers, important in one way or another, are given special treatment. Technical adaptations of products are for example sometimes offered to some customers, whereas other firms can only buy from a standard product range. The relation to a certain buying firm is, as we mentioned earlier, built up successively. Often there are some kinds of self-generated aspects in the process which means that it develops in both volume and stability. The process must therefore be controlled in order to avoid binding the seller to inappropriate buying firms. For the seller the solution to this problem is therefore not to make one or a few decisions regarding the customers with whom he will interact and the level of interaction, but more or less continually pay attention to this matter and analyse the nature of the interaction process with different customers.

The second question concerns the handling of each relationship (the handling problem). Here it is important to regard both social and physical exchange. Social exchange relates to the creation of confidence.[4] One aspect here is to give customers information about important conditions of the seller's own firm and obtain information about the customer. If, for instance, a firm wants to demonstrate a high need solving ability, its marketing department must be competent to handle technical questions up to a certain level and also have routines for involving technical experts in the interaction when its own technical competence is inappropriate. A firm which tries to demonstrate a high transfer ability must have a broad experience in transport economies, logistics, and so forth.

Arrangements like these are thought to give high social exchange which implies an efficient physical exchange (e.g. regarding deliveries of actual products, financial arrangements, etc.).

Physical and social exchange are also related to each other in such a way that a more complex physical exchange must be combined with a more extensive social exchange.

The discussion up to this point identified two important aspects of industrial marketing – need-solving ability and transfer ability. In relation to these aspects the industrial goods producer is confronted with two problem areas – the limitation problems and the handling problems. Both of these problem areas ought to be a focus for further research. In this chapter we now limit the discussion to a specific aspect of the handling problems – the seller's possibilities of influencing decision-makers in the buying firm. We call this aspect the seller's influence tactics. The seller always has the ability to change the buyer's perception of a certain situation. This does not mean that the seller tries to communicate inadequate information because professional buyers will in the long run see through such a ploy. Instead the seller should try to adapt the buyer's perception to what he believes is a reasonable assessment of the situation. The next section will be devoted to this question.

ALTERNATIVE INFLUENCE TACTICS

In accordance with the introductory discussion each customer is assumed to be more or less unique in industrial markets. In an analysis of the influence tactics of an industrial goods purchaser it is consequently inappropriate to start the analysis with an average picture of the customers. Instead the starting-point should be the relationship with the individual customer. In some situations, however, several customers can be influenced in the same way, making aggregations possible. Irrespective of this fact we define the influence tactics in relation to the individual customer. Thus an industrial goods producer will have a number of tactics which are similar in some respects and different in others.

The theoretical argument is supported by the empirical fact that industrial goods producers often have specialized organizational units which are responsible for activities directed toward more important customers.

By influencing the perceived uncertainty of the buyer in different ways it will be possible for the selling firm to bring about various types of behaviour effect. The perceived uncertainty can be either increased or decreased depending on the contents of the influence tactics. In different marketing situations different combinations of increases and decreases in the three uncertainty dimensions discussed earlier are more or less efficient. Before discussing various combinations in detail, i.e. influence tactics with various contents, we treat each uncertainty dimension separately.

By giving the buyer new technical information the seller may modify the buyer's actual perception of the product and increase his perceived need uncertainty. In consequence decision-makers may try to broaden the decision base internally, and interact with firms which can be expected to fulfil the increased functional demand.

A seller can also try to reduce the perceived need uncertainty of a buyer by emphasizing that the problems to be solved are not as complex as the buyer believes. From an influence point of view it is, in other words, possible both to increase and to diminish the perceived need uncertainty. Probably it is much more difficult to achieve the latter in practice.

If the seller can give such information that the buying firm perceives greater differences and/or greater changes on the market than was previously the case, the perceived market uncertainty of the buyer increases. The buyer's attention will consequently be focused on the market and he will make more extensive comparisons between prices, qualities, payment conditions, and so forth. On the other hand, if the seller provides information which emphasizes the uniformity of the market the opposite effect will probably be achieved. In this case the buyer does not conceive the idea of broadening his knowledge of the market situation.

The seller may also emphasize the abilities of the firm to carry through its delivery commitments. He can reduce thereby the perceived transaction uncertainty of the buyer. This can be achieved by building up a buffer stock for the customer or by developing a joint transport and stock system. Tactics intended to increase the buyer's perceived transaction uncertainty toward the seller are not meaningful; this can, however, be the purpose of the information tactics of the competitors.

We conclude that the seller, by influencing the uncertainty perceptions of the buyer in these three dimensions, can cause certain desired behavioural reactions. The influence tactics of an industrial seller toward a certain customer describe how the seller simultaneously influences the buyer in all the three uncertainty dimensions. The influence tactics can be described in the matrix presented in Table 1. Three levels of change are distinguished. The seller can either try to keep the uncertainty perception of the purchaser constant or to increase or decrease it. The matrix makes it possible to distinguish a fairly large number (27) of influence tactics. Some of them are frequent, some are more or less exceptions.

Table 1 Descriptive matrix for influence tactics

Direction of change	Increase	Constant	Reduce
Need uncertainty			
Transaction uncertainty			
Market uncertainty			

APPLICATIONS

So far we have discussed how the influence tactics of the industrial goods producer can be described. We shall now use this descriptive model as a norm in order to guide industrial marketing managers in their planning of information activities. Different influence tactics are of varying efficiency depending on the nature of the marketing situation. We can identify two basic marketing situations, which require opposite influence tactics. In one very common marketing situation the firm has well established relations with the customers and is primarily concerned with the development and the stabilization of those relations. In the other situation, which is also very common, there are strong relations between a competitor and potential customers and the important task is to break these relations in order to have the opportunity to establish new relations. In the first situation the influence tactics should attempt to reduce the customer's perceived uncertainty which is expected to lead to increased stability and closer cooperation between the two firms. In the other situation influence tactics which seek to increase perceived need uncertainty and market uncertainty are preferable. A situation is thereby created where the customer will be interested in more information about alternative sellers and will in some cases test new sources. In the first situation it was advantageous to stabilize the relationship with the customer by reducing the uncertainty perception of the buyer. In the other it is appropriate to unsettle the situation by an increase in the uncertainty.

These two marketing situations are fairly clear-cut and the proposed influence tactics rather obvious. The cases in the next section partly illustrate these clear-cut situations and the influence tactics observed correspond to the results from the theoretical analysis. However, more detailed normative discussions of the effectiveness of different influence tactics in different marketing situations must derive from a much broader data base. Our descriptive model can then be used in order to generate hypotheses regarding the effectiveness of specific tactics in particular marketing situations.

In the following case studies we describe and classify actual influence tactics. In each case we have observations in the matrix described above.

Before presenting the cases it is necessary to outline the measurement of the tactics, i.e. the manner of locating the tactical behaviour of a firm in our matrix. On an unambitious level it is possible to let a marketing manager make intuitive judgements of the firm's activities. A more ambitious approach is to let the researcher pass judgement after exhaustive discussions with marketing people about the context of various marketing activities.

In the following cases we used the latter approach. Activities in real marketing situations are described in detail on the basis of interviews with marketing managers and supplementary written material. The descriptions are focused on the seller's marketing activities. The descriptions of the cases were written together with the actual firms whereas all comments and discussions of the influence tactics are our own. This is the reason why our concepts are used in the discussions and the comments on each case. The cases describe average influence tactics for each selling firm. In accordance with the discussions in this chapter there is a unique tactic in relation to each customer. However, it was impossible to obtain information about these individual tactics and an average tactic for a group of important customers was measured instead.

THREE CASES

Söderberg and Haak and structural alloy steel

The case

In September 1974 Söderberg and Haak (SH) started the marketing of structural alloy steel in Sweden.[5] The market was new to SH. The firm had, however, long enjoyed a strong position as a steel wholesaler. As the expansion opportunities in this market were considered unsatisfactory, SH was systematically searching for new steel products which could be expected to fit the firm's structure with regard to organization, marketing methods, handling equipment, and so on. Structural alloy steel was considered to have the desired synergy effects in relation to the other activities. The special steel is used in mechanical engineering works for products which are exposed to high quality demand such as cogwheels, shafts, etc. The total Swedish market is estimated as 50 000 tons per year. The biggest user is the car industry. As the firms in that industry and some other big engineering firms are major users of structural alloy steel they buy the steel direct from the producers. SH's potential customers were therefore the great number of firms which can be characterized as small and medium-sized engineering firms. This group can be estimated to include more than 10 000 firms. An investigation showed that fewer big customers of alloy steel than expected were already steel customers of SH. The available data did not allow a more precise estimate of the market.

Four Swedish steel works dominated the market. SKF was the biggest with 50% of the market. Bofors and Uddeholm, who had coordinated their marketing, could be considered as a unit with around 20% of the market. Fagersta was the smallest with a market share of less than 10%. The rest of the demand was covered through imports. To a great extent this took the form of direct buying by the car industry from continental steel works.

The market was regarded as "sleeping". Advertising and other kinds of mass communication were modest. The communication mainly contained quality arguments. It was emphasized that structural alloy steel was a technically rather complex product where it was essential that the supplier provide both technical advice and technical service. According to the common opinion among customers this could only be offered by a steel producer and not by a wholesaler such as SH.

SH entered this market with an aggressive and somewhat strident voice. Their behaviour was in stark contrast to the communication style of their four Swedish competitors. For their part SH wished to tell the market that something new was happening, that there was a new way of thinking. A new mode of distribution was in fact introduced to the market. In contrast to the steel works, SH emphasized the width of their product line and the speed of delivery as important decision variables from the customer's point of view. The price was in no way stressed. SH preferred rather to maintain the same price level as the Swedish steel works.

SH employed five salesmen who had specialized in structural alloy steel and possessed previous experience of the market. They were also trained to give the customers technical advice. During the first period their work was to visit and inform customers about the product line and emphasize "traditional" wholesale arguments, i.e. the width of the product line and the efficiency of distribution.

Classification of the influence tactics

At the time of SH's entry the structural alloy steel market was stable with a number of established seller–buyer relations. Sellers on this market had always stressed their need solving ability, whereas SH, as a wholesaler, emphasized the transfer ability. Indirectly SH also implied that the level of need solving ability claimed by the steel producers was in most cases exaggerated.

The problem faced by SH was how to break these stable buyer–seller relations, so that SH could establish their own relations. The customer is assumed to have had a medium need uncertainty, a low market uncertainty and a low transaction uncertainty at the time of SH's entrance. The SH advertising campaign was an attempt to make the buyer perceive a higher market uncertainty by informing him about a new and different alternative. Of course, the hope was to initiate processes in the customers' organizations meaning that new supplier alternatives would be considered, and that the interest in changes toward these new alternatives would increase.

SH did not push the need uncertainty dimension too hard but tried to make a modest reduction of the potential customers' need uncertainty. They also sought to get technical competence regarded as necessary in relation to the customers' need uncertainty.

The buyer's perceived transaction uncertainty in relation to SH was intended to be reduced. The buyers had known their former suppliers for a long time and generally considered them safe from a delivery point of view. Compared to them SH were new, even if they were old in neighbouring product markets. SH invested in equipment for material handling and a wide initial stock which covered all important dimensions and sizes.

SH's influence tactics are summed up in Table 2.

Table 2 The influence tactics of Söderberg and Haak

Direction of change	Increase	Constant	Reduce
Need uncertainty			×
Transaction uncertainty			×
Market uncertainty	×		

ASEA synchronous motors

The case

Synchronous motors are generally produced to order at ASEA in Västerås. The size of the effects of the motors varies between 50 and 500 kW and the price between 15 000 and 2 million Sw. Cr. The total ASEA sales of synchronous motors are about 80 million Sw. Cr. per year.

The functional demands on the motors are very high and they have to be adapted to the specific demands of different users. To obtain a high load capacity the motors must have a mechanical strength and the coils must be well insulated so that they can endure vibrations for instance. The motors are generally a very important part of the customers' production system as a breakdown can stop the whole production process and cause very high costs. The rising demand concerning performance and reliability means that the motors are more and more differentiated, at the same time as the producers try to reduce the number of variants by increased standardization, e.g. with regard to size.

The supply of synchronous motors is characterized by a small number of big international firms and a great number of local producers. For instance Siemens, General Electric, General Electric Company, and Hitachi are important international competitors to ASEA. All four generally have bigger market shares than ASEA on most markets. Siemens, for instance, has a very high market cover and also excellent service.

Some other international firms, which, from a market share point of view are smaller than ASEA, are Brown Bovery Company, AEG, and Westinghouse. Their competitive profile is also somewhat different from the profile of the four biggest. They bid on separate occasions and offer shorter delivery time or lower price.

ASEA is regarded as a technically advanced firm with highly reliable products. Information from ASEA is also accepted as correct as regards functional characteristics, delivery times, etc. The price of ASEA's products is thus somewhat high and ASEA heavily emphasize in their marketing the long term economic consequences of a motor rather than its price. In recent years ASEA has made heavy investments in order to raise the capacity and reduce the delivery times. The characteristics of customers are very different with regard to size, industry and knowledge. Some customer firms have a wide knowledge and experience base, while others are much less experienced. On the whole there are very stable relations between ASEA and its customers. The ten biggest customers within each product range are very loyal to ASEA and usually represent 50–90% of the sales.

As usual in industrial marketing most marketing resources are allocated to personal selling. The selling activities together with other competitive means such as pamphlets are controlled by the desire to give relevant technical information. The sales force informs about ASEA in general, about the product line, about its products in comparison with products of the competitors, and so on. An important part of the information, which is especially emphasized in contacts with new and inexperienced customers, consists in the discussion of difficulties and problems in connection with motors. The salesmen – who are generally technicians – thus raise problems which have occurred earlier and which ASEA has attempted to solve. In this way the salesmen try to make the customers realize problems which they have not met and note that more aspects than price and functional effect should be considered in the decision to buy.

In addition to ASEA's normal service division there are some service technicians who are experts on synchronous motors. At present they are primarily utilized as trouble-shooters, i.e. they are called in when problems arise at the customers.

Classification of influence tactics

From the above description it is clear that ASEA emphasizes the functional characteristics of its products at the same time as attempts are made to raise the degree of standardization. This means that ASEA neither wants, nor is able to manufacture, motors which are adapted to the specific demand of each customer. The need-solving ability can be characterized as the means. ASEA has tried to increase the transfer ability during the last few years by making investments in new plants in order to reduce delivery times.

The influence tactics are the same for all customers with respect to market uncertainty and transaction uncertainty. Firstly ASEA makes no attempt to influence the perceived market uncertainty in any direction, i.e. the tactics are neutral in this dimension. Secondly, ASEA always tries to reduce the perceived transaction uncertainty by emphasizing the safety and reliability of its deliveries. However, in the third dimension – need uncertainty – there are different tactics for different customers. ASEA tries to increase the perceived need uncertainty of those customers who are inexperienced and/or have low technical competence.

Experienced buyers on the other hand know all the possible problems and therefore already have a high need uncertainty. ASEA does not try to influence these customers in the need uncertainty dimension. The tactics to induce the customer to perceive a high need uncertainty are built on the principle that a high need uncertainty means that the customer will make heavy technical demands on the seller, which will favour ASEA which is assumed to have this technical competence.

ASEA's influence tactics are summed up in Table 3.

Table 3 The influence tactics of ASEA's synchronous motors in relation to some customers

Direction of change	Increase	Constant	Reduce
Need uncertainty	×		
Transaction uncertainty			×
Market uncertainty		×	

ASEA Quintus presses

The case

The Quintus department of ASEA markets presses for hydrostatic extrusion, plate forming and isostatic pressing. An isostatic press consists of a pressure vessel in which the material to be pressed is enclosed and subjected to a high uniform pressure from a pressure medium. ASEA's Quintus isostatic press consists of a pre-stressed cylinder having straight inner walls and nonthreaded enclosures which are kept in position by an outer frame. The cylinder consists of a steel core which has been wound with high strength wire, pre-stressed to such a degree that the steel core is always kept under compression even at maximum compaction pressure. Due to the combined effect of pre-stressing, the absence of axial forces in the mantle of the cylinder and the straight cylinder wall the stress configuration obtained is very favourable especially from the fatigue point of view.

Two types of isostatic presses are manufactured:

- Presses for cold isostatic pressing where the pressure medium is a fluid. Cold Quintus isostatic pressing equipment is available with pressure vessels for pressures up to 6300 bars, inside diameters up to 1400 mm and inside heights up to 3150 mm.
- Presses for hot isostatic pressing where gas, usually argon, is used as pressure medium. In a hot isostatic press, pressing is effected by a combination of high pressure and high temperature.

Quintus hot isostatic pressing equipment is available with pressure vessels for pressures up to 3200 bars and furnaces for temperatures up to 1750°C. The maximum diameter of the hot zone is 1290 mm and the maximum length 2550 mm.

The isostatic pressing process is used for producing billets, tungsten carbide parts such as tool bits, press tools and rolls for cold-strip mills, jet engine parts of special alloys, and so forth.

The prices of the presses vary between 0.5 and 10 million Sw. Cr. with a mean around 3 million. The total market for these types of press is 20–40 presses annually. ASEA delivers around half of them.

The two biggest competitors are National Forge and Autoclave, both in the USA. The state-owned Carbox is a small Swedish competitor. Autoclave is the strongest of the American firms in the smaller dimensions.

Swedish authorities were quick to formulate rigorous safety requirements for equipment in Sweden. To meet these demands without additional safety precautions in the form of concrete bunkers the ASEA presses are more technically advanced in this safety respect and as a consequence the prices on the ASEA presses are somewhat higher than those of their competitors.

National Forge has almost the same product programme as ASEA but the prices are usually somewhat lower. In the final stage of negotiation there is generally a difference of 10% to the advantage of National Forge. There is very hard competition for the big projects, while for the small projects ASEA is sometimes the only manufacturer approached.

ASEA is generally considered to have the best technical solutions but, as stated above, at a somewhat higher price.

The customers are normally private industrial firms working with powder technology where they are looking for material characteristics and/or production methods which cannot be attained by conventional techniques.

Those who handle the purchases are usually very advanced technically and always know their requirements with respect to temperature and pressure uniformity. They are often new customers as only a few have bought several presses. The explanation is that the technique of isostatic pressing is so new that there has not been any need for replacement purchases.

The most important means to influence the customers is the salesmen. The first contacts with a new customer are usually made by the field salesmen who belong to the organization of the sales companies and to some extent are specialized on the Quintus presses. These salesmen try to form an opinion about the need of the customer and usually obtain the information which ASEA needs to be able to submit a preliminary offer. These are usually within ±10% of the final offer with respect to both technical performance and price. The customers generally ask for offers from several suppliers and on the basis of these offers the final specifications are made. During this process extensive discussions are held between the customer and the supplier. Besides the field salesmen, one or several of the specialists at the production unit in Västerås take part in these discussions. There are altogether 14 such specialists – all of them with technical education to university level. During these contacts ASEA emphasizes the technical solution and the safety of the equipment. The time from the first contact to the final order varies between eight months and three years. During this period several tests and technical investigations are often made.

ASEA has a high pressure laboratory where the pressure and test conditions desired by the customer can be tested. The tests are sometimes made free of charge, i.e. as a sales promotion activity, but usually the customer has to pay for them.

ASEA spends very limited amounts on the advertising of this product. They participate in exhibitions, in particular those with advanced technical character.

Classification of the influence tactics

Information to customers is characterized by ASEA's emphasis on their need-solving ability. This emphasis is made in the information of the salesmen as well as in information pamphlets. The development of the ASEA high pressure laboratory emphasizes the need-solving ability too. ASEA designs the product direct according to the need of the customer and also helps in identifying and specifying this need. The transfer ability is not emphasized in the same way, only through ASEA's general reliability.

The influence tactics are characterized by the fact that ASEA does not try to influence need uncertainty and market uncertainty. It is probably difficult to increase the perceived need and market uncertainty of the customers for this type of product, as the buyers normally perceive a high need uncertainty and are well aware of the differences between the suppliers. As ASEA's long-term strategy aims at creating a high need-solving ability there is no reason to try to reduce the perceived uncertainty in these two dimensions. On the other hand ASEA always tries to reduce the perceived transaction uncertainty by emphasizing reliability.

The influence tactics are summarized in Table 4.

Table 4 The influence tactics of ASEA's Quintus presses

Direction of change	Increase	Constant	Reduce
Need uncertainty		×	
Transaction uncertainty			×
Market uncertainty		×	

THE THREE CASES – SOME CONCLUSIONS

In all three cases the observed influence tactics had the expected effects from the selling firm's point of view. Söderberg and Haak actually succeeded in breaking stable buyer–seller relations and in building up new relationships. ASEA (case 2) succeeded in stabilizing and developing already existing relations. These two cases are similar insofar as both illustrate industrial buying with a high degree of rebuy situations. The problem for the selling firm with the entry onto a new market is to be considered a serious source. In order to be considered as an alternative, an efficient tactic is to increase the market uncertainty and thereby induce search processes for new alternatives (Söderberg and Haak). If you already are a working supplier you will have to develop existing relations by efficiently solving current problems (of function, delivery, etc.). If the firm is highly competent technically an appropriate tactic in situations where the need uncertainty is modest will be to try to increase the need uncertainty by identifying possible problems and thereby inducing the buyer to choose a technically advanced firm (ASEA case 2).

In case 3 there was a clear-cut picture. There was no doubt that purchasers perceived a high need uncertainty and that they also knew the existing differences between actual suppliers. In other words there are few opportunities to change this accepted picture. In a certain situation, however, it might be appropriate to emphasize technical problems in order to increase the need uncertainty. In buyer–seller relations ASEA always tries to show that it has the competence to handle the complex situation perceived by the buyer.

Söderberg and Haak were confronted with exactly the same situation but on a much lower technical level. They really had to show the customers that they as a wholesaler had the technical competence to solve the technical problems. Söderberg and Haak also tried to effect a modest reduction of the buyers' perceived need uncertainty.

The discussions in this chapter raise a number of questions which should be the focus for further research. An important one concerns the degree to which the organization design is a key variable in shaping adequate influence tactics. As mentioned before, organization design is probably an important variable in order to control the process of building up relationships with customers.

Another important research question is to discuss more explicitly the normative implications of the influence tactics model presented here. It will be necessary to develop more definite measurements of the fit between the influence tactics and the marketing situation.

NOTES

* The authors are grateful for the constructive comments of Lars Hallén, Lars-Gunnar Mattsson, Ivan Snehota of the University of Uppsala, Ove Brandes and Leif Melin of the University of Linkoping. The study has been financially supported by the Svenska Handelsbanken Foundation for Social Science Research.

1. See e.g. Boyd and Massey (1972), Howard (1973), Hill, Alexander and Cross (1975) and Kotler (1976).
2. The theoretical background for this interaction approach is presented in Håkansson and Östberg (1975). The present chapter is part of the research programme outlined there. The ideas from these two papers have formed the basis of a research project dealing with international industrial marketing which involved Jean-Paul Valla, University of Lyon; David Ford, University of Bath; Malcolm Cunningham and Peter Turnbull, University of Manchester, Institute of Science and Technology; and the Group for Industrial Marketing, University of Uppsala.
3. For a more detailed discussion of these questions, see Håkansson and Östberg (1975).
4. The social exchange concept is described in Håkansson and Östberg (1975).
5. This case is a summary of Wootz (1977).

REFERENCES

Boyd, H. W. and Massey, W. F. *Marketing Management*. Harcourt Brace Jovanovich, New York (1972).
Håkansson, H. and Östberg, C. Industrial Marketing: An Organizational Problem? *Industrial Marketing Management* **4**, 113–123 (1975).
Håkansson, H. and Wootz, B. Supplier Selection in an International Environment – An Experimental Study. *Journal of Marketing Research*, **Vol. XII**, 46–51 (1975a).
Håkansson, H. and Wootz, B. *Changes in the Propensity to Import – An Interaction Model on the Firm Level*. Department of Business Administration. University of Uppsala (1975b).
Håkansson, H. and Wootz, B. Företags inköpsbeteende (English translation of the Swedish title: Organizational Buyer Behavior). Studentlitteratur, Lund (1975c).
Håkansson, H. Studies in Industrial Purchasing with special reference to Determinants of Communication Patterns. *Acta Universitatis Upsaliensis*: University of Uppsala (1975).
Hill, R. M., Alexander, R. S. and Cross, J. S. *Industrial Marketing*. Richard D. Irwin, Homewood, Illinois (1975).
Howard, J. A. *Marketing Management, Operating, Strategic and Administrative*. Richard D. Irwin, Homewood, Illinois (1973).
Kotler, P. *Marketing Management, Analysis, Planning and Control*. Prentice-Hall, Englewood Cliffs, New Jersey (1976).
Wootz, B. Studies in Industrial Purchasing with special reference to Variations in External Communication. *Acta Universitatis Upsaliensis*: University of Uppsala (1975).
Wootz, B. Söderberg and Haak. MTC case series, Stockholm School of Economics (1976).

2.2 The development of buyer–seller relationships in industrial markets*

David Ford

INTRODUCTION

It has frequently been noted that buyer–seller interdependence is a crucial characteristic of industrial marketing,[1] i.e. that industrial firms establish buyer–seller relationships which are often close, complex and frequently long-term. Despite this, the nature of these relationships has, until recently, received scant attention in the literature.[2] Instead, marketing writers have been more concerned with analysis of the (albeit complex) process by which buying firms arrive at individual purchase decisions, and the ways in which the seller can influence this process in its favour.

This paper examines the nature of buyer–seller relationships in industrial markets by considering their development as a process through time. It is based on ideas generated from the IMP project[3] and is particularly concerned with the following factors:

- What is it that makes a buyer establish and develop relationships with one or a few suppliers, as an alternative to "playing the market"?
- How do the relationships between buying and selling firms change over time? What are the factors which aid or hinder the development of close relationships? Which of these are within the control of the two companies?
- What are the implications of close buyer–seller relationships for the two organizations involved? What problems can they lead to? How are the day-to-day dealings between the companies affected by, and how do they affect, the overall relationship?

THEORETICAL BASIS

Buyer–seller relations can be examined with reference to the interaction approach as developed by the IMP Group[4] as well as concepts drawn from the "New Institutionalists" within economics.[5]

The interaction approach

This sees buyer–seller relationships taking place between two *active* parties. This is in contrast to the more traditional view of marketing which analyses the *reaction* of an aggregate market to a seller's offering. The interaction approach considers that either buyer or seller may take the initiative in seeking a partner. Further, both companies are likely to be involved in adaptations to their own process or product technologies to accommodate each other. Neither party is likely to be able to make unilateral changes in its activities as buyer or seller without consultation, or at least consideration, of the possible reactions of their individual opposite numbers. Thus, industrial marketing and purchasing can properly be described as the "management of buyer–seller relationships".

The nature of relationships

Not all of the dealings between industrial buying and selling firms take place within close relationships. There are clear differences between the supply of paper clips and automotive components, or lubricating oil and factory buildings. The product and process technologies of the two companies are important factors in determining the nature of buyer–seller relations. Also important are the buyer and seller market structures which exist and hence the availability of alternative buyers and sellers.

Companies will develop close relationships rather than play the market, where they can obtain benefits in the form of cost reduction or increased revenues. These benefits are achieved by tailoring their resources to dealing with a specific buyer or seller, i.e. by making "durable transaction specific investments".[6] These investments mark major *adaptations* by a company to the relationship. By definition, they are not marketable, or at least their value in other transactions is less than in the specialized use for which they were intended. Therefore these adaptations mark a *commitment* by the buyer or seller to the relationship. They can be seen most clearly in such things as a supplier's development of a special product for a customer, a buyer's modification of a production process to accommodate a supplier's product or the joint establishment of a stock facility in a neutral warehouse. On the other hand, companies can be involved in "human capital investments",[7] i.e. alterations in procedures, special training, or allocation of managerial resources. These human adaptations produce savings by the familiarity and trust which they generate between the parties.

Overall relationships and individual episodes

The complexity of buyer–seller relations and the importance of mutual adaptations means that the analysis of relationships must be separated between the overall relationship itself and the individual *episodes* which comprise it. Thus, each delivery of product, price negotiation or social meeting takes place within the context of the overall relationship. Each episode is affected by the norms and procedures of the relationship as well as the atmosphere of co-operation or conflict which may have been established. Additionally, each episode affects the overall relationship and a single episode can change it radically, e.g. a relationship can be broken off "because" of a single failure in delivery. In fact, this failure is more likely to be the culminating episode in a worsening relationship. Thus, only a partial analysis of buyer–seller relations is achieved by researching individual episodes, e.g. a particular buying decision. On the other hand, an incomplete picture is obtained by examining the overall atmosphere of a relationship, for example in terms of power and dependency. Thus it is important to analyse both individual episodes and the overall relationship, as well as to understand the interaction between the two.[8]

The development of buyer–seller relationships

This article is less concerned with the reasons for the choice of buyer or seller partners (although this is acknowledged as a question of considerable importance!). Instead, it analyses the process of establishment and development of relationship over time by considering five stages in their evolution. We should also note that the process described here does not argue the inevitability of relationship development. Relationships can fail to develop or regress depending upon the actions of either party or of competing buyers or sellers. Throughout the examination, the bilateral nature of relationships will be stressed, particularly the similarity of the buyer's and seller's activities. The five stages are illustrated in Table 1. Throughout the analysis we consider the variables of Experience, Uncertainty, Distance, Commitment and Adaptations.

Table 1 The development of buyer–seller relationships in industrial markets – summary

	1 Pre-relationship stage	2 Early stage	3 Development stage	4 Long-term stage	5 Final stage
	Evaluation of new potential supplier	Negotiation of sample delivery	Contract signed or delivery build-up	After several major purchases or large scale deliveries	In long-established stable markets
Evaluation initiated by: Particular episode in existing relationship		Experience Low	Increased	High	
General evaluation of existing supplier performance		Uncertainty High	Reduced	Minimum Development of institutionalization	Extensive institutionalization – Business based on Industry Codes of Practice
Efforts of non-supplier					
Other information sources					
Overall policy decision		Distance High	Reduced	Minimum	
Evaluation conditioned by: Experience with previous supplier		Commitment Actual: low Perceived: low	Actual: increased Perceived: demonstrated by informal adaptations	Actual: maximum Perceived: reduced	
Uncertainty about potential relationship					
"Distance" from potential supplier		Adaptation High investment of management time. Few cost-savings	Increasing formal and informal adaptations Cost-savings increase	Extensive adaptations, Cost-savings reduced by institutionalization	
Commitment					
Zero					

Stage 1: The pre-relationship stage

Previous authors have stressed the *inertia* of buying companies, when it comes to seeking new sources of supply.[9] Buyers may continue with existing sources with relatively little knowledge or evaluation of the wider supply markets available to them. We will take as our starting point the case of a company which has grown to rely on a main supplier for a particular product purchased on a regular basis, as in the case of equipment, or continuously as with a component.

In these circumstances a decision to evaluate a potential new supplier can be the result of a particular episode in an existing relationship. For example, a UK producer of consumer durables started to evaluate alternative suppliers following a major price increase by a company, which had until then supplied all its requirements for a certain product.

Other reasons which may cause evaluation of new potential suppliers include: a regular vendor analysis in which the performance and potential of existing suppliers is assessed; the efforts of a non-supplying company to obtain business, perhaps based on a major change in its offering, e.g. a new product introduction; some change in requirements or market conditions experienced by the buyer, e.g. a UK car manufacturer began evaluating overseas sources for windscreens following the move towards tempered glass for which there was a European capacity shortage.

Alternatively, the evaluation of potential suppliers can be the result of a general policy. For example, widespread industrial troubles in the UK in 1974 ("the three-day week") caused one manufacturer to adopt the policy of obtaining approximately 40% of its components from overseas. It then started a search to find and evaluate potential sources of supply to carry out this policy.

A company's evaluation of a potential new supplier will take place without any commitment to that supplier at this stage. The evaluation will be conditioned by three factors: experience, uncertainty and distance. Experience in existing and previous relationships provides the criteria by which the potential and performance of a new partner will be judged – a partner of which the company has no experience. The buyer will face uncertainty about the potential costs and benefits which are likely to be involved in dealing with a new supplier. The costs can be separated into those involved in making a change to a particular partner, e.g. in a buyer modifying its own product to suit that of a new seller. Additionally, there are the opportunity costs involved in the continuing relationship, when compared with alternative partners, e.g. in a buyer having to accept less frequent deliveries.

The distance which is perceived to exist between buyer and seller has several aspects:

- *Social distance:* the extent to which both the individuals and organizations in a relationship are unfamiliar with each others' ways of working.
- *Cultural distance:* the degree to which the norms, values or working methods between two companies differ because of their separate national characteristics.
- *Technological distance:* the differences between the two companies' product and process technologies.
- *Time distance:* the time which must elapse between establishing contact or placing an order, and the actual transfer of the product or service involved.
- *Geographical distance:* the physical distance between the two companies' locations.

Technological distance is likely to be great in evaluations for the purchase of innovative products. Social distance will be considerable in all new relationships as the companies know little of each other. This is combined with large cultural and geographical distance when the companies are dealing across national boundaries.[10] Finally, the companies will be considering a purchase which is unlikely to take place for a considerable time, with consequent apprehension that it will not come to fruition as desired.

We can now see the effects of these variables of Experience, Uncertainty, Distance and Commitment in the early stages of dealings between the companies.

Stage 2: The early stage

This is the time when *potential* suppliers are in contact with purchasers to negotiate or develop a specification for a capital goods purchase. This stage can also involve sample delivery for frequently purchased components or supplies. The stage can be characterized as follows.

Experience

At this early stage in their relationship, both buyer and seller are likely to have little experience of each other. They will only have a restricted view of what the other party requires of them, or even of what they hope to gain from the relationship themselves. No routine procedures will have been established to deal with issues as they arise, such as sample quality, design changes, etc. These issues can only be resolved by a considerable investment of management time at this stage. This investment of human resources is likely to precede any investment in physical plant.

Uncertainty

Human resource investment will be made at a time of considerable uncertainty, when the potential rewards from the relationships will be difficult to assess and the pattern of future costs is undetermined.

Distance

There will have been little opportunity to reduce the distance between the parties at this early stage in their dealings.

Social distance.   There will be a lack of knowledge between buyer and seller companies as well as an absence of personal relationships between the individuals involved. This will mean that many of the judgements made of each company will be on their reputation, as a substitute for experience of their abilities.

Geographical–cultural distance.   Geographical distance is, of course, beyond the control of the seller except in so far as it can be reduced by the establishment of a local sales office or by sending staff out to the customer on a residential basis. Cultural differences can only be reduced by employment of local nationals. The lack of social relationships means that there is nothing to reduce the effects of geographical and particularly cultural distance. This can result in a lack of trust between the companies. For example, a supplier may believe that he is simply being used as a source of information and that the customer has no intention of placing major orders or building a relationship. Further, the distrust of an individual supplier can cause a purchaser to place emphasis on cultural stereotypes – e.g. a customer may attach importance to the alleged "discipline" of German suppliers, as opposed to a lack of faith in "undisciplined" British suppliers.

Technological distance.   Inexperience of a supplier's product will emphasize any differences which may exist between the product or process technologies of the two companies.

Time distance.   In the early stage of a relationship, companies are likely to be negotiating about agreements or transactions which may only come to fruition at some considerable time in the future. This maximizes the buyer's concern about whether he will receive the product in the form specified and at the promised price and time. Similarly, the seller will be concerned as to whether orders being discussed will ever materialize in the way it expects.

Commitment

Both companies will be aware of the risks involved and will have little or no evidence on which to judge their partner's commitment to the relationship. In fact, it is likely that the actual commitment of both parties will be low at this time. Thus, perceptions of the likely commitment of the other company are strongly influenced by factors outside the relationship such as the number and importance of its other customers or suppliers.

The actions of seller and buyer in the future will be influenced by their initial assessment of the performance and potential of their partner. Their judgement of the place and importance of this relationship within the company's portfolio of suppliers or clients will also be important. Thus, a US engineering manufacturer clearly separates those "development suppliers" from others, very early in their dealings. It is these suppliers who receive the customer's investment of time, money and expertise to build the relationship. It may be that one of the partners may seek to develop the relationship, while the other remains passive. Also, efforts at development may founder, either because of the unwillingness of the partner or the incompetence of the initiator in overcoming the problems inherent in the early stages of a relationship.

We can now consider the development of a relationship beyond the early stage in terms of the tasks of building experience, increasing commitment and the associated reduction in uncertainty and distance.

Stage 3: The development stage

The development stage of a relationship occurs as deliveries of continuously purchased products increase. Alternatively, it is the time after contract signing for major capital purchases. Staged deliveries may be being made or the supplier may have started work on the item. Both buyer and seller will be dealing with such aspects as integration of the purchased product into the customer's operations of pre-delivery training, etc.

Experience

The development stage is marked by increasing experience between the companies of the operations of each other's organizations. Additionally, the individuals involved will have acquired some knowledge of each other's norms and values.

Uncertainty

The uncertainties which exist for both parties in the relationship will have been reduced by experience. In particular, the adaptations required to meet the wishes of the partner company will have become more apparent and the costs involved in these adaptations will also become clearer. Each company will be better able to judge the adaptations to meet its own requirements. These include those made by itself and those which it should require from its partner.

Distance

Social distance. This is reduced by the social exchange which takes place between the companies. As well as increasing their knowledge of each other, these personal relations establish trust between individuals. Nonetheless, this trust cannot be based upon social relationships alone. It also requires personal experience of the other company's satisfactory performance in exchange of product or services and finance.

Geographical and cultural distance. The reduction in social distance also contributes to a lessening of the effects of geographical and cultural distance. However, in a relationship between companies in different countries, it is possible that the seller company may reduce geographical and cultural distance through the establishment of a local office and employment of local nationals as business builds up.

Technological distance.   The adaptations which companies make to suit each other reduce the technological distance between them. Thus, their respective products, production and administrative process become more closely matched with each other. This produces consequent savings for one or both parties.

Time distance.   The experience of transactions means that the time distance between negotiation and delivery is eliminated in the case of continually delivered products. However, in the case of irregular purchases of for example, capital goods, then each cycle of order and delivery can be marked by similar time distances. Nevertheless, the importance of this distance decreases as the companies' mutual experience and trust of each other builds up.

Commitment

Much of a company's evaluation of a supplier or customer during the development of their relationship will depend on perceptions of their commitment to its development. Efforts to reduce social distance are one way for the supplier to demonstrate commitment. Commitment can also be shown in other ways:

It can be indicated by "adapting" to meet the needs of the other company, either by incurring costs or by management involvement. It is useful to separate these adaptations into *formal* adaptations which are contractually agreed between the companies and *informal* adaptations which may be arranged subsequently, to cope with particular issues which arise as the relationship develops. It is possible that the formal adaptations between companies may be dictated by the nature of the industry, e.g. that special products must always be developed for individual customers. On the other hand, a supplier's informal adaptations beyond the terms of a contract are often an important indicator of commitment.[11] For example, one large UK buying organization lists a major criterion in assessing the commitment of suppliers to be their "flexibility", for example in arranging a rapid increase in supply to cope with a sudden demand change.

In the international context, a company can demonstrate its commitment to a general market. This can be done by setting up a sales or buying office in that market. For example, a UK manufacturer and a French company had not progressed beyond the stage of exchanging "letters of intent" to buy. This was despite being in contact with each other for over two years. It was clear that the buyer doubted the supplier's commitment to it or the market, because of its unwillingness to establish a French office or assign specific personnel to the relationship during its development.

Finally, a company can emphasize commitment to a relationship by the way it organizes its contact with its partner. This includes both the status of personnel involved and the frequency of contact. For example, a British buyer of packaging machinery formed an unfavourable impression of the commitment of a Swedish supplier because of the lack of seniority of the people with which it had to deal and the slow speed of response in their contacts.

The process of development of an inter-company relationship is associated with an increasing level of business between the companies. Over time, many of the difficulties existing in the early stages of relationship are removed through the processes we have described in the development stage. However, development does not continue indefinitely. The relationship can be discontinued by either party on the basis of their assessment of its potential, the performance of the other party, or of the actions of outsiders. Even if this does not occur, the character of a relationship will change gradually. The changes which slowly develop are of vital significance to both buying and selling firms and we now turn to their description.

Stage 4: The long-term stage

It is not possible to put a timetable on the process by which a relationship reaches the long-term stage. This stage is characterized by the companies' mutual importance to each other. It is reached after large-scale deliveries of continuously purchased products have occurred or after several purchases of major unit products.[12]

Experience

The considerable experience of the two companies in dealing with each other leads to the establishment of standard operating procedures, trust, and norms of conduct. For example, a UK supplier of components to a German truck producer has arrangements for deliveries against three-month "firm" and six-month "tentative" orders. Prices are negotiated on an annual basis with an effective date of 1 January . . . "although we often don't get round to firming them up until well in the spring, so we just apply them retrospectively". Similarly, a UK producer of marine diesel engines will start construction of an individual unit costing up to £100 000 on the basis of a verbal order from a main customer. Formal orders often follow much later.

Uncertainty

Uncertainty about the process of dealing with a particular partner is reduced to a minimum in the long-term stage. Paradoxically, this reduction in uncertainty can create problems. It is possible that routine ways of dealing with the partner will cease to be questioned by this stage. This can be even though these routines may no longer relate well to either parties' requirements. We refer to this phenomenon as *institutionalization*. For example, discount structures may have become unrelated to developing delivery patterns, product variety may involve increased production costs for the seller whilst the buyer may be able to use a much narrower range of product.

These institutionalized patterns of operation make it difficult for a company to assess its partner's real requirements and so it may appear less responsive or uncommitted to the relationship. Institutionalized practices may also allow a company to drift into overdependence on a partner or incur excessive costs in its dealings. One company may exploit the other's institutionalized practices and lack of awareness and hence reduce its own costs at the expense of the partner. Finally, institutionalized practices of one relationship can affect a company's whole organization and hence its development of other relationships. For example, a supplier of high-grade alloys had become very heavily involved with a large domestic customer. It then attempted to transfer its experience with this customer to others in different market segments overseas. So many aspects and operations within this relationship had become institutionalized, or taken for granted, that the supplier was unable to modify its procedures to suit new customers.

Distance

Social distance. This is also minimized in the long-term stage. There are three particular features to the close relationship established by this stage.

Firstly, an extensive contact pattern will have developed between the companies. This may involve several functional areas and its aim will be to achieve an effective matching and adaptation of the systems and procedures of both supplier and customer. However, in the long-term stage the interactions by the different functions may become separated. For example, the technical problem solving between a supplier and its customers can become quite separate from the commercial transactions which take place. This can lead to problems of co-ordination and control if different departments are not to work in conflict with each other. For example, a German engineering company had 40 of its staff in constant contact with 12 people in a UK supplier. In view of this, the customer appointed a section head to "manage" the relationship. It was his responsibility to ensure that all of the separate interactions with the supplier were mutually compatible and in line with the overall policy of the buying company.

Secondly, strong personal relationships will have developed between individuals in the two companies. The strength of these can be seen by the extent of mutual problem solving and informal adaptations which occur. However, it may be difficult for an individual to separate these personal relationships from the business relation. Difficulties can arise when company interests are subordinated to those of the personal relationships. This has its most extreme form in the phenomenon of "side-changing" where individuals act in the interests of the other company and against their own, on the strength of their personal allegiances.

Thirdly, in the long-term stage, companies may become personified in an individual representative. Indeed, it may be the seller's policy to identify closely a relationship with the person of the local representative. This may be of value in establishing a presence in an overseas market. However, it inevitably involves problems if this individual has to be replaced or acts in his own interests rather than those of the company. For example, a UK exporter of machinery had to re-negotiate spares prices charged to its main French customer. These had previously been fixed by the supplier's local representative at a very low level. This had been done because the representative was greatly concerned about the effects of losing this business in his own position.

Technological distance. Successive contracts and agreements between the companies lead to extensive formal adaptations. These closely integrate many aspects of the operations of the two companies. This close integration is motivated by cost reduction for both companies as well as increased control over either their supply or buyer markets. De Monthoux has emphasized the barriers to the entry of other companies to which this close integration leads.[13]

Commitment

By the long-term stage, both seller and buyer companies' commitment to the relationship will have been demonstrated by the extensive formal and informal adaptations which have occurred. Nevertheless, the seller company faces two difficulties over commitment at this stage.

Firstly, it is likely to be difficult for a company to balance the need to demonstrate commitment to a client against the danger of becoming overly dependent on that client. This was expressed by a UK supplier faced with a major customer as follows: "We want them to think they are still important to us. At the same time we also want them to believe that they must work for our attention in competition with other customers".

Secondly, a customer's perception of a supplier's commitment to a relationship may differ from the actual level. This is because the required investment of resources has largely been incurred before the long-term stage is reached. It is also possible that the level of business between the companies has stabilized. Thus, paradoxically, when a supplier is at his most committed to a long-term and important client, he may *appear* less committed than during the development stage.

We have now come "full circle" in the description of relationship development. We have reached that stable situation before evaluation of potential new suppliers which was our starting point. In this, a company may continue with existing sources of supply or customers with little knowledge or evaluation of the available supply or customer markets. However, before concluding, it is worthwhile to mention a final stage which buyer–seller relationships may enter.

Stage 5: The final stage

This stage is reached in stable markets over long periods of time. It is marked by an extension of the institutionalization process to a point where the conduct of business is based on industry codes of practice. These may have relatively little to do with commercial considerations, but correspond more to a "right way to do business", e.g. the avoidance of price cutting and restrictions on changes in the respective roles of buyer and seller. It is often the case that attempts to break out of institutionalized patterns of trading in the final stage will be met by sanctions from other trading partners or the company's fellow buyers or sellers.[14]

MARKETING IMPLICATIONS

We have described how the development of buyer–seller relationships can be seen as a process in terms of:

- The increasing experience of the two companies;
- The reduction in their uncertainty and the distance between them;
- The growth of both actual and perceived commitment;
- Their formal and informal adaptations to each other and the investments and savings involved.

We can now turn to some of the implications of this process for the marketing company. The most obvious implication is that a company cannot treat its market in some overall way. Not only must it segment that market according to the different requirements of companies, it must also see its potential market as a network of relationships. Each of these must be assessed according to the opportunity they represent and how the relationship can be developed. The company's marketing task then becomes the establishment, development and maintenance of these relationships, rather than the manipulation of a generalized marketing mix. Further, this management of relationships must take place with regard to the company's skills and the costs involved, as well as the allocation of its resources between different relationships according to the likely return.

Establishing relationships

The existing relationships between buying and selling companies in an industrial market are a powerful barrier to the entry of another company. The barrier consists of the inertia in existing relationships, the uncertainties for the customer in any change of supplier, the distance which exists between buyer and a potential seller, and the lack of awareness or information about possible alternative partners. These factors are particularly significant in the case of overseas purchases,[15] where buyers may form stereotypes of national characteristics.

The marketer should be involved in the following activities to overcome these problems:

Market analysis

An analysis is required, which goes beyond determining which markets or sectors to enter. This analysis must examine the relationships held by potential customers and existing competitors. Customers may be categorized into those with long-established supplier relationships for the product, or those in the development or early stages. It is difficult to generalize at which stage relationships are easiest to break into, although different approaches will be required depending on this stage. Thus, a potential customer in the early stages of a relationship with a supplier may be facing problems which require considerable management involvement. This may mean that the company is in a position to evaluate alternatives and is aware of the inadequacies of its existing relationship. In contrast, a company which has begun to adapt and become committed to a supplier may be unwilling to face further uncertainty by considering a change. Thus, in the case of a satisfactorily developing or long-term relationship, it is likely that a new supplier will only be considered if there is some failure or particular inadequacy in an existing supplier. For example, we have pointed out that a buyer's perception of a supplier's commitment can decrease in the long-term stage and that problems may arise through institutionalized practices.

The analysis we refer to will indicate the required approach to different potential customers. Breaking into existing, early-stage relationships may involve emphasis on a broad range of factors, e.g. product specification, prices and delivery. Also, the approach may be to the senior management which is likely to be involved at this stage. The approach to customers with more established relationships involves determining the *specific* problems they are facing. Also, the seller must examine whether an attempt to solve these problems is within its capabilities. The company must question whether the adaptations it must make will provide adequate returns. Finally, it must tailor its approach to the individuals within the customer's organization who are in the areas of the relationship where problems have arisen.

Developing relationships

We have discussed the importance of commitment and distance reduction in the development of relationships. These involve a supplier in human and capital costs – in an overall market. It is worth noting that commitment to a market normally involves investment, in the form of local offices, etc., *before* business has developed. This contrasts with the attitudes of many industrial exporters who seem only prepared to invest in a sales or service operation *after* sales have been achieved.

The development of relationships can also be considered as a problem of strategy and organization. We must distinguish between the "strategic management" of relationships and the "operational management" of a single relationship. Strategic management involves the assessment of any one relationship within the company's strategy in a particular market or markets. Further, strategic management covers a portfolio of relationships. It is concerned with the interplay between them, their respective importance and the consequent resource allocation between them. It is difficult for those people involved in detailed interaction with a customer to see the relationship in perspective or to see the possible effects of institutionalization on it. It is because of this that the strategic management function should be carried out by marketing staff who are not involved in the day-to-day operation of relationships.

A company's marketing structure should also follow from the nature of its relationships. A functional organization within marketing may be appropriate for a firm with a large number of small clients. However, the complexity of the interaction with major clients emphasizes the importance of co-ordination of all aspects of a company's dealings with a client. There is a clear role for a "relationship manager" as in the German buying company referred to earlier. This is someone of sufficient status to co-ordinate all aspects of the company's relationships with major clients at the operational level. This individual is the major "contact man" for the company. He takes overall responsibility for the successful development of a relationship. This is based on his assessment of appropriate resource allocation to that relationship and his orchestration of the interactions between *all* functions – product development, production, sales, quality, and finance, etc. This requires more than the kind of authority usually given to an industrial salesman or "key account executive". In fact, the relationship manager should be independent of those departments which he co-ordinates in managing his portfolio of important relationships. Relationship management is most likely to be seen in operational form in industrial export marketing. Paradoxically, the limited resources often allocated by the seller company to export business mean that one man is involved directly or indirectly in all contacts – hence providing effective co-ordination. The relationship manager has a vital function in the case of irregularly purchased products, e.g. capital equipment. In this case, there is a clear need to *maintain* the relationship between purchase opportunities, either using sales staff or by his own contact.

Our research indicates that industrial companies are more likely to invest marketing resources at the operational than at the strategic level, perhaps because of their more immediately apparent results. This means that many companies are better staffed in the sales areas than under such designations as market planning or market development managers. Thus, staff are often pulled between the separate tasks of day-to-day operations and longer-term strategic planning. Under these circumstances it is not surprising that strategic planning is inadequately covered in the company.

Maintaining relationships

We have noted that perhaps the most significant aspect of long-term relationships is the problem of institutionalization. This can make a seller unresponsive to the changing requirements of its customers. The separation of operational and strategic management within the company's marketing is the key to reducing these problems. Strategic management includes a company's market analysis and points to differences in market sector and customer characteristics. Hence, it reduces the danger of transferring inappropriate marketing practices from one market to another. Strategic management involves a re-examination of the company's existing operations to see if they continue to be relevant to particular client relationships and market conditions. Finally, strategic management determines the resource allocation between different relationships according to their potential and stage of development. The over-emphasis on operational marketing within many companies means that they do not have the staff or the time to re-examine those activities which have been taken for granted in the company's long-term relationships.

Final remarks

In conclusion, it is important to emphasize that companies should examine their existing relationships whether home or overseas to see which of the stages described here they fall into. This examination should be a preliminary to an assessment of each relationship, as follows:

1. What is the likely potential of this relationship?
2. What resources are required to fulfil this potential?
3. Where do the threats to this development come from?
4. Where does this relationship fit within the context of the company's overall operations and resource allocation in that market?
5. Are the current efforts devoted to the relationship appropriate to this overall strategy?
6. Are we over-committed to this customer?
7. Finally, are our ways of dealing with this customer appropriate both to its needs and our strategy or are they dealings based on habit or history?

NOTES

* The author acknowledges the contribution of Anna Lawson who read earlier drafts of this article.

1. For example: Webster, F. E. *Industrial Marketing Strategy*. Wiley, New York (1979).
2. Exceptions include: de Monthoux, P. B. L. G. Organizational mating and industrial marketing conservation – some reasons why industrial marketing managers resist marketing theory. *Industrial Marketing Management*, **4**, 25–36 (1975); Blois, K. J. Vertical quasi-integration. *Journal of Industrial Economics*, **XX**, July, 253–72 (1972): Håkansson, H. and Wootz, B. A framework for industrial buying and selling. *Industrial Marketing Management*, **3**, 28–39 (1979).
3. For details see: Cunningham, M. T. International marketing and purchasing of industrial goods: features of a European research project. *European Journal of Marketing*, **14**(5/6), 322–38 (1980).
4. *Ibid.*
5. See for example: Williamson, O. E. *Markets and Hierarchies: Analysis and Anti-Trust Implications*. Free Press, New York (1975).
6. Williamson, O. E. Transaction cost economics: the governance of contractual relations. *Journal of Law and Economics*, **22**(2), October, 232–62 (1979).
7. *Ibid.*
8. For a discussion of the methodological implications of analysis of episodes and relationships see: Ford, I. D. A methodology for the study of inter-company relations in industrial market channels. *Journal of the Market Research Society*, **22**(1), 44–59 (1980).
9. See for example: Cunningham, M. T. and White, J. G. The determinants of choice of supply. *European Journal of Marketing*, **7**(3), 189–202 (1973).

10. For use of a similar concept of distance in international business see: Johanson, J. and Wiedersheim-Paul, F. The internationalization of the firm – four Swedish case studies. *Journal of Management Studies*, October, 305–22 (1975). For an attempt to analyse the effect of distance on purchase behaviour see: Håkansson, H. and Wootz, B. Supplier selection in an international environment – an experimental study. *Journal of Marketing Research*, **XII**, 46–51 (1975).

11. Suppliers' informal adaptations are often referred to in the purchasing literature as "Supplier Value Added".

12. This does not mean that a single supplier has been responsible for all of a customer's requirements of a continuously purchased product or every purchase of a major item.

13. de Monthoux, *op cit.*

14. For further discussion of institutionalized practices in long-established markets see: Ford, I. D. Stability factors in industrial marketing channels. *Industrial Marketing Management*, **7**, 410–27 (1978).

15. See: Håkansson, H. and Wootz, B. Supplier selection in an international environment. *Journal of Marketing Research*, **XII**, February, 46–51 (1975).

2.3

How do companies interact?*

David Ford, Håkan Håkansson and Jan Johanson

INTRODUCTION

The past 10 to 15 years have seen a growth in the number of studies within what has become known as the "Interaction Approach", see for example Håkansson (1982) and Turnbull and Valla (1986). These studies have examined aspects of the interaction and relationships between companies in industrial and/or international markets and have had the objective of increasing understanding of the behaviour of buying and selling companies in those markets. This article is an attempt to go one step further than previous studies by exploring some ideas which have emerged over these years about the basic nature of interaction between companies. One of our purposes is to develop a model which identifies the strategic options available to companies in their interactions with others. This does not mean that we believe that there exist a number of clear-cut interaction strategies which a company can choose between. On the contrary we think that, for several reasons, inter-company interaction is basically ambiguous rather than clear cut. Furthermore, we believe that this ambiguity is an important element in an company's interaction.

A starting point

Our starting point is that every working company exists within a complex network of interactions between companies as they exchange with each other information, expertise, goods and services, payments and loans, etc. A company can be viewed as a node in an ever-widening pattern of interactions, in some of which it is a direct participant, some of which affect it indirectly and some of which occur independently of it. This web of interactions is so complex and multifarious as to deny full description or analysis. Indeed, the interaction between a *single* buying and selling company can be complex enough, as shown by the following illustration.

Salespeople and sales managers from a selling company seek contacts with personnel in a potential customer. Contact is likely to be with buyers but also may be with production or other technical personnel. The sellers try to demonstrate the qualities of their products and their company's capability to manufacture and deliver them and to support the customer with technical services, spare parts, etc. They may bring to the customer various technical specialists in order to discuss and analyse any particular problems of the customer which may require modification of products or production processes. They may also bring in logistical expertise in order to analyse delivery and scheduling questions. If a deal is reached then new and more practical problems are likely to be encountered during production. To solve them, still more personnel are involved. Even after delivery new problems may emerge and need to be handled, future requirements are anticipated and further negotiations may be started. In this example the producer was the most active partner and the influence of any third party was neglected. In contrast a customer company, for example a manufacturer of consumer goods, may approach a number of potential suppliers of producer goods, services or finance. Similar interactions will take place, where the buyer seeks to explain its requirements, assess the suppliers and show its own value as a customer for those suppliers.

Companies interact, react, re-react etc., with each other both in words and other forms of action such as purchases, deliveries, and payments. These interactions may be frequent or infrequent, regular or irregular, explicit or implicit, conscious or unconscious. Each interaction may be individually more or less important, but collectively they comprise a comprehensive picture both of the company and of the reasons for its existence. Thus there are good reasons to try to deepen our understanding of this interaction.

THE NATURE OF COMPANIES' INTERACTIONS

Within companies a number of inter-related activities are performed. These activities are in turn interwoven with activities in a larger industrial system. All of these demand resources of various kinds; physical – plant, machinery and raw materials; human – skills, knowledge and experience of the organizational members; financial, etc. These resources are in themselves essentially *passive* and fragmented.

It is the company's interaction with others which leads to an *activation* and an integration of its resources. The company's control of these resources, its use of them in activities, its adding to and changing of its resource base is a response to interactions and anticipated interactions. The interaction with others is, in this way, the force that unifies the company and gives it the *capability* to perform its activities. The effects of this force are not the same in all situations. They depend on variations both in the interactions and in the company itself. The company can respond to inter-action differently and it can influence the other parties in the interaction in different ways.

Thus, all companies are continuously involved in a wide range of interactions, for example in the acquisition of production inputs or finance, the sale of products or services, joint product development activities, systems selling or co-operation within a trade association. Because of this the company exists in an "interacted environment". This may be compared with Weick's (1979) concept of the "enacted environment". It is against this background that we view companies as sets of interrelated interactions, through which capabilities are developed and employed. Similarly, wider industrial systems are seen as networks of inter-related interactions. In such networks several interdependent companies interact in order to influence and adapt each other's future activities and resources. This implies that the companies have both common and conflicting interests. It may be in the interest of companies which are dependent on each other to develop matching activities and capabilities. To that extent they have common interests. On the other hand, which company is to bear the costs of the adaptations and developments necessary for interaction to take place successfully is not predetermined. Thus, all intercompany relations have elements of both mutual and conflicting interest and their relative importance depends on how the companies view each other.

Intercompany interactions are performed by human beings. They have intentions when inter-acting and they make interpretations of the interaction and the intentions of others (Giddens, 1975; Klint, 1985). Every interaction is based on intentions and is interpreted from at least two sides. Through these interpretations the interaction is given meaning by the parties. In the rest of this article we will concentrate on these meanings and more or less disregard the form of interaction, noting however that the form of interaction is often chosen in order to underline its meaning. This approach means that we shall view interaction as a process of giving and receiving information, rather like streams of questions and answers given to each other by the parties involved.

A fundamental characteristic of interaction is that it is at least bilateral and sometimes multi-lateral; there are at least two parties involved at each moment. The parties are aware of each other's existence and try to understand and influence each other. As we have stated, in all interactions there are intentions and interpretations from at least two sides. Furthermore, as the parties are aware of each other they are also aware of the importance of trying to give a favourable picture of their own intentions. The situation is made more complicated in some ways by the fact that the parties have memories and thus also interpret current interaction on the basis of previous experience. However, this previous experience can also simplify interaction as it increases predictability and leads to standard procedures, often based on trust.

As the interaction is often complex and between several persons from each party there will be numerous intentions and interpretations involved. This complexity requires that each company has the necessary capacity to turn its intentions into acts as well as to interpret what intentions lie behind the acts of its counterparts. Unfortunately, both sides usually have limited capacities to act and to interpret and this leads to an unclear situation. The parties do not usually have a clear, consistent and common view of where they stand with each other and what are each others' intentions. For these reasons each new interaction is seen as a test of the relationship between the parties and a way of learning about each other. The flow of "questions" and "answers" between the parties calibrates the relationships between them repeatedly and adjusts their activities and capabilities to this calibration. Furthermore, the meaning of an interaction is not given by the interaction itself but by its relations to previous interactions as well as to other interactions the parties are involved in with other actors. Thus, every interaction is unique at the same time as it is influenced by the whole network of interactions. Thus, interaction is both particular and universal (Belshaw, 1965, p. 114).

Against this background we suggest that analyses of company interaction should focus on four aspects of interaction which capture the general features described above. These aspects are interesting from the interaction parties' points of view because they are important to their own company's development. Additionally, the aspects can to some extent be used consciously by the parties and each has a measure of discretion in handling them. Each aspect can be discussed through a question and the answers to that question:

- What can you do for me?
- How do you see me?
- What are you prepared to do for me, compared to what you do for others?
- Which variations are there in these "whats" and "hows"?

The aspect of interaction which relates to the handling of the first question centres on the *capability* aspect of interaction. It describes the relationship between the parties in terms of what they can do for each other and concerns the functions which they fulfil. We are concerned with both the width and the importance of these functions. In examining capability we see both counterparts *together* forming a functional entity and are concerned with the functional interdependence between their capabilities.

The second aspect of interaction, dealing with the second question, focuses on the social relations between the parties. It is labelled *mutuality* and is based on the assumption that different parties, at least to some extent, share common goals or interests. Mutuality describes how the parties handle the relations between their respective and common interests. Interaction may be dominated by the self-interests of the parties, such as in one-off price negotiation. In contrast, it may be based on a view of mutual interest, such as in joint negotiations with a third party. We are also concerned with the ways in which the parties demonstrate their interest in each others' well-being. Thus mutuality involves a view of the interacting parties as a social entity and deals with the basic social interdependence between them.

The third aspect of interaction, which handles the third question, is an attempt to characterize the interaction in terms of direction and uniqueness: it relates the interaction between the parties to their interactions with other actors. This aspect is called *particularity*. In some extreme cases interaction between two parties is unique and directed solely towards each other – there is a high degree of particularity. This would be seen, for example, in a company's negotiations with the government body which controls its operations. At the other extreme there may be no interaction which is particular to a company and any one of its counterparts. All counterparts are dealt with as a group and interaction is of standard form, as in the case of a large supplier and its many small customers. Of course many parties will want to be seen as more or less particular. However, they are seldom likely to be prepared to pay for the higher costs which follow such special treatment.

Inconsistency refers to the ambiguity or lack of clarity in interaction. This ambiguity is in the "messages" passed to the counterpart concerning, for example, the company's wishes or intentions. Interaction can be inconsistent over time or there can be inconsistency between different interactions with the same partner undertaken by different personnel. In this way, the concept focuses on the possible coexistence of conflict and co-operation within the interaction. Thus, co-operation is possible between parties which have conflicting interests as well as conflicts which can occur between those with interests in common. Inconsistency also implies the opportunity for short-term expediency or changes in individual acts without changes to principal policies. In this way, inconsistency captures the dynamic nature of interaction. We can refer to inconsistency in both intentions and interpretations and the concept has important bearings on the other three aspects of interaction already discussed. Inconsistency is an important but neglected aspect of interaction. It is probably one of the most difficult aspects to handle managerially as it goes against most normal managerial advice which stresses "clear and consistent policies" (Porter, 1985). Inconsistency is, however, an important key to change and development in interaction and the management of inconsistency is central to inter-company interaction.

The four aspects of interaction are closely related to each other in various ways and will now be discussed in more detail. First we discuss the two aspects which are primarily concerned with the *effects* of interaction – capability and mutuality. Then we discuss the two other aspects, particularity and inconsistency, which are more concerned with the *implementation* of interaction.

Capability

We noted earlier that it is through interaction with others that the resources of a company are integrated and activated. Interaction between companies takes place because each seeks to gain from the other and from their association with each other. For interaction to be worthwhile, the interacting parties must form together something that is meaningful and they must have a function for each other. In this way, interaction takes place in the form of continuous questioning: What can you do for me? Can you do this or that for me? What can I do for you? Through this process, the essentially passive resources of a company – financial, physical plant, technological or managerial – are translated into capabilities for a specific partner or partners. Clearly, a company must be able to analyse and describe itself in terms of the needs of counterparts which it has the capability to satisfy. Similarly, those resources which have no value to any counterpart remain passive and do not constitute worthwhile capabilities, nor are they likely to be of value to the company itself. Certain capabilities can be more or less unique to a single company – and hence counterparts may have greater or less difficulty in finding similar alternatives.

The resources of a company may be wide or narrow in range. Irrespective of this, a counterpart may seek interaction with that company because of a single capability which it recognizes as significant, for example the low price of its product or its speed of delivery. It may be quite uninterested in the company's resources for technical problem solving. Alternatively, interaction can take place because of a combination of capabilities which the company possesses or seeks to offer. These variations in resources are illustrated in Figure 1 in a simple two-by-two matrix which also shows some of the implications of these factors for the nature of interaction. For example, cell 2 approximates to perfect competition in that interaction is based on a single capability, e.g. the ability to deliver a standard product, which is widely available for a standardized price. Perhaps the buyer may seek to move away from this position so that interaction involves more capabilities – product modification, improved delivery for a correspondingly higher price. This would move the interaction into cell 3 and would probably require both parties to enhance their capabilities for each other by "particularity". Cell 1 may approximate to the situation of a monopoly supplier or monopsonistic buyer. Interaction is based on a single capability by either party, but only one

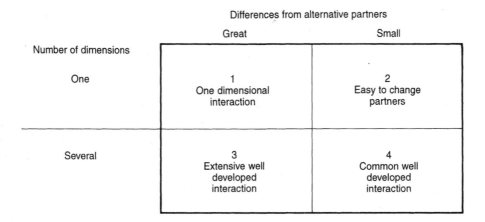

Figure 1 Interaction variations.

company has that capability, or companies each have significantly different capability from each other. Examples would include the superior product technology of a supplier or the great sales potential of a customer. Over time, it may be that further capabilities are required in the interaction, in which case it moves into cell 3. Conversely, if the significant single capability on which the interaction is based becomes more common then the interaction moves back into cell 2. Finally, cell 4 refers to the complex, widespread interaction that we might expect to find in much of industrial marketing and purchasing. Here the differences between companies' capabilities may be relatively small and dealings are based on a number of abilities. Management under these circumstances seek to improve its efficiency in providing the capabilities required or may try to move from this cell to cells 1 or 3 through capability development.

Thus, not only does interaction employ the capabilities of a company, it may also lead to their change or development over time. Interaction or anticipated interaction enables the organization to learn what is required by counterparts, as well as what it can expect in return. Through this the company will seek to add or to develop its resources in particular directions. In many cases, companies will seek to initiate contact with others, mainly as means of developing their capabilities. An example of this would be when a small supplier seeks work with a larger or higher technology company, so that the process of meeting the client's requirements will enhance its own skills or product quality. Over time, too, a company has choices in relation to its capabilities. If a particular type of interaction, or interaction with a specific counterpart is valuable to it then the company may choose to invest more of its resources in that interaction – hence enhancing its capabilities there, through developing new products, or applying more management time, etc. Alternatively, the company can minimize or reduce its investment. Thus it will *extract* its own resources from the interaction whilst at the same time seeking to maximize the capabilities of its counterpart which it uses. An example of this is the often discussed tactic of "milking" a declining product through higher prices and a lack of product improvement investment.

Mutuality

The concept of mutuality rests on the importance of collective goals or common interests between more than one company. Mutuality is a measure of how much a company is prepared to give up its own individual goals or intentions in order to increase the positive outcomes of others and, through this, increase its own ultimate well-being. This inevitably involves trade-offs between short-term opportunism and longer-term gain. Mutuality can be seen both in bilateral interaction and between larger groups of companies. For example, many industrial customers will share technology with suppliers on the basis that both will benefit through enhancement of the suppliers' capabilities. Alternatively, manufacturers will sometimes supply goods on consignment to a distributor, if the distributor faces cash-flow problems. These examples can be contrasted with the view of buyer–supplier interactions which are seen by the participants as a zero sum game, typically concentrating on price negotiation. An example of strong mutuality between larger numbers of companies is provided by the members of trade associations who will sometimes agree to common marketing practices in their joint interests as "the industry". Sometimes, this activity goes beyond the law, in such arrangements as market sharing or price fixing.

Mutuality costs nothing to show at the spoken level – in for example the promises of a salesperson. However, mutuality can only really be demonstrated over time. Similarly, the extent of the mutuality demonstrated on specific occasions is often long remembered. For example there were customers within the European paper and pulp industry who in the late 1970s still remember and used in argument how different suppliers had acted towards them during the scarcity period of the Korean War, 25 years previously.

Mutuality is the mirror of the trust which exists between parties. One way in which this trust can be demonstrated is through the commitment shown to the counterpart by use of the company's various capabilities in interaction. This is often seen in the case of sellers who adapt product, price or delivery schedules, often on an informal basis. It is through these adaptations or "Transaction Specific Investments" (Williamson, 1979) that close relationships are developed over time (Ford, 1980). In well-established relationships, mutuality is more or less taken for granted and the relationship can withstand short-term problems which may arise. This is an analogous situation to that of a marriage. Here also, once the parties feel that mutuality has been lost then the relationship is in danger or, alternatively, it will take a long time for mutuality to be re-established.

Mutuality is not the opposite of conflict. In contrast, the existence of many conflicts requires a certain minimum level of mutuality. It is common for companies to have an overall idea of mutual interest whilst simultaneously being in conflict over what should be their respective contributions towards its achievement. Conflict can exist when one party to interaction is prepared to operate on the basis of a higher level of mutuality than is the other. Thus, conflict in this case often takes the form of argument over short-term as opposed to long-term gain, or is expressed in terms of accusations of "selfishness".

Finally, a company may wish to reduce the mutuality on which interaction is based. The adaptation and commitment involved may become burdensome when compared with the rewards. Thus, the company may seek to substitute immediate self-interest instead of joint and, by implication, longer-term interest.

Particularity

The concept of particularity is based on the existence of the complex, interlocking network of interaction in which a company exists. Because of this, interaction with one counterpart may indirectly affect others. For example, the amount of product development capability employed by a manufacturer towards the requirements of a particular customer will directly affect the amount available for solution of other customers' problems. Interactions are always relative in the sense that they are compared to each other. If one customer is treated in some special way then others may request the same type of special treatment.

The extent of particularity in interaction is often strongly influenced by the specific situation or wider network in which it takes place. For example, a customer buying certain electronic products from a single supplier will inevitably have to develop production processes compatible with these and incompatible with the products of other suppliers. However, companies do have a certain discretion in particularity. An obvious example of this is the price structure which companies adopt and whether or not they are prepared to negotiate special prices for individual customers. Discounts are often seen by customers as illustrations of the selling company's priority structure and we have found companies which have developed very complicated price structures in order to make it more or less impossible for customers to calculate the price level for others – hence disguising their particularity. Network structure influences the importance of particularity. The more tight and well-structured a network, with close and well-established interaction between the companies, then the more likely that this interaction is based on strong particularity. Particularity often increases over time as adaptations are made to suit each other's requirements. In this way particularity becomes imposed on the company by the enacted environment and hence is a constraint.

However, the company can also choose to use particularity as a type of strategic variable. For example, it can decide to give certain counterparts special treatment depending on their perceived value, while others only get standard treatment. It can, in the same way, choose to differentiate between counterparts in certain dimensions while keeping others standardized – for example it may vary the delivery or services but not the products to certain customers. Furthermore, the company can choose to give special treatment in certain situations but not in others, such as dealing differently with orders of different sizes.

Particularity is often closely related to costs, when companies make specific investments dedicated to their interaction with a counterpart. The issue is therefore often formulated in terms of whether or not a special approach to interaction will pay off over time. Many companies, however, seek to find ways to give special treatment without increasing the costs, that is to find standardized methods to produce individual solutions. This has been referred to in the general context of marketing as the "industrialization of service" (Levitt, 1976).

Inconsistency

It is self-evident that companies consist of individuals and subgroups, and it is these who are involved in the company's interactions. This provides a starting point for our examination of inconsistency because it means that a company can never present a wholly unified approach in its interactions. We refer to this as "interpersonal inconsistency". Each person involved in interaction between companies will have his or her own expectations of his or her counterpart. Some individuals will be more committed to interactions with a particular company than will others. For example, it is possible that a company's salesperson could devote great efforts to finding out the precise requirements of a customer and to tailoring his or her own offering to meet these. At the same time these requirements could appear self-indulgent to the company's production-planning department. Similarly, individuals may approach interaction on the basis of their own personal interests rather than those of the company. Thus, salespeople may feel a sense of commitment to serve the interests of a customer, based on personal ties, even though this may be against the instructions given by their own company. This phenomenon is often referred to as "side-changing".

As well as interpersonal inconsistency, a company will also demonstrate "intertemporal inconsistency". We would expect that different considerations will be important to the company at various times in its interactions. Thus when it is first trying to establish contact with a new potential customer we would expect a supplier to be more solicitous in initial interactions than with a customer with whom it has been dealing for many years and which it has come to take for granted. Ford (1980) has discussed this phenomenon in terms of institutionalization in the development of relationships. There is a parallel between this inconsistency and what is referred to by Cyert and March (1963) in the intra-organizational context as "sequential attention to goals".

The discussion so far may have indicated that inconsistency is an unfortunate, but unconscious or unavoidable, factor associated with interaction. However, in our view, companies are intricate webs of inter-related activities and resources. Through interaction these are embedded in wider networks of similarly intricate, inter-related activities and resources. This is a complex, ever-changing world which is impossible to survey from outside, but possible to understand and influence, at least partially, from inside. In such a world inconsistency may make it possible to explore and test different developments. Inconsistencies in interaction may also help in rearranging relationships with other companies. Inconsistency may also be a way to handle both conflicting and common interests. Hence, inconsistency in interaction may be fruitful for the company. And even if it may be difficult to plan it may very well be supported consciously. A company in negotiation with another may use two people, one of whom plays the "hard man" and one who is more conciliatory. Similarly, the interactions between the respective research and development departments of two companies may be allowed to be based on greater mutuality than those between the corresponding salesperson and buyer. Further we would expect a company to change its interactions with a customer when its relative importance as a source of revenue increased or decreased.

Inconsistency is important to both sides in an interaction – both the company performing a particular activity and the corresponding party which is trying to interpret the action. The action will include elements of inconsistency and there will be inconsistencies in the counterpart's interpretation. An activity which is notionally based on mutuality will include elements of self-seeking. Any such action may be interpreted as friendly by some representatives of the counterpart, but by others as unfriendly.

Inconsistency is a powerful concept in interpreting inter-company interaction. We often speak of "companies interacting" and thus we reify the organization. We would argue that it is appropriate to describe the dealings of organizations at the level of the collectivity. Nevertheless, an adequate understanding of company behaviour can only be provided by also analysing the company as a collection of interactions by individuals and subgroups which are more or less inconsistent with each other and over time.

THE INTER-RELATIONSHIP BETWEEN THE DIMENSIONS: THE DYNAMIC CHARACTER OF INTERACTION

The four dimensions are closely related to each other. Inconsistency is, for example, a dimension that can be used to characterize a company's activities in the three other dimensions (mutuality, particularity and capability). Mutuality and particularity can in the same way be seen as two dimensions of a company's capability. Furthermore, as already described, mutuality and particularity are related to each other in several ways. However, this interconnectedness is not at such a level that there are reasons to integrate the four dimensions into one total dimension. Instead it can be seen as an indication of the dynamic character of the interactions.

The four dimensions may be used to characterize interaction which in turn is very much time related. The dynamics of interaction are shown by the fact that it can be perceived as a learning process. The actors take part in mutual learning where they successfully get to know when and how they should utilize each other. Each participant will increase his or her knowledge and experience, not just of the interaction itself but of the characteristics and expectations of his or her counterpart. The similar development of trading relationships in traditional society has been described by Belshaw (1965):

> The exchanges are accompanied by forms of words and ceremonial acts, all of which reinforce the notions of honourable gift giving and mutual dependence between persons who in most instances would be strangers in other circumstances. But since the institution has been passed on from generation to generation so has been the interlinkage of partners in a relationship which is itself passed on and developed through generations.

Nevertheless, the development of a relationship is in no way deterministic. Williamson (1979) has discussed those circumstances where relationship development is likely to occur. For our purposes here, we can simply note that these relationships may be close, complex and long-term – as in the case of a components supplier to the automotive industry. Alternatively they may be intense, but only at irregular intervals as in the case of purchase of capital equipment, or distant and irregular as in the case of the contact and relationship between competitors in some industries. Therefore interaction over time provides the opportunity for both mutuality and conflict. Relationships may develop, stagnate or be close or distant depending upon variations in commitment and expectations. For a further discussion of relationship changes over time see Ford and Rosson (1982).

This means that a relationship is defined in terms of the existing and previous pattern of interaction. As well as interaction defining a relationship, it is the relationship itself and the participants' experience of it which provides the context for all subsequent interaction. This means that no single element or episode in the dealings between companies can be considered in isolation.

SOME MANAGERIAL ISSUES

This article has suggested that the interaction between a company and its counterparts is a process of managing mutuality, particularity, and the company's capabilities, whilst at the same time coping with and positively using inconsistency in its dealings with others. It is through interaction that a company's capabilities are used and developed and from which it receives rewards. Crucial decisions for the company concern the extent of the capabilities it will apply to interaction with a particular counterpart and its willingness to invest in capability development for long-term reward. Decisions on the development of interaction have long-term implications. For example, the decision to devote resources to a particular project of a potential customer means that those resources cannot be applied elsewhere and, perhaps more importantly, that further resources or investment may be made necessary at later stages of this interaction.

Some of these issues can be addressed through Figure 2. This matrix illustrates the inter-relationships between different aspects of interaction. Cell 1 raises central questions about the extent to which a company should tailor its capabilities towards interaction with a particular counterpart. This issue is of major concern to those sellers faced with a single customer responsible for a large part of its production. The particularity of a company's capabilities has long-term implications because of the non-transferability of many investments made in interactions, e.g. tailored product development or dedicated production facilities. Because of this, companies must be concerned about the extent to which mutuality is related to particularity (cell 2).

Considerations here involve the extent to which *both* parties have invested their capabilities with a common view of mutual benefit. If we return to our example of the selling company, then often such a company will closely watch the attitude and actions of a customer to measure its commitment to a continuing relationship, as well as the level of its own investment (cell 1).

Cells 3 and 4 concern inconsistency in capability and mutuality in interactions. Here we must again differentiate between inconsistency as an unfortunate consequence of differences in approach between different members of a company's staff, or over time *and* inconsistency as conscious strategy. In the former case, a company must analyse whether it is giving the right message to its partner through its interaction. For example, after a salesperson has secured an order on the basis of

	Particularity	Inconsistency
Capability	1	3
Mutuality	2	4

Figure 2   Inter-relationships between variables.

arguing his or her company's commitment to a customer, then production staff or service personnel may give the impression that the company is not committed to this client. Further, it is possible for a company to waste its capabilities by seeking to apply them to too many counterparts or by failing to be seen to maintain commitment over time to an important counterpart.

Conscious inconsistency is an important strategic choice. For example, a company may seek to withdraw some of the capabilities it offers to a counterpart in order to draw its attention to their importance. One specialized metal manufacturer faced with a single customer who accounted for much of its sales used this tactic to strike a balance between making the customer feel important, but not taking the supplier for granted. Similarly, a selling company must examine its charging basis as a tactic in mutuality. For example, it may sometimes be appropriate for a company to accept the development charges for a project on the basis that the success of the project is in both parties' interests. At other times, the company must emphasize the importance of its reward and insist on payment for its development costs.

These four aspects of interaction raise a host of issues for managerial decision making. We argue that a primary focus for analysis of these decisions is to view companies in the context of their network of interactions. This is instead of taking a narrower perspective which focuses on the company alone and views it as a (more or less) unilateral decision maker and controller of its resources. It is through interaction with other companies that resources are mobilized and strategy implemented and indeed through which the very nature of a company is defined.

NOTE

* An earlier version of this article was presented at the second open IMP International Research Seminar, Uppsala, September 1985.

REFERENCES

Belshaw, C. S. *Traditional Exchange and Modern Markets.* Prentice Hall, Englewood Cliffs, NJ (1965).

Cyert, R. M. and March J. G. *A Behavioral Theory of the Firm.* Prentice Hall, Englewood Cliffs, NJ (1963).

Ford, D. The development of buyer–seller relationships in industrial markets. *European Journal of Marketing*, **14** (5/6), 339–53 (1980).

Ford, D. and Rosson, P. The relationship between export manufacturers and their overseas distributors. In *Export Management, An International Context*, pp. 257–75. Praeger, New York (1982).

Giddens, A. *New Rules of Sociological Method.* Anchor Press, Essex (1975).

Håkansson, H. (ed.) *International Marketing and Purchasing of Industrial Goods: An Interaction Approach.* Wiley, Chichester (1982).

Klint, M. B. *Mot en konjunturanpassad kundstrategi – om den sociala relationens roll vid marknadsforing av massa och papper.* [Towards a customer strategy allied to the business cycle: about the role of the social relationship in the marketing of pulp and paper]. Ph.D. thesis with an English summary, Department of Business Administration, University of Uppsala (1985).

Levitt, T. The industrialization of service. *Harvard Business Review*, September/October (1976).

Porter, M. E. *Competitive Advantage. Creating and Sustaining Superior Performance.* The Free Press, New York (1985).

Turnbull, P. W. and Valla, J. P. (eds). *Strategies for International Industrial Marketing.* Croom Helm, London (1986).

Weick, K. E. *The Social Psychology of Organizing*, 2nd edn. Addison-Wesley, Reading, Mass. (1979).

Williamson, O. E. Transaction-cost economics; the governance of contractual relations. *Journal of Law and Economics*, **22** (2), 232–62 (1979).

2.4 The burden of relationships or who's next?

Håkan Håkansson and Ivan Snehota

Intercompany relationships have recently attracted a great deal of attention in the business literature. Benefits to companies from developing "close relationships" with customers, suppliers and other counterparts, possible allies, are usually emphasised. These benefits are certainly important and deserve to be explored further. At the same time one cannot avoid noticing that there is a lack of studies of the problems or difficulties with close relationships. Of course, there are a large number of studies analysing market solutions, i.e. the case with no relationships, but that is another question. We mean that business relationships entail costs and problems that warrant some attention. While business relationships can be a valuable resource for a company they bring in, at the same time, severe limitations to what the company can do. Close relationships can easily turn into a burden for one or both of the involved partners (as we so well know from personal experience). Relationships thus have both a huge benefit and a huge burden potential. In order to understand relationships better we have to look at both sides. The chapter explores and illustrates the "burden" of relationships, focusing both on basic factors and episodes that make the burdening consequences large and acute. It is argued that the burden of relationships is the other side of the benefit potential. It means that the risk for a relationship to become a burden can never be escaped, it is the automatic consequence of the development of a fruitful relationship. And the potential burden is no argument against the need to develop relationships but it is important to realise this in order to have realistic expectations.

BUSINESS AND RELATIONSHIPS

The interest shown in business literature recently of intercompany relationships testifies to their perceived importance. There seem to be at least two quite different reasons for the growing attention. One is the wave of various formal co-operative ventures between companies over the last decade. These formalised ventures have led to various forms of inter-company organisational arrangements that have been studied quite extensively. Another is the increasing number of studies showing that most companies, especially in the so called business-to-business markets, are highly dependent on the exchange with a limited number of customers and suppliers with whom they often develop extensive relationships.

The study of what have been labelled as "business relationships" has proven their existence and importance and has broadened our understanding of their development processes. Still the very notion of relationship is not univocal, a point to which we will return later. On the whole the research studies point to the potential benefits from developing "good" and "close" business relationships. A "good" relationship is usually characterised by more or less marked co-operative intent of the two companies (e.g. Ring and Van de Ven, 1994). It has been shown that business relationships can be a source of valuable technical know-how, they can be an important factor in developing the technical capabilities of a company, they can be important to create the market position of the company or they can be leveraged to approach new customers.

The concern with the benefit potential of business relationships appears well motivated. On the basis of our own research we are firmly convinced that companies in many cases can exploit the potential benefits from business relationships better than they do. However, at the same time, we cannot avoid noticing that the "dark" side of relationships, for example the large development costs and the way these limit what a firm can do or achieve, has to be much more penetrated. There are very few examples of such analysis (an exception is Blois, 1995). We will in this chapter make a first attempt to have a closer look at these aspects. The focus will be on the burden of relationships.

THE BURDEN OF RELATIONSHIPS

At first glance, relationships appear to turn into a burden as a consequence of changes exogenous to the relationship itself; something that happens in the context and turns the relationship to a burden (the appearance of a "third" party – a new alternative). Then the attention of the involved parties is turned to the negative consequences and the relationship becomes a burden. That seems invariably true in business as in relationships in general. However, the situation is a little more complex as the following discussion will show.

A first important observation is that a relationship valuable in some dimensions might be negative in some other dimension. A close relationship with a customer that is very beneficial for the technical development in the selling company might be negative in terms of excessive costs. An example of the opposite would be a conflictual relationship with a supplier that is very rewarding from an economic point of view. Developing close relationships does not guarantee a positive balance of the outcomes, more that both positive and negative consequences are enlarged. The conclusion must be that most relationships have some negative effects, i.e. always contain a certain burden.

A second observation is that there are at least three types of circumstances when the burden of a relationship feels more acute. A first situation is when one of the parties wishes, for whatever reason, to exit the relationship and such a wish is not shared by the counterpart. The abandoned party will in this case feel cheated because it will lose the investments made earlier without getting anything in return. The abandoned party might retain and exercise some sanction power that will further amplify the negative consequences. It might be the start of a war!

A second situation is when both parties would like to exit a relationship but it is impossible due to a high interdependency (joint investments etc.). The two parties have to continue to live (deal) with each other despite all the negative "feelings". A third situation is when two parties would like to develop a relationship but external factors or parties make it impossible. The burden is then related to the loss of the potential positive outcomes.

Consequently, a relationship can be a burden in quite different situations: when it is broken, when is has to continue or when it can not be developed.

From the discussion above it is clear that the burden of relationships is related both to the content of them and to the counterpart. A conclusion must be that a relationship which is perceived as good at a certain point in time can become a burden both through the development within the relationship and through the development of other relationships. Looking closer into the characteristics or relationships reveals that there are at least five different quandaries that can cause a relationship to become a burden. These five will be discussed one by one.

Unruliness – the loss of control

Developing a relationship leads to giving up some degree of freedom. It entails giving up the control over some of the company's own resources, activities and intentions, sharing these with the counterpart. This aspect is present in all relationships even though it is not always recognised. It is

Partly this problem depends on the resource demands from every relationship, which has as a consequence that there are limited expectations and the fact that relationships are undetermined. Every actor has to believe that the counterpart will prioritise just its demands. Other close relationships will be seen as competing in one way or another if they are not directly connected to the focal one.

We hinted at the problems caused by exclusiveness when commenting on the Vegan case and the fact that only a limited number of relationships can be developed at a time. The case of a Swedish equipment producer Inteq (Axelsson and Wynstra, 1995) can be a good example. Inteq had for a long time been the main supplier to a large Swedish and a large American customer. When another large American company – a competitor to the American customer – takes over the Swedish customer it decides that the Swedish company must use its own supplier. The relationship with Inteq is rather abruptly brought to an end. Another example of this effect could be the case of a Swedish wood supplier, Glulam (Waluszewski, 1995), who develops a close relationship with a Dutch furniture manufacturer. By doing so it is jeopardising its relationship with the previous wholesale distributor who it still needs in order to sell other products.

Regardless of its causes, the effects on the parties is the same. The exclusiveness of relationships leads easily to conflicts whenever a new close relationship is developed.

Stickiness – you never know when and from whom there will be requests

Developing a relationship with a counterpart automatically gets you closer to the friends of the counterpart. You get connected in one way or another to a whole set of other actors. The effect may come in terms of unexpected visits or demands from these third parties and at very different moments in time. Becoming part of a "new" network can be a strain as all those new acquaintances belonging to it might not be the ones you would like to be connected to. The friends of your friend might not be those who you would like to have as friends. They might be unfriendly, inefficient, just boring or may come with unexpected demands. In business relationships a customer or a supplier might in the short term be interesting due to its offer or demand but can in the longer time perspective become a burden due to its other relationships. As a customer it can demand development of products which in the long run are "dead ends". As a supplier it might offer competitive prices but not keep up at all with the technical development due to the fact that its other customers are very unsophisticated.

The problems that "stickiness" can cause in business relationships have been felt very much by companies in the construction industry in Sweden during the last recession. Quite a number of them got into large financial troubles not because of inefficiency in their own production but due to the problems their customers had in their customer relationships.

Furthermore, there is connectedness over time. In a sense relationships never die. Being connected to a certain partner in a certain period becomes part of one's identity, which affects possibilities for developing and maintaining relationships on other occasions with other partners. The effects from connected relationships may arise unexpectedly a long way into the future.

THE RELATIONSHIP PREDICAMENT

Focusing on possible problems resulting from developing close relationships with business partners, we are faced with a rather gloomy picture. The loss of control, uncertain outcomes, high costs, preclusion from other opportunities, and unexpected backlashes seem to be more or less automatic consequences of close relationships. Any of these problems is of such magnitude that it can bring a company (or an individual) to the verge of desolation, despair and total ruin. Especially when, as often is the case, the company is highly dependent on a very limited number of relationships, the burden of relationships can be very heavy indeed.

Unlike the picture painted by some others who promise large rewards to those who engage in close relationships, we are faced with a relationship predicament. There may be huge rewards from relationships but their burden can be substantive and they cannot be escaped. Business relationships are assets to companies, but also liabilities.

Scrutinising the negative consequences of close relationships naturally raises the question whether these can be avoided. Can we find a way to only get the positive consequences of a relationship? Our understanding, based on the above discussion of common relationship draw-backs, is that they cannot be avoided, but maybe mitigated. They are invariably present as a relationship develops between two parties. Only by refraining from engaging in relationships can the burden of relationships be avoided. Once a relationship is developed there is always a risk that it might become a burden. It has to do with the very meaning of a relationship.

The notion of a business relationship is not univocal. Those who tend to emphasise that "good" relationships are the solution to various problems, tend to give relationships mainly a psycho-logical, attitudinal meaning. The notion is then used to signify social interaction, i.e. the "co-operative intent". Relationships are then in themselves attached positive connotations. However, if we let the notion of relationships cover the mutual interdependencies of behaviours, the "total" interaction, the notion will become much more value-neutral. It will mean mutual orientation and conditioning of behaviours, which in a business context will be interaction with technical, economic and administrative content besides the social one.

This varied usage of the term becomes clear from casual observations of attitudes and behaviour of companies. There are companies that do not perceive and conceive of dealings with others as relationships but as normal business conduct.

Unaware of interdependencies they appear to handle them well, they exploit the advantages of long term dealings with counterparts (relationships) and contain the negative consequences. Other companies aware of relationships perceive them as adversarial and "negative" and a necessary evil but seem to cope with the situation successfully. Others still aware of the importance of relationships put their efforts into developing "good" relationships with their partners, concentrat-ing on the social level, and nevertheless struggle with difficulties. The awareness of the need to be careful in handling business relationships is hardly enough to solve the problems of a business. The interest must be on creating a positive balance of outcomes.

Our own research suggests that companies have a choice in the way they participate in different relationships. However, most do not have a choice in terms of staying outside relationships. In the sense in which we use the notion of relationships (party specific interdependencies), these are to many companies a given, a very condition of their existence and development. They are often a distinctive feature of the context in which the companies operate. Take a typical example of a company in business markets – a supplier to the automotive industry. This company is always dependent on very few customer relationships. The only choice is how to take part in these relationships. It is the insight that depending on how the relationship evolves, which at least partly can be influenced by the single party, the potential burden will take on different nature and occurrence. The company does not have to meet them unprepared.

Last but not least, whether interdependencies from developing a relationship will on balance turn out to be burdening or rewarding for the parties depends both on the development of the relationship in itself and on how the relationship is embedded into the larger web of relationships. A relationship can become a burden because of the costs incurred within it but also because of effects on other existing or potential relationships. The rewards can in the same way come directly from the relationship or from its connections to other relationships. Clearly, there is a multiplicity of effects and the final results will very much depend on getting the positive outcomes to outweigh the negative ones. Sometimes this is impossible and then the question becomes "Who's next?"

WHO'S NEXT?

As the burden of relationships cannot be escaped and is likely to be heavy, a natural question is: should a company (or a person) have relationships at all? This question is, sadly enough, meaningless. Because without relationships there is no life in the long run. No business is an island in the same way as no man is an island. Life without interdependencies is not meaningful. Developing relationships is clearly to create interdependencies but it is also the most important means of handling interdependencies. It is the means of handling the texture of interdependencies that shape the very existence and development of companies, as well as that of the individuals.

The very same aspects of relationships we listed as sources of problems and the cause of them becoming a burden make relationships an effective instrument for handling the problem of interdependence. The very same aspects make them rewarding. The loss of control, giving up the freedom consequent to establishing a relationship is just the reverse of sharing the burden of interpreting the context and choosing the appropriate course of action. It gives an actor the possibility of transcending its own "imprisoning" boundaries.

The inherent undeterminedness of relationships makes them ways of escaping the gauge of history. It provides the two parties with the possibilities of creating their own world and their own future. Together they can build history, they can innovate and create unique combinations and thereby achieve unique performance.

The energy and costs required in order to develop a relationship become against the background of the undeterminedness and the connectedness an investment in opening up possibilities. The costs are not only sacrifices, they are the necessary investments for a rewarding future. The larger these investments the larger the potential for future rewards.

The mechanism of priority causing preclusion has as the reverse effect – inclusion. A life without friends is not just empty, it will also be extremely costly for a company. If it has to distrust all its exchange partners and always be prepared to get a knife in the back, then too much energy will go to safeguarding.

The stickiness of the relationships is what provides for future opportunities, favourable circumstances well ahead and far away from the ones enacted within the existing relationships.

Finally, considering the value of business relationships, the rewards and burden they entail, it is the rewards that spur the development of a relationship. Only when there is no expectation of any further major rewards will they tend to become felt as a burden. The "who's next" will become compelling.

REFERENCES

Asberg, M. and Håkansson, H. (1995) "Swelag" in H. Håkansson and I. Snehota (eds), *Developing Relationships in Business Networks*, pp. 97–119, Routledge, London.

Axelsson, B. and Wynstra, F. (1995) "Inteq: positioning in a changing global network" in H. Håkansson and I. Snehota (eds), *Developing Relationships in Business Networks*, Routledge, London.

Blois, K. (1995) *Relationship marketing in organisational markets – when is it appropriate*, Working paper, Oxford.

Ford, D. and Thomas, R. (1995) "Omega" in H. Håkansson and I. Snehota (eds), *Developing Relationships in Business Networks*, pp. 221–31, Routledge, London.

Pelz, J. and Snehota, I. (1995) "Svitola SpA" in H. Håkansson and I. Snehota (eds), *Developing Relationships in Business Networks*, pp. 251–60, Routledge, London.

Ring, S. P. and Van de Ven, A. (1994) "Developmental Process of Co-operative Interorganizational Relationships", *Academy of Management Review*, 19 (January), pp. 90–118.

Spencer, R. and Mazet, F. (1995) "Vegan" in H. Håkansson and I. Snehota (eds), *Developing Relationships in Business Networks*, pp. 148–63, Routledge, London.

Waluszewski, A. (1995) "Glulam" in H. Håkansson and I. Snehota (eds), *Developing Relationships in Business Networks*, pp. 78–97, Routledge, London.

2.5 Don't all firms have relationships?

Keith Blois

INTRODUCTION

The current enthusiasm for "relationship marketing" brings with it a number of problems. In particular this paper will suggest that, unless a counter-intuitive definition of a "relationship" is used, it is impossible for firms not to have relationships – indeed that a firm does not have the choice as to whether or not it has relationships. Instead the paper will suggest that what is important is that a firm should determine, given its particular circumstances, what types of relationships are appropriate with each of its customers.

WHAT SORT OF "RELATIONSHIPS" DO FIRMS NEED?

With practising managers, consultants and, not least, academics all looking for ideas which will provide them with a competitive advantage, "fads" are a well recognised feature of management thinking. Whether or not "relationship marketing" will turn out to be a fad it has already entered into the "rhetoric" of management (Keltner, 1995) and yet, while like all fads it has an initially intuitive appeal, at present the concept lacks clarity. For example, in consumer markets the term is often used where a relational data base is used to underpin a supplier's marketing activities with the customers not necessarily being conscious that they are participants in a relationship marketing campaign. In comparison in many organisational markets relationship marketing involves the establishment of "a relationship" which is explicitly recognised by both buyer and seller. However, in spite of this lack of clarity, many assertions are being made about the importance of "relationship marketing" with influential writers stating that "companies must move from a short-term *transaction-orientated* goal to a long-term *relationship-building* goal". (Kotler, 1992)

In fact, unless a counter-intuitive definition of "relationship" is used, everybody and all organisations have some relationships (Anderson and Narus, 1991). However, the depth of these relationships will vary from those where "a relationship" might be said to exist, that is where both the supplier and the customer recognise, accept and act upon their mutuality of interest (Blois, 1995), through to situations where, although the customer and supplier do have a relationship (because they do business with each other), it is one where the characteristics are those of discrete exchange. It has been suggested (Blois, forthcoming) that an observer watching two organisations' behaviour as they conduct an exchange can only make an assessment of the current state of their relationship when:

(1) they have knowledge of the contractual terms under which the exchange is being conducted;
(2) they can observe the exchange process over extended periods of time; and,
(3) the participants give explanations of the reasons why the observed actions were undertaken.

The reason for proposing this is that it is arguably the way that those matters which do not fall within a contract are handled that indicates the quality of a relationship, for while in any exchange situation it may be impossible to specify *ex ante* the response which will be made to unpredicted contingencies, both parties have an expectation *ex ante* of the criteria which would determine an appropriate or equitable fulfilment of the exchange. In other words the exchange will be governed by some accepted principle and this principle will be used to select behaviour in all situations – whether unpredicted or not – where there is more than one possible response. Thus in a discrete exchange contract law would be appealed to; in other exchanges custom and practice might be invoked as the guiding principle; in others some form of dispute resolution mechanism might be used; etc. However, in "a relationship" the over-riding guiding principle would be the maintenance of the two parties' goal interdependence.

There are, however, two difficulties with such a guiding principle. The first is that, as implied above, the give and take that the application of such a principle requires often only produces equitable responses over a period of time. Therefore a great deal of trust may be required by one or both parties. Thus a supplier, with limited capacity, who has developed a new design might be asked by a customer to permit a competitive supplier to use that design so that final customer demand can be met. The customer might promise to compensate the first supplier in some way when the next round of contracts are placed. For the supplier to agree to such a proposal requires it both to trust in the customer's good intentions and to believe that circumstances will be such that the customer will be able to honour their commitment. However, many factors outside the customer's control may make it impossible for the customer to do this.

The second difficulty is that organisations do not make decisions – people do in the name of organisations. So, except where there is a tight legal contract, the interpretation of such "give and take" arrangements relies on the behaviour of individuals. But individuals leave organisations and also change jobs within their organisations and such changes may have an effect on both the company's culture and its relationships for two reasons. First, interactions with the customer's staff may be changed. Second, it may affect the type of mutual trust between members of a management team which would enable, say, a marketing manager, if he or she believed it to be essential for the sake of a relationship with a customer, to agree to a change which will require alterations to the production schedules without first referring to the production manager.

It is important to recognise that, while it is interpretations of events by individuals and the decisions that they consequently make which determine how a relationship evolves, it is the interpretation of those decisions by individuals in other organisations which determines the reputation of that organisation. Thus if two organisations are establishing or have established a relationship it is the interaction of their two cultures which creates the relationship and this is not only mediated by the behaviour of individuals but is the creation of individuals' interpretation of events.

In spite of the uncertainty as to what "a relationship" is, the current interest in relationship marketing may encourage a greater recognition that costs are incurred when building and maintaining relationships, and therefore the investments made into a relationship should be carefully evaluated. It may also consequentially create a greater awareness that relationships are "market investments" (Johanson and Mattsson, 1985) or assets but that they have positive and negative aspects with their value being determined by the relative importance of these aspects. Clearly, even with regard to a specific individual customer, the assessment of the balance between these positive and negative aspects may vary between suppliers for a whole variety of reasons. The examples of NECX, which does not have "relationships" in the sense that some writers (e.g. Kotler, 1992 and Gronroos, 1994) propose is *the* model, and of the KGF Bank (fictitious name), which maintains a variety of relationships, demonstrate a number of these features.

NECX INC. – SUCCESSFUL BECAUSE IT AVOIDS "RELATIONSHIPS"?

It is often helpful to take extreme examples to make a point. NECX is such an example. It demonstrates that the types of customer relationships which are appropriate for one highly successful business may not be close; may not be high on mutual commitment; and, may only involve limited co-ordination – all of which have been identified (see below) as features found in "relationships".

It will also show that the types of relationship which are best for NECX are in part determined by its own organisational structure and consequently the way in which its costs are built up.

Owned by two individuals, who started it from a domestic kitchen in 1980, by 1995 NECX was the world's largest independent distributor of integrated circuits and computer products with a turnover of about $450 million; no debt (other than to suppliers); and, no equity from outsiders. It acts as an intermediary between chip makers and purchasers world-wide – sometimes being a broker and sometimes a dealer (Damore, 1995) and makes its profits by being a supplier of last resort to whom customers turn when they cannot get supplies from their regular sources. Indeed it is where "the panic-stricken turn when the official distributors fail them" (Charbuck, 1994). It will meet such customer's requirements in one of two ways. Either it is holding the item in stock on a speculative basis or, if it is not, then it will seek out a supplier which does hold stocks of the item, buy the item and after repackaging it resell it. The core of its activities is its large electronic trading floor (which bears a striking resemblance to the fast-paced environment of a traditional stock exchange) where the world-wide availability and pricing of semiconductors are continuously reflected on a big board as over 75 multilingual, professional traders work the open market 24 hours a day 7 days a week.

NECX has a policy of repackaging all items before selling them with the aim of maintaining as high a degree of anonymity between its customers and its sellers as is possible. The reason given for doing this is that anonymity protects both the buyers, who are having difficulties in maintaining their output because of supply difficulties, and the sellers, who have surplus stocks, from being identified. More importantly though it makes it difficult for NECX to be by-passed by a customer in future going direct to the supplier(s) or vice versa.

From the descriptions given of the nature of "relationships" (see below) it is arguable that it is inappropriate for NECX to establish "relationships" with its customers. NECX exists purely because there are uncertainties of both supply and demand and it makes its profits by its ability to "wheel and deal". In fact it behaves opportunistically in the sense that it charges a price which reflects the urgency of the customer's need while having bought at a price which reflects the supplier's desire to off-load unwanted stock – stock which rapidly becomes obsolescent. It is arguable that NECX would feel inhibited in "exploiting" shortage situations if it had "relationships" with its customers. However, it must be stressed that there is nothing unethical about making money in this way and for a firm to position itself as a supplier of "last resort" is a perfectly respectable thing to do. Indeed the customers of such firms are glad that they exist and that they know of them – though they are even more glad that they rarely have to make use of their services! While some suppliers of "last resort" have regular purchase arrangements with their suppliers, where a firm operates in the same way as NECX then its suppliers are also happy that they exist but are also glad that they do not have to use them too often.

Thus compared with companies manufacturing chips (e.g. Intel or Siemens) not only is NECX not a manufacturer but it makes its profits by offering a very different service. The manufacturers will have organisations designed to be efficient at supplying the market's requirements based upon their forecast of demand and while doubtless they can cope with some variations in demand they can only do this within limits. In particular they are unlikely to be able economically to meet sudden large increases in demand while unexpected falls in demand will leave them with surplus stocks of rapidly dating items. In comparison NECX exists to cope with the uncertainties of both supply and demand. Although from time to time it holds stocks of chips on a speculative basis, its ideal is to know where there are surplus supplies of chips so that when approached by a potential customer it can make a trade.

NECX's assets include knowing where it can obtain chips surplus to others' requirements and being known by firms which may face unforeseen shortages. However, it is questionable if it wishes to have "a relationship" with any customer for there is nothing to suggest that doing so would be economically beneficial. In terms of the costs of its operation there may be some benefits arising from knowing a customer's style of business, credit worthiness, reputation, etc. For example, early in its life NECX suffered a loss of $80 000 on a single trade due to lack of knowledge of one its customer's other business connections (Charbuck, 1994: 236). Yet these benefits seem unlikely to have the same potential significance as those which manufacturing firms obtain from relationships (Kalwani and Narakesari, 1995) when set against the disadvantages of having a "relationship". For NECX such disadvantages would include restraints on its ability to get the best price for a chip for two reasons. First, a "relationship" client would not expect the supplier to behave opportunistically by exploiting a shortage situation. Second, where more than one customer needs an item which is in short supply, the supplier would feel obliged to give priority to its "relationship" customer even though other customers might be willing to bid a higher price to obtain supplies.

KGF BANK COMMITTED TO RELATIONSHIP MANAGEMENT

The KGF Bank, which has publicly committed itself to a relationship management strategy, reviews its relationships with the firms in its market each year and categorises them into one of seven categories. The review is based on an analysis of the effort which the bank has expended and the revenue obtained from each customer in the previous twelve months plus estimates of the potential revenue for the next twelve months. The sevenfold classification draws attention to a number of aspects of relationship management and marketing. In particular the following issues are raised: the variety of relationship forms which are available; the need to recognise the customer's viewpoint; and. the "light and dark side" of relationships. The seven categories are:

No wish to be a supplier. Potential customers may fall into this category for many reasons. For example, it might be that the bank's view of the customer's standards of behaviour, activities, etc. leads it to feel that association with such a customer might have a negative effect on its reputation. Thus there are financial institutions in the City of London which have effectively "black-listed" certain potential customers because they are concerned about their inclination to follow what is euphemistically called "sharp practice".

Prospecting. Here the bank's knowledge of the customer is very limited and it is still seeking to understand the customer's business and its strategies at the simplest level. For example does the prospect organise the purchase of financial products through a central office or does it delegate responsibility to the management of each of the territories in which it has offices? Only when the bank has a thorough understanding of these matters is it able it to put together a product offering which may look attractive to that client. Part of the activity when prospecting is for some of the bank's employees to make contact with their counterparts in the prospect's organisation and through this for the bank to become accepted as a competent, helpful and imaginative potential supplier.

A competitive supplier. Here the bank is already supplying at least one product to the customer and it knows that, not only are its competitors supplying similar products, but that the customer's policy is to continue to split the available business between two or more suppliers. Furthermore, while the product is only one of several which the bank could supply, the customer discourages attempts by any of its suppliers to cross-sell other products. The customer is perceived to prefer an "arms-length" relationship.

A valued niche supplier. In this case the bank still only sells one or two products out of the range which the customer is known to purchase but, where it is a supplier, it is the largest (sometimes the sole) supplier of these products. The bank therefore has a close relationship with a part of the customer's organisation but because the customer discourages cross-selling it cannot easily use this as a basis for obtaining additional business. This because its knowledge of the customer's financial requirements is not detailed enough to enable it to present a package of financial products which together take account of the customer's detailed financial strategy.

A valued diversified supplier. The bank in this situation supplies several products to the customer but it may not be the dominant supplier of any one and certainly not of more than one product. The customer does not discourage the bank from seeking to increase its share of the supply of any of these products. There are opportunities for cross-selling either on a product or a geographic basis and the bank has the possibility of developing the relationship into that of being *a major supplier* but this will require the investment of a considerable amount of managerial effort usually over a period of time.

A major supplier. Here the bank is the dominant supplier of a number of products which the customer sees as being of particular importance to its financial strategy. The customer expects the bank to consider how the products it is offering together support its financial strategy. To be able to do this the bank's staff need to have very close relationships with the customer's staff in individual sections but also its senior staff must have sufficient access to the customer's senior financial team to be able to understand the customer's financial strategy in depth. The bank appoints a client manager who is responsible for the whole relationship and who has "authority" over other staff (including those more senior than him) who may be responsible for the individual products being supplied.

A strategic partner. When this stage has been reached the bank is perceived by the client as *the* automatic place from which to seek advice and the bank almost has the right of first refusal for any new business opportunity. Furthermore the bank is perceived by the financial community to occupy this position and is thus automatically associated with the success or the failure of the client's financial strategy. A relationship manager is appointed to manage the relationship but the intent is to manage the relationship back to being *a major supplier* because of the perceived disadvantages of such a close relationship (see below).

WHAT IS A "RELATIONSHIP"?

It still seems that "(t)he perception of RM (viz Relationship Marketing), however, varies between authors" (Gummesson, 1994) and that there is not agreement regarding what can be defined as "relationship marketing". Furthermore some writers use terms such as "relational marketing" and "relationship exchange" which often seem similar if not synonymous. Yet, because these terms are not always defined, this may be an unwarranted assumption which further complicates the situation.

Where definitions of "relationship marketing" are given they do not indicate the activities which might be used in implementing a "relationship marketing" policy. Neither do they indicate the required inputs or features which would enable an observer to determine if such a policy was being followed. For example, some writers make it clear that "relationship marketing" has as its aim "the dual focus of getting and keeping customers" (Christopher, Payne and Ballantyre, 1991). Others, state that the essence of relationship marketing is the supplier's creation of commitment and trust between itself and a customer with the intent of "establishing, developing, and maintaining successful relational exchanges" (Morgan and Hunt, 1994). Certainly the statement that relationship marketing's "operational contents are unclear" (Gummesson, 1994) still holds true and little work seems to have been undertaken on establishing what the activities are which lead to the creation and maintenance of "a relationship".

Most definitions emphasise "long-term" or "lasting" relationships but sometimes they appear to be the *aim* of establishing a relationship while in other cases they are portrayed as the *result* of a relationship. Many writers now stress the need for mutual commitment and trust. Commitment being a desire to maintain a relationship which is often indicated by an on-going "investment" into activities which are expected to maintain the relationship. "Trust" is less clearly defined with some writers equating it with reliability (though whether or not there is a fundamental difference between "trusting" and "relying" is a matter of dispute), but in general being taken to mean an acceptance of vulnerability to another's possible, but not expected ill will (or lack of good will). The view stated being that commitment and trust are key components of a relationship because they encourage partners:

(1) to make investments into the relationship;
(2) to resist taking advantage of alternatives which provide short-term benefits; and,
(3) not to behave opportunistically with regard to the relationship. (Morgan and Hunt, 1994).

WHAT TYPE OF RELATIONSHIP?

It has been has suggested that the customer's view of the desirability of entering into a "relationship" will be affected by its perception of the likely size of the transaction costs involved (Blois, 1996). Customers, it is suggested, will seek that form of relationship which they believe will minimise the need for them to incur high transaction costs. A further perspective has been introduced (Håkansson and Snehota, 1995) through the emphasis that while there are benefits in any relationship there are also disadvantages and that, when determining how close a relationship to seek to develop with another organisation, a firm must recognise that there are trade-offs to be made. A firm cannot operate in total isolation but, if it wishes to maintain some independence, it must not become involved in a relationship which completely smothers it.

Håkansson and Snehota (1995) have suggested that there are five negative factors or disadvantages which result from being in a relationship. These are:

Loss of control. Developing a relationship inevitably means giving up, to some degree, control over such matters as resources, activities and even intentions.

Indeterminedness. A relationship is changing all the time. Its future is uncertain and is, in part, determined by its history but also by current events and the parties' expectations of future events.

Resource demanding. It takes effort to build and maintain a relationship. This can be viewed as an investment and a maintenance cost (Blois, 1995).

Preclusion from other opportunities. Given that resources are limited and that building and maintaining a relationship is resource demanding, then there is always a need to prioritise the use of resources and it may not be possible to pursue all of the individually attractive opportunities. Furthermore some potential relationships, which in isolation may look attractive, may be irreconcilable with an existing relationship.

Unexpected demands. The other party in a relationship will also have other relationships. This means that establishing a relationship actually means being linked, if only passively, into a network of relationships. The "membership" of such a network may bring with it obligations or expectation by others of specific behaviours.

The degree to which each of these factors exists will vary according to the nature of the relationship and, as has been made clear, the degree to which each is a disadvantage will vary within individual relationships. Thus a particular relationship may not lead to much loss of control but may make substantial resource demands. However, there is a reverse side to the coin and some of the benefits derived from relationships arise from these five factors. Yet the difference between a benefit and a problem is frequently very slight and will be contingent upon specific circumstances. Thus, "preclusion from other opportunities" may be perceived as a golden cage or a prison depending upon, for example, the alternatives open at any time.

NECX AND ITS RELATIONSHIPS

It is clear that NECX cannot have "a relationship" with its partners (either suppliers or customers) in the sense that some writers refer to relationships. The nature of its business is such that it:

(1)   would not wish to make an investment in a relationship because it must feel free to go where it can obtain the lowest purchase price and the highest selling price;

(2)   would not be concerned with attaining a "return on investment" in a relationship because it must feel free to take a short-term view as that is when arbitrage opportunities exist; and,

(3)   must be free to behave opportunistically.

Indeed NECX makes money by exploiting its suppliers' and its customers' unpredicted contingencies – its exchanges are certainly not guided by the over-riding guiding principle of the maintenance of both parties' goal interdependence. There would seem to be little benefit to NECX in allowing relationships to develop with either its customers or its suppliers which would lead to any of the five features identified becoming dominant issues (Håkansson and Snehota, 1995). Thus:

Loss of control. If NECX developed relationships with one or more customers it might compromise its ability to sell at the highest attainable price. As this is the basis on which it make its profits such a constraint would be a serious disadvantage.

Indeterminedness. It would seem inevitable that for NECX any relationship it develops will be very uncertain. Suppliers would ideally not wish to have output surplus to their customers' requirements. Customers would ideally prefer not to face the uncertainty and cost of seeking emergency supplies. Neither of these two groups would thus wish to commit themselves to deal with NECX in the future.

Resource demanding. Given the indeterminedness of their relationship there is no economic logic in NECX investing much in relationships with individual customers.

Preclusion from other opportunities. The basis on which NECX makes its profits is the freedom to behave opportunistically and NECX cannot afford to enter into any relationship which would preclude it from dealing with any supplier and/or customer which offers the opportunity of making a profit.

Unexpected demands. Given NECX's need not to be limited in its dealings with suppliers and customers, it would not wish its relationship with another organisation to place it under any obligation either to deal or not to deal with another firm in that organisation's "network".

Furthermore NECX's organisation and way of trading make it very difficult for close relationships to develop between its staff and either its customers' or its suppliers' personnel. Given that it is individuals' interpretation of events and the decisions that they consequently make which determine how a relationship evolves, this lack of consistent personal interaction makes the development of anything other than very limited trust most unlikely thus making "a relationship" almost impossible.

    Yet NECX must and does have relationships – the problem is not whether or not relationships exist but with the generality of the terms used to discuss "relationships". For example, the basis on which NECX makes its profits is to behave opportunistically with regard to imbalances of supply and demand. Yet the anonymity that it provides is only of value if both its customers and suppliers trust NECX to maintain it and not to make inappropriate use of its knowledge of their affairs by, say, letting a customer's competitors know that it is in difficulties because of a shortage of component supply. There must also be trust between itself and its suppliers that not only will an order be honoured but also that the quality of the chips supplied will be acceptable – there is not time (nor the necessary organisational structure) to allow NECX to check quality. Again its customers must trust NECX only to deal with trustworthy suppliers.

    Strategically a company should determine what type of relationships are ideally appropriate to its circumstances but in reaching that decision it must take account of the type of relationship which its customers find acceptable. So it is also important to consider whether or not NEXC's customers would wish to have a "relationship" with NECX for, whatever NECX's preferences, account must be taken of the type of relationship which its customers would find attractive. However, it does not seem unreasonable to presume that most of NECX's customers will not wish for a "relationship" for this could constrain their ability to use NECX only as and when it suited them, i.e. when their regular suppliers are unable to meet their requirements. Yet they would wish to have the type of relationship within which they are recognised by NECX to be trustworthy customers.

Where a supplier finds that a customer's view is not congruent with that which it holds then it must adapt its own position to meet that customer's viewpoint. The alternative is to take steps which will lead the customer to find some alternative arrangement acceptable. For firms with a limited number of customers this process may result in them managing several different types of relationship – perhaps even a different one for each customer (Macdonald, 1995). Given the way that NECX is organized neither of these approaches is feasible and so NECX recognises that there are some potential customers with whom it will never do business.

THE KGF BANK'S VIEW OF RELATIONSHIPS

As was indicated above, the bank reviews client relationships every twelve months using some historic information relating to costs and revenues plus forecasts of the next twelve months' activity. However, an important element in the reclassification procedure is the inclusion of a number of qualitative inputs. First, what is known of the client's view of relationships? The range of positions adopted by clients is very wide. For example, there are some who seem to have no policy – in such cases is it worth the bank trying to first demonstrate and then develop the value of close customer/supplier contact? Some clients seem to resist attempts to develop close relationships – where this is the case then it may be appropriate for the bank to remain a *competitive supplier* or a *valued niche supplier*. To try to change the customer's position will, at best, involve costly activity probably over a long period, at worst might annoy the client. Other clients seem keen on building "relationships" but what are they seeking from such relationships? Do they really see relationships as being based upon "mutually recognised goal interdependence"?

A second qualitative input is an assessment of the bank's resources – especially its staff resources. There would be little point in seeking to develop *a major supplier* relationship if the staff with appropriate experience are not available to act as client managers. The availability of staff of the correct calibre is a major difficulty for such banks and in consequence they often face the problem of allocating scarce resources in response to estimates of the potential revenue. Alternatively it might have difficulties in balancing the various levels of management required to handle the mix of relationships open to it. This so-called "leverage problem" (i.e. the average proportion of time required to manage an account by professionals of different seniority) is the classic cost problem in professional services. The issue then becomes one of allocating scarce resources in response to estimates of the potential revenue. This may mean that, although there would seem to be an opportunity to become *a major supplier*, the bank will decide that it is better to maintain an effective but less "deep" relationship with a client until such time as it is able to develop or recruit the appropriate staff to meet the customer's needs.

The third qualitative factor is the dark and light side of relationships. As the discussion of strategic *partnerships* indicated, while the bank may obtain the substantial benefit of being given first refusal on any new business it can also face problems. For example, if such a customer runs into financial difficulties then the bank's reputation may be tarnished through "guilt by association". In other cases such customers have presumed because of their close relationship that the bank will support them financially without first obtaining formal agreement. In both such cases it can be very difficult for the bank to publicly disassociate itself from the customer's actions.

Indeed for each of the above categories of relationship there is a different balance between the potential dark and light side. Thus while acting as *a competitive supplier* the bank is disadvantaged by its limited understanding of its client's financial strategy and consequently may not be able to offer the best solution to a particular problem faced by the client. However, unless a decision has already been taken to seek to build the client relationship to one of the closer forms of relationship, within a *competitive supplier* relationship the bank can both offer what it regards as an appropriate level of service and also obtain the best financial return possible. In comparison, within a "relationship" the bank would need to be much more sensitive to the client's views and avoid any tendency to act opportunistically. Again where the bank is in a *major supplier* relationship while there may be many advantages there will almost certainly also be restrictions on its ability to deal with that customer's competitors.

For this bank the implementation of its commitment to a relationship management strategy is not a simplistic "we will have *relationships*". Rather it is a complex decision process where: the client's views are taken into account; the bank's resource base; and, the benefits and risks of different types of relationships are carefully balanced to assess what type of relationship the bank feels best fits its strategic plans. In other words the bank regularly adjusts the depth of its relationship with each of its customers and consequently the bank's response to an unexpected contingency arising from a customer's behaviour cannot be predicted without knowing from which customer the matter arises.

WHERE DOES THIS LEAVE US?

NECX is an unusual but by no means unique organisation but the inappropriateness of it developing "relationships" is apparent. Obviously it does have relationships with all those with whom it does business but these are not close relationships in the sense implied by many writers on the topic of "relationships". The case of NECX acts as a reminder that there is an almost unlimited variety of forms of relationship open to an organisation and this is reinforced by the KGF Bank's position. There are cases where it is appropriate for a firm to develop relationships, within which there is a high degree of trust and considerable commitment, with some or all of its customers. On the other hand there are companies like NECX which keep their commitment to all their customers to a minimum and which only seek to develop trust with regard to certain aspects of their relationships. Thus while NECX's customers must be prepared to trust it with regard to the quality of the supplies it obtains for them from an anonymous source, they do not expect NECX to do other than behave opportunistically with regard to price.

The KGF Bank shows that relationships between a supplier and some of its customers can be very deep and close across all the dimensions which might be used to describe a relationship. Yet relationships with other customers may be less deep on some but not all of these dimensions and others point to the need to recognise that the dimensions mentioned in the literature, such as "trust", can themselves be sub-categorised.

There are no easy solutions to the question as to what type of relationship a supplier should seek to develop with its customers. However, if nothing else within organisational markets the current interest in "relationship marketing" does act as a reminder that a supplier should regularly consider what type of relationship with each significant customer best suits its circumstances. This requires a thorough understanding of:

- both the dark and the light side of relationships;
- the customers' viewpoints; and,
- the costs of building and maintaining different types of relationships.

Then, depending upon the relative importance of individual customers, the supplier may need to develop an organisational structure which will enable it to manage a range of different types of relationships.

MANAGERIAL IMPLICATIONS

These two examples suggest that there are four issues which require management's attention when considering its relationships with customers. First, what is the customer's opinion of the desirability of developing a close relationship with its suppliers? Some customers have clearly expressed policies in this regard. Where this is not the case, and particularly when approaching a customer for the first time, a supplier should make an assessment of the customer's likely position. Failure to do this may lead to an inappropriate approach to the customer which, at best, may lead to a wasteful use of resources and, at worst, cause the customer considerable irritation.

Second, suppliers must determine the organisational structure which they need to put into place to effectively manage their relationship with a customer. Unfortunately this may differ for each customer and a supplier can find that to set up the ideal structure for each customer would involve extremely elaborate and costly organisational arrangements. In such circumstances some degree of compromise between the ideal and the economic must be found. For example segmenting the market on the basis of the type of relationships customers would prefer may be necessary – with all the trade-offs that segmentation schemes necessarily involve.

Third, the supplier must carefully evaluate the resources required to maintain whatever form of relationship it decides to develop and maintain with its various customers. Particularly as a result of down-sizing this is now a major problem in many firms. The difficulty is that more than ever before management needs to evaluate the alternatives to which a resource could be allocated. For example, to maintain a particular type of relationship with one customer might require a certain number of days of technical advice each year. If this is the case then it must be decided whether that number of days is available and, if not, whether they could be made available by, say, recruiting? If they are or can be made available then what alternative uses might they be put to?

Fourth, suppliers need to recognise that all relationships involve an element of risk. These risks need to be identified and evaluated so that the degree of commitment that is appropriate from their point of view can be determined. A matrix linking the risk of a relationship perceived by the supplier with the value added to the customer by the supplier's activities (see Figure 1) may provide a useful way for a supplier to start to evaluate this.

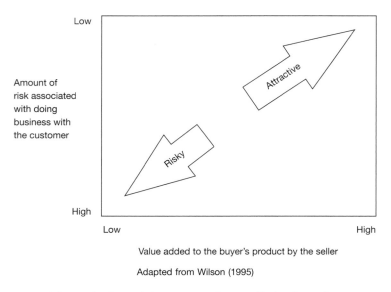

Adapted from Wilson (1995)

Figure 1 Potential partners – the supplier's viewpoint.

The argument being that customers' procurement policies range from adversarial through to relational. Where a customer adopts an adversarial procurement posture then there is considerable risk for the supplier and this will be accentuated where the supplier is adding little in value terms to the customer's activities. However, where a customer is not opposed to a relationship policy then this is less risky for the supplier and if, in addition, the supplier's product adds substantial value to the customer's activities it seems reasonable to assume that the customer will be more careful to assure itself of such supplier's capabilities. Where these are satisfactory then the supplier will enjoy an element of monopoly power. Thus the top right corner of the matrix appears the most attractive from the supplier's point of view.

CONCLUSIONS

Firms are linked together in a "dense network of co-operation and affiliation" (Richardson, 1972). To suggest or even imply that firms do not have relationships is to ignore this fact. Every organisation should recognise: that relationships cost time and effort to establish; relationships need managing; and, that the type of relationship which is appropriate should be determined in the light of the supplier's understanding of its customer's evaluation of the potential benefits of the available forms of relationship. The risk of viewing relationships as if they *must* involve commitment and an almost blanket trust is to ignore the rich diversity of relationships which not only exist but are appropriate in different contexts.

REFERENCES

Anderson, J. C. and Narus, J. A. (1991), "Partnering as a Focused Market Strategy", *California Management Review*, Vol. 33:3, Spring, pp. 95–113.

Blois, K. J. (1996), "Relationship Marketing in Organizational Markets – assessing its costs and benefits", *Journal of Strategic Marketing*, Vol. 4:3, pp. 181–191.

Blois, K. J. (1996), "Relationship Marketing in Organizational Markets – when is it appropriate?", *Journal of Marketing Management*, Vol. 12:1–3, pp. 161–175.

Blois, K. J. (forthcoming). "Are Business to Business Relationships Inherently Unstable?" *Journal of Marketing Management*.

Christopher, M., Payne, A., and Ballantyre, D. (1991), *Relationship Marketing*. Butterworth-Heinemann Ltd., Oxford.

Churbuck, D. C. (1994). "Fish and chips", *Forbes* (September 12), pp. 235–236.

Damore, K. (1995) "Spot market offers sense of renewal", *Computer Reseller News*, No. 635 (19th June) pp. 45–47.

Gummesson, E. (1994), "Making Relationship Marketing Operational", *International Journal of Service Industry Management*, Vol. 5, pp. 5–20.

Johanson, J. and Mattsson, L.-G. (1985), "Marketing investments and market investments in industrial networks", *International Journal of Research in Marketing*, Vol. 2, pp. 185–195.

Gronroos, C. (1994), "Quo Vadis, Marketing? Towards a Relationship Marketing Paradigm", *Journal of Marketing Management*, Vol. 10, pp. 347–360.

Håkansson, H. and Snehota, I. (1995), "The Burden of Relationships or Who's Next?" *Proceedings of the IMP 11th. International Conference* (Manchester) pp. 522–536.

Kalwani, M. U. and Narakesari, N. (1995). "Long-term Manufacturer–Supplier Relationships: Do They Pay Off for Supplier Firms?" *Journal of Marketing*, Vol. 59, pp. 1–16.

Keltner, B. (1995), "Relationship Banking and Competitive Advantage: Evidence from U.S. and Germany", *California Management Review*, Vol. 37 (Summer), pp. 45–71.

Kotler, Philip (1992), "It's Time for Total Marketing", *Business Week ADVANCE Executive Brief*, 2.

Krep, D. M. (1996), "Corporate Culture and Economic Theory" pp. 221–275 in P. J. Buckley and J. Mitchie (eds), *Firms, Organizations and Contracts*, Oxford University Press, Oxford.

Macdonald, S. (1995), "'Too Close for Comfort?': The Strategic Implications of Getting Close to the Customer", *California Management Review*, Vol. 37:4, pp. 8–27.

Morgan, R. M. and Hunt, S. D. (1994), "'The Commitment–Trust Theory of Relationship Marketing", *Journal of Marketing*, Vol. 58:3, pp. 20–38.

Richardson, G. B. (1972), "The Organization of Industry", *Economic Journal*, Vol. 82, pp. 883–896.

Wilson, David T. (1995), "An Integrated Model of Buyer–Supplier Relationships", *Journal of the Academy of Marketing Science*, Vol. 23:4, pp. 335–345.

2.6 Business dancing – the nature and role of interfirm relations in business strategy*

Ian F. Wilkinson and Louise C. Young

INTRODUCTION

The concept of "relationship marketing" represents part of a larger theme fast gaining centre stage in many business disciplines. This is the recognition that a firm's performance depends not only upon its own efforts, skills and resources but also on the efforts, skills and resources of other organizations which provide it with valued inputs. These other organizations include suppliers of materials and components, suppliers of machinery and specialists services, channel organizations that help link a firm to its customers and organizational customers themselves. The development and management of relations with these organizations thus becomes a key focus of strategic attention, for it is through these relations that key resources are accessed and value created and delivered to customers.

In this paper we consider the nature of the relationships that exist between firms and how they can be managed. In particular, relationships are examined in terms of their degree of cooperativeness and competitiveness. We draw on some of the results of a program of research carried out in Australia to study interfirm relations in order to illustrate various types of interfirm relations that exist. We then suggest an alternative to the oft-used marriage metaphor for analysing and guiding relationship management. Instead we propose a dancing analogy. We argue that this offers a richer base for considering the variety of interfirm relations that exist and persist in business systems and avoids the often implicit notion that relations must necessarily develop towards a uniform type of mature state, the "successful marriage", which is usually characterized in terms of a long-term committed relationship. Finally, we consider the implications of our analysis for the management of interfirm relations.

THE CO-OPERATIVE AND COMPETITIVE NATURE OF BUSINESS RELATIONSHIPS

Business relationships and individual interactions are often conceptualized as either competitive or cooperative in nature (Argyle, 1991). In cooperative interactions both parties can gain from the interaction while in competitive interactions the relevant goals of both parties cannot be simultaneously satisfied (Deutsch, 1949; Stern, 1971). It is often argued that cooperation and competition are either mutually exclusive or inversely related. Thus high or low levels of cooperation and competition cannot exist simultaneously in relationships.

Life cycle models of relationship development such as those proposed by Ford (1980) and Dwyer, Schurr and Oh (1987) imply an inverse relationship between cooperation and competition. In early phases of relationships parties are "distant" from one another, compete for benefits and

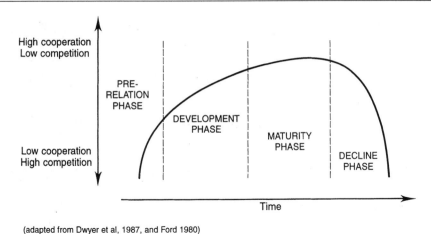

(adapted from Dwyer et al, 1987, and Ford 1980)

Figure 1 A relationship life cycle model.

take advantage of opportunities which may present themselves. In later phases, relations are characterized by increasing commitment and cohesion stemming from the increasing scope and scale of cooperation and the diminished or absent competition. In the final stage relations may decline or their patterns of interaction become institutionalized. This development pattern is depicted in Figure 1.

An alternative view is that within a relationship cooperative and competitive aspects are likely to coexist (Nisbet, 1972). As Deutsch (1962) observes, "people may be promotively interdependent with respect to particular goals and not others. Firms manufacturing the same product may be cooperative with regard to expanding the total market but competitive with regard to the share of it each attains" (p. 278). An example would be a relation where parties cooperate to achieve reliable quality, delivery, and acceptable price but compete for the most favourable payment terms. Each party may wish to hold the money involved in their transactions as long as possible with the seller wanting cash on delivery, the buyer wanting 90 days interest free credit. Parties may continue to compete for more advantageous financial terms within the context of an otherwise cooperative relationship.

Competition may be built into the legal and social norms and expectations which are themselves a type of cooperative structure. For example, the market may be structured in a way which precludes more than a certain amount of cooperation between trading parties (e.g. anti-collusion laws or price fixing legislation) and require the relation to be regulated by the market. Or, competition between suppliers may be structured as a tendering process based on lowest price, as exists in some government departments.

FOUR TYPES OF INTERFIRM RELATIONSHIPS

In this section we describe four types of interfirm relations in terms of their cooperative and competitive characteristics. This analysis is based on some of the results of the Interfirm Relations Research Program (IRRP) which aims to develop a general methodology and questionnaire for studying all types of interfirm relations. The methodology and questionnaire have been refined through a number of studies and a large and diverse data base of interfirm relations has been created. To date over 1000 interviews concerning over 600 interfirm relations have been conducted. (More details about the IRRP research program are to be found in Young, 1992; Young and Wilkinson, 1989a, 1989b, 1992.)

As part of this research multiple item measures of various aspects of a firm's trust and cooperation in a relationship were developed. These in turn were used to identify two underlying dimensions of firms' behaviour that could be used to classify relationships. These have been labelled relationship cooperativeness and competitiveness.

Relationship cooperativeness is made up of three components. The first is a measure of the trust and cooperativeness of the respondent firm, including their concern for the interests and welfare of the trading partner and various indicators of their own cooperative behaviour. The second component is a measure of the trust and cooperativeness of the trading partner, including the level of trust in the trading partner and a belief that they act in a fair and honest way. The third component measures the positive motivation of the trading partner, including their perceived concern for the interests and welfare of the respondent's firm. Relationship competitiveness comprises measures of the extent to which the respondent firm and the trading partner try to gain advantage at the other firm's expense.

Relationships were classified into high and low cooperative and competitive groups based on whether they scored above or below average on each of these dimensions. This results in a four way classification of relations. In the following, case studies are used to illustrate some of the main characteristics of each type of relationship.

Low cooperation and low competition

Relations with low levels of cooperation and competition are likely to be those where there is a non-crucial relationship in place between the parties, i.e. there is limited or no interdependence between the trading parties. This lack of interdependence could stem from a relationship being in its infancy or near its end such that few ties have been established or remain. An example of a relationship with very low overall competition and cooperation scores is that of a large financial institution that has been providing a tyre retailer with a line of credit for twelve months. Two different respondents in the financial institution agreed that the retailer's incompetent management led the firm to trading losses. The relationship is unlikely to continue because the retailer's liquidity problems were so severe that he is perceived to be likely to go under.

Neither the financial institution nor the retailer behave particularly cooperatively or competitively. The retail firm's lack of competence and declining opportunities decrease both their cooperative and competitive options. They too may perceive themselves as likely to go under and may have already "given up". The respondent's lack of cooperation and competition seems to stem from the lack of importance of this customer to the financial institution. The retailer represents a minuscule percentage of the respondent's total business and their success or failure means little to the respondents. The respondents have obviously already written this relationship off and are, psychologically at least, in the "dissolution" stage of relationship development (as per the classification of Dwyer et al., 1987).

But relations with less extreme but still below-average overall cooperation and competition scores may well be ongoing and of the mutually convenient, uninvolved, "transaction-based" type. These would include relations where firms are essentially unimportant to each other due to multi-sourcing, competitive bidding or only have intermittent need of one another.

An example of a relationship with moderately below-average cooperation scores and competition scores is that of a fast-food chain with a printer supplying promotional material. The printer in this instance is competent and has a history of successful interactions with the respondent firm. But purchaser policy precludes establishment of highly committed relationships. The printing firm is a member of a pool of similarly competent print suppliers, used always on a quote-for-job basis. Their best efforts will achieve them no more than "always-a-share" of the available business (Jackson, 1985). This situation is not unusual, as a buyer's policy is often to keep a small number of competent suppliers available (and thus in business). Such a policy would seem likely to lead to low but stable cooperation and competition in a relationship which can continue indefinitely.

Low cooperation and high competition

A combination of low cooperation and high competition is often seen as the classic "poor" and/or eroding relationship. An example is a relationship between an Australian importer and a Fijian clothing manufacturer registering very high levels of competition and very low levels of cooperation. The three-year relationship was described as difficult to coordinate with much negotiation needed; formal and informal rules and regulations from a variety of sources are used to organize the interactions between these two firms. There is much conflict in the relationship, in particular with respect to financial arrangements and delivery of goods. This appears to be exacerbated by very poor communication from both parties. The poor exchange of information occurs both deliberately as parties withhold information for advantage or to "get even", and due to geographic (and perhaps psychic) distance.

Both parties are very self-interested. They frequently let each other down in the pursuit of their own objectives. The respondent firm frequently coerces its trading partner to get its way. Yet threats are unlikely to be effective. The manufacturer is not dependent on the respondent and so threats lack "teeth". It is exasperation rather than their best interests which lead the respondents to threaten, as they are highly dependent on this manufacturer. They perceive that it is likely the relationship will end in the foreseeable future – primarily to their cost. There are no alternative suppliers for them.

Relationships of this type are under stress and there is consequently pressure to change. Sometimes the relationship can cease, as is occurring in the first example. In other instances relationships continue because of contractual agreements which require that they do so. Resignation characterizes a relationship with moderate to high competition and moderate to low cooperation scores. Two transportation companies operating in the leisure and tourism industry entered into a quasi joint venture which now exists solely because there is a ten-year agreement tying the two firms together. The "wronged" respondent firm is merely biding their time until they can end the relationship with a partner they describe as incompetent and opportunistic. The respondent firm behaves neutrally, providing only the minimum cooperation specified in the contract and they take advantage of whatever opportunities present themselves with the aim of strengthening their future market position and weakening that of their trading partner, who will be a competitor at the end of the joint venture.

Rather than end, relationships may "improve" their character by increasing their cooperativeness, and/or decreasing their competitiveness, thus becoming a different relationship type. Some firms not now in the low cooperation-high competition group report past behaviour indicating that the relationship used to be low in cooperation and high in competitiveness but is no longer. For instance, this has been reported by firms who have introduced some sort of quality management into their relationships. A supplier to the automotive industry discussing a moderately good (and improving) relationship using a just-in-time supply system reported a relationship history of considerable competitiveness and minimal cooperation that had gradually and painfully evolved to being more cooperative and less competitive. This evolution from a "bad" past to a "better" present often is characterized by strong mutual dependence which leads to a strong motivation to make things work.

High cooperation and high competition

High cooperation and high competition relationships are generally perceived by respondents to be effective. Sixty-six per cent of the relations in this group are described as good working relationships. Only 8% are perceived as not good or poor. This would indicate that the enhanced social and operational functioning often associated with high cooperation can outweigh or overcome many of the problems often thought to be associated with high competition.

Sometimes competitiveness is not perceived to be a problem but rather part of the normal practices of doing business. A firm distributing pipes prides themselves both on working well with their customers and on being loyal to their own interests, i.e. achieving everything they can for their company. They assume their trading partners do likewise and accordingly have set up systems and procedures which minimize the effect of other firms' opportunistic actions on themselves. However, this opportunism (their own and their partner's) is not perceived to be inappropriate or conflict-inducing but rather sound business practice. This is reflected in moderately high levels of cooperation and competition in the relationship discussed with a major customer.

Often above-average "competitiveness" scores are based on respondents reporting that their trading partner behaves in their own interests to the detriment of the relationship. But the score may reflect unacceptable behaviour or behaviour which has become part of the norms of a stable relationship. The manufacturing manager of a company producing consumer appliances describes a somewhat competitive and cooperative relationship with a supplier of their components in this way: "we have been doing business for so long we know each other inside out; there is tremendous involvement with each other now and (it) has been so for a long time."

Why is this relationship competitive as well as cooperative? The purchaser is now much larger, more powerful and more innovative than their relation partner. But the reverse was true 30 years ago when they commenced trading. Each firm has differing ways in which they wish to evolve and to respond to market conditions (as well as different overall conditions to respond to). They each attempt to incorporate their own approach into the relationship. The respondent firm recognizes that their supplier will either not benefit from or will not perceive the benefits of the management techniques and marketing initiatives the respondent firm continues to introduce. The supplier almost always has to be compelled into any change. But this seems to be accepted as just part of the process of their doing business, has been going for quite a while and is anticipated to continue. In other words, a combination of high competition and cooperation can be embedded in the relationship culture as long as it remains within acceptable bounds and occurs within a history of effective interactions.

The relationship between a distributor of video tapes and a retailer which has been in operation for six years is one with very high cooperation and competition scores. One informant in the distributor firm categorized the relationship as "good" and the other as "moderately good." The firms are highly interdependent and committed and both firms are reported as fairly satisfied with the relationship. The relationship has improved through time with mutual respect and trust increasing. It continues to improve slowly and is described as one of the best by a senior executive and above-average by a middle manager in the company.

This relationship is characterized by moderately high levels of conflict. There are frequent disagreements about payment and price and some disagreements about product nature and quality. It often requires considerable negotiation before they reach agreements. The firms behave opportunistically towards one another at least some of the time. The respondent firm occasionally increases prices and/or decreases product quality without advance warning to the retailer. Both firms mislead one another on occasion. However, the informants report that their conflicts with their trading partner are satisfactorily resolved.

Why do firms so interconnected, possessing ties of strong mutual trust and respect, continue to behave in these competitive ways? Or, how could norms of mutual trust and respect arise in this type of atmosphere? One possible reason is that the interdependence between these firms seems to be based on shared history rather than the unique contributions the respondents can and do make to one another. They have worked together well in the past and as a result think they will continue to do so. However, the trading partner's competitors are perceived as similar in quality to potential relation partners and there are no unique systems of procedures which tie these firms together. Therefore, the ties may not be as strong as might be the case when deeply entrenched systems and procedures and shared technology bind firms.

The second reason is that the relationship appears to exist in a "win–lose" culture. Some of the business opportunities available involve loss to the trading partner; and these opportunities are not passed by. There is no indication of the perception of mutual opportunities (i.e. win–win). This competitive culture and the behaviour associated with it are probable reasons for the high levels of conflict which characterize the relationship.

The underlying reason for this cooperation–competition mix and the nature of the dependence and culture associated with it may in part be the result of the degree of change and adapt both firms have had to deal with during the relationship's history. The video market has increased dramatically since the initiation of this relationship, as has the competition. Both firms have grown considerably in size, in particular the retailer who, during the life of the relationship, has started franchizing outlets. While both firms' prospects are seen as good, the environment is not now nor has it ever been stable.

The firms are tied together by their shared history of successful interaction and ability to overcome their conflicts. They do this in volatile industry conditions where good relationships are likely to be difficult to achieve and to maintain. This difficult environment most probably contributes to the high levels of competitiveness. The fact that the firms try hard and are able to successfully interact in such adverse conditions in turn probably contributes to the high levels of cooperativeness. Since the respondents perceive the relationship to be improving and very likely to continue in the foreseeable future (and because the market is becoming increasingly stable), one possible outcome for this relationship is that it will become increasingly cooperative and less competitive in the longer term.

Low competition and high cooperation

The low competition and high cooperation relationship is often envisaged as the "ideal" relationship that firms will try to develop towards. These relationships appear to be similar to those depicted as mature relations in models of relationship development (Dwyer *et al.*, 1987; Ford, 1980) in that they are committed, usually long term and highly effective.

For example, high cooperation and low competition is found in the relationship between a manufacturer of industrial safety equipment and a supplier of its packaging material. This relationship has been in operation for 25 years with the informant being involved for the past twenty years. This is a highly committed relationship with very strong personal, though not social, links between the respective firms. Both firms are highly satisfied with the relationship.

This is a relationship between a small firm supplying a substantial amount of their output (35%) to a significantly larger customer. While there is a contract between the firms, this is relatively unimportant. The relationship is coordinated by understandings based on past interactions, although the rules and regulations of their market do play a role. Mostly however the transactions are largely routine with rates and delivery times being easily renegotiated periodically. The firms are highly interdependent and would find it difficult to replace one another. And there is no desire to do so. The respondent characterizes the success of the relationship as due to their trading partner being "a small firm extremely responsive to our (evolving) needs." This is a highly stable and mature relationship which will almost certainly continue far into the future.

The most predictable evolution and greatest stability seems to be associated with relationships which are low in competition and high in cooperation. Their life expectancy is uniformly good. Over 95% are expected to continue indefinitely. The nature and evolution of relationships of this type often resembles the descriptions of the development of cooperative relations set out in previously mentioned models of relationship development (Dwyer *et al.*, 1987; Ford, 1980). The nature of the relationship nurtures it and the ties that bind them together grow ever-stronger and more meaningful to the participants.

However, relationships may evolve to this state via a circuitous route. An example is that of a small advertising agency with its building company client. The relationship was described as being excellent for a number of years; then market conditions conspired to push the client company from a minor to major player in its industry. Their changed requirements and expectations were extremely difficult for the agency to adapt to. The relationship survived and again prospers, probably due to its strong past ties, but went through very high levels of competition for a number of years as the firms struggled to retain and adapt their relationship.

RELATIONSHIP DEVELOPMENT PATHS

The preceding examples highlight both the range of cooperative and competitive combinations possible in relationships and the routes by which relationships may develop. A summary is provided in Figure 2 which shows the position of the case studies described in the previous section according to their cooperativeness and competitiveness scores. Also shown are the direction(s) from which each relationship is reported to have come. This has been ascertained from a series of open-ended questions about the degree, nature and scope of change in the relationship.

Figure 1 shows that respondents' reports of the way in which their relationships have developed do not conform in any clear way to the patterns suggested in the models of relationship development. Most respondents report their relationships as moving from the low cooperation and low competition quadrant to either the high cooperation-low competition or the low cooperation-high competition quadrant. The exception is the printer-fast food chain relationship, which reports the amounts of cooperation and competition increasing but remains in the low cooperation-low competition quadrant.

The high cooperation and high competition relationships appear to have developed from either highly cooperative and not competitive relations in the past on the one hand, or highly competitive

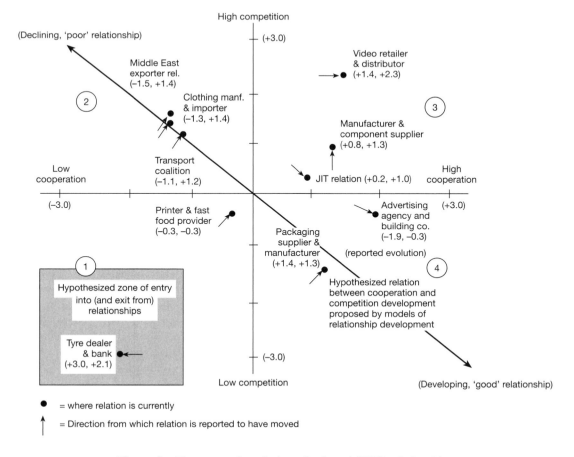

Figure 2 The reported evolution of selected IRRP relationships.

and not cooperative patterns of past behaviour on the other. In the former cases the respondents report that high levels of competition developed subsequently as a result of difficult environmental circumstances. In the latter cases high levels of cooperation developed due to better management of interdependence, such as the development of effective conflict resolution mechanisms and/or the introduction of quality management techniques.

Only two respondents report relationships developing according to the life cycle models. The advertising agency relationship became both less cooperative and more competitive for a period of time before reversing itself and becoming more cooperative and less competitive. The relationship with just-in-time purchasing in place similarly reported both a decrease in competition and an increase in cooperation as they worked towards a more effective management of their interdependence.

A CHOICE OF METAPHORS – DANCING VERSUS MARRIAGE

A commonly used metaphor to characterize interfirm relations is that of a marriage, e.g. Levitt (1986), Dwyer, Schurr and Oh (1987), Business International (1990). We contend that this metaphor is limited in its ability to capture the full range and diversity of interfirm relations described. The tendency is to portray relations unidimensionally in terms of a life cycle of development towards the "perfect marriage" which tends to be seen as a strong, cooperative, committed, trusting relation. The alternative to marriage usually proposed is that of "affairs" when one plays the field in terms of short term superficial encounters. Some have argued that a variety of different types of marriages can be successful. For example the "shotgun wedding" versus "the arranged marriage" versus the "career couple" can achieve success in strategic alliances (Business International, 1990). However these distinctions are more about the reasons for formation of the partnership or the character of the participants than about the nature of the alliance itself. The dance metaphor, we suggest, is more capable of capturing essential facets of relations as revealed in our studies.

First, the concept of business dancing captures the central notion of the role of cooperation. Value comes from firms working with other firms rather than from their separate actions. The issue becomes that of working with existing partners to jointly achieve more, instead of seeking permanent or transient partners which will maximize one's own rewards.

Second, the dancing metaphor leads to a process view of relationships rather than a structural view. Dancing involves an active cooperation, not a formal type of connection. A relationship is described in terms of the interaction between partners rather than the form of the link between them. In business, firms are held together through ongoing patterns of interaction that shape the nature of the attitudes and perceptions of the partners and can become institutionalized in various ways in the organizational structures or rules governing behaviour. These rules in turn shape further interaction.

Third, there are an infinite number of types of dances requiring various types and degrees of coordinated action varying from the close coordination of ballroom dancing to the looser disco dancing. Dances can be in dyads or involve larger numbers of partners as in formation and line type dancing. You cannot marry everyone but you can dance in many ways with many others. So it is with business. Many types of relations emerge in business reflecting the different types of coordinated action required, from the routine mechanical relations for standard items to strongly coordinated relations involving co-developed resources, technology, products and services.

Fourth, the different types of dances reflect the variety of coordination and cooperative tasks required in industry as a result of different technological and environmental conditions. The rules of the dance mimic the inherent logic of the processes that must be effected in a value chain. Further, the other dancers on the floor shape the problems confronted in much the way that a particular business relation is influenced by the other relations to which it is connected in both a cooperative and competitive way.

In Table 1, the dance metaphor is used to dramatize the various types of interfirm relations suggested in the above analysis. Of course this is only illustrative and speculative but it serves to capture some of the essence of relations in a novel way. Eight types of relationships are presented. The four types identified in our typology are further differentiated according to whether cooperation and competition levels are extreme or moderate. Each type is portrayed in terms of both the

Table 1 Contrasting the marriage and dance metaphors

Relation type	Connection type	Type of dance	Character of dance	Quality of relationship
1A Extreme Low Cooperation– Low Competition	Just met or getting divorced	Walking on or off the dance floor	Warm up or cool down exercise – not really dancing with your partner	Commencing or finishing
1B Moderate Low Cooperation– Low Competition	Placid and occasional affair	Line dancing	Coordinated and in unison but not partnering	Arms length – fairly indifferent, neither good nor bad
2A Extreme Low Cooperation– High Competition	Stormy affair – quarrels and throwing things or marriage by proxy (great distance between parties)	Salsa – lots of screaming and fire	Repeatedly (and perhaps deliberately) steps on foot, partners may deliberately send false signals when they lead	Likely to be poor and declining
2B Moderate Low Cooperation– High Competition	Affair or unhappy marriage may be no possibility of divorce, may be in "counselling" to try to improve	Inept "New Vogue"	Going through the set motions (not very well)	Poor relation in process of change, could be for the better or the worse
3A Extreme High Competition– High Cooperation	Tempestuous but devoted marriage	Latin medley, (including the tango)	Lots of unexpected tempo changes, maybe a crowded dance floor, requires an expert couple	Good relationship despite dynamic environment and probable self-interest
3B Moderate High Competition– High Cooperation	Dual career marriage – joint and conflicting interests	Ballet as well as ballroom	At least as concerned about one's solo parts as the duo's	Good relationship which normalizes some opportunism
4A Extreme Low Competition– High Cooperation	Marriage made in heaven	Waltz or rumba	Smooth and semi-spontaneous glide, cheek-to-cheek with someone you love	Highly committed and good quality relationship
4B Moderate High Competition– Low Cooperation	Newly weds or semi-committed relationship[1]	Cha-cha or new vogue	Beginners with talent or parties (re)establishing partnership, they undertake simple steps or those predetermined by rules	Relationship in process of developing higher levels of commitment

[1] A number of different types of marriages (or affairs) could be considered as semi-committed, e.g. the "old married couple" who undertake separate but complementary tasks and interact indifferently and/or infrequently, the "arranged marriage" where partnerships have been formulated outside the dyad by third party (perhaps government or other network members), or "shotgun weddings" where parties have unwillingly contracted a relationship to ensure survival.

link involved using the marriage metaphor as well as in terms of a type of "dance" or coordinated action required.

The marriage metaphor captures to some extent the differences between the low cooperation–high competition relationships (which correspond to affairs) and low competition–high cooperation relationships (which correspond to marriages). In order to distinguish between other types of relations different types of marriages and affairs are suggested. Thus marriages are specified to be "tempestuous" (3A) or "made in heaven" (4A) and affairs as "stormy" (2A) or "placid" (1B).

The dance metaphor allows a large range of types of interaction to be easily envisaged. Dances are faster–slower (e.g. the salsa in 2A versus the waltz in 4A); are easier or more difficult (e.g. a new vogue dance of 1B requiring one lesson to learn the sequence of steps versus the ballet in 3B requiring years of concentrated training); require more or less physical and psychic contact (e.g. the tango in 3A versus the cha-cha in 4B); and, perhaps most importantly, are characterized by more or less interdependence (e.g. the line dance in 1B which requires rules to ensure everyone dances in unison but no partner, versus a ballet duet where a failure to catch your partner could result in a crippling injury). The quality of the dance varies depending on the specific skills of each partner (e.g. talent, fitness, and ability to lead/follow) and on their combined skills (e.g. compatible steps and styles).

In dancing, as well as in relationships, history matters. Partners develop partnership-specific skills within the course of relations. Long term partners such as the Olympic ice dancers Torville and Dean will retain only some of their abilities if they terminate their partnership and form new ones. Within a partnership many patterns of evolution are possible but these depend to some extent on past history. Parties can, through time, change the type of dancing they do together and/or add different types of dances to their repertoire. Partners move from one dance to another. But skill, based on past experience, largely influences the additional dances they may successfully attempt. Partners over time become more expert and are able to do more complicated dances together (and with other partners). But not all development paths are possible for partners. The relationship's history dictates the choices available.

RELATIONSHIP MANAGEMENT IMPLICATIONS

Overall the foregoing results and discussion support and reinforce the "interaction approach" that has been developed by the European based Industrial Marketing and Purchasing Group (Håkansson, 1982; Ford, 1990; Axelsson and Easton, 1992). Several types of implications for relationship management emerge.

First, relationship management is not so much about one party developing and imposing a structure on the relationship to their advantage but about managing an ongoing process of action and interaction taking place on multiple levels between organizations. The traditional distinction between marketing and buying behaviour approaches to business markets is replaced by an integrated approach in which both aspects are closely interwoven. Further, interpersonal relations and social interaction play an important role in facilitating or inhibiting relations and should be seen as part of the overall management process.

This integrated relationship orientation is not encompassed by some extension of the marketing mix paradigm, such as adding another P for people or politics, or by a more sensitive application of existing elements of the mix. It calls for us to stop "P–ing" on the customers and to focus instead on interacting and cooperating with them.

Relationship management is not something that one firm does to another in a stimulus response manner, but a two-way process in which initiatives can be taken by either party with each responding to the problems and opportunities of the other. In terms of our dance metaphor we must recognize that following is as important a part of the skill of dancing as leading and the two styles must match to be mutually supportive. Similarly, relationship management is as much about "being manageable", including being responsive to the initiatives of others and facilitating their relating to you, as about managing others, i.e. being the initiator. An emphasis on being manageable is particularly relevant when the perspective of the less powerful actor in a relationship is taken. However, the perspective often taken in discussion is that of the powerful actor, initiating things and dictating terms and conditions. The less powerful actor situation requires equal attention as many firms are likely to find themselves in this situation. Moreover, research suggests that less powerful firms can play an important role in introducing change to networks of relations (Easton, 1992).

Relationship management is as much about creating value through relationships as it is about protecting and safeguarding the value of existing assets and resources. Value is created through jointly planning and mutually adapting products, processes, people and resources. These adaptations result in what are termed relationship specific investments or assets, which bond the parties together and make them mutually dependent. The focus of attention in much of the literature tends to be on the potential problems created by such investments and assets due to one firm being able to exploit the dependency of another. For example, the transaction cost literature is largely devoted to the problem of designing relationships between exchange partners (or governance structures in their terms), which protect against such risks. Obviously these risks cannot be ignored but here we stress that relationship specific investments are an important potential outcome of a relationship, rather than being something that pro-exists "outside" the relationship and determines the way the relationship should be designed. Relationship specific assets such as mutual trust and respect, mutual understanding, and personal relationships as well as more tangible adaptations of products and processes arise though a process of working together over time. They are an integral part of the relationship, not something protected by the relationship. They are not easily or quickly developed or replaced and yet they can have an important bearing on the strength and viability of a company.

Our results indicate that there is no one, ideal type of relationship. High performing relationships are to be found of all of the four types described. For example, as previously noted, relationships high in both cooperation and competition are often perceived as effective. The appropriate type of relationship obviously depends on the objectives of the parties involved, the tasks to be performed and the environment in which the relationship operates. This does not always dictate the development of strongly committed, long term cooperative relations (Low, 1994). Performance evaluation in a relationship is also relative rather than absolute. It depends on the expectations and comparisons available to those involved and these are provided by history and the environment. History matters in that the problems and issues confronted over time in a relationship and how they have been dealt with will influence both perceptions of benefit and expectations of benefit. The environment of relationships establishes more general norms and standards of behaviour expected. The case of video industry relationships is an example of an environment creating limited expectations of non opportunistic behaviour.

Following on from the previous point, there is not one best way of managing and directing relationships as they are not all headed in the same direction and do not operate from similar starting places. Elsewhere we have suggested four broad types of strategies firms can adopt in dealing with situations in which the behaviour of another firm affects the outcomes of the firm's own behaviour (Wilkinson and Young, 1994). Each one results in quite different types of relations between the firms involved. (a) A firm can spend resources to better predict the behaviour of the other firm and adjust its behaviour accordingly. In complex dynamic environments such predictions can become costly and unreliable. (b) A firm can attempt to control the behaviour of the other firm through the exercise of power. This strategy is only available to the powerful and, depending on the way power is exercised, can have adverse effects on the future development of the relationship. (c) A firm can attempt to reduce its dependence on another firm. This could be done by switching to standardized product or service inputs that are available from many firms and relying on arms length market dealing. Alternatively, vertical integration could be used to internalize the activities of the supplier, bringing it under direct control. Of course, technological and market constraints can limit the feasibility of either of these approaches. (d) Lastly, a firm can seek to cooperate with the other firm to jointly plan and implement strategies for mutual advantage. It is this latter type of strategy that has been the subject of much recent attention in the business literature. Evidence of all four types of strategies and the relationships that result are to be found in the foregoing analysis.

Two further issues affecting the development of relationship management strategies are highlighted by our research and analysis. First, it should be noted that firms may not be able to choose their relationship partners freely and this will affect the nature and quality of the relationship management strategies available. Lack of choice can arise because of an absence of other firms capable of providing the necessary inputs or because firms may be locked in to particular relations as a result of past contracts or agreements. Second, our research indicates that cooperativeness and competitiveness should be regarded as separate dimensions of relations rather than opposites. This means that strategies to increase cooperation and reduce competition are not simple alternatives to each other. A balance of both is needed.

As a final point it should be noted that the focus here has been on the nature and management of relations between pairs of firms. But relationships do not occur in isolation from each other. Firms are connected to other firms both directly and indirectly through networks of relationships. These networks are the means by which resources are developed and accessed and products and services created and delivered to end customers. They both constrain firms' behaviour but also provide opportunities. Firms have to consider both their micro and macro positions in the network and how the two affect each other (Mattsson, 1984; Johansson and Mattsson, 1992). Micro positions concern the management of individual relations, whereas macro positions refer to a firm's position in the network as a whole. The macro position is not a simple aggregation of micro positions and changes in relations in one part of the network can have profound implications for relations in other parts. Hence, the management of individual relations must take into account the effects on other relations. One consequence of this is that evaluating relations becomes more problematic, because relations can act as conduits or bridges to other firms and relations. Hence the value of a particular relationship and its performance cannot be assessed without considering its network context. Similarly, effective decisions about commencing and terminating relations are made by considering the structure of the network and one's position within it. A focus on networks leads to new ways for understanding and developing business strategy, as well as several challenging research opportunities that are only now beginning to be explored.

NOTE

* Presented at the First International Colloquium in Relationship Marketing, Monash University, Australia, August 1993.

REFERENCES

Argyle, M. *Cooperation: The Basis of Sociability*. Routledge, London (1991).

Axelsson, B. and Easton, G. (eds) *Industrial Networks: A New View of Reality*. Routledge, London (1992).

Business International *Making Alliances Work*. Business International Ltd., Economist Group, London, March (1990).

Deutsch, M. A theory of cooperation and competition. *Human Relations*, **2**, 129–51 (1949).

Deutsch, M. Cooperation and trust: some theoretical notes. In Jones, M. R. (ed) *Nebraska Symposium on Motivation*, University of Nebraska Press, Lincoln (1962), pp. 275–319.

Dwyer, F. R., Schurr, P. H. and Oh, S. Developing buyer seller relations. *Journal of Marketing*, **51** (2), 11–28 (1987).

Easton, G. Industrial networks: a review. In Axelsson, B. and Easton, G. (eds) *Industrial Networks: A New View of Reality*. Routledge, London, (1992), pp. 1–27.

Ford, I. D. The development of buyer seller relations in industrial markets. *European Journal of Marketing*, **14**, 339–53 (1980).

Ford, I. D. *Understanding Business Markets: Interaction, Relationships and Networks*. Academic Press, London (1990).

Håkansson, H. (ed). *International Marketing and Purchasing of Industrial Goods by the IMP Group*. John Wiley, Chichester (1982).

Jackson, B. B. *Winning and Keeping Industrial Customers*. Lexington Books, Lexington, Massachusetts (1985).

Johansson, J. and Mattsson, L.-G. Network positions and strategic action – an analytical framework. In Axelsson, B. and Easton, G. (eds) *Industrial Networks: A New View of Reality*. Routledge, London (1992), pp. 205–217.

Levitt, T. *The Marketing Imagination*. The Free Press, New York (1986).

Low, B. Long-term relationships in industrial marketing: reality or rhetoric? Paper presented at 10th IMP Conference, Groningen September 29–October 1 (Department of Marketing Working Paper Series 94/2, University of Western Sydney, Nepean) (1994).

Mattsson, L.-G. An application of a network approach to marketing: defending and changing market positions. In Dholkia, N. and Arndt, J. (eds) *Changing the Course of Marketing: Alternative Paradigms for Widening Marketing Theory*. JAI Press, Greenwich, Connecticut (1984).

Nisbet, R. A. Cooperation. In *International Encyclopedia of Social Sciences*, Vol. 3. Collier–Macmillan, New York (1972), pp. 384–90.

Stern, L. W. Antitrust implications of a sociological interpretation of competition, conflict, and cooperation in the marketplace. *The Anti Trust Bulletin*, **16** (3), 509–30 (1971).

Wilkinson, I. F. and Young L. C. The space between: the nature and role of interfirm relations in business. AMA Research Conference on Relationship Marketing, Emory University, Atlanta, Georgia (1994).

Young, L. C. The nature and role of trust and cooperation in marketing channels. *Ph.D. thesis*, School of Marketing, University of New South Wales (1992).

Young, L. C. and Wilkinson, I. F. The role of trust and cooperation in marketing channels: a preliminary study. *European Journal of Marketing*, **23** (2), 109–22 (1989a).

Young L. C. and Wilkinson, I. F. 1989 Survey of interfirm relations – preliminary findings. Report 89/3, Interfirm Relations Research Program, School of Marketing, University of New South Wales (1989b).

Young, L. C. and Wilkinson, I. F. Toward a typology of interfirm relations in marketing systems. 8th I.M.P. Conference, Lyon, France (1992).

Part 3
Understanding Business Networks

In order to understand what goes on inside a business we need to know about its relationships. In order to understand its relationships we need to know about the network of which they form part. Analysis at the network level can provide insights into business behaviour that cannot be gained by observing individual relationships. At the network level we can start to make sense of such things as complex joint ventures and consortia, how technology evolves *between* companies and how companies attempt to combine the technologies of many other companies with their own increasingly concentrated skills.

This part of the book includes a number of readings that try to explain what networks are all about. But of course, once we move from discussion of a single relationship or of a company's portfolio of relationships then things get more complex. So the readings chosen for this section are intended to provide a clear structure that can form the basis for later discussion of business marketing and purchasing.

The first reading by Geoff Easton provides a general review of the area. This reading relates some of the ideas on networks by the IMP group to other research traditions and also discusses a number of different views of business networks. The first view is the one mentioned above, that networks are sets of *relationships*. The second is of networks as some sort of *structure* for the activities that go on between firms. The third view sees networks as the aggregation of the separate *positions* of different firms. The idea of network position will recur a number of times in the book. Easton also discusses the *processes* that occur in networks. The second reading also forms a building block for later pieces. In this one Håkan Håkansson and Jan Johanson provide a simple model of what happens in business networks using three terms that are common in the network literature; *activities, actors* and *resources*.

Following from this general introduction to ideas on networks, the third reading by Håkan Håkansson and Ivan Snehota discusses what some of these ideas mean for companies. They draw the conclusion that looking at inter-company networks will lead to changes in many traditional assumptions about how we can manage in business markets and how we judge effectiveness in them. This reading shows how a network perspective changes our understanding of the boundaries around companies, of the processes of strategy and the nature of companies themselves. The fourth reading is also by Håkansson and Snehota and is taken from a book which reports on the IMP2 project into business networks. It is included at this stage because it shows how ideas on the nature of a single business relationship are linked to the pattern of a number of relationships of each company, as well as to a wider network. The paper draws conclusions on what this means for the managerial task in business markets.

Readings five and six are both by Jan Johanson and Lars-Gunnar Mattson. The first develops ideas on network position further and the second takes a network approach to the issue of company internationalisation. The reading is useful for its examination of different positions that a company might have in an international network and also because it contrasts the network approach to understanding the process of internationalisation with other, more traditional views. Reading seven, by Jim Anderson, Håkan Håkansson and Jan Johanson presents a strong conceptualisation of the connectedness of individual business relationships within complex networks. It illustrates this conceptualisation with two case examples. Reading eight by Aino Halinen, Asta Salmi and Virpi Havila is an important analysis of the dynamics of business networks, also illustrated with case material. The final reading in this section by Håkan Håkansson and David Ford draws lessons for managers operating in business networks by pointing out and explaining a number of paradoxes about those networks.

CONTENTS

3.1 Industrial netw a

Geoff Easton

INTRODUCTION

Research in the area which encompasses organisational marketing, business to business marketing and organisational buying behaviour has developed in two quite different traditions. The first, and original, approach has, to a large extent, taken its lead from consumer marketing, has by and large opted for study of either buyers or sellers and is generally associated with writers in the United States. The second tradition has its home in Europe, has been influenced by work outside the marketing area and focuses on the "space" between organisations. Neither exhibits monolithic paradigms; both traditions have had room for a variety of approaches. Within the European tradition, and a twenty-year history allows the use of the word, the industrial network approach has emerged as a separate and viable paradigm in its own right. It shares with other approaches a belief that the existence of relationships, many of them stable and durable, among firms engaged in economic exchange provides a compelling reason for using interorganisational relationships as a research perspective. It differs from other approaches mainly in terms of its scope. It is concerned to understand the totality of relationships among firms engaged in production, distribution and the use of goods and services in what might best be described as an industrial system. The boundaries of such a system are problematic and will probably vary depending upon the purposes for which the boundary is being drawn. The focus of research is, ultimately, the network and not the firm or the individual relationship, although firms and relationships must be studied if networks are to be understood.

Much of the work on industrial networks has been published but in far-flung places that are often difficult to access. What is surprising, and gratifying, is that it is available at all to an international audience since the bulk of the work has been done in Sweden by Swedes. The objective of this review it to provide a stepping off point for the remainder of the book. To do so it must be relatively comprehensive yet succinct. It has not been an easy task. For such a young paradigm there exist a remarkable number of alternative views and perspectives, sometimes espoused by the same author at different times. In addition since these are views of the same phenomena from different angles they are irreconcilable and cannot be integrated and I have not attempted to do so. However the paradigm is socially rather cohesive and there are many shared assumptions.

The problem of multiple perspectives is not an uncommon one especially in the social sciences. Morgan (1986) has championed the cause of a metaphorical mode of analysis. In *Images of Organisation* he apportions the literature on organisations among a series of metaphors. More recently Mintzberg (1988) has described five alternative metaphors for strategy. A similar approach will be taken here. Four metaphors for industrial networks are used to structure the chapter. They are: networks as relationships; structures; processes; and positions. However, first, to set the scene, the history and provenance of the industrial networks approach is described. The final section is concerned with the normative implications of network ideas and areas of application.

The industrial network approach has a number of progenitors although the exact relationships to their offspring is not always clear. At an early stage, studies of distribution channels both in Europe and the United States were concerned with the relationships between channel members and dealt with issues of power and control which are also held to be important for industrial networks. The nature of the functions, retailing/distribution, meant that a relatively narrow approach to inter-organisational activities could be taken and the assumption of a homogeneous channel could be justified. This assumption is not made in the industrial network approach. In a parallel field of study, research into the process of internationalisation has dealt with similar issues, i.e. how do firms organise to export and manufacture abroad. The interaction approach, which was a product of the first, pan-European, IMP study used as the basic unit of analysis the dyadic relationship between buyers and sellers of manufactured products in different countries (Håkansson, 1982b). The IMP group successfully demonstrated the existence of stable long-term buyer–seller relation-ships and were able to characterise their richness and diversity in a four element analytical framework. Industrial networks, by definition, comprise many such relationships and so any account of them not only has to sacrifice some of the descriptive richness of the interaction approach but also has to concentrate on those aspects which have particular implications for network operation.

The resource dependence model provides another perspective on inter-organisational relation-ships (Pfeffer and Salancik, 1978). Unlike the interaction approach it is concerned with a focal organisation but attempts to describe the multiplicity of relationships of any industrial or com-mercial organisation. The basic assumption is that organisations use these relationships in order to gain access to the resources which are vital to their continuing existence. Firms access resources not only through suppliers and customers but also through banks, shareholding institutions, govern-ment, distributors, consultants, associations, etc. The resource dependence model mainly focuses on the way in which firms handle individual relationships. It sees the behaviour of firms as the resultant of two opposing forces; the competing and often contradictory desires of stakeholders within organisations and the external requirements of the organisations to which and from which resources flow. The resource dependence model brings to the study of industrial systems a vision of the multiplicity of relationships and the dominant role of resources in determining behaviour. However it differs from the industrial network perspective by concentrating on the actions of a single firm. The network, or more accurately net, is viewed through the eyes of that firm and the working of the network is seen to be of secondary importance. In other words the units of analysis are very different.

The second IMP study has, in some ways, a similar focus. It is concerned with individual relationships as in the first study but has moved on to examine each relationship in the context of the other relationships a particular firm may have. It therefore operates at a higher level of aggregation than the first programme of work and might be said to provide one form of link between studies of firms buying and selling and the full blown network level of analysis.

By contrast theories of social exchange are primarily interested in explaining the operation of network phenomena: "The primary focus of social exchange theory is the explanation of the emergence of various forms of social structure, including networks and corporate groups" (Cook and Emerson, 1984). The central construct of social exchange theory is that of connection. "Two exchange relationships are connected to the extent that exchange in one relationship is contingent, positively or negatively, upon exchange in the other relationship." This concept allows us to move beyond the dyad, sequentially, to invoke and model system-wide effects. It defines the idea of indirect relationships where A may affect C through B simply because there are connected exchange relationships between all three parties. Viewing an industry as a network of inter-connected exchange relationships implies adopting a systemic focus and level of explanation. In practice the approach of social exchange theory has been to test simple analytical models of network behaviour using experimental methods. It is thus rather distant from the empirical and naturalistic approach adopted by workers in the industrial network tradition. Nevertheless the debt is a very real one. Social exchange theory argues that complex network behaviour can result from the interplay of relatively simply defined exchange relationships. It is an aggregative approach and one which has influenced at least one strand of network methodology as well as providing a building block for theoretical developments.

By contrast, research into communication and social networks has been largely inductive in character (Rogers and Kincaid, 1981). The unit of analysis is commonly the individual in a social context and the network is defined in terms of the patterns of communication and/or social interactions occurring regularly between and among those individuals. The problems have occurred not in data collection but in analysis. The large numbers of links which may exist in such a network make the discernment of patterns particularly difficult. In response a whole series of matrix manipulation techniques have been developed. While these are only just beginning to be used to characterise industrial networks, network studies have influenced the language and orientation of the industrial network approach. In particular they share the view that networks should be treated as a whole, that network boundaries are problematic and that network models must be dynamic in nature.

Defining a paradigm is often helped by making clear what it is not. The industrial network approach has used traditional, and not so traditional economics, as stalking horses. In particular the notions of pure competition with atomistic and unconnected firms striking individual and instant deals with one another, in the face of competitors doing the same thing, is rejected. If strong relationships exist among buyers and sellers then the facile switching among easily available alternatives which is assumed in economic analysis no longer applies. History becomes important. Inertia is introduced into the system and the rules of optimum resource allocation fail as relational constraints start to bite and motives other than short term profit maximisation begin to dominate.

The branch of economics described as industrial organisation theory may be said to address similar issues to those dealt with by the industrial networks approach. In particular it is concerned with the structure of industries and the relationships among firms in those industries. However, once again, the relationships between suppliers and customers are assumed to be atomistic and, in this model, marginal to the central issue of rivalry among the competitors that defines, somewhat narrowly, the boundaries of the industry. Indeed in Porter's articulation of industrial organisation theory customers are identified as "extended rivals" in that they constrain the focal organisation in direct relation to the power they are capable of drawing upon.

The development of institutional economics which gives transaction costs a major role in determining vertical market mechanisms, comes closest to addressing the same issues as the industrial network approach (Williamson, 1975). It assumes that transactions between suppliers are not without friction and that, as a result, costs arise which are dependent on the particular nature of the transactions. These costs, in turn, help determine which organisational form – free markets, vertical integration or bilateral governance – is most likely to emerge assuming firms seek to minimise costs. Johanson and Mattsson (1986), however, argue that the similarities are more superficial than profound. The transaction cost approach focuses on the single relationship not the network. It assumes equilibrium under cost minimisation and economic rationality (albeit bounded). Most fundamentally it has little to say about the most interesting case, at least from a network view, that of bilateral governance. This omission is somewhat rectified in Williamson's later work when it is admitted that bilateral governance may be a stable organisational form (Williamson, 1985).

Similarly the model of marketing which derives from microeconomic assumptions is also rejected for most organisational markets. It is no longer sensible to assume seller dominated markets where the firm, as the focal unit, sets the mix parameters and the faceless market responds. Instead the market is seen to have a face. Many individual customers may be distinguished and dealt with separately which, in turn, creates a new and different set of marketing (and buying) problems. While the industrial network approach acknowledges these issues it is important to recognise a major difference in orientation. The focus is upon the network and not the individual firm. The goal is primarily description and explanation not prescription. A network perspective has profound normative implications but they spring from the approach rather than drive it.

Having described the roots, real or imaginary, of the industrial network approach we will now examine it from four different angles in the expectation that by doing so we may come to an understanding of its nature and essence.

NETWORKS AS RELATIONSHIPS

If there are no "relationships", using the word in a rather general sense, between buying and selling organisations in an industrial system then the free market models beloved of economists should reign. In other words relationships among firms are the *sine qua non* of an industrial network approach. One approach to industrial networks is therefore to regard them as aggregations of relationships. While modelling the network is the ultimate goal it could be argued that one line of attack is to start at the most basic level and build. However there is nowhere in evidence the naive belief that the process of aggregation is likely to be simple or additive. "Adding together" relationships provides massive opportunities for systemic structures to emerge which overlay the simple and apparent linkages. Nevertheless relationships are important in determining network properties and a knowledge of their behaviour has important implications for understanding networks. The interaction approach provides a rich model of relationships between firms buying from and selling to one another. Much of this richness has, of necessity, to be discarded when an aggregate approach to relationships is required. In this section only those characteristics of single relationships which are thought to have relevance for the structure and processes of networks are discussed.

One analysis of interfirm behaviour distinguishes between relationships and interactions (Johanson and Mattsson, 1987). The relationship elements of the behaviour are rather general and long-term in nature. Interactions, by contrast, represent the here and now of interfirm behaviour and "constitute the dynamic aspects of relationships" (Johanson and Mattsson, 1987). Thus there is an interplay between the two variables. Interactions, in their turn, are said to comprise exchange processes and adaptation processes. The former represent the day-to-day exchanges of a business, social or informational nature that occur between firms. The latter comprises the processes by means of which firms adjust products, production and routines.

Relationships, in their various manifestations, will be discussed first. They may be presented as comprising four elements: mutual orientation; the dependence that each has, or believes it has, upon the other; bonds of various kinds and strengths, and the investments each has made in the relationship. Clearly each of these elements is strongly interrelated with the others and is itself capable of being further decomposed and elucidated.

One of the preconditions for the existence of an interfirm relationship is what has been termed mutual orientation. "This implies that the firms are prepared to interact with each other and expect each other to do so" (Mattsson, 1988). Cooperation is required and this depends, at least in terms of one view of cooperation, on the relationships between the firms' objective. "Vigorous relationships presuppose the existence of a certain complementarity between the objectives of the parties" (Hagg and Johanson, 1983). The cooperation may be instrumental in that each firm seeks to gain different ends from the same means, e.g. access to a new process and a new market entry from the same development programme. Alternatively the objectives might be commonly held, e.g. advancing a new technology.

Complementarity of objectives is a rather abstract rationale for entering into a relationship. Why would a firm seek, consciously or unconsciously, to develop relationships? A number of instrumental reasons can be identified and these appear to fall into two main categories. The first exploits the complementarities of an individual partner. "[R]elationships allow of a more effective acquisition of resources and sale of product" (Hagg and Johanson, 1983). By knowing a partner firm better and appreciating what they can do and have to offer, it is possible both to reduce costs and increase sales. Needs can be matched more exactly. Adaptations may be made which both reduce costs of production or transfer and increase effectiveness of exchanges. Knowledge may be created between firms by combining the existing knowledge and skills they both possess. Relationships also provide continuity and stability with an increased ability to plan, reduce costs and increase effectiveness.

The second set of rationale for entering into a relationship concern a firm's ability to exploit network access. A relationship implies a measure of control over another organisation and, through that organisation, the environment. The consequent reduction in uncertainty and increase in stability may be very valuable objectives for many organisations. Similarly a relationship offers access to third parties who may have resources that are either valuable or essential to survival. One such resource is information and relationships can serve as data conduits and provide firms with a perspective on what is taking place in distant parts of the network. Alternatively, through relationships, partners may be mobilised against third parties, i.e. competitive suppliers.

Dependence is the second element which was used to describe relationships and in some senses may be regarded as the price a firm may have to pay for the benefits that a relationship bestows. Dependence is partly a matter of choice and partly a matter of circumstances. An extreme example is the case of dealing with a monopolist or a monopsonist. Since there are by definition no alternatives, circumstances dictate a strong degree of dependence. However in the long-term a firm may choose to make changes in its operations such that it is no longer dependent upon a single source. Alternatively, even where choice exists a firm may decide to trade off the benefits of flexibility for the benefits, described above, which can accrue from a strong relationship.

Dependence brings with it the problems of power and control. If firms are mutually dependent then they may have difficulty dealing with other relationships but should be able to manage the focal relationship reasonably well. However, if the power is asymmetrically distributed then the relationship will not only be difficult to manage but the benefits for the junior partner less easy to realise.

The third element of a relationship is the bond which may be said to exist between firms. A bond implies a measure of tying, albeit unspecified, between partner firms which is implicit in all that has already been discussed. Firms are bonded together and are not usually entirely free to dissolve those bonds at will. The strength of a bond is a difficult parameter to measure. One suggestion for an operational procedure is to define it as the capacity to withstand a disruptive force (Easton and Araujo, 1986). They identified different disruptive situations corresponding to the application of different kinds of force to a bond. Some bonds might well be able to withstand some kinds of force better than others, e.g. responding to changing needs of a partner compared with responding to the arrival of an alternative partner. In network terms strong bonds provide a more stable and predictable structure and one which is more likely to be able to withstand change. Weakly bonded networks are likely to be rather volatile. Patterns of strong and weak bonding provide one measure of the structure of networks in a way analogous with communication networks.

A related characteristic of network relationships is longevity. The original IMP study demonstrated the existence of long-term relationships but the sampling frame did not allow estimation of the overall longevity of different types of relationship (Håkansson, 1982b). Gadde and Mattsson (1987) carried out a more complex analysis of relationship duration within the context of other relationships. They concluded that while individual relationships might endure, the changes to the total system of supplier relationships were rather large. Gradual changes were made, rarely a simple one for one exchange, and these accumulated so that at the end of a relatively few years the whole supplier structure had radically altered. These results would no doubt be reflected in network dynamics. Thus we would expect network structures to be stable but not static; they would gradually change in response to changes external and internal to the network. Nor should it be assumed that the nature of relationships will remain constant even though measures of product flow are the same. What is being exchanged may have little relationship to how it is being exchanged.

The relationship between longevity and strength is not a simple one. Even a strongly bonded network will change if the external forces are powerful enough. A weakly bonded network may continue to exist in the same form in benign and unchanging conditions.

Similarly it can be argued that relationships may spring into being fully fledged and rather quickly should the circumstances be appropriate (Easton and Smith, 1984). Thus the applicability of the network concept is not entirely dependent upon the existence of long-term relationships. Similarly the stronger the relationship the more closely will the relationship be expected to determine the behaviour of firms towards one another. But weak relationships are still a far cry from no relationships and while the structure and processes of "weak" networks will differ from those of "strong" they are still, it is argued, best treated as networks. In other words where any form of relationship may be held to exist among firms in an industrial system a network approach will be appropriate.

Bonds thus far have been treated as unitary phenomena and there are arguments for so doing. However it was also thought to be helpful in some of the earlier writing on industrial networks to decompose the elements of a bond, or to describe different types of bond (Mattsson, 1984). Bonds may be thought of as having, variously, economic, social, technical, logistical, administrative, informational, legal and time based dimensions.

The economic element of a relationship is largely self evident and, when discussing industrial systems, may be regarded as the *sine qua non* for the existence of a network. Other types of networks may not be fundamentally economic in nature. Clearly the portfolio of products and services offered and the price agreed to consummate the exchange, are important and highly visible evidences of a relationship. The economic rationale for strong bonding is clearly dependent upon the satisfaction with the terms of the current exchange and the presence or absence of alternatives. More formal economic bonds may also exist as where firms invest in one another or in joint ventures or provide extended credit facilities. However the very existence of noneconomic exchange aspects of a relationship serves to down play the contribution of price in determining the behaviour of the two parties. Indeed the stronger the bond the less importance economic factors, at least as conventionally defined, have in the processes of exchange (Hagg and Johanson, 1983). It should also be pointed out that there are a number of types of relationship in a network where direct economic exchange is absent though other forms of relationship (primarily informational) may exist, e.g. between competitors.

Social exchange has been identified as a significant factor in the overall strength of interfirm relationships. Mattsson (1988) cites Blau's description of the process. "Social exchange relations evolve in a slow process, starting with minor transactions in which little trust is required because little risk is involved and in which both partners can prove their trustworthiness, enabling them to expand their relation and engage in major transactions" (Blau, 1968). And familiarity breeds affection. Social relations between firms are the resultant of the relations of the individuals involved. There is no guarantee that relations will be uniform although social pressures within a firm may induce conformity. It is also possible that social bonds will transcend and even replace economic bonds as the *raison d'être* for the relationship to continue. Social relationships extend beyond individual firms. Networks will usually have a social dimension characterised by patterns of individual social contacts (Hamfelt and Lindberg, 1987). They may also have what might be described as a culture, i.e. commonly held beliefs about the basis of social activity within the network.

Technical bonds stem from the characteristics of the products and services exchanged. Firms adjust products and processes to their partner's requirements, subject to the constraints of technology and economics. They also acquire technical knowledge some of which may be rather specific to one relationship. Partners adjust logistically to each other in respect of the physical transfers of product or execution of services. Such adjustments may be rather permanent or relatively flexible in nature. Administrative systems vary from organisation to organisation.

However they have to interface where there is a continuing relationship. Again procedures may have to be adapted or else sub-routines or heuristics developed to cope.

Information is the common currency of interfirm relations. All of the other dimensions described operate through the communication of information, from the formal transmission of orders and invoices to the tone of voice used in a telephone conversation. Stocks of information, i.e. knowledge, may also be regarded as an investment that a firm can make in respect of a particular partner. Information clearly forges its own networks (Rogers, 1984). The collection of information is one of the primary uncertainty reduction activities that firms adopt and networks provide a necessary vector. The relative ease of exchange and transmission means that it can flow around a network very quickly when the communication nodes are in place and connected. In this sense it differs from the slower responses that are characteristic of the social or technical dimensions.

Firms may be bound legally by contracts or by rather more general articles of involvement or ownership. Such bonds are highly visible but may be less binding than they appear. Indeed the need to invoke a legal framework suggests that other types of bonding may not be working particularly well. Firms must also learn to adjust to what might be called the rhythms of their partners. There are characteristic activities, e.g. new product developments, which have a particular time horizon and urgency for the organisation concerned. Partner organisations have to learn what the time patterns of various crucial activities are and how to adjust to them or have them adjusted.

It is clear that other dimensions and subdivisions of existing dimensions could be used to better characterise bonds. However the process is not without penalties. In particular such an analytical approach courts the danger of ignoring the necessarily holistic nature of bonds:

> The different types of bonds are not independent of each other. Thus social bonds of more than minimal strength and content might e.g. be necessary for the development of knowledge based bonds which in turn might be a prerequisite for strong technical bonds. (Mattsson, 1984).

This whole/part problem occurs throughout the network literature largely because of the scope of the phenomena it is expected to describe.

The fourth element of relationships identified by Johanson and Mattsson is investment. "Investments are processes in which resources are committed in order to create, build or acquire assets which can be used in the future" (Johanson and Mattsson, 1986). In this case the investment is in a specific relationship. The returns to such an investment might include "The rendering more effective of the current transactions, accumulation of knowledge, control possibilities *vis-à-vis* the other party" (Hagg and Johanson, 1983). Such an investment may have all the hallmarks of a traditional investment, i.e. the purchase of a new machine solely for the purpose of supplying a particular customer. This is often termed hard investment. More likely the resources are people and their time. Soft investment of this kind may include such things as acquiring knowledge of the technical, administrative or logistical characteristics of a partner. It may also be time spent in establishing good social relationships. In one sense any resource committed above and beyond that required to execute the current exchanges may be regarded as an investment. As a result it is difficult to distinguish between investments and recurrent costs (Hagg and Johanson, 1983).

The recurrent costs of exchange activities are close to what some institutional economists call transaction costs. They are the costs of doing business with someone else. In economists' terms they represent the friction in the system which impedes optimum resource allocation. For transaction costs economists, minimum costs determine the form of relationship that firms will adopt. However in the industrial network approach costs are simply one way of describing exchanges in the contexts of relationships.

Relationship specific investments are not the only kinds of investment firms make and therefore they will both affect and be affected by those other investments. Again distinguishing among kinds of investment will not be easy. Buying a new machine, for example, may represent an investment in a new technology, a specific market and in several customer relationships. Where the investment is highly relationship specific it may have a very low or zero alternative value, e.g. the time spent wining and dining a specific technical salesman. On the other hand few human activities are without some transfer or learning value. Given the mutuality of relationships it is evident that investment by one partner depends upon the existence of complementary assets in the other. It is pointless investing in knowledge of a particular technical application if the partner firm is simply not interested in using it.

One final aspect of relationships not discussed by Johanson and Mattsson is that of atmosphere. Inherent in any relationship is the tension between conflict and cooperation (Ford, Håkansson and Johanson, 1986). It is inherent because in any relationships the partners will be concerned that they are receiving an equitable share of the benefits which accrue from the existence of the relationship. Conflict may also arise from absence of mutuality because of changes in the objectives of either party or because the processes of exchange are not being managed to the satisfaction of one or both parties.

Relationships form the context in which transactions take place. Transactions, as described earlier, may be divided into exchanges and adaptation procedures. The latter are closely associated with the investment element of relationships. Adaptation is a continuous process which results in changes in products or services bought or sold, in processes of manufacture or in routines and administrative procedures and which implies resource commitment. The resulting adaptations are investments in specific relationships. The returns to adaptation investment are strengthening of bonds between firms, easier resolution of conflicts, confirmation that continuing adaptation is possible and development of mutual knowledge and orientation (Johanson and Mattsson, 1987).

Adaptation processes are, in turn, related to exchange processes. "The more intensive the exchange process among firms, the stronger will be the reasons to make adaptations. The type of adaptations is also related to the characteristics of the exchange, including frequency, complexity, and regularity" (Johanson and Mattsson, 1987). Similarly exchange processes are intimately connected to relationships. Relational elements strongly influence the processes of exchange, for example a firm will not order a product from a partner firm that it knows the firm finds difficult to produce. Conversely continuing exchanges provide the only medium firms have to change the form of their relationship. For example social exchanges may be strengthening social bonds at the same time as product exchanges are weakening technical bonds.

Implicit in this analysis is the notion that strongly bonded relationships define networks. While this may be true in general it is arguable that other kinds of relationships exist in networks which can have a significant effect on their operation. Easton and Araujo (1986) distinguished weak, potential and residual exchange relationships as well as pointing out the existence of potentially influential noneconomic exchange relationships, e.g. those between competitors. Weak relationships may, for example, have the power to affect network outcomes through their use as communication conduits (Granovetter, 1973). Potential and residual relationships change the context in which a focal relationship operates since they offer visible alternatives. It is not necessary to have economic exchanges between firms for there to be direct effects on their behaviour.

Indirect relationships are another very different form of relationship though a crucial one since they provide a very direct link between dyadic relationships and networks. An indirect relationship is most simply described as the relationship between two firms which are not directly related but which is mediated by a third firm with which they both have relationships. Two rather important kinds of indirect relationships are vertical, firm to customer's customer, and horizontal, firm to competitor through mutual customer.

Taking a focal firm viewpoint it is clear that a firm will have, except in the sparsest of networks, more indirect than direct relationships. This adds considerably to the problem of relationship management. However it is equally likely that some law of "distance" will apply such that the more distant and indirect the relationship the less impact it will have. Indirect relationships also specify the routes by means of which firms gain access to resources. One could, for example, imagine a situation where an indirectly connected secondary ring of firms might be capable of insulating the focal firm from the rest of the network. In a similar way indirect relationships provide the context for direct relationships and are capable of strongly influencing them (Mattsson, 1986).

An important element in indirect relationships is the nature and operation of the firm which connects two other firms indirectly. Certain types of intermediary, for example, customers as compared with suppliers, may influence the indirect relationships in rather different ways. Particular kinds of firm may perform the task of network node rather differently and thus strongly affect the operation of the net to which they belong. Whatever the influence, the process of transmission of information, resource, power, etc. will not be unaffected by the route taken.

Mattsson (1986) identifies seven dimensions which can be used to characterise indirect relationships. They include distance from a focal firm; vertical or horizontal nature; complementary or competitive; narrow or wide connection; the strength, kind and content of the direct bonds concerned; the interdependency of the direct relations concerned and the value added of a focal firm's direct relationship. Such a characterisation provides a link between descriptions of the operation of direct relationships and the operation of networks. For example the predominance of widely or narrowly connected indirect relationships will fundamentally affect the structure of a network. In a sense a focus on indirect relationships provides the microstructure and micro-processes of networks. It remains to be seen whether this intermediate form of analysis provides a useful route to descriptions of aggregate network phenomena.

NETWORKS AS STRUCTURES

If the firms in an industrial system are interdependent rather than independent then networks will have structure. Interdependence introduces constraints on the actions of individual firms which create structure "in the large". Where there is no interdependence, as is assumed in some economic models, then an industrial system will be unstructured and stochastic in nature. The greater the interdependence the clearer the structure of the network becomes and the more important it is in determining the behaviour of individual firms. Structure in this context is based upon firms as the elements of structure.

A basic assumption of the industrial network approach is that networks are essentially hetero-geneous in nature (Hagg and Johanson, 1983). Again this contrasts with the homogeneity assumptions of much economic writing. The sources of heterogeneity are easy to describe, less easy to model. Industrial systems exist to match heterogeneous resources to heterogeneous demands. It is indisputable that resources available to create products and services are heterogeneous in nature. This is not just a recognition of variety among resources but also the fact that such resources are themselves multi-dimensional in character. One might also expect that individuals or individual firms would have dissimilar needs or, failing that, would accept that such needs could be met in a variety of different ways (Alderson, 1965). The third element of heterogeneity lies in the firms involved in the network transforming resources to meet needs. Each firm is individual in its structure, employee preferences, history, resources, investments, skills, etc. The role it chooses, or may be forced, to play in the transformation process will be determined partly by factors such as these. In addition the relationships such firms have, will themselves create new possibilities which may in turn generate new forms of relationship and provide an additional source of heterogeneity as well as stabilising the structure so created. Uncertainty reduction is one motive for forming strong relationships though it has been argued that networks also create uncertainty albeit of a different kind. Specialisation, learning by doing, and the existence of transaction specific invest-ments support heterogenisation. Thus interdependence is not only a source of heterogeneity, it is also a result of it. They are mutually reinforcing.

Such a view of networks has a number of implications. The first is that for a given set of resources and a given set of needs there are a large, possibly infinite, number of network structures which are capable of carrying out the transformation process. That is not to say that all are equally likely to occur in practice. Conversely, as will be argued later, it should not be assumed that there exists some objective function for the network, defined for example in terms of entropy, efficiency or effectiveness, which would predict which structure would be the optimum and therefore emerge as the most preferred. That is not to argue that networks do not change. What is clear is that in networks, as in organisations, structure and process are intimately related.

One way of characterising the structure of a network is by the division of work among the firms in the network. If a series of transformation activities have to be carried out in order to transform resources into products and services for final consumption by customers at whatever point in the network then individual firms will have responsibility for those activities. Clearly one could envisage a rather monolithic network where there are few firms carrying out the bulk of transformation. Alternatively the network might have a large number of firms each carrying out a small proportion of the required conversion activities with a concomitant increase in exchange activities. The balance between conversion and exchange activities may be regarded as another measure of network structure.

One structural issue in network analysis is that of boundaries. Mattsson (1988) comments "We can regard the global industrial system as one giant and extremely complex network since there exist always some path of relationships that connect any two firms." However he goes on to say "for obvious analytical reasons, this total network must be subdivided according to criteria such as interdependence between positions due to industrial activity chains, geographical proximities etc." In general such subdivisions have been called nets though the usage is by no means consistent. Perhaps there is a reluctance to accept the "universal" network. More likely it is a question of level of aggregation. Networks defined as equivalent in scope to industrial systems are as large as any analyst is likely to be able to comprehend let alone analyse. Nets provide a lower level of analysis. It should, however, be recognised that all boundaries are arbitrary.

Nets may be identified in terms of the strength of complementarity among the members of the net (Hagg and Johanson, 1983). They may be thought of as local concentrations in the network. They have natural boundaries in the sense that relationships among members are stronger than relationships between members and non members. Nets may be characterised along different dimensions: product, geography, process, technology, etc. From this definition it is clear that a firm may be a member of more than one net which adds another dimensionality problem to the analysis of networks. A net may also be defined by the activities of a single powerful organisation. In fact Mattsson (1984) suggests that the term net be used to describe only this situation. It corresponds to the organisation set concept used by Aldrich (1981). Clearly there are arguments for both definitions. However it is important that the terminology should be clarified. Researchers will wish to use different net definitions depending upon their research objectives. However it should also be recognised that networks, being in part social constructions, will also be perceived by their participants in different ways. Networks are socially constructed and there are likely to be disagreements among participants and multiple models of structure.

Social network analysis has developed a number of concepts, all of which have operational measures, which describe what are regarded as key structural characteristics. Mattsson (1986) has applied four of these concepts to industrial networks. Structuredness refers to the general level of interdependence in a network. In a tightly structured network firms have strong bonds and clearly demarcated activities. Individual firms are heavily constrained and exits and entries to the network are infrequent. Loosely structured networks have the opposite characteristics. Homogeneity describes the similarity of firms in terms of their bond types, relative importance of firms and the functions each firm may undertake. Where a small number of firms have a dominating influence on the network then it may be said to be hierarchical though the form of the resulting hierarchies may be many and various. Exclusiveness refers to the extent to which a network is insulated from other networks. There are many other measures of network structure which could be employed. However *ad hoc* measures bring with them the danger of atheoretical analysis. Perhaps their use should await a clearer articulation of one or more network theories which can make predictions about structure and its relationship to other network variables.

NETWORKS AS POSITION

The network as position perspective is partial but powerful. In addition it has links to other areas of business analysis such as industrial economics and strategy. It represents a different level of analysis since the focus is at least partly upon single firms rather than the network. To provide some measure of comparability, a network in this perspective may be thought of as an aggregation of interlocking positions though it is likely that the proponents would not describe it in these terms. Mattsson (1984) defines a position as a role "that the organisation has for other organisations that it is related to, directly or indirectly". This statement has echoes of the definition of social role. "Thus this implies that the firm is expected by other firms to behave according to the norms associated with the position" (Mattsson, 1984). Other organisations, in effect, define the position of a focal organisation through the relationships that they have with it. Håkansson and Johanson (1984a) describe a related concept, strategic identity "which refers to the views about the firm's role and position in relation to other firms in the industrial network".

Position is inherently a dialectical concept. The net clearly constrains and circumscribes the behaviour of the focal firm. However it also offers opportunities in terms of access to the resources of the rest of the network. There is a balance between constraint and opportunity and a key normative issue is the way in which firms manage this balance. In addition the resource dependence model suggests that firms will make conflicting demands upon the focal firm. Such demands have to be reconciled or dealt with in some fashion if a tenable, i.e. balanced position is to be maintained. There are tensions in the relationships, which keep the firm in its position. Positions are also balanced as between the past and the future. History determines the current position but the future offers opportunities for change.

Mattsson (1984) outlines four characteristics of position. Function describes the function firms are held to perform, the activities they are expected to undertake, for example, a limited line wholesaler. The identity of the net of firms that the focal firm has relationships with is a second feature of position. If the net changes the expectations change and so does the position. A third aspect of position is the relative importance of the firm in its net, measured by size or other correlates of power. Positions may be defined at different levels of analysis. Mattsson distinguishes macro- and micropositions. The former refers to relationships between individual firms and is therefore largely a recasting of the bonding or interaction concepts to make them more compatible with network description. The latter describes the firm's relationship to the network as a whole. Strength of relationship was later added as a fifth variable (Mattsson, 1987a).

In later work Johanson and Mattsson (1986) used micro- and macropositions as superordinate variables and described them in the following terms:

> The micropositions are characterised by: a) The role of the firm in relation to the (other) firm(s) b) its importance to the other firm, and c) the strength of the relationship with the other firm. The macropositions are characterised by: a) the identity of the other firms with which the firm has direct relationships and indirect relationships in the network b) the role of the firm in the network and, c) the strength of the relationships with other firms.

The separation of the two concepts allows us to speculate about the way in which micropositions build to macropositions. Originally Mattsson suggested that macropositions might be thought of as "aggregates or weighted averages of micropositions". However in later work this simple model is discarded. "Thus the macroposition, while referring to the whole network, is not an aggregation of the micropositions in the network" (Johanson and Mattsson, 1986). This is almost self evident since macropositions are affected by the whole network interdependencies while micropositions are not. It is to be expected that there will be strong interrelationships between the two kinds of position.

For example taking on a new type of customer (a new microposition) may change other firms' expectations about the functions a focal firm can perform and its importance in the network (a macroposition change). Mattson (1984) discusses a variety of ways in which micro and macro-positions may be related.

Positions in networks are primarily concerned with the nature of network connections. Thus they provide a language to talk about network changes. Fundamentally, a change in the position of one firm will change, to a greater or lesser extent, the position of other firms in the network. Such changes need not be confined to those firms in direct relationship with the initiating firm. Position changes can spread out from the initiating firm through the whole network by way of a cascade of position changes. However it should not be thought that position changes are easy to achieve or even always possible. Firms may be in preferred positions and defend those positions by any means at their disposal including making other microposition changes to nullify the initiated change. Firms also have desired positions to which they may be seeking to achieve and which may be threatened by the proposed changes.

Mattsson provides a link to strategy by identifying four strategic situations in relation to network position: entering and exiting an established network, defending and changing existing positions. He goes on to describe specific strategies that firms might adopt in the last two situations. The analyses are complex and contingent. For example position changes may be marginal or structural, firm or other initiated, acceptable or unacceptable. Mattsson (1987a) goes further and argues that all strategies involve network position change whether or not this particular focus provides the best way of understanding or implementing them. The approach provides real insights into what might be called the microprocesses of network change. It corresponds to the strategy as position perspective as characterised by Mintzberg (1988) but contrasts strongly with the alternative positional, competitive models used by Porter.

NETWORKS AS PROCESS

Change is a central feature of much that is written about industrial networks. Networks are concerned with relationships and these cannot be conceived of in anything but dynamic terms. It is hardly surprising that the processes by which networks function have been a major preoccupation of workers in this field. There is no clear focus but a number of issues can sensibly be discussed under this heading.

Coordination of firms in an industrial system may be conceived as being effected by three kinds of mechanisms. Economists have argued for the invisible hand of the market. In particular, price formation provides the signals which determine which firms produce what products. The processes which achieve this coordination are difficult to model since the markets are by no means perfect and simple assumptions will not suffice. Nevertheless market mechanisms do exist, because firms can make choices, and may be said to have a coordinative role. Firms are not, however, mechanistic in their response to external stimuli nor are they simple in structural or process terms. They provide a form of coordination which is internal, self directing and managerial. It has been called the visible hand. Those activities which are under the control of a single firm are coordinated by them to their own plans towards their own ends, sometimes in conflict with market mechanisms, at other times replacing them. In the latter case we call this a hierarchy, *vide* transaction cost theory.

Where strong inter-organisational relationships exist, a third form of coordination emerges: network processes. Coordination is not achieved by some grand master plan or quasi hierarchy since the firms concerned are too independent and the activities too numerous and diverse to control. But neither, in general, are firms so independent from one another that the market dictates and controls their actions. The reasons for the existence of strong relationships between firms and the constraints they place upon them, have already been described. Where such relationships exist they exert a coordinative influence on the system through the need for coordination at the level of the dyad. Significant structural changes cannot occur without the breaking of strong bonds and this introduces inertia into the system. More important, the direction of change is governed by the pattern of relationships that the participant firms judge, on a resultant rather than a collective basis, to be most favourable. This is a form of coordination which is neither market nor hierarchy not yet an intermediate form. It is an alternative mode which operates by different mechanisms.

Network processes are dominated by the distribution of power and interest structures. Some firms in the network have access to more and better resources than others. This may be a result of historical accident (location, invention, synergy, etc.) or may be due to far sighted management of the resource base. Whatever the cause, the effect is to render some firms more powerful than others, i.e. many relationships are asymmetrical with respect to power. In addition not all firms have the same interests especially since an interest vector will be the resultant of the interests of the actors within the firm. The power/interest distributions dictate the way in which the network both operates and develops. A single powerful firm may dominate a part of a network and part of its interest structure may be a desire to remain in control at the expense of other possible goals. Conversely a network where the power is rather evenly distributed offers many opportunities for development. This is especially true if the interest structures of participants coincide or, more usually, where feasible trade-offs, between the cooperation required to coordinate and the conflict over the distribution of surpluses, can be made.

Two dialectical processes in networks are competition and cooperation. The picture of relationships provided by the network approach emphasises cooperation, complementarity and coordination. Firms buying and selling from one another have to have a minimal level of cooperation in order to complete even a single exchange. In practice, the existence of strong bonding demonstrates a high level of cooperation. Even those firms judged as market competitors by traditional standards, being indirectly linked through customers, may find themselves cooperating in order, for example, to develop new products as a benefit for the network as a whole. Firms therefore find themselves in the position of having to make fine judgements about their modes of operation. In single relationships, nets and networks they have to decide the trade-off between cooperation, necessary in order to create benefit, and competition over the control, ownership or share of the resources so created.

Hagg and Johanson (1983) argue that competition in the traditional sense is replaced by rivalry for the control of resources. Such rivalry may occur at any level of aggregation. For example the fiercest competition may occur between networks rather than within them. There is no sense in which such rivalry will necessarily lead to optimal allocation of economic resources. An alternative but complementary view is that competition in networks is a function of the overlap of organisational domains. Complete overlap implies competition; partial overlap implies networking (Thorelli, 1986).

Networks are stable but not static. The continuing processes of interaction between firms are stabilised since they take place within the context of existing relationships. However such relationships are also changing, partly in response to events external to the relationships and partly because of the transactions which help to define them. In addition new relationships are formed and old relationships disappear. Evolution is the main mode; revolution is possible but unusual. Network inertia and interdependencies slow and shape change (Johanson and Mattson, 1986). Thus networks do not have lifecycles. They transform over time, merge, shift in focus and membership. Stability also provides a platform for change. The continuous interaction between firms offers, on the one hand, the opportunity for innovation and, on the other, the existence of a known and predictable environment in which it can be realised.

Industrial systems exist to create products and services. Innovation is a major force in networks and much of the empirical work on industrial networks has been done on new product development (Håkansson, 1987). It is argued that invention and innovation occur in networks not within but between firms. Even when the "Newton syndrome" seems to be at work it is often the problems or opportunities presented by other organisations which provide the necessary inspiration. More often it is the working through of mutual problems between supplier and customer which creates the novel solution. Either supplier or customer may take the lead in this process. Each brings a complementary set of skills, knowledge and resources to the problem.

For the invention to become a reality, network mobilisation must occur. It is not enough that the technical knowledge is available. Novelty requires changes in network structures as well as changes within the firms involved, i.e. self mobilisation. Firms must adapt old relationships and internal activities and develop new relationships. Mobilisation requires resources and if such resources are not available or, more likely, will not be made available by network participants then the innovation will fail. It is also apparent that they must be the right resources in the right combinations. In a network where innovation dominates, limitation of resources forces firms into increasing technical specialisation. This means that they, in turn, become increasingly reliant upon other firms which have complementary resources with whom they are driven to coordinate their research activities. Thus innovation leads to strongly bonded networks. Håkansson (1987) identifies these three aspects of innovation in a network perspective as knowledge development, resource mobilisation and resource coordination.

At a more general level any change in a network requires resources to be mobilised. In particular existing actors not only need to have the necessary resources but also the will and interest to deploy them. On the other hand any firm, however apparently powerless, may initiate change if it can draw upon the resources of the whole network by virtue of the acceptability of the change. 'If the power for change is to suffice then both knowledge and demand must be mobilised in a particular direction' (Håkansson and Waluszewski, 1986).

One fundamental issue remains about which there is strong disagreement. What are the forces which drive network changes? Håkansson and Johanson (1984a) argue that "it is meaningless to speak about optimal activity systems or configurations." Changes to improve network efficiency do occur but there is no mechanism by which the optimal direction can be discerned. Networks do not tend to optimal efficiency configurations. Mattsson (1986) suggests that "lack of balance between resources is an important driving force for investment processes to be initiated in different firms". This suggests that resource distribution in networks may tend towards some sort of equilibrium. Thorelli (1986) sees entropy as the driving force leading to the disintegration of networks. Resources are consumed and structures created in an attempt to arrest the process.

IMPLICATIONS AND APPLICATIONS

The industrial networks approach, from whichever perspective it is viewed, offers a totally different view from that of traditional marketing and buying behaviour approaches. To start with it integrates these two separate fields of endeavour. It eschews markets and adopts relationships. It is positive and does not smuggle normative principles into its models. There are, however, normative implications which might contribute to the management of exchange processes under the general heading of relational marketing (or purchasing). They are, in a sense, external to the industrial networks approach but provide an interpretation of it by taking a focal firm viewpoint.

From a functional marketing or purchasing stand-point the emphasis lies in the management of relationships. Such a relationship may be dominated or initiated by either partner. The key issues are choice of partners, resource allocation among them and the management of individual relationships. The first issue is largely a strategic one and will be discussed later. The second issue has been described as the limitation problem. A firm has only limited resources; it must choose how much, and in what fashion, it will devote to each relationship, potential or actual. A portfolio approach to this issue has been both suggested (Campbell and Cunningham, 1984) and criticised (Easton and Araujo, 1985). The interesting question is how firms actually make the trade-offs. The third issue concerns how an individual relationship is managed. What the industrial network approach adds to the interaction approach is the knowledge that the focal relationship (a) cannot be managed in isolation from the other relationships a firm has and (b) represents a conduit to other relationships through which resources may be accessed.

In terms of strategy the networks as positions perspective provide not only useful insights but also a contrast with the Porterian position. Porter recognises extended rivalry and describes strategy in terms of strategic positions in relationship to the rival forces. The network position characterises these forces in terms of the organisations with which the focal firm has relationships and, in addition, handles both conflict and cooperation among them. The strategic alternatives have already been described in the position section. The general picture is of a firm at the centre of a web of relationships which both constrain it and provide opportunities. By changing patterns of relationships, itself no easy task, a firm can change position, acquire more control over its own destiny and better achieve what the stakeholders require. The central concept is one of balance and positional sense; a tightrope walking act.

There are, in addition, industrial policy implications of a network approach. Hagg and Johanson (1983, ch. 5) provide a useful summary. Perhaps the most salient change suggested is a move away from treating the individual firm as the unit of analysis. Nets and networks provide a more powerful focus since they recognise the fact that a policy intervention must take into account the relationship among the target firms. Further, governments may only be able to achieve their policy objectives by seeking to strengthen, weaken or restructure relationships *per se*.

The industrial networks approach has been applied to a wide variety of the phenomena of industrial life and reference has been made throughout this chapter to a number of relevant studies. However particular emphasis has been laid on the twin processes of internationalisation and technological development. In the former case an industrial network approach offers an alternative to the traditional economic and more recent transaction cost approaches. It argues that internationalisation follows the existing patterns of relationships (Håkansson and Johanson, 1988). The importance of networks in invention and innovation has been demonstrated (Håkansson, 1987). It is argued that these processes occur between firms and not solely within them. For an innovation to succeed the network must be capable of being mobilised. The resources must be available in the network and under the control of, or accessible to, the actors with an interest in the success of the innovation.

CONCLUSION

This review has been a process of gathering together relevant material, restructuring and explaining the industrial network approach. No attempt has been made to provide a critical analysis. It is, however, easy to predict what criticisms it would attract from outside the paradigm. Where is the systematic evidence for the cornerstone assumption, that strong relationships among firms in industrial systems, prevail? Is it not simply a rather general approach incapable of being operationalized and tested? Why is the language of industrial networks so diffuse, contradictory and hence difficult to learn? Each of these criticisms can be answered, at least partially, and in some detail. However they would reflect different aspects of a rather more general answer. The industrial network approach is both new and rich. The paradigm is less than a decade old. The infant is precocious. It needs time to mature. But already it challenges the orthodoxy of traditional perspectives in a number of disciplines. It provides an alternative and plausible view of the world it seeks to describe. It depicts a new reality.

REFERENCES

Alchian, A. A. and Demsetz, H. (1972) 'Production, Information Costs and Economic Organisation', *American Economic Review*, 62, p. 783.

Aldrich, H. E. (1979) *Organisations and Environments*, Englewood Cliffs, NJ, Prentice Hall.

Aldrich, H. E. (1981) *The Origins and Persistence of Social Networks. Social Structure and Network Analyses*, Beverly Hills, Calif., Sage.

Aldrich, H. E. and Whetten, D. A. (1981) 'Organisation-sets, Action sets and Networks. Making the most of simplicity' in P. C. Nystrom and W. H. Starbuk (eds) *Handbook of Organisational Design*, Vol. 1, Oxford, Oxford University Press pp. 385–408.

Alderson, W. (1957) *Marketing Behaviour and Executive Action*, Homewood, Ill., Richard D. Irwin.

Alderson, W. (1965) *Dynamic Marketing Behaviour. A Functionalist Theory of Marketing*, Homewood Ill., Richard D. Irwin.

Alexander, R., Surface, S. and Alderson, W. (1940) *Marketing*, Boston, Mass., Ginn and Company.

Arndt, J. (1979) 'Overview: The Impact of Stakeholder Publics in Shaping the Future of Marketing' in G. Fisk, J. Arndt, and K. Gronhaug (eds), *Future Directions for Marketing* Cambridge, Mass., Marketing Science Institute, pp. 76–7.

Arrow, K. (1974) *Limits of Organisation*, New York, W. W. Norton and Co.

Astley, W. G. (1984) 'Toward an Appreciation of Collective Strategy'. *Academy of Management Review*, 9, 3, pp. 526–35.

Astley, W. G. (1985) 'The Two Ecologies: Population and Community Perspectives on Organisational Evolution', *Administrative Science Quarterly*, 30, pp. 224–41.

Astley, W. G. and Fombrun, C. (1983) 'Collective Strategy: Social Ecology of Organisational Environments', *Academy of Management Review*, 8, pp. 576–87.

Averitt, R. T. (1968) *The Dual Economy: The Dynamics of American Industry Structure*, New York, W. W. Norton and Co.

Axelrod, R. (1984) *The Evolution of Cooperation*, New York, Basic Books.

Axelsson, B. (1982) 'Wilmanshyttans uppgang och fall. En kommentar till angreppssattet i en foretags-historisk studie' ('The Rise and Fall of Wilmanshyttan Steel Works. A Commentary on the Approach in a Company History Study'), *Acta Universitatis Upsaliensis*, 15, Liber.

Axelsson, B. (1987) 'Supplier Management and Technological Development' in H. Håkansson (ed.) *Industrial Technological Development: A Network Approach*, London, Croom Helm.

Axelsson, B. and Håkansson, H. (1979) 'Wikmanshyttans uppgang och fall. En analys av ett stalforetag och dess omgivning under 75 ar' ('The Rise and Fall of the Wikmanshyttan Steel Works. An Historical Analysis of a Steel Company during 75 years'), Studentlitteratur.

Axelsson, B. and Håkansson, H. (1984) *Inkap for Konkurrenshraft (Purchasing for Competitive Power)*, Liber.

Barney, J. B. and Ouchi, W. G. (1986) *Organisational Economics* San Francisco, Calif., Jossey Bass.

Berg, P. O. (1985) 'Organisation Change as a Symbolic Transformation Process' in P. J. Frost *et al. Organization Culture*, New York, Sage.

Bjorklund, L. (1988) *International Projekforsaljning (International Systems Selling)*, Research Report, EFI., Stockholm School of Economics, Sweden.

Blau, P. M. (1964) *Exchange and Power in Social Life*, New York, John Wiley.

Blau, P. M. (1968) 'The Hierarchy of Authority in Organisations', *American Journal of Sociology*, 73, pp. 453–67.

Blois, K. J. (1972) 'Vertical Quasi-integration', *Journal of Industrial Economics*, 20, pp. 253–72.

Bonoma, T. (1976) 'Conflict, Cooperation and Trust in Three Power Systems', *Behavioural Science*, 21, pp. 499–514.

Bucklin, L. P. (1960) 'The Economic Structure of Channels of Distribution' in B. Mallen (1967) *The Marketing Channel: A Conceptual Viewpoint*, New York, John Wiley and Son, pp. 63–6.

Burt, R. S. (1980) 'Testing a Structural Theory of Corporate Cooptation: Interorganisational Directorate Ties as a Strategy for Avoiding Market Constraints on Profits', *American Sociological Review*, 45, pp. 821–41.

Campbell, N. C. G. (1984) 'The Structure and Stability of Industrial Networks. Developing a Research Methodology. Research Developments in International Marketing', 1st IMP International Research Seminar, UMIST, Manchester.

Campbell, N. C. G. (1985) 'Network Analysis of a Global Capital Equipment Industry', 2nd IMP International Research Seminar, University of Uppsala, Sweden.

Campbell, N. C. G. and Cunningham, M. T. (1984) 'Customer Analysis for Strategy Development in Industrial Markets', *Strategic Management Journal*, 4, pp. 369–80.

Caves, R. (1982) *Multinational Enterprise and Economic Analysis*, Cambridge, Cambridge University Press.

Cavusgil, S. T. and Nevin, J. P. (1981) 'The State-of-the-Art in International Marketing. An Assessment' in B. M. Enis and K. J. Roerring (eds) *Review of Marketing*, Greenwich, Conn., JAI Press.

Contractor, F. J. and Lorange, P. (1988) 'Why Should Firms Cooperate? The Strategy and Economics Basis for Cooperative Ventures' in F. J. Contractor and P. Lorange, *Cooperative Strategies in International Business*, Lexington, Mass., Lexington Books.

Cook, K. S. (1977) 'Exchange and Power in Networks of Interorganisational Relations', *Sociological Quarterly*, 18, pp. 62–82.

Cook, K. S. (1981) *Network Structure from Exchange Perspectives in Social Structure and Network Analyses*, Beverly Hills, Calif., Sage, pp. 177–200.

Cook, K. S. and Emerson, R. (1978) 'Power, Equity and Commitment in Exchange Networks', *American Sociological Review*, 43: pp. 712–39.

Cook, K. S. and Emerson, R. (1984) 'Exchange Networks and the Analysis of Complex Organisations', *Research in the Sociology of Organisations*, Vol. 3, Greenwich, Conn., JAP Press pp. 1–30.

Cox, R. and Goodman, C. (1956) 'Marketing of Housebuilding Materials', *Journal of Marketing*, 11, 1, pp. 36–61.

Cummings, T. G. (1984) 'Transorganisational Development', *Research in Organisational Behaviour*, Vol. 6, Greenwich, Conn., JAI Press, pp. 367–422.

Cunningham, M. T. (1987) 'Interaction, Networks and Competitiveness: A European Perspective of Business Marketing', European–American Symposium 'World Wide Marketplace for Technology Based Products', University of Twente, Enschede, The Netherlands.

Cyert, R. M. and March, J. G. (1963) *A Behavioural Theory of the Firm*, Englewood Cliffs, NJ, Prentice Hall.

Dahl, R. A. (1957) 'The Concept of Power', *Behavioural Science*, 2, pp. 201–15.

Dahmen, E. (1988) 'Development Blocks in Industrial Economics', *Scandinavian Economic Review*, 1, pp. 3–14.

Di Maggio, P. (1986) 'Structural Analysis of Organisational Fields', *Research in Organisational Behaviour*, Vol. 8, Greenwich, Conn., JAI Press, pp. 335–70.

Easton, G. (1988) 'Marketing strategy and Competition', *European Journal of Marketing*, 22, 1, pp. 31–49.

Easton, G. (1990) 'Relationships Among Competitors', in G. Day, B. Weitz and R. Wensley (eds) *The Interface of Marketing and Strategy*, Greenwich, Conn., JAI Press.

Easton, G. and Araujo, L. (1985) 'The Network Approach: An Articulation', 2nd International IMP Research Seminar, University of Uppsala, Sweden.

Easton, G. and Araujo, L. (1986) 'Networks, Bonding and Relationships in Industrial Markets', *Industrial Marketing and Purchasing*, 1, 1, pp. 8–25.

Easton, G. and Smith, P. (1984) 'The Formation of Inter-Organisational Relationships in a Major Gasfield Development', Research Seminar on Industrial Marketing, Stockholm School of Economics, Sweden.

Emerson, R. M. (1962) 'Power Dependence Relations', *American Sociological Review*, 27, pp. 31–40.

Emerson, R. M. (1972) 'Exchange Theory, Part II: Exchange Relations in Networks', in J. Berger, M. Zedditch and B. Andersson (eds) *Sociological Theories in Progress*, Boston, Mass., Houghton Mifflin, pp. 58–87.

Engwall, L. (1985) 'Fran vag vision till komplex organisation. En studie av Varmlands Folkblads ekonomiska och organisatoriska utveckling' (from a Vague Vision to a Complex Organisation. A Study of the Economic and Organisational Development of the Varmlands Folkbald'), *Acta Universitatis Upsaliensis*, 22, University of Uppsala, Sweden.

Engwall, L. and Johanson, J. (1989) 'Banks in industrial networks', Working Paper, Department of Business Studies, University of Uppsala, Sweden.

Evan, W. M. (1966) ' "The Organisation-Set" Toward a Theory of Interorganisational Relations', in J. Thompson (ed) *Approaches to Organisational Design*, Pittsburg, Pa. University of Pittsburg Press.

Fiocca, R. and Snehota, I. (1986) 'Marketing e alta tecnologia', *Sviluppo e Organizzazione*, 98, pp. 24–31.

Fombrun, C. J. and Astley, W. G. (1983) 'Beyond Corporate Strategy', *Journal of Business Strategy*, 3, pp. 47–54.

Ford, D., (1978) 'Stability Factors in Industrial Marketing Channels', *Industrial Marketing Management*, 7, pp. 410–22.

Ford, D., Håkansson, H. and Johanson, J. (1986) 'How do Companies Interact?', *Industrial Marketing and Purchasing*, 1, 1, pp. 26–41.

Forrester, J. (1961) *Industrial Dynamics*, Boston, Mass., MIT Press.

Forsgren, M. (1985) 'The Foreign Acquisition Strategy – Internationalisation or Coping with Strategic Interdependencies in Networks?', Working Paper, Department of Business Administration, University of Uppsala, Sweden.

Forsgren, M. (1989) *Managing the Internationalisation Process. The Swedish Case*, London, Routledge.

Fullerton, R. (1986) 'Understanding Institutional Innovation and System Evolution in Distribution', *International Journal of Research in Marketing*, 3, pp. 273–82.

Gadde, L.-E. and Mattsson, L.-M. (1987) 'Stability and Change in Network Relationships', *International Journal of Research in Marketing*, 4, pp. 29–41.

Gadde, L.-E., Håkansson, H. and Oberg, M. (1988) 'Change and Stability in Swedish Automobile Distribution', Report prepared for the 2nd Annual Forum of the International Motor and Vehicle Program, Boston, Massachusetts Institute of Technology.

Gattorna, J. (1978) 'Channels of Distribution Conceptualisations: A State-of-the-Art Review', *European Journal of Marketing*, 12, 7, pp. 471–512.

Glaser, A. and Strauss, B. (1967) *The Discovery of Grounded Theory*, Chicago, Ill., Aldine.

Giete, J. (1984) 'High Technology and Industrial Networks', International Research Seminar on Industrial Marketing, Stockholm School of Economics, Sweden.

Granovetter, M. S. (1973) 'The Strength of Weak Ties', *American Journal of Sociology*, 78, 6, pp. 1360–80.

Granovetter, M. S. (1984) 'A Theory of Embeddedness', Department of Sociology, State University of New York.

Granovetter, M. S. (1985) 'Economic Action and Social Structure: The Problem of Embeddedness', *American Journal of Sociology*, 91, 3, pp. 481–510.

Grinyer and Spender (1979) 'Recipes, Crises and Adaptation in Mature Business', *International Studies of Management and Organisation*, 9, pp. 113–33.

Hagg, I. and Johanson, J. (1983) 'Firms in Networks', Business and Social Research Institute, Stockholm, Sweden.

Håkansson, H. (1982a) 'Teknisk Utveckling och Marknadsforing' ('Technical Development and Marketing'), *MTC* 19, Stockholm, Stockholm School of Economics, Liber.

Håkansson, H. (ed.) (1982b) *International Marketing and Purchasing of Industrial Goods: An Interaction Approach*, Chichester, Wiley.

Håkansson, H. (ed.) (1987) *Industrial Technological Development: A Network Approach*, London, Croom Helm.

Håkansson, H. (1989) *Corporate Technological Behaviour: Cooperation and Networks*, London, Routledge.

Håkansson, H. and Johanson, J. (1984a) 'Heterogeneity in Industrial Markets and its Implications for Marketing' in I. Hagg and F. Wiedersheim-Paul (eds) 'Between Market and Hierarchy', Department of Business Administration, University of Uppsala, Sweden.

Håkansson, H. and Johanson, J. (1984b) 'A Model of Industrial Networks', Working Paper, Department of Business Administration, University of Uppsala, Sweden.

Håkansson, H. and Johanson, J. (1988) 'Formal and Informal Co-operation Strategies in International Industrial Networks' in F. J. Contractor and P. Lorange *Co-operative strategies in International Business*, Lexington, Mass., Lexington Books.

Håkansson, H. and Ostberg, C. (1975) 'Industrial Marketing – An Organisational Problem', Industrial Marketing Management, 4, pp. 113–23.

Håkansson, H. and Snehota, I. (1989) 'No Business is an Island. The Network Concept of Business Strategy', *Scandinavian Journal of Management Studies*, 4, 3, pp. 187–200.

Håkansson, H. and Waluszewski, A. (1986) 'Technical Development in a Dense Network', 3rd International IMP Research Seminar, IRE, Lyon.

Hall, R. (1977) *Organisations: Structure and Process*, 2nd edn, Englewood Cliffs, NJ, Prentice Hall.

Hallen, L. (1984) 'Market Approaches in European Perspective', in P. Turnbull and J. P. Valla *Strategies in International Industrial Marketing: A Comparative Analysis*, London, Croom Helm.

Hamfelt, C. and Lindberg, A.-K. (1987) 'Technological Development and the Individual's Contact Network' in H. Håkansson (ed.) *Industrial Technological Development: A Network Approach*, London, Croom Helm.

Hammarkvist, K.-O. (1983) 'Markets as Networks', Marketing Education Group Conference, Cranfield, UK.

Hammarkvist, K.-O., Håkansson, H. and Mattsson, L.-G. (1982) *Marknadsforing for konkurrenskraft (Marketing for Competitive Power)*, Malmo, Liber.

Hampdon. G. M. and Van Gent, A. P. (eds) *Marketing Aspects of International Business*, Boston, Mass., Kluwer-Nijhoff.

Hannan, M. T. and Freeman, J. H. (1977) 'The Population Ecology of Organisations', *American Journal of Sociology*, 82, pp. 929–64.

Harrigan, K. (1983) *Strategies for Vertical Integration*, Lexington, Mass., Lexington Books.

Harrigan, K. (1985) *Strategies for Joint Ventures*, Lexington, Mass., Lexington Books.

Hawley, A. (1968) 'Human Ecology' in D. L. Sills (ed.) *The International Encyclopedia of the Social Sciences*. Vol. 4, New York, Macmillan and Free Press, pp. 328–37.

Hegert, M. and Morris, D. (1988) 'Trends in International Collaborative Agreements' in F. J. Contractor and P. Lorange *Co-operative Strategies in International Business*, Lexington, Mass., Lexington Books.

Henderson, J. M. and Quandt, R. E. (1971) *Microeconomic Theory*, 2nd edn, New York, McGraw-Hill.

Hettne, B. and Tamm, G. (1974) *Mobilisation and Development in India. A Case Study of Mysore State*, SIDA.

Hughes, T. P. (1983) *Networks of Power, Electrification in Western Society, 1880–1930*, Baltimore, Md., Johns Hopkins University Press.

Hultbom, C. (1990) 'Internal Exchange Processes. Buyer–Seller Relationships within Big Companies', Unpublished Ph.D. dissertation, Department of Business Studies, University of Uppsala, Sweden.

Hulten, S. (1985) 'What Can Theories of Industrial Change Contribute to the Understanding Of International Markets as Networks?', 2nd International IMP Research Seminar, University of Uppsala, Sweden.

Imai, K. (1987) 'Network industrial organisation in Japan', Working paper prepared for the workshop on 'New Issues in Industrial Economies' at Case Western Reserve University, Cleveland, OH, on 7–10 June.

Jansson, H. (1985) 'Marketing to Projects in South East Asia. A Network.' Working Paper 1985/3, Department of Business Administration, University of Uppsala, Sweden.

Johanson, J. and Mattsson, L.-G. (1984) 'Marketing Investments and Market Investments in Industrial Markets', International Research Seminar in Industrial Marketing, Stockholm School of Economics, Stockholm, Sweden.

Johanson, J. and Mattsson, L.-G. (1985) 'Marketing and Market Investments in industrial networks', *International Journal of Research in Marketing*, 2, 3, pp. 185–95.

Johanson, J. and Mattsson, L.-G. (1986) 'Interorganisational Relations in Industrial Systems: A Network Approach Compared with a Transaction Cost Approach', Working Paper, University of Uppsala, Sweden.

Johanson, J. and Mattsson, L.-G. (1987) 'Interorganisational Relations in Industrial Systems: A Network Approach Compared with a Transaction Cost Approach', *International Studies of Management Organisation*, 17, 1, pp. 34–48.

Johanson, J. and Mattsson, L.-G. (1988) 'Internationalisation in Industrial Systems – A Network Approach', in N. Hood and J.-E. Vahlne (eds) *Strategies in Global Competition*, London, Croom Helm.

Johanson, J. and Sharma, D. (1985) 'Swedish Technical Consultants; Tasks, Resources and Relationships – A Network Approach', International Research Seminar on Industrial Marketing, Stockholm School of Economics, Stockholm, Sweden.

Kaynak, E. and Savitt, R. (eds) (1984) *Comparative Marketing Systems*, New York, Praeger.

Killing, K. P. (1982) 'How to Make a Global Joint Venture Work', *Harvard Business Review*, 61, 3, pp. 120–7.

Killing, J. P. (1983) *Strategies for Joint Venture Success*, New York, Praeger.

Kinch, N. (1988) 'Emerging Strategies in a Network Context: The Volvo Case', *Scandinavian Journal of Management Studies*, October.

Kranzberg, M. (1986) 'Technology and History: "Kranzberg's Laws"', *Technology and Culture*, 7, pp. 185–95.

Kutachker, M. (1982) 'Power and Dependence in Industrial Marketing' in H. Håkansson (ed.) *International Marketing and Purchasing of Industrial Goods: An interaction approach*, Chichester, Wiley.

Kutachker, M. (1985) 'The Multi-Organizational interaction approach to Industrial Marketing', *Journal of Business Research*, 13, pp. 383–403.

Laage-Hellman, J. (1984) 'The Role of External Technical Exchange in R&D: An Empirical Study of the Swedish Special Steel Industry', M.T.C. Research No. 18, Marketing Technology Centre, Stockholm, Sweden.

Laage-Hellman, J. (1987) 'Process Innovation through Technical Cooperation', in H. Håkansson (ed.) *Industrial Technological Development; A Network Approach*, London, Croom Helm.

Laage-Hellman, J. (1988) 'Technological Development in Industrial Networks', Working paper, Department of Business Administration, University of Uppsala, Sweden.

Laage-Hellman, J. (1989) 'Technological Development in Industrial Networks', Unpublished Dissertation, Department of Business Administration, University of Uppsala, Sweden.

Laage-Hallman, J. and Axelsson, B. (1986) 'Bioteknisk Foll i Sverigeforskninasuolam, forskninasinriktning, samartetsmonster. En studie av det bioteknisk Follnatverket 1970–1985' (Biotechnological R&D in Sweden. Research Volume, Direction of Research, Patterns of Cooperation. A study of the Biotechnological R&D Network 1970–1985), STU Information 536, Styrelsen for Teknisk Utveckling, Stockholm, Sweden.

Larsen, J. K. and Rogers, E. M. (1984) *Silicon Valley Fever*, New York, Basic Books.

Levine, S. and White, P. E. (1961) 'Exchange as a Conceptual Framework for the Study of Interorganisational Relationships', *Administrative Science Quarterly*, 5, pp. 583–601.

Lorenzoni, G. and Ornati, O. A. (1988) 'Constellations of Firms and New Ventures', *Journal of Business Venturing*, 3, pp. 41–57.

Lundgren, A. (1985) 'Datoriserad Bildbehandling i Sverige' ('Computerized Image processing in Sweden'), Working Paper, EFI, Stockholm School of Economics, Stockholm, Sweden.

Lundgren, A. (1987) 'Bildbehandlingens framvaxt', Working Paper, Stockholm School of Economics, Stockholm, Sweden.

Mallen, B. (ed.) (1967) *The Marketing Channel: A Conceptual Viewpoint*, New York, John Wiley and Son.

March, J. M. (1966) 'The Power of Power' in D. Easton (ed.) *Varieties of Political Theory*, Englewood Cliffs, NJ, Prentice Hall.

Marret, C. (1971) 'On the Specification of Interorganisational Dimensions', *Sociology and Social Research*, 56, pp. 83–9.

Mattsson, L.-G. (1969) *Integration and Efficiency in Marketing Systems*, EFI, Stockholm, Nordstedt & Soner.

Mattsson, L.-G. (1975) 'System Interdependencies – A Key Concept in Industrial Marketing', 2nd Research Seminar in Marketing, FNEGE, Senanque, France.

Mattsson, L.-G. (1981) 'Interorganisational Structures in Industrial Markets: A Challenge to Marketing Theory and Practice', Working Paper 1980/1, Department of Business Administration, University of Uppsala, Sweden.

Mattsson, L.-G. (1984) 'An Application of a Network Approach to Marketing: Defending and Changing Market Positions' in N. Dholakia and J. Arndt (eds) *Changing the Course of Marketing. Alternative Paradigms for Widening Marketing Theory*, Greenwich, Conn., JAI Press.

Mattsson, L.-G. (1986) 'Indirect Relationships in industrial networks: A Conceptual Analysis of their Significance', 3rd IMP International Seminar, IRE, Lyon, France.

Mattsson, L.-M. (1987a) 'Management of Strategic Change in a "Markets-as-Networks" Perspective' in A. Pettigrew *The Management of Strategic Change*, Oxford, Blackwell.

Mattsson, L.-G. (1987b) 'Conceptual Building Blocks of Network Theory', Working Paper, Stockholm School of Economics, Stockholm, Sweden.

Mattsson L.-G. (1988) 'Interaction Strategies: A Network Approach' AMA Marketing Educator's Conference, Summer, San Francisco, Calif.

McCammon, B. (1964) 'Alternative Explanations of Institutional Change and Channel Evolution' in B. Mallen (ed.) (1967) *The Marketing Channel: A Conceptual Viewpoint*, New York: John Wiley and Son, pp. 75–81.

McCammon, B. and Little, R. W. (1965) 'Marketing Channels: Analytical Systems and Approaches' in G. Schwartz (ed.) (1970) *Science in Marketing*, New York, John Wiley and Son, pp. 321–85.

McVey, P. (1960) 'Are Channels of Distribution What the Textbooks Say?', *Journal of Marketing*, XXIV, 3, pp. 61–5.

Mintzberg, H. (1988) 'Opening up the Definition of Strategy' in J. B. Quinn, H. Mintzberg and R. M. James (eds) *The Strategy Process*, Englewood Cliffs, NJ, Prentice Hall International.

Morgan, G. (1986) *Images of Organisation*, Beverly Hills, Calif., Sage.

Nelson, R. R. and Winter, S. G. (1982) *An Evolutionary Theory of Economic Change*, Cambridge, Mass., Harvard University Press.

Nieschlag, R. (1954) 'Die Dynamik der Betriebsformen im Handel', Rheinisch-Westfahalches Institut fur Wirtschaftsforschung, Essen, Schriftenreihe, Neue Folge nr 7.

Nilsson, A. (1987) 'Distributionssystems for Finpapper', ('Distribution Systems for Fine Paper'), Working Paper, EFI Stockholm School of Economics, Stockholm, Sweden.

Pascale, R. T. (1984) 'Perspectives on Strategy: "The Real Story Behind Honda's Success"' ' *California Management Review*, 26, 3, pp. 47–72.

Pettigrew, A. (1985) *The Awakening Giant: Continuity and Change in Imperial Chemical Industries*, Oxford, Basil Blackwell.

Pfeffer, J. (1978) *Organisational Design*, Arlington Heights, Ill., AHM Publishing Co.

Pfeffer, J. (1987) 'Bringing the Environment Back in The Social Context of Business Strategy' in D. Teece *The Competitive Challenge: Strategies for Industrial Innovation and Renewal*, Cambridge, Mass., Balinger Publishers.

Pfeffer, J. and Lebjebici (1973) 'Executive Recruitment and the Development of Interfirm Organisations', *Administrative Science Quarterly*, 18, pp. 449–61.

Pfeffer, J. and Salancik, G. (1978) *The External Control of Organisations*, New York, Harper and Row.

Piori, M. and Sabel, F. (1984) *The Second Industrial Divide: Possibilities for Prosperity*, New York, Basic Books.

Porter, M. J. (1980) *Competitive Strategy: Techniques for Analysing Industries and Competitors*, New York, The Free Press.

Reich, L. S. (1985) *The Making of American Industrial Research; Science and Business at G. E. and Bell, 1876–1926*, Cambridge, Cambridge University Press.

Rogers, E. M. (1982) *Interorganisational Coordination*, Ames, Ia., Iowa State University Press.

Rogers, E. M. (1984) 'Organisations and Networks; Illustrations from the Silicon Valley Microelectronics Industry', International Research Seminar on Industrial Marketing, Stockholm School of Economics, Stockholm.

Rogers, E. M. and Kincaid, D. L. (1981) *Communication Networks: Toward a New Paradigm for Research*, New York, The Free Press.

Root, F. (1978/82) *Foreign Market Entry Strategies*, New York, AMACON.

Rosenberg, D. L. (1982) *Inside the Black Box: Technology and Economics*, Cambridge, Cambridge University Press.

Scherer, F. M. (1980) *Industrial Market Structure and Economic Performance*, 2nd edn, Boston, Mass., Houghton Mifflin.

Schumpeter, J. A. (1955) *The Theory of Economic Development*, Cambridge, Mass., Harvard University Press.

Scott, R. W. (1987) *Organisation: Rational, Natural and Open Systems*, 2nd edn, Englewood Cliffs, NJ, Prentice Hall.

Silverman, D. (1970) *The Theory of Organisations*, London, Heinemann.

Smith, P. and Easton, G. (1986) 'Network Relationships: A Longitudinal Study' 3rd International IMP Research Seminar, IRE Lyon, France.

Thorelli, H. B. (1986) 'Networks: Between Markets and Hierarchies', *Strategic Management Journal*, 7, 1, pp. 37–51.

Thompson, J. D. (1967) *Organisations in Action*, New York, McGraw-Hill.

Tichy, N. and Fombrun, C. (1979) 'Network Analysis in Organisational Settings', *Human Relations*, 32, 11, pp. 923–65.

Turnbull, P. W. and Valla, J.-P. (1986) *Strategies in International Industrial Marketing*, London, Croom Helm.

Van de Ven, A. (1976) 'On the Formation and Maintenance of Relations among Organisations', *Academy of Management Review*, 4, 4, pp. 24–36.

Van de Ven, A. and Ferry, D. L. (1980) *Measuring and Assessing Organisations*, New York, John Wiley.

Van de Ven, A. and Walker, G. (1984) 'Dynamics of Interorganizational Coordination', *Administrative Science Quarterly*, Dec. pp. 598–621.

Venkataraman, N. and Camillius, J. L. (1984) 'Exploring the Concept of "Fit" in Strategic Management', *Academy of Management Review*, 9, 3, pp. 513–25.

von Hippel, E. (1978) 'Successful Industrial Products from Customer Ideas', *Journal of Marketing*, 42, pp. 39–49.

von Hippel, E. (1986) 'Cooperation between Competing Firms. Informal Know-how Trading', Working Paper no. 1959–86, Sloan School of Management, March.

Walker, G. (1988) 'Network Analysis for Cooperative Interfirm Relationships' in F. J. Contractor and P. Lorange *Co-operative Strategies in International Business*, Lexington, Mass., Lexington Books.

Waluszewski, A. (1987) 'CTMP-Processen. Fran vedkravande till vedsnala processor', Department of Business Studies, University of Uppsala, Sweden.

Waluszewski, A. (1989) 'Framvaxten av en ny mekanisk massateknik – en utrecklingshistoria' ('The Emergence of a New Mechanical Pulping Technique – A Development Story'), Unpublished dissertation, Department of Business Studies, University of Uppsala, Sweden.

Weick, K. E. (1969) *The Social Psychology of Organizing*, 1st edn, Reading, Mass., Addison-Wesley.

Weick, K. E. (1970) 'Educational Organisations as Loosely Coupled Systems', *Administrative Science Quarterly*, 21, 1, pp. 1–19.

Weick, K. E. (1979) *The Social Psychology of Organizing*, 2nd edn, Reading, Mass., Addison-Wesley.

Weick, K. E. (1984) 'Small Wins: Redefining the Scale of Social Problems', *American Psychologist*, 39, pp. 40–9.

Weitz, B. (1985) 'Introduction to Special Issue on Competition in Marketing', *Journal of Marketing Research*, 22, pp. 229–36.

Wibe, S. (1980) 'Change of Technology and Day to Day Improvements', Umea Economic Studies, Umea University, Sweden.

Williamson, O. E. (1975) *Markets and Hierarchies*, New York, The Free Press.

Williamson, O. E. (1985) *The Economic Institutions of Capitalism*, New York, The Free Press.

Wind, Y. (1979) 'The Journal of Marketing at a Cross Road', *Journal of Marketing*, 43, pp. 9–12.

Yamagashi, T., Gilmore, M. and Cook, K. (1988) 'Network Connections and the Distribution of Power in Exchange Networks', *American Journal of Sociology*, 93, 4, pp. 835–51.

Zaltman, G., Le Masters, K. and Heffring, M. (1982) *Theory Construction in Marketing*, New York, John Wiley.

3.2

A model of industrial networks

Håkan Håkansson and Jan Johanson

SUMMARY

1   Alderson proposed micro-functionalism as opposed to macro-functionalism in the analysis of the market system. Instead of starting from defining the macro-function of the larger system, the micro-functional approach is set to identify the functions performed by the elements of the system, without defining any overriding purpose for the broader system as a whole.

2   A similar approach has been advocated by Axelrod (1984:38 ff.) when analysing the outcome of interactive behaviour.

3   The importance of rules and routines as means of coping with complexity is a theme not new to behavioural theorists. It raises the broad issue of formation of effective rules of conduct and of the role they play in 'rational behaviour'. It is relatively recent in the management literature, traditionally building on a conception of rationality that calls for assessment of each choice situation strictly on its own merits.

STARTING POINTS

This chapter outlines a model of industrial networks. The main aim of the model is to make possible an integrated analysis of stability and development in industry. While stability is generally seen as the opposite to change and development this model views stability as vital for industrial development. A second aim of the model is to provide a basis for studies of the roles of actors and sets of actors in industrial development processes, given the relation between industrial stability and development.

   The model's basic classes of variables are actors, activities and resources. These variables are related to each other in the overall structure of networks. This overall structure is mainly a matter of definition. Actors are defined as those who perform activities and/or control resources. In activities actors use certain resources to change other resources in various ways. Resources are means used by actors when they perform activities. Through these circular definitions a network of actors, a network of activities and a network of resources are related to each other (see Figure 1).

ACTORS

Actors control activities and/or resources. Individuals, groups of individuals, parts of firms, firms, and groups of firms can be actors. Thus, in an industrial network, there are actors at several organisational levels. Actors at lower levels can be part of actors at higher levels, independent of level, actors have five characteristics. First, they perform and control activities. They determine, alone or jointly, which activities to perform, how these activities are to be performed, and which resources are to be utilised when performing the activities. Second, through exchange processes

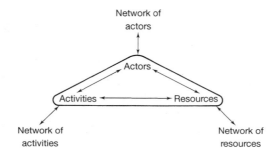

Figure 1 Basic structure of the model.

actors develop relationships with each other. Each actor is embedded in a network of more or less strong relationships, which gives the actor access to other actors' resources.

Third, actors base their activities on control over resources. Such control can be direct or indirect. Direct control is based on ownership. Indirect control is based on relationships with other actors and the associated dependence relations with those actors. Relationships with other actors give indirect control over resources directly controlled by those actors to the extent that those actors are dependent on the focal actor. Within the constraints formed by ownership, control is also a function of knowledge. The existence of actors at several levels means that it is usually unclear which actors control which resources. Different actors may have different views about the control over a certain resource. Likewise opinions may differ widely as to the extent of control by a certain actor. The degree and nature of such differences in perceptions are important characteristics of industrial networks.

Fourth, actors are goal oriented. Irrespective of the goals of specific actors the general goal of actors is to increase their control over the network. The emphasis on the control goal follows from the assumption that control can be used to achieve other goals. Through their direct or indirect control, resources can be mobilised for other purposes. Network control is reached through control over resources and/or activities. Increased control over resources is a matter of increasing the control of resources directly, of increasing the indirect control over other resources via relationships, and of reducing indirect control by other actors through relationships, that is increasing autonomy. Control of activities is a matter of control over resources and of knowledge.

Fifth, actors have differential knowledge about activities, resources and other actors in the network. This knowledge is primarily developed through experience with activities in the network. Consequently, the knowledge of nearer parts of the network is greater than knowledge of more distant parts. The actors know different parts of the network, and even if they have experience of the same parts such experience may not be identical.

Network control is not evenly distributed over the actors in a network. The efforts of the actors to increase control affects the control of other actors. Increased control of one actor is always achieved at the expense of the control of at least one other actor. The actors have, to some extent, conflicting interests. On the other hand, increased control of one actor may, and generally will, lead to increased control of some other actors in the network. To some extent actors in a network also have common interests.

Thus, in a network, there are a number of conflicting and common interests as well as efforts to provide for those interests. In this struggle the actors use their knowledge of the network as well as their relationships with other actors in order to increase their control. Furthermore, as the actors are at different organisational levels this struggle takes place not only between actors but also within actors.

ACTIVITIES

An activity occurs when one or several actors combine, develop, exchange, or create resources by utilising other resources. Because actors have different characteristics two main kinds of activities are distinguished, transformation activities and transfer activities. Through transformation activities resources are changed in some way. Transformation activities are always directly controlled by one actor. Transfer activities transfer direct control over a resource from one actor to another. Transfer activities link transformation activities of different actors to each other. They are never controlled by only one actor and they affect and are affected by the relationship between the actors involved.

Single activities are linked to each other in various ways. They constitute parts of more or less repetitive activity cycles where a number of interdependent activities are repeated. A complete activity cycle always contains both transformation and transfer activities. Either certain transfer activities are performed in order to make possible certain transformation activities or certain transformation activities are performed in order to make possible certain transfer activities. A complete activity cycle is never controlled by a single actor.

Some activity cycles are tightly coupled to each other while others are more loosely coupled. A sequence of tightly coupled activity cycles constituting a logical whole forms a transaction chain. Many activities are part of several activity cycles, and consequently, of several transaction chains. The different activity cycles of which an activity is part need not have the same regularity or periodicity; some of them may be more regular than others. And some are more frequently repeated than others. Actors performing single activities learn to perform those activities in a way which is to some extent dependent on the nature of the activity cycles and the transaction chains of which it is part. This experiential learning creates routines and informal rules which give the activities a certain institutionalised form. A basic stability is created.

Activities in the network are coupled to each other in various ways and to various degrees. Generally a certain activity is tightly linked to some other activities and loosely linked to others. Consequently there are a great number of relationships between activities. Direct relations exist between two activities which are directly coupled to each other, whereas indirect relations exist when activities are coupled to each other via intermediate activities. Specific relationships exist when two activities are linked to each other through specific actors whereas general relations between activities imply that the link between them is independent of specific actors.

From the perspective of the network, single activities by specific actors are almost never indispensable. They can always be dispensed with. This means that if a specific activity disappears the network can remain functionally intact because the surrounding activities are adjusted so that they take over the function of the absent activity. Furthermore, it is always possible to conceive of changes in the performance of single activities as well as in the couplings between them which would not affect the functioning of the network. Clearly, all such changes are associated with costs of adjustment which are not, however, necessarily born by those performing the activities.

The activity network is always imperfect in the sense that new activities, changes in old activities, or rearrangement of activities can make it more efficient. This is valid for whole networks as well as for any section of a network, even those controlled by single actors. Such changes are always occurring. Consequently, it is meaningless to speak about optimal activity systems or configurations.

RESOURCES

Performing transformation and transfer activities requires resources. Resources are combined and thus combination requires resources. All resources are controlled by actors, either by single actors or jointly by several actors. Resources are heterogeneous. They have attributes in an unlimited number of dimensions. This means that the possibilities for the use of a specific resource can never be fully or finally specified. There are always further possibilities to use the resource in a different

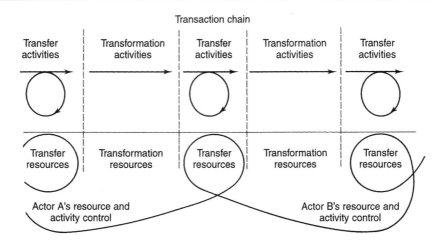

Figure 2 Transaction chain.

way or in a different setting. It is not possible to decide definitely how a certain resource can be combined with other resources. The result of combinations can always be elaborated.

Performing transformation activities requires transformation resources and performing transfer activities requires transfer resources (see Figure 2). Transfer and transformation resources are mutually dependent on each other. The use and value of a specific resource is dependent on how it is combined with other resources. Those dimensions of a resource which are utilised and the value which is given a resource are dependent on the activity cycles in which it is utilised and on their functions in various transfer chains as well as their functions in the network.

Knowledge and experience of resources are important. First, when heterogeneous resources are combined their joint performance increases through experiential learning and adaptation. This is valid in the small scale when very specific resources are combined when performing specific activities. It is also valid in the large scale when bundles of resources controlled by one actor are combined with other bundles of resources. Second, when heterogeneous resources are combined new knowledge emerges which creates possibilities for new and improved combinations. New insights into the handling of resources can break existing activity cycles and transfer chains and contain the seeds for development and change in industrial networks. Thus, when resources are heterogeneous, change induces further change. This holds both for those resources which are used in the activities and those which perform and influence activities. It is also valid both for transformation resources and transfer resources.

Resources can be characterised, first, by the actors controlling the resource. They can be controlled directly by one actor or jointly by several actors. Indirectly the resources can be controlled by those actors who have relationships with the actor directly controlling the resource. The less available a resource the more important is the control over it and the more efforts will be spent on getting control over it. If there is a surplus of the resource, control is of no interest to the actors. A second characteristic is the utilisation of the resource in activities. How many dimensions of the resource are used and how standardised is the utilisation in each of the dimensions? We can conceive a scale with the resource used in one dimension in a standardised way as one extreme and in multiple dimensions in unique ways as the opposite extreme. Standardisation and uniqueness refer to how the resource is used by one actor as compared with the use of the resource by other actors. A third characteristic is the versatility of the resources. To what extent and at what cost can the resource be used in other activity cycles and in other transfer chains?

THE NETWORK

For each of the three basic classes of variables, we have outlined relations between the elements. These elements form structures that can be described as networks. Actors develop and maintain relationships with each other and to understand the situation of an actor requires knowledge about the nature of the actor's relationships with other actors as well as an idea about the wider network of relationships around. In the same way the industrial activities are related to each other in patterns which can be seen as networks. Similarly resources are related to each other in networks and furthermore, the three networks are closely related to each other. They are interwoven in a total network. The three networks are bound together by forces, in terms of which the total network can be analysed. Important forces are as follows:

1 Functional interdependence: actors, activities and resources together form a system where heterogeneous demands are satisfied by heterogeneous resources. They are functionally related to each other.
2 Power structure: on the basis of control of activities and resources there are important power relations between the actors. The performance of the activities is to some extent organised on the basis of these power relations.
3 Knowledge structure: the design of the activities as well as the use of the resources is bound together by the knowledge and experience of present and earlier actors. And the knowledge of those actors is related one to another.
4 Intertemporal dependence: the network is a product of its history in terms of all memories, investments in relationships, knowledge, routines, etc. Changes of the network must be accepted by at least large parts of the network. Therefore all changes will be marginal and closely related to the past.

This last point suggests that stability and development within the network are closely related. Development in certain areas needs stability in others, and vice versa. Development of activities can be a means to secure stability in the power structure. Stable relationships can be important when one actor tries to develop the use of certain resources.

Actors in the network can act. Thus, the model is voluntaristic. On the other hand, the action possibilities are circumscribed by the relations between actors, activities and resources. But these relations are also the means for important changes in the network. Relationships make it possible to mobilise large parts of the network when great changes are required.

In summary, the network model described here suggests mechanisms whereby stability and change in industrial systems not only co-exist but are actually dependent one upon the other.

REFERENCES

Alderson, W. (1957) *Marketing Behaviour and Executive Action*, Homewood, Ill., Richard D. Irwin.
Alderson, W. (1965) *Dynamic Marketing Behaviour. A Functionalist Theory of Marketing*, Homewood Ill, Richard D. Irwin.

3.3

No business is an island: the network concept of business strategy

Håkan Håkansson and Ivan Snehota

INTRODUCTION

Looking back over what has happened in the study of business organization over the last 20 years, we can see that two major trends emerge quite clearly. Firstly, there has been a growing interest in business strategy and how it is managed. Secondly, a shift can be noticed in the focus of organizational theory away from the internal processes of organizations and towards the organization–environment interface. Both trends have produced valuable new insights and have advanced our understanding of the behaviour of business organizations.

There is an interesting contraposition between the two fields of research. Organizational theory studies which focus on the interface between the organization and its environment have tended to conclude that the individual organization is often embedded in its environment and that its behaviour is thus greatly constrained if not predetermined, which means that it is not a free and independent unit. In contrast to this, research on strategy management has been concerned with the opportunities for directing and managing the behaviour of the individual organization, consequently assuming that the organization possesses a certain degree of freedom of choice. Cross-fertilization between the two fields of research has so far been limited, possibly because of this difference in perspective.

The purpose of this article is to explore the contribution that could be made to a conceptual frame of reference for business strategy management by one of the research programmes which focuses on the organizational–environment interface, and to which a network approach has been applied. We start by examining some of the assumptions underlying the current "strategy management doctrine". The network model of the organization–environment interface is then reviewed and three central issues of the strategy management doctrine are discussed from the viewpoint of the network model: (1) organizational boundaries, (2) determinants of organizational effectiveness, and (3) the process of managing business strategy.

THE CONCEPT OF BUSINESS STRATEGY

The conceptual frame of reference of business strategy management is not easy to grasp. It consists of a large and growing body of quite varied contributions from such groups as industrial economists (Chandler, 1962; Porter, 1980, 1985), organizational theorists (Hall and Saias, 1980; Miles and Snow, 1984; Mintzberg, 1987; Pfeffer, 1987) and management theorists and consultants (Ansoff, 1965; Hofer and Schendel, 1978; Henderson, 1979; Ohmae, 1982). These multifaceted contributions are pretty heterogeneous in their approach as well as in the areas covered. In their current forms they can only be loosely linked together in what will be referred to below as the doctrine of business strategy management.

The concept of strategy as applied to business studies has only been appearing with any great frequency since about 1960 (Chandler, 1962; Ansoff, 1965). Since that date, it has gained wide acceptance, although "strategy" remains an ambiguous and elusive concept. Its meaning in the military context, "the art of so moving and disposing troops as to impose upon the enemy the place and time and conditions for the fighting preferred by oneself" (*Oxford English Dictionary*) does not seem to lend itself easily to business organizations. In particular, it is argued, because resources of business organizations (i.e. their "troops") are largely fixed in place and time (Pennings, 1985, p. 2) it is difficult to dispose resources in time and space. In business organization contexts "strategy" has sometimes been defined with a certain degree of opportunism. Its definition often remains implicit, open to intuitive interpretation. (Among others Ansoff (1965) avoided any definition of strategy). Explicit definitions of strategy are nevertheless quite numerous. The content assigned to the concept varies from one author to another, but the essence of the many definitions converges in the concept of strategy as "the pattern in the stream of decisions and activities . . . (Mintzberg and McHugh, 1985, p. 6) . . . that characterizes the match an organization achieves with its environment . . . and that is determinant for the attainment of its goals . . ." (Hofer and Schendel, 1978, p. 25). The emphasis is on the pattern of activities which has an impact on the achievement of the organizational goals in relation to its environment.

Research on business strategy has been concerned primarily to understand what makes a business organization effective in its environment, and to explore the organizational processes required to enhance this effectiveness. It is usually assumed that the criterion of effectiveness in the case of business organizations is the accumulation of monetary wealth over time, achieved by way of exchange with other parties in the environment. The accumulation of resources is supposed to be the prerequisite for the survival of the organization. The dominant idea in the conceptual core of business strategy research has been partly derived from biology ("survival of the fittest"). The effectiveness of the organization, its potential for accumulating resources, is assumed to be a function of matching the characteristics of the environment with the capabilities of the organization. A positive balance in the exchange of resources with the environment is ensured by adapting to this environment. The idea of "fit" between the capabilities of the organization and the characteristics of the environment (in particular customers and competitors, referred to as the "market") is the central theme in the strategy management doctrine (Miles and Snow, 1984; Venkatraman and Camillus, 1984).

The fit with the environment is assumed to be good, if the organization outperforms other organizations in competing for the resources held by other entities in the environment. To outperform others is usually equated with offering "superior value" to one's counterparts in the exchange process (Porter, 1985, p. 3; Levitt, 1980). It is assumed that this "superior value" is based on overall efficiency in transforming inputs into outputs. This efficiency permits a company to "dominate" parts of its environment (Rhenman, 1973; Norman, 1977, p. 26).

Strategy management is seen as a process of adapting the pattern of activities performed by the organization to the external environmental conditions in which the organization operates. Managing strategy thus means managing the process whereby the pattern of activities to be performed by the organization is conceived (i.e. strategy formulation), and then creating the conditions necessary to ensure that these activities are carried out (i.e. strategy implementation). It is often stressed that, because the environment is always changing, this has to be a continuous process.

Three assumptions are generally made explicitly or implicitly about the nature of the process of adapting to the environmental conditions in the current strategy management doctrine.

First, the environment of an organization is faceless, atomistic and beyond the influence or control of the organization. Whatever happens to the task environment of the organization stems from forces outside the organization itself. Even it it is sometimes admitted that "political networking" with competitors, for example, may provide a way of exerting influence over some part of the environment, the basic assumption is still that the environment cannot be controlled. Consequently opportunities do exist in the environment, and they are there to be identified and exploited. They cannot be created or enacted; rather, the organization can exploit them by adapting itself to its environment. It is implied that a dividing-line exists between the organization and its environment. The environment exists, even without the organization.

Secondly, the strategy, the pattern of critical activities, of a business organization results from the deployment of resources controlled hierarchically (contractually) by the organization. Controlled resources are allocated in certain combinations, providing products/services to be exchanged with the environment. Further resources can be obtained by means of exchange with the environment, across the boundaries of the organization. In the supposedly competitive and "non-controllable" environment, the effectiveness or exchange potential of an organization will depend on its relative efficiency in combining its internal resources. Internal resources can be reallocated in order to adapt to environmental conditions, thus enhancing effectiveness.

Thirdly, environmental conditions change continuously, so that frequent if not continuous adaptation is required of the organization. There is a group of individuals (management) in the organization which is concerned by definition with managing organizational effectiveness. It is assumed that this group can and does interpret environmental conditions, after which it formulates and implements a future strategy. It decides and crafts the pattern of activities to be executed by the organization.

All three assumptions have been challenged, directly or indirectly by several streams of research, particularly in organization theory. Hannan and Freeman (1977) with their concept of the collective dependence of organizations, Pfeffer and Salancik (1978) who talk about the resource dependence of organizations, Weick (1969) who discusses the ex-post rationality of organizations, and Hall and Saias (1980) and Mintzberg (1987) who examine the nature of the strategy formulation process, are but a few examples of those who advocate the adoption of different assumptions regarding a number of issues.

In this paper we will examine in particular the position adopted by the proponents of the network model of the organization–environment interface. This proposition draws on the work of the organizational theorists referred to above, but it also constitutes a somewhat more elaborate set of propositions, particularly about the market behaviour of business organizations.

NETWORK MODEL OF ORGANIZATION–ENVIRONMENT INTERFACE

What is referred to below as the network model is the outcome of a fairly broad research programme dealing primarily with the functioning of business markets, which originated in the mid-1970s at the University of Uppsala. The research programme has spread to a few other research institutions, mainly in Europe. The programme can be described as a collection of studies with a largely common frame of reference (Hägg and Johanson, 1982; Hammarkvist et al., 1982; Mattsson, 1985; Kutschker, 1985; Ford et al., 1986; Turnbull and Valla, 1986; Thorelli, 1986; Håkansson, 1982, 1987, 1989).

The network model of the organization–environment interface stems originally from casual observations that business organizations often operate in environments which include only a limited number of identifiable organizational entities (actors). These entities are involved in continuous exchange relationships with the organization. In such cases each individual party exerts considerable influence on the organization. This situation is encountered most often by industrial companies operating in business markets which include a limited number of suppliers, competitors and customers. However, some more extensive empirical studies (Turnbull and Valla, 1986; Håkansson, 1989) suggest that this type of situation may be the rule rather than the exception for a wider population of business organizations in general. The propositions of the network model refer to situations and cases in which the environment of the organizations is of a concentrated and structured kind, i.e. it is constituted by a set of other active organizations.

When the entities constraining and impinging on the behaviour of the organization are few in number, they are usually treated as unique counterparts, i.e. each one is endowed with a distinct identity. As a result of an organization's interactions and exchange processes with any of these, relationships develop that link the resources and activities of one party with those of another. The relationships (linkages) are generally continuous over time, rather than being composed of discrete transactions. They are often complex, consisting of a web of interactive relations between individuals in both organizations.

Within the framework of such an interorganizational relationship, a complex set of interdependencies gradually evolves. Activities within one party are connected with activities carried out in the other. Activities are carried out by actors pursuing their own goals and possessing their own perceptions of the interacting party's activity pattern, among other things. Activities undertaken by the parties in a relationship cannot, therefore, be connected without the active and reciprocal involvement of both parties. The establishment and development of an interorganizational relationship requires a "mutual orientation" (Ford *et al.*, 1986).

Relating the activities of the two parties to one another entails adaptations and the establishment of routines on both sides. Given the distinctive nature of the parties, the interdependencies in the relationship become further strengthened. Through their relationship either party can gain access to the other's resources. To some degree actors can therefore mobilize and use resources controlled by other actors in the network. An organization's relationships with others represent the framework and form for the exchange process with other parties.

The interaction between the parties in a relationship entails more than just passive adaptation. While the two parties are interacting, their problems are confronted with solutions, their abilities with needs, etc. Reciprocal knowledge and capabilities are revealed and developed jointly and in mutual dependence by the two parties. Distinct capabilities are thus generated and have meaning in an organization only through the medium of other parties. They are unique to each party, since no two sets of related organizations are alike. In this sense the identity of an organization is created in interaction with its major counterparts.

When the environmental conditions of a business organization are of the kind described, when it is gravitating towards a set of other active organizations, then analogous environmental conditions can be assumed for the whole set of organizations with which the focal organization is interacting. The organization is then embedded in relationships with identifiable counterparts. This web of relationships can be called a network. One of the salient properties of such a network consists of the interdependencies between the different relationships (Cook and Emerson, 1978). These interdependencies exist as regards activities, resources and actors. The activities in two different relationships can complement each other, if they are part of the same activity chain. Or they may be in competition. Similarly resources used, accessed or exchanged in one relationship can complement or compete with those used, accessed or exchanged in another relationship in which the organization is involved. Actors can use the existence of complementarity or competitiveness in their relationships in different ways, as they interact with one another. This can create not only triangular relationships, but even "dramas" involving four, five, six, or more participating business organizations.

The performance and effectiveness of organizations operating in a network, by whatever criteria these are assessed, become dependent not only on how well the organization itself performs in interaction with its direct counterparts, but also on how these counterparts in turn manage their relationships with third parties. An organization's performance is therefore largely dependent on whom it interacts with.

Before we can summarize the propositions of the network model, we must mention the concept of the environment of the organization. What appears to give a business organization its identity and to define its field of operations in the network view, cannot be fruitfully covered by the concept of the "environment", or by the more circumscribed concept of the "relevant environment". The environment is not a meaningful concept in these situations; more meaningful is the set of related entities. Moreover, the (inter)dependence of an organization on other entities makes it difficult to disconnect the organization from its network, since a business organization without its interactive environment loses its identity. It therefore seems useful to adopt the concept of the "context" of an organization rather than its environment, when we want to refer to the entities that are related to the organization. The context is enacted, it is created by the organization itself, and in a sense it even constitutes the organization itself. The propositions of the network model can at this point be summarized as follows:

1. Business organizations often operate in a context in which their behaviour is conditioned by a limited number of counterparts, each of which is unique and engaged in pursuing its own goals.
2. In relation to these entities, an organization engages in continuous interactions that constitute a framework for exchange processes. Relationships make it possible to access and exploit the resources of other parties and to link the parties' activities together.
3. The distinctive capabilities of an organization are developed through its interactions in the relationships that it maintains with other parties. The identity of the organization is thus created through relations with others.
4. Since the other parties to the interaction also operate under similar conditions, an organization's performance is conditioned by the totality of the network as a context, i.e. even by interdependencies among third parties.

When and if organizations operate under the conditions described above, then acceptance of the propositions of the network model calls for a review of the assumptions underlying the business strategy management doctrine. We will undertake such a review in the following discussion. Our intention is to contribute to the development of a frame of reference for the strategy management doctrine, relevant to organizations operating under the kind of conditions for which the network model has proved its descriptive adequacy. We shall try to see how far the present frame of reference for business strategy can be enriched to become a more effective conceptual tool for intervention in the funtioning of an organization if and when the organization is operating under the circumstances assumed by the network model.

ORGANIZATIONAL BOUNDARIES

The definition of a "boundary", when applied to any social system, is naturally quite arbitrary (Hall and Fagen, 1956) and depends on the intentions and aims of the observer. When the perspective of management is adopted, as in the strategy management doctrine, the intention is to embrace within the boundaries of the organization those resources and activities that can be controlled and influenced by the organization, and to leave outside those that cannot be influenced. This control is assumed to be necessary in order to adapt and relate effectively to the environment. An organization's boundaries should thus be set as coterminous with the limits to its activity control: "the organization ends where its discretion ends and another begins" (Pfeffer and Salancik, 1978, p. 32).

The conventional view is that the boundaries are given by the hierarchical (proprietary or contract) control of resources (including individual actors). This view implies what can be referred to as a "membership criterion" for the definition of the boundaries of an organization. Such a criterion gives an apparently clear dividing-line between the organization and its environment, in effect between internal and external factors. Apart from the problem of the type of contractual arrangement that permits "hierarchical" control and discretion in the exercise of deliberate choice behaviour (Cheung, 1983), the issue that remains to be dealt with is whether such a view permits us to capture, within the boundaries of the organization, all the resources and activities that have a significant impact on its effectiveness. In a network perspective, this is hardly the case.

Where the network view of the organizational context holds, some of the organization's relationships with other organizations in the network constitute in themselves one of the most – if not the most – valuable resources that it possesses. Through these relationships with other parties, resources and activities are made available and can be mobilized and exploited by the organization in order to enhance its own performance. Access to the other party's resources – resources that complement those of the focal organization – constitutes an important asset (Fiocca and Snehota, 1986). According to a somewhat more extreme view of the assets of a business organization, it is claimed that the "invisible" or "intangible" assets assume a central role in organizational effectiveness, since they are the differentiating factor in performance that gives an organization its distinctive identity (Itami, 1987; Vicari, 1988). The invisible assets, consisting largely of knowledge and abilities, fame and reputation, are mainly created in external relationships. Furthermore they cannot be separated from these relationships.

Quite apart from the resource argument, another aspect emphasized in the network view of the organizational context has considerable bearing on the problem of boundary-setting, namely the interrelatedness that prevails in networks and the possible impact on the focal organization of relationships among third parties. The concept of interrelatedness is inherent in the network view. The magnitude of these effects on the behaviour of the organization has been stressed, for example, in some studies of technology development processes. The importance of resources and activities "external" to the traditional boundaries of the organization, and the interrelatedness with relationships to third parties, has been documented in studies that focus on the process of technology diffusion and technology development (von Hippel, 1982; Håkansson, 1987; Waluszewski, 1988; Imai, 1987) and in some of the research on growth patterns in new-venture organizations (Aldrich *et al.*, 1987; Lorenzoni and Ornati, 1988).

In view of the role of "external" resources and interdependencies stressed in the network view of business organizations, it becomes meaningless and conceptually impossible to disconnect the organization from its context. The organization appears without boundaries in as much as it is to a certain degree constituted by resources and activities controlled by other parties forming the network, and exists only in the perceptions of other parties. It develops its distinctive capabilities in relationships with others. The organization is constrained in the exercise of its discretion, as much as it constrains the discretion of those with whom it interacts. The organization exists and performs in a context rather than in an environment, in as much as it has a meaning and a role only in relation to a number of interrelated actors. This makes it difficult to define "where the discretion of an organization, and thus organization itself, ends and another begins".

In comparison with the conventional view of an organization's boundaries, this approach means on the one hand that some of the resources and activities traditionally considered "internal" can hardly be controlled and influenced by the organization, while a number of what have been considered "external" resources and activities do actually constitute an integral part of the organization itself and are subject to its influence and control. The "membership" criterion, while legally clear and important in determining the outcome of exchange, does not permit a focus on the variables determining an organization's effectiveness.

The purpose of setting the boundaries of an organization in the business strategy management doctrine is to focus on the variables which determine the effectiveness of the organization and which are also subject to the influence of the organization (that can be managed). In this management perspective it is essential to make the distinction between controllable and non-controllable variables. If this is to be done with a view to identifying the determinants of the organization's performance then the boundaries of an organization should be defined more broadly so as to include the critical connected activities and the resources that can be mobilized as a result of the ongoing network relationships – in other words, the context of the organization. How much of the context constitutes the organization depends of course on the degree of interdependence within the context. To assess the interdependencies we need to look a little more closely at the question of organizational effectiveness.

ORGANIZATIONAL EFFECTIVENESS

The issue of organizational effectiveness is central to the whole business strategy management doctrine. The content of a strategy, the activity patterns that affect the achievement of goals, can only be defined by reference to the factors that determine the organization's effectiveness. Assuming that survival is the overriding goal of the organization, which in the case of a business organization is based on the accumulation of monetary wealth through exchange, the effectiveness of the business organization is determined by its "bargaining position". An organization's bargaining position is "the ability of the organization to exploit its environment in the acquisition of scarce and valuable resources" (Yuchtman and Seashore, 1967, p. 898). The effectiveness of a business organization is thus given by its capacity to acquire resources through exchange with other parties in its context.

After relating effectiveness to "bargaining position" we have to ask ourselves how a certain bargaining position is reached by an organization and what are the determinants of this position. In organizational theory, the bargaining position is often interpreted in terms of organizational power, in the sense of a capacity to influence the behaviour of related actors. Few issues have been discussed with as much heat and as little result as the issue of interorganizational power. Hoping to avoid entanglement in the intricacies of this concept that have little bearing on our subject, we will resort to a slightly different view of the bargaining position.

In order to elaborate the idea of the bargaining position, it seems necessary to examine the nature of exchange transactions. A few disciplines such as economics, social anthropology and marketing have been concerned with this topic. The common view of the nature of exchange transactions is that the object of any exchange between two parties is some form of activity or performance, e.g. products and goods, services, money. The purpose of exchange is the acquisition of "performance" regardless of the form in which it is represented. What is acquired by the exchange is not goods or services or money, but what these things can do for the party engaged in the exchange (Levitt, 1980; Belshaw, 1965). Even when the purpose appears to be the acquisition of resources, the underlying rationale is the acquisition of activities (utility or performance). The outcome of an exchange process is thus determined by what the objects of the exchange can accomplish for the exchanging parties; it is therefore individual and subjective. (It should be noted that this view contains some elements of the notion of "distinct counterparts" rather than generic environment or market.

The traditional view of economists and organizational analysts is that an organization's capacity to reach a favourable bargaining position, a position that permits a positive balance in exchange with the environment, depends mainly on the organization's efficiency in transforming input resources into output. It is said to be so, since in a certain situation the expected value of the organization's output (product, service, etc.) is assumed to be the same for all kinds of different counterparties. What can be obtained through exchange is, therefore, largely outside the control of the individual organizational unit. The unit can only exercise a certain amount of control over the cost side of the transformation. The bargaining position is thus assumed to be dependent on the arrangement of resources and activities internal to the firm (within the narrow boundaries). The fit of the activities of the organization with the characteristics of the environment is achieved by rearranging the activities and resources internal to the organization. It is conceded, mainly by those who adopt the management perspective and in particular by marketing theorists, that to a certain degree organizations can choose their environments, especially their customers, thus improving their bargaining position (Abel and Hammond, 1979). But it is still assumed that the move is achieved autonomously and unilaterally by the organization by making adjustments in its internal resources. The bargaining position of the organization is therefore conceived as determined by the deployment of the organization's own assets.

Two concepts that appear in the network model – "network position" and "strategic identity" (Johanson and Mattsson, 1985; Håkansson and Johanson, 1988) – could be useful to anyone exploring the issue of the bargaining position and the effectiveness of the organization. Both concepts have been used to stress some of the characteristics of the exchange processes in the network setting. To a party engaged in a transaction relationship with an organization, the expected value of the exchange is given by the amount of resources that can be accessed and the activities which the organization can perform for the focal party within the relationship. To the individual party the value of the performance available through the relationship is a function of the position that the organization assumes in that party's network. This "microposition" (Johanson and Mattsson, 1985) is the bargaining position of the organization *vis-à-vis* one specific counterpart. It depends on the efficiency of the resource deployment of the organization, and also on the effectiveness of the organization in relating to other entities constituting the network. It reflects the perceived potential of the organization to constitute a link with parts of the network that the focal party cannot access or relate to, or at least not with reasonable efficiency.

The composite of the micropositions – the macroposition – is qualitatively different. It reflects the role of the organization in its own network. Again, it is dependent on the capacity of the organization to constitute a link with resources and activities among the parties making up the network. It is therefore given partly by what is done within the organization itself and partly by what the organization does in relationships with others.

The network position, on the other hand, is a relative concept. Since no two parties' positions are alike, the network position means different things to different parties related to the focal organization. Moreover, the performance of an organization in a relationship is perceived and evaluated by another party on the basis of previous experience and present expectations. It is thus enacted rather than given by the amount and type of resources directly controlled. It exists only if perceived and recognized by the parties in the context. Recognition is dependent on the outcome of the interaction processes in an organization's relationships. The concept of "strategic identity" (Håkansson and Johanson, 1988) is thus included in the network model. Such a view seems to provide a slightly different picture of the means for achieving fit with the context. It suggests that the fit is obtained largely by establishing and maintaining relationships with other parties. For a relationship to come into existence requires that some action at least is taken by the other party. The action, or reaction, of the other party can only be triggered by the perceived exchange potential of the focal actor. The perception of exchange potential between the actors is largely determined by social interaction, and is therefore enacted rather than predetermined and given.

This leads us to regard the effectiveness of the organization as given, not by the organization's "adapting" to the environment but by its "relating" to the context. These "relating" activities include the quasi-integration of activities; the connection of resources in order to branch out into several actor levels, both to gain influence over others and to become dependent on others; and the influencing of one's own and other parties' perceptions of important dimensions in the context. While "adapting" necessarily leads to a focus on the internal processes of the organization, "relating" induces a shift in focus to its context. It is through its relationships with others that the distinctive capabilities of an organization are acquired and developed. It is therefore the activities taking place between the organization and the other parties, rather than activities within the organization itself, which are the determinants of the bargaining position and of the overall effectiveness of the organization in achieving its goals.

The concept of strategy, the pattern of activities determining effectiveness, thus acquires a different content from the one assumed in the prevailing strategy doctrine. Activities connected with positioning in the network and performed within the framework of external relationships – i.e. the process of relating – assume the primary role. The concepts of fit and misfit, which refer to states only, thus lose a great deal of their analytical power.

Such a view of strategy content has a significant bearing on the issue of management strategy, or the management of organizational effectiveness. We will now explore this further below.

MANAGING THE EFFECTIVENESS OF AN ORGANIZATION

The traditional view of how the effectiveness of an organization is managed seems to concentrate mainly on *what* is to be managed and *how* it is to be done, and to a lesser degree on *who* does it. What is to be managed in order to enhance the effectiveness is, of course, related to the concept of effectiveness itself. Consequently the allocation of the organization's resources and its efficiency in transforming inputs into outputs are traditionally considered key issues. Positioning *vis-à-vis* the environment is said to be achieved by the type of output generated. The adaptation of output and internal efficiency are therefore the means to achieving a fit with the environment.

How is this done? Treatment of this issue has often been vague, except for the normative recommendations of the strictly managerial approach. The prevailing interpretation of the process is that strategy is first conceived and formulated on a basis of an assessment of the current and projected state of the environment and of the organizational resources. The assessment permits the identification of the adaptations that will be required of the organization, and which will subsequently be implemented (see among others Hofer and Schendel, 1978; Galbraith and Nathanielson, 1978). This process is continuous, or at least frequently recurring. It can be more or less explicit and formal, depending on the complexity and culture of the organization and the rate of change in its environment.

This view of the process of managing effectiveness could be called "the planning approach". It implies that decisions are taken after the scanning of environmental conditions, changes and opportunities; a plan of action is then formulated and implemented. It assumes that the management of the pattern of activities involves drafting a master plan of the pattern, which is then followed. Getting the organization to follow the plan may cause problems, but these can be solved by clear target setting, incentives and control. This view of the strategy management process has been challenged from quite different standpoints (Weick, 1969; Peters and Waterman, 1982; Kagono *et al.*, 1985). Its critics have invoked the bounded rationality of complex organizations in a complex and dynamic environment as their main objection.

When it comes to the question of who manages organizational effectiveness, the various opinions are delivered in disguise, especially and somewhat surprisingly in organizational theory. A clearcut but less convincing position has been offered elsewhere. It is generally suggested, sometimes implicitly, that strategy formulation and implementation are the concern of a group of individuals in the organization, namely management, whose primary function is to interpret the environment, to formulate strategy, and to make the adaptations required of the organization in order to pursue this strategy.

The network model seems to generate another approach to the question of effectiveness management in organizations. It was claimed above that relating to the context is the central issue of the strategy. Relating to the context, that is to say creating a distinctive identity, is something that has to be managed. Given the relativity of the context concept, the context itself is conceived not as given beforehand or predetermined, but as enacted: it cannot be assessed. Strategic identity, the basis of effectiveness, is achieved by the interaction behaviour of individuals in relationships. Interaction is the stream of events that ultimately determines effectiveness and constitutes strategy. Thus the effectiveness of an organization – its strategy – is based on interactive behaviour. How can interactive behaviour be directed and managed?

Within a relationship interaction takes place between actors who are pursuing their own goals and acting purposefully. In such a setting, reacting to other actors' actions can be more important than acting itself. And the reactive behaviour in the process of interaction is something that can hardly be planned. Rather, the behaviour of actors in these circumstances can only be guided by norms and values based on past experience, possibly in the form of organizational routines (Nelson and Winter, 1982, p. 124). The pattern of activities that determines effectiveness can thus be directed and managed by values and norms of behaviour, not by prescriptions about the pattern.

This brings us back to the concept of context. The context of an organization is a social symbolic reality in which an organization chooses to exist, and does so by "framing" it (Berg, 1985). The framing of a context, i.e. assuming its structural and dynamic properties, is the basis of any attempt to create an identity for an organization and to position it in the context. The framing of a context can only be achieved by interpreting and rationalizing past experience. This ex-post rationalization constitutes the organization's learning which, when formulated into norms and routines, guides the behaviour of the different actors in the organization (March and Olsen, 1976; Weick, 1969; Mintzberg, 1987; Kinch, 1988). Organizational effectiveness is thus managed by framing the context rather than by designing (planning) a future pattern of activities.

The framing of a context at the organizational level is a social process. It is carried out by individuals but is coded and stored collectively. The individuals who implement the socialization of the context-framing are thus those who *de facto* manage the effectiveness and the strategy of the organization. They may not necessarily be identical with those who plan and design the pattern of activities, but it is the management of the organization which is accountable for the results achieved through exchange.

CONCLUDING REMARKS

Throughout the above discussion we have been addressing one broad issue: what contribution can be made to the conceptual frame of reference of the business strategy doctrine on a basis of the insights gained by adopting a network view of business organization. A few areas in which the business strategy doctrine could be developed in the case of organizations operating under "network conditions" have been identified and discussed.

We have touched upon the problems of defining the boundaries of an organization, of assessing organizational effectiveness and finally of managing organizational effectiveness. We have claimed that when a network view is adopted some not inconsiderable changes are required in all the three areas with respect to the basic assumptions of the business strategy model. All our arguments stem from a basic proposition about the situations described by the network model: continuous interaction with other parties constituting the context with which the organization interacts, endows the organization with meaning and a role. When this proposition applies, any attempt to manage the behaviour of the organization will require a shift in focus away from the way the organization allocates and structures its internal resources and towards the way it relates its own activities and resources to those of the other parties that constitute its context. Such a shift in focus entails a somewhat different view of the meaning of organizational effectiveness: what does it depend on and how can it be managed?

By applying the network concept to the analysis of the behaviour of the business organization, we open up another broader issue that we have not addressed here, concerning the assumptions that are made about the very scope of the concept of the business organization. We have been referring throughout to the concept of the business organization as it is used in the literature of strategy management, with its roots in the microeconomic theory of the firm. The firm or organization is viewed primarily as a production function, which is thus concerned mainly with the control and allocation of internal resources according to the criterion of efficiency. This view has also been institutionalized in the legal system, for example, in terms of laws regarding ownership (i.e. the legal boundary of the company), accounting, tax regulations, and so on. It has led to a fairly narrow perspective on the basic issues addressed by the strategy management doctrine. There have been other attempts to broaden and adjust this perspective apart from our own, but hardly any attempts to change it radically.

When we look back over the implications of the network model we get the impression that if the network view is adopted, it will constitute a challenge to the prevailing view of the business organization as a production function. The network model leads to quite a different view of the range and role of the business organization. The emphasis on the linking of activities and resources within a network as a primary task of the business organization seems to suggest that enterprise should be conceived as a transaction function rather than a production function. Such a concept of enterprise could lead naturally to a shift in focus, away from the control of resources towards the integration of resources, and away from the management of acting towards the management of reacting. Although we feel that such a new concept of enterprise is called for, it still seems to be pretty far off.

REFERENCES

Abel, D. F. and Hammond, J. S. *Strategic Market Planning*. Prentice Hall, Englewood Cliffs, NJ (1979).

Aldrich, H., Rosen, B. and Woodward, W. A social role perspective of entrepreneurship, Working paper. UNC School of Business Administration (1987).

Ansoff, I. H. *Corporate Strategy*. McGraw-Hill; New York (1965).

Belshaw, C. S. *Traditional Exchange and Modern Markets*. Prentice Hall, Englewood Cliffs, NJ (1965).

Berg, P. O. Organization change as a symbolic transformation process. In P. J. Frost *et al.* (eds), *Organization Culture*. Sage, New York (1985).

Buzzel, R. D. and Gale, B. T. *The PIMS Principles*. The Free Press, Macmillan, New York (1987).

Chandler, A. D., Jr. *Strategy and Structure*. MIT Press, Cambridge, MA (1962).

Cheung, S. N. C. The contractual nature of the firm. *Journal of Law and Economics*, April, 2–21 (1983).

Cook, K. S. and Emerson, R. M. Power, equity and commitment in exchange networks. *American Sociological Review*, 721–39 (1978).

Fiocca, R. and Snehota, I. Marketing e alta tecnologia. *Sviluppo e Organizzazione*, 98, 24–31 (1986).

Ford, D. I., Håkansson, H. and Johanson, J. How do companies interact? *Industrial Marketing and Purchasing*, 1, 26–41 (1986).

Galbraith, J. R. and Nathanielson, D. A. *Strategy Implementation, The Role of Structure and Process*. West Publishing, St. Paul, MN (1978).

Hägg, I. and Johanson, J. (eds), *Företag i nätverk – ny syn på konkurrenskraft* (Firms in Networks – A New Perspective of Competitive Power), SNS, Stockholm (1982).

Håkansson, H. (ed.) *International Marketing and Purchasing of Industrial Goods. An Interaction Approach*, John Wiley, Chichester (1982).

Håkansson, H. (ed.) *Industrial Technological Development. A Network Approach*. Croom Helm, London (1987).

Håkansson, H. *Corporate Technological Behaviour. Cooperation and Networks*. Routledge, London (1989).

Håkansson, H. and Johanson, J. Formal and informal cooperation strategies in international industrial networks. In F. J. Contractor and P. Lorange (eds), *Cooperative Strategies in International Business*. Lexington Books, MA (1988).

Hall, A. D. and Fagen, R. E. Definition of system. *General Systems: The Yearbook of the Society for the Advancement of General Systems Theory*. (1956), pp. 18–28.

Hall, D. J. and Saias, M. A. Strategy follows structure. *Strategic Management Journal*, 149–63 (1980).

Hammarkvist, K.-O. Håkansson, H. and Mattsson, L-G. *Marknadsföring för konkurrenskraft* (Marketing for Competitive Power). Liber, Malmö (1982).

Hannan, M. T. and Freeman, J. The population ecology of organizations. *American Journal of Sociology*, 929–65 (1977).

Henderson, B. D. *Hendersson on Corporate Strategy*. Boston Consulting Group Inc. Abt Books, Cambridge, MA (1979).

Hofer, C. W. and Schendel, D. *Strategy Formulation, Analytical Concepts*. West Publishing, St. Paul, MN (1978).

Imai, K. Network industrial organization in Japan. Working paper prepared for the workshop on "New Issues in Industrial Economics" at Case Western Reserve University, Cleveland. 7–10 June 1987.

Itami, H. *Mobilizing Invisible Assets*. Harvard University Press, Boston, MA (1987).

Johanson, J. and Mattsson, L.-G. Marketing investments and market investments in industrial networks. *International Journal of Research in Marketing*, 185–95 (1985).

Kagono, T., Nonaka, K., Sakakibara, K. and Okumura, A. *Strategic vs Evolutionary Management: A U.S.-Japan Comparison of Strategy and Organization*. North Holland, Amsterdam (1985).

Kinch, N. Strategic illusion as a management strategy. Working Paper. Dept of Business Administration, University of Uppsala (1988/2).

Kutschker, M. The multi-organizational interaction approach to industrial marketing. *Journal of Business Research*, 383–403 (1985).

Levitt, T. Marketing success through differentiation – of anything. *Harvard Business Review*, January/February (1980).

Lorenzoni, G. and Ornati, O. A. Constellations of firms and new ventures. *Journal of Business Venturing*, 41–57 (1988).

March, J. G. and Olsen, J. P. *Ambiguity and Choice in Organizations*. Universitetsforlaget, Bergen, Norway (1976).

Mattsson, L.-G. An application of a network approach to marketing. Defining and changing market positions. In J. Dholakia and J. Arndt (eds), *Alternative Paradigms for Widening Marketing Theory*. JAI Press, Greenwich, CT (1985).

Miles, R. E. and Snow, C. C. Fit, failure and the hall of fame. *California Management Review*, **3** (Spring), 10–28 (1984).

Mintzberg, H. Crafting strategy. *Harvard Business Review*, July/August, 66–75 (1987).

Mintzberg, H. and McHugh, A. Strategic formulation in an adhocracy. *Administrative Science Quarterly*, 160–97 (1985).

Nelson, R. R. and Winter, S. G. *Evolutionary Theory of Economic Change*. Harvard University Press, Cambridge, MA (1982).

Norman, R. *Management for Growth*. John Wiley, Chichester (1977).

Ohmae, K. *The Mind of the Strategist*. McGraw-Hill, New York (1982).

Pennings, J. M. (ed.) *Organizational Strategy and Change*. Jossey-Bass, San Francisco (1985).

Peters, T. J. and Waterman, R. H. *In Search of Excellence*. Harper and Row, New York (1982).

Pfeffer, J. Bringing the environment back in the social context of business strategy. In D. Teece (ed.), *The Competitive Challenge. Strategies for Industrial Innovation and Renewal*. Ballinger, Cambridge, MA (1987).

Pfeffer, J. and Salancik, G. R. *The External Control of Organizations. A Resource Dependence Perspective*. Harper Row, New York (1978).

Porter, M. E. *Competitive Strategy*. Free Press, Macmillan, New York (1980).

Porter, M. E. *Competitive Advantage*. Free Press, Macmillan, New York (1985).

Rhenman, E. *Organization Theory for Long Range Planning*. Wiley, London (1973).

Thorelli, H. B. Networks: between markets and hierarchies. *Strategic Management Journal*, 37–51 (1986).

Turnbull, P. and Valla, J. P. (eds), *Strategies for International Industrial Marketing*. Croom Helm, London (1986).

Venkatraman, N. and Camillus, J. C. Exploring the concept of "fit" in strategic management, *Academy of Management Review*, **3**, 513–25 (1984).

Vicari, S. Risorse immateriali e comportanto incrementale. Working Paper no. 1 88. SDA Bocconi, Milan (1988).

von Hippel, E. Appropriability of innovation benefit as a predictor of the source of innovation, *Research Policy*, **2**, 95–115 (1982).

Waluszewski, A. CTMP-fallet. Processutveckling inom skogsindustrin (The CTMP-case. Process Development within the Forest Industry). Working Paper. Dept of Business Administration, University of Uppsala (1988).

Weick, K. E. *The Social Psychology of Organizing*. Addison Wesley, Reading, MA (1969) (2nd edn, 1979).

Yuchtman, E. and Seashore, S. E. A system resource approach to organizational effectiveness, *American Sociological Review*, 891–903 (1967).

3.4

Analysing business relationships

Håkan Håkansson and Ivan Snehota

Faced with the empirical evidence of long-lasting relationships in business, the scholars of management have reacted in rather different ways. At first the phenomenon was largely ignored. It is only during the last decade or so it has received some attention from researchers (e.g. Arndt, 1979; Håkansson, 1982; Astley, 1984). More recently we have witnessed an upsurge in interest for business relationships, especially among academics in the US (e.g. Webster, 1992; Miles and Snow, 1992; Nohria and Eccles, 1992; Alter and Hage, 1993; Achrol, 1991). Some have argued that what we labelled as business relationships is a relatively new phenomenon while earlier business was conducted much more on an arm's-length basis. Others, often practitioners and those studying the so-called business markets, have claimed that relationships have always been an important part of the business landscape and that today we are simply becoming more aware and are telling the practitioners to do what they have been trying to do for many years.

Indeed, business relationships do not easily find a convincing explanation in the traditional, transaction-focused framework of economics that inspires management studies. It requires redrawing the conceptual framework, which always is difficult and risky. The purpose of developing an analytical framework with respect to a phenomenon is to provide guidance for acting on it. In management studies an analytical framework is supposed to help identify the problems to be handled, to structure the situation assessment in order to identify the intervening variables, and to identify alternative courses of action. To make a step in that direction we need first to understand how relationships between companies develop and what forces they are subject to. Relationships are a complex phenomenon.

When we propose a conceptual framework we have to single out the variables that are critical in the explanation of the phenomenon. We have to focus on some aspects and to exclude many others. The value of a theory for the praxis lies in that it dismisses a number of possible explanatory variables. A broad descriptive framework of the substance and functions of business relationships will be outlined in this chapter. A few dimensions that can be used to assess and analyse business relationships will be proposed. The choice of these is always a critical step as it determines what will be observed and put in focus in the further analysis.

THE CONCEPT OF RELATIONSHIP

While intuitively appealing, the notion of "relationship" may be difficult to grasp. What makes dealings between two companies in a market become a relationship? It is not easy to define what a relationship is. Tentatively we can say that a relationship is mutually oriented interaction between two reciprocally committed parties. One reason why we choose the notion of relationship in analysis of intercompany interaction is that it evokes the concepts of mutual orientation and commitment over time. Mutual orientation and commitment are common in interactions between companies, if we judge from the empirical studies discussed earlier. Another reason is the high degree of interdependency between business organizations, as their very existence depends on exchange with other economic subjects. A relationship often arises between two parties because of the interdependence of outcomes, even if it can arise for other reasons. As it entails mutual commitment over time a relationship creates interdependence which is both positive and negative for the parties involved. A relationship develops over time as a chain of interaction episodes – a sequence of acts and counteracts. It has a history and a future. In this way a relationship creates interdependence as much as it is a way to handle interdependence.

We believe that exchange interaction between companies in industrial markets can be fruitfully described in terms of relationships essentially for two reasons: one is that actors themselves tend to see their interactions as relationships, another is that the interaction between companies over time creates the type of quasi-organization that can be labelled a relationship (Blois, 1972).

The research findings discussed in chapter 1 indicate that mutual orientation and commitment over time, as well as interdependence, are typical of the exchange interaction between companies in industrial markets. The interaction between, for example, suppliers and industrial customers appears as a series of acts and counteracts creating interdependencies and affecting their behaviours. Mutual commitment and interdependence of companies in the industrial market constrains their behaviour as much as it creates opportunities; relationships are mutually demanding besides being mutually rewarding. Time has to be explicitly considered in order to identify the forces shaping the behaviour. The combination of a process over time and the interdependencies make the relationships produce something unique by interlocking activities and resources of the two companies. Relationships produce something that neither of the two can produce in isolation and something that cannot easily be duplicated. That is why we choose to conceive the interaction between businesses in industrial markets as relationships. This is what is at the core of the "relationship" view of business markets.

The empirical research on business relationship discussed earlier shows that, despite certain similarities, there is a large variation between different relationships. Relationships always have some unique features. We observed earlier that no two relationships are alike. Still, there is a certain pattern in the effects they produce. There are two dimensions that appear to capture the effects and which can be used to categorize business relationships: one regards who is affected by the relationships, the other what is affected. We will call the former the function and the latter the substance of business relationships.

What makes the relationship concept slippery is that it cannot be conceived as "just a relationship". A relationship is a result of an interaction process where connections have been developed between two parties that produce a mutual orientation and commitment. A relationship is thus not a given, but a variable that can take on different values. That is why we have to go beyond the consideration that relationships exist between companies and are important. We need to look at the elements being connected in a relationship and the effects the connections produce. This is the reason for choosing to describe business relationships in the two dimensions of substance and function.

The first dimension regards what the relationship affects on the two sides – the "substance" of a business relationship. Three different layers of substance can be identified in a business relationship. First, there is an activity layer. A relationship is built up of activities that connect, more or less closely, various internal activities of the two parties. A relationship links activities. Clearly the activity links affect the outcomes of the relationship for the parties. Second, there is a resource layer. As a relationship develops, it can connect various resource elements needed and controlled by two companies. A relationship can tie together resources. Relationships consist then to various degrees of resource ties. As a relationship makes various resource elements accessible for the parties it also constitutes a resource that can be used and exploited. Third, there is an actor layer. As a business relationship develops, actors become connected. Bonds between actors are established which affect how the actors perceive, evaluate and treat each other.

The three layers of substance can be taken as three different effect parameters that are determinants of the values involved in a relationship and thus of its outcome. They add up to a relationship. A relationship between two companies can be characterized by the relative importance of the three layers. The more effects there are in the three layers in a relationship, the "thicker" and the more complex it will be. Major relationships between companies tend to have complex substance. Still, there is a large variety in their substance, dependent on the existence, type and strength of the activity links, resource ties and actor bonds.

In sum, a relationship between two companies has a profile in terms of activity links, resource ties and actor bonds:

- *Activity links* regard technical, administrative, commercial and other activities of a company that can be connected in different ways to those of another company as a relationship develops.
- *Resource ties* connect various resource elements (technological, material, knowledge resources and other intangibles) of two companies. Resource ties result from how the relationship has developed and represents in itself a resource for a company.
- *Actor bonds* connect actors and influence how the two actors perceive each other and form their identities in relation to each other. Bonds become established in interaction and reflect the interaction process.

The existing activity links, resource ties and actor bonds can be used to characterize the nature of a relationship that has developed between two companies. If we are to assess, predict or explain the importance and role of a relationship, they need to be examined.

The second dimension regards the effects a relationship has for different actors – what we have chosen to call the "functions" of business relationship. A relationship between two companies has different functions because it affects and is affected by different parties and other relationships.

We believe three different functions can be distinguished. First, a relationship has effects for the dyad in itself, i.e. the conjunction of two actors. A relationship is a place where some kind of interaction takes place, and something is produced; where activity links, resource ties and actor bonds are established. This kind of effect can be more or less pronounced in a relationship between two companies. Second, a relationship has a function for each of the two companies; it is likely to affect them in different ways and is affected by them. A relationship is one of the resources the company can exploit and use in combination with other resources (other relationships) available to the company. What is produced in a relationship can be used for different purposes and with different effects by either of the two companies. Third, as relationships are connected, what is produced in a relationship can have effects on other relationships and thus on other companies than those directly involved. A certain relationship is also subject to effects from other relationships and actors as it is an element of the larger structure and has a function in it. All the three types of effect originate and are intervening in business relationships.

Thus, if we are to find out what effects a relationship has and is subject to we have to take into account three different functions:

- *Function for the dyad* This originates in the conjunction of the two companies; their activities, resources and actors. Activity links, resource ties and actor bonds in a relationship integrate various elements and thereby some unique outcomes and effects are produced.
- *Function for the individual company* A relationship has effects on each of the companies, on what it can do internally and in other relationships. These depend on how what is produced in the dyad can be connected to other internal elements of the company and its other relationships.
- *Function for third parties* Being a building element in the larger network structure, what is produced in a relationship can affect and is affected by other relationships that involve other parties. The effects on third parties and from third parties and their relationships on the relationship in any of the three layers of substance depend on how tight the connectedness of relationships is in the overall network.

The three functions are closely interwoven but they can be more to less pronounced in a certain relationship. However, whenever analysing a relationship between two companies and its development potential, all three functions concur and therefore deserve attention.

We have examined in this section the premise that intercompany interaction can be conceived in terms of relationships as they show the traits of mutual orientation and commitment. We believe it is fruitful to consider intercompany interaction as relationships, but have argued that in doing so we need to go beyond and look into the substance and functions of the relationships. The argument we used is that if we are to use "relationship" as an analytical concept we need to find the underlying generative structures of relationships. In order to capture the variety of business relationships we proposed two dimensions: the substance and function. We posited that the substance of a business relationship becomes manifest in activity links, resource ties and actor bonds that arise as two companies become connected. The functions of a relationship can be conceived in terms of the effects a relationship between two companies produces for the dyad, for each of the involved parties and for third parties.

THE SUBSTANCE OF BUSINESS RELATIONSHIPS

We have observed that the substance of the relationships between companies in business markets can have facets and layers that vary with respect to the kind of effects they produce. In this section we will discuss more extensively the three earlier identified layers of activities, resources and actors. For the sake of simplicity we will start by treating the three separately, although in practice they are very closely related.

Activity links

A relationship between two companies may affect the way the two companies perform their activities, that is, their activity structure. Compared to individuals, companies are much more complex as to the variety and volume of activities performed. Thousands of different activities are performed and coordinated within a company. Every company thus takes the (often complex) form of a coordinated activity structure. When two companies build up a relationship, certain of their different technical, administrative or commercial activities can become linked to each other. A business relationship grows as a flow of exchange episodes in which some activities are undertaken by either of the companies. These activities in a relationship link a number of other activities in the two companies. The internal activity structures in either of the two companies may need to be adapted. Also in other directions the activity links are important; as the activity structures of the two companies change over time the interaction activities in a relationship may need to be modified and adjusted. The linking of activities reflects the need for coordination and will affect how and when the various activities are carried out. That, in turn, will have consequences for both the costs and effectiveness of the activities.

Activity links have to reflect not only sequential but also horizontal (parallel) interdependencies of activities. Parallel activities are linked, for example, when a buying company tries to influence suppliers delivering complementary products to adapt to each other. The needs of parallel coordination and thus parallel activity links are particularly strong in certain industries such as, for example, construction or investment equipment businesses, where unit or small batch technologies prevail. Sequential activity links seem critical in industries where process technology is dominant. Both types of links are common in many other industries with large-scale manufacturing.

Linking activities can be regarded as a way to create a unique performance. By linking the activities of a company with those of its counterparts the company's performance is affected because of the effects either on its own activity structure or on the activity structure of the counterpart. Activity links are a factor in the productivity of the companies involved. They also affect, however, the productivity in the whole network.

As both companies have other relationships in which activity links can be important, an activity link in a relationship "links other links" in the activity pattern. A business relationship is thus a link in what might be conceived as an activity chain in which activities of several companies in a

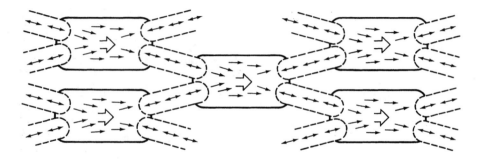

Figure 1 Activity structures, links and pattern over five companies.

sequence are linked to each other (as exemplified in Figure 1). Activities of a sub-supplier can affect those of a supplier which will in turn have effects on those of a buying company which in turn is reflected in those of its customers. These activity chains are quite robust in many industries, as for example in the automotive industry where the buying departments can be involved down to the third-tier level in the supplier network. In these industries the effects of change in an activity link may be very large. In other industries the sequential interdependence of activities tends to be weaker.

As the activity structures of companies become linked and coordinated through and by activity links in relationships, a complex activity pattern emerges in which different companies carry out different parts. Developing new relationships and activity linkages changes the overall pattern. Conversely, changes elsewhere in the activity pattern affect the activity links between two companies. This effect is palpable when new technological paradigms are being accepted by at least a subset of the network of which the two companies are part.

The wider activity pattern of which the company with its relationships is a part is often difficult to map as the activity links are mostly known only to those directly involved. This may be a problem for an outsider or newcomer who, in order to be accepted, has to find out what this pattern looks like and what interdependencies exist between various activities.

The activity aspect is present in all business relationships, but its importance can vary both with the ambitions that the two companies have in the relationship and with the complexity of their own activity structures. Companies are often involved in relationships with others where a substantial portion of the activities (in terms of volumes, frequencies, etc.) is performed and thus holds the key to the total costs and performance of the company. The flexibility of the pattern is very much dependent on the way the company has linked up with different counterparts. Even though the activity links are intangible, their effect on business relationships is often clearly manifest. If properly handled, they can be exploited by some companies for their own advantage.

In order to describe, explain or predict the effects of a relationship and how it is likely to develop, the assessment of activity links is an important starting point. The type and the strength of activity links are among the critical dimensions in our conceptual framework.

Resource ties

A relationship between two companies has effects on the way the companies are utilizing resources. Within a relationship different resource elements of the two actors can be tied together. A business enterprise consists of an assortment of different resources – manpower, equipment, plant, knowledge, image and financial means – that sustain its activities. Industrial companies in particular are as a rule large and complex resource units. In a relationship between two companies some of the resources needed for their activities can be accessed and acquired. The resources sought by the parties respectively are of different types. Expectations, of either party, to get access

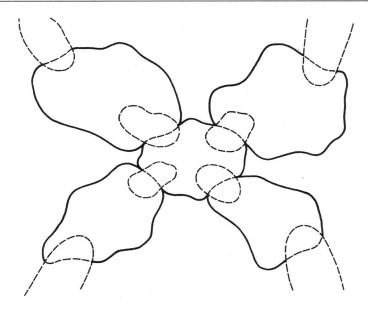

Figure 2 Resource ties, resource collections and resource constellation over five companies.

to various types of resources are a common ingredient of a business relationship. Apart from the tangible resources in the form of products, various intangible, often vaguely defined, resources such as technical, commercial or administrative know-how can be of interest.

Relationships between companies are, however, not just a way to acquire and access resources. In a relationship some of the resources of the two companies are brought together, confronted and combined. The interface between the resources of the two companies, over time, can become both broad and deep; it can embrace different types of resources and activate these to various degrees. The effect on the resources will be that they become specifically oriented towards each other, that is, various resource ties will emerge. The resources of the two companies will be tied together. New resource combinations are thus likely to arise as a relationship develops. As different elements of the two companies, tangible as well as intangible, become integrated they constitute resources of new quality. As relationships are valuable bridges to access resources, they can also be regarded in themselves as resources. A relationship is a resource which ties together various resource elements. The process required to develop a business relationship has some characteristics that make it similar to an investment process. It usually is costly, and the costs precede the future benefits; when a relationship is developed it becomes an asset that must be taken care of and utilized in an efficient way.

On the whole the availability of resources provides opportunities and constraints on the activities that can be undertaken by a company. The relationships that a company develops to others are important for the collection of resources available, which affects what the individual company can do. They make it possible to mobilize and access the resources of others for a company's own purpose and advantage.

There are some resource ties among most of the interacting actors (resource providers), within a certain context. The result is a kind of aggregated resource structure – a resource constellation. In such a structure resource ties are but one of the structural elements – a piece of resource in a larger resource constellation. Resource ties in a relationship are an element of the aggregated structure. They can thus become both a valuable asset and a constraint for other third companies when different resources of the resource constellation can be connected. The extent and type of resource ties in a relationship can vary, and because of the economic consequences on productivity and innovation are the second central dimension in a relationship analysis.

Actor bonds

A relationship between two companies affects the two units in a way similar to that between two persons. Bonds between two actors may alter their way of seeing and interpreting situations, as well as their identities both in relation to each other and to others. Being seen as a "close friend" to a company known as advanced or powerful helps in other relationships. The perceived identity thus affects the possibilities to act. There are some specific problems with business relationships between collective actors as companies, as the interpersonal relationships in their organizations do not sum up in a simple linear way.

Bonds arise in a relationship between two companies as they direct a certain amount of attention and interest towards each other – they become mutually committed. To become mutually committed amounts to giving and being given some priority. Giving priority is closely interwoven with a building up of identity. Actor bonds have an effect on what the parties know about each other and what they can exchange. Identities in relation to each other but also to some third parties might change. Every act and counter-act in a relationship is based on an assumed identity by the counterpart. The assumed and created identities reflect actors' bonds, giving rise to or ending certain relationships, or meaning that they are never even attempted.

There are different clues to the assumed identity of a company; some stem from the direct past interaction experience, others from what is known, or believed to be known, about the counterparts. The process of shaping identities in a relationship is close to that of learning. Learning (and "teaching") is central within relationships. The interdependencies of outcomes for the parties to a relationship in a specific situation are not always fully understood by those involved, and perhaps

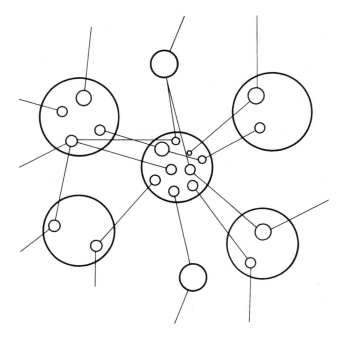

Figure 3   Actor bonds, organizations and the web of actors.

never can be. What and how a party learns about the interdependencies affects very much how it perceives the identity of the counterpart. In the relationship the two sides get to know each other's ambitions and perceptions, which increases the possibilities to utilize each other in some future situations.

Yet, neither mutual commitment nor identities are based on certainties; no amount of "learning" can ever fully dissipate the uncertainties. There is always a margin for beliefs and trust that in the end become essential for the commitment. The development of trust is a social process typical for relationship development. Neither the beliefs nor the trust are dependent solely on the direct interaction experience; other clues are also used. Perceived relationships of the counterpart to other third parties are one of those clues.

The interaction behaviour of either of the parties thus depends also on other relationships in which they are involved, that is, on the whole set of different roles, or identities, that a company assumes in its various relationships. The existence of a certain relationship will have effects on how others perceive the two companies involved in the relationship. Each of the two, in their relationships to other parties, will to some extent represent also its counterpart. The relationship between them will be perceived by some others as a fact, as something to which one should adapt. The relationship acquires and constructs some kind of joint, or collective, identity of which the parties are an integral part and that becomes a phenomenon with a life of its own – if not wholly independent of its components, at least with a distinct identity.

Commitment, identity and trust are processes that constrain and at the same time enable the behaviour of the actors in relation to each other. To be committed, to have a certain identity, to be trusted, means that an actor has to comply with some specific rules. We use the notion of "bonds" to indicate these restrictions.

As bonds are established between actors, an organized structure of actors emerges. Bonds in a relationship are but a portion of a wider web of actors. The bonds affect the actors' present and future interaction in the relationships. The peculiarity of the aggregated structure is its dependence on the processes of learning and perception and thus its continuing fluidity. The web of actors changes as the individual actors learn and adjust their bonds. At the same time, bonds affect the learning.

A particular property of the network form of organization is its indeterminateness. The set of actor bonds making up the structure is not given, as it is not related to some overriding purpose for the structure as a whole. Relationships arise for different and varying reasons; some evolve and others tend to decay. New relationships are created linking previously unconnected actors, others dissolve and cease to exist. Being a part in a larger structure, any relationship is both a source of change and a source of stability in the whole network structure.

When focusing on business relationships we have up to now abstracted organizations into a notion of a collective actor. This is not without problems. First, several individuals are usually involved in carrying out the activities that add up to a business relationship between two companies. Those involved pursue goals that are not identical and the interaction is subject to perceptual and other behavioural limits of the individuals involved. Individuals interact on the basis of their perceptions, they acquire their personal identity and position towards others as they learn and develop in conjunction. Second, all larger companies consist of several units. There are departments, business units, divisions, companies and groups of companies. As we will see later, relationships are influenced by who is defined as the "actor". In certain situations it is thus clear that a company must be seen as a multi-actor while in others it can be considered a single actor.

In summary, the bonds developed between companies in business relationships affect their behaviour and identities. The actor bonds are the third layer of substance of business relationships. In order to make any analysis of a certain relationship between two companies, the nature and strength of these bonds have to be taken into account.

Interplay between the layers of substance in business relationships

Every business relationship is an integrated entity and our ambition is not to decompose it into three different ones. When we propose to distinguish the three layers of substance it simply serves the purpose of identifying possible variations in the effects of intercompany relationships. Our ambition is to capture the differences in relationships important for the economic consequences.

There are relationships between companies which mainly consists of actor bonds. An example can be a customer who has a supplier of electronic components "just to keep in touch", to monitor what is happening, with a limited volume of exchange and coordination. In other relationships both actor bonds and resource ties have been developed but without many activity links. An example can be from the same electronic component industry when a supplier relationship becomes critical for the customer because of the need to access the test or development facilities, and resource ties develop. Another type can be relationships where the activity links are strong while bonds between actors and resource ties are weak. An example here can be the type of relationships that sub-suppliers of relatively simple products in the automotive industry have to their customers. The differences may reflect the type of industrial activity or company-specific circumstances. Most often, however, they reflect a more or less conscious choice on the part of the companies involved, or just neglect of the existing possibilities.

The possibilities of developing closer and economically more effective links, ties and bonds in existing relationships are often large. Thus, every relationship can be developed in one or several of the substance dimensions. Links, bonds and ties existing between two companies are, as a rule, but a few of the possible connections. There are always potential interconnections that can be substantiated as they become perceived and enacted.

The three layers are not independent; there is an interplay between the actor bonds, activity links and resource ties (see Figure 4). Actors carry out activities and activate resources. Activities are resource-consuming and evolve as the capabilities of actors develop. Resources limit the range of activities an actor can pursue. The existence of bonds between actors is a prerequisite for them to

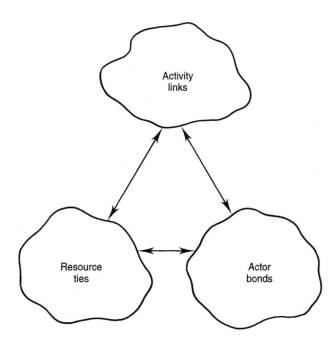

Figure 4   Interplay of the three substance layers of business relationships.

actively and consciously develop strong activity links and resource ties. Activity links make it likely that bonds can develop, and so on.

The interplay of bonds, ties and links is at the origin of change and development in relationships. Actor bonds evolve, resource ties and activity links change and the three become mutually adjusted. The interplay of the three dimensions is a driving force in the development of business relationships. Changes in connections account for much of the dynamics in business relationships.

Strong activity links direct the attention of actors to possible uses of resource elements that can be accessed at the other company or through it. Strong resource ties tend as a rule to lead to strengthening of activity links. There is a tendency towards some kind of balance in activity links, resource ties and actor bonds as the substance of a relationship develops in an incremental way and solutions are sought by the companies in the vicinity of the existing ones. The balance can, however, be on very different levels.

What connections will be acted upon and what level will be reached depends on different factors. First, it will depend on how the interaction evolves between the parties. Second, it will be influenced by the characteristics and ambitions of the actors that reflect their situation and circumstances. This will to a large extent be an effect of the set of relationships these actors have developed. Third, there are the features of the aggregate structure – the network – and how the relationship is related to other existing relationships to and between actors directly or indirectly connected. That brings us back to the issue of the functions of business relationships.

FUNCTIONS OF BUSINESS RELATIONSHIPS

When discussing the substance of business relationships we concentrated on the various layers that can be used by different parties, for different purposes, under different circumstances. We thus came across what we will call different functions of business relationships.

A starting point for a discussion of the functions of business relationships is offered in the micro-functional perspective on market exchange proposed by Alderson (1965). Adopting a micro-functional perspective on business relationships permits identification of at least three different functions of business relationships that were to some extent implied in our earlier discussion.

First, a relationship has a function as the junction of the two companies; it has a function for the dyad. Second, a relationship has a more or less clear function for each of the two parties involved, depending on how it connects to the other relationships they have. Third, a relationship between two companies can also have a function for some third parties either directly or indirectly connected to the two parties directly involved. We could use the notion of first-, second- and third-order functions of a business relationship in order to distinguish different levels of analysis. All the three levels are required to capture the factors affecting the development of the substance profile of a business relationship and the effects it has. They are thus needed in order to assess the economic consequences of a business relationship.

The function for the dyad

A business relationship is developed as the two companies establish connections in the activity, resource and actor layer. If successful, the resources, activities and actors of the two companies are blended and melted together in a unique way. The substance of the dyad, the activity links, resource ties and actor bonds, will not be just the sum of what the two parties turn towards each other; it will become something qualitatively different. The relationship is a "quasi-organization" that amounts to more than simply the sum of its elements because of the existing links, ties and bonds. There is a "team effect" (Alchian and Demsetz, 1972). Jointly, the two companies can perform activities and utilize resources which none of them could accomplish in isolation. What they can accomplish depends on how the relationship develops.

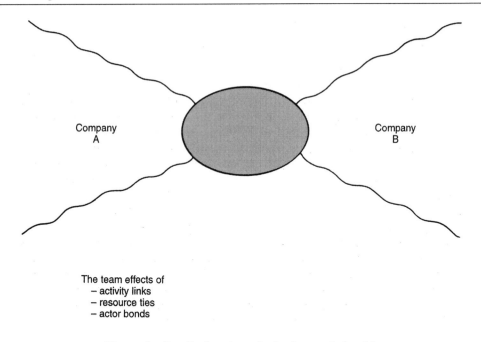

The team effects of
– activity links
– resource ties
– actor bonds

Figure 5 Dyadic function of a business relationship.

A relationship between two companies does not become automatically a perfect "team" (or quasi-organization), but the potential is always there. The team effects have to be tried out. They develop as the parties involved experiment with various connections and learn about their effects. The quality of the relationship is the extent to which this function will be exploited.

The degree to which team effects will come into being depends on the substance of the relationship in all three dimensions. In order to carry into effect the dyadic function at least some substance is needed. There has to be a significant development of activity links, resource ties or actor bonds if a relationship between two companies is to become a quasi-organization and the team effects are to materialize.

The function of a business relationship as a quasi-organization (i.e. for the dyad) acquires importance in proportion to how many new resources are created, novel combinations of activities emerge, knowledge is gained. Only the conjunction of the parties can produce these effects. As the activities, resources and actors become linked in a team it tends to provide a unique performance. The function of intercompany relationships for the dyad is its being the locus of the team effects.

From the above description it should be clear that the more the dyadic function of a relationship is understood and emphasized, the greater is the magnitude of the team effects that can be appropriated by the two companies. It provides either of the parties in the relationship with an opportunity to develop its capabilities, resources and/or activities. Exploiting these is a matter of tuning the marketing and purchasing function of the companies.

The single actor function

We argued that relationships are important for the performance of companies. Each of a company's main relationships offers some benefits but also entails substantial costs. A relationship affects the performance potential of a company by effects on its activity structure, the collection of resources it can use and its organizational structure. Given these effects relationships are an important factor in the development of capabilities of a company and thus for the economic outcomes of its operations.

For a business unit existing within a context where the counterparts are individually important, the impact of relationships is rather evident. Relationships affect the resource collection a company can use. They also affect the possibilities of carrying out certain production and development activities within the company, that is, its activity structure and its activity potential. Finally, each relationship affects the organization of the company. The total set of relationships to others a company has determines in this way the competence of the company as well as its productivity and innovativeness. Coping with relationships can be seen as a broad learning and attribute-developing process. Relationships offer the possibility of developing the competence, productivity and innovativeness of the company and are in this respect valuable assets.

The effects of a certain relationship stem from the combination (complementarity and related-ness) of the relationship with the activity structure, resource collection and organization of the company and with the set of other relationships it has. These effects are not simply cumulative of the dyadic effects of the single relationships. They originate in the quality and properties of the whole set of the relationships and their substance. That is, they depend on the type of activity links, resource ties and actor bonds that intersect the company. There are important synergies in some dimensions and contemporaneously important constraints in other dimensions.

Costs and benefits of engaging in a relationship are related to the consequences that a relationship has on the innovativeness, productivity and competence that stem from the impact it has on the activity structure, the set of resources that can be accessed, but also for the perceived goal structure of the actor.

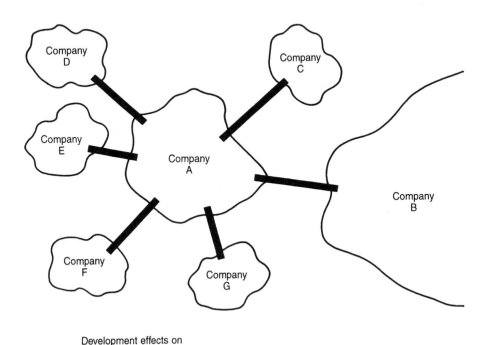

Development effects on
 – activity structure
 – resource collection
 – organizational structure

Figure 6   Single actor function of a relationship.

The company develops by exploiting the potential offered by the dyadic function. How successful it will be will depend on its ability to perceive and handle the connectedness in the relationships in which it is directly involved.

A business relationship has different effects on the two companies in a relationship. While the potential of effects cannot be overrated it may be, and often is, a source of possible tension and conflict in a relationship, especially when the goals of the two differ greatly and are imposed in the interaction.

The "network function"

As relationships are connected, change in the substance of a relationship may affect other relationships and thus companies other than the two involved. Every relationship has the network function; activity links are important in the activity pattern, resource ties in the resource constellation and actor bonds in the web of actors. At the same time, opposite effects are possible from the network structure on the single relationship.

A third party (like the companies C and D in Figure 7) can react to the change in a relationship between two actors (companies A and B in Figure 7) in different ways. They can try to exploit the development by adjusting their own activity links and resource ties in their own relationships in accordance with how the relationship between A and B looks in these dimensions. Alternatively, they can choose to work against the connections created in the relationship (between A and B), attempting to adjust and develop their own relationships (bonds, links and ties) in such a way that the focal relationship will become less influential in the overall structure.

Any relationship is because of its substance a constituent element of the wider network in which relationships are interconnected. Activity links, resource ties and actor bonds in a relationship are connected, directly or indirectly, to some others. The aggregated structure is an organized web of conscious and goal-seeking actors; it is also an organized pattern of activities as well as an organized constellation of resources.

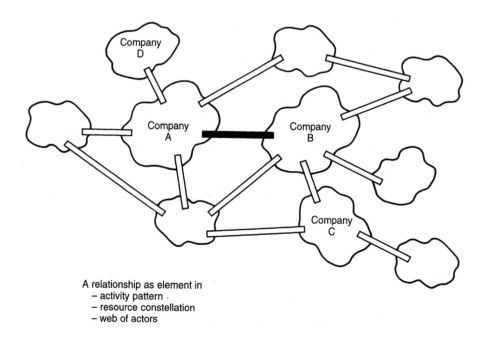

Company D

Company A

Company B

Company C

A relationship as element in
– activity pattern
– resource constellation
– web of actors

Figure 7   Network function of a relationship.

We observed that the structure of business networks has certain peculiar organizational attributes. The actors (companies) have no common goal, but there exist some shared beliefs about the activity pattern as well as the resource constellation. A network has no clear boundaries, nor any centre or apex. It exists as an "organization" in terms of a certain logic affecting the ordering of activities, resources and actors. It can be seen as an "organization" as it affects how companies are reciprocally related and positioned. As a form of organization it will only be kept together as long as the network logic is accepted by enough actors.

Change in the substance of any of the relationships affects the overall structure. Since a change in any relationship affects the position of those involved, the whole set of interrelated relationships is subject to change and that has consequences for the outcome of a relationship for those involved. A dyad, a relationship, is a source as well as a recipient of change in the network.

The network is usually seen as a structure of actors. However, a challenging idea is to see it on a lower level. Then the position of all elements (actors, activities, resources and their bonds, links and ties) is given by the existing relations. The structure takes shape as relations between its elements evolve. It is thus a product of past connections between its elements and the emergent structure elicits developing connections. It impinges, directly and indirectly, on the possibilities to establish new and disrupt existing relations. It affects all layers of substance in a relationship. All relations get modified as structural constraints and possibilities are perceived (learned) by the actors.

The essence of the network function of business relationships is that as they arise they form a structure of actor bonds, activity links and resource ties where third parties are integrated. How the relationships develop and unfold is important for the features of the actors' organization, activity pattern and resource constellation and thus on the properties of the network structure such as its stability. The emergent structure has in any given moment a limiting effect on its actors at the same time as it provides the base for future development.

The balance of functions of business relationships

The different functions of business relationships reflect the various effects of the substance of a given relationship. What is implied is that the outcomes of a relationship for a company over time will not depend simply on its own acts in specific interaction episodes but also on how the counterpart acts and will react and on how others, third parties connected to the two parties, have been, are and will be acting. The effects of a business relationship originate in activity links, resource ties and actor bonds and affect the dyad, the individual company and the network.

The magnitude of the effects will vary, for the specific relationship, with the circumstances and be dependent on the substance of the relationship, on how central the relationship is for the two involved companies and on how tightly the network is structured. The dyadic function of business relationships is value-creating and is a condition for the positive effects for the single actor. The network functions reflect the interdependence of individual and collective action.

There is a problem of balance with regard to the functions of business relationships. Too much emphasis on the functions for the single actor may become counterproductive, as it may destroy the dyadic team function. Too much emphasis on the dyadic function could also turn out to be counterproductive; being overly altruistic may be harmful for the self-interest. Disregard for the network functions can produce disastrous effects or mean that a company does not recognize certain development opportunities being offered or constraints which arise. It is up to management in each company to handle and take care of the various business relationships in a way that is favourable not just for itself but for important counterparts and third parties. Thus, coping with the relationships requires some concern and control of who is benefiting from them.

DEVELOPMENT OF BUSINESS RELATIONSHIPS

The core of our argument is that business relationships are developed by the companies and thus voluntarily created, but when they come into existence they become a constraining element for the same companies. The development of relationships between companies in industrial markets cannot thus escape a pattern created by their own development. There is a path dependence in the development of business relationships and networks. Every actor within the network structure will have some discretion in certain areas and at the same time be entirely locked into others. The network of business relationships is both a prison and a tool.

Our discussion of the substance and functions of intercompany relationships exposed the complexity of effects that a relationship can produce and be subject to as it develops. All these have a bearing on the possibilities of a company to develop a relationship and may explain why certain relationships are weakened or interrupted. The complexity of effects and underlying factors of relationship development is difficult to reduce to manageable proportions. Yet it has to be done. It is needed in order to cope with relationship development. We will therefore outline an analytical scheme that sums up our earlier discussion and use it to identify the critical factors in the development of business relationships and the critical issues in coping with relationships. We will start by putting together the two dimensions of substance and function of business relationships.

Development and role of business relationships

A relationship develops between two companies as some activity links, resource ties or actor bonds are formed between two companies. These links, ties and bonds make up a relationship that can be conceived as a "quasi-organization". These connections are productive on their own merit; they are a source of value. How valuable they are depends on how each of the layers is taken care of and on their interplay. This can be schematically illustrated as shown in Figure 8.

The development of a relationship (of activity links, resource ties and actor bonds) between two companies cannot be unilateral, it requires co-alignment of two parties. How it will develop depends on how each of the parties act and react in the relationship. Once established, a relationship has a life of its own, it gets its own substance as a dyad. It is improved or deteriorates as a result of actions taken by the parties.

Every business relationship is developed by two companies with certain requirements and capabilities. Both the requirements and capabilities result from existing relationships of each of the

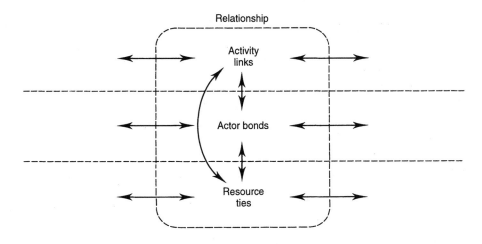

Figure 8   Relationship as a dyad.

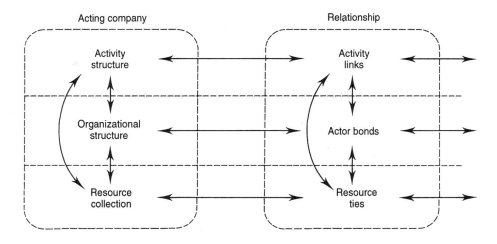

Figure 9 Relationships and the company.

companies. The activity links, resource ties and actor bonds in a relationship between two companies affect the activity structures, the collections of resources and the organizational structures of the companies involved. At the same time the activity structures, resource collections and organizational structures of the companies will influence what kinds of links, ties and bonds can develop in a relationship. This kind of reciprocal conditioning is schematically illustrated in Figure 9.

The effect of a relationship on the company will depend on its internal features, but also on the other relationships the company has. The economic consequences of a relationship will depend on how the productivity, innovativeness and competence of the company and thus its overall capabilities are affected by the activity links, resource ties and actor bonds that arise in a relationship. The development of a relationship has an effect on and at the same time is dependent on the capabilities of the company, that is, on its development potential.

The effects of a relationship between two companies are not limited to the two companies directly involved and their relationships. Other parties and relationships may be affected. An

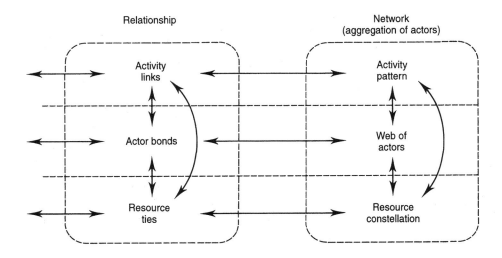

Figure 10 Relationships in a network.

activity link is but a link in a broader activity pattern spanning several companies, a resource tie is but an element of a broader resource constellation that companies can mobilize, and an actor bond is but a part of a web of actors. Again there is a two-way conditioning between the relationship and the network structure, illustrated in Figure 10. Development of a relationship between two companies thus has an organizing effect on the overall network structure and every relationship has a role in it.

The scheme of analysis

Putting together the two dimensions we can outline a broad analytical scheme to identify where and what effects are likely to occur as a relationship evolves, is established, develops or is interrupted. We believe the scheme outlined in Figure 11 can be used in two ways: first, it can be used as a conceptual framework to analyse the effects of change in a relationship and/or to identify the factors that affect the possibilities of development of a relationship. Second, it can be used as a heuristic device in coping with relationships in business. It can be used to single out the critical issues in coping with relationships, to assess the state of a relationship and its development potential. It can thus be used to identify where and how to intervene in relationships in order to get some desired effects. The scheme can be used to identify the dynamic effects in the development of a business relationship. It summarizes the main variables of relationship development discussed in this chapter.

It can be used in order to distinguish possible effects of change, for whatever reason, in a relationship. Any change in a relationship can have three types of effects. One is the direct effect changing the potential of the relationship. This will depend on how it affects the interplay of the different layers of the relationship (column 2). Another type of effect is on the companies involved and their cost-revenue parameters (column 1). A third more indirect effect takes place as the change might lead to different reactions, causing more or less of an "explosion" in the overall network (column 3). The scheme can be used for analysing all three types of effect.

The scheme can also be used to identify the impact of change on the development of a relationship. Any change (in any of the cells of the matrix) can affect the development of a certain

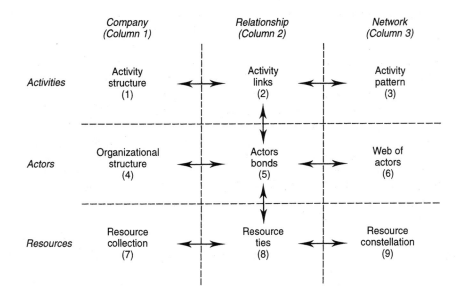

Figure 11 Scheme of analysis development effects of business relationships.

relationship. If, for example, one or both of the companies are changing some activities this might have effects in both the horizontal and vertical dimensions of the scheme. It might have a direct effect in terms of increased or decreased efficiency in the performance of the internal activities of the company (cell 1). It might also have some direct effects for some third parties who have to adapt to the new link with accompanying positive or negative effects on its outcome (cell 3). The change might also have an indirect effect. It can give cause to make further changes within the relationship in terms of new ties (cell 8) or bonds (cell 5). It can also give cause to make adjustments in relationships to third parties (cell 3). One change can in this way cause a number of reactions which might be both expected (wanted) and unexpected (surprises) for the party initiating the change.

The value of the scheme in Figure 11 is limited from an explanatory point of view, as it only identifies where effects might occur. It does not say anything about which changes shall produce certain effects. It provides just the frame that indicates the main direction of effects and their type. The scheme does not provide guidance in order to assess the likelihood or the magnitude of impact of changes in a relationship or elsewhere in the network. These require a further analysis that permits assessment of the strength of connections in the various layers of substance of the relationships and the economic consequences of these. However, it provides the guidance in directing such an analysis.

COPING WITH RELATIONSHIPS

Coping with relationships, exploiting them economically, requires an awareness of their effects and insight to the interdependence that accounts for their dynamics. The conceptual framework developed in this chapter can, we believe, be of some help for this purpose. It can be used to formulate some broad normative implications for management.

Compared with the more traditional view of determinants of a company's performance, the relationship perspectives yield rather different implications. The main points in our argument so far are as follows:

- In numerous companies, relationships have an overwhelming impact on their economic performance. When that is the case, i.e. when single specific relationships matter, they have to be managed.
- Companies cannot unilaterally control and decide the development of relationships; they are but part of relationships and of a larger whole that affects both their outcomes and their development potential. Awareness of this interdependence is needed in order to cope with relationships successfully.
- The time dimension becomes more important as conduct and its outcomes are rooted in the past and its effects become manifest in time. Interdependence and awareness of interdependence in the company and its counterparts will be decisive to the outcome of joint action. Insight into the dynamics of business networks is required in order to cope with relationships effectively.

The scheme of analysis developed from our discussion of the substance and functions of business relationships (see Figure 11) can be used to identify the critical issues in coping with relationships in business.

There are three areas where effects of relationship are important and need to be coped with: marketing and purchasing; capability development; and strategy development. These can be illustrated schematically, as in Figure 12. Marketing and purchasing is about relationship development. Capability development is about coping with the effect of relationships on the development potential of a company. Strategy development is about positioning the company in the overall network through the development of its relationships.

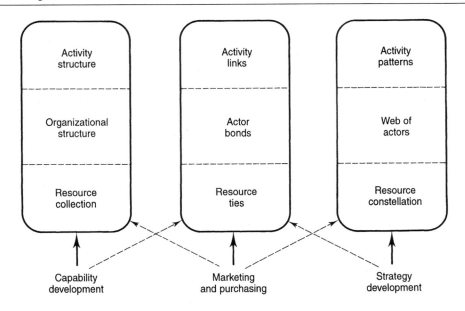

Figure 12 Critical issues in coping with business relationships.

Marketing and purchasing

Critical relationships to customers, suppliers and eventually other third parties have to be maintained and possibly developed. The issue here is how "team" effects can be produced or, in other words, the functioning of the quasi-organization that the major relationships constitute.

The main management task is to keep the customer and supplier relationships "productive". In terms of our scheme of analysis it is a matter of coping with the interplay of the various substance layers in relationships and the mutuality of the interaction process. To intervene in a relationship is to develop (or to interrupt) activity links, resource ties and actor bonds in interaction with the counterpart. That requires an understanding of connections and assessment of their effects, as well as monitoring of changes and their likely impact on the relationship.

The primary task of marketing and purchasing function is thus close to what we called development of the function of relationships as a dyad.

Capability development

This area is about exploiting the possible positive effects of business relationships on the activity structure, resource collection and organization of the company and on other relationships of the company. It is also about containing the possible negative effects in the same dimensions. The effects of relationships will depend on possible connections of links, ties and bonds to those of other relationships.

Business relationships have, among other things, important effects on the development of the technical competence and capacity of the company. On the whole they seem to affect the productivity, innovativeness and competence – that is, all the components of a company's capability and thus its performance. The capabilities of a company reflect how successful it has been in combining relationships and its internal features.

Strategy development

This area is about manoeuvring for a favourable position for the company in the business network. The position affects the economic outcome of a company's relationships over time and the possibilities of developing and maintaining relationships to various other parties. The position of a company with respect to others (its relationships) reflects its capacity to provide values to others (productiveness, innovativeness, competence). It is also a determinant of the possibilities of developing its capability by drawing on the capacity of others.

The critical issue for management here is monitoring the changes in the network structure that affect the position and thus the capability and capacity of the company. Changes must be assessed in terms of their likely impact on the position of the company with respect to the wider activity pattern, resource constellation and web of actors. Strategies need to be devised to meet the changes or to produce changes in the network. The overall position of a company is a composite of position with respect to the relevant resource constellation, activity pattern and structure of actor bonds.

Handling the single relationships, that is, managing the dyadic function, is a condition for exploiting the potential of relationships and for taking economic advantage of business relationships. It is a condition for developing capabilities and for the strategy development in a company. Conversely, to pursue a change in the strategy of the company requires that the development effects on the relationships are monitored and adjusted.

Handling relationships, their development, their impact on the company and on its strategy affects the economic performance of companies, as we have stated several times. The problem is that the effects may offset one another and they can become manifest at different times. The economic consequences of actions taken in a relationship can thus hardly be quantified precisely. What is evident, however, is that they are significant both in terms of impact on the short-term economic efficiency and in terms of the longer-term effectiveness. That calls for a final consideration on the use of the scheme. We have observed several times that the effects of relationships are complex and can hardly be mapped in detail. Dynamics of business relationships would make such a map, possible in principle, obsolete the moment it is produced.

An accurate assessment in every specific case and situation is beyond the capacity of any company. No company is likely to be able to assess all the effects of the interdependencies in a specific situation, even if aware of their nature. So much more so because the effect will depend on how others will choose to behave, and the effects that will become evident over time are highly uncertain. Yet, if the outcome of the relationships is somehow to be managed, that is, controlled and influenced in favour of the individual company, awareness of the effects and insight into the interdependence is needed. The problem we face is how to cope with complexity of factors affecting the outcomes when an *a priori* assessment of relevant effects is ruled out. In general terms it has been argued that purpose-directed behaviour under such circumstances calls for the adoption of behavioural rules that do not necessarily derive from a cognitive elaboration of the specific situation as it is met, but rather from an individual elaboration of past experience (e.g. Weick, 1969; Starbuck, 1985, March 1988) or from the generalized collective experience somehow transmitted to the subject (Hayek, 1967; Kelley and Thibaut, 1978).

Awareness of the effects of and insight into the interdependencies can contribute to the formation of the behavioural rules that guide effective behaviour. The identification of the main variables of relationship development can serve to elaborate the experience and thus the adoption in a company of an effective "relationship strategy".

REFERENCES

Achrol, R. S., 1991, 'Evolution of the Marketing Organization: New Forms for Turbulent Environments', *Journal of Marketing*, Vol. 55 (Oct.), pp. 77–93.

Alchian, A. A. and Demsetz, H., 1972, 'Production, Information Costs, and Economic Organization', *The American Economic Review*, Vol. 62, pp. 777–795.

Alderson, W., 1965, *Dynamic Marketing Behavior*. Homewood, Ill.: Richard D. Irwin Inc.

Alter, C. and Hage, J., 1993, *Organizations Working Together*. Newbury Park, Cal.: Sage.

Arndt, J., 1979, 'Toward a Concept of Domesticated Markets', *Journal of Marketing*, Vol. 43 (Fall), pp. 69–75.

Astley, G. W., 1984, 'Toward an Appreciation of Collective Strategy', *Academy of Management Review*, Vol. 9, No. 3, pp. 526–535.

Blois, K. J., 1972, 'Vertical Quasi-integration', *Journal of Industrial Economics*, Vol. 20, No. 3, pp. 253–272.

Håkansson, H., (ed.), 1982, *Internal Marketing and Purchasing of Industrial Goods – An Interaction Approach*. New York: Wiley.

Hayek, F. A., 1967, *Studies in Philosophy, Politics and Economics*. London: Routledge and Kegan Paul.

Kelley, H. H. and Thibaut, J. W., 1978, *Interpersonal Relations: A Theory of Interdependence*. New York: Wiley.

March, J. G., 1988, *Decisions and Organizations*. Oxford: Basil Blackwell.

Miles, R., and Snow, C., 1986, 'Organizations: New Concepts for New Forms', *California Management Review*, Vol. 28, pp. 62–73.

Nohria, N. and Eccles, R. G. (eds), 1992, *Networks and Organizations: Structure, Form, and Action*. Boston, Mass.: Harvard Business School Press.

Starbuck, W. H., 1985, 'Acting First and Thinking Later: Theory Versus Reality in Strategic Change', in Pennings, J. M. (ed.), *Organizational Strategy and Change*. San Francisco, Cal.: Jossey-Bass.

Webster, F. E., 1992, 'The Changing Role of Marketing in the Corporation', *Journal of Marketing*, Vol. 56, Oct. pp. 1–17.

Weick, K. E., 1969, *The Social Psychology of Organizing*. Reading, Mass.: Addison-Wesley.

3.5 Network positions and strategic action – an analytical framework

Jan Johanson and Lars-Gunnar Mattsson

INTRODUCTION

The basic idea in the industrial network model is that firms are engaged in networks of business relationships. The network structure, that is the ways in which the firms are linked to each other, develops as a consequence of the firms transacting business with each other. At the same time, the network structure constitutes the framework within which business is carried out. This chapter develops and discusses a notion of strategic action in industrial networks. Strategic action is interesting not only in its consequences for firms, but also because of its implications for the dynamics of industrial systems.

There are three specific attributes of the network model which are central to the argument developed in this chapter. First, it views networks as sets of connected relationships between actors. Further, a distinction is made between two levels in the industrial system; the network of exchange relationships between industrial actors and the production system where resources are employed and developed in production. Resources and activities form the production system. The network of exchange relationships is viewed as a structure governing the production system. Second, the concept of network position is used to describe how the individual actors in the network are related to each other in a network structure. Third, both the means and ends of strategic action are closely linked to the position concept.

The choice of these three characteristics may be justified on the following grounds.

1. The separation of the actors in the network from the resources and activities in the production system is analytically helpful first of all because the concept of strategic action presupposes actors. Actors have intentions, they make interpretations of conditions in the industrial system and they act. It is also useful because there is not necessarily a one-to-one correspondence between a production system and a network of relationships. For example an actor in a network may be engaged in exchange relationships covering several production systems or control different, widely separated clusters of resources in one production system. Correspondingly a production system may involve several actors who have no business relationships with each other.
2. The use of the position concept is not only a way to move from a dyadic to a network analysis, but it also provides a conceptual understanding of how the individual actor is related to, or rather embedded in, the environment.
3. The use of the position concept as both means and ends of strategic action makes it possible to give such action meaning in relation to the conditions for structural change in industrial networks. This is another way of saying that the individual actor's opportunities and constraints depend on the network and on the results of earlier strategic action. Thus, the notions

of embeddedness and of investments in networks are given strategic meaning (cf. Pfeffer (1987) and Johanson and Mattsson (1985)).

The chapter proceeds as follows. First, the industrial system model is described. Since some of the conceptual building blocks are quite similar to what should already be common ground, we concentrate on the specifics. Second, we make a somewhat deeper analysis of the position concept before, in the third and final section, discussing strategic action as efforts to change or preserve network positions.

THE INDUSTRIAL SYSTEM

In production systems, resources are employed, combined and transformed in industrial production. Coordination and direction of activities in the production systems takes place through governance structures. The production system together with the governance structure constitutes the industrial system. The term production is taken in a wide sense to include all the different kinds of activities needed to create and use products and services (R&D, manufacturing, marketing, distribution, purchasing, etc.). The resources are dependent on each other in the sense that the outcome of the use of one resource is dependent on how another is used. The resources are more or less heterogeneous and specialised. The more they are specialised the stronger are the dependencies between actors. In the extreme case when two resources are completely specialised in a use where they are combined, they are completely complementary and there is a very high positive dependence between them. At the opposite extreme two specialised resources may be complete substitutes, in which case there is a high negative interdependence. On the whole, an operating production system can be characterised in terms of dependence between resources according to an industrial logic where resources are more or less complementary and/or substitutable inputs into, and outputs from, production.

Resource specialisation and interdependencies are, however, not solely determined by some technical imperative. In any specific situation they are a consequence of earlier use of the resources and of the structure of the production system. Resources are more or less heterogeneous, implying that they have properties in a number of different dimensions, so that over time, they can be used in different ways, combined in different ways, and transformed in different ways. Thus two heterogeneous resources which are combined can usually, through experience in use, become more specialised in their combined use leading to higher joint productivity, higher degrees of complementarity and increased interdependence between them.

In such production systems, where there are innumerable, different, and changing resource interdependencies, there is a strong need for some kind of coordination between resources not only to economise their use, but also to create changes of an innovative nature. Traditionally two different governance modes are assumed to bring about this coordination: the hierarchy and the market (Williamson, 1985). In the hierarchy, one supreme actor controls all the resources and brings about coordination. In the market model coordination takes place through price signals which inform the autonomous actors about the availability of, and need for, resources. In the present model it is assumed that the production system is governed through a network of exchange relationships between semi-autonomous actors. The actors are engaged in and develop exchange relationships with each other and can in this way handle the interdependencies between the resources they control (see Figure 1).

We assume a circular causal relation between the network level and the production level. Through the exchange relationships the actors learn about each other and develop some trust in each other. On that basis they adapt and develop their resource use to increase the productivity which also leads to increased resource interdependence between them. At the same time, as a result of interdependence, the actors develop their relationships, thus linking them closer to each other. Consequently, unless no other factors intervene, through current activities the specific dependencies

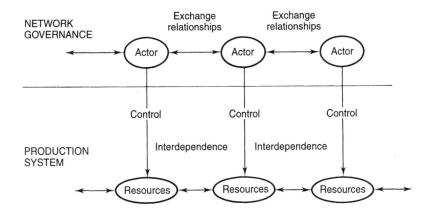

Figure 1   Network governance in the industrial system.

and relationships will become gradually stronger and closer. However, as the specific relationship is embedded in a network of such relationships and since this focal dependence is only one in an intricate fabric of such dependencies there are always such intervening factors affecting the causal circle. Sometimes such forces are channelled via the network, sometimes they operate through the dependencies in the production system (see Figure 2).

The exchange relationship is a mutual orientation of two actors towards each other. They are prepared to interact with each other in order to coordinate and develop interdependent resources that each actor controls. They interact to get access to some of the resources controlled by the other actor. These exchange relationships develop over time and resources are used to establish, maintain and develop them. Exchange relationships in networks may become lasting, especially if the heterogeneous resources controlled by the actors become adapted to each other and become highly specialised.

Exchange relationships also link actors indirectly to other actors with whom they do not have any such relationships. Evidently, actors in the industrial system also use resources which are interdependent without the actors having exchange relationships with each other. This is typically the case with competing actors. Similarly there may be interdependencies between actors with complementary resources, e.g. complementary suppliers who have no exchange relationship with each other. If actors consider such interdependencies important they may start interaction with each other, thus developing an exchange relationship. Correspondingly, actors may have more or less "sleeping" relationships with each other, for historical or other reasons without any resource dependencies between the resources they control. Such a relationship may be used to combine resources, thus creating new productive resource interdependence.

A basic characteristic of networks is that relationships are connected, i.e. exchange in one relationship is conditioned by exchange in others (Cook and Emerson, 1978). The connections may

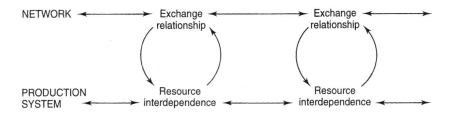

Figure 2   Interlinked causal relationship/interdependence circles.

be positive or negative. A positive connection between two relationships implies that exchange in one relationship has a positive effect on exchange in the other. This is, for instance, the case with relationships handling a sequence of interdependencies along a production chain. Correspondingly, two competing suppliers to a customer are usually negatively connected via that customer. The two cases are examples of simple connections via the resource interdependencies in the production system. It is apparent that connections in a network may be much more indirect and complex so that two distant relationships in a network are connected with each other in multiple ways, some of which are positive and some negative.

However, the connections between relationships may also take place exclusively via the actors at the network level. In this case they are of a subjective nature and are a matter of intentions, strategies, views, and the "network theories" of the actors (Weick, 1979). Thus, an actor may, taking a long-term view of a market, consider two relationships as complementary in some sense, for instance in terms of technical development. Similarly the actor may see two relationships as substitutes for each other in a foreign market entry. Thus, although there are no interdependencies on the production level the two relationships may be negatively connected. Obviously, actor-mediated connections are much more ambiguous, fluid and invisible than those which are resource interdependence mediated. Nevertheless, they exist and have important implications for network development.

Since there are no objective criteria by which to decide which exchange relationships to include in networks and which to exclude, the boundaries of a specific network are necessarily fuzzy. However certain interdependence criteria may be used. A production system can be delimited on the basis of resource interdependencies in relation to some focal products, technology, country, region, etc. The inclusion of relationships is then a matter of determining who are the actors who control relevant resources. The excluded relationships can then be regarded as belonging to other networks and as a means of providing links between networks. If, for example, the focal production system exists in a certain geographic area, relationships with actors outside that area should reasonably be considered as links to other networks. On the other hand, if there are strong interdependencies between resources in that area and resources in other areas, the focal production system should not be delimited on an area basis. One test of such delimitations is whether there are important exchange relationships with actors in other networks. Thus, if the exchange relationships included coordinated resources which according to a specific industrial logic belong to a specified focal production system, a test of the suitability of such a definition is if any excluded exchange relationships coordinate resources that have important influences on the included relationships.

Since we are interested in industrial development and structural change, influences from actors outside the focal network, that is the network governing the focal production system, could be important. As an example it is sufficient to mention internationalisation of competition. Even if it is apparent that the whole world is connected we need, for analytical reasons, to consider production system boundaries. Thus, analytically there exist many networks and a specific actor may be engaged in several networks. To take another example, if we define a focal production system to exclude some of the resource interdependencies which one actor coordinates through exchange relationships, then this actor is defined as being involved in more than one network. This actor's resource interdependencies among several production systems might suggest that the delimitation of the production system as well as network should be "multi-industrial".

The actors in a network may view the network, its extensivity and the nature of its exchange relationships in quite different ways and also differently from the description that might be provided by an outside analyst who is not an actor. First, the network is extensive and includes exchange relationships in which the actor is not directly involved. Second, even in those relationships where the actor is involved, the counterparts may view the relationships in different ways. Third, network analysis deals not only with the present but also with the past and the future which means that the interpretations are influenced by different memories and different beliefs about the future. Since the actors form cognitive structures through experience and interpretations linked to theories about "reality", perceptions will be influenced by which conceptual framework the actors use (Zaltman *et al.*, 1982). Whether the actor's "theory" is that the industrial system is governed by a network or by a market mechanism will obviously be of importance. This means that there is a potential normative value in the idea that a network has less clear boundaries than a "market structure" based on a traditional industrial organisation model. The actor with a network perspective will focus some attention on influences from "outside" actors and might therefore extend the network boundaries and thereby perhaps increase the possibilities for effective strategic action.

POSITIONS IN NETWORKS

Each actor is engaged in a number of exchange relationships with other actors. These relationships define the position of the actor in the network. Since positions can be defined for all the actors in the network, the concept can be used to characterise network structure and network distance between actors. A basic attribute of exchange relationships is that they are established and developed over time and so this process can be viewed as an investment process (Håkansson, 1982b). Thus, network positions are the result of investments in exchange relationships (Johanson and Mattsson, 1985). Positions are a consequence of the cumulative nature of the use of resources to establish, maintain and develop exchange relationships. The position of an actor also connects the separate, individual relationships with each other. The position characterises the actor's links to the environment and is therefore of strategic significance. The positions of all the actors in the network are also a major characteristic of the environment in which the actor is embedded. Furthermore, the position strongly influences the basis for an actor's development of exchange relationships in the future, i.e. forms the base for the actor's strategic actions (Mattsson, 1984).

A distinction can be made between a limited and an extended definition of positions. The limited definition refers purely to the network level. According to the limited definition, the position of an actor is a matter of the exchange relationships of the actor and the identities of the counterparts in those relationships. The identities of the counterparts are, in consequence, a matter of their relationships to others. This corresponds to the way in which positions are used in sociometric network analyses and makes it possible for us to use all the usual measures for characterising network positions: interconnectedness, distance, etc. (Di Maggio, 1986). When operationalising the limited definition it is possible to view relationships as integer variables that only take the values zero and one. It is, however, also possible to view relationships as continuous metric variables, defined on the same scale, with values between zero and one depending on the strength of the relationship. Further, relationships may be conceived of as vectors with values depending on the strength of a number of bond dimensions – legal, social, etc.

The extended definition, however, refers, in addition, to the role the actors have in the production system. Thus, according to the extended definition, the position of an actor includes also the productive processes – in a broad sense – in which it is involved and its direct and indirect network interdependencies. The production role has two dimensions, one qualitative and one quantitative. The qualitative dimension describes which function the actor has in the production system. In a sequential chain linking the separate resources, the individual actor has one or more specific functions, for which the resources it controls are specialised. The quantitative dimension character-ises the relative importance that the resources of the actor have in relation to the resources of other actors, i.e. how much of the total quantity of substitutable resource are controlled by the actor. A network position gives an actor some power over resources controlled by other actors. This power is in no way absolute since exchange relationships by definition depend on voluntary mutual orientation and not on coercion.

Clearly, the positions of different actors in a network are more or less interrelated. This is the direct result of the basic assumption that networks are sets of connected exchange relationships. Connectedness means that exchange in one relationship is conditioned – facilitated or hindered – by exchange in another. Connectedness can occur on the production level. Through direct and indirect resource interdependencies the positions of two actors are interrelated. This type of position interrelation may be described as objective. It is a matter of the industrial logic. The stronger the resource interdependencies, the stronger are the position interrelations. This means that the closer two actors are in a production chain, the stronger are their position interrelations. This means also that the more specialised the production of the actors is in relation to each other in a network, the stronger are their position interrelations. It means also that the more closed the production system is in relation to other production systems, the stronger are position interrelations in the system. Furthermore, positions of different actors may be positively or negatively connected to each other in the sense that when the position of one is strengthened the position of the other is strengthened or weakened. This can also be seen as a matter of the industrial logic.

However, interrelations between positions can also occur at the network level, which means that they are a matter of intentions and interpretations of the actors. They are of a subjective nature. It seems reasonable to assume that the longer the time perspective the less important are the objective interdependencies driven by an industrial logic and the more important are the intentions and interpretations of the actors. Thus, in a long-term perspective, position interrelations become more of a subjective matter. The knowledge and the values of the actors are therefore important factors. Likewise it seems reasonable to assume that the smaller the investments in the production systems, the more important are the subjective views of the actors of the interrelations between positions. This does not mean that there are fewer position interrelations in soft industrial systems such as R&D or service industry systems than in manufacturing industry systems or that there are fewer position interrelations in the long term, only that they are more ambiguous. Generally, however, it can be assumed that the position interrelations are stronger the closer the actors are connected at the network level, as they will tend to have more analogous "network theories".

To sum up, the position of an actor is described by the characteristics of its exchange relationships. A limited, basic definition is that the position is a matter of with which actors the focal actor has exchange relationships. An extended definition of a position also involves the role of the actors in the production system. The role comprises the function accorded by the industrial logic and the relative importance of the actors.

The position of an actor changes all the time, not only because new exchange relationships are developed, old ones interrupted and others change in character, but also because the counterparts' positions are changing and, furthermore, the positions of third parties, with whom the focal actor has no direct relationships, are also changing. This follows from the definition of positions as being a matter of the identities of counterparts. But the ways in which position change may differ depending on whether the changes take place on the actor (network) or on the resource (production system) level.

STRATEGIC ACTION

In the general strategy literature, strategic actions are usually characterised as efforts by actors to influence their relationship with their environment. In the network approach this general notion is translated to mean that strategic actions are efforts by actors to influence (change or preserve) their position(s) in network(s). The following discussion is about such strategic action by one focal actor. Strategic objectives are defined in terms of network positions. Obviously, almost all actions in networks have some effect on network positions. This is, for instance, the case with action in an exchange relationship concerning current production. When two actors carry out exchange they develop their exchange relationships thus modifying their positions as well as those of other actors in the network. In this chapter, however, only action which aims primarily at the positions is considered strategic. Plainly, it is difficult to make a distinction between such position-directed action and more production-directed action.

This view of strategic action means that strategic action by a focal actor aims not only at increasing that post-action network effectiveness. It is also a matter of developing the base from which future action can proceed. Within the framework of the limited definition of network positions, strategic action aims at influencing actors, relationships and network structures. It can be directed at the relationships of the focal actor, it can be directed at relationships between other actors in the network, or it can be directed at relationships with other networks. These goals may be achieved by breaking old relationships, establishing new ones, changing the character of existing, or preserving relationships endangered by adverse actions by other actors. The strategic action may also aim to influence actor perceived mediated connections between relationships, such as whether and to what extent actors view relationships as complementary or competing. This is a matter of influencing their "network theories". Such action may aim at influencing the "network theories" of a specific actor or a specific set of actors in a network. It may also aim at influencing or creating a dominant "network theory" in a network. This may imply attempts to make the "network theories" of different actors in the network more consistent. It may, however, also represent efforts to disconnect the network into two or more separate nets, where, for instance, the focal actor is the only link between the nets or where the focal actor has a strong position in one of the nets. Alternatively it may aim at connecting different sections more closely or at connecting different networks with each other.

Working within the framework of the extended definition of network positions, strategic action may also aim at restructuring the web of dependencies in the production system. An overall objective of such restructuring may be to develop the focal actor's role in the production system in a particular direction. Such action may, for instance, include weakening the dependence of the focal actor or reducing the dependence of a focal net on resources in certain other networks. This may include transforming specific dependencies between actors into more general dependencies which are not related to specific actors. The strategic action can also be designed to strengthen inter-dependencies in a production system in order, for instance, to create a specific dominant sequential chain of interdependencies. Correspondingly, it may aim at creating a set of dependencies around a certain resource controlled by the focal actor. Such actions may mean that general market dependencies are transformed into specific actor dependencies.

Using the limited definition of positions the base for strategic action by a focal actor are its (1) network positions, (2) resources, and (3) "network theory". The three bases of strategic action are not unrelated. Thus the quantity and quality of the resources influence the resource inter-dependencies which are closely related to the exchange relationships and consequently the network positions. The network position influences the network theory since that theory is to a large extent based on information channelled through the exchange relationships. Of the three types of strategic base the network position has a special status, since the strategic objectives are also defined in terms of network positions.

Let us finally illustrate the framework by discussing briefly strategic action in relation to the internationalisation of a focal firm. Such a strategic development involves, to an increasing degree, relationships cutting across national network boundaries. The focal firm brings internationalisation by establishing relationships with firms in other national networks. The first step may or may not involve control of production resources inside the new national network. Further internationalisation moves may include development of exchange relationships and positions in still more national networks and increased interdependency between the firm's positions in the different networks. The internationalisation of the firm can be seen as a consequence of strategic action by the firm to the extent that the moves are not the result of continuous development of current production activities or of actions taken by other actors.

The bases for internationalisation are, first, the firm's position, which can be used in various ways. Some of the exchange relationships in the old domestic network may be connected to existing or potential exchange relationships in the new network, depending to what extent these other firms have positions in those networks. Alternatively, the position of the actor in the old network can be communicated to actors in the new network thereby influencing their network theories so as to make them interested in becoming positively connected to the focal firm. A special case is that of actors who mutually exchange access to each other's positions in their respective networks. Observe, however, that the position in the old network can be a constraint on movement into new networks to the extent that commitments made in the old exchange relationships cannot be kept if new exchange relationships are added.

A second way that a firm may internationalise is that the firm's own resources can be made interdependent with resources controlled by actors in the other network. Quantitative and qualitative adjustments may or may not have to be made in order to establish and develop exchange relationships. Adjustments involve investments in new resources by the firm and purchase of already existing resources controlled by other actors. Another way to achieve the changes in resource structure is through explicit coordination with another firm.

Third, the firm's network theory not only directs the strategic action towards specific efforts to influence resources and positions, but can also be communicated to other actors in the network and thereby influence their action. For example, if the firm's network theory assumes expectations of network structure changes implying increasing interdependence between positions in different networks, i.e. internationalisation, this view can influence other actors with whom joint strategic action is desired or it can be used to affect dominant network theories in the new networks.

So far the discussion concerns the situation when a focal firm starts moving into new networks. Let us now look at a situation when both the focal firm and many other actors have positions in many national networks. The interrelated nature of network positions in different networks makes it even more important to consider the network theories of actors in the further internationalisation moves. Strategic actions, involving explicit linkages between a focal firm's and one or more other actors' network positions, are to a large extent based on communication of network theories and may result in changes from negative to positive or from positive to negative connections between positions. So-called strategic alliances are a good example of this process in operation. They may create or handle interdependencies between production resources, but they also limit the number of potential alliances in the networks since some actors become appropriated. The survival of strategic alliances depends less on the extent to which resource coordination in the production system succeeds than on how network theories of both the involved and third actors develop.

Buying another firm is frequently referred to as a strategic action. An important issue in such a purchase is whether the buying firm can get control of the other firm's exchange relationships. In other words can the focal firm take over the position as well as the resources. Depending on the network theory in the focal firm, the major aim of the acquisition may be to get control of the exchange relationships, to change their character, or to change the connections between exchange relationships. Control of exchange relationships through acquisitions is, however, never certain, since there are always two actors involved.

As national networks become increasingly interdependent an obvious change in the actors' network theories is to regard the network boundaries as obsolete and to consider other boundaries as more relevant. Such changes in network theories might, for example, imply that the actors regard their positions as even more interdependent since they belong to the same network. Measures of network positions such as quantitative and qualitative aspects of resource interdependencies will become different when network boundaries change.

REFERENCES

Alchian, A. A. and Demsetz, H. (1972) 'Production, Information Costs and Economic Organisation', *American Economic Review*, 62, p. 783.

Aldrich, H. E. (1979) *Organisations and Environments*, Englewood Cliffs, NJ, Prentice Hall.

Aldrich, H. E. (1981) *The Origins and Persistence of Social Networks. Social Structure and Network Analyses*, Beverly Hills, Calif., Sage.

Aldrich, H. E. and Whetten, D. A. (1981) 'Organisation-sets, Action sets and Networks. Making the most of simplicity' in P. C. Nystrom and W. H. Starbuk (eds) *Handbook of Organisational Design*, Vol. 1, Oxford, Oxford University Press pp. 385–408.

Alderson, W. (1957) *Marketing Behaviour and Executive Action*, Homewood, Ill., Richard D. Irwin.

Alderson, W. (1965) *Dynamic Marketing Behaviour. A Functionalist Theory of Marketing*, Homewood Ill., Richard D. Irwin.

Alexander, R., Surface, S. and Alderson, W. (1940) *Marketing*, Boston, Mass., Ginn and Company.

Arndt, J. (1979) 'Overview: The Impact of Stakeholder Publics in Shaping the Future of Marketing' in G. Fisk, J. Arndt, and K. Gronhaug (eds). *Future Directions for Marketing* Cambridge, Mass., Marketing Science Institute, pp. 76–7.

Arrow, K. (1974) *Limits of Organisation*, New York, W. W. Norton and Co.

Astley, W. G. (1984) 'Toward an Appreciation of Collective Strategy'. *Academy of Management Review*, 9, 3, pp. 526–35.

Astley, W. G. (1985) 'The Two Ecologies: Population and Community Perspectives on Organisational Evolution'. *Administrative Science Quarterly*, 30, pp. 224–41.

Astley, W. G. and Fombrun, C. (1983) 'Collective Strategy: Social Ecology of Organisational Environments', *Academy of Management Review*, 8, pp. 576–87.

Averitt, R. T. (1968) *The Dual Economy: The Dynamics of American Industry Structure*, New York, W. W. Norton and Co.

Axelrod, R. (1984) *The Evolution of Cooperation*, New York, Basic Books.

Axelsson, B. (1982) 'Wilmanshyttans uppgang och fall. En kommentar till angreppssattet i en foretags-historisk studie' (The Rise and Fall of Wilmanshyttan Steel Works. A Commentary on the Approach in a Company History Study'), *Acta Universitatis Upsaliensis*, 15, Liber.

Axelsson, B. (1987) 'Supplier Management and Technological Development' in H. Håkansson (ed.) *Industrial Technological Development: A Network Approach*, London, Croom Helm.

Axelsson, B. and Håkansson, H. (1979) 'Wikmanshyttans uppgang och fall. En analys av ett stalforelag och dess omgivning under 75 ar' ('The Rise and Fall of the Wikmanshyttan Steel Works. An Historical Analysis of a Steel Company during 75 years'), Studentlitteratur.

Axelsson, B. and Håkansson, H. (1984) *Inkap for Konkurrenshraft, (Purchasing for Competitive Power)*, Liber.

Barney, J. B. and Ouchi, W. G. (1986) *Organisational Economics* San Francisco, Calif., Jossey Bass.

Berg, P. O. (1985) 'Organisation Change as a Symbolic Transformation Process' in P. J. Frost *et al. Organization Culture*, New York, Sage.

Bjorklund, L. (1988) *International Projekforsaljning (International Systems Selling)*, Research Report, EFI., Stockholm School of Economics, Sweden.

Blau, P. M. (1964) *Exchange and Power in Social Life*, New York, John Wiley.

Blau, P. M. (1968) 'The Hierarchy of Authority in Organisations', *American Journal of Sociology*, 73, pp. 453–67.

Blois, K. J. (1972) 'Vertical Quasi-integration', *Journal of Industrial Economics*, 20, pp. 253–72.

Bonoma, T. (1976) 'Conflict, Cooperation and Trust in Three Power Systems', *Behavioural Science*, 21, pp. 499–514.

Bucklin, L. P. (1960) 'The Economic Structure of Channels of Distribution' in B. Mallen (1967) *The Marketing Channel: A Conceptual Viewpoint*, New York, John Wiley and Son, pp. 63–6.

Burt, R. S. (1980) 'Testing a Structural Theory of Corporate Cooptation: Interorganisational Directorate Ties as a Strategy for Avoiding Market Constraints on Profits', *American Sociological Review*, 45, pp. 821–41.

Campbell, N. C. G. (1984) 'The Structure and Stability of Industrial Networks. Developing a Research Methodology. Research Developments in International Marketing', 1st IMP International Research Seminar, UMIST, Manchester.

Campbell, N. C. G. (1985) 'Network Analysis of a Global Capital Equipment Industry', 2nd IMP International Research Seminar, University of Uppsala, Sweden.

Campbell, N. C. G. and Cunningham, M. T. (1984) 'Customer Analysis for Strategy Development in Industrial Markets', *Strategic Management Journal*, 4, pp. 369–80.

Caves, R. (1982) *Multinational Enterprise and Economic Analysis*, Cambridge, Cambridge University Press.

Cavusgil, S. T. and Nevin, J. P. (1981) 'The State-of-the-Art in International Marketing. An Assessment' in B. M. Enis and K. J. Roerring (eds) *Review of Marketing*, Greenwich, Conn., JAI Press.

Contractor, F. J. and Lorange, P. (1988) 'Why Should Firms Cooperate? The Strategy and Economics Basis for Cooperative Ventures' in F. J. Contractor and P. Lorange, *Cooperative Strategies in International Business*, Lexington, Mass., Lexington Books.

Cook, K. S. (1977) 'Exchange and Power in Networks of Interorganisational Relations', *Sociological Quarterly*, 18, pp. 62–82.

Cook, K. S. (1981) *Network Structure from Exchange Perspectives in Social Structure and Network Analyses*, Beverly Hills, Calif., Sage, pp. 177–200.

Cook, K. S. and Emerson, R. (1978) 'Power, Equity and Commitment in Exchange Networks', *American Sociological Review*, 43: pp. 712–39.

Cook, K. S. and Emerson, R. (1984) 'Exchange Networks and the Analysis of Complex Organisations', *Research in the Sociology of Organisations*, Vol. 3, Greenwich, Conn., JAI Press pp. 1–30.

Cox, R. and Goodman, C. (1956) 'Marketing of Housebuilding Materials', *Journal of Marketing*, 11, 1, pp. 36–61.

Cummings, T. G. (1984) 'Transorganisational Development', *Research in Organisational Behaviour*, Vol. 6, Greenwich, Conn., JAI Press, pp. 367–422.

Cunningham, M. T. (1987) 'Interaction, Networks and Competitiveness: A European Perspective of Business Marketing', European–American Symposium "World Wide Marketplace for Technology Based Products", University of Twente, Enschede, The Netherlands.

Cyert, R. M. and March, J. G. (1963) *A Behavioural Theory of the Firm*, Englewood Cliffs, NJ, Prentice Hall.

Dahl, R. A. (1957) 'The Concept of Power', *Behavioural Science*, 2, pp. 201–15.

Dahmen, E. (1988) 'Development Blocks in Industrial Economics', *Scandinavian Economic Review*, 1, pp. 3–14.

Di Maggio, P. (1986) 'Structural Analysis of Organisational Fields', *Research in Organisational Behaviour*, Vol. 8, Greenwich, Conn., JAI Press, pp. 335–70.

Easton, G. (1988) 'Marketing strategy and Competition', *European Journal of Marketing*, 22, 1, pp. 31–49.

Easton, G. (1990) 'Relationships Among Competitors', in G. Day, B. Weitz and R. Wensley (eds) *The Interface of Marketing and Strategy*, Greenwich, Conn., JAI Press.

Easton, G. and Araujo, L. (1985) 'The Network Approach: An Articulation', 2nd International IMP Research Seminar, University of Uppsala, Sweden.

Easton, G. and Araujo, L. (1986) 'Networks, Bonding and Relationships in Industrial Markets', *Industrial Marketing and Purchasing*, 1, 1, pp. 8–25.

Easton, G. and Smith, P. (1984) 'The Formation of Inter-Organisational Relationships in a Major Gasfield Development', Research Seminar on Industrial Marketing, Stockholm School of Economics, Sweden.

Emerson, R. M. (1962) 'Power Dependence Relations', *American Sociological Review*, 27, pp. 31–40.

Emerson, R. M. (1972) 'Exchange Theory, Part II: Exchange Relations in Networks', in J. Berger, M. Zedditch and B. Andersson (eds) *Sociological Theories in Progress*, Boston, Mass., Houghton Mifflin, pp. 58–87.

Engwall, L. (1985) 'Fran vag vision till komplex organisation. En studie av Varmlands Folkblads ekonomiska och organisatoriska utveckling' (from a Vague Vision to a Complex Organisation. A Study of the Economic and Organisational Development of the Varmlands Folkbald'), *Acta Universitatis Upsaliensis*, 22, University of Uppsala, Sweden.

Engwall, L. and Johanson, J. (1989) 'Banks in industrial networks', Working Paper, Department of Business Studies, University of Uppsala, Sweden.

Evan, W. M. (1966) ' "The Organisation-Set" Toward a Theory of Interorganisational Relations', in J. Thompson (ed.) *Approaches to Organisational Design*, Pittsburg, Pa. University of Pittsburg Press.

Fiocca, R. and Snehota, I. (1986) 'Marketing e alta tecnologia', *Svihippo e Organizzazione*, 98, pp. 24–31.

Fombrun, C. J. and Astley, W. G. (1983) 'Beyond Corporate Strategy', *Journal of Business Strategy*, 3, pp. 47–54.

Ford, D. (1978) 'Stability Factors in Industrial Marketing Channels', *Industrial Marketing Management*, 7, pp. 410–22.

Ford, D., Håkansson, H. and Johanson, J. (1986) 'How do Companies Interact', *Industrial Marketing and Purchasing*, 1, 1, pp. 26–41.

Forrester, J. (1961) *Industrial Dynamics*, Boston, Mass., MIT Press.

Forsgren, M. (1985) 'The Foreign Acquisition Strategy – Internationalisation or Coping with Strategic Interdependencies in Networks?', Working Paper, Department of Business Administration, University of Uppsala, Sweden.

Forsgren, M. (1989) *Managing the Internationalisation Process. The Swedish Case*, London, Routledge.

Fullerton, R. (1986) 'Understanding Institutional Innovation and System Evolution in Distribution', *International Journal of Research in Marketing*, 3, pp. 273–82.

Gadde, L.-E. and Mattsson, L.-M. (1987) 'Stability and Change in Network Relationships', *International Journal of Research in Marketing*, 4, pp. 29–41.

Gadde, L.-E., Håkansson, H. and Oberg, M. (1988) 'Change and Stability in Swedish Automobile Distribution', Report prepared for the 2nd Annual Forum of the International Motor and Vehicle Program, Boston, Massachusetts Institute of Technology.

Gattorna, J. (1978) 'Channels of Distribution Conceptualisations: A State-of-the-Art Review', *European Journal of Marketing*, 12, 7, pp. 471–512.

Glaser, A. and Strauss, B. (1967) *The Discovery of Grounded Theory*, Chicago, Ill., Aldine.

Giete, J. (1984) 'High Technology and Industrial Networks', International Research Seminar on Industrial Marketing, Stockholm School of Economics, Sweden.

Granovetter, M. S. (1973) 'The Strength of Weak Ties', *American Journal of Sociology*, 78, 6, pp. 1360–80.

Granovetter, M. S. (1984) 'A Theory of Embeddedness', Department of Sociology, State University of New York.

Granovetter, M. S. (1985) 'Economic Action and Social Structure: The Problem of Embeddedness', *American Journal of Sociology*, 91, 3, pp. 481–510.

Grinyer, P. and Spender, J. C. (1979) 'Recipes, Crises and Adaptation in Mature Business', *International Studies of Management and Organisation*, 9, pp. 113–33.

Hagg, I. and Johanson, J. (1983) 'Firms in Networks', Business and Social Research Institute, Stockholm, Sweden.

Håkansson, H. (1982a) 'Teknisk Utveckling och Marknadsforing' (Technical Development and Marketing'), *MTC* 19, Stockholm, Stockholm School of Economics, Liber.

Håkansson, H. (ed.) (1982b) *International Marketing and Purchasing of Industrial Goods: An Interaction Approach*, Chichester, Wiley.

Håkansson, H. (ed.) (1987) *Industrial Technological Development: A Network Approach*, London, Croom Helm.

Håkansson, H. (1989) *Corporate Technological Behaviour: Cooperation and Networks*, London, Routledge.

Håkansson, H. and Johanson, J. (1948a) 'Heterogeneity in Industrial Markets and its Implications for Marketing' in I. Hagg and F. Wiedersheim-Paul (eds) 'Between Market and Hierarchy', Department of Business Administration, University of Uppsala, Sweden.

Håkansson, H. and Johanson, J. (1984b) 'A Model of Industrial Networks', Working Paper, Department of Business Administration, University of Uppsala, Sweden.

Håkansson, H. and Johanson, J. (1988) 'Formal and Informal Co-operation Strategies in International Industrial Networks' in F. J. Contractor and P. Lorange *Co-operative Strategies in International Business*, Lexington, Mass., Lexington Books.

Håkansson, H. and Ostberg, C. (1975) 'Industrial Marketing – An Organisational Problem', *Industrial Marketing Management*, 4, pp. 113–23.

Håkansson, H. and Snehota, I. (1989) 'No Business is an Island. The Network Concept of Business Strategy', *Scandinavian Journal of Management Studies*, 4, 3, pp. 187–200.

Håkansson, H. and Waluszewski, A. (1986) 'Technical Development in a Dense Network', 3rd International IMP Research Seminar, IRE, Lyon.

Hall, R. (1977) *Organisations: Structure and Process*, 2nd edn., Englewood Cliffs, NJ, Prentice Hall.

Hallen, L. (1984) 'Market Approaches in European Perspective', in P. Turnbull and J. P. Valla *Strategies in International Industrial Marketing: A Comparative Analysis*, London, Croom Helm.

Hamfelt, C. and Lindberg, A.-K. (1987) 'Technological Development and the Individual's Contact Network' in H. Håkansson (ed.) *Industrial Technological Development: A Network Approach*, London, Croom Helm.

Hammarkvist, K.-O. (1983) 'Markets as Networks', Marketing Education Group Conference, Cranfield, UK.

Hammarkvist, K.-O., Håkansson, H. and Mattsson, L.-G. (1982) *Marknadsforing for konkurrenskraft (Marketing for Competitive Power)*, Malmo, Liber.

Hampdon, G. M. and Van Gent, A. P. (eds) *Marketing Aspects of International Business*, Boston, Mass., Kluwer-Nijhoff.

Hannan, M. T. and Freeman, J. H. (1977) 'The Population Ecology of Organisations', *American Journal of Sociology*, 82, pp. 929–64.

Harrigan, K. (1983) *Strategies for Vertical Integration*, Lexington, Mass., Lexington Books.

Harrigan, K. (1985) *Strategies for Joint Ventures*, Lexington, Mass., Lexington Books.

Hawley, A. (1968) 'Human Ecology' in D. L. Sills (ed.) *The International Encyclopedia of the Social Sciences*, Vol. 4, New York, Macmillan and Free Press, pp. 328–37.

Hegert, M. and Morris, D. (1988) 'Trends in International Collaborative Agreements' in F. J. Contractor and P. Lorange *Co-operative Strategies in International Business*, Lexington, Mass., Lexington Books.

Henderson, J. M. and Quandt, R. E. (1971) *Microeconomic Theory*, 2nd edn., New York, McGraw-Hill.

Hettne, B. and Tamm, G. (1974) *Mobilisation and Development in India. A Case Study of Mysore State*, SIDA.

Hughes, T. P. (1983) *Networks of Power, Electrification in Western Society, 1880–1930*, Baltimore, Md., Johns Hopkins University Press.

Hultbom, C. (1990) 'Internal Exchange Processes. Buyer–Seller Relationships within Big Companies', Unpublished Ph.D. dissertation, Department of Business Studies, University of Uppsala, Sweden.

Hulten, S. (1985) 'What Can Theories of Industrial Change Contribute to the Understanding Of International Markets as Networks?', 2nd International IMP Research Seminar, University of Uppsala, Sweden.

Imai, K. (1987) 'Network industrial organisation in Japan', Working paper prepared for the workshop on 'New Issues in Industrial Economics' at Case Western Reserve University, Cleveland, OH, on 7–10 June.

Jansson, H. (1985) 'Marketing to Projects in South East Asia. A Network.' Working Paper 1985/3, Department of Business Administration, University of Uppsala, Sweden.

Johanson, J. and Mattsson, L.-G. (1984) 'Marketing Investments and Market Investments in Industrial Markets', International Research Seminar in Industrial Marketing, Stockholm School of Economics, Stockholm, Sweden.

Johanson, J. and Mattsson, L.-G. (1985) 'Marketing and Market Investments in industrial networks', *International Journal of Research in Marketing*, 2, 3, pp. 185–95.

Johanson, J. and Mattsson, L.-G. (1986) 'Interorganisational Relations in Industrial Systems: A Network Approach Compared with a Transaction Cost Approach', Working Paper, University of Uppsala, Sweden.

Johanson, J. and Mattsson, L.-G. (1987) 'Interorganisational Relations in Industrial Systems: A Network Approach Compared with a Transaction Cost Approach', *International Studies of Management Organisation*, 17, 1, pp. 34–48.

Johanson, J. and Mattsson, L.-G. (1988) 'Internationalisation in Industrial Systems – A Network Approach', in N. Hood and J.-E. Vahlne (eds) *Strategies in Global Competition*, London, Croom Helm.

Johanson, J. and Sharma, D. (1985) 'Swedish Technical Consultants; Tasks, Resources and Relationships – A Network Approach', International Research Seminar on Industrial Marketing, Stockholm School of Economics, Stockholm, Sweden.

Kaynak, E. and Savitt, R. (eds) (1984) *Comparative Marketing Systems*, New York, Praeger.

Killing, K. P. (1982) 'How to Make a Global Joint Venture Work', *Harvard Business Review*, 61, 3, pp. 120–7.

Killing, J. P. (1983) *Strategies for Joint Venture Success*, New York, Praeger.

Kinch, N. (1988) 'Emerging Strategies in a Network Context: The Volvo Case', *Scandinavian Journal of Management Studies*, October.

Kranzberg, M. (1986) 'Technology and History: Kranzberg's Laws', *Technology and Culture*, 7, pp. 185–95.

Kutschker, M. (1982) 'Power and Dependence in Industrial Marketing' in H. Håkansson (ed.) *International Marketing and Purchasing of Industrial Goods: An interaction approach*, Chichester, Wiley.

Kutschker, M. (1985) 'The Multi-Organizational interaction approach to Industrial Marketing', *Journal of Business Research*, 13, pp. 383–403.

Laage-Hellman, J. (1984) 'The Role of External Technical Exchange in R&D: An Empirical Study of the Swedish Special Steel Industry', M.T.C. Research No. 18, Marketing Technology Centre, Stockholm, Sweden.

Laage-Hellman, J. (1987) 'Process Innovation through Technical Cooperation', in H. Håkansson (ed.) *Industrial Technological Development; A Network Approach*, London, Croom Helm.

Laage-Hellman, J. (1988) 'Technological Development in Industrial Networks', Working Paper, Department of Business Administration, University of Uppsala, Sweden.

Laage-Hellman, J. (1989) 'Technological Developments in Industrial Networks', Unpublished Dissertation, Department of Business Administration, University of Uppsala, Sweden.

Laage-Hallman, J. and Axelsson, B. (1986) 'Biotekfnisk Foll i Sverigeforskninasuolam, forskninasinriktning, samartetsmonster. En studie av det bioteknisk Follnatverket 1970–1985' (Biotechnological R&D in Sweden. Research Volume, Direction of Research, Patterns of Cooperation. A study of the Biotechnological R&D Network 1970–1985), STU Information 536, Styrelsen for Teknisk Utveckling, Stockholm, Sweden.

Larsen, J. K. and Rogers, E. M. (1984) *Silicon Valley Fever*, New York, Basic Books.

Levine, S. and White, P. E. (1961) 'Exchange as a Conceptual Framework for the Study of Interorganisational Relationships', *Administrative Science Quarterly*, 5, pp. 583–601.

Lorenzoni, G. and Ornati, O. A. (1988) 'Constellations of Firms and New Ventures', *Journal of Business Venturing*, 3, pp. 41–57.

Lundgren, A. (1985) 'Datoriserad Bildbehandling i Sverige', ('Computerized Image processing in Sweden'), Working Paper, EFI, Stockholm School of Economics, Stockholm, Sweden.

Lundgren, A. (1987) 'Bildbehandlingens framvaxt', Working Paper, Stockholm School of Economics, Stockholm, Sweden.

Mallen, B. (ed.) (1967) *The Marketing Channel: A Conceptual Viewpoint*, New York, John Wiley and Son.

March, J. M. (1966) 'The Power of Power' in D. Easton (ed.) *Varieties of Political Theory*, Englewood Cliffs, NJ, Prentice Hall.

Marret, C. (1971) 'On the Specification of Interorganisational Dimensions', *Sociology and Social Research*, 56, pp. 83–9.

Mattson, L.-G. (1969) *Integration and Efficiency in Marketing Systems*, EFI, Stockholm, Nordstedt & Soner.

Mattson, L.-G. (1975) 'System Interdependencies – A Key Concept in Industrial Marketing', 2nd Research Seminar in Marketing, FNEGE, Senanque, France.

Mattsson, L.-G. (1981) 'Interorganisational Structures in Industrial Markets: A Challenge to Marketing Theory and Practice', Working Paper 1980/1, Department of Business Administration, University of Uppsala, Sweden.

Mattsson, L.-G. (1984) 'An Application of a Network Approach to Marketing: Defending and Changing Market Positions' in N. Dholakia and J. Arndt (eds) *Changing the Course of Marketing. Alternative Paradigms for Widening Marketing Theory*, Greenwich, Conn, JAI Press.

Mattsson, L.-G. (1986) 'Indirect Relationships in industrial networks: A Conceptual Analysis of their Significance', 3rd IMP International Seminar, IRE, Lyon, France.

Mattsson, L.-M. (1987a) 'Management of Strategic Change in a "Markets-as-Networks" Perspective' in A. Pettigrew *The Management of Strategic Change*, Oxford, Blackwell.

Mattsson, L.-G. (1987b) 'Conceptual Building blocks of Network Theory', Working Paper, Stockholm School of Economics, Stockholm, Sweden.

Mattsson L.-G. (1988) 'Interaction Strategies: A Network Approach' AMA Marketing Educator's Conference, Summer, San Francisco, Calif.

McCammon, B. (1964) 'Alternative Explanations of Institutional Change and Channel Evolution' in B. Mallen (ed.) (1967) *The Marketing Channel: A Conceptual Viewpoint*, New York: John Wiley and Son, pp. 75–81.

McCammon, B. and Little, R. W. (1965) 'Marketing Channels: Analytical Systems and Approaches' in G. Schwartz (ed.) (1970) *Science in Marketing*, New York, John Wiley and Son, pp. 321–85.

McVey, P. (1960) 'Are Channels of Distribution What the Textbooks Say?', *Journal of Marketing*, XXIV, 3, pp. 61–5.

Mintzberg, H. (1988) 'Opening up the Definition of Strategy' in J. B. Quinn, H. Mintzberg and R. M. James (eds) *The Strategy Process*, Englewood Cliffs, NJ, Prentice Hall International.

Morgan, G. (1986) *Images of Organisation*, Beverly Hills, Calif., Sage.

Nelson, R. R. and Winter, S. G. (1982) *An Evolutionary Theory of Economic Change*, Cambridge, Mass., Harvard University Press.

Nieschlag, R. (1954) 'Die Dynamik der Betriebsformen im Handel', Rheinisch-Westfahalches Institut für Wirtschaftsforschung, Essen, Schriftenreihe, Neue Folge nr 7.

Nilsson, A. (1987) 'Distributionssystems for Finpapper', ('Distribution Systems for Fine Paper'), Working Paper, EFI Stockholm School of Economics, Stockholm, Sweden.

Pascale, R. T. (1984) 'Perspectives on Strategy: "The Real Story Behind Honda's Success" ' *California Management Review*, 26, 3, pp. 47–72.

Pettigrew, A. (1985) *The Awakening Giant: Continuity and Change in Imperial Chemical Industries*, Oxford, Basil Blackwell.

Pfeffer, J. (1978) *Organisational Design*, Arlington Heights, Ill., AHM Publishing Co.

Pfeffer, J. (1987) 'Bringing the Environment Back in The Social Context of Business Strategy' in D. Teece *The Competitive Challenge: Strategies for Industrial Innovation and Renewal*, Cambridge, Mass., Balinger Publishers.

Pfeffer, J. and Lebjebici (1973) 'Executive Recruitment and the Development of Interfirm Organisations', *Administrative Science Quarterly*, 18, pp. 449–61.

Pfeffer, J. and Salancik, G. (1978) *The External Control of Organisations*, New York, Harper and Row.

Piori, M. and Sabel, F. (1984) *The Second Industrial Divide: Possibilities for Prosperity*, New York, Basic Books.

Porter, M. J. (1980) *Competitive Strategy: Techniques for Analyzing Industries and Competitors*, New York, The Free Press.

Reich, L. S. (1985) *The Making of American Industrial Research; Science and Business at G. E. and Bell, 1876–1926*, Cambridge, Cambridge University Press.

Rogers, E. M. (1982) *Interorganisational Coordination*, Ames, Ia., Iowa State University Press.

Rogers, E. M. (1984) 'Organisations and Networks; Illustrations from the Silicon Valley Microelectronics Industry', International Research Seminar on Industrial Marketing, Stockholm School of Economics, Stockholm.

Rogers, E. M. and Kincaid, D. L. (1981) *Communication Networks: Toward a New Paradigm for Research*, New York, The Free Press.

Root, F. (1978/82) *Foreign Market Entry Strategies*, New York, AMACON.

Rosenberg, D. L. (1982) *Inside the Black Box: Technology and Economics*, Cambridge, Cambridge University Press.

Scherer, F. M. (1980) *Industrial Market Structure and Economic Performance*, 2nd edn, Boston, Mass., Houghton Mifflin.

Schumpeter, J. A. (1955) *The Theory of Economic Development*, Cambridge, Mass., Harvard University Press.

Scott, R. W. (1987) *Organisation: Rational, Natural and Open Systems*, 2nd edn, Englewood Cliffs, NJ, Prentice Hall.

Silverman, D. (1970) *The Theory of Organisations*, London, Heinemann.

Smith, P. and Easton, G. (1986) 'Network Relationships: A Longitudinal Study' 3rd International IMP Research Seminar, IRE Lyon, France.

Thorelli, H. B. (1986) 'Networks: Between Markets and Hierarchies', *Strategic Management Journal*, 7, 1, pp. 37–51.

Thompson, J. D. (1967) *Organisations in Action*, New York, McGraw-Hill.

Tichy, N. and Fombrun, C. (1979) 'Network Analysis in Organisational Settings', *Human Relations*, 32, 11, pp. 923–65.

Turnbull, P. W. and Valla, J.-P. (1986) *Strategies in International Industrial Marketing*, London, Croom Helm.

Van de Ven, A. (1976) 'On the Formation and Maintenance of Relations among Organisations', *Academy of Management Review*, 4, 4, pp. 24–36.

Van de Ven, A. and Ferry, D. L. (1980) *Measuring and Assessing Organisations*, New York, John Wiley.

Van de Ven, A. and Walker, G. (1984) 'Dynamics of Interorganizational Coordination', *Administrative Science Quarterly*, Dec. pp. 598–621.

Venkataraman, N. and Camillius, J. L. (1984) 'Exploring the Concept of "Fit" in Strategic Management', *Academy of Management Review*, 9, 3, pp. 513–25.

von Hippel, E. (1978) 'Successful Industrial Products from Customer Ideas', *Journal of Marketing*, 42, pp. 39–49.

von Hippel, E. (1986) 'Cooperation between Competing Firms. Informal Know-how Trading', Working Paper no. 1959–86, Sloan School of Management, March.

Walker, G. (1988) 'Network Analysis for Cooperative Interfirm Relationships' in F. J. Contractor and P. Lorange *Co-operative Strategies in International Business*, Lexington, Mass., Lexington Books.

Waluszewski, A. (1987) CTMP-Processen. Fran vedkravande till vedsnala processor', Department of Business Studies, University of Uppsala, Sweden.

Waluszewski, A. (1989) 'Framvaxten av en ny mekanisk massateknik – en utrecklingshistoria' ('The Emergence of a New Mechanical Pulping Technique – A Development Story'), Unpublished dissertation, Department of Business Studies, University of Uppsala, Sweden.

Weick, K. E. (1969) *The Social Psychology of Organizing*, 1st edn, Reading, Mass., Addison-Wesley.

Weick, K. E. (1970) 'Educational Organisations as Loosely Coupled Systems', *Administrative Science Quarterly*, 21, 1, pp. 1–19.

Weick, K. E. (1979) *The Social Psychology of Organizing*, 2nd edn, Reading, Mass., Addison-Wesley.

Weick, K. E. (1984) 'Small Wins: Redefining the Scale of Social Problems', *American Psychologist*, 39, pp. 40–9.

Weitz, B. (1985) 'Introduction to Special Issue on Competition in Marketing', *Journal of Marketing Research*, 22, pp. 229–36.

Wibe, S. (1980) 'Change of Technology and Day to Day Improvements', Umea Economic Studies, Umea University, Sweden.

Williamson, O. E. (1975) *Markets and Hierarchies*, New York, The Free Press.

Williamson, O. E. (1985) *The Economic Institutions of Capitalism*, New York, The Free Press.

Wind, Y. (1979) 'The Journal of Marketing at a Cross Road', *Journal of Marketing*, 43, pp. 9–12.

Yamagashi, T., Gilmore, M. and Cook, K. (1988) 'Network Connections and the Distribution of Power in Exchange Networks', *American Journal of Sociology*, 93, 4, pp. 835–51.

Zaltman, G., Le Masters, K. and Heffring, M. (1982) *Theory Construction in Marketing*, New York, John Wiley.

3.6

Internationalisation in industrial systems – a network approach

Jan Johanson and Lars-Gunnar Mattsson

INTRODUCTION

International interdependence between firms and within industries is of great and increasing importance. Analyses of international trade, international investments, industrial organisation and international business behaviour attempt to describe, explain and give advice about these interdependencies. The theoretical bases and the level of aggregation of such analyses are naturally quite varied.

In this chapter we discuss explanations of internationalisation of industrial firms with the aid of a model that describes industrial markets as networks of relationships between firms. The reason for this exercise is a belief that the network model, being superior to some other models of "markets", makes it possible to consider some important interdependencies and development processes on international markets. The models that we have selected for some comparative analyses are the transaction cost based "theory of internalisation" for multinational enterprise and the "Uppsala Internationalization Process Model" emphasising experiential learning and gradual commitments. While the former is a dominating theoretical explanation of multinational enterprise (Buckley and Casson, 1976), the latter seems to be the most cited explanation of a firm's foreign market selection and mode of international resource transfer over time (Bilkey, 1978; Johanson and Vahlne, 1977).

We will first present some empirical data in support of some basic assumptions of the network model. We will then describe this model, commenting especially on the investment nature of marketing activities. Internationalisation of the firm and of the network is also given a conceptual interpretation. We are then in a position to analyse four cases concerning internationalisation of the firm and of the network: The Early Starter, The Lonely International, The Late Starter, and The International Among Others. Finally, we will comment on some research issues raised by our analysis.

CUSTOMER–SUPPLIER RELATIONSHIPS IN INDUSTRIAL MARKETS: SOME EMPIRICAL FINDINGS

A number of studies in industrial marketing and purchasing have demonstrated the existence of long-term relationships between suppliers and customers in industrial markets (e.g. Blois, 1972; Ford, 1978; Guillet de Monthoux, 1975; Håkansson and Ötberg, 1975; Levitt, 1983; Wind, 1970). It has also been emphasised by a leading marketing scholar that "for strategic purposes, the central focus of industrial marketing should not be on products or on markets, broadly defined, but on buyer–seller relationships" (Webster, 1979; 50). Such relationships have also been noted in studies in contractual relations (Macneil, 1978; Williamson, 1979) and in studies of technical development (von Hippel, 1978).

In an extensive international research project, industrial customer–supplier relationships were investigated. Interviews were made with industrial suppliers in Germany, France, Britain, and Sweden about the relations to their most important customers in the four countries and in Italy. Interviews were conducted with managers who had personal experience of the customers (Håkansson, 1982). Business transactions with important customers generally took place within well-established relationships. The average age of the 300 relations investigated was around 13 years (Hallén, 1986). The relationships were important to the two parties involved. In export relationships the suppliers were "main supplier" – in the sense that they provided at least half of the customer's needs for the products concerned – in about half of the cases. In the domestic relationships the suppliers were more often main suppliers – in around 80 per cent of the relationships.

The customers were also important to the suppliers. In the German sub-sample in which data about the customer's share of the supplier's sales are available, the average share of the customers investigated was 5.5 per cent. If we (somewhat arbitrarily) define a relationship as important to the customer if the supplier provides at least half of the need, and important to the supplier if the customer purchases at least 1 per cent of the supplier's sales, then 35 per cent of the relationships are classified as mutually important, 25 per cent as important to the supplier only, 18 per cent as important to the customer only, and 22 per cent as not important.

One of the reasons for the existence of long-term relationships is that suppliers and customers need extensive knowledge about each other if they are to carry on important business with each other. They need knowledge not only about price and quality, which may be very complex and difficult to determine; they also need knowledge about deliveries and a number of services before, during and after delivery. Much of that knowledge can in fact only be gained after transactions have taken place. Besides, they need knowledge about each other's resources, organisation and development possibilities. Knowledge about all these issues is seldom concentrated in one person in the firms. Not only marketers and purchasers, but also specialists in manufacturing, design, development, quality control, service, finance, and so on may take part in the information exchange between the companies. Contacts on several levels in the organisational hierarchies may be required. Such contacts may include personnel on the shop floor, top management and, of course, middle and lower management. The average total number of interacting persons in the relationships is between seven and eight from each party. Such contacts take time to establish: it takes time to learn which persons in a company possess certain types of knowledge, and which have the potentiality to influence certain conditions. On many occasions direct experience is the only possible way to learn so much about each other that the information exchange between the parties works efficiently. Such experiences certainly take time to acquire, and the parties invest in knowledge about each other.

Around 40 per cent of the relationships include contacts on the general management level. Specialists from manufacturing are involved on the customer side in 60–70 per cent of the relationships. Specialists on design and development take part in about 50 per cent of the relationships, and in both cases the supplier side is most involved. On the whole there are quite complex contact and interaction patterns in the relationships between the firms. Another aspect of the relationships is that significant business transactions require that the parties have confidence in each other's ability and willingness to fulfil their commitments. It takes time and effort to build such levels of confidence. The perceived social distance to the customers indicates the investments in confidence in the relationships. In 60–70 per cent of the relationships the respondent considered the relation as involving "close personal relations" or "friendly business relations" rather than more "formal business relations". Evidently these important relationships are also usually rather close, implying that they result from investments in the relationships.

Suppliers and customers are also often linked to each other through various types of technical and administrative arrangements. They may adapt products, processes, scheduling, delivery routines and logistical systems to the needs and capabilities of the specific counterpart. In the

German sub-sample some data are available about this type of investment in customer–supplier relationships. In the eight German customer relationships investigated, on average 2.5 inter-firm production system adaptations were made. In almost every relationship some adaptation of this kind was made. The adaptations were somewhat more common in domestic than they were in export relationships.

Against the background of this type of evidence, we assume that firms in industrial markets are linked to each other through long-lasting relationships. The parties in the relationships are important to each other; they establish and develop complex, inter-firm information channels, and they also develop social and technical bonds with each other. Generally, domestic relationships seem to be more developed and stronger than export relationships. However, many export relationships are also important and long-lasting. We assume that the relationships are important for the functioning of industrial markets and for the market strategies of industrial firms.

MARKETS AS NETWORKS – A GENERAL DESCRIPTION

The network approach in the form described in this section has been developed by a group of Swedish researchers whose background is research on distribution *systems*, internationalisation *processes* of industrial firms, and industrial purchasing and marketing behaviour as *interaction* between firms (Mattson (1985) describes this background). The approach is developed in a general way in Hägg and Johanson (1982) and Hammarkvist, Håkansson and Mattsson (1982). This section builds on those publications, and on Johanson and Mattsson (1985, 1986).

The industrial system is composed of firms engaged in production, distribution and use of goods and services. We describe this system as a network of relationships between the firms. There is a division of work in the network which means that the firms are dependent on each other, and their activities therefore need to be co-ordinated. Co-ordination is not brought about through a central plan or an organisational hierarchy, nor does it take place through the price mechanism as in the traditional market model. Instead, co-ordination occurs through interaction between firms in the network, where price is just one of several influencing conditions (cf. Lindblom, 1977). The firms are free to choose counterparts and thus "market forces" are at play. To gain access to external resources and make it possible to sell products, however, exchange *relationships* have to be established with other firms. Such relationships take time and effort to establish and develop, processes which constrain the firms' possibilities to change counterparts. The need for adjustments between the interdependent firms in terms of the quantity and quality of goods and services exchanged, and the timing of such exchange, call for more or less explicit co-ordination through joint planning, or through power exercised by one party over the other. Each firm in the network has relationships with customers, distributors, suppliers, and so on (and sometimes also directly with competitors), as well as indirect relations via those firms with suppliers' suppliers, customers' customers, competitors, and so on.

The networks are stable *and* changing. Individual business transactions between firms usually take place within the framework of established relationships. Evidently, some new relationships are occasionally established and some old relationships are disrupted for some reason (e.g. competitive activities), but most exchanges take place within earlier existing relationships. However, those existing relationships are continually changing through activities in connection with transactions made within the relationship. Efforts are made to maintain, develop, change and sometimes disrupt the relationships. As an aspect of those relationships, *bonds* of various kinds are developed between the firms. We distinguish here between technical, planning, knowledge, social, economic, and legal bonds. These bonds can be exemplified by, respectively, product and process adjustments, logistical co-ordination, knowledge about the counterpart, personal confidence and liking, special credit agreements, and long-term contracts.

We stress complementarity in the network. Of course, there are also important competitive relations. Other firms want to obtain access to specific exchange possibilities either as sellers or as buyers, and co-operating firms also have partially conflicting objectives. The relationships imply that there are *specific inter-firm dependence relations* which are of a different character compared with the general dependence relations to the market in the traditional market model. A firm has direct and specific dependence relations to those firms with which it has exchange relationships. It has indirect and specific dependence relations with those firms with which its direct counterparts have exchange relationships – that is, the other firms operating in the network in which it is engaged. Because of the network of relationships the firms operate in a complex system of specific dependence relations which is difficult to survey.

To become established in a new market – that is, a network which is new to the firm – it has to build relationships which are new both to itself and its counterparts. This is sometimes done by breaking old, existing relationships, and sometimes by adding a relationship to already-existing ones. Initiatives can be taken both by the seller and by the buyer. A supplier can become established in a network which is new to the firm, because a buying firm takes the initiative.

This model of industrial markets implies that the firm's activities in industrial markets are *cumulative processes* in which relationships are continually established, maintained, developed, and broken in order to give satisfactory, short-term economic return, and to create positions in the network, securing the long-term survival and development of the firm. Through the activities in the network, the firm develops relationships which secure its access to important resources and the sale of its products and services.

Because of the cumulative nature of the market activities, the market *position* is an important concept. At each point in time the firm has certain positions in the network which characterise its relations to other firms. These positions are a result of earlier activities in the network both by the firm and by other firms, and constitute the base which defines the development possibilities and constraints of the firm in the network. (See Mattsson (1985) for an analysis of the position concept and its use in a discussion of market strategies.) We distinguish here between *micro-positions* and *macro-positions*. A micro-position refers to the relationships with a specific individual counterpart; a macro-position refers to the relations to a network as a whole or to a specific section of it. A micro-position is characterised by:

1. the role the firm has for the other firm;
2. its importance to the other firm; and
3. the strength of the relationship with the other firm.

A macro-position is characterised by:

(1) the identity of the other firms with which the firm has direct relationships and indirect relations in the network;
(2) the role of the firm in the network;
(3) the importance of the firm in the network; and
(4) the strength of the relationships with the other firms.

The macro-positions are also affected by the interdependencies in the whole network as well as by the complementarity of the micro-positions in the network. Thus, in the context of the whole network, the macro-position is not an aggregation of micro-positions.

Example: Firm A's micro-position in relation to firm B. (1) It is a secondary supplier of fine paper and of knowhow about printing purposes. (2) The sales volume is 100, A's share of B's purchases of fine paper is 30 per cent and A is an important source of technical information. (3) The knowledge bonds are strong, but social bonds are rather weak due to recent changes in personnel in both A and B.

Example: Firm A's macro-position. (1) Lists exist of suppliers, customers, competitors and other firms in the network to whom the firm is directly or indirectly related. (2) It has the role as a full line distributor of fine paper in southern Sweden. (3) Its market share is 50 per cent, making it the market leader. (4) It enjoys strong knowledge, planning and social bonds to its major customers, and strong economic and legal bonds to its suppliers.

The positions describe the firm's relations to its industrial environment and thereby some important strategic possibilities and restrictions. All the other firms in the network have their own positions and likewise have future objectives regarding those positions. Desired changes or defence of positions thus describe important aspects of the firm's strategy. The strategies of firms can be complementary to each other, or competitive, or both. Important dimensions of the network structure are related to the set of positions of the organisations that are established there. The *degree of structuring* of the network is the extent to which positions of the organisations are interdependent. In tightly structured networks, the interdependence is high, the bonds are strong, and the positions of the firms are well defined. In loosely structured networks, the bonds are weak and the positions are less well defined.

The global industrial network can be partitioned in various ways. Delimitations can be made concerning geographical areas, products, techniques, and so on. We use the term "net" for specifically defined sections of the total network. When the grouping is made according to national borders we distinguish between different "national nets". Correspondingly we refer to "production nets" when the grouping is made on the basis of product areas. A production net contains relationships between those firms whose activities are linked to a specific product area. Thus, it is possible to distinguish a "heavy truck net" including firms manufacturing, distributing, repairing and using heavy trucks. This heavy truck net differs from the corresponding "industrial branch" as it also comprises firms with complementary activities, whereas the individual branch comprises firms with similar, mostly competing, activities. The firms in the net are linked to each other and have specific dependence relations to each other.

Within the framework of a product area with its production nets, different national production nets can be distinguished. Thus, in the heavy truck field we can speak of a Swedish, a Danish, a West German, an Italian, etc. heavy truck net, comprising the firms or operations in each country engaged in manufacture, distribution service and use of heavy trucks.

To sum up: we have described markets as networks of relationships between firms. The networks are stable *and* changing. Change and development processes in the networks are cumulative and take time. Individual firms have positions in the networks, and those positions are developed through activities in the network and define important possibilities and constraints for present and future activities. Marketing activities in networks serve to establish, maintain, develop and sometimes break relationships, to determine exchange conditions and to handle the actual exchange. Thus, important aspects of market analyses have to do with the present characteristics of the positions, the relations and their development patterns, in relevant networks for the firm. Important marketing problems for both management and for researchers are related to *investments*, since activities are cumulative; to *timing* of activities, because of interdependencies in the network; to *internal coordination* of activities, since "all" the firm's resources are involved in the exchange and since the micro-positions are interdependent; and to *co-operation* with counterparts, since activities are complementary.

INVESTMENTS IN NETWORKS

Investments are processes in which resources are committed to create, build or acquire assets which can be used in the future, assets which can be tangible or intangible. Examples of the former are plants and machinery, while examples of the latter are production and marketing knowledge, and proprietary rights to brand names. We call these assets *internal assets*: they are controlled by the firm and are used to carry out production, marketing, development and other activities.

A basic assumption in the network model is that the individual firm is dependent on resources controlled by other firms. The firm gets access to these external resources through its network positions. Since the development of positions takes time and effort, and since the present positions define opportunities and restrictions for the future strategic development of the firm, we look at the firm's positions in the network as partially controlled, intangible *"market assets"*. Market assets generate revenues for the firm and serve to give the firm access to other firms' internal assets. Because of the interdependencies between firms, the use of the asset in one firm is dependent on the use of other firms' assets. Thus, in addition, the investment processes, including their consequences, are interdependent in the network. (The reasoning in this section is developed at greater length in Johanson and Mattson (1985).)

INTERNATIONALISATION ACCORDING TO THE NETWORK APPROACH

According to the network model, the internationalisation of the firm means that the firm establishes and develops positions in relation to counterparts in foreign networks. This can be achieved (1) through establishment of positions in relation to counterparts in national nets that are new to the firm, i.e. *international extension*; (2) by developing the positions and increasing resource commitments in those nets abroad in which the firm already has positions, i.e. *penetration*; and (3) by increasing coordination between positions in different national nets, i.e. *international integration*. The firm's degree of internationalisation informs about the extent to which the firm occupies certain positions in different national nets, and how important and integrated are those positions. International integration is an aspect of internationalisation which it seems motivated to add to the traditional extension and penetration concepts, against the background of the specific dependence relations of the network model. Since position changes mean, by definition, that relationships with other firms are changed, internationalisation will according to the network model direct attention analytically to the investments in internal assets and market assets used for exchange activities. Furthermore, the firm's positions before the internationalisation process begins are of great interest, since they indicate market assets that might influence the process.

The network model also has consequences for the meaning of internationalisation of the market (network). A production net can be more or less internationalised. A high degree of internationalisation of a production net implies that there are many and strong relationships between the different national sections of the global production net. A low degree of internationalisation, on the other hand, means that the national nets have few relationships with each other. Internationalisation means that the number and strength of the relationships between the different parts of the global production network increase.

It can also be fruitful to distinguish between the internationalisation of production nets, implying more and stronger links between the national sections of the global production net; and the internationalisation of national nets, implying that they are becoming increasingly interconnected with other national nets. The difference is a matter of perspective: in the former case, attention is focused on a production net, in the latter on a national net. The distinction is interesting, because there may be important differences between the degree of internationalisation of different national nets. In one country the production net may be highly internationalised, whereas the corresponding net may not be very internationalised in another country. The distinction is also interesting, because in some situations internationalisation of the global production net affects all the national sections of the global production net. In other situations only some specific national nets with their production nets are internationalised. This may be the case when two or more national economies are integrated.

AN APPLICATION OF THE NETWORK MODEL TO ANALYSES OF THE INTERNATIONALISATION OF INDUSTRIAL FIRMS

What are the reasons explaining why firms internationalise their activities? Let us assume that the driving forces for increased internationalisation are that the firm wants to utilise and develop

		Degree of internationalisation of the market (the production net)	
		Low	High
Degree of internationalisation of the firm	Low	The Early Starter	The Later Starter
	High	The Lonely International	The International Among Others

Figure 1 Internationalisation and the network model: the situations to be analysed.

its resources in such a way that its long-run economic objectives are served. Firms then internationalise if that strategy increases the probability of reaching the general objectives. According to the network model, the firm's development is to an important extent dependent on its positions: it can use its market assets in its further development. Thus, the internationalisation characteristics of both the firm and of the market influence the process. The firm's market assets have a different structure if the firm is highly internationalised than they do if it is not. Furthermore, the market assets of the other firms in the network have a different structure if the market has a high or low degree of internationalisation. We will therefore make a comparative analysis of four different situations, as set out in Figure 1.

The analysis of the four situations thus concerns internationalisation processes in the three dimensions, extension, penetration and integration; and how these processes can at least partially be explained by reference to the network model. After this exercise we will make a comparison with what the internalisation model and the internationalisation model offer in the same types of situations.

The Early Starter

The firm has few and rather unimportant relationships with firms abroad. The same holds for other firms in the production net. Competitors, suppliers and other firms in the domestic market, as well as in foreign markets, have few important international relationships. In this situation the firm has little knowledge about foreign markets and it cannot count upon utilising relationships in the domestic market to gain such knowledge. As ventures abroad demand resources for knowledge development and for quantitative and qualitative adjustments to counterparts in the foreign markets, the size and resourcefulness of the firm can be assumed to play an important role. The strategy, often found in empirical studies, that internationalisation begins in nearby markets using agents rather than subsidiaries can be interpreted as (1) minimisation of the need for knowledge development; (2) minimisation of the demands for adjustments; and (3) utilisation of the positions in the market occupied by already-established firms. The firm can utilise the market investments that the agent in the foreign market has made earlier, thereby reducing the need for its own investment and risk taking. As the volume sold in the foreign market increases, the increase in the market assets may justify investment in production facilities in the foreign market.

The alternative strategy, to start with an acquisition or greenfield investment, would require a greater investment in the short run, but might perhaps enhance the long-term possibilities for knowledge development and penetration in the market. This is a strategy which is possible mainly for firms which have already become large and resourceful in the home market before internationalisation.

The importance of agents and other middle men is reinforced by the presumptive buyers' lack of experience of international operations. If those buyers happened to be at all conscious of foreign supply alternatives, they would probably be somewhat reluctant. This means that the supplier must let some third party – an agent – guarantee the firm's delivery capability, or itself invest in confidence-creating activities – for example, getting "reference customers", keeping local stocks, building a service organisation or even a manufacturing plant in the foreign market. This means further market investments.

Initiative in the early internationalisation of the firm is often taken by counterparts – that is, distributors or users in the foreign market. Thus, the foreign counterpart uses its own market assets to establish a new firm within its own network. Whether the firm, with this introduction as base, can develop its position in the market is very uncertain, and may depend on the degree of structuring of the network and on the positions of the "introducer". If the "introducer" is a leading distributor in a tightly structured network, the conditions are favourable for rapid penetration by the firm, given that the adjustments to the network are made. An obstacle may be that the demands for quantities become so high that the production capacity of the firm is too small. This may require increased engagement in the market through the establishment of production units. To reduce the risk of overcapacity, the parties may have to enter into long-term supply contracts, a process which is quite consistent with a tightly structured network.

As already discussed, the need for resource adjustment may become quite heavy in connection with a first step abroad. Such adjustments can be assumed to imply investments and it must be important to minimise the resource adjustment requirement in connection with early steps abroad. This holds for quantitative resource adjustments in connection with the capacity increases which the added market may demand, and it also holds for qualitative resource adjustments which may be required because of the possibility of new market needs deviating from earlier ones. Obviously, it may be possible to complement the resources through external sources. To the extent that such resource completions are made in the domestic market, they probably imply the same type of problems. They mean commitments which may be difficult to fulfil if the foreign engagement is a failure. On the other hand, they are probably risk reductions if they can be made in the actual foreign market. It is, however, not likely that a firm which has no experience of foreign operations would have qualifications for organising resource completions in the foreign market – that is, to establish positions in relation to local suppliers.

Another problem is that some resource adjustments can be made possible by giving up control over the operations in exchange for the flexibility needed to reduce risk taking in connection with foreign ventures. Such ventures may be carried out if the old owner transfers control of the firm to someone who is able to complement the firm's resources. In the absence of internationalisation of the environment, the extension to additional foreign markets will also be determined in general by the need for knowledge development and the need to create, or use already-existing, market assets. If conditions in markets which are new to the firm are similar to the conditions in the home market (and/or in the foreign markets in which the firm began its internationalisation), then there is a greater likelihood that these markets will be the next ones. If, however, the network is tightly structured, or if there is a lack of effective "introducers" on the foreign market that is "next in line", from a knowledge and adjustment point of view we expect to find extension patterns with other characteristics.

As the firm becomes more internationalised, it changes from an Early Starter situation to becoming a Lonely International.

The Lonely International

How is the situation changed if the firm is highly internationalised while its market environment is not? To start with, in this situation the firm has experience of relationships with and in foreign countries. It has acquired knowledge and means to handle environments which differ with respect to culture, institutions, and so on, and failures are therefore less likely. The knowledge situation is more favourable when establishing the firm in a new national net.

The second advantage is that the international firm probably has a wider repertoire of resource adjustments. The need for resource adjustments is likely to be more marginal and less difficult to handle. This holds for both quantitative and qualitative adjustments even if the former are perhaps more strongly affected by the greater size which attends internationalisation than they are by the internationalisation *per se*. In particular it is easier for the international firm to make various types of resource completions in the foreign markets. This is a special case of the general advantage of international firms, because of much greater resource combination possibilities. Note that resource combinations also include those external resources to which the positions give access. The firm which is highly internationalised may also use its market investments to get a rapid diffusion of its new products. It may use its positions partially to control the internationalisation moves of competitors, but may also involuntarily stimulate such moves (see below).

With regard to the structuring of the national nets, it can be assumed that the international firm will experience less difficulties than others in entering tightly structured nets. It already possesses good knowledge about many kinds of national markets. Further extension is not so dependent on similarities between markets as it is for the Early Starter. Experience and resources give the firm a repertoire which allows it to make the heavy market investments which are required to enter a tightly structured production net. It also has better possibilities for taking over firms with positions in the structured net or establishing relationships with such firms. It can also give its counterparts access to other national nets: for example, the international firm has greater possibilities than others to engage in barter trade.

Initiatives for furthering internationalisation do not come from other parties in the production nets, since the firm's suppliers, customers and competitors are not internationalised. On the contrary, the Lonely International has the qualifications to promote internationalisation of its production net, and consequently of the firms engaged in it. The firm's relationships both with and in other national nets may function as bridges to those nets for that firm's suppliers and customers. Perhaps they have a similar effect on competitors (cf. Knickerbocker, 1973). Firms which are internationalised before their competitors are forerunners in the internationalisation process and may enjoy advantages for that reason, in particular in tightly structured nets, because they have developed network positions before the competitors.

To exploit the advantages of being a Lonely International, the firm has to co-ordinate activities in the different national nets. International integration is therefore an important feature in the development of the highly internationalised firm. However, the need to co-ordinate is probably less than for the International Among Others.

The Late Starter

If the suppliers, customers and competitors of the firm are international, even the purely domestic firm has a number of indirect relations with foreign networks. Relationships in the domestic market may be driving forces to enter foreign markets. The firm can be "pulled out" by customers or suppliers, and in particular by complementary suppliers, e.g. in "big projects". Thus, market investments in the domestic market are assets which can be utilised when going abroad. In that case it is not necessary to go from the nearby market to more distant markets and the step abroad can already be rather large in the beginning. In addition, nearby markets may be tightly structured and already "occupied" by competitors. Thus, the extension pattern will be partly explained by the international character of indirect relations and the existence of entry opportunities.

Is the market penetration process of the firm affected by the degree of internationalisation of the production network where it is operating? The need for co-ordination is greater in a highly internationalised production net, which implies that establishment of sales subsidiaries should be made earlier if the firm is a Late Starter than if it is an Early Starter. The size of the firm is probably important: for example, a small firm going abroad in an internationalised world probably has to be highly specialised and adjusted to problem solutions in specific sections of the production nets.

Starting production abroad probably is a matter of what bonds to the customers are important. If joint planning with customers is essential it may be necessary to start local production early. Similarly, if technical development requires close contacts with the customers, it may be advantageous to manufacture locally. On the other hand, it may be better to use relationships with customers in the domestic market for development purposes, especially if these customers are internationalised (as they to some extent are, by definition, in the Late Starter case). However, such customers also have access to alternative, internationally based counterparts for their own development processes which might reduce the importance of their domestic suppliers.

The situation is different for large firms. As firms which have become large in the domestic market often are less specialised than small firms, their situation is often more complex than in the case of the small firm. One possibility is that of becoming established in a foreign production net through acquisition or joint venture. Of course, this is associated with great risks to a firm without experience of foreign acquisitions or joint ventures, particularly if other firms in the production net are internationalised. In general, it is probably more difficult for a firm which has become large at home to find a niche in highly internationalised nets. Unlike the small firm, it cannot adjust in a way which is necessary in such a net, nor has it the same ability as the small firm to react on the initiatives of other firms – which is probably the main road to internationalisation in a net in which other firms are already international.

The Late Starter has a comparative disadvantage in terms of its lesser market knowledge as compared with its competitors. Furthermore, as suggested above, it is often difficult to establish new positions in a tightly structured net. The best distributors are, for example, already linked to competitors. More or less legally, competitors can make the late newcomer unprofitable, by means of predatory pricing. In addition in comparison with the Early Starter the Late Starter probably has a less difficult task with regard to trust. Firms in the foreign markets already have experience of suppliers from abroad.

In a highly internationalised world the firms are probably more specialised. Consequently, a firm which is a Late Starter has to have a greater customer adaptation ability or a greater ability to influence the need specifications of the customers. However, the influence ability of a Late Starter is probably rather limited. The comparison between the Early Starter and the Late Starter illustrates the importance of timing as a basic issue in the analysis of strategies in networks.

The International Among Others

In this case both the firm and its environment are highly internationalised. A further internationalisation of the firm only means marginal changes in extension and penetration, which, on the whole, do not imply any qualitative changes in the firm. It is probable, however, that international integration of the firm can lead to radical internationalisation changes.

Both with regard to extension and penetration the firm has possibilities to use positions in one net for bridging over to other nets. A necessary condition for such bridging is that the lateral relations within the firm are quite strong. Some kind of international integration is required, not only in the "vertical", hierarchical sense, but also in the lateral, decentralised sense (Galbraith, 1973). As extension takes place in a globally interdependent network, the driving forces and the obstacles to this extension are closely related to this interdependence. Models of global oligopolies fit the argument here. Entries are made in those sections of the global production net which the competitors consider their main markets in order to discourage the competitor from making threatening competitive moves in other markets. In such a situation the entry may meet some resistance, but it is difficult for the competitors to use predatory pricing.

For the Early Starter, penetration through production in a foreign market was mainly a result of a need to bring about a balance between internal resources and external demands and possibilities in the specific market. For the International Among Others, the situation is different. The operations in one market may make it possible to utilise production capacity for sales in other markets. This may lead to production co-ordination by specialisation and increased volumes of intra-firm international trade. When the markets are expanding, it is possible in that case to put off capacity increases in one market, while capacity increases are made in another market before the positions in that market motivated such expansion. The surplus capacity could be linked to the wider international network, and this requires strong international integration of the firm.

Establishment of sales subsidiaries is probably speeded up by high internationalisation, as the international knowledge level is higher and there is a stronger need to co-ordinate activities in different markets. The need for coordination places heavy demand on the organisation. The competitors can utilise weaknesses in one market if they are not likely to meet counter-attacks in markets in which the firm is strong. Co-ordination gains in procurement, production and R&D are more likely than if the internationalisation of the firm and of the network is low. National differences are smaller, innovations are diffused more rapidly, and indirect business relations via the "third country" become more important to utilise. The market investments in one country will probably be more important as the external resources to which the relationships give access are more dispersed internationally.

The many positions which the International Among Others occupies in internationally linked networks give it access to, and some influence over, external resources. This means that the possibility for "externalisation" increases. The international manufacturing firm may thus increasingly tend to purchase components, sub-assemblies, etc. rather than do the manufacturing itself. Such subcontracting is sometimes required by host governments, but may also be a way to make the multinational enterprise more effective. Since important customers or joint-venture partners in one country are also by definition international, the International Among Others is faced with opportunities for further extension or penetration in "third countries". Thus, a Swedish firm might increase its penetration in a South American market because of its relationship in Japan with an internationalising Japanese firm. Other examples of such international interdependence are "big projects" in which design, equipment supply, construction, ownership and operation can all be allocated to firms of different national origin, but with internationally more or less dispersed activities. In such production nets, further internationalisation is probably predominantly dependent on the firm's configuration of network positions and on its ability not only to co-ordinate its own resources in different parts of the world, but also to influence, through its market assets, the use of resources owned by other firms.

The advantage of being able to co-ordinate operations in international networks is still more evident when changes take place in the environment. Assume that such changes spread from country to country: the international firm is then likely to have better possibilities to discover such changes as well as better opportunities to take advantage of them. A third advantage may be that the international firm can dominate and influence the international diffusion process and thus affect the development – but this probably requires size as well. Changes also occur in the localisation of economic activity. The internationally co-ordinated firm has better opportunities to detect and adjust to such changes. It can, for example, use its earlier established positions in an expanding national market to increase its penetration in that market and perhaps also its extension to other national markets within an expanding region of such markets. A driving force for further internationalisation by the International Among Others is to increase its ability to adjust to (or perhaps to influence) the geographical reallocation of activities in the production net.

The International Among Others predominantly faces counterparts and competitors who are themselves internationally active and markets that are rather tightly structured. This means that major positions changes in this situation will increasingly take place through joint ventures, acquisitions and mergers, in contrast with the other three cases that we have analysed. If, finally, we compare with the Early Starter situation, internationalisation for the International Among Others will be much less explicable by reference to the need for knowledge development and the similarities between the foreign markets and the home market. Instead, the driving forces and the restrictions are related to the strategic use of network positions.

THE NETWORK APPROACH COMPARED WITH TWO OTHER MODELS

The theory of internalisation

The theory of internalisation (Buckley and Casson, 1976; Rugman, 1982) currently seems to be generally accepted as an explanation of multinational enterprise. The theory assumes that a multinational enterprise has somehow developed a firm-specific advantage in its home market. This is usually in the form of internally developed, intangible assets giving the firm some superior production, product, marketing and/or management knowledge. If this asset cannot be exploited and safeguarded effectively through market (or contractual) transactions, an "internal market" has to be created. Expansions outside the firm's domestic market, given that local production is advantageous, will then take place through horizontal and/or vertical integration. The firm either establishes or buys manufacturing plants outside its home market. Thus, the multinational enterprise exists because of "market failures" or high "contracting costs". The firm wants to protect its intangible assets and to be able to control the price others pay for the use of these assets. There are, however, also costs of internalising in the form of internal administrative systems and risk-taking. These costs of internalisation will be lower, the less different the foreign market is from the home market. Thus, the internalisation model will predict that internalisation starts in "nearby" markets (Caves, 1982, chapter 1). It should be noted that the internalisation model is not intended to explain processes: rather, it tries to explain a specific economic institution, the multinational enterprise. It does say something, however, about the driving forces for internationalisation and the modes of international resource transfer.

We believe that the explanatory power of the internalisation model is greater in the situations in which the environment is not internationalised. The application of the model to the Early Starter situation is somewhat less than straightforward, though, since in the beginning the Early Starter is not a multinational enterprise and it exports products rather than manufacturing them abroad. However, we might extend the reasoning underlying the internationalisation model to include not only manufacturing, but also marketing activities. Given such an interpretation, if the advantages of local manufacturing are small, then it seems reasonable to expect the firm to export its intangible assets "embedded in products", and that the marketing activities in the foreign market are carried out by a sales subsidiary rather than by an independent agent (unless the contracting costs are less than the cost of internalising). The internationalisation model could be used to explain why firms enter a market using a sales subsidiary and not an independent agent, while the internationalisation model discussed below could be used to explain why agents precede sales subsidiaries. While the first model emphasises the need for exploiting and protecting internally created intangible assets, the second model emphasises the need for gradual development of market knowledge and the need to learn from interaction with other firms during the process.

In addition, the further expansion into the Lonely International case seems to fit with basic assumptions in the internalisation approach. The intangible assets constitute a firm-specific advantage that can be exploited in many markets through the operations of a multinational enterprise. However, it if takes a long time from the beginning of the internationalisation process to the status of Lonely International, the question arises as to how the firm can further develop its firm-specific advantage and not merely preserve and exploit it. It seems to be an implicit assumption in the internalisation approach that the firm's development activities are "internal". In the network approach, development activities are to an important extent dependent on the relationships with other firms, and thus on the network positions of the firm. Since internationalisation is a process by which network positions are established and changed, internationalisation as such influences the further development of the products, production processes, marketing behaviour, etc.

We said earlier that firms in networks invest in relationships with other firms. The positions thus created are in this chapter regarded as market investments, or in other words, as a form of intangible assets. These assets give partial access to external resources. Thus, the multinational enterprise increasingly enjoys direct relationships with customers and users in foreign markets rather than the indirect relations through agents or licensee's enjoyed by the less internationalised firm, operating only in its home market. This leads to a further observation linked to the network model. The highly internationalised firm may use its network positions effectively to "*externalise*" some of its activities, without losing control of its crucial intangible assets. The manufacturing value added by multinational industrial firms might decrease because of increased "subcontracting". We believe that this is especially true in the International Among Others case.

If both the firm and its environment are highly internationalised, it seems that a model which aims to explain multinational enterprise loses some of its relevance for analysis of further internationalisation. We might, of course, still be helped by the transaction cost approach in our attempts to understand just what institutional form penetration, expansion and integration actually take. However, the approach does not consider the cumulative nature of activities, the use of external assets, the development potential of network relationships, or the interdependence between national markets.

The (Uppsala) internationalisation model

The internationalisation process described as a gradual step-by-step commitment to sell and to manufacture internationally as part of a growth and experimental learning process is a model that is associated with the research on the internationalisation of Swedish manufacturing industry that has been carried out at the University of Uppsala (see, for example, Hörnell *et al.*, 1973; Johanson and Wiedersheim-Paul, 1974; and Johanson and Valine, 1977). Focusing especially on export behaviour Bilkey (1978) conceptualised, and found evidence for, the exporting process as a sequential learning process by which the firm goes through stages of increasing commitment to foreign markets. This "stage model" has lately come under some criticism, even if its general acceptance in the research community as a valid description seems to be high. Reid (1983) argues that the model is too deterministic and general: according to him, the firm's choice of entry and expansion modes are more selective and context-specific, and can be explained by heterogeneous resource patterns and market opportunities. Firms will therefore use multiple modes of international transfers. Reid suggests that a transaction cost approach is superior to the experiential learning model. Hedlund and Kverneland (1984, p. 77) also criticise the model, concluding that the "experiences of Swedish firms in Japan suggest that establishment and growth strategies on foreign markets are changing towards more direct and rapid entry modes than those implied by theories of gradual and slow internationalisation processes".

We believe that the internationalisation model is less valid in situations in which both the market and the firm are highly internationalised. The firms which started their internationalisation during the early twentieth century were usually in the Early Starter situation. The studies of Swedish industrial firms, on which the Uppsala model is based, describe and explain this situation and its transition to the Lonely International stage. There is no explicit consideration in the model of the internationalisation of the firm's environment. We would therefore expect the internationalisation model to be most valid in the Early Starter case and least valid in the International Among Others stage. Both the network approach and the internationalisation model stress the cumulative nature of the firm's activities. The latter, however, is a model focusing on the internal development of the firm's knowledge and other resources, while the network approach also offers a model of the market and the firm's relations to that market.

In the Late Starter situation, we therefore expect the internationalisation model to be less valid than the network model because of the importance of indirect international relations in the home market and because of the probably quite heterogeneous pattern of entry opportunities when foreign markets are compared. In the International Among Others case, the internationalisation model seems to lose much of its relevance. Reid's, and Hedlund and Kverneland's arguments seem to be valid. Since by definition the firm and its counterparts and competitors have positions in a large number of markets, penetration and integration aspects of internationalisation seem to be more important strategic moves than further extension. In such a global perspective, specific national market differences will likely have less explanatory power.

To sum up: we believe that both the internalisation and the internationalisation models leave out characteristics of the firm and the market which seem especially important in the case of "global competition" and co-operation in industrial systems.

SOME CONCLUDING REMARKS CONCERNING RESEARCH ISSUES

Against the background of the above discussion, we believe that more research in two, closely related, fields will serve to increase knowledge about the internationalisation of business: firstly, network internationalisation processes; and secondly, use of market assets in international competition.

Network internationalisation

Studies of network internationalisation may focus on internationalisation of national nets or of production nets. Such studies should describe and analyse the roles of different types of industrial actors in the process. They should also investigate the implications of the cumulative nature of network processes. More specifically, we advocate research into foreign market entry strategies in different situations with regard to network internationalisation. According to the network we can distinguish entry strategies which differ with regard to the character and number of relationships the entry firm seeks to establish with other firms in the network. We can also study which of the actors in the network take initiatives in different entry processes and in networks which are more or less internationalised. Furthermore, the entry strategies may differ with regard to the ambitions of the entry firm in adopting or influencing the network structure in the entry market.

The network approach also implies that the strategic discretion is constrained by the character of the network in which the firm is operating or into which it intends to enter. This indicates that during the internationalisation of a network, the timing of the operations of a firm is important. It can also be expected that, because of the cumulative nature of network processes, the sequential order of activities in international markets is important and should be given more attention in research. Perhaps, however, the problem of timing is next to impossible to solve. From a strategic point of view the most interesting research issue, then, is that of analysing how to build preparedness for action when the time is ripe. Presumably, preparedness is largely a matter of having relationships with other parties.

This view on industrial markets implies that there are strong interdependencies between different sections, i.e. national nets, of the global networks: hence, integration of operations is important. At the same time, the view implies that action has to be taken close to other actors in the market, often in response to their actions. Strategies can probably not be planned and designed by remote headquarters, and their implementation requires some kind of lateral relation between organisational units operating in different national nets. Research about the organisation problem of integrating operations in international networks is required.

Use of market assets in international competition

We have emphasised the strategic importance of market assets and suggest research about their use in international competition. In particular, there is scope for work on the use of the market assets of one country as they affect competition with other countries. We think it would be interesting to study how market assets in one country are used when entering other country markets. Such studies should concern not only the use of domestic market assets in the first step abroad, but also the use of foreign market assets when entering third-country markets. They could focus on different types of market assets, or the country of the assets utilised – in terms of networks – or the target markets.

Another interesting research issue is the use of market assets in global competition. Such research could focus on the use of relationships with more or less multinational companies in global competition. Relationships with suppliers, customers, distributors or consultants are of different importance when competing in various types of production nets and national nets.

Finally, the strategic importance of market assets implies that fruitful research can be made about control of foreign market assets. Whereas internal assets are usually controlled hierarchically with ownership as the base, control of market assets must have other bases. Research has demonstrated that such factors as access to critical resources, information or legitimacy are often important as bases of control. The significance of those factors may differ considerably in different contexts. Both conceptual and empirical research is required.

REFERENCES

Bilkey, W. J. An attempted integration of literature on the export behavior of firms. *Journal of International Business Studies*, Spring, 93–8 (1978).

Blois, K. J. Vertical quasi-integration. *Journal of Industrial Economics*, **20** (3), 253–72 (1972).

Buckley, R. J. and Casson, M. C. *The Future of Multinational Enterprise*. Macmillan, London (1976).

Caves, R. E. *Multinational Enterprise and Economic Analysis*. Cambridge University Press, Cambridge (1982).

Ford, D. Stability factors in industrial marketing channels. *Industrial Marketing Management*, **7** (6), 410–22 (1978).

Galbraith, J. *Designing Complex Organizations*. Addison-Wesley, Reading, Mass (1973).

Guillet de Monthoux, P. Organizational mating and industrial marketing conservatism – some reasons why industrial marketing managers resist marketing theory. *Industrial Marketing Management*, **4** (1), 25–36 (1975).

Hägg, I. and Johanson, J. (eds) *Företag i Nätverk*. SNS, Stockholm (1982).

Håkansson, H. (ed.) *International Marketing and Purchasing of Industrial Goods: An Interaction Approach*. Wiley, Chichester (1982).

Håkansson, H. and Östberg, C. Industrial marketing – an organizational problem? *Industrial Marketing Management*, **4**, 113–23 (1975).

Hallén, L. A comparison of strategic marketing approach. In P. W. Turnbull, and J. P. Valla (eds), *Strategies for International Industrial Marketing: A Comparative Analysis*. Croom Helm, London (1986).

Hammarkvist, K.-O., Håkansson, H. and Mattsson, L.-G. *Marknadsföring för Konkurrenskraft*. Liber, Malmö (1982).

Hedlund, G. and Kverneland, Å. Investing in Japan – *The Experience of Swedish Firms*. Institute of International Business, Stockholm School of Economics, Stockholm (1984).

Hörnell, E., Vahlne, J.-E. and Wiedersheim-Paul, F. *Export och utlandsestableringar*. Almqvist and Wiksell, Uppsala (1973).

Johanson, J. and Mattsson, L.-G. Marketing investments and market investments in industrial networks. *Industrial Journal of Research in Marketing* **2** (3), 185–95.

Johanson, J. and Mattsson, L.-G. International marketing and internationalization processes – A network approach. In S. Paliwoda and P. N. Turnbull (eds), *Research in International Marketing*. Croom Helm, London (1986).

Johanson, J. and Vahlne, J.-E. The internationalization process of the firm – a model of knowledge development and increasing foreign market commitments. *Journal of International Business*, **8** (Spring–Summer), 23–32 (1977).

Johanson, J. and Wiedersheim-Paul, F. The internationalization of the firm – four Swedish case studies. *Journal of Management Studies*, **3** (October), 305–22 (1974).

Knickerbocker, F. T. *Oligopolistic Reaction and Multinational Enterprise*. Division of Research, Harvard Graduate School of Business Administration, Cambridge, Mass. (1973).

Levitt, T. *The Marketing Imagination*. The Free Press, New York (1983).

Lindblom, C.-E. *Politics and Markets*. Basic Books, New York (1977).

Macneil, I. R. Contracts: adjustment of long-term economic relations under classical, neoclassical, and relational contract law. *Northwestern University Lay Review*, **72** (6), 854–905 (1978).

Mattsson, L.-G. An application of a network approach to marketing: defending and changing market positions. In N. Dholakia and J. Arndt (eds), *Alternative Paradigms for Widening Marketing Theory*. JAI Press, Greenwich, CT (1985).

Reid, S. Firm internationalization, transaction costs and strategic choice. *International Marketing Review*, Winter, 44–56 (1983).

Rugman, A. M. (ed.) *New Theories of the Multinational Enterprise*. Croom Helm, London (1982).

Von Hippel, E. Successful industrial products from customer ideas. *Journal of Marketing*, **42**, 39–49 (1978).

Webster, F. E., Jr. *Industrial Marketing Strategy*. Wiley, New York (1979).

Williamson, O. E. Transaction cost economics: the governance of contractual relations. *Journal of Law and Economics*, 233–61 (1979).

Wind, Y. Industrial source loyalty. *Journal of Marketing Research*, **8**, 433–6 (1970).

3.7 Dyadic business relationships within a business network context

James C. Anderson, Håkan Håkansson and Jan Johanson

In recent years, several models and frameworks have contributed significantly to our understanding of working relationships between firms in business markets (e.g. Anderson and Narus, 1990; Anderson and Weitz, 1989; Dwyer, Schurr, and Oh, 1987; Frazier, 1983; Hallén, Johanson, and Seyed-Mohamed, 1991). Each approach focuses on the dyadic relation between two firms. Some recent developments in business practice, however, strongly suggest that the connections between a firm's dyadic relations are of growing interest.

"Deconstructed" firms are emerging, in which firms focus on a subset of the value-adding functions traditionally performed within a firm (e.g. research and development, design, manufacturing) and rely on coordinated relationships with other firms to provide the remainder of the value-chain activities needed for a market offering (Verity, 1992). Another development is the "value-adding partnership" (Johnston and Lawrence, 1988, p. 94), which is "a set of independent companies that work closely together to manage the flow of goods and services along the value-added chain," enabling groupings of smaller firms to compete favorably against larger, integrated firms. A final development to note is the "virtual corporation," a transitory network of firms organized around a specific market opportunity, lasting only for the length of that opportunity (Byrne, Brandt, and Port, 1993).

A crucial question is how these developments in business practice should be regarded conceptually as well as managerially. A ready answer, drawing on recent work by organizational theorists (e.g. Miles and Snow, 1992; Snow, Miles, and Coleman, 1992) and European marketing scholars largely associated with the International Marketing and Purchasing Group (e.g. Ford, 1990; Håkansson, 1987; Mattsson, 1987), is to move from dyadic business relationships to business networks. Yet this answer is deceptively simple – no particular conceptualization is implied. For example, business networks can be regarded as sets of connected firms (e.g. Astley and Fombrun, 1983; Miles and Snow, 1992) or alternatively, as sets of connected relationships between firms (e.g. Cook and Emerson, 1978; Håkansson and Johanson, 1993). And, even when this latter view is held, consideration of the individual relationships and what occurs within them often is scant, with the relationships themselves rapidly diminished to links within a network that is of focal interest. This is surprising because if business networks are to possess advantages beyond the sum of the involved dyadic relations, this must be due to considerations that take place within dyadic business relationships about their connectedness with other relationships. Therefore, we intend to provide further conceptual development of dyadic business relationships that captures the embedded context within which those relationships occur. As an integral part of this, we formulate business network constructs from the perspective of a focal firm and its partner in a focal relation that is connected with other relationships. In doing so, we also advance the conceptualization of business networks as sets of connected relationships.[1]

We first examine the environment of the firm. We then discuss dyadic business relationships and networks and follow this with two recent case studies of business networks that, taken together with business network concepts, provide inductive grist for further conceptual development. We next conceptualize some network constructs that can be incorporated within dyadic business relationship models. Our intent is to provide a means of representing the connectedness of dyadic business relationships within these kinds of models. To furnish some empirical support that these proposed constructs are sufficiently well delineated and generate some suggested measures for them, we conduct a substantive validity assessment. We conclude with a prospectus for research on business relationships within business networks.

THE ENVIRONMENT OF THE FIRM

One critical specification in all approaches developed to analyze managerial problems involves the interface between the firm and its environment. Classically, there has been an assumption of a clear boundary between the two, in which *environment* has been defined as "anything not part of the organization itself" (Miles, 1980, p. 195). Firms have been viewed as "solitary units confronted by faceless environments" (Astley, 1984, p. 526). A firm's relationship with its environment is one of adapting to constraints imposed by an intractable externality (Astley and Fombrun, 1983).

This conceptualization of the environment of the firm has been questioned in both economics and organizational theory.[2] Resource dependence theory and related perspectives (Astley, 1984; Pfeffer, 1987; Pfeffer and Salancik, 1978) have argued that because firms' environments "are primarily socially constructed environments . . . the boundary between organizations and their environments begins to dissolve" (Astley, 1984, p. 533). Thus, the perspective changes to one of a firm interacting with its perceived environment (Pfeffer, 1987; Pfeffer and Salancik, 1978).

Drawing on this and related work (e.g. Thibaut and Kelley, 1959), a stream of research in marketing has stressed the importance of dyadic busines relationships (e.g. Anderson and Narus, 1990; Anderson and Weitz, 1989; Dwyer, Schurr, and Oh, 1987; Frazier, 1983; Hallén, Johanson, and Seyed-Mohammed, 1991). Yet the existence of relationships themselves questions the very meaning of the boundary between a firm and its environment. A relationship gives each firm a certain influence over the other (Anderson and Narus, 1990), which means that each firm is gaining control of at least one part of its environment while giving away some of its internal control. Relationships also indicate that firms do not treat the environment in a generalized or standardized way but interact with specific "faces" (Håkansson and Snehota, 1989; Thorelli, 1986).

The existence of relationships gives some specific faces to the environment of a firm, but this raises another question: How should the environment of these relationships be regarded? Should this environment be looked on as some faceless force, or should it instead be regarded as having some specific, organized character? Although past work in marketing has largely and implicitly regarded the studied relationships as existing within some faceless environment, we argue for the latter. In the next section, we elucidate the perspective of a firm within a focal relationship that is itself connected to other relationships and the nature of the environment as it relates to this.

BUSINESS NETWORKS AND DYADIC BUSINESS RELATIONSHIPS

Business networks recently have been of interest to a group of marketing academics in Europe (e.g. Ford, 1990; Gaddé and Mattsson, 1987; Håkansson and Johanson, 1993): Seeking a compatible framework, these researchers generalized the social exchange perspective on dyadic relations and social exchange networks (e.g. Cook and Emerson, 1978; Emerson, 1972) to dyadic business relationships and networks. Here, we examine the nature of business networks and firms within business networks and, in doing so, present the principal concepts for each.

Business networks

The developments in business practice mentioned at the outset are examples of what can be called *business networks*. A business network can be defined as a set of two or more connected business relationships, in which each exchange relation is between business firms that are conceptualized as collective actors (Emerson, 1981). Connected means the extent to which "exchange in one relation is contingent upon exchange (or non-exchange) in the other relation" (Cook and Emerson, 1978, p. 725). Moreover, two connected relationships of interest themselves can be both directly and indirectly connected with other relationships that have some bearing on them, as part of a larger business network. As illustrated in Figure 1, a focal relationship is connected to several different relationships that either the supplier or the customer has, some of which are with the same third parties.[3]

What functions do the relationships fulfil it we look on them from a network point of view? To answer this question, we can take as a starting point the concept of the firm as an actor performing activities and employing resources (cf. Demsetz, 1992; Henderson and Quandt, 1971). According to this view, the function of business relationships can be characterized with respect to three essential components: *activities, actors*, and *resources*. We can also draw a distinction between primary and secondary functions. By *primary functions*, we mean the positive and negative effects on the two partner firms of their interaction in a focal dyadic relationship. The *secondary functions*, also called *network functions*, caputre the indirect positive and negative effects of a relationship because it is directly or indirectly connected to other relationships. However, in a given relationship, secondary functions can be as important as the primary ones, or even more so.

The primary functions of the relationships corresponding to activities, resources, and actors are efficiency through interlinking of activities, creative leveraging of resource heterogeneity, and mutuality based on self-interest of actors. Activities performed by two actors, through their relationship, can be adapted to each other so that their combined efficiency is improved, such as in just-in-time exchange (Frazier, Spekman, and O'Neal, 1988). The two parties also can learn about each other's resources and find new and better ways to combine them; that is, the relationship can have an innovative effect (Lundvall, 1985). Finally, in working together, two actors can learn that by cooperating, they can raise the benefits that each receives (Axelrod, 1984; Kelley and Thibaut, 1978).

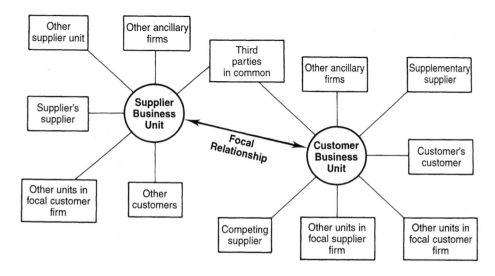

Figure 1 Connected relations for firms in a dyadic relationship.

Secondary or network functions are caused by the existence of connections between relationships. With regard to the three components, the secondary functions concern *chains of activities* involving more than two firms, *constellations of resources* controlled by more than two firms, and *shared network perceptions* by more than two firms. By adapting activities in several relationships to each other, thus raising the complementarity of sequences or other interdependent activities, activity chains stretching over several firms are created. Similarly, resources developed in a relationship not only are important to those engaged in that relationship, but also may have implications for resources of parties engaged in connected relationships. Thus, innovations developed as a result of interaction in several relationships may support each other. Finally, by getting close to its partners, a focal firm may have its views shaped by, and shape the views of, its partners' partners.

Relationships are dyads, but the existence of the secondary functions means that they also are parts of networks. A business network is built up by business relationships, but the latter are also caused by the secondary functions, reflecting the business network. However, a critical point is that there is no simple one-to-one relation between the relationship and the network, which can be seen by considering their dynamic features (cf. Aldrich and Whetten, 1981; Van de Ven, 1976). Developing relationships can have stabilizing and/or destabilizing consequences. If the development builds further on the earlier principles of the network, it will strengthen it. If, on the other hand, the development is a contradiction to the earlier structure, then it can be a first step toward network extension or consolidation (Cook, 1982; Emerson, 1972) – that is, a new network.

Firms within business networks

Network context and strategic network identity. Evidently, actors have bounded knowledge about the networks in which they are engaged (Emerson, 1981; Håkansson and Johanson, 1993). This is due to not only the network extending further and further away from the actor but also the basic invisibility of network relationships and connections. The network setting extends without limits through connected relationships, making any business network boundary arbitrary. For the purpose of analysis, however, it is possible to define *network horizons*, which denote how extended an actor's view of the network is. The network horizon can be expected to be dependent on the experience of the actor as well as on structural network features. This implies that the network horizon of an actor changes over time as a consequence of doing business. At the same time, it clearly demonstrates that any business network boundary is arbitrary and depends on perspective.[4]

The part of the network within the horizon that the actor considers relevant is the actor's *network context* (Håkansson and Snehota, 1989). The network context of an actor is structured, we posit, in the three dimensions identified in the discussion of primary and secondary functions of relationships: the *actors*, who they are and how they are related to each other; the *activities* performed in the network and the ways in which they are linked to each other; and the *resources* used in the network and the patterns of adaptation between them. The contexts are partially shared by the network actors, at least by actors that are close to each other.

In this ambiguous, complex, and fluid configuration of firms that constitute a network, in which the relations between firms have such importance, the firms develop *network identities* (Håkansson and Johanson, 1988). Network identity is meant to capture the perceived attractiveness (or repulsiveness) of a firm as an exchange partner due to its unique set of connected relations with other firms, links to their activities, and ties with their resources. It refers to how firms see themselves in the network and how they are seen by other network actors.

Because network identity is represented as a perception, it is crucial to specify the vantage point of the perceiver. A firm's network context provides the vantage point for its perceptions of the network identities of other firms within the network. And, significantly, even though network contexts of different firms may be partially shared, they are always unique in at least some respects. Thus, because network identity depends at least partly on the network context of the viewer, a focal firm has a distinct, though perhaps congruent, identity to each other firm in the network.[5] Similarly, a firm's perception of its own network identity is based on its own network context. We call this the firm's *strategic network identity*. This captures the overall perception of its own attractiveness (or repulsiveness) as an exchange partner to other firms within its network context. It is a reference point against which the firm perceives and judges its own and other firms' actions (Ring and Van de Ven, 1994).

Because identities are context related, they are described in the same dimensions. Each identity communicates a certain orientation toward other actors; it conveys a certain competence, because it is based on each actor's perceived capability to perform certain activities (Albert and Whetten, 1985); and it has a certain power content, because it is based on the particular resources each actor possesses (Cook *et al.*, 1983; Yamagishi, Gillmore, and Cook, 1988).

These actor orientations, activity competencies, and resources possessed are largely actualized and made apparent through exchange interaction in a firm's set of connected relations (cf. Goffman, 1959). At the same time, these connected relations impart additional meaning about a focal firm's actor orientations, activity competencies, and resources. For example, a firm will be viewed as strong in resource terms if it is seen as being able to mobilize and leverage the substantial resources of a connected partner. In summary, an actor is seen as "belonging" together with some others, having a certain competence in relation to those others, and being more or less strong in resource terms. This network identity, which can be more or less clear, conscious, and uniform, is itself a reference point against which all of a focal firm's acts are perceived and judged (Ring and Van de Ven, 1994).

Network context and environment. In what ways can we usefully distinguish between the concept of a network context and the previous, related concept of environment? Recently, for example, in presenting alternative forms of the marketing organization that are responsive to turbulent environments, Achrol (1991) appears to use the terms *environment* and *network* interchangeably. In contrast, our view is that the firm is embedded within a business network context that is itself enveloped by an environment.[6] Under this view, at least two useful distinctions between environment and network emerge: the different ways in which boundaries of the firm are regarded and different conceptual clarities in characterizing disparate impacts on a focal firm (or focal business relation).

In contrast with the classical specification, a network perspective better captures the notion that the boundary between the firm and its environment is much more diffuse. The environment is not completely given by external forces but can be influenced and manipulated by the firm, and there will also exist external, known actors that are influencing some of the firm's internal functions. Importantly, the network approach does not suggest merely that it is not meaningful to draw a clear boundary between the firm and its environment, but that much of the uniqueness of a firm lies in how and with whom it is connected (Håkansson and Snehota, 1989).

A difficulty in understanding what is meant by environment, let alone how it differs from a network, is that it has been discussed in numerous ways (cf. Miles, 1980). Moreover, in a given discussion, to capture *disparate impacts* on the firm, *levels* of environment are often assumed or posited (Miles, 1980). As a particularly germane example, in their analysis of the marketing environment of channel dyads, Achrol, Reve, and Stern (1983) distinguish between primary task environment, secondary task environment, and macro environment. The primary task environment is composed of a focal dyad's immediate suppliers and customers, in which any impact can be traced back to specific firms – to the "direct exchange network," as it is referred to at one point (Achrol, Reve, and Stern, 1983, p. 59). The primary task environment, in turn, is assumed to be affected by the secondary task environment, which comprises actors that are indirectly connected to the focal dyad (through exchange relations with actors in the primary task environment). Achrol, Reve, and Stern (1983) contend that the secondary task environment falls beyond the scope of their political economy framework and that its impact on the dyad can be best characterized in terms of abstract qualitative dimensions. The relatively amorphous effects of the macro environment are manifested only through their impact on the qualitative dimensions of the secondary task environment.

We conjecture, as Achrol, Reve, and Stern (1983) seem to do, that the primary task environment is structured as a network. We differ, however, in the way we deal analytically with the parts of the environment that are outside this "direct exchange network." Given our basic social exchange framework, it is logical to consider those parts or aspects of the environment that the actor perceives as relevant (Håkansson and Snehota, 1989). Thus, the concept of network context, which may encompass indirectly connected exchange relations in addition to the direct exchange network, appears to offer a natural delimiter of network from environment. Finally, similar in spirit to Achrol, Reve, and Stern (1983), we posit that the impacts of the relatively amorphous or imperceptible parts of the secondary task and macro environments, which we refer to simply as the environment, are mediated through the network context.[7]

TWO BUSINESS NETWORK CASES

A basic conclusion from the previous discussion is that every relationship should be viewed as being part of a network. The identity of the firm is embedded in the network through its relationships, which are connected to each other. This naturally leads to consideration of how network embeddedness contributes to the understanding of dyadic business relationships. As grist for inductive theory development (Deshpandé, 1983; Leonard-Barton, 1990), we present two European case studies of business networks.

Development of new saw equipment.   A network – labeled the *wood saw network* – was studied in Håkansson (1987). The focal relationship was between a saw equipment producer and a sawmill but, as depicted in Figure 2, several other relationships were connected. Cooperation was required to develop band saw equipment that could be used for cutting frozen timber, a necessity for the equipment to be used in Sweden. By working together with its components supplier, the equipment supplier managed to provide an initial solution technically.

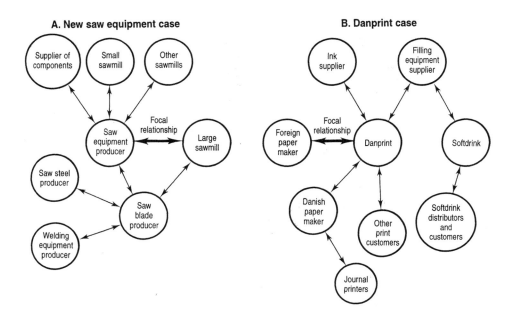

Figure 2   Two business network cases.

In the next phase, this solution was tried out together with two customer firms – one small sawmill located nearby with which the supplier had worked on other projects and a large sawmill that was viewed as an opinion leader. The latter was interested because it had several large investment projects coming up. The first prototype, a small band saw, was developed successfully and tested with the small customer. But when this solution was transferred to the larger customer, cracks developed in a bigger prototype, and there were even some serious breakdowns in which the whole band saw broke off. Weaknesses in the steel and especially in the welding seams in the band saws were regarded as the problems. So the large sawmill initiated technical cooperation with a saw blade producer in the belief that it would be possible to eliminate these problems by making changes in the saw blade producer's production process. However, it was found that it was necessary for the saw blade producer to get adaptations in the steel it bought from a saw steel company as well as acquiring new equipment for the welding operation. These efforts were not wholly successful, so the saw equipment producer had to make further adaptations to its equipment. The total process took several years to accomplish but was, in the end, very successful.

Danprint. Danprint is a small Danish printer that has supplied labels to a big Danish soft drink producer, Softdrink, for many years (Sjöberg, 1991). The labels were printed on a simple paper produced by one of the mills of a Danish paper maker, which also supplied other papers from its other mills to Danprint. Although simple, the paper was quite special in that it had a certain yellow shade that was strongly associated with Softdrink's image among its distributors and customers. Due to its wood content, the paper also was well-adapted to Softdrink's equipment for cleaning and filling return bottles. These relations appear in Figure 3.

Danprint, however, was only a marginal buyer of this product in comparison with journal printers. When they changed to another, more "elegant" paper, the paper maker had to close the

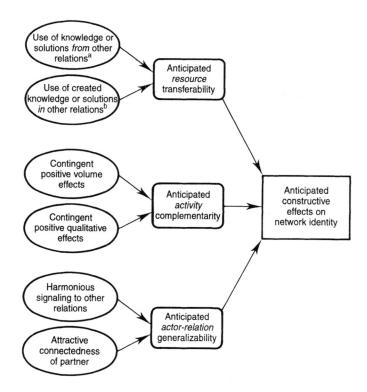

Figure 3   The constituent facets of the construct: anticipated constructive effects on network identity.

mill where Danprint's paper was made. Worse still, the paper maker could not produce a paper with Softdrink's specifications in any of its other mills. After some search, Danprint found a foreign paper mill that, after some cooperation, could produce a paper with almost the same yellow color as the original paper. This new paper was more expensive than the old, but rather than taking the risk of relaunching the drink with a new label, Softdrink accepted the higher price.

But the guarantee of Softdrink's filling equipment supplier concerning the speed and functioning of its equipment was not valid unless they, too, found the paper acceptable. Consequently, some cooperative activities between Danprint and the equipment supplier were required to gain this acceptance. In parallel, Danprint also engaged in cooperation with its ink supplier to be able to print on the new paper to the satisfaction of Softdrink and its connected distributors and customers. Moreover, Danprint learned from the cooperation with the foreign mill the exact prescription of and procedure for testing this yellow paper. On the basis of this new know-how, Danprint returned to their old Danish paper maker in a stronger position and induced this supplier to produce and supply the new paper in competition with the foreign mill.

Consider now Danprint's situation when it engaged in cooperation with the foreign paper maker (this is the focal relationship in Figure 3). Several network effects can be discerned. First, Danprint had to take their relationship with Softdrink into consideration. The primary anticipated effect was development of a paper that could be used in Softdrink's filling equipment to the satisfaction of Softdrink and its connected equipment supplier, distributors, and customers. Second, Danprint wanted to demonstrate to Softdrink that it was dependable even when considerable efforts were required. The relationship with Softdrink was important not only because of the sales volume involved; Softdrink was prestigious, and the relationship with it showed other Danprint customers that it was a capable print supplier.

Danprint also had to consider their relationship with the Danish paper maker, which still was its main supplier of other papers. Switching to the foreign supplier might harm other activities in their relationship. Yet cooperation with the foreign supplier could lead to a new product solution that could be transferred to the Danish relation, thus strengthening their long-run relationship.

Moreover, when engaging in cooperation with the foreign paper maker, Danprint had reason to consider the possibilities to coordinate these activities with those in relationships with the filling equipment and ink suppliers and to develop complementary solutions.

Some observations. Taken together, these cases provide a worthwhile, practical basis for considering and developing constructs that capture the embedded context within which dyadic business relationships occur. They also show some points of departure from the social network literature. Before developing some network constructs, we note some aspects of these cases.

The cases show both interesting similarities and differences. In both, the focal relationship is affected by the broader context of connected relationships. Activities or resources of other actors in this way are partly determining what is achieved in the focal relationships. Because of this, consideration of secondary or network functions will be especially critical in developing constructs. One important difference between the cases is that in the new saw equipment case, the connected relations provide positive, complementary development sources. In the Danprint case, several of the connected relations function as restricting connections.

The cases also show that these connections cannot be seen simply as positive or negative, as suggested in Cook and Emerson's (1978) analysis of social exchange networks. Rather, a relationship, in different ways, can be both positively and negatively connected with another relationship at the same time. Danprint's relationship with the foreign paper mill was, to some extent, negatively and positively connected to its relation with the Danish paper maker. And, apart from this, though some connections are rather easy to estimate quantitatively, others are entirely a matter of perceptual judgment or interpretations. Finally, the cases also stress the importance of time dependence in the analysis of business networks and the connections between dyadic relationships. Two firms might be positively connected in one time period but negatively connected in another. The dyadic relationships develop over time within a network context, which is also evolving as time goes by.

CONSTRUCTS THAT CAPTURE THE EMBEDDED CONTEXT OF DYADIC BUSINESS RELATIONSHIPS

An essential commonality of a dyadic business relationship perspective and a business network perspective is a consideration of the interdependencies that exist between firms doing business with one another and the resultant need for cooperation. Unquestionably, cooperation emerges as the pivotal construct from the two cases. Our intent here is to conceptualize, in a fundamental way, some network constructs that contribute to or have an effect on cooperation in dyadic business relations. Then, to illustrate how these constructs might be incorporated in dyadic relationship models, we sketch out some construct relationships with cooperation and what we view as its critical consequence: commitment. We conclude this section with a substantive validity assessment of our proposed constructs.

In positing constructs that capture network properties, a critical difference between perspectives that must be resolved is the focus on relationship *states* (e.g. the state of cooperation in the relationship) in the dyadic relationship perspective versus the focus on *activities* in the network perspective. How are activities and resources translated into perceptions of relationship states? Our reconciliation of this difference in perspectives is that activities requiring resources are undertaken in pursuit of outcomes, which, when evaluated by actors, provide judgments of relationship states. Viewed in this way, network properties underlie the network constructs that we conceptualize.

Constructs that capture the focal relationship's connectedness

Most often, models of dyadic business relationships have the implicit assumption of *ceteris paribus* in all other relations. The cases reveal that this is probably not a realistic assumption. As one instance of connectedness, the guarantee of Softdrink's filling equipment supplier was invalidated without its acceptance of label changes. Thus, antecedent constructs in dyadic perspective models can provide only a partial understanding of consequent constructs of interest (e.g. cooperation, relationship commitment) in that no constructs have been put forth that reflect the influence of this connectedness on the decisions and activities of a focal firm in a dyadic relationship of interest.

We offer two constructs that capture the connectedness of the focal relationship, as perceived by each partner firm. The first is *anticipated constructive effects on network identity*, which can be defined as the extent to which a focal firm perceives that engaging in an exchange relation episode with its partner firm has, in addition to effects on outcomes within the relation, a strengthening, supportive, or otherwise advantageous effect on its network identity. Given the conceptualization of network effects and network identity, three constituent facets can be distinguished: anticipated resource transferability, anticipated activity complementarity, and anticipated actor-relationship generalizability. These constituent facets, along with their principal aspects, appear in Figure 3.

Anticipated resource transferability refers to the extent to which knowledge or solutions are transportable. As its principal aspect use of knowledge or solutions from other relations indicates, resources needed for developing the focal relationship may exist already in some other relationship. A solution, or at least its basic principles (Hallén, Johanson, and Seyed-Mohamed, 1991), can be taken from this other relationship and employed in the focal relationship. Furthermore, cooperation in the focal relationship may develop resources that can be combined with resources from other relationships. Alternatively, the other principal aspect, use of created knowledge or solutions in other relationships, indicates that resources developed through exchange in a focal relationship can strengthen network identity when they can be utilized in one or more other relationships. The relationship between the saw equipment producer and the small mill can be seen as an instance of anticipated resource transferability.

Anticipated activity complementarity captures the notion that the value of the outcomes from activities undertaken in connected exchange relationships may be contingent on activities performed in the focal relationship; thus, these focal relationship activities have a strengthening effect on the firm's network identity. As its principal aspects indicate, these positive effects can be volume based or qualitative in nature. An increase in volume may have positive scale effects in other relationships, such that the costs of performing the same types of activities in all other relationships are lowered. In a similar way, qualitative changes in activities performed in a focal relationship may have qualitative effects in other relationships. The cooperative activities between Danprint and the equipment supplier to uphold the fill-rate guarantee for Softdrink illustrate activity complementarity of contingent positive volume effects, whereas Danprint and the ink supplier working together on printing quality can be seen as an example of contingent positive qualitative effects.

Anticipated actor-relationship generalizability refers to the possibility that cooperation with a certain actor may have broader implications for other actors. As its principal aspect harmonious signaling to other relations indicates, when a focal firm cooperates with another firm in such a way that it is visible to other actors, it sends a message that it is willing and capable of having cooperative relations (Hill, 1990). Therefore, this harmonious signaling can alter or reinforce other firms' network perceptions of the focal firm in an advantageous way. Consider, for example, the signals from Danprint to its other print customers that it is prepared to make strong cooperative efforts to solve technical problems. Its other principal aspect, attractive connectedness of partner, captures the notion that by getting closer to a certain partner firm, the focal firm also gets closer to its partner's other partners. Thus, the relationship with the well-known and prestigious Softdrink was a central element in Danprint's network identity.

In summary, anticipated constructive effects on network identity, with its constituent facets, aims at capturing the effects of positive connections between the focal relationship and all other relationships from the focal firm's point of view. These connections are not of marginal import. On the century, a firm's uniqueness can be found in its way of interrelating its set of relationships.

Participation in the focal relationship also can be expected to have harmful consequences on the focal firm's relations with other firms. Accordingly, our second construct is *anticipated deleterious effects on network identity*, which can be defined as the extent to which a firm perceives that engaging in an exchange interaction episode with the partner firm has, in some way, negative, damaging, or otherwise harmful effects on its network identity. Given the conceptualization of network effects and network identity, three constituent facets of this construct can be distinguished: anticipated resource particularity, anticipated activity irreconcilability, and anticipated actor-relationship incompatibility. These constituent facets, along with their principal aspects, appear in Figure 4.

Anticipated resource particularity, with its principal aspects of tying up resources from use in other relationships and adaptations detrimental to other relationships, captures the potentially problematic nature of using resources in more than one relation (cf. the related but more narrow concept of asset specificity (Williamson, 1985)). A focal firm simply may have limited resources for exchange.[8] Thus, the involvement of those scarce managerial resources may require reallocating resources from other relationships, which get less attention, with a subsequent harmful effect on the focal firm's network identity. Other customers of the saw equipment producer – sawmills having other production problems – may have seen the whole project as a waste of time and efforts.

Anticipated activity irreconcilability refers to the difficulty or impossibility of integrating activities in different relations with each other. As its principal aspects indicate, these negative effects can be volume based or qualitative in nature. Activity patterns often must be tailored to the requirements of the focal relationships (Hallen, Johanson, and Seyed-Mohamed, 1991), yet these

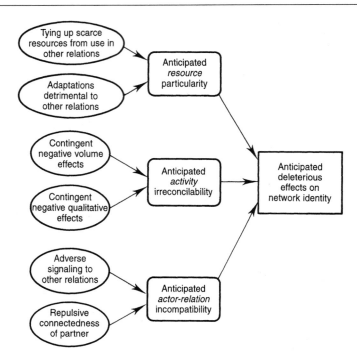

Figure 4 The constituent facets of the construct: anticipated deleterious effects on network identity.

activity patterns may be harmful and disturbing to other relationships. For example, Danprint could not change to a new paper if this was not accepted by Softdrink's filling equipment supplier.

Finally, *anticipated actor-relationship incompatibility* represents the unwanted "baggage" that may come from engaging in a focal relationship, in which relations with specific actors can be perceived as a threat by other actors or regarded by them as noxious in some way. Other affected firms may even take sanctions against the focal firm. Its principal aspect, adverse signaling to other relations, refers to the possibility that cooperation with a certain actor may convey to other firms that the focal firm is moving in a strategic direction that is inimical to their own best interests. Danprint's working together with the foreign supplier may have been construed as an adverse signal by the Danish paper maker. Its other principal aspect, repulsive connectedness of partner, represents the potential problems for the firm with negative connectedness of its partner. For example, it was reported that Mitsubishi has been reluctant to engage in cooperative relations with Daimler-Benz because Mitsubishi has a strong supplier relationship with Boeing whereas Daimler-Benz is part of the Airbus consortium, an ardent competitor of Boeing (Brull and Mitchener, 1993).

In summary, a focal business relationship, in addition to desired effects on outcomes within that relationship, inevitably may have some downsides as well with respect to a focal firm's network identity. Moreover, anticipated constructive effects on network identity and anticipated constructive effects on network identity are likely to be present to a varying extent in each business relationship. The saw equipment producer working together with the two saw mills and Danprint working together with the foreign paper maker each had, to some extent, both constructive and deleterious effects. Much like influence over and influence by the partner firm (Anderson and Narus, 1990), they represent separate constructs, not opposite ends of a single continuum.

Outcomes given comparison level and comparison level for alternatives as network constructs

How do firms evaluate the outcomes they obtain from working together? Under a dyadic relationship perspective, Anderson and Narus (1984) suggest that the outcomes (economic and social) that each firm obtains within an exchange relation are judged relative to the firm's own *comparison level* (CL) and *comparison level for alternatives* (CL_{alt}), which are standards that represent, respectively, expectations of benefits from a given kind of relationship based on experience with similar relations, and the benefits available in the best alternative exchange relation (Thibaut and Kelley, 1959). How would the meaning of these change in moving to a network perspective?

We can reconceptualize CL as a standard representing the synthesis of all perceived *connected* relationships for a firm in its network context. In contrast, CL_{alt} can be reconceptualized as a standard representing the synthesis of all directly or nearly substitutable relations for a firm in its network context. In most business-to-business settings, relations are only nearly substitutable in that some adaptation will be needed, even though it may be rather minor (Hallén, Johanson and Seyed-Mohamed, 1991). Thus, the concept of network context defines the pertinent network structure, which, significantly, provides the firm's judgment frame (Tversky and Kahneman, 1981) for evaluating its outcomes from each dyadic relationship and making decisions about allocating resources in the next period.[9] Put simply, network context provides the evoked set for judgments about a firm's dyadic relationships, and CL and CL_{alt}, capture this in their respective, integrative ways.

The constructs of interest, though, are *outcomes* given CL and *outcomes* given CL_{alt}. Even as we move to a network context for the focal relationship, outcomes still refer to the economic and social rewards obtained minus costs incurred by each firm in what it does in the focal relationship and thus are akin to the primary functions of relationships discussed previously (and the potentially enhanced results produced by them). That is, outcomes that occur within the focal relationship are judged against CL and CL_{alt}. Although what a firm does in a focal relationship may also affect outcomes in other connected relationships, as in the Danprint case, these outcomes *are* not reflected in outcomes given CL and CL_{alt}. Instead, these connectedness effects on outcomes that occur in a firm's other relations are captured by the constructs of anticipated constructive and deleterious effects on network identity and thus are akin to the secondary functions of relationships discussed previously.[10]

This link of social exchange concepts to network concepts provides an underpinning for them that has been, by and large, implicit in social exchange theory writings (cf. Thibaut and Kelley, 1959, chapters 6 and 7). And although the concepts of outcomes given CL and CL_{alt} have not been discussed in marketing as business network concepts, clearly their meaning is dependent on the presence of other business relationships that are in some way connected with the focal business relationship. Network context thus provides an explicit conceptual mechanism for a more complete understanding of what other relations constitute the defining sets for CL and CL_{alt}.

Posited construct relationships with cooperation and commitment

Although a comprehensive model of dyadic business relationships is beyond our scope here, we present some posited construct relations simply to illustrate how the constructs we have proposed might be incorporated in such models. To understand them better, we first provide brief conceptualizations of the constructs of cooperation and commitment.

Cooperation can be defined as similar or complementary coordinated activities performed by firms in a business relationship to produce superior mutual outcomes or singular outcomes with expected reciprocity over time (Anderson and Narus, 1990). Surprisingly, cooperation seldom has been studied explicitly as a construct (see Anderson and Narus (1990) for a recent exception). Yet in recent work in interorganizational theory and marketing, several processes and studied constructs can be construed as compatible with our conception of cooperation. In their interorganizational process model for transactional value analysis, which is offered as a preferred alternative to transaction cost analysis, Zajac and Olsen (1993) discuss a "processing" stage in which value-creating exchanges occur. Ring and Van de Ven (1994) view cooperation more broadly as characterizing a particular kind of interorganizational relationship. However, the "execution" stage in their process framework, in which the actors engage in mutually pre-agreed activities requiring resources, appears to capture what we mean as cooperation.

In marketing, several recently studied constructs can be viewed as cooperation. Heide and John (1990) studied the construct of joint action, in which two firms in a close relationship carry out "focal activities in a cooperative or coordinated way" (p. 25). Cooperation can be viewed broadly as occurring within the relationship maintenance process outlined by Heide (1994) and is more specifically reflected in the flexible adjustment process construct studied. In the relationship development framework of Dwyer, Schurr, and Oh (1987), cooperation is a part of the initiation and expansion phases. Finally, in work that embraces a transaction cost perspective, the constructs of specific investments (Heide and John, 1990) and idiosyncratic investments (Anderson and Weitz, 1992) can be interpreted as dedicated activities and resources employed in cooperation between firms.

Relationship commitment captures the perceived continuity or growth in the relationship between two firms (Achrol, 1991; Anderson and Weitz, 1992). A closely related construct is relationship continuity (Anderson and Weitz, 1989; Heide and John, 1990), which reflects each firm's "perception of the likelihood that the relationship will continue" (Anderson and Weitz, 1989, p. 311). Growth in the relationship refers to a broadening and deepening of the exchange relation. The relationship can broaden through the extent of joint value created between firms (Zajac and Olsen, 1993). It deepens through having established role behavior increasingly supplemented with "qua persona behavior . . . as personal relationships build and psychological contracts deepen" (Ring and Van de Ven, 1994, p. 103). Ring and Van de Ven (1994) and Dwyer, Schurr, and Oh (1987) each argue that relationship commitment, through its increasingly unique economic and social psychological benefits to each partner, forecloses comparable exchange alternatives for each firm.

Considering construct relationships, we posit positive causal paths from anticipated constructive effects on network identity to cooperation and relationship commitment. The cases provide ample support for these hypothesized effects. Of course, whether the constructive effects on relationship commitment are direct and indirect or are solely mediated through cooperation remains an empirical question.

Contemplating the construct of anticipated deleterious effects on network identity, a negative, causal path is hypothesized from it to cooperation. By its nature, this construct would appear to hamper cooperation in the focal relationship. But, on further thought, this negative effect might not be as predictable as the positive effect of anticipated constructive effects on network identity on cooperation. This is because adverse effects on network identity might be compensated by the focal firm changing cooperation in other relations. Instead of decreased cooperation in the focal relationship, deleterious effects might be compensated by increased cooperation in those other relationships. Danprint's cooperating with the filling equipment supplier is an instance of such cooperation.

A negative causal path is also hypothesized from anticipated deleterious effects on network identity to relationship commitment. In support of this, Kogut, Shan and Walker (1992) found that new biotechnology firms become increasingly unwilling to make commitments to relations that are counter to their established set of relations. Similar to our previous prediction, whether the deleterious effects are direct and indirect or are solely mediated through cooperation remains an empirical question. A final consideration in our posited relationships for anticipated constructive and deleterious effects on network identity is that changes in significant relationships will have both strong positive and negative network effects. This coexistence of strong reasons both for and against cooperation suggests the need to have separate constructs that capture anticipated constructive effects and anticipated deleterious effects on network identity.

Considering outcomes given CL and CL_{alt}, we hypothesize positive, causal paths from them to cooperation. To the extent that past outcomes exceed expectations and/or alternatives, the focal firm is motivated to sustain the relationship with its partner. Cooperative activities represent a primary means for each firm to maintain, or improve on, its outcomes (Zajac and Olsen, 1993).

Finally, as implied, we posit a positive causal path from cooperation to relationship commitment. Interestingly, however, although process frameworks typically have cooperation and commitment leading to one another over time, specification of their causal ordering in a given exchange episode has varied (cf. Anderson and Weitz, 1992; Heide and John, 1990). The work of Axelrod (1984) supports the position that for a given exchange episode, cooperation causes commitment. In studying trench warfare in World War I, Axelrod (1984, p. 85) concludes, "The cooperative exchanges of mutual restraint actually changed the nature of the interaction. They tended to make the two sides care about each other's welfare."

Substantive validity assessment

To provide some initial empirical support that the constructs we have proposed are sufficiently well delineated and to generate some suggested measures for them, we conducted a substantive validity assessment (cf. Anderson and Gerbing, 1991). As Anderson and Gerbing (1991) discuss, their pretest method for substantive validity assessment provides not only predictions on the performance of measures in a subsequent confirmatory factor analysis, but also feedback "*on the adequacy of the construct definitions as well*" (p. 739, emphasis in original). So, our primary intent in employing this substantive validity pretest method was to gain this feedback.

The seven constructs studied were network identity, anticipated constructive effects on network identity, anticipated deleterious effects on network identity, outcomes given comparison level, outcomes given comparison level for alternatives, cooperation, and relationship commitment. We followed the Anderson and Gerbing (1991) methodology precisely. Single-sentence definitions were written for each construct that captured their theoretical meaning using everyday language (Angleitner, John, and Lohr, 1986). As an example, consider network identity.[11]

> *Network identity* captures the perceived attractiveness (or repulsiveness) of a firm as an exchange partner due to its unique set of connected relations with other firms, its links to their activities, and its ties with their resources.

Because our primary interest was in anticipated constructive and deleterious effects on network identity, 16 measures were written for each of them, and 4 measures were written for each of the other 5 constructs for a total of 52 measures. Twenty-four Swedish managers participating in a management development program served as research participants and assigned each item to the concept that they decided it best indicated. Substantive validity coefficients (c_{sv}) were calculated for each item and tests of their statistical significance were conducted.

In our context, statistically significant values of c_{sv} would indicate that a construct was sufficiently well defined; research participants were able to assign intended measures of a construct to it meaningfully. Overall, 36 of the 52 items (.692) have significant ($p < .05$) c_{sv} values. Of greater interest, 7 of 16 items for anticipated constructive effects and 15 of 16 items for deleterious effects on network identity have significant c_{sv} values. The difference in number of significant items suggests either that writing negative or harmful effects measures is easier to do or that research participants are more sensitive to these effects in relationship practice (perhaps because of painful past experience) and thus are able to make item assignments more accurately. Moreover, these results provide strong initial support for our proposed constructs and their definitions.

Considering the remaining constructs, the number of items having significant c_{sv} values were as follows: network identity, 3 of 4; outcomes given comparison level, 3 of 4; outcomes given comparison level for alternatives, 1 of 4; cooperation, 4 of 4; and relationship commitment, 3 of 4. In Table 1, we provide some suggested measures for our proposed constructs generated from this assessment. Because of our discussion of them within a business network context, we also include suggested measures for network identity, outcomes given CL, and outcomes given CL_{alt}.

A PROSPECTUS FOR RESEARCH

We provide some conceptual development of dyadic business relationships embedded within business networks. The perspective we have taken differs from others. We are interested in managers' perceptions and imputed meanings of the connectedness of a focal relationship to other relationships and its effects on their firm's decisions and activities. To further study what we discuss, we propose a prospectus for research that encompasses both theory development and testing and management practice.

Theory development and testing research

Two complementary research approaches are outlined to provide empirical support for the proposed constructs and their posited effects: directed case studies to guide and refine theory development, and survey research using key informants and structural equation modeling.

Table 1 Suggested measures for proposed business network constructs

Anticipated Constructive Effects on Network Identity
What we gain from working with this customer will be useful in other relations. (c_{sv} = .70, p < .001)[a]
By working closely with this customer, our firm becomes more attractive to our suppliers.
   (c_{sv} = .67, p < .001)
Our way of doing business with this customer has positive consequences on our activities with other
   customers. (c_{sv} = .50, p < .05)
Because this customer is a demanding one, competence developed in working with it can be used to
   enhance the productivity in all our firm's relations. (c_{sv} = .50, p < .05)

Anticipated Deleterious Effects on Network Identity
Institutionalizing quality programs with this one customer may make it difficult to work together with
   other firms. (c_{sv} = .92, p < .001)
Too close a relationship with this particular customer may destroy the balance among our firm's exchange
   partners. (c_{sv} = .79, p < .001)
Collaborating with this specific customer may be rewarding in some ways, but harmful to our reputation
   with certain other firms. (c_{sv} = .75, p < .001)
Although working close together with this customer will likely provide some benefits, important other
   customers and supplier may not be happy about this. (c_{sv} = .71, p < .001)

Network Identity
Our firm can attract the most competent suppliers. (c_{sv} = .71, p < .001)
Due to our supplier relations, our firm is regarded as one of the most attractive suppliers to our present and
   potential customers. (c_{sv} = .54, p < .05)
Our firm has the capability to influence the development in our field. (c_{sv} = .42, p < .05)

Outcomes Given Comparison Level
What we have achieved in our relationship with this customer has been beyond our predictions.
   (c_{sv} = .63, p < .01)
The financial returns our firm obtains from this customer are greatly above what we envisioned.
   (c_{sv} = .50, p < .05)
The results of our firm's working relationship with this customer have greatly exceeded our expectations.
   (c_{sv} = .46, p < .05)

Outcomes Given Comparison Level for Alternatives
Working together with this particular customer puts less strain on our organisation than does working with
   other potential partners. (c_{sv} = .50, p < .05)

[a] The measure's substantive validity coefficient value and its associated probability level are given in parentheses.

Directed case studies. Qualitative field research such as field-depth interviews and case studies play an essential part in refining the construct definitions we have given and elaborating the content domains of each construct. Directed case-study research may suggest the need for additional constructs or alteration in the structures of the constructs we have proposed.

To develop our knowledge, detailed case studies of development processes within different types of networks are needed. These case studies should cover substantial time periods and be based on material from several of the firms as well as from different functions within the firms. Leonard-Barton (1990) recently has described a dual methodology for field case study of these kinds of complex phenomena. With her approach, a single real-time longitudinal case study is combined synergistically with multiple retrospective case studies to enhance the internal and external validity of the research findings.

Key informant and structural equation modeling research. Field survey research employing key informant reports and structural equation modeling is well accepted by marketing academics in the channels and business marketing areas. The issue of single versus multiple informants (Phillips, 1981) is especially critical in studying networks, given that individual actors appear to have bounded knowledge about their firms' networks (Emerson, 1981). Thus, a multiple informant approach would appear to be necessary – but this has been problematic in practice (cf. Anderson and Narus, 1990). However, the firm hybrid-consensual methodology recently described by Kumar, Stern and Anderson (1993) appears to offer a means of gaining perceptual agreement among the multiple informants for each firm with respect to phenomena of interest.

Another issue to consider is the inherent trade-off between the breadth of structural equation model that a researcher might desire to capture the complexity of network phenomena and practicality (cf. Bentler and Chou, 1987). Being mindful of this, our conceptualization has focused on four constructs, and for two of these – outcomes given CL and outcomes given CL_{alt} – we simply have provided business network underpinnings to constructs that have already appeared in models of business relationships (Anderson and Narus, 1984, 1990). Thus, researchers wanting to understand the effects of connectedness would need to add only two new constructs to their models: anticipated constructive effects on network identity and anticipated deleterious effects on network identity. Although we have articulated the constituent facets and principal aspects for each of these constructs, only the constructs themselves and their indicators (e.g. the generated measures appearing in Table 1) should be incorporated in structural equation models of dyadic business relationships.[12]

Management practice research

The inherently ambiguous, complex, and fluid nature of business networks place unfamiliar and often perplexing demands on managers. In our experience, two areas greatly in need of management practice research are analyzing and building business networks.

Analyzing business networks. To understand what business networks mean for their firms, managers first must be able to define germane networks and then analyze them in some consistent way. Networks can be defined meaningfully at different levels of granularity, depending on the analytical purpose. The concepts of network horizon, network context, and network identity can be applied at each level with correspondingly different substantive meanings. Whatever network context is selected, definition of the network should focus on the set of significant relationships. For example, Håkansson (1989) has found that the ten largest suppliers and the ten largest customers account for an average of 72% and 70% of the total volume bought and sold, respectively, by a business unit. Finally, because we regard business networks as sets of connected business relationships rather than as sets of connected firms, secondary functions of relationships should be of predominant interest for analysis and study by managers.

Building business networks. Managers who understand the potential of business networks for their firms naturally would like to know how to build one in practice. Snow, Miles and Coleman (1992) argue that, in constructing business networks, certain managers operate as brokers, creatively marshaling resources controlled by other actors. They sketch out three broker roles that significantly contribute to the success of business networks: the *architect*, who facilitates the building of specific networks yet seldom has a complete grasp or understanding of the network that ultimately emerges; the *lead operator*, who formally connects specific firms together into an ongoing network; and the *caretaker*, who focuses on activities that enhance network performance and needs to have a broader network horizon. Research is needed to understand how performance of these roles and what other factors (e.g. resources and activities) contribute to successful business networks.

CONCLUSION

In business-to-business settings, dyadic relationships between firms are of paramount interest. Emerging practice strongly suggests that to understand these business relationships, greater attention must be directed to the business network context within which dyadic business relationships take place. Drawing on business network research and social exchange theory, we have provided a fundamental conceptualization to capture network properties and relationship connectedness within dyadic business relationship models. Granovetter (1992) cautions that it is easy to slip into "dyadic atomization," a type of reductionism in which an analyzed pair of firms is abstracted out of their embedded context. By building out from focal dyadic relationships to consider effects of their embedded network contexts, we attempt to enrich the study of exchange relationships in marketing, which largely has had a dyadic atomization character.

Because of the extraordinarily complex nature of network phenomena, without doubt, refinement and elaboration are needed. As means for accomplishing this, we have proposed some directions for research that embrace the complementary strengths of two methodological approaches. Although research on business networks is challenging, it has the potential to make significant contributions to not only business marketing theory, but evolving business practice as well.

NOTES

1. Let us further clarify our intent by stating what we are *not* pursuing. Our interest is not in explicating networks and their structural properties (e.g. cliques, actor equivalence), as, for example, has been done recently by Iacobucci and Hopkins (1992) in their presentation of a set of related statistical models for network analysis. Rather, our interest is in managers' perceptions and imputed meanings of the connectedness of a focal relationship to other relationships, as they act as key informants on its effects on their firms' decisions and activities.

2. In recent development of transaction cost economics, Williamson (1991a, 1991b) discusses the existence of hybrid forms of economic organizations between (faceless) markets and hierarchies, in which co-operative adaptation is required between two organizations. Nonetheless, questions remain about the applicability of transaction cost economics to embedded contexts (cf. Granovetter, 1985) and contexts of recurrent and relational contracts, in which reliance on trust among the organizations is high (cf. Ring and Van de Ven, 1992). Thus, for our purposes, approaches based in social exchange theory (Homans, 1958; Thibaut and Kelley, 1959), such as resource dependence theory (Pfeffer and Salancik, 1978), appear to be more useful.

3. Our perspective can be usefully compared and contrasted with Aldrich and Whetten's (1981, p. 386) concept of an *organization-set*, which they define as "those organizations with which a focal organization has direct links." Although our perspective might be viewed as the sum total of the organization-sets for each of the two firms engaged in the focal dyadic relationship, we believe that this misses our emphasis on the *dyadic relationship* as the unit of primary interest within business networks, rather than the individual firms themselves.

4. Because of this, the social network concept of *centrality* (Cook *et al.*, 1983; Emerson, 1981), whose definition depends on some objective delimiting of a network, appears problematic for a business network setting (cf. Aldrich and Whetten, 1981).

5. Although network identities are distinct, two firms must establish a congruent understanding of each other's network identity for a relation between them to prosper (Ring and Van de Ven, 1994).

6. Shortell and Zajac (1990, p. 168) recently have observed, "We prefer to demystify the discussion of organizational environments by viewing the environment of a health care organization as simply the collection of other specific organizations that are interconnected to or interdependent with it . . . In other words, when a health care organization 'looks out' with concern at its turbulent environment, what it sees are other organizations 'looking out' at it!" Consistent with our own position, they then recognize the existence of environmental forces that are nonorganizational in nature, which are viewed as less germane to the focal organization.

7 Although Emerson (1972) and Cook (1982) discuss network extension and network consolidation as mechanisms for balancing network dependence, these concepts also can be employed to capture the dynamic character of the network and its environment. Network extension occurs when relatively amorphous forces (which alternatively might be viewed as latent actors) become manifest actors with which the firm has a direct or connected relation, either because of their impact on the network or because of proactive search by network actors for the resources and activities these new actors can contribute within the network. Conversely, network contraction occurs when relations with actors whose resources and activities no longer contribute to the network are ended, with the terminated actor receding to a relatively imperceptible force in the environment.

8. Support for negative effects due to limited resources for exchange can be found in the recent experimental studies of Molm (1991). Subjects in negatively connected exchange relations, in which exchange with one partner meant nonexchange with another, had a tendency to follow nonexchange by a partner with punishment for that partner in the next exchange opportunity. Great caution must be taken, though, in generalizing the findings from experimental studies of social exchange networks to business networks because several of the conditions and assumptions in such studies (e.g. that resources have fixed values, are constant across longitudinal exchange sequences, have the same value to each actor) make them less relevant, or even problematic, for business networks (cf. Aldrich and Whetten, 1981). For a noteworthy exception, in which the value of resources was not held constant for actors in a network, see Yamagishi, Gillmore, and Cook (1988).

9. Because time dependence is an important feature of relationships and network content and the analysis focuses on ongoing exchange processes, CL, and to a lesser extent CL_{alt}, are based on the firms' past, present, and perhaps even expected future outcomes from the relevant relationships.

10. Some readers may wonder why we have not simply defined overall outcomes given CL and CL_{alt} for a focal firm at a network context level; that is, omnibus constructs that capture both the outcomes in the focal relationship and the outcomes in all other relations in its network context. This, in some ways, would subsume the constructs of anticipated constructive and deleterious effects on network identity and appear to be in keeping with Thibaut and Kelley's (1959; Kelley and Thibaut, 1978) consideration of larger groups, such as triads. Our conceptualization for a business context departs from Thibaut and Kelley's (1959) social context for at least two reasons. First, Thibaut and Kelley consider only groups, so that, by definition, the actors are completely interconnected. By contrast, within a business network context, some actors germane to each member of a focal dyad will not be directly connected to the other member. Thus, CL and CL_{alt} for the group have more cohesive meanings than for a business network context. Second, in the Thibaut and Kelley analysis, which largely focuses on triads of friends, an actor simply changes groups when exercising CL_{alt} for the group. It would be much more difficult, if not impossible, for a focal firm to move to a new network context, which has a completely different set of connected business relationships.

Apart from these conceptualization differences, omnibus constructs would blur a critical conceptual and managerial distinction between outcomes that occurred in a focal relationship and those related outcomes that occurred outside it in the connected relationships. Thibaut and Kelley (1959, chapter 4; Kelley and Thibaut 1978, chapter 11) appear to support this distinction in their discussion of facilitation and interference in interaction in the focal dyad due to other relationships. Finally, even when considering triads, Thibaut and Kelley (1959, chapter 11) recognize the existence of CL and CL_{alt}, for each of the three constituent dyads of the triad and, interestingly, discuss outcomes given CL_{alt} for the individual's best dyad as the limiting condition for that individual remaining in the triad (CL_{alt}, triad), much as being alone might be the best alternative to being in a given dyad.

11. The complete set of construct definitions employed are available from the first author.

12. Note that we have given a formative specification in Figures 3 and 4 for the relationships of the constituent facets and principal aspects to the constructs, such that these facets and aspects might be viewed as causal indicators (cf. MacCallum and Browne, 1993). So, in empirical research on these structures, we concur with MacCallum and Browne's (1993) recommendation to incorporate effects indicators for each construct, which overcomes identification problems. Importantly, from our perspective, they then are represented as endogenous constructs rather than composites.

REFERENCES

Achrol, R. S. Evolution of the marketing organization: new forms for turbulent environments. *Journal of Marketing*. **55** (October), 77–93 (1991).

Achrol, R. S., Reve, T. and Stern, L. W. The environment of marketing channel dyads: a framework for comparative analysis. *Journal of Marketing*, **47** (Fall), 55–67 (1983).

Albert, S. and Whetten, D. A. Organizational identity. In Cummings, L. L. and Staw, B. M. (eds), *Research in Organizational Behavior*, JAI Press, Greenwich, CT (1985), pp. 263–95.

Aldrich, H. and Whetten, D. A. Organization-sets, action-sets, and networks: making the most of simplicity. In Nystrom, P. C. and Starbuck, W. H. (eds), Oxford University Press, New York (1981), pp. 385–408.

Anderson, E. and Weitz, B. Determinants of continuity in conventional industrial channel dyads. *Marketing Science*, **8** (Fall), 310–23 (1989).

Anderson, E. and Weitz, B. The use of pledges to build and sustain commitment in distribution channels. *Journal of Marketing Research*, **29** (February), 18–34 (1992).

Anderson, J. C. and Gerbing, D. W. Predicting the performance of measures in a confirmatory factor analysis with a pretest assessment of their substantive validities. *Journal of Applied Psychology*, **76** (October), 732–40 (1991).

Anderson, J. C. and Narus, J. A. A model of the distributor's perspective of distributor–manufacturer working relationships. *Journal of Marketing*, **48** (Fall), 62–74 (1989).

Anderson, J. C. and Narus, J. A. A model of distributor firm and manufacturer firm working partnerships. *Journal of Marketing*, **54** (January), 42–58 (1990).

Angleitner, A., John, O. P. and Lohr, F. It's *what* you ask and *how* you ask it: an itemmetric analysis of personality questionnaires. In Angleitner, A. and Wiggins, J. S. (eds), *Personality Assessment Via Questionnaires*. Springer, Berlin (1986), pp. 61–108.

Astley, W. G. Toward an appreciation of collective strategy. *Academy of Management Review*, **9** (3), 526–35 (1984).

Astley, W. G. and Fombrun, C. J. Collective strategy: social ecology of organizational environments. *Academy of Management Review*, **8** (4), 576–87 (1983).

Axelrod, R. *The Evolution of Cooperation*. Basic Books, New York (1984).

Bentler, P. M. and Chou, C. Practical issues in structural modeling. *Sociological Methods and Research*, **16** (August), 78–117 (1987).

Brull, S. and Mitchener, B. The alliance demands patience: five years on, Daimler and Mitsubishi are still talking. *International Herald Tribune* (December 15), 11 and 15 (1993).

Byrne, J. A., Brandt, R. and Port, O. The virtual corporation. *Business Week* (February 8), 98–103 (1993).

Cook, K. S. Network structures from an exchange perspective. In Marsden, P. V. and Lin, N. (eds), *Social Structure and Network Analysis*, Sage Publications, Beverly Hills (1982), pp. 177–99.

Cook, K. S. and Emerson, R. M. Power, equity, commitment in exchange networks. *American Sociological Review*, **43** (October), 721–38 (1978).

Cook, K. S., Emerson, R. M., Gillmore, M. R. and Yamagishi, T. The distribution of power in exchange networks: theory and experimental results. *American Journal of Sociology*, **89** (2), 275–305 (1983).

Demsetz, H. *The Emerging Theory of the Firm*. Acta Universitatas Uppsaliensis, Uppsala, Sweden (1992).

Deshpandé, R. "Paradigms lost": on theory and method in research in marketing. *Journal of Marketing*, **47** (Fall), 101–10 (1983).

Dwyer, F. R., Schurr, P. H. and Oh, S. Developing buyer–seller relationships. *Journal of Marketing*, **51** (April), 11–27 (1987).

Emerson, R. M. Exchange theory, Part I: Exchange relations and network structures. In Zelditch, M. and Anderson, B. (eds), *Sociological Theories in Progress*, 2. Houghton Mifflin, Boston (1972), pp. 58–87.

Emerson, R. M. Social exchange theory. In Rosenberg, M. and Turner, R. (eds), *Social Psychology: Sociological Perspectives*. Basic Books, New York (1981), pp. 30–65.

Ford, D. (ed.) *Understanding Business Markets: Interaction, Relationships and Networks*. Academic Press, San Diego (1990).

Frazier, G. L., Interorganizational exchange behavior in marketing channels: a broadened perspective. *Journal of Marketing*, **47** (Fall), 68–78 (1983).

Frazier, G. L., Spekman, R. E. and O'Neal, C. R. Just-in-time exchange relationships in industrial markets. *Journal of Marketing*, **52** (October), 52–67 (1988).

Gaddé, L.-E. and Mattsson, L.-G. Stability and change in network relationships. *International Journal of Research in Marketing*, **4**, 29–41 (1987).

Goffman, E. *The Presentation of Self in Everyday Life*. Doubleday, New York (1959).

Granovetter, M. Economic action and social structure: the problem of embeddedness. *American Journal of Sociology*, **91** (November), 481–510 (1985).

Granovetter, M. Problems of explanation in economic sociology. In Nitin, N. and Eccles, R. G. (eds), *Networks and Organizations: Structure, Form, and Action*. Harvard Business School Press, Boston (1992), pp. 25–56.

Håkansson, H. (ed.) *Industrial Technological Development*. Routledge, London (1987).

Håkansson, H. *Corporate Technological Behavior: Co-operation and Networks*. Routledge, London (1989).

Håkansson, H. and Johanson, J. Formal and informal cooperation strategies in international industrial networks. In Contractor, F. J. and Lorange, P. (eds), *Cooperative Strategies in International Business*. Lexington Books, Lexington, MA (1988), pp. 369–79.

Håkansson, H. and Johanson, J. Industrial functions of business relationships. In Deo Sharma, D. (ed.), *Advances in International Marketing*, Vol. 5. JAI Press, Greenwich, CT (1993), pp. 15–31.

Håkansson, H. and Snehota, I. No business is an island: the network concept of business strategy. *Scandinavian Journal of Management*, **5** (3), 187–200 (1989).

Hallén, L., Johanson, J. and Seyed-Mohamed, N. Interfirm adaption in business relationships. *Journal of Marketing*, **55** (April), 29–37 (1991).

Heide, J. B. Interorganizational governance in marketing channels. *Journal of Marketing*, **58** (January), 71–85 (1994).

Heide, J. B. and John, G. Alliances in industrial purchasing: the determinants of joint action in buyer–supplier relationships. *Journal of Marketing Research*, **27** (February), 24–36 (1990).

Henderson, J. M. and Quandt, R. E. *Microeconomic Theory*, 2nd ed. McGraw-Hill, New York (1971).

Hill, C. W. L. Cooperation, opportunism, and the invisible hand: implications for transaction cost theory. *Academy of Management Review*, **15** (3), 500–13 (1990).

Homans, G. C. Social behavior as exchange. *American Journal of Sociology*, **63** (May), 597–606 (1988).

Iacobucci, D. and Hopkins, N. Modeling dyadic interactions and networks in marketing. *Journal of Marketing Research*, **29** (February), 5–17 (1992).

Johnston, R. and Lawrence, P. R. Beyond vertical integration – the rise of the value-adding partnership. *Harvard Business Review*, **88** (July/August), 94–101 (1988).

Kelley, H. H. and Thibaut, J. W. *Interpersonal Relations: A Theory of Interdependence*. John Wiley & Sons, Inc., New York (1978).

Kogut, B., Shan, W. and Walker, G. The make-or-cooperate decision in the context of an industry-network. In Nitin, N. and Eccles, R. G. (eds), *Networks and Organizations: Structure, Form, and Action*. Harvard Business School Press, Boston (1992), pp. 348–65.

Kumar, N., Stern, L. W. and Anderson, J. C. Conducting interorganization research using key informants. *Academy of Management Journal*, **36** (December), 1633–51 (1993).

Leonard-Barton, D. A dual methodology for case studies: synergistic use of a longitudinal single site with replicated multiple sites. *Organization Science*, **1** (August), 248–66 (1990).

Lundvall, B. Å. *Product Innovation and User–Producer Interaction*. Aalborg University Press, Aalborg, Denmark (1985).

MacCallum, R. C. and Browne, M. W. The use of causal indicators in covariance structure models: some practical issues. *Psychological Bulletin*, **114** (November), 533–41 (1993).

Mattsson, L.-G. Management of strategic change in a "markets-as-networks" perspective. In Pettigrew, A. (ed.), *The Management of Strategic Change*. Basil Blackwell, London (1987), pp. 234–56.

Miles, R. E. and Snow, C. C. Causes of failure in network organizations. *California Management Review*, **34** (Summer), 53–72 (1992).

Miles, R. H. *Macro Organizational Behavior*. Scott, Foresman and Company, Glenview, IL (1980).

Molm, L. D. Affect and social exchange: satisfaction in power-dependence relations. *American Sociological Review*, **56** (August), 475–93 (1991).

Pfeffer, J. Bringing the environment back in: the social context of business strategy. In Teece, D. J. (ed.), *The Competitive Challenge: Strategies for Industrial Innovation and Renewal*. Ballinger Publishing, Cambridge, MA (1987), pp. 119–35.

Pfeffer, J. and Salancik, G. R. *The External Control of Organizations: A Resource Dependence Perspective*. Harper & Row, New York (1978).

Phillips, L. W. Assessing measurement error in key informant reports: A methodological note on organizational analysis in marketing. *Journal of Marketing Research*, **18** (November), 395–415 (1981).

Ring, P. S. and Van De Ven, A. H. Structuring cooperative relationships between organizations. *Strategic Management Journal*, **13**, 483–98 (1992).

Ring, P. S. and Van De Ven, A. H. Developmental processes of cooperative interorganizational relationships. *Academy of Management Review*, **19** (January), 90–118 (1994).

Shortell, S. M. and Zajac, E. J. Health care organizations and the development of the strategic management perspective. In Mick, S. S. *et al.* (eds) *Innovations in Health Care Delivery: Insights for Organizational Theory*. Jossey-Bass Publishers, San Francisco (1990), pp. 144–80.

Sjöberg, U. Produktförandringar i nätverk. Ett fall från pappersindustrin. (Product changes in networks: a case from the paper industry): Working paper, Uppsala University, Department of Business Studies (1991).

Snow, C. C., Miles, R. E. and Coleman, H. J. Jr. Managing 21st century network organizations. *Organizational Dynamics*, **20** (Winter), 5–19 (1992).

Thibaut, J. W. and Kelley, H. *The Social Psychology of Groups*. John Wiley & Sons, Inc., New York (1959).

Thorelli, H. B. Networks: between markets and hierarchies. *Strategic Management Journal*, **7** (January/February), 37–51 (1986).

Tversky, A. and Kahneman, D. The framing of decisions and the psychology of choice. *Science*, **211** (January), 453–58 (1981).

Van de Ven, A. H. On the nature, formation, and maintenance of relations among organizations. *The Academy of Management Review*, **1** (October), 24–36 (1976).

Verity, J. W. Deconstructing the computer industry. *Business Week* (November 23), 90–100 (1992).

Williamson, O. E. *The Economic Institutions of Capitalism*. The Free Press, New York (1985).

Williamson, O. E. Comparative economic organization: the analysis of discrete structural alternatives. *Administrative Science Quarterly*, **36** (June), 269–96 (1991a).

Williamson, O. E. Strategizing, economizing, and economic organization. *Strategic Management Journal*, **12**, 75–94 (1991b).

Yamagishi, T., Gillmore, M. R. and Cook, K. S. Network connections and the distribution of power in exchange networks. *American Journal of Sociology*, **93** (January), 833–51 (1988).

Zajac, E. J. and Olsen, C. P. From transaction cost to transaction value-analysis: implications for the study of interorganizational strategies. *Journal of Management Studies*, **30** (January), 131–45 (1993).

3.8

From dyadic change to changing business networks: an analytical framework[*]

Aino Halinen, Asta Salmi and Virpi Havila

INTRODUCTION

Networking has recently become part of industrial reality in developed economies and, simultaneously, various network perspectives have become popular in business research (for reviews of network literature see Araujo and Easton, 1996; Iacobucci, 1996; Nohria and Eccles, 1992). In this paper we will investigate the dynamics of business networks by taking the so-called IMP Group's network approach to industrial markets as our starting point (see Turnbull *et al.*, 1996). Within this predominantly Nordic and European research tradition, industrial markets are described as networks of inter-firm relationships. Companies build exchange relationships with other companies, and through these become connected to broader networks of business relationships.

In accordance with the network model proposed by Håkansson and Johanson (1985) and Håkansson and Snehota (1995a), we view business networks as structures formed by three basic elements and connections between them: business actors, activities and resources. Actor bonds, activity links and resource ties bind the companies together, creating interdependence between them and stability in the market. From the viewpoint of an individual company, the network that it perceives the most relevant and to which it is connected forms the context for its business operations (see, for example, Anderson *et al.*, 1994). The network constrains the company's activities but also provides new possibilities and opportunities to achieve desired goals. The business network thus incorporates the forces of both stability and change.

The network approach views any company's business context in a holistic rather than fragmented way. It pays particular attention to the connectedness of business relationships and the borderless nature of the network in which each company is embedded. As different parts of a network are linked, change may emerge and shift from any one part to another – an occurrence that the network view can reveal better than traditional organization theory or marketing approaches. The network approach offers conceptual tools to the study of dynamics in business markets. It pinpoints the importance of both direct and indirect, close and distant relationships for understanding change and allows us to see that relationships may function in various important roles in the generation and transmission of change.

The dynamics and change in business networks have recently aroused increasing interest among researchers of industrial marketing. Research has covered a broad range of issues, from the development and change of individual business relationships (e.g. Ford, 1980; Halinen, 1997; Wilson and Mummalaneni, 1986) to change processes in marketing channels (Wilkinson, 1990), small nets (triads) (Easton and Lundgren, 1992; Smith and Laage-Hellman, 1992) or in networks more generally (Håkansson and Henders, 1995; Håkansson and Snehota, 1995; Mattsson and Hultén, 1994).

While there is increasing interest in the dynamics of business networks, we still know very little about how networks change and what the underlying forces behind their change are. Incremental evolution has been seen as the main mode of network change. Change is regarded as a result of a continuous networking process, the connecting of actor bonds, activity links and resource ties within a business network (Håkansson and Snehota, 1995b, pp. 283–4). Radical changes or revolutions have been viewed as possible but unusual (Easton, 1992, p. 24). In most recent discussions, the possibility of revolutionary change has been brought up more openly, and authors have resorted to, for example, the punctuated equilibrium paradigm to form an understanding of network evolution (Easton and Araujo, 1994; Salmi, 1995).

The aim of this paper is to elaborate on the process of change in business networks. An analytical framework is proposed for understanding and investigating network change. In the development of the framework, we wish to emphasize two points that we consider still to be neglected in present studies of network change. First, we argue that the mechanism of change in networks is circular rather than unidirectional. In contrast to traditional research approaches, where the focus is on environmental effects on companies and business relationships, we place particular emphasis on the impact that a dyad may have on other connected relationships. By focusing on how change may spread via relationships, we make good use of the particular strengths of the network approach. Moreover, we argue that by employing existing change theories (see Van de Ven, 1992; Van de Ven and Poole, 1995), we are better able to understand the nature of network change and the forces that lie behind it. We found the punctuated-equilibrium model to be especially useful in the network context.

The structure of the paper is as follows. First, we shall examine *the mechanism of change*, emphasizing the central role of business relationships, i.e. dyads and their role as both generators, recipients and transmitters of change in networks. Secondly, we shall focus on *the nature of network change*, both as an incremental and radical shift. Thirdly, we shall examine *the forces of change* in business networks. The mental process of 'enactment' and the intentionality and interdependence of business actors are seen as important explanations of both network change and stability. It is further suggested that the concept of the critical event encompasses radical change in particular. Finally, the proposed ideas are summarized in an analytical framework of change in business networks. Along the way, our conceptual elaboration is illustrated by evidence from earlier empirical research.

THE MECHANISM OF CHANGE IN BUSINESS NETWORKS

The network approach to industrial markets emphasizes the role of a business-relationship dyad in understanding change in business networks (e.g. Anderson *et al.*, 1994; Håkansson and Snehota, 1995). In an ongoing business relationship, the two parties are usually seen to adapt to each other – that is, change their behaviour *vis-à-vis* one another. Continuous changes in the relationship occur due to the interaction between the parties. Change may concern actor bonds, activity links and/or the resource ties which exist between firms.

Single dyads play a central role in the change mechanism of business networks. Substantial changes are initiated and carried out in interaction between the companies. It is obvious that the development of a business network is also influenced by various forces external to it, for example, general economic conditions. Such changes will, however, be transformed into or at least combined with endogenous change through the networking process, where relationships function as transmitters or transformers of these changes (Håkansson and Snehota, 1995b, p. 272).

The change occurring in a single dyad may have different consequences on other connected relationships. We suggest that part of the change always remains within a business-relationship dyad, whereas some part of change may also affect other relationships and actors in a network. The former we call confined change and the latter connected change.

Confined change

Network theorists have emphasized the coexistence of stability and change in business networks. The stability of existing business relationships provides a platform for continuous interaction and change (Easton, 1992, p. 23). The overall pattern of business relationships seems to be relatively stable, even though existing business relationships change in content and strength (Håkansson and Snehota, 1995b, p. 269).

Confined changes characterize this seemingly 'stable situation' in a network. They remain within a dyad and are not received or acted upon by other actors in the network. Various types of change may be confined to a business relationship. For example, the number of persons involved may increase or decrease, the perceived trust between the parties may deepen or weaken or the activities performed in cooperation may change in character with no effects on other relationships.

Figure 1 presents a case of confined change. It depicts a small network of connected business relationships. The relationships between B and its customers C_1, C_2 and C_3 have changed character between Time 1 and Time 2, which is illustrated by the change in thickness of the three lines. These changes, however, have occurred within the dyads and have not spread from one dyad to another. Such changes occur throughout the network due to the parties' interaction.

In the following, the case of a Swedish component manufacturer and its sales subsidiaries and customers in the German market is used as an empirical illustration of confined change (see Havila, 1996).

The Swedish component manufacturer (A) used a sales subsidiary (B) of another Swedish company in Germany to take care of its customer contacts in the German market. This stable situation (see Figure 1) endured for about ten years, during which time various changes occurred within individual relationships in the network. In B's relationships with customers C_1, C_2 and C_3, for instance, contact patterns were changed. The field salesman, who had previously taken orders from customers, lost his key role of keeping in touch with customers when the company decided on an organizational change. Another salesman located at the office was to be responsible for orders,

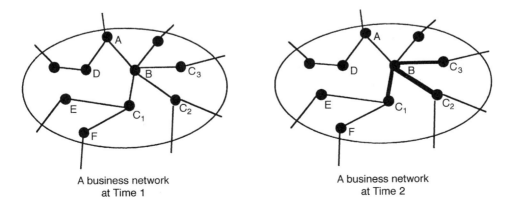

A business network
at Time 1

A business network
at Time 2

Figure 1   Illustration of confined change in a business network.

which gave him much more influence over customer relationships. This change can be characterized as a confined change that was not transmitted to or received by other relationships.

Connected change

As soon as a change in one business relationship also influences some other business relationship(s), it can be characterized as *connected change*. We define connected change as a change in one relationship that is received and acted upon by other actors in the network. The notion of connected change includes the idea that a dyad may function both as a receiver and transmitter of change. Håkansson and Snehota (1995a, pp. 39–41) call this the 'network function' of a business relationship. Easton and Lundgren (1992), on the other hand, provide an enlightening analysis of the various ways in which an individual company may receive or transmit change.

Figure 2 illustrates connected change. A change in the relationship between A and D affects the relationships that C_1 maintains with B, D, E and F. Parties to these relationships act upon the change they perceive in the relationship between A and D by making changes in their own relationships.

The case of the Swedish component manufacturer can again be used as an example. After a seemingly stable period, the Swedish manufacturer (A) decided to use an additional marketing channel – a sales subsidiary of its own (D) – that had not previously sold such components in Germany (see Figure 2). As a consequence, customer C_1 received an offer from both the sales subsidiary B and from A's own subsidiary D. The offer from D had no inbuilt margin and was thus 10 per cent lower. C_1 found it very peculiar that the same product was sold at two different prices and began to purchase more product from an Italian (E) and a Swiss (F) component manufacturer. As a result, C_1's relationships with E and F grew stronger, while those with B and D (and thus with A) weakened. This incident also started a price war in the German component market, which in the end led to the Swedish manufacturer losing its market share. This network change originated from the channel decision of one actor: the Swedish manufacturer. The company's reaction to various different change forces that it encountered in its business context had significant consequences on several relationships in the European component market. The network approach helps to put the initial event in its broader context, and analyse its influence on other connected relationships.

A change which is spread to another business relationship may cause a 'domino effect' among several connected business relationships (see Hertz, 1993, p. 271). Because of various network interdependencies, indirect relationships relatively distant from the focal dyad may be affected. Smith and Laage-Hellman (1992) note that there are several transformation possibilities open to

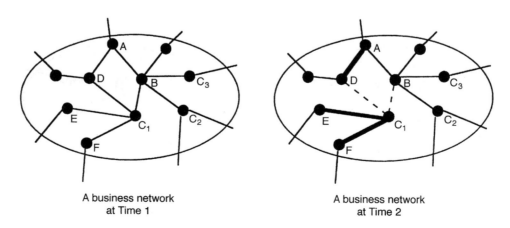

A business network at Time 1

A business network at Time 2

Figure 2   Illustration of connected change in a business network.

actors within connected relationships. The connected parties can react to the change in different ways, so that changes in the connected relationships need not be of the same kind as the change in the focal dyad (Håkansson and Snehota, 1995a, p. 39). The character of a relationship may change or in an extreme case the relationship is dissolved and new relationship(s) may be established instead.

As we see it, change always emerges at the level of dyads, where it is potentially generated, received and transmitted to other business relationships. The role of a dyad in network change is thus threefold: it generates change by itself, but also functions as a recipient and a transmitter of change with respect to other relationships in the network. From the perspective of business dynamics, this type of connected change is of particular interest.

INCREMENTAL AND RADICAL CHANGE IN NETWORKS

Network change has usually been regarded as an evolutionary process. The focus has rested on change through gradual and incremental steps as network actors interact and adapt to each other. However, the recent waves of acquisitions, mergers and bankruptcies in various fields of business have shown that discontinuities and revolutionary change can also happen in business networks and should therefore be examined in models of network evolution.

In order to include both gradual and revolutionary change in the analysis of business networks, we shall utilize the punctuated-equilibrium model. According to this model, systems evolve through the alternation of periods of equilibrium, in which persistent underlying structures permit only incremental change, and periods of revolution, in which these underlying structures are fundamentally altered (Gersick, 1991). The punctuated-equilibrium paradigm of change has aroused particular interest in the social sciences and organization research (Gersick, 1991; Tushman *et al.*, 1986; Van de Ven, 1992), and it also seems fruitful for the study of business-network dynamics (see Easton and Araujo, 1994; Salmi, 1995).

The punctuated-equilibrium model offers three concepts that are particularly useful for network analysis: a deep structure, periods of stability[1] and revolutionary periods.

Deep structure refers to the underlying structures of the system.[2] According to Gersick (1991, p. 15), deep structure is 'a network of fundamental, interdependent "choices" of the basic configuration into which a system's units are organized, and the activities that maintain both this configuration and the system's resource exchange with the environment'. In the business-network context, we define deep structure as the fundamental choices which sets of business actors have made concerning who they are connected to. The deep structure includes the actor bonds, activity links and resource ties the network actors have built between each other over time.

During *periods of stability*, the basic organization and activity patterns of the system remain essentially the same and only incremental changes occur. This does not imply a static situation, however. The system is in the process of continuous movement and adjustment (Gersick, 1991). Periods of stability are relatively long term and thus represent the 'usual' standing of a network. Empirical evidence of stability in business networks is predominant. In fact, the IMP Group's network approach largely emerged from an empirical notion of stability of industrial market structures. During the periods of stability, the relationships – that is, actor bonds, activity links and resource ties – between actors remain, but their character may change.

The punctuated-equilibrium model proposes that the longer periods of stability are punctuated by sudden and *revolutionary changes*. These are 'relatively brief periods when a system's deep structure comes apart, leaving it in disarray until the period ends, with the "choices" around which a new deep structure forms' (Gersick, 1991, p. 20). In network terms, the underlying structures of actor bonds, activity links and resource ties are fundamentally altered during revolutionary periods. Such periods imply radical change in individual dyads. Change can be considered radical when a relationship between two actors is broken or a new relationship is established. This may happen, for instance, when one actor disappears from the network together with connections to other actors, or a new actor enters the network, so initiating new relationships. The punctuated-equilibrium model also suggests that systems do not shift from one kind of structure to another through incremental steps but through frame-breaking change (Gersick, 1991, pp. 19–22). It is likely that this period of destruction involves great uncertainty and a feeling of discomfort for the individual actors involved (see, for example, Halinen, 1997, p. 281; Salmi, 1995, p. 197).

We thus suggest that the evolution of business networks involves both incremental and radical change. The two types of change are viewed here as empirical categorizations. Confined change at the level of dyads may manifest itself either as gradual and incremental, or instant and radical. Where the change also affects other connected business relationships and thus becomes a network change, it may similarly appear as incremental or radical. Incremental change in a business network involves changes in the nature and content of single relationships, while radical change means that relationships are dissolved or new relationships built.

THE FORCES OF CHANGE BEHIND NETWORK DYNAMICS

At different time periods a business network may be in either a stable or revolutionary state. The punctuated-equilibrium model suggests that different explicatory factors are at work in these states. Time is thus used as an avenue for incorporating different explanations of change processes (see Van de Ven and Poole, 1995, p. 531). We call these different explanations *forces of stability and change*. We suggest that different intertwined forces underlie and create network dynamics. The network approach emphasizes the interdependence of actors, activities and resources as a major force. It also stresses the intentionality of individual actors over environmental influence: business actors are goal-oriented and aim to control the network and their interaction with each other (see, for example, Håkansson and Johanson, 1992).

Stability is an inherent feature of a network, for which several reasons can be found. To begin with, industrial systems follow an industrial logic (Johanson and Mattsson, 1992, p. 207), and technical and resource interdependencies cause rigidity in the network. Increasing market concentration, high costs of change (switching costs) and risk-reducing strategies have also been suggested as reasons for stability (Turnbull *et al.*, 1996, p. 44). Salmi (1995) recently found that institutional interdependencies cause rigidity. Various institutional rules for 'correct' network behaviour emerge as an outcome of interaction between network actors. Moreover, the inclination of both individuals and organizations to stick to former behaviour patterns and resist change has a stabilizing effect. As we see it, all the stabilizing forces are manifested in *inertia*, that is a tendency to maintain the deep structure of the business network. Due to inertia, the business network experiences only incremental changes.

From the perspective of network dynamics, the forces of change are even more interesting. The network is never in a state of equilibrium, but, due to interaction between business actors and their different intentions, tensions and forces of change are always present. Since radical changes also occur in business networks, it is logical to ask what triggers these changes. In terms of the punctuated-equilibrium model, we should consider what factors trigger revolutionary periods and are able to dismantle the deep structure of a business network. We will now turn to this issue by introducing the concept of the critical event. The nature of critical events as manifestations of change forces is discussed and illustrated by way of findings from recent network research.

Critical events and 'enacted' reality

The concept of *the critical event* (or critical incident) has been used in studies of business relationships, when referring to those events that have a decisive effect on relationship development (Elsässer, 1984, p. 163; Halinen, 1997, p. 272; see also Hertz, 1993, p. 246). For the purpose of understanding network dynamics, 'critical event' is defined here as an incident that triggers radical change in a business dyad and/or network. It is a manifestation of the change forces inherent in networks. A critical event has the potential to break the deep structure of a dyad, that is the connection between two parties. To develop a radical change in a business network, the effects of the event have to be received in several relationships.

A critical event should be seen as an impulse that sets the stage for radical change (see Gersick, 1991, p. 22). The need for such change may have developed over time as various conflicting forces – some cementing inertia, others inducing change – create tensions and the potential for instability. Whether a revolutionary period is started or not depends ultimately on the actions and intentions of the companies in the network. It is not the mere event itself that is critical but the way the parties of a focal and other dyads react to it. A critical event is the impulse that allows tensions to be released and the network to reconfigure. It may also be the 'last straw' in a series of developments that finally leads to major company action. Just as for societal revolutionary change (for example, the destruction of the Berlin Wall), the seeds of the change may have been sown some time ago and the pressure for radical change evolved during a long but seemingly stable period of incremental change.

The perceptions and intentional behaviour of business actors are thus decisive for change. Industrial reality is continuously 'constructed' by the human actors involved in the business (see Berger and Luckmann, 1967). The mental process of enactment can be regarded as a key explanation for both stability and change (Melin, 1989, p. 168). What can be considered a critical event is ultimately an empirical question. It is business actors and their interpretations that determine what is critical and what is not. The actions taken by companies in their business relationships, and the degree to which these actions are received and acted upon in other connected relationships, ultimately determine whether any frame-breaking changes occur in a business network. The degree of revolutionary change may also differ according to the number of actors and relationships that become part of it.

Types of critical event

Critical events may arise from dyads in different parts of the business network or ultimately from outside it, from the broader business environment and society as a whole (see Anderson *et al.*, 1994, p. 4; Håkansson and Snehota, 1995b, p. 271; Melin, 1989, p. 167). In the following, we discuss the potential critical events that emerge from interaction between companies, and from the broader environment.

Critical events arising from interaction in the dyad. Critical events arising from business relationships characterize the role of dyads as generators of change. To begin with, certain events occurring in interacting companies become potentially critical for a dyad. The impact of personnel changes in the upper echelons of the organization has been particularly emphasized (Easton and Araujo, 1994, p. 387; Gersick, 1991, p. 23). These changes are likely to be preceded by a crisis or at least a stated need for changing the company's strategy (Gersick, 1991, p. 23; Salmi, 1995, p. 191; Tushman *et al.*, 1986, p. 38). Shifts in organizational structures have also been identified as critical events. In her study of advertising agency–client relationships, Halinen (1997) found that an organizational change in a client company, caused by rapid international expansion of the company and various conflicting interests within it, functioned as a critical event in the development of the company's advertising agency relationship.

Several events that occur within a dyad – that is, through interaction between two business actors – may prove to be critical. All the entrepreneurial and strategic actions of companies fall into this category. Entrepreneurial actions always require the change or development of business relationships (Håkansson and Snehota, 1995b, p. 273), and strategies are related to a company's interaction with and positioning towards other actors in the network (Melin, 1989, p. 169). For instance, changes in a company's business, marketing and purchasing strategies are potential critical events. An empirical case of a Swedish manufacturer and its French customer shows how a shift in the marketing strategy of a customer triggered radical change (Havila, 1996). A ten-year-old, well-established relationship was suddenly dissolved when the French customer (a component manufacturer) decided to focus on a new and less demanding customer segment and lowered the quality standards of its products. The high-quality, semi-finished materials that the company had bought from the Swedish manufacturer were no longer needed and the relationship came to an end.

Acquisitions, mergers, bankruptcies and partner-switching may also be identified as potential critical events for a relationship and the broader business network (for empirical support see, for example, Hertz, 1993). In all of the events mentioned, a dyad is the generator of radical network change, on the condition that other actors in the network perceive the event as critical and act upon it.

Critical events arising from the business environment.   Critical events may arise from general economic, political, social and technological conditions. For instance, changes in technology, institutional conditions or industrial structures, and their influence on actors in business networks, have recently been analysed (Mattsson and Hultén, 1994). Environmental events concern several network actors simultaneously.

Economic recession is one environmental change force behind a variety of critical events. It has a sweeping effect on business networks where actors are dependent on each other through various activity links and resource ties. The impact of economic problems in one industry is rapidly transferred to other industries. Economic downturns have, for instance, affected companies' advertising expenditures and as a consequence the advertising and media companies' business conditions. The 1990–93 recession in the Finnish economy led to a series of bankruptcies and a fundamental restructuring of the advertising industry. For an individual business relationship, a recession with its side-effects may turn out to be critical and lead to the dissolution of the relationship (see Halinen, 1997).

We want to emphasize, however, that while environmental forces seem to have a general impact on networks, they are always transmitted within the network through individual relationships. In the network context, environmental forces are channelled through business relations with other specific parties, rather than operating as a kind of general market force influencing the firm (Håkansson and Johanson, 1993, p. 44; Nohria, 1992, p. 5). Together with other change forces, they may materialize into events that the business relationship actors perceive as critical. Empirical support can be found, for instance, in the study carried out by Salmi (1995) that analysed a Finnish company's coping with a large-scale environmental change process, namely the economic reform of the former Soviet Union. According to the study, the fundamental and unique change forces relating to the transformation of an economic system were channelled through the interorganizational relations which the focal company maintained. The company perceived these change forces as a stream of events in its business relations, and some although not all of the events were considered critical and led to radical change in the company's relations.

We have used the network concepts to describe how the environmental forces actually function and affect business relationships. When business actors throughout the network react to environmental pressures, the change per se only takes place in individual dyads, from which it is then mediated to other connected dyads. The dyad functions as a recipient of change and, potentially, as a transmitter of change to other relationships in the network. To the extent that critical events occur, the outcome may be a radical network change.

A FRAMEWORK OF CHANGE IN BUSINESS NETWORKS

Our propositions concerning the mechanism, nature and forces of change are summarized in an analytical framework of network change, presented in Figure 3. In this framework we focus on connected change, the most interesting form from the perspective of network dynamics. We suggest using this framework as an analytical tool for understanding network dynamics and making empirical investigations. Key elements in our framework are: (1) dyadic change and network change; (2) radical change circle and incremental change circle; and (3) transfers from one circle to another.

We see the two units, dyad and network, as being important to the understanding of network dynamics (the left and right halves of Figure 3). Change always emerges at the level of dyads. It may be confined to a single relationship or spread to others and thus become a network-level change. We have also argued that change may be incremental or radical. Incremental dyadic change refers to change in the character of a relationship, whereas radical change means that a relationship is terminated or established. Similarly, network change may be incremental, involving changes in the character of relationships, or radical and frame-breaking.

We have distinguished between two important concepts that reflect the impact of various change forces behind network dynamics: inertia and critical events. Inertia, defined as the tendency to maintain the deep structure of the network, manifests the various interdependencies between companies and thus keeps the network in a stable state, where only incremental change and adjustments occur. By contrast, critical events that result from the interplay of different change forces trigger radical change in dyads and break connections, that is actor bonds, activity links and resource ties. What is perceived as critical and in need of prompt action depends on the perceptions and intentions of business actors.

The framework identifies different change patterns in business networks. We suggest that two circles of change dominate network evolution: *the incremental change circle*, owing to inertia, and *the radical change circle*, triggered by critical events (see the inner and outer circles in Figure 3).

The incremental change circle involves the idea that incremental changes in a dyad tend to cause only incremental changes in a business network and vice versa. Actions taken by business partners

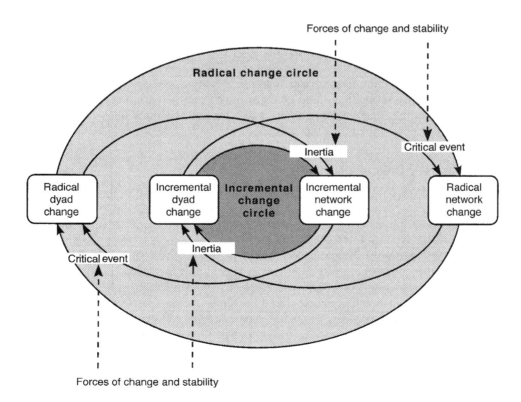

Figure 3 An analytical framework of change in business networks.

or events occurring in the business environment are perceived as minor issues that require only small incremental changes in relationships with other actors – thus, a period of stability prevails. Technical and institutional interdependencies, among other stabilizing forces, create inertia that keeps the circle viable.

The radical change circle, on the other hand, suggests that radical change in a dyad is likely to lead to radical changes in the surrounding network as well, and vice versa. The interplay of various change forces becomes manifest in critical events that are perceived and acted upon by other actors in the network. It is easy to find examples: for instance, in times of economic recession, fundamental changes spread from one industry to another due to strong connections, as described earlier.

Most interesting from the perspective of network dynamics is, however, *a transfer from the incremental change circle to the radical or vice versa*. There seem to be situations where radical changes take place within an individual dyad, while the business network remains basically the same. For instance, when a marginal customer decides to stop ordering from one big wholesaler and starts to buy from another, the breakdown of one relationship causes only minor changes in the character of other connected relationships.

Another option in Figure 3 is that of an incremental dyadic change leading to a radical network change. Depending on the connected relationships, a relatively small change in one dyad may eventually trigger dramatic changes in the business network. This happens if the small initial change is perceived as important by other actors, and consequently promotes major responses. The case of the Swedish manufacturer that changed its channel strategy in Germany provides a good example of this.

Here we have stressed the role of dyads as generators of change, because of the important role of the enactment process in explaining network dynamics. However, change is not only unidirectional but circular, and therefore dyads may also be seen as recipients of change. This means that incoming impulses from the network may also lead to a transfer from the incremental change circle to the radical change circle (i.e. incremental network change becomes radical dyadic change) and vice versa. This is illustrated by the corresponding arrows in the lower half of Figure 3.

In fact, both the transfers from one change circle to another and the circular change effect make network change a far more complicated issue than it may at first seem. Different patterns of change may be realized in a business context and changes may have their origins in distant parts of the network, which makes the issue challenging to handle for both business managers and researchers alike.

CONCLUSIONS AND IMPLICATIONS

The strengths of the IMP Group's network approach, as we have shown in this paper, lie mostly in the perspective it takes of business markets as borderless webs of connected business relationships. Clearly, the network approach is most fruitful for investigations of several business actors simultaneously, or the dynamics of business markets more generally. It offers tools to analyse how change impulses originating in different parts of the network spread and affect business relationships. By viewing the business context as a web of specific business actors rather than a faceless environment, and by stressing perception processes, the network approach increases our understanding of how change is actually generated and transmitted in business markets. It thus provides better options for tackling the process of change than conventional marketing perspectives limited to an actor or dyad with some reference to the impact of the environment.

Current understanding of the dynamics of business networks leaves room for improvement. In this conceptual paper we have attempted to deepen this understanding by making better use of the existing theories of change, particularly of the punctuated-equilibrium model. We have proposed several concepts to describe network change and developed a comprehensive analytical framework that compiles the mechanism, nature and forces of change in business networks.

A number of ideas have been put forward to contribute to the development of network theory. We started by emphasizing the central role of business-relationship dyads for understanding the mechanism of network change. We promoted the idea of change as confined, occurring only within a dyad; or connected, with spill-over effects to other relationships in the network. We also advanced the idea of radical change in business networks. The concept of the critical event was introduced to pinpoint incidents that emerge from the interplay of various change forces and trigger fundamental reconfiguration of the network. The mental process of enactment is proposed to be a key explanation for both stability and change in networks. Depending on the perceptions of individuals – how they view the business context and its interdependencies, and possibilities to achieve their business goals in this context – some events are considered critical and requiring prompt action from the company, while others are perceived as minor, allowing inertia to come to the fore.

The proposed framework also allows for further elaboration of the change patterns in business networks. Two major circles of network change were distinguished: the radical change circle – involving radical change of a dyad and network – and the incremental change circle, where incremental change in a dyad perpetuates incremental changes in the network, and vice versa. Moreover, transfers from one circle to another are of particular interest from the perspective of network dynamics, as they indicate alternation of stable and revolutionary periods in networks. These transfers, and the circular change effect from dyad to network and network to dyad, add to the complexity of change and create considerable challenges for both researchers and managers in their attempt to deal with change.

We believe that our analytical framework can be used as a source of inspiration for future research on network dynamics and a basis for empirical investigations. We have already addressed the need to incorporate radical change into the analysis of network evolution. The framework also raises a number of more specific questions to be considered in future studies; for example, to what extent and under which conditions do changes in business-relationship dyads remain confined and never become connected with other relationships? How typical are the circles of radical and incremental change and transfers from one circle to another? More theoretical and empirical research is also needed to analyse the interplay of forces of change and forces of stability that ultimately create network dynamics.

Although our paper does not offer direct managerial implications, it does raise interesting research questions concerning managerial behaviour. For instance, future studies could analyse how managers interpret and distinguish critical from minor events. Another interesting research theme would be the role of enactment and managerial intentions in creating a radical change in a network.

NOTES

* We would like to thank the anonymous *JMS* reviewers for their useful comments. We are also grateful to Professors Geoff Easton, Jan Johanson and Ivan Snehota for very constructive comments on earlier drafts of this paper. This research was partially supported by grants from the Joint Committee of the Nordic Social Science Research Councils (NOS-S), the Foundation of Marketing Technology Center (MTC), the Foundation for Economic Education (Liikesivistysrahasto), and the Academy of Finland.

1. A network of business relationships is never in a state of equilibrium or optimum (see, for example, Håkansson and Snehota, 1995b, p. 271). Therefore, in the context of business networks we refer to periods of stability rather than periods of equilibrium (cf. Gersick, 1991).
2. Authors discussing the punctuated-equilibrium model refer to the term 'system'. In our case, this relates to the discussion of network boundaries. In network studies, the term 'system' should be seen to refer to a net or network that has been delimited according to the specific needs of analysis.

REFERENCES

Anderson, J. C., Håkansson, H. and Johanson, J. (1994). 'Dyadic business relationships within a business network context'. *Journal of Marketing*, **58**, 4, 1–15.

Araujo, L. and Easton, G. (1996). 'Networks in socioeconomic systems. A critical review'. In Iacobucci, D. (Ed.), *Networks in Marketing*. Thousand Oaks: Sage, 63–107.

Berger, P. L. and Luckmann, T. (1967). *The Social Construction of Reality* (reprinted in 1971). London: Penguin Books.

Easton, G. (1992). 'Industrial networks: a review'. In Axelsson, B. and Easton, G. (Eds), *Industrial Networks – A New View of Reality*. London: Routledge, 3–27.

Easton, G. and Araujo, L. (1994). 'Discontinuity in networks; initiators, issues and initiatives'. In Biemans, W. G. and Ghauri, P. N. (Eds), *Meeting the Challenges of New Frontiers. Proceedings of the 10th IMP Annual Conference*. Groningen: University of Groningen, 381–97.

Easton, G. and Lundgren, A. (1992). 'Changes in industrial networks as flow through nodes'. In Axelsson, B. and Easton, G. (Eds), *Industrial Networks – A New View of Reality*. London: Routledge, 89–104.

Elsässer, M. (1984). *Marknadsinvesteringar. Två fallstudier av etablering på utlåndsk marknad*. Stockholm: Liber Förlag.

Ford, D. (1980). 'The development of buyer–seller relationships in industrial markets'. *European Journal of Marketing*, **14**, 5/6, 339–54.

Gersick, C. J. G. (1991). 'Revolutionary change theories: a multilevel exploration of the punctuated equilibrium paradigm'. *Academy of Management Review*, **16**, 1, 10–36.

Håkansson, H. and Henders, B. (1995). 'Network dynamics: forces and processes underlying evolution and revolution in business networks'. In Möller, K. and Wilson, D. (Eds), *Business Marketing: An Interaction and Network Perspective*. Boston: Kluwer Academic Publishers, 139–54.

Håkansson, H. and Johanson, J. (1985). 'A model of industrial networks'. Working paper, Uppsala University, Department of Business Administration, Uppsala.

Håkansson, H. and Johanson, J. (1992). 'A model of industrial networks'. In Axelsson, B. and Easton, G. (Eds), *Industrial Networks – A New View of Reality*. London: Routledge, 28–34.

Håkansson, H. and Johanson, J. (1993). 'The network as a governance structure: interfirm cooperation beyond markets and hierarchies'. In Grabher, G. (Ed.), *The Embedded Firm*. London: Routledge, 35–51.

Håkansson, H. and Snehota, I. (Eds) (1995). *Developing Relationships in Business Networks*. London: Routledge.

Håkansson, H. and Snehota, I. (1995a). 'Analysing business relationships'. In Håkansson, H. and Snehota, I. (Eds), *Developing Relationships in Business Networks*. London: Routledge, 24–49.

Håkansson, H. and Snehota, I. (1995b). 'Stability and change in business networks'. In Håkansson, H. and Snehota, I. (Eds), *Developing Relationships in Business Networks*. London: Routledge, 269–329.

Halinen, A. (1997). *Relationship Marketing in Professional Services. A Study of Agency–Client Dynamics in the Advertising Sector*. London: Routledge.

Havila, V. (1996). 'International business-relationship triads: a study of the changing role of the intermediating actor'. Doctoral dissertation no. 64, Uppsala University, Department of Business Studies, Uppsala.

Hertz, S. (1993). The internationalization processes of freight transport companies. Doctoral dissertation, Stockholm School of Economics, The Economic Research Institute, Stockholm.

Iacobucci, D. (Ed.) (1996). *Networks in Marketing*. Thousand Oaks: Sage.

Johanson, J. and Mattsson, L.-G. (1992). 'Network positions and strategic action – an analytical framework'. In Axelsson, B. and Easton, G. (Eds), *Industrial Networks – A New View of Reality*. London: Routledge, 205–17.

Mattsson, L.-G. and Hultén, S. (Eds) (1994). *Företag och marknader i förändring – Dynamik i nätverk*. Stockholm: Nerenius & Santérus Förlag AB.

Melin, L. (1989). 'The field-of-force metaphor'. In *Advances in International Marketing*, vol 3. Greenwich, CT: JAI Press, 161–79.

Nohria, N. (1992). 'Is a network perspective a useful way of studying organizations?'. In Nohria, N. and Eccles, R. G. (Eds), *Networks and Organizations: Structure, Form, and Action*. Boston, MA: Harvard Business School Press.

Nohria, N. and Eccles, R. G. (Eds) (1992). *Networks and Organizations: Structure, Form, and Action*. Boston, MA: Harvard Business School Press.

Salmi, A. (1995). 'Institutionally changing business networks. An analysis of a Finnish company's operations in exporting to the Soviet Union, Russia and the Baltic States'. Doctoral dissertation, Publications of Helsinki School of Economics and Business Administration A-106, Helsinki.

Smith, P. C. and Laage-Hellman, J. (1992). 'Small group analysis in industrial networks'. In Axelsson, B. and Easton, G. (Eds), *Industrial Networks – A New View of Reality*. London: Routledge, 37–61.

Turnbull, P., Ford, D. and Cunningham, M. (1996). 'Interaction, relationships and networks in business markets: an evolving perspective'. *Journal of Business & Industrial Marketing*, **11**, 3/4, 44–62.

Tushman, M. L., Newman, W. H. and Romanelli, E. (1986). 'Convergence and upheaval: managing the unsteady pace of organizational evolution'. *California Management Review*, **29**, 1, 29–44.

Van de Ven, A. H. (1992). 'Suggestions for studying strategy process: a research note'. *Strategic Management Journal*, **13**, 169–88.

Van de Ven, A. H. and Poole, M. S. (1995). 'Explaining development and change in organizations'. *Academy of Management Review*, **20**, 3, 510–40.

Wilkinson, I. F. (1990). 'Toward a theory of structural change and evolution in marketing channels'. *Journal of Macromarketing*, **10**, 2, 18–46.

Wilson, D. T. and Mummalaneni, V. (1986). 'Bonding and commitment in buyer–seller relationships: a preliminary conceptualisation'. *Industrial Marketing and Purchasing*, **1**, 3, 44–58.

3.9 How should companies interact in business networks?

Håkan Håkansson and David Ford

INTRODUCTION

The words relationships and networks have recently received a great deal of attention from both academics and practitioners. Strategists have been concerned with joint ventures, strategic alliances and strategic networks. The term relationship marketing has become a buzzword for marketers and purchasers have discussed supply chain models and supplier networks.

These preoccupations seem to point to some basic changes in how companies relate to their environment and in the problems they face. More generally, the words network and relationship indicate that there is some kind of special organisational form at an aggregate level above that of individual companies. This leads to the interesting question, "If such an organisational form exists then what kind of problems and issues does it pose for companies and how can they respond?" This question forms the focus for this article.

WHAT IS A NETWORK?

In its most abstract form a network is a structure where a number of nodes are related to each other by specific threads. A complex business market can be seen as a network where the nodes are business units – manufacturing and service companies and suppliers of finance, knowledge and influence and the relationships between them are the threads. Both the threads and the nodes in the business context have their own particular content. Both are "heavy" with resources, knowledge and understanding in many different forms (Håkansson, 1997). This heaviness is the result of complex interactions, adaptations and investments within and between the companies over time. The network is not a world of individual and isolated transactions between companies. Instead, each node or business unit, with its unique technical and human resources is bound together with many others in a variety of different ways through its relationships.

The existence of business relationships

The existence of tangible relationships between companies, that are connected together to form a "quasi-organisation" or complex networks has been observed in a range of studies over the past 25 years. Examples include Håkansson (ed.) 1982, Henders, 1992, Raesfeld-Meeijer, 1997, Ford (ed.) 1997, Axelsson and Easton, 1992, Gadde and Håkansson, 1993, Halinen, 1996, Iacobucci, 1996, Laage-Hellman, 1997, Naude and Turnbull, 1998. The relationships are likely to be complex and long-term and their current form is the outcome of previous interactions between the business units. Relationships enable companies to cope with their increasing technological dependence on others and the need to develop and tailor offerings to more specific requirements. Technologies are both developed and exploited within them (Lundgren, 1995, Ford and Saren, 1996). The characteristics of companies' relationships influence what happens inside the companies themselves.

The existence of connections between relationships

Business relationships are connected to each other. This can be illustrated by the simple example of three companies related through two business relationships. The interaction between any two of the companies, whether to buy or sell, or to co-operate in product development, will depend on what happens in relation to the third party. If company A is a supplier and B and C are two customers, then any development between A and customer B will have an negative or positive effect on its relationship with the other customer C. Similarly, if A is a customer and B and C are both suppliers then what happens between A and one of the suppliers will affect A's relationship with the other. If the three companies are in a chain, so that A supplies B, who supplies C then interaction in either of the two relationships will affect the other. When any resources or activities are shared between relationships there will be either a positive or a negative connection between them. What happens in one relationship will always affect all connected relationships, sometimes marginally, but often substantially.

This means that the development of any one relationship between two companies will depend on a number of factors: On what has happened in the past in the relationship; on what each of the two parties has previously learned in its other relationships; on what currently happens between the companies in the relationship and in others in which they are involved; on the expectations of both companies of their future interactions; on what happens in the wider network of relationships in which they are not directly involved.

This means that no one interaction, whether it is a sale, purchase, advice, delivery or payment can be understood without reference to the relationship of which it is a part. Similarly, no one relationship can be understood without reference to the wider network. Each company gains benefits and incurs costs from the network in which it is embedded and from the investments and actions of all of the companies involved.

Managerial questions about relationships and networks

This view of companies, relationships and networks leads to a number of important questions for managers, as follows:

What kind of special opportunities and restrictions does a network bring to a company? This leads to consideration of how a company should manage and vary its interactions with counterparts and how each of its relationships is related to others. One concern is how the company and its counterparts can use their relationships to their advantage and how these relationships restrict the pursuit of their individual aspirations. A company is, in fact, examining opportunities and restrictions when it seeks to bring order into the value and costs involved in the many relationship choices open to it.

What is the interplay for a company in a network between influencing others and being influenced by them? This question concerns the interface between the node and the threads. In particular, managers must face the issue of what it really means to them to have important business relationships. These relationships provide the opportunity to influence others, but they are also the means by which a company can be influenced by them. Much managerial analysis and decision-making is concerned with trying to understand a company's interface with both immediate and more distant counterparts, as well as the respective contributions to their operations of different relationships.

What are the effects both on the network and on the company itself of any ambition it might have to control the development of the network? This third question relates to the position that the company holds in the network and to the network structure. It is also concerned with how the characteristics, aims and activities of all of the companies and relationships in the network affect that total structure. Behind each of these three managerial questions is an important paradox in the nature of business networks or relationships. We will examine these three paradoxes and consider their implications for managers and how they might cope with them.

> ## OPPORTUNITIES AND LIMITATIONS IN NETWORKS: THE FIRST NETWORK PARADOX
>
> Strong relationships are at the heart of a company's survival and the basis of its growth and development. But a well-developed network of relationships also ties a company into its current ways of operating and restrict its ability to change. Thus managers face the paradox that a network is both the source of life for a company and the cage that imprisons it.

This paradox is closely related to the way that a node is built into a network. A node is directly related to the existence of threads. The content of the node is the result of internal investments. The content of the threads is the result of investments by *both* of the counterparts. The greater the investments the more substantial will be the content. The total network is formed by investments and the life of a node is the result of the interplay between internal investments and those that are made in the threads. The development of the threads is an outcome of investments in both the nodes as well as in the threads themselves. The development of the threads gives opportunities to both nodes, but the existence of the threads also imposes restrictions on them. The stronger the threads are – the more content there is within them – the more important they will be in giving life to the node, but the more they will also restrict the freedom of the node to change.

The first network paradox and the business world

The first network paradox means that companies within a network are not wholly free to act according to their own aims, or to circumstances as they arise. They do not operate in isolation from others, or in response to some generalised environment as "one-against-all". Instead, each companies' considerations, actions and the things that happen to them can only be fully understood within a structure of individually significant counterparts and relationships. Both companies and their relationships are "heavy" with the experience and resources that have been built up through previous interactions and investments. The history of a business network is the process through which time and money have been devoted to build, adapt, develop, understand, relate and combine different human and physical resources together. A business network has a specific and intense structure with economic, technical and social dimensions. Together, these dimensions describe a world that is much more full than empty.

Opportunities and limitations for a company are related both to the resources invested in relationships and to the companies' internal capabilities. There are two main and partly contradictory consequences of this: The first has to do with the fact that a network consists of more or less unique parts. Each company's relationships and resources can be developed and combined with others in a large number of different ways. This creates major opportunities for innovation, to the benefit of both the companies that seize them and perhaps for others as well. A change in a network always involves changes in both companies and relationships. This means that a company seeking change is always dependent on the approval and actions of others to achieve the change, when introducing a new service, altering a logistics patterns or developing a new product. But, a company can mobilise part of the network in the direction it wishes, if its action is designed appropriately and seen to be positive by those whose support it needs. On the other hand no company and no relationship in a network has been built or operates independently of others. A business network is seldom the result of one "designer", although some companies will believe that they are responsible for its design. Generally, the network is the outcome of the deliberations, aims and actions of a number of the participants. Similarly, no company is the "hub" of the network or is likely to have complete control over it, although some will act as if they were in control. Such a view is likely to be the outcome of a lack of understanding of the nature of networks and the perspectives of others in them. All decisions, all actions and all changes occur within the context of the structure of the network. This structure of existing companies and relationships influences both what can be done and how it can be done (Anderson, Håkansson and Johanson, 1994). Thus, the network of existing relationships is also a severe limitation on a single company.

This limitation affects the costs of making a change in a network for both those involved in the change and may have effects elsewhere in the network. These effects are often not readily observable, such as the effects of a change in a company's inventory policy on the component manufacturers of its suppliers, or the effects of a development agreement between two companies in a different country. In contrast, sometimes the costs of change are immediately apparent. For example, one Swedish company makes an internal administrative charge of £5000 on any department seeking to establish a relationship with a new supplier. This charge sends a clear message to staff that establishing a new relationship involves both cost and effort, so there must be very good reasons to do so. Whatever form the costs of change take, they contribute to the inertia in a network. The effects of this inertia will be obvious to any company outside the structure that tries to get into it, even though it is not observable to others on the outside.

An illustration of the first network paradox

An illustration is provided by the network of companies and relationships involved in the Internet. Among these are software and hardware suppliers, fee-based Internet Service Providers, access suppliers such as fixed-line telecoms companies, E-commerce traders, such as Amazon.com etc and end-users of these services. Each has a network position, consisting of its own resources and those that exist within its relationships. These resources, technical, economic and social, are the source of each company's strength and the basis for its growth and development in a rapidly evolving market. For example, relationships between hardware and software suppliers and service providers enable them to offer innovative product and service features to end-users. But each of these network positions also represents an investment in the current structure and ways of thinking. Because of this, existing relationships restrict a company's ability to react to or to emulate new entrants with new ways of operating, based on different resources and without the constraints of already established network positions.

Managerial implications of the first network paradox

There are several important consequences of this first paradox for any decision-maker within a company. Firstly, it indicates that the diversity of the network gives every decision-maker myriad opportunities to act and the freedom to do almost whatever it wants. But its ability to act and the effects of its actions are constrained by the existing structure of the network. Change by companies and change within companies occurs through changes to the structure of the network. The existence of the structure and its inertia makes action in the network more difficult, but also more important. Secondly, the only way that a company can achieve change is through the network. This requires persistence in convincing others of the benefits of that change *and managing their expectations*. A company must give others a picture of the intended direction of a change and find ways to combine changes in internal resources and relationships that relate to their motivations and resources. The more difficult it is to achieve change, the more important are the individual actions of the company.

Thirdly, because change in a network is initially dependent on the existing structure and resources, it is more difficult for a company to achieve change by seeking new counterparts. The company must first find a suitable counterpart. Even if it can do this, the knowledge and understanding that exists in previous relationships will not be present. So both must be able to see the potential benefits of the new relationship and be prepared to incur the costs, make the necessary investments and accept its effects on their companies' existing relationships. Managers have to accept that change must often be accomplished within existing relationships, where some investments have already been made and where costs and benefits are more apparent. This is often the case with the development of new products or services. The key questions for both marketing and purchasing in business networks are thus more often about how to interact with *existing* counterparts than about how to choose new ones (Wynstra, 1997).

Fourthly, a network of relationships also develops a common knowledge and understanding between the parties about each other and the ways that they can and should interact. This is both a strength and an impediment to change. The costs and time involved in building relationships and in adjusting to a different way of behaving may mean that it makes sense for a company to develop those new relationships where the need for new knowledge is minimised, or where some commonality exists, perhaps because each company has the same related relationships already. It also means that a company can reduce its costs and enhance its benefits by seeking similar relationships and standardising them by content, level of commitment or the requirements of either side. Fifthly, the first paradox should also affect a manager's view of the nature of technological change and its effect on the world around him. Technological knowledge is embedded both within the companies and the relationships of a network. Change in a network is not the result of a single technology, but of the development, synthesis and application of many different technologies, both new and existing across the network. Neither the development nor the application of new technologies occurs in a single company. It is the network that provides the "bundle" of different new and existing technologies, necessary for any innovation (Ford and Saren, 1996). But the existing structure of the network acts as a brake on innovation because of its investment in existing ways of working and because of the requirement to enlist the co-operation of those with which the innovator does not have a relationship (Håkansson, 1989, 1994).

INFLUENCING AND BEING INFLUENCED IN A NETWORK: THE SECOND NETWORK PARADOX

A company's relationships are the outcomes of its strategy and its actions. But the paradox is that the company is itself the outcome of those relationships and of what has happened in them. Thus a network is both a way to influence and to be influenced. Both situations exist simultaneously and both premises are equally valid.

The interconnection between the threads and the node is a critical one and they each determine the other. The interconnection can be examined by the more obvious view that the node is something that was created first and then developed its own threads. Alternatively, we can see the node as a cross-roads between threads that has its existence defined by those threads. But, without nodes there are no threads and without threads the nodes have no value or function for each other. A thread that provides a link to a node is without value if that node has no special feature. Developing a node always involves developing its threads and a thread cannot be developed without affecting the nodes to which it is linked. It is meaningless to try to determine which of them comes first. In this way, nodes and threads are completely interdependent. There is an obvious direction from the node to the thread but there is at the same time an obvious direction from the thread to the node.

The second network paradox and the business world

If we translate this paradox to a business context then the interesting question is posed, "What is a business relationship and how is it related to a company?" If we claim that a company develops its own relationships then we see those relationships as tools used by the company. This way of examining the interface between the company and the relationships is a typical managerial approach and it points to the importance of a company's development of its relationships. But such a view can over-emphasise a company's ability to act in a network and can easily become ego-centric. If, on the other hand we suggest that a company is developed by or through its relationships then we emphasise the importance of having the right counterparts. Consequently, listening, reflecting and reacting to others become central activities. These are not typical managerial actions, but companies in a network have to live with both ways of behaving.

An illustration of the second network paradox

An example of the second paradox is provided by the Swedish telecoms company Ericsson and the largest Swedish tele-phone operator, Telia. The two companies have had a close relationship for 100 years and this has had profound effects on both of them. They developed their first automatic exchanges together in the 1920s. The later AXE exchange, developed by Ericsson in co-operation with Telia had a major effect on its international success. Later, mobile phones were developed within this relationship. From this perspective the relationship has *formed* both Ericsson and Telia. However, the relationship has to operate in a way that suits each of the companies and their overall strategies. For example when launching a new release of the GSM-system for mobile phones, Ericsson has to take into account a number of major users, of which Telia is only one. For Telia, the release has to be compatible with the new releases they are getting from other suppliers, such as Nokia.

Managerial implications of the second network paradox

A common view of business strategy is of a self-generated pattern or plan. Through this a company marshals its *own* goals, actions and resources into a cohesive whole in the light of its interpretation of the current and potential environment. But the second network paradox highlights that a company's characteristics are also the outcome of its interactions and relationships and that its future is dependent on what happens in those relationships (Håkansson and Lundgren, 1997). No company has sufficient resources itself to satisfy the requirements of any customer. It is dependent on the skills, resources, actions and intentions of suppliers, distributors, other customers and sometimes competitors, to satisfy those requirements. Similarly, no company can develop or exploit its own resources except in conjunction with those of others. Interdependence between companies means that the strategy process is interactive, evolutionary and responsive, rather than independently developed and implemented. The "strategizing" task is about identifying the scope for action, within existing and potential relationships and about operating effectively with others within the internal and external constraints that limit that scope.

A second implication of this paradox concerns which of the parties in a relationship will most affect its development. The party that is *least* committed to a relationship is likely to control it negatively by restricting its development. Conversely, the *positive* development of a relationship is likely to be driven by the party that is most committed to it. The development of a relationship is never determined unilaterally, even in those situations where one party appears overwhelmingly powerful or committed. A relationship does not develop without effort and it is certainly important that someone believes in it and is prepared to work for it (Huemer, 1998).

The third implication of this paradox concerns the extent of effects in a network. The close connection between a company and a relationship means that all actions in the two are inter-dependent. The second network paradox emphasises that if a manager looks at a network of companies then he will undoubtedly get a very restricted picture of the reality he faces. If he looks at a network of relationships then he will get a quite different picture. For a full picture he needs to look at both.

Finally, the second network paradox has implications for individual managers. The co-determination of companies and relationships in a network means that the more important are a company's relationships then the more important will be the actors who interact in them. This emphasises the importance for each company to manage all of its interactions carefully and for each individual person to interact self-consciously.

**CONTROLLING AND BEING OUT OF CONTROL IN NETWORKS:
THE THIRD NETWORK PARADOX**

Companies try to control the network that surrounds them and to manage their relationships to achieve their own aims. This ambition is one of the key forces in developing networks. But, the paradox is that the more that a company achieves this ambition of control, the less effective and innovative will be the network.

Each thread of a node is important to that node, not so much on its own, but as part of a larger structure. Each thread connects two nodes. It provides contact for both of them, but may well have a different role for each. One reason for this is that each node has other threads and has to relate each of them to the others. The total network structure is dependent on how all of the threads are related to each other. The effect of any one thread on the nodes is affected by these inter-dependencies with other threads. But it is the nodes that connect the threads and handle these interdependencies. The connecting of threads by the nodes is a key ingredient in network development. This development depends on the "stronger" ties that usually exist in more well-established relationships. It also depends on the "entrepreneurial" development of *potential* relationships and "weak ties" that can provide links to other parts of a network (Granovetter, 1973, Burt, 1992, Wilkinson and Young, 1999). From the perspective of the network as a whole, it is important that at least several nodes are active in this way.

The third network paradox and the business world

Each company will try to develop its position in the network relative to other companies, by influencing the knowledge and understanding within other companies and the direction in which each relationship develops. However, the more successful a company is in forcing its thinking onto the network, the more it and those around it are likely to encounter long-term problems. If the development process becomes directed from one centre it will become more integrated and may have fewer overt conflicts, but the network may cease to exist and become more of a hierarchy (Williamson, 1975, 1981). A uni-directed network will have less ability to embrace relationships that are not compatible with each other or which are developing in different directions. These may subsequently be important in ways that were impossible to forecast beforehand (Wilkinson and Young, op. cit). A second issue concerns knowledge and understanding in a more general sense. It is through the links between relationships that common ideas of "what-everyone-knows" are developed in a network. These norms or cultural patterns can strongly influence views of the actions or entry of outsiders. In this way, relationships can act as an impediment to change and innovation.

An illustration of the third network paradox

For a long time IBM tried to control its network, especially on the customer side. The company set strict roles for the software companies who had the rights to sell IBM-computers and IBM was able to develop a very efficient geographically-based organisation for production and sales. IBM had no plans to change this organisation, until it became apparent that it had become static and that the networks of other companies had been developing much faster. IBM lost out because a controlled network cannot develop faster than the company that controls it. Such a company has little incentive to change as long as it has control. The developments between advanced customers and other producers of hardware and software forced IBM to change its own internal organisation to become much flatter and much more diversified. In order to cope with the variety in the surrounding network, the organisation has had to become much messier, with fewer strict rules and more freedom for individuals to take initiatives.

Managerial implications of the third network paradox

Firstly, this paradox reinforces the need for a manager to analyse his company's position in terms of its specific relationships and its own and others' resources, rather than in terms of a set of products, markets and competitors. Secondly, it highlights the problems for managers if they take a self-centred view of the network. A network will look very different from the perspective of different companies, each with their own motivations, resources and understandings. A company that only sees the network from its own perspective will fail to understand its dynamics and the interface between the well-being of others and itself. The third network paradox also has strong implications for the conventional view of business strategy. All companies seek to manage their relationships to their own ends. But it is dangerous for a company to seek to manage its relationships so as to achieve overall control of a network. If this were ever to be achieved then the only source of wisdom and innovation in the network would be the company itself. Instead, each company must seek to manage *in* that network. In doing so the company is accepting that conflict is both inevitable in a network and is a source of change. The strategy process in complex networks is not a sequence through which companies *analyze* an environment, then *develop* a strategy and then *implement* that strategy in isolation from those around them. In practice, a company's analysis is concerned with making sense of the limitations and opportunities that the company has to act. That action is a complex pattern of reaction and re-reaction to the events and actions of others. Strategic management is about the development of orientation and approach in each episode, relationship and network situation. Strategy in complex networks consists of attempting to influence others where possible and to benefit from their resources and, more importantly from their initiatives and their creativity

HOW SHOULD COMPANIES INTERACT IN BUSINESS NETWORKS?

We started this paper with the clear question: How should companies interact in complex networks? A clear answer to this must be based on an awareness of the limitations both of business researchers and of businesses themselves. Business researchers can aim to construct tools to help managers to understand their world, not tell them what decisions to take or what to do. Business researchers cannot predict the direction of development of a network, nor forecast the final effects of any network action. This is because of the large number of ways each participant can act and react. Developing relationships is similar to the testing process in a laboratory and is something that can be done more or less thoughtfully and efficiently. Managers also have to accept that their current network position may not be optimal from the perspective of each single issue that they face. But changing a network position is a major strategic activity that can only be achieved in the long run. Networks are built on variety, but despite this they do have systemic properties. This means that the answers to managers' questions about their interactions will always depend on the specific situation and context. There are no nice neat solutions or standardised approaches to strategic network success. The paper has shown the value of thinking through what lies behind the actions of themselves and others and the dynamics of the network itself. Thus, the basis for interaction should be the formulation of new questions rather than looking for optimal solutions, as follows.

Opportunities and threats

Managerial questions about the opportunities and threats facing a company relate to the "heaviness" and the "variety" of the network and to the first network paradox of the simultaneous liberating and restricting characteristics of networks. Variety means that a company should interact to continuously learn and develop the way it is embedded in its relationships and the network. Variety requires ever-new *conceptualisations* of situations, relationships and business units. Heaviness emphasises the costs of changes and the importance of using the resources that are already available to the company in its existing relationships. Inertia limits innovation, but it also creates a firm basis from which developments can take place.

Influencing and being influenced

Questions about influence relate to the second network paradox of the simultaneous influence of a company on its relationships and of those relationships on itself. A company should use its interactions as a way to learn about the link between its own resources and those in its relationships – between the node and the threads. This is not simply saying that a company should try to understand its dependence on others in a network. And understanding cannot be achieved by viewing the world as a set of competitors, customers and suppliers. Instead a company should interact to try to understand how the network functions *from the perspective of these specific others* and how they see their own position and its own.

Control in the network

Questions about how to manage a company's interactions relate to the third network paradox, that control if ever achieved, can be destructive. This means that companies should not aim to achieve some "final" control over the surrounding network (or their supply chain or value chain!). Of course, a company's task is to try to modify its own network position and to influence what happens in their own and others' relationships. This falls well short of control. The management task is to encourage and help others to continuously clarify *their* understanding of the network. It is their actions, based on *their* perspectives that provide the dynamics of a network. These dynamics and the company's participation in them lead to change in the company's position and bring advantage to it. Interaction in business networks leads to a process of learning and systematising action. This takes advantage of the variety in the network and capitalises on the economy of network stability.

REFERENCES

Anderson, J., Håkansson, H. and Johanson, J. (1995), 'Dyadic Business Relationships Within a Business Network Context', *Journal of Marketing*, Vol. 58 (October), 1–15.

Axelsson, B. and Easton, G. (1992), *Industrial Networks: A New View of Reality*, London, Routledge, 1996.

Burt, R. (1992), *Structural Holes: The Social Structure of Competition*, Cambridge, Mass, Harvard University Press.

Dubois, A. (1998), *Organising Industrial Activities Across Firm Boundaries*, London: Routledge.

Easton, G. and Håkansson, H. (1996) 'Markets as Networks: Editorial Introduction,' *International Journal of Research in Marketing*, Vol. 13, No. 5, Dec., pp 407–13.

Ford, D. (ed.) (1997), *Understanding Business Markets*, 2nd edition, London: Dryden.

Ford, D., Gadde, L.-E., Håkansson, H., Lundgren, A., Snehota, I., Turnbull, P. and Wilson, D. (1998), *Managing Business Relationships*. London: Wiley.

Ford, D. and Saren, M. (1996), *Technology Strategy for Business*, London: Thomson.

Gadde, L.-E. and Håkansson, H. (1993), *Professional Purchasing*, London: Routledge (also published in Swedish).

Goldstein, J. (1994), *The Unshackled Organisation: Facing the Challenge of Unpredictability through Spontaneous Reorganisation*, Portland, Oregon, Productivity Press.

Granovetter, M. (1973), "The Strength of Weak Ties", *American Journal of Sociology*, Vol. 78, 1360–1380.

Håkansson, H. (ed.) (1982), *International Marketing and Purchasing of Industrial Goods*, New York: Wiley.

Håkansson, H. (1989), *Corporate Technological Behaviour. Cooperation and Networks*, London: Routledge.

Håkansson, H. (1994), Networks as a mechanism to develop resources, in Beije et al. (eds) *Networking in Dutch Industries*, Garant Uitgivers.

Håkansson, H. (1997), Organization Networks, in Sorge, A. and Warner, M. (eds) *The IEBM Handbook of Organizational Behaviour*, London: International Thompson Business Press.

Håkansson, H. and Johanson, J. (1993), Network as a Governance Structure, in Grabher, G., *The Embedded Firm. The Socio-Economics of Industrial Networks*, London: Routledge.

Håkansson, H. and Lundgren, A. (1997), Paths in Time and Space – Path dependence in industrial networks, in Magnusson, L. and Ottosson, J. (eds) *Evolutionary Economics and Path Dependence*, Cheltenham: Edward Elgar.

Håkansson, H. and Snehota, I. (1995), *Developing Relationships in Business Networks*, London: Routledge.

Halinen, A. (1997) *Relationship Marketing in Professional Services*, London: Routledge.

Harrison, D. (1998), 'Strategic Responses to Predicted Events: The case of the banning of CFCs'. Unpublished doctoral dissertation, University of Lancaster.

Hedaa, Laurids (1997), 'Sat ud af spillet. Case: Tele Danmark Forlag' – Paper published by the Personal Management Institute, Copenhagen: Samfundslitteratur.

Henders, B. (1992), 'Positions in Industrial Networks', Unpublished PhD dissertation, University of Uppsala, Sweden.

Huemer, L. (1998), *Trust*, Umea, Sweden, Borea Bokforlag.

Iacobucci, D. (ed.) (1996), *Networks in Marketing*, Thousands Oaks, CA: Sage.

Laage-Hellman, J. (1997), *Business Networks in Japan. Supplier–customer interaction in product development*, London: Routledge.

Lundgren, A. (1995), *Technological Innovation and Network Evolution*, London: Routledge.

Naude, P. and Turnbull, P. W. (eds.) (1998), *Network Dynamics in International Marketing*, Oxford: Pergamon.

Raesfeld-Meeijer, A. (1997), 'Technological Cooperation in Networks. A Socio-Cognitive Approach', Ph.D-dissertation, University of Twente.

Senge, P. M. (1990), *The Fifth Discipline*, New York, Doubleday Currency.

Tunisini, A.-L. (1997), 'The Dissolution of Channels and Hierarchies', Ph.D-dissertation no 69, Department of Business Studies, University of Uppsala.

Turnbull, P. and Zolkiewski J. (1997), Profitability in Customer Portfolio Planning, in Ford (ed.), op cit, 305–325.

Wilkinson I. F. and Young L. (1999), On Co-operating: Firms, Relations and Networks, Unpublished Research Paper, University of Western Sydney.

Williamson O. E. (1975), *Markets and Hierarchies*: *Analysis and Anti-Trust Implications*, New York, Free Press.

Williamson O. E. (1981), 'The Modem Corporation: Origins, Evolution, Attributes', *Journal of Economic Literature*, Vol 19 (Dec), pp. 1537–1568.

Wynstra, F. (1997), Purchasing and the Role of Suppliers in Product Development. Lic, thesis no 32, Department of Business Studies, University of Uppsala.

Part 4
Marketing in
Business Networks

The first three parts of this book try to build a conceptual basis for analysing business relationships and inter-company networks. The final two parts concentrate on how this conceptual basis can be used to understand business marketing strategy and purchasing strategy. The IMP approach has emphasised that if researchers are to achieve an understanding of what happens in a business network they need to examine *both* the marketing and purchasing sides of relationships. Also, it is important for marketing and purchasing managers to be familiar with the problems and approaches of their counterparts and to see how a relationship is viewed by their counterparts and how it fits into their plans. For these reasons we would emphasise that both of these parts of the book are of equal value to marketers and purchasers.

The readings in Part Four have been chosen to illustrate a number of different aspects of business marketing strategy. The first two readings, by Malcolm Cunningham with Elling Homse and Nigel Campbell respectively, set the scene by examining the vital issues in business marketing of effectively analysing a portfolio of customers, allocating the company's resources between them and managing the patterns of its contacts with them. The third reading by Peter Turnbull and Judy Zolkiewski was specially written for this book. This reading provides a comprehensive overview of ideas on how a marketer can manage a portfolio of business relationships.

The next reading by Kristian Moller and Arto Rajala tackles the important but usually neglected issue of organising for business marketing and the paper by David Ford and Ray McDowell uses case examples to show how companies can assess the *value* to them and to their customers of different actions in their relationships. Reading six by Thomas Ritter examines how skills or "Network Competence" can be used to operate effectively in business networks and explains what is necessary to achieve that competence. A further tool for analysis is provided by Pete Naude and Francis Buttle in reading seven when they examine the views of managers on what makes for "quality" in a business relationship. One aspect of quality and value in a relationship is provided by the adaptations that each side may make to suit its counterpart's requirements. These adaptations are examined in detail by Ross Brennan and Peter Turnbull in Reading eight. Finally, David Ford and Mike Saren examine how a company can analyse its own technologies and point to ways in which these can be effectively exploited in a business network.

CONTENTS

4.1 Controlling the marketing–purchasing interface: resource development and organisational implications

Malcolm Cunningham and Elling Homse

INTRODUCTION

Supplier–customers interdependence is a feature of many concentrated industrial markets. Marketing and purchasing in such circumstances can be construed as an exchange process leading to the adaptive behaviour of both parties over time. This is achieved through the mechanisms of organizational interaction. At the core of these exchange processes between suppliers and customers is the person-to-person dyadic relationship involving a salesman and a buyer. Supporting this narrowly based dyad is a complex network of inter- and intra-organizational personal contacts.

In this article we consider the organizational and resource allocation issues arising from the patterns of personal contacts between suppliers and their customers. The ideas and empirical data have evolved from the "interaction approach" of the IMP (International Marketing and Purchasing) research group's five-country study of supplier–customer relationships in European industrial markets (Håkansson, 1982).

First, we examine these personal contacts within the context of interaction theory. This leads on to a discussion of the roles which personal contacts play in developing and maintaining supplier–customer relationships. Third, we investigate some of the factors determining the resource allocation to different customers. Fourth, we analyse the networks of supplier–customer contacts, focusing upon their frequency, breadth and the managerial levels involved. Finally, we develop a taxonomy of patterns of contacts between suppliers and customers and consider the management issues involved.

Interorganizational personal contacts represent a scarce human resource in which is vested much of the expertise, credibility and authority of the participating companies. This raises several managerial questions for a supplier company:

- How should human resources be allocated among different markets and customers? What is the correct balance between technical, marketing and senior managerial staff required to have personal contact with customers?

- How frequently, and at what venue (customer or supplier) should personal contacts occur to achieve the objectives?
- What factors should determine the amount of resources which must be deployed to handle various supplier–customer relationships?

No simple answers to such questions have so far emerged from previous research. Here we present some evidence of current practice and offer explanation for these resource allocation decisions.

THE INTERACTION CONTEXT OF PERSONAL CONTACTS

The interaction model of buyer–seller relationships proposed by the IMP research group (Håkansson, 1982) focuses attention upon the different categories of variables affecting the processes of interaction between individuals and also between formally and informally constituted organization groups in the supplier and customer companies.

Four major groups of variables provide the framework for describing and analysing supplier–customer relationships. First, the interaction processes involved in exchanging goods, services, information, etc.; second, the parties to the exchange, comprising individuals, groups and formal organizations; third, the economic and market environment surrounding the exchange; and, fourth, the atmosphere characterizing the relationship between the supplier and the customer. The interaction model recognizes that personal contacts between the two companies are a frequently used mechanism for initiating, developing and maintaining such relationships.

A major task of the industrial marketer is to manage the interface between the business and its customers in a competitive environment. On one side of the supplier–customer interface is the customer's purchasing decision-making unit (DMU) of which the buyer is but one part (Webster and Wind, 1972). The mirror image of this DMU is the supplier's sales-service-design team who are frequently in personal contact with customers (see Figure 1).

Figure 1 illustrates four types of interorganizational contacts. First, a single dyadic relationship existing between salesman and buyer; second, a series of interfunctional contacts between personnel in different supplier and customer functional departments; third, the contacts between the senior managers of functional departments and, fourth, contacts between the general management in the two companies.

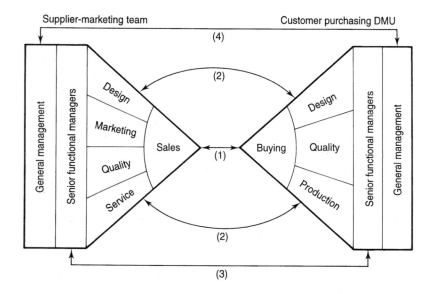

Figure 1   Interface between parties in supplier–customer relationships.

THE ROLES OF PERSONAL CONTACTS IN SUPPLIER–CUSTOMER RELATIONSHIPS

Interpersonal contacts between supplier and customer companies are identified in the IMP interaction model as performing vital roles in problem solving, in exchanging social values and information and in demonstrating commitment to, and credibility with, the other party. Ford (1984) pointed out the strong association which exists between buyers' assessments of the professional and commercial skills of their suppliers and the extent of the perceived commitment, adaptability and capability of suppliers to reduce the "distance" that can exist between them and their customers. This followed his earlier ideas (Ford, 1981), developed from the interaction model which took the form of a multi-stage paradigm demonstrating how such characteristics as commitment, uncertainty, distance reduction and adaptations change as the buyer–seller relationship proceeds through developmental stages over time. Clearly, personal contacts are one means of accomplishing this "distance reduction".

Based upon Ford's ideas, the stepwise evolution of the patterns of inter-organizational contacts between a supplier and customer can be represented as in Figure 2. The emphasis in this diagrammatic portrayal is on how the perceived distance between the two parties (social distance, technological distance, cultural distance and geographical distance) is reduced in stages as the personal contacts change from a simple salesman–buyer relationship to a multi-functional network of contacts. This stage is characterized by limited experience, high uncertainty, low commitment and limited information exchange (Figure 2a). The next stage is characterized by increasing experience, increasing confidence, perceived high commitment and moderate information exchange (Figure 2b). The long-term relationship stage is characterized by interdependence, extensive experience, high resource commitment, extensive adaptations and reciprocal information exchange. The functional departments develop bonds which are of comparable strength to those between salesman and buyer.

Personal contacts as a mechanism for the reduction of "psychic" or cultural distance between exporters and importers have been researched by others (Hallen and Wiedersheim-Paul, 1982). They focus upon the acquisition of market knowledge, the development of close business connections and the transmission/reception of information between buyers and sellers.

However, based on their analysis of over 100 supplier–customer relationships in international markets, interorganizational personal contacts were found to serve other roles than those of distance reduction (Cunningham and Turnbull, 1982). These roles were identified as:

- Information exchange;
- Assessment;
- Negotiation and adaptation;
- Crisis insurance;
- Social bonding;
- Ego enhancement.

These widely varying roles may be achieved by different forms, structures and patterns of personal contacts. For example, reducing distance and demonstrating commitment may be fulfilled either by a small number of very senior staff in infrequent interaction, or by a large number of junior personnel in frequent contact.

Adopting an alternative perspective (that of the buyer) the roles of personal contacts can be considered according to their contribution to gaining and retaining business from customers in a highly competitive environment. An analysis of the attitudes and experiences of over 400 buyers of industrial goods in Europe revealed that there are eight major groups of factors which characterize relationships between suppliers and customers (Turnbull and Cunningham, 1981). Buyers can compare the relative capabilities of competing suppliers on these factors. These eight factors are closely related to the key marketing tasks which the supplier must perform in order to be an acceptable supplier and on which they will be evaluated by members of the customer's purchasing

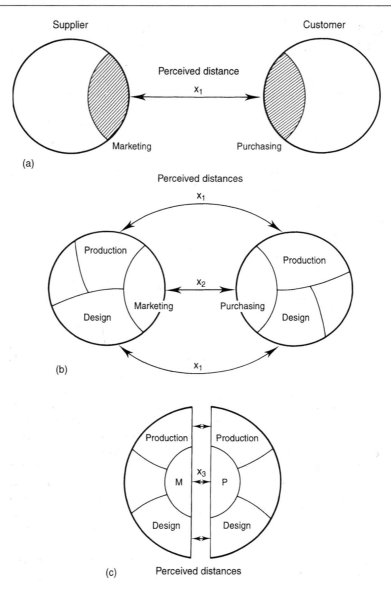

Figure 2 (a) The early stage of the relationship. (b) The development stage. (c) The long-term relationship stage.

DMU. These eight factors and the marketing tasks characterizing successful supplier–customer relationships are summarized in Table 1.

It is in performing the tasks described in Table 1 and particularly in communicating them effectively and convincingly to customers that the role of personal contacts can best be appreciated.

These tasks represent the core requirements which are most likely to meet customers' needs. However, the particular strategy being pursued by suppliers in different markets in different competitive environments and with selected target customers are clearly going to impinge on the way in which the scarce human resources of the supplier are going to be deployed. Competitive marketing strategies based on superior technical innovations call for a different mix of resources

Table 1   Characteristics of supplier–customer relationships

1.	*Customer orientation*	Suppliers must analyse customer needs, be international in outlook, show interest in the customer's problems and be sensitive to the way foreign firms operate
2.	*Technological expertise*	The technical competence of marketing staff must be complemented by the willingness of suppliers to offer new technology and innovative products to the customer in order to solve any technical problems
3.	*Commercial competence*	The supplier organization should be able to provide adequate and speedy responses to requests for information and be able to handle complaints
4.	*Flexibility and adaptability*	A willingness to adapt products, manufacturing processes, payment systems, delivery dates and administrative procedures
5.	*Supply performance capability*	The supplier must demonstrate an ability to provide a reliable delivery, quality assurance, after-sales service and information
6.	*Price competitiveness*	A price representing good value for money; accompanied by a willingness to negotiate on price and to recognize the other cost consequences of purchase in addition to an initial price
7.	*Organizational effectiveness*	The organization structure and co-ordination of the supplier's marketing, technical and manufacturing expertise has to be compatible with the customer's needs. This has important implications for the interorganizational personal contacts between the two companies in order to facilitate communications and negotiations
8.	*Social integration*	An atmosphere of co-operation, trust, commitment, closeness and legitimate exercise of power is a key feature of relationships with suppliers

from those required to implement strategies of being the lowest price supplier or strategies which are dependent upon offering guaranteed delivery reliability.

RESEARCH METHODOLOGY

The research reported here is based on an analysis of the intercompany personal contacts between 49 British suppliers of industrial goods and their customers in France, Germany, Italy, Sweden and the UK. It is part of a larger data base generated from 876 personal interviews with marketing and purchasing executives in five European countries. A full description of the research methodology is to be found in Håkansson (1982). The data relating to personal contacts between supplier and customer companies were obtained by focusing upon a small number of identifiable and important specific customers. No claim for representativeness of all its customer relationships for each company is made. Rather, the research is exploratory to gain a deeper understanding of relationships in industrial markets, especially across national boundaries as in export marketing and international purchasing.

The form in which the data were summarized and coded for computer analysis is as shown in Figure 3. The supplier company personnel were identified by consultation with the marketing/sales executive primarily responsible for handling the customer relationship. By a similar process of enquiry the customer personnel were identified. Subsequently, the matrix or network of inter-company contacts was mapped out. Finally, the frequency of contact, site location and topics dealt with through these personal contacts were elicited. Figure 3 illustrates one such supplier–customer relationship.

Nature and frequency of intercompany contact pattern

Nature purpose of contact (N)
1 = Commercial negotiations
2 = Technical negotiations
3 = General commercial information exchange
4 = General technical information exchange
5 = Commercial problem solving
6 = Technical problem solving
7 = Technical training and advice
8 = Progressing (delivery and technical)
9 = Other (appendix var 365)

Frequency of contact (F)
1 = Very frequent (weekly or more)
2 = Frequent (once every 3 months or more but less than weekly)
3 = Infrequent (less than every 3 months but more than once a year)
4 = Very infrequent (once a year or less)

Customer functions

	1 General mgt		2 Prodn		3 Quality		4 R&D eng		5 Finance		6 Mkting		7 Prchsing		8 Other		9 Other	
Supplier functions	N	F	N	F	N	F	N	F	N	F	N	F	N	F	N	F	N	F
1 Gen. mgt	34	4																
2 Prodn																		
3 Quality					6	3												
4 R&D eng					46	2	46	2					46	3				
5 Finance																		
6 Jun mkt.	34	4			6	3	246	2			3	4	135	2	8	4		
7 Sen mkt.							4	3					3	3				
8 Sal. abr.																		
9 Other***															8	3		

Note: Supplier personnel and functions are listed on the vertical axis and the customer equivalent on the horizontal axis. Where data are recorded in a cell of this matrix then the respective supplier and customer personnel are in face-to-face contact. The data record the many purposes of their meetings and the frequency with which these occur. For example, in this illustration general managers from both companies meet once a year for a general exchange of commercial and technical information (N = 3.4; F = 4).

Figure 3 Interorganizational personal contact pattern.

From these data the subsequent analysis of personal contacts covering the three dimensions of frequency, breadth and organizational level was made.

FACTORS INFLUENCING THE ALLOCATION OF RESOURCES TO CUSTOMERS

In the introduction to this article, we posed several important questions to be faced by managers in supplier companies when handling customer relationships. It is possible to investigate current practice in individual markets to shed light on these issues. In doing so we draw on concepts arising from the interaction model. It has already been argued that the stage of a supplier–customer relationship is likely to be a major determinant of the resources involved. In the following section we focus on three major factors: market structure (a feature of the environment of relationships), customer importance (derived from the value of product exchanges involved in the interaction process) and product complexity (arising from technology of the supplier/customer parties).

Market structure

Although other researchers have argued that interaction between suppliers and customers is affected by the recognition of their mutual interdependence and interest in gaining access to each other's resources (Melin, 1977), no effective measure of interdependence was proposed. Interdependence is clearly influenced by market structure which determines the available choice and power of prospective partners in a market. We can easily speculate that market structure will have a major impact upon the amount of interaction and, therefore, on the human resources committed to develop or defend special relationships in industrial markets. For example, we see from Figure

Number of suppliers

	Few	Many
Number of customers Few	Mutual interdependence Cell 1	Customer dominated Cell 2
Many	Supplier dominated Cell 3	Relative independence Cell 4

Figure 4   Market structure and supplier–customer relationships.

4 that in concentrated markets, where few suppliers and few customers exist (such as in cell 1), there is likely to be a "pairing off" between some customers and their preferred suppliers. Less equally balanced supplier–customer relationships, as in cells 2 and 3 of the matrix, are characterized by one party exercising power over the other. Finally in cell 4 the mutual commitment between suppliers and customers may be low and there is greater freedom for both parties to change partners, with the consequential lower switching costs.

Customer importance

Clearly the economic importance of the customer is one vital factor in resource allocation. Yet the resource investment in personal contacts between suppliers and customers cannot be simply correlated with the amount of business being transacted with a customer. For instance, information and social exchange often precedes financial and product exchange and there is a significant time lapse between resources (investment) and business (financial return).

Product and transaction complexity

Exchanges between suppliers and customers are not all of equal complexity and so the amount of resources allocated to a customer is likely to be affected by the technological complexity of the product and of the commercial complexities of the contract being negotiated. Perceived risk occurs in buying and this risk is significantly affected by the transaction complexity. It is in highly complex exchanges that interpersonal contacts are a much valued mechanism used by suppliers and customers alike to reduce the perceived risk. Such contacts clearly serve as a vital part of the continuous information gathering (inputs) of buyers and of the long-term communications mix (outputs) of suppliers.

How do British suppliers to European markets allocate their human resources between customers?

Our research findings allow us to look at the influence of markets, customers and product technology on this resource allocation question.

Some interesting insights are to be found by analysing some of the data in such a way as to compare domestic with foreign customers. We also choose two product categories from the large number in our sample and use two alternative measures of customer importance (sales value and proportion of total sales revenue of the supplier). The data are presented in Table 2.

Table 2 Resource allocation to different customers and product markets

	Product A customers		Product B customers	
	Domestic customers	Foreign customers	Domestic customers	Foreign customers
Average value of sales to each customer	£9m	£0.5m	£1.4m	£0.3m
Customer purchases as a percentage of supplier's total sales	29%	1.5%	5%	0.9%
Index of resources allocation to each customer	15.5	5.3	5.2	1.7

In Table 2 an index of resources allocated to each customer relationship is shown for the relatively complex Product A and the technologically simpler Product B. The index was compiled to take into account only human resources involved in personal contact with customers. The index incorporates the number of staff, the number of functional areas, their frequency of contact and the management level in the organizational hierarchy of personnel involved in the supplier–customer relations.

As might be expected, domestic customers for both categories of products represent the more important customers and receive a higher allocation of resources than do foreign customers. However, foreign customers receive a proportionately higher resource than their current financial importance would suggest. It will also be seen that domestic customers for Product A receive *three* times more resources than their equivalents for the less technically complex Product B. But each Product A domestic customer is approximately six times more important than each Product B domestic customer.

Therefore product complexity appears to be a less important factor than the importance of the customer (either in terms of financial volume or export potential) in allocating personal contact resources.

NETWORKS OF SUPPLIER–CUSTOMER CONTACTS

So far, it has been argued that the personal contacts allocated to customers and markets are determined by such factors as the value of the order, the stage which the supplier–customer relationship has reached, the complexity of the product or contract, and the tasks to be performed to meet customers' requirements or to gain differentiated advantage in the eyes of the customers. They are also idiosyncratic in so far as they depend upon the specific strategy being pursued by suppliers. These interorganizational contacts span many functions, involve varying frequency of visits and take place at many levels in the hierarchy of the supplier and customer firms. Figures 1 and 3 portray the network of contacts involved.

The measurement or evaluation of the human resources which suppliers allocate to handle customer relations can be considered under three headings or dimensions:

- The frequency of interpersonal contacts.
- Their breadth across different functions.
- The level in the organization at which they occur.

The frequency of interpersonal contact

Very frequent personal contact may be needed for a number of reasons such as performance monitoring, demonstrating commitment, information gathering and social bonding. The frequency with which the partners meet is one important indicator of the amount of resources being committed to the relationship by the parties. It is also an important measure of the quantity (but not necessarily the quality) of actual exchanges that take place between companies.

Table 3 Frequency of interpersonal contacts in supplier–customer relationships

	All relationships (n = 59)	In domestic markets (n = 18)	In export markets (n = 41)
Average number of meetings per annum at suppliers' premises	1.5	2.6	0.9
Average number of meetings per annum at customers' premises	8.7	16.6	5.2
Average frequency of meetings in total (per annum)	10.2	19.2	6.1

It would seem natural to refer to the frequency of contacts in terms of the number of meetings between suppliers and customer personnel. However this is an inadequate measure of the resource commitment because research evidence suggests that there is probably an inverse relationship between the frequency of visits and the time spent on each visit.

It was found that a high correlation exists between the distance or cost of travel and the time spent with the customer on each visit, particularly as far as foreign customer visits are concerned in comparison with domestic ones. The concentration or dispersion of customers in different markets determines the supplier's approach to cost effective planning of customers' visits.

A summary of the frequency with which interpersonal contacts occur between British suppliers and their customers is shown in Table 3. For the 59 relationships analysed, meetings occur 10 times per annum though the vast majority of these take place at the customer's premises. As one would expect, the frequency of meetings with domestic customers is much greater (approximately 20 times per annum) than with foreign customers (six times per annum). It is of interest to note that the foreign customers pay visits to their British suppliers almost once each year.

The breadth of contact

We use the term breadth of contact to indicate the number of areas or subjects covered by the pattern of personal relationships. A narrow relationship may be concerned only with the minimum commercial contacts needed for the exchange of product and payment to be effected.

A broad relationship brings together supplier and customer staff to discuss commercial and technical matters, special arrangements for the storage and movement of goods, quality control procedures, market situation, product and process departments, future plans and strategies and so forth. Relationships can be considered as developing through different levels of integration. A broad personal contact pattern can perhaps best be described as reflecting a "highly integrated" relationship.

We have defined the breadth of the contact pattern in terms of the diversity of content of personal exchanges rather than any "physical" characteristics of the pattern. As defined, this dimension is complex to observe and analyse. However, there are several "proxy" measures which are much more readily observable. The best measures are probably the number of functional departments, people and organization levels involved in the relationship.

In Table 4 we present a summary of the breadth of personal contacts in 59 relationships between British suppliers and their customers. Overall, across all markets, on average eight supplier staff are interacting with nine customer staff. At least three different departments are involved in both the supplier and customer organizations.

The breadth of contact varies widely depending upon whether the relationship is between a British supplier and its British customer or whether relationships are in export markets. For domestic markets 14 supplier staff from more than four functional departments interact with 13 customer staff in almost four departments on average. In marked contrast, relationships in foreign

Table 4 Breadth of personal contact in supplier–customer relationships

	All relationships (n = 59)	In domestic markets (n = 18)	In export markets (n = 41)
Average number of supplier staff involved	8	14	5
Average number of customer staff involved	9	13	6
Average number of supplier functions involved	3.2	4.2	2.8
Average number of customer functions involved	3.3	3.7	3.2

markets involve five supplier staff and six customer staff representing approximately three functional departments in their respective companies.

The level of contact

The level of contact refers to the position in the organization hierarchy of those involved.

It is evident in a number of the relationships studied that a matching of levels took place. If customer contact was made by a supplier representative of a particular status, customer staff on a similar level would be available for him to see. In order to establish a point of direct contact with a customer at director or general management level, the involvement of similar high level staff in the supplier company was also needed.

In some of the more involved relationships, a matching of status at a number of levels takes place. The research also produced evidence of different forms of interpersonal contacts between staff at various levels in the supplier and customer companies. First, the simple chief executive to chief executive dyadic contact. Second, the matched status, multi-level contacts as shown in Figure 5a. Third, the multi-status contacts as shown in Figure 5b. Fourth, the multi-status, multi-functional, multi-level contacts as shown in Figure 5c.

In this instance the supplier–customer relationship involved 16 interpersonal contacts between six major supplier functions (marketing, finance, quality control, design, manufacturing and service) at the middle and lower hierarchical levels, reinforced by general management contacts with senior and middle management personnel in the customer company.

In our research we analysed the levels of interpersonal contacts in 59 relationships involving British suppliers and customers. Due to disparities between organization structures in companies it was only feasible to standardize the data to represent three hierarchical levels. These are categorized as senior, middle and junior levels. The senior level includes functional directors, such as Purchasing or Engineering Director and also general management or managing director positions. In Table 5 we present abbreviated data which show that at some time during the year 50% of all the relationships involved personal contacts by senior management in the supplier companies and 39% of relationships involved senior customer staff. Domestic relationships made

Table 5 Level of contact in supplier–customer relationships

	All relationships (n = 59)	In domestic markets (n = 18)	In export markets (n = 41)
Relationships involving suppliers' senior general management and directors	50%	77%	32%
Relationships involving customers' senior general management and directors	39%	50%	34%

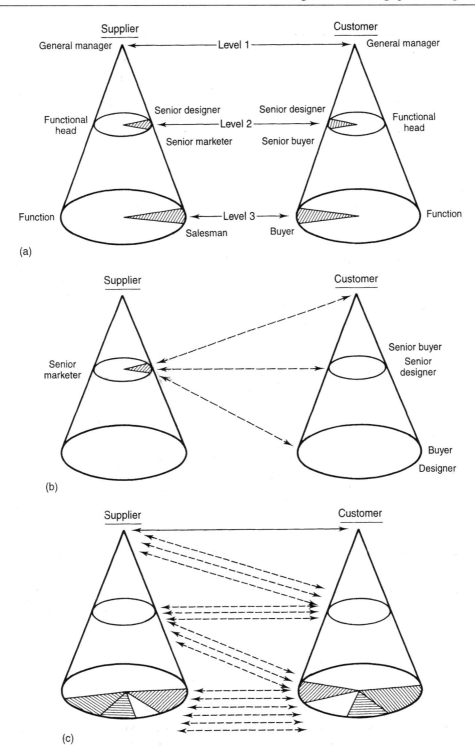

Figure 5 (a) Matched status, multi-level contact. (b) Multi-status contacts (c) Multi-status, multi-functional, multi-level contacts.

greater demands on senior management, 77% for suppliers and 50% for customers than did the foreign relationships (32 and 34% respectively).

A TAXONOMY OF PATTERNS OF INTERORGANIZATIONAL CONTACTS

Important issues of control and co-ordination of personal contacts between suppliers and customers arise from our research. In this final section we present some evidence of the various organizational mechanisms in use in supplier–customer relationships. Here we are more speculative than definitive and further research is needed into these organizational forms observed.

The contacts established between supplier and customer companies usually centre on the marketing and purchasing departments respectively. Often a particular customer is the special responsibility of a Customer Account Manager, or a sales representative who handles all customers in a certain industry or geographical territory. In the purchasing organization, sectional managers often have responsibility for the relationship with suppliers of certain categories of products. Here we examine certain categories of control and co-ordination.

Marketing and purchasing controlled contact patterns

The concepts of boundary spanning units and boundary spanning activities are commonly used in organizational theory. In some companies all direct contact with supplier or customer staff is made by the marketing or purchasing departments. They are the only functions which "break through" the boundary that surrounds the organization and separates it from the supply or customer environment, and they conduct all boundary spanning activities in relation to these parts of the environment.

Relationships with customers where all direct contact is channelled through the marketing department we shall refer to as "marketing controlled". Similarly, where only purchasing staff interact directly with a supplier, the relationship is "purchasing controlled". Figures 6a, b and c show a marketing controlled, a purchasing controlled, and a marketing and purchasing controlled pattern of personal contacts, respectively. The concept of "breaking through" the organization boundary is reflected in the graphical presentation of these relationships.

Several "pure" marketing controlled contact patterns were found in the present study in interviews with unit or small batch manufacturers of capital plant. Such companies often had separate contracts departments specializing in developing tailor-made product offerings to suit a particular customer's needs. In the companies studied, the contracts department staff were rarely involved in direct personal contact with the potential customer. In a similar manner, it was evident in many of the large automotive components suppliers that a considerable amount of "behind the scene" engineering work was carried out for specific customers, but with little or no direct personal contact between the supplier engineers doing this work and their opposite numbers in the customer companies.

Marketing and purchasing co-ordinated contact patterns

The marketing and purchasing functions may co-ordinate rather than control completely the personal interactions that take place between supplier and customer. In a marketing co-ordinated relationship there may be direct personal contact between other supplier functions and various customer departments, but in all such contacts, marketing staff are also involved.

Typically, such relationships are when the sales representative "brings along" a member of the engineering department, for example, and together they visit the customer's engineering personnel. Figures 7a, b and c illustrate a marketing co-ordinated, a purchasing co-ordinated and a both marketing and purchasing co-ordinated relationship, respectively.

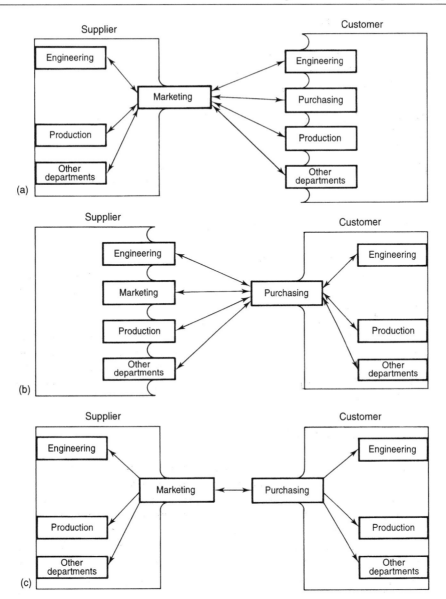

Figure 6   (a) A marketing controlled contact pattern. (b) A purchasing controlled contact pattern.
(c) A marketing and purchasing controlled contact pattern.

Stratified contact patterns

When the pattern of personal contacts between supplier and customer staff is neither controlled nor co-ordinated by either marketing or purchasing staff, we have a stratified contact pattern. This term was chosen because, when depicted diagrammatically, the impression is one of different "layers" or "strata" of contacts. This is shown in Figure 8.

For a stratified contact pattern to occur, both the supplier and the customer organization have to be highly specialized in terms of functional departments. In addition, it would appear that one of the following three conditions has to be present – good internal communications, an explicit

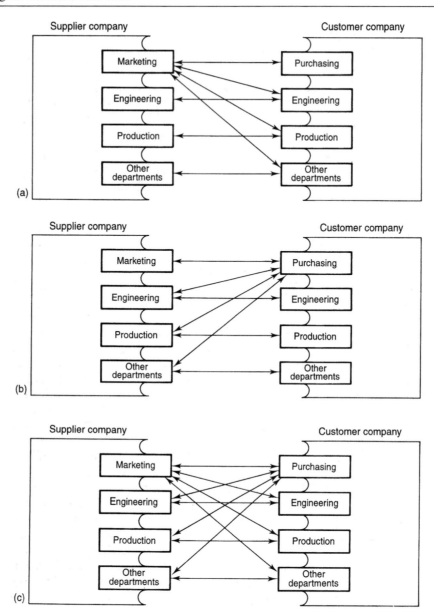

Figure 7 (a) A marketing co-ordinated contact pattern. (b) A purchasing co-ordinated contact pattern. (c) A marketing and purchasing co-ordinated contact pattern.

strategy for dealing with the counterpart company or an open relationship based on trust, integrity and loyalty.

SUMMARY AND DISCUSSION

The relationships which we have analysed are not intended to be representative of what occurs generally in British home and export markets. They were deliberately selected to allow a further and better understanding of the more important supplier–customer relationships in medium/high

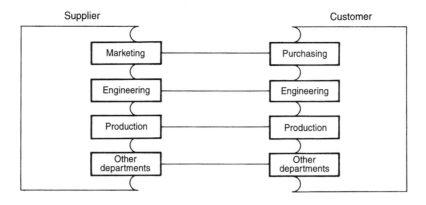

Figure 8 A stratified contact pattern.

technology industrial markets. They are most likely to be "representative" of key accounts with major customers in concentrated and highly competitive international markets. Overall, marketing and purchasing executives in 49 companies were interviewed and illustrations are given from these organizations. A more detailed study of 59 supplier–customer relationships was carried out and the results have been presented in summary form.

Interface contacts in industrial markets between suppliers and customers rarely take the form of simple dyadic relationships between salesman and buyer or, indeed, of salesmen's face-to-face meetings with different members of the customer's DMU. Several personnel in different functional departments in supplier companies are involved in a network of contacts with their counterparts in the customer firm and this embraces multiple levels in the organizational hierarchy. These contacts develop into a variety of extremely complex patterns as the stages of a supplier–customer relationship evolve over time. Many different roles formed by these contacts were identified through interviews and case study analysis in specific relationships. From a supplier's perspective they account for a substantial deployment of scarce and costly human resources but from a customer's perspective they are instrumental in achieving a reduction of the perceived "distance" between his organization and that of a potential supplier. Additionally, the research data point to eight major groups of factors or criteria which buyers take into account in evaluating their current and potential suppliers. These include Customer Orientation, Technical Expertise, Commercial Capability, Adaptability, Supply Reliability, Price Competitiveness, Organizational Effectiveness and Social Integration. The personal contacts between the two organizations are a vital means for the supplier to demonstrate his company's competitive ability on these criteria.

Three measures of resource implications of the network of interpersonal contacts between supplier and customer staff have been used to portray the essential features of organizational relationships in industrial markets. These are the frequency, breadth and hierarchical level.

First, the *frequency of contact*. On average, face-to-face meetings between supplier and customer staff occur almost weekly in domestic markets and once every two months with foreign customers. The meetings take place both at the customer's and at the supplier's premises, though the vast majority (over 85%) are when supplier staff call on customers.

Second, the *breadth of contact* represents the range of issues dealt with in the relationship. In a broad relationship, exchanges between representatives cover commercial matters as well as issues relating to technical development, production, quality, logistics, administration, long-term plans and strategies, etc. Although the breadth of contact refers essentially to the content of exchanges, both the number of people and the number of functions involved in the relationship are good "proxy" measures of the resources involved.

The complexity and resource implications of supplier–customer relationships is in evidence from the results showing that, for each customer, an average of eight supplier staff and nine customer staff are involved in the network of interpersonal contacts. In domestic markets 14 suppliers and 13 customer staff, on average, are involved. Contacts by such supplier functions as sales, design, quality control, manufacturing and finance take place and, in general, four functions from both supplier and customer companies are brought into domestic market relationships and three functions from each organization in export market relations.

Third, the *level of contact* refers to the position of the organizational hierarchy of those involved. A matching level in the two companies often occurs.

At least three levels of management in supplier and customer companies are committed to many key account customer relationships. Each higher level represents an increasingly scarce and costly resource. In 77% of major domestic relationships the senior general managers or directors are occasionally called upon to make personal contacts with customers but only 32% of foreign relationships get the allocation of senior management time in face-to-face meetings. Customers likewise commit senior management to be involved in relationships with suppliers though not to the same extent. Customer senior management are more involved in domestic than foreign supplier relationships.

Finally, a taxonomy of patterns of supplier–customer contacts was derived from the empirical evidence; these patterns reflect various mechanisms used for the *control and co-ordination of contacts*. There is a certain similarity between the extent of formalization and the degree of control. However, the former refers more to the "atmosphere" and the content of exchanges, whereas the latter deals more with the "physical" pattern of personal contacts.

A *controlled* contact pattern is where all contacts are physically channelled through a single department or individual, typically through the marketing or purchasing department which has personal contacts with the other company. In a *co-ordinated* contact pattern, many different departments have direct personal contacts with the other company, but there is one department or person, usually a buyer or sales representative, who is involved personally in all other contacts that take place.

In a *stratified* contact pattern there are no persons or functions either controlling or co-ordinating personal contacts.

Pure examples of these patterns are relatively rare. It is therefore more meaningful to refer to the degree of control, co-ordination or stratification.

The *resources deployed* and the pattern of intercompany personal contacts reflect the importance of the specific relationship within the overall strategy of each of the two parties. Each partner will be involved in many other relationships in the market. The major factor determining the resources allocated to individual customer relationships is the economic importance of the customer, as perceived by the supplier. The structure of the market, the mutual interdependence of supplier and customer and the complexity of the transaction in different stages of the relationship are important determinants of the deployment of resources by suppliers. The actual pattern of personal contacts at the interface will reflect elements of opportunism and resource constraints.

The complexity, resource implications and organizational problems of managing interpersonal contacts between supplier and customer are clear from the foregoing discussion and results. Most companies develop procedures and controls for ensuring that different categories of customers are called upon at specified intervals by marketing and sales staff. Rarely is it appreciated that other scarce human resources in technical, manufacturing and quality control functions as well as in senior general management levels in the supply company can become committed in an *ad hoc* manner to a company's array of customers and prospects in both domestic and foreign markets. Some of the factors affecting the allocation of a supplier's human resources are under the company's direct control, others occur because of environmental and competitive forces in the market. There is a clear requirement for management to identify these key factors and ensure that their resources are being directed at appropriate markets and customers in order to establish and defend vital relationships.

REFERENCES

Cunningham, M. T. and Turnbull, P. W. Interorganizational personal contact patterns. In Håkansson, H. (ed.), *International Marketing and Purchasing of Industrial Goods: An Interaction Approach*. Wiley (1982) pp. 304–16.

Ford, D. The development of buyer–seller relationships in industrial markets. *European Journal of Marketing*, **14**, (5/6) (1981).

Ford, D. Buyer-seller relationships in international industrial markets. *Industrial Marketing Management*, **13**, (101–12) (1984).

Håkansson, H. (ed.). *International Marketing and Purchasing of Industrial Goods: An Interaction Approach*, Wiley (1982), Ch. 2, pp. 10–27.

Hallen, L. and Wiedersheim-Paul, F. Psychic distance and buyer–seller interaction. *Organization Marked og Samfunn*. **16**, (5) 305–24 (1982).

Melin, L. *Strategisk Inkopsverkamhet–Organization och Interaktion* (Strategic Purchasing Actions–Organization and Interaction) (with summary in English). University of Linkoping, Linkoping, Sweden (1977).

Turnbull, P. W. and Cunningham, M. T. *International Marketing and Purchasing: A Survey of Attitudes of Marketing and Purchasing Executives in Five European Countries*. Macmillan (1981).

Webster, F. E. Jr. and Wind, Y. A general model of organizational buying behaviour. *Journal of Marketing*, **36**, (2), 12–19 (1972).

4.2 Customer analysis for strategy development in industrial markets

Nigel Campbell and Malcolm Cunningham

INTRODUCTION

Assessment of a company's strategic position must include an analysis of the company's situation in the markets which it serves. Normally, this analysis focuses on the company's products relative to competitors with questions such as: what are the sales trends, profits and market shares of different products in different market segments?

To do this analysis business planners have available an array of tools such as the well-known product portfolio matrix (Henderson, 1970), the product-positioning matrix (Hofer and Schendel, 1978) and the product/performance matrix (Wind, 1982). Such tools neglect trends in purchases by individual customers, and profits and market shares by customer. This may be a weakness, particularly in concentrated industrial markets which have a small number of key customers.

This paper suggests that, in many industrial markets, a company should develop its strategy from an analysis of existing customers. The analysis should highlight the current allocation of resources to different customers and customer groups and identify the company's position with key customers relative to competition in different market segments. The purpose of the analysis is to improve the allocation of scarce technical and marketing resources between different customers to achieve the supplier's strategic objectives. It leads to a reappraisal of a supplier's competitive strength with different customers, and it also ensures that relationships with key customers are managed more effectively.

In contrast to Porter (1980) who lays stress on the need to counteract buyers' bargaining power, this paper emphasizes the scope for developing relationships of mutual interdependence and shared objectives. This approach has its origin in a major research study which is briefly described in the next section.

METHODOLOGY

The new approach to industrial marketing and purchasing which underpins this paper is based on a continuing effort by the IMP research group (Håkansson, 1982) to understand the nature of buyer/seller relationships in industrial marketing. The major part of the IMP project was an international cross-sectional study with companies selected to represent different types of products and different production technologies in a 3 × 3 matrix (see below). This matrix enabled the research group to investigate the influence on supplier/customer relationships of the nature of the supplier's product and the nature of the customer's production process. Product complexity, product essentiality, frequency of purchase, consequences of product failure, and extent of adaptations by each partner, were among the factors investigated.

Buyer's production technology

	Unit production	Batch or mass production	Process manufacture
Raw materials			
Components and parts			
Capital equipment			

Seller's product technology

Some 300 companies drawn from 15 different industries in five countries were involved in the research. Interviews were conducted with marketing and purchasing managers, who were directly involved in, or knew about, particular relationships.

The ideas presented here came from further research carried out to complement the previous IMP project. An intensive study over a two year period was conducted in the packaging industry in one European country. The research, using a "direct" approach (Mintzberg, 1978), focused on the marketing strategy of a leading company through a detailed analysis of its relationships with 63 customers. Information about customer relationships was obtained from company records (sales and profit histories, age of relationships, resource allocation) and from semi-structured interviews with the 27 senior managers who had contact with customers. Several managers were interviewed more than once. Wherever possible each relationship was considered in the context of trading relations between other suppliers and customers in the same market segment. Altogether data were collected from the supplier for 167 trading relationships in 10 market segments. In addition, a cross-section of customers and non-customers was interviewed which generated additional information about their supplier relationships. In several cases, interviews were conducted with the buyer and seller on both sides of the same relationship.

The "interaction" approach to marketing and purchasing strategy which emerged from this research emphasizes the active role of both buyer and seller. Their interaction can lead to co-operation or conflict, and the implications of this approach for marketing and purchasing strategy are reported by different members of the IMP group in Håkansson (1982).

THE NEED FOR CUSTOMER ANALYSIS

That there is a need for customer analysis may seem self-evident. In fact there are a number of particular reasons why a customer analysis, in addition to a market and product analysis, is particularly relevant to industrial markets.

In industrial markets, a company's customers are often its greatest assets. Corey (1976, p. 5) says that "the development of strong, multidimensional and constructive working relationships with one's customers is the key to industrial marketing success". In addition, researchers beginning with Wind (1982) and including Cunningham and Kettlewood (1976) and Håkansson (1982) have testified to the importance of source loyalty and long term relationships. One consequence is that, particularly in mature markets, it is difficult to break into new customers. This means that the supplier should avoid any erosion of loyalty by his existing customers. He must maintain his competitive strength with key customers on a regular basis.

Industrial concentration is high and probably increasing. Sawyer (1981) reports figures for the five firm concentration ratios derived from the British Census of Production for 1975. For 118 industries, at the three digit SIC level, the largest five firms produced, on average, 50.6% of the net output. A similar high concentration is found in American industry (Mueller and Hamm, 1974) and in the European Community (Locksley and Ward, 1979) and, although slight, there seems to be a continuing upward trend. With the largest four or five firms accounting for such a high proportion of activity in many industries, an emphasis on customer analysis seems greatly overdue.

Empirical evidence shows that suppliers tend to follow the growth and development of customers often by adding new products, and even new technologies, to continue to serve the needs of that customer. Indeed, Parkinson (1980) states that close co-operation between suppliers and customers enhances technical innovation, and Achiadelis *et al.* (1971) have proposed that a thorough knowledge of customers' needs increases the probability of successful marketing of new products.

Although the argument above has concentrated on industrial markets, it also applies to many consumer markets, where manufacturers develop or sell "retailer branded" or "own label" products to a few large retailers and distributors. Indeed, Arndt (1979) has suggested that the 1980s will be an era of "domesticated" marketing. With the need for a customer analysis established, the next section describes the three steps proposed.

THE THREE STEPS PROPOSED

Step 1: Life cycle classification of customer relationships

Despite its limitations the product life cycle is a useful concept. Why not apply the same idea to customers? Porter (1980) points out that, as an industry matures, customers tend to become more price sensitive. Their own margins are squeezed and they become more expert purchasers. To counteract this tendency the supplier must either develop new substitute products, or find ways to lower his production costs. He must allocate his resources appropriately to different customer groups. Table 1 suggests a simple classification of customers to each category.

Management should have all the information available except possibly customer profitability and the use of strategic resources. The concept of strategic resources is the same as that used by Hofer and Schendel (1978). It includes the financial, technical, marketing and production resources, which are devoted to developing future business, rather than maintaining existing business. The classification of customer relationships is derived from the work of Cunningham and Homse (1982) and it owes a debt to Drucker (1963), who proposed a similar analysis for products. Before describing each customer category it is necessary to emphasize that only customers for one product or one relatively homogeneous product group should be included in the same table. Where a company manufactures several different products, separate tables are needed. Thus, a company which is a regular customer for product A may appear as tomorrow's customer for a new product B.

Table 1 Life cycle classification of customer relationships

Criteria for classification of customers	Customer categories			
	Tomorrow's customers	Today's special customers	Today's regular customers	Yesterday's customers
Sales volume	Low	High	Average	Low
Use of strategic resources[a]	High	High	Average	Low
Age of relationship	New	Old	Average	Old
Supplier's share of customer's purchases	Low	High	Average	Low
Profitability of customer to supplier	Low	High	Average	Low

[a] The technical, marketing and production resources devoted to developing future business rather than maintaining existing business.

Tomorrow's customers

These are the customers that the company is trying to gain, or regain, at home or abroad. They may be customers in a new market area, opened up as a result of technical developments, or they may be vital "reference point" customers in an export market. Sales to these customers are low, but strategic resources are allocated to improve the current sales position and to develop the relationship.

Today's special customers

These customers usually purchase large quantities: they are old-established and the company is continually engaged in development work with them. Frequently a supplier and its special customers have adapted to each other in various ways, mutual trust and commitment are at a high level and many people from each side are in regular contact. For example, such relationships exist between British Leyland and Lucas, between British Steel and Davy Engineering; Black and Decker and Marks and Spencer have policies of developing such special relationships with suppliers, and reports from Japan suggest that the structure is favoured there (Campbell, 1982).

Today's regular customers

These customers also purchase large quantities and the relationships are old-established, but the exchanges are less intimate, the customers are less loyal and more price sensitive; development work tends to be intermittent.

Yesterday's customers

These customers are often numerous, but, although the relationships are old-established, each contributes only small sales volume and they receive little or no technical development work. Customers in this category are those in market segments now abandoned, or those whose requirements are now more like "commodities". The company continues to serve them, but without any great enthusiasm. However, they provide useful additional volume for little effort.

The number of customers and the proportion of sales in each category will differ from company to company. In the packaging company studied the proportions were as in Table 2. This company pursues an innovation strategy so that considerable resources are devoted to developing tomorrow's customers. The company also has two very special and important customers with whom relationships are especially close.

In any one year the number of customer companies and the proportion of sales in each category is not, by itself, very significant. The value comes from carrying out the exercise regularly and from monitoring the progress of tomorrow's customers. To justify the development expenses committed to them they must move to become either special or regular customers. The length of time before such a move takes place will vary depending on the industry. The time also varies depending on the circumstances under which the customer took on the new supplier. Contrast the following two

Table 2 A packaging company's customer analysis

Category of customer	Number of customers	Percentage of sales	Percentage of technical development expenditure
Tomorrow's customers	7	1	39
Today's special customers	2	43	38
Today's customers	38	44	23
Yesterday's customers	175	12	–
Total:	222	100	100

situations. In the first, the customer's demand for the product is expanding; he is seeking additional sources of supply, and so he approaches the supplier. If the supplier is familiar with what is required, he will be able to meet the specification quickly, and the time from the start of the relationship to regular supplies may last only a matter of months. By contrast, assume that the second situation involves a proposal from the customer for the development of a substitute product which will save him money. If the application is outside the supplier's current knowledge, he must learn the requirements, and devote research and development time to establishing whether his technology will provide a solution. This process may take years.

To summarize, this classification provides management with a useful overview of its customers. It shows how the strategic resources, which will ensure the future health of the business, are allocated among customers. Management can ask whether the resources devoted are sufficient and, by following their progress, verify that prospects yield a reasonable return. The existence of special relationships with some customers is highlighted as well as the customer's dependence on them. Is the loyalty of such customers in danger of being eroded? What can be done to strengthen the relationships? Or, are market conditions such that management should try to disengage from such customers, whose position in their own markets is weakening?

Step 2: Customer/competitor analysis by market segment

The life cycle classification of customers provides a general overview. The allocation of critical resources is highlighted and management can take decisions to retain or modify the amount. The next stage is to introduce competition and this is done by the use of a customer/competitor chart for each market segment. A typical chart is presented in Figure 1 for one of the food markets in which the packaging company operates.

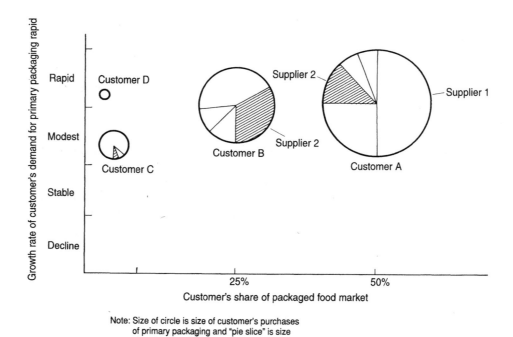

Note: Size of circle is size of customer's purchases
of primary packaging and "pie slice" is size
of each competitor's share.

Figure 1 Customer/competitor analysis: primary packaging for a range of packaged foods.

The horizontal axis simply measures the customer's share in his market. Thus in Figure 1 customer A has about 50% of the market, customer B has 25%, and there are two smaller companies. The vertical axis is a measure of the growth rate in the customer's demand for the product. This is not the same as the customer's sales growth, as it also reflects changes that may occur in usage of the product, owing to design changes at the customer or, because of penetration of the market by substitutes.

The size of each circle is a measure of the volume of the supplier's product purchased by each customer and the size of the "pie slice" represents the share of each competitor. Detailed market share information of this kind is not easy to obtain. Buyers are often reluctant to divulge the split of their business between suppliers. To get round this reluctance, the supplier needs to seek information from several sources – from technical and production staff of the customer, from other non-competitive suppliers, from other more open customers, and so on. In this way, suppliers can build up a reasonably accurate picture. In Figure 1, customer B purchases about half as much as customer A; supplier 1 has a dominant position with customers A and C, but does not sell to B; supplier 2, on the other hand, has a strong position with customer B, but a weaker one with A and C. The explanation for this pattern is bound up with the historical development of the trading relationship of each company.

To be useful, management should procure a customer/competitor chart for one product or one homogeneous product group. The product should serve the same customer function and be manufactured by the same basic technology for all customers on the chart. Thus, in Figure 1 the function is the primary packaging of a food product and the competitors all use the same technology. In other words, the chart does not mix different types of packaging (glass, plastic bags, cartons, etc.). Although Figure 1 is for a homogeneous product range it still masks differences between individual members of the range. Management can prepare separate charts where the additional analyses would yield greater insights.

The customer/competitor chart must also have a geographical boundary. Should it include only domestic customers and competitors, leaving out overseas companies? The choice depends on what is relevant and what is practically available in the way of data. It is best to make the geographical spread as wide as possible.

The value of the customer/competitor chart is to assess opportunities and threats. In Figure 1 supplier 1 has no sales to customer B. Should supplier 1 attack this customer? If it did, would supplier 2 retaliate and attack its large market share with customer A? Such questions are highlighted by the customer/competitor chart, as it enables management to see the strength of its position compared to competitors. Charts prepared over a number of years will indicate whether competitors are increasing their penetration.

In carrying out the customer/competitor analysis management may find it helpful to think broadly about the type of buyer/seller relationships which operate in their market segments. Buyer/ seller relationships can take a wide variety of forms, but three general categories can be distinguished, as shown in Figure 2 and Table 3 (Campbell and Cunningham, 1983).

Relationships are characterized by dependence when either the buyer or the supplier dominates. Relationships are buyer dominated when there are many suppliers and few buyers; when the share the buyer takes of the supplier output is high; and when the buyer has a low need for the supplier's skills, but the buyer's requirements are specialized, so that suppliers must make an investment (in special facilities or knowledge). There are many examples of such buyer dominated relationships between the automotive companies and their smaller suppliers. Independent relationships arise when there are few suppliers and few customers; when each party is dependent on the other; and when the buyer needs the supplier's skills, because the purchase is customized in some way. The supplier dominated and independent categories have opposite characteristics to those identified above for buyer dominated and interdependent relationships.

This type of analysis can also help management in the third and final step of the analysis.

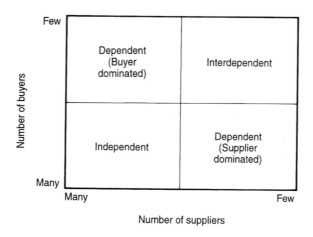

Figure 2   Power balance in buyer/seller relationships.

Table 3   Power balance in buyer/seller relationships

| Criteria for classifying buyer/seller relationships | Categories of buyer/seller relationships | | | |
| | Dependent | | | |
	(Buyer dominated)	(Supplier dominated)	Interdependent	Independent
Number of suppliers	Many	Few	Few	Many
Number of customers	Few	Many	Few	Many
Share of supplier's output taken by the buyer	High	Low	High	Low
Share of buyer's requirements purchased from the supplier	Low	High	High	Low
Buyer's need for supplier's skills	Low	High	High	Low
Buyer's need for customized product	High	Low	High	Low

Step 3: Portfolio analysis of key customers

This final step involves the analysis of key customers. Management can choose which customers to include. Key customers are likely to be existing large customers plus those on which strategic resources are expended. First, the key customers are analysed together, and then the most important ones analysed individually. The customer portfolio in Figure 3 is an analysis of the key customers of the packaging supplier using a variation of the familiar growth share matrix. The co-ordinates are the competitive position of the company with the customer on the horizontal axis, and the growth rate of the customer's market on the vertical axis. Competitive position is measured by the share the supplier holds of the customer's purchases relative to the share held by the largest competitor. The positions are plotted on a log scale to accommodate the wide variations. Within the matrix the size of the circles represents the sales volumes of each customer. Thus, Figure 3 shows that the company has one key customer in cell 4 whose business is growing steadily and where the company's share of purchases is very high. The company also holds a very high share of the purchases of customers on the borderline between cells 7 and 10. However, the markets in which these companies operate are not growing. On the right hand side of Figure 3, the company has a weak competitive position because of its low share of the customer's purchases.

The main purpose of Figure 3 is to show the position of the largest customers, but it can also be used to indicate the position of tomorrow's future prospects. These are represented by dots rather

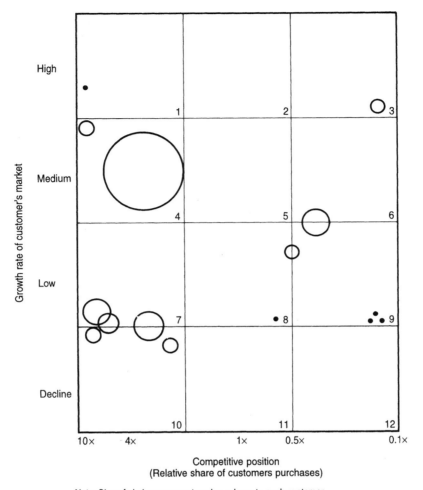

Figure 3 Portfolio of key customers.

than circles as sales are negligible at present. There are three dots in cell 9, one in cell 8 and only one in cell 1. Thus, the supplier is devoting some of its strategic resources to developing sites with customers whose markets are not growing. The supplier justified this because its objective was to develop a substitute, which, if successful, would lead to substantial business. Nevertheless, the company would have preferred more prospects in the top left hand corner of the portfolio. The management implications of Figure 2 are discussed in the conclusions.

Although Figure 3 gives useful information about key customers, clearly this is not sufficient where the largest customer itself represents 45% of sales, as in the case of the packaging company studied. A more detailed breakdown is needed as shown in Figure 4 where the customer is split up into a series of subcustomers. This part of the analysis is similar to that proposed by Fiocca (1982). Figure 4 shows that the largest customer really consists of four separate businesses which have been classified on the horizontal axis using the life cycle categories. The vertical scale shows, as before, the real growth in the customer's purchases. The size of the circle is drawn to represent the size of the customer's purchases. A "pie slice" can be added to represent the share held by the supplier company.

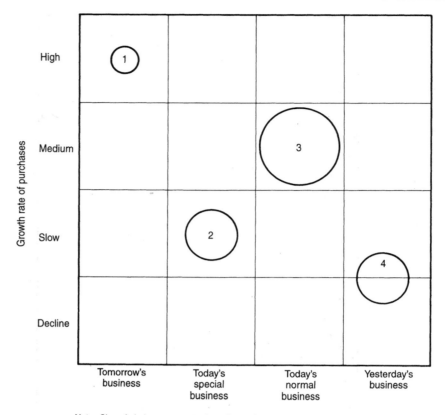

Note: Size of circles represents the volume of customer's purchases.
Numbers refer to the different products of the supplier company sold to the customer.

Figure 4   Analysis of a key customer.

For the life cycle classification and for the customer/competitor chart only customers who bought products with similar usages manufactured by the same technology were included together; for the analysis of key customers the reverse is true. The chart should display all the different products sold to that customer. Figure 4 shows that there is a small but developing business for product 1; a slow growing, but specialized business for product 2; a large and steadily growing, standard business for product 3; and an average, slightly declining, business for product 4.

With the aid of these two analyses management can obtain a clear picture of its strategic position with key customers.

CONCLUSIONS

This paper has put forward proposals to help managers in industrial companies analyse their customers in a way which will highlight critical issues. The analysis concentrates on customers rather than products because of the small number of key customers in so many markets. The emphasis on customers is compatible with the way forward thinking management intuitively carry out their activities, but not in the way in which company planning is undertaken. The presentation here makes explicit and logical what is latent and unco-ordinated practice in many firms.

The analysis comprises three stages which start with a life cycle classification of customer relationships designed to give prominence to those to whom the company is allocating strategic funds in the hope of developing future business, and to emphasize those on whom the company is very dependent. An analysis of the allocation of strategic resources leads to a number of useful questions. Are sufficient resources being devoted to developments with customers? Is the allocation right? Is the company obtaining the expected co-operation from customers? What sales are forecast to flow from the development underway during the planning period? What has been the record of success with previous development projects? Management may want to probe these questions in the light of their initial investigations. In addition, management can look at the number and importance of special customers and discuss whether the company is too dependent on them. To throw further light on such questions the next stage in the analysis allows management to take a closer look at its competitive position with different customers, in particular end-use markets.

The customer/competitor chart allows management to evaluate its competitive position in each market segment and assess threats and opportunities. A review of charts prepared in previous years enables a company to observe the impact of competition, and of changes in the relative importance of different buyers.

The final stage of the analysis takes the key customers, who have appeared in different market segments, and groups them into a customer portfolio along the lines of the growth/share matrix. Management can assess the strengths and weaknesses of the company's position with its key customers and question the choice of key development customers. The most important and largest customers are then subjected to a further analysis of their component parts to ensure that the overall relationship with the customer is being managed satisfactorily.

The overall emphasis in this paper is on the need for segmentation and market share calculation down to the level of the individual customer. This is all the more necessary given the inertia in buyer/seller relationships and the discretion which the buyer has in dealing with a supply market. Suppliers can waste much time and money in attempting to gain business from a customer who has no intention of switching from his preferred supplier. Management may have to accept a small share of the business and concentrate on producing, for this customer, an acceptable product with the minimum of service at as low a cost as possible (Campbell, 1982). Special developments, with higher margins, may have to seek more friendly opportunities elsewhere.

The emphasis on customer analysis has its origin in the IMP Group's approach to industrial marketing and purchasing. Many leading firms operating in concentrated and highly competitive markets recognize the crucial importance of the effective management of supplier–customer relationships, and the need to provide guidelines for the allocation of scarce resources to different customers.

The analysis proposed here was developed as a result of the experience of working with one company. The company concerned is a market leader in a mature market with a diversity of end user segments. It is to be hoped that other research will take up the challenge of developing and improving these proposals.

REFERENCES

Achiadelis, B., Jarvis, P. and Robertson, B. Project Sappho: a study of success and failure in industrial innovations. *Report to the Science Policy Research Council.* Science Policy Research Unit, University of Sussex, Brighton (1971).

Arndt, J. Toward a concept of domesticated markets. *Journal of Marketing*, **43**, 69–75 (1979).

Campbell, N. C. G. Organizational buying behaviour: an interaction approach. *Organizational Buying Behaviour Workshop*, EIASM, Brussels, December 1982.

Campbell, N. C. G. and Cunningham M. T. Interaction strategies for the management and buyer/seller relationships. *Journal of Marketing*, in review (1983).

Corey, E. R. *Industrial Marketing: Cases and Concepts*, 2nd edn. Prentice Hall, Englewood Cliffs (1976).

Cunningham, M. T. and Homse, E. An interaction approach to marketing and purchasing strategy. In Håkansson, H. (ed.), *International Marketing and Purchasing of Industrial Goods: An Interaction Approach*. Wiley, Chichester (1982).

Cunningham, M. T. and Kettlewood, K. Source loyalty in the freight transport market. *European Journal of Marketing*, **10**, 60–79 (1976).

Drucker, P. K. Managing for business effectiveness. *Harvard Business Review*, **41**, May–June (1963).

Fiocca, R. Account portfolio analysis for strategy development. *Industrial Marketing Management*, February, 53–62 (1982).

Håkansson, H. (ed.) *International Marketing and Purchasing of Industrial Goods: An Interaction Approach.* Wiley, Chichester (1982).

Henderson, B. D. *The Product Portfolio*, Perspective Series, Boston Consulting Group, Boston (1970).

Hofer, C. W. and Schendel, D. *Strategy Formulation: Analytical Concepts.* West Publishing, St Paul (1978).

Locksley, G. and Ward, T. Concentration in manufacturing in the EEC. *Cambridge Journal of Economics*, **3**, 91–7 (1979).

Mintzberg, H. An emerging strategy of direct research. *Administrative Science Quarterly*, **24**, 582–9 (1979).

Mueller, W. F. and Hamm, L. G. Trends in Industrial market concentration 1947–1970. *Review of Economics and Statistics*, **56**, 511–20 (1974).

Parkinson, S. T. User–supplier interaction in new product development, Ph.D. Dissertation, University of Strathclyde, Glasgow (1980).

Porter, M. E. *Competitive Strategy.* The Free Press, New York (1980).

Sawyer, H. C. *The Economics of Industries and Firms.* Croom Helm, London (1981).

Wind, Y. *Product Policy: Concepts, Methods and Strategy.* Addison-Wesley, Reading, Mass. (1982).

4.3 Relationship portfolios – past, present and future[1]

Judy Zolkiewski and Peter W. Turnbull

INTRODUCTION

Relationship management has long been at the heart of success in business-to-business management strategy and marketing. However, the increasing impact of technology change, evidenced by the dramatic growth in E-Commerce, ever developing globalisation of markets, and other environmental change, is leading many business leaders and marketing academics to question whether traditional business relationships will continue to be at the core of competitive advantage. For instance, will business marketers revert to the reliance on the marketing mix approach with price being the dominant market motivator, or will relationship management continue to be the route to success, as relationships, based on interpersonal interaction, trust and commitment, become the only differentiator in an electronic network?

It is our belief that because of the nature of relationships and the enduring features identified in the interaction approach (Håkansson, 1982, Turnbull and Valla, 1986, Ford, 1980), relationships will continue to be a major determinant of purchase behaviour and the ongoing management of business-to-business markets. As Turnbull and Valla (1986) point out, effective marketing is not simply about the management of relationships; relationship management is also central to other management challenges, such as industrial channel positioning, market segmentation and competitive position. Therefore, we contend that there will be a continuing need for effective relationship management strategies.

The managerial challenge however, is how to differentiate between the often large number of business relationships that a firm has. As the firm develops its position in markets, a complex set of relationships – a network[2] – will evolve. These relationships have to be understood and managed over time; some will be handled electronically, some almost entirely on a person-to-person contact basis, and others by a mixture.

Central to the effective and efficient management of these sets of relationships – the relationships portfolio – must be an integrated information system that includes both internal and external analysis of the marketing environment and the real dynamics of the relationships set. A particular important, yet often neglected aspect of this 'intelligence' is the need for a real understanding of the benefits, costs and profitability of each relationship the firm manages.

In FMCG markets the use of strategic marketing planning tools that are based upon portfolio analysis, such as the BCG (Boston Consulting Group) matrix, is commonplace. However, where market share and market growth may be very high and relatively static respectively (as is often the case in business-to-business markets) the applicability of such analysis is doubtful. Business-to-business markets are often characterized by small numbers of players and high degrees of dependency. It is in this context that customer and supplier relationship portfolio planning has developed. In these circumstances portfolio analysis can be a very useful aid in the development of relationship strategy.

Research into business networks; Axelsson and Easton (1992), Håkansson and Johanson (1992), Håkansson and Snehota (1995), Möller and Wilson (1995), Iacobucci (1996), is also important because it recognizes the influence upon a firm's strategy and tactics of *all* the different 'actors' in the network surrounding that firm. As a consequence of this it becomes important to recognize the role of relationship portfolio analysis for all the relationships in the network, not just customer relationships. Relationship analysis can also be of strategic significance for supplier relationships and the other relationships that surround a firm.

In the following sections we critically review a range of portfolio models and discuss their application. Examples of empirical investigations into their use are given. This is followed by a discussion of how portfolios can be used to operationalize network theory. Finally, the managerial implications of using these models are raised.

CONCEPTUAL REVIEW

The majority of relationship portfolio models[3] that have been conceptualized are based in either customer or supplier relationship modelling. The models which have been developed include both two and three-dimensional axes along with single, two and three-step analysis phases. For a full review of these models see Zolkiewski and Turnbull (2000). Their review suggests that the models proposed by Fiocca (1982) and Shapiro et al. (1987) have been the most widely adopted as the basis for further research.

However, in the published research two major drawbacks to the use of the Fiocca (1982) model have been identified. This means that it has limited potential for use in strategic marketing management. The first problem relates to the mixture of subjective and actual values needed to calculate the portfolio dimensions. This is especially problematic when the main point of using such analysis should be to produce data which can be used for comparison. Additionally, Fiocca (1982) does not take into account factors that can be critical in doing business internationally such as distance and cultural factors. These reservations have been confirmed by Turnbull and Topcu (1994) who tested the Fiocca (1982) matrix using detailed case study data from a Turkish industrial minerals manufacturer and encountered problems with both the subjectivity of the analysis scales and the way the axes were interpreted.

Secondly, Yorke and Droussiotis (1994) point out that the model does not recognize the importance of considering customer profitability and, in fact, simply assumes that different cells can be associated with different levels of profitability. This assumption that customers are profitable simply because management perceive them to be is a general problem in much analysis. In reality, customers are often found to be not as profitable as managers believe them to be (once full account is taken of real selling costs).

Another model, which uses mainly subjective data, is that developed by Krapfel, Salmond and Spekman (1991). This model uses the concepts of 'relationship value' and 'interest commonality' as its dimensions and encourages managers to think about the importance of the relationships in which the company is involved.

The model proposed by Shapiro et al. (1987) (Figure 1) provides an alternative focus, it views customers as profit centres and uses only quantitative data. Four types of costs were used to define the cost-to-serve axis: presale, production, distribution and postsale service costs. By combining this calculation with the net price charged, they found that such analysis identified a wide range of profit margins both by customer and type of product sold. Figure 1 shows the 'labels' that Shapiro et al. (1987) ascribe to customers in each quadrant of the matrix, each type representing different profit contribution profiles.

Shapiro et al. (1987) suggest that many suppliers believe that if they analyze the breakdown of their accounts most accounts will fall into the 'carriage trade' and 'bargain basement' quadrants. Yet, when analysis is actually performed, it will usually show that over half a suppliers' accounts fall into the 'passive' and 'aggressive' quadrants.

They also observe that the position of any one account is likely to change over time, often starting in the 'carriage trade' segment and migrating towards another segment. They argue that this dispersion of customer profitability can be managed by following an action plan, which

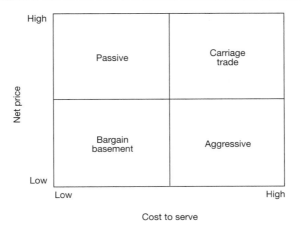

Figure 1 Customer classification matrix (Shapiro et al., 1987, p. 104).

involves: repeated analysis, pinpointing costs, preparing profitability dispersions, focusing strategy and providing support systems. However, they leave the interpretation of low and high values to the discretion of the analyst, which could cause difficulty when comparable data sets are required, especially if management make subjective judgements as to these values.

The usefulness of the Shapiro classification matrix was demonstrated by Rangan, Moriarty and Swartz (1992) who showed that the grid can be successfully used to segment customers in mature industrial markets. The matrix provides a more refined mechanism for calculating customer profitability than other models, such as Yorke and Droussiotis (1994) and Dubinsky and Ingram (1984). For instance, Dubinsky and Ingram (1984) calculate *present profit contribution* as follows:

$$\text{contribution margin} = \frac{(\text{net sales to a particular customer} - \text{cost of goods sold})}{(\text{gross margin} - \text{direct selling expenses of salesperson})}$$

and contrast it with *potential profit contribution*. Their calculations do not take into account ongoing maintenance/support costs nor do they seem to cater for R&D.

In view of the limited empirical research extant it can be concluded that further empirical research is needed to test the model dimensions for robustness and validity. The section below describes one such investigation of the models.

THE RESEARCH

Methodology

This research empirically tested the Shapiro et al. (1987) and Krapfel, Salmond and Spekman (1991) relationship portfolio analysis models. These models were chosen because they included dimensions that were identified as being important in the discussion above, namely customer profitability and value.

The results are derived from a case study in a Computer Systems provider that operated in a wide range of industrial markets, including utilities, electricity generation, oil and gas production and distribution and process industries. The company provided real-time control and monitoring systems to those industries and had an annual turnover of £20 million. The systems, both the hardware and software aspects, were designed and developed within the group. Hardware was bought in from another division of the company and other computer manufacturers such as

Hewlett-Packard and DEC. Applications software was developed in-house and incorporated into software provided by others.

Customers from one particular operations group, the Oil, Gas and Process Industries group, were investigated during the case study because they formed a convenient data sample. Ten projects for four different customers, all of which had been completed within a three-year period, were used in this study. These were chosen because:

- They comprised the majority of the work undertaken by one office during the period being studied.
- They included a wide range of project values, from around £50,000 to £2,000,000, which is generally representative of the business undertaken by the company.
- The clients were considered to be important, long-term customers by the company.

For reasons of confidentiality, these projects are identified as A to J in the following calculations. Projects A to E and I were for customer 1; the relationship with the parent group of customer 1 was established in the mid 1970s, while the relationship with this group had been in place since the late 1980s. The relationship with the group was complicated by interfaces with different operational groups and third party contractors.

Project F was for customer 2; the relationship with the company had been in place for about 15 years (since the early 1980s). Projects G and J were for customer 3; this relationship was established approximately 6 years before (1988/89, making it the 'newest' relationship in the study). Project H was for customer 4; another longstanding customer who had been doing business with this company for over 10 years (since 1982/3).

The methodology used was based on cost and profit analysis on a project-by-project basis. The calculation methods used are outlined below. It should be noted that it is not possible to describe the complexities of the research analysis and how certain measures were determined and the underlying assumptions for some of these here. This methodology is, however, fully described in Zolkiewski (1994).

Cost and relationship value measurement

Shapiro et al. identify four areas of costs to suppliers that were examined: presale costs, production costs, distribution costs and postsale service costs. In the study these costs were determined from the management accounts, sales force records etc., and, when costs had not been individually recorded, detailed interviews were carried out with the personnel involved. The management accounting system produced very accurate information for 'direct' costs and very general information for 'indirect' costs; in this case 'indirect' costs covered many of the presale and postsale costs, which meant that much care had to be taken in estimating these results.

The following were identified as presale costs and included in the calculations:

- Sales time and expenses
- Costs of bidding
- Use of new technology/contribution to R&D
- Contracts time and expenses
- Management time and expenses

Because of the complex technical nature of the systems provided by the group and the demands for detailed sales proposals made by customers it was necessary to take into account these costs, which can be anywhere in the range from £2,000 to £50,000. The control systems market was one in which technology was rapidly changing, and as such the group had to make considerable investments in R&D to maintain its position in the market and ensure that its customers' investments in technology were protected. Since 1991 spend on R&D had been monitored in the same way as the spend on customer projects. This provided data that was used to estimate the costs of the developments used in systems supplied. However, such estimates are fraught with difficulties, especially if investment in R&D is considered in the long-term and can only be regarded as arbitrary. (Discussion of how to apportion the cost of R&D in an environment such as this is beyond the scope of this discussion.)

The production costs for the projects being studied included both time and materials and were taken directly from the management accounts, where they were recorded in great detail because they were considered to be direct costs by the company.

Distribution costs are negligible in this type of business and were included as a direct cost in all offers made to customers. Hence they were not considered as a separate cost in these calculations.

The following postsale costs were identified and included in the calculations:

- Management time and expenses
- Contracts time and expenses
- Support time and expenses
- Sales time and expenses
- User Conference

The User Conference was held once a year for existing customers of the company and provided a forum for customers to describe the systems they have introduced and the company to gives details of its future plans and developments.

Relationship value was calculated (in the manner defined by Krapfel, Salmond and Spekman, 1991): as 'a function of four factors: criticality, quantity, replaceability and slack . . .

$$RV_i = f(Cj,Qj,Rj,Sj)$$

RV_i is the value of the relationship to the seller
Cj is the criticality of the goods purchased by the buyer
Qj is the quantity of the seller's output consumed by this buyer
Rj is the replaceabilty of this buyer (i.e. the switching cost of accessing other buyers)
Sj is the cost savings resulting from the buyer's practices and procedures.

RESULTS AND ANALYSIS

Results of costs to serve calculations

The results of the cost to serve calculations for the projects being studied were very interesting. The management accounts only recorded the production and direct costs for individual projects and the managers at the company in question did not make any efforts to calculate the presale and postsale costs for individual projects or customers. This finding supports Shapiro et al.'s postulation that managers do not know the real cost to serve individual customers. The figures show that presale and postsale costs can form a significant percentage of the costs, as shown in Table 1.

The high value of pre- and postsale costs is something that managers cannot afford to neglect, especially as in one case these costs are more than 20 per cent of the total cost to serve. In the above sample pre- and postsale costs formed an average of 10 per cent of the cost to serve (ranging from a low of 4 per cent to a high of 23 per cent). Hence, it is clear that they should be given serious attention.

However, the manner in which pre- and postsale costs are recorded can prove to be extremely difficult to implement in a technically complex product context. The amount of time spent by R&D staff, sales engineers, managers etc., on the various projects can be difficult to determine exactly, especially as the relationships are long term and involve a range of projects.

Table 1 Cost to serve and profitability calculations for projects A to J to September 1993

| Project | Customer | Cost to serve | | | | Total costs | Pre- & postsale costs as a % of cost to serve | Selling price (£) | Cost to serve as a % of selling price | Profit margin (£) gross contribution | Profit margin % |
		Presale costs	Production costs	Distribution costs	Postsale costs						
A	1	57,180	615,154	0	3,062	675,396	8.9	733,230	92.1	57,834	7.9
B	1	14,165	107,860	0	4,415	126,440	14.7	188,600	67.0	62,160	33.0
C	1	13,299	133,039	0	1,910	148,248	10.3	191,732	77.3	43,484	22.7
D	1	36,327	545,486	0	5,316	587,129	7.1	674,257	87.1	87,128	12.9
E	1	16,462	102,958	0	1,229	120,649	14.7	164,163	73.5	43,514	26.5
F	2	26,059	363,936	0	2,159	392,154	7.2	353,111	111.1	−39,043	−11.1
G	3	14,025	226,840	0	573	241,438	6.1	332,894	73.5	91,456	27.5
H	4	9,812	64,029	0	9,227	83,068	22.9	54,765	151.7	−28,303	−51.7
I	1	71,080	1,734,506	0	8,657	1,814,243	4.4	1,701,534	106.6	−112,709	−6.6
J	3	34,485	663,652	0	9,216	707,353	6.2	795,000	89.0	87,647	11.0

Note that projects F, H and I were loss-making projects.

Also, the manner in which costs such as R&D are apportioned could be subject to great debate, as, very often, R&D expenditure is directed towards the needs of both existing and potential customers. Another problem area is the manner in which the costs of bidding are apportioned; in the examples above the costs of bidding have only covered bids to existing customers. How the costs of bidding unsuccessfully to potential customers are accounted for is not easy to determine – writing off these costs in a separate area could be disastrous especially if these costs were larger than the total profit from existing customers.

Whatever the difficulties associated with calculating cost to serve, it surely must be important for the cost to serve values to be given due consideration by management, as they can give very important indications as to the true profitability of either individual projects or the overall profitability of different customers. Another aspect of the cost to serve figures which can be analysed is whether individual projects within the overall customer relationships have low or high costs to serve. In addition to this data being needed to prepare the customer classification matrix it also gives a summary of the effort needed to support different projects and/or customers.

Results of the relationship value calculations

Table 2 gives the relationship value functions for the projects studied. Clearly, this information is 'softer' or more judgemental than the more specific cost data and requires certain assumptions to be made as described by Zolkiewski (1994). Not surprisingly, given the choice criteria of the sample, all the projects studied have been classified as having a high interest commonality because they are all either repeat or follow-on purchases.

Table 2 Relationship values

Customer	C_j	Q_j	R_j	S_j	RV_i
1	High	High	High	Low	High
2	High	Low	High	Low	Low
3	High	High	High	Low	High
4	High	Low	High	Low	Low

Although the projects studied could be placed on the grid, they were only positioned in two of the quadrants (partner and friend). Turnbull and Zolkiewski (1997) were not surprised by these results because of the long-term nature of the relationships they were studying. However, they found that the process of assessing relationship value did have some utility as it provided another dimension which could be used to assess customers.

Portfolio analysis

Table 1 summarizes the net price and cost to serve values for the projects studied and Figure 2 shows how the projects can be positioned on the Shapiro et al. matrix. Projects B, E and G are defined as having a low cost to serve.[4] In the first instance it could be assumed that low cost to serve would ensure that the project was extremely profitable and in the examples chosen this is indeed the case. It would, therefore, seem to be a logical management aim to achieve a low cost to serve and consequently highly profitable projects. However, such an aim must be treated with extreme caution as it may not always be good to have a low cost to serve, indeed the effort required to establish long term relationships may often require a high initial investment, as suggested by Turnbull and Wilson (1989), i.e. a high cost to serve in the first instance. Indeed B, E and G were all follow-on purchases and the initial projects in the sequence, I and J, both have a high cost to serve.

Because of the nature of the business and the fact that only long-term relationships were studied, it is not surprising to find that the majority of projects were classified as being 'carriage trade'.

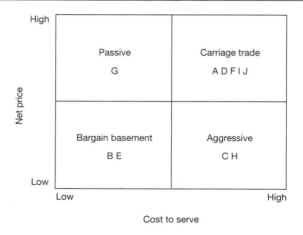

Figure 2 Results for Shapiro et al. classification.

However, the positioning of some projects in each of the three remaining quadrants shows that customer behaviour does change within a relationship and also varies from customer to customer. Hence, it is important for both managers and sales and marketing personnel to realize that a customer's reaction should not be taken for granted.

Another interesting observation on the positioning of the various projects on the grid is that the positions of some of the projects are not where the management in the company concerned predicted. For example, the group manager indicated that customer 2 (project F) was one of the most 'aggressive' customers that he dealt with, which leads to the prediction that projects for the customer would have a low net price and a high cost to serve and therefore be classified as aggressive on the Shapiro et al. matrix. However, project F has been classified by the researchers as 'carriage trade'. This leads to the question of whether the arbitrary definition of low and high net price has caused the mispositioning on the matrix or even if the nomenclature used by Shapiro et al. (i.e. aggressive) would lead to general confusion by non-specialist managers trying to use the classification matrix as a marketing tool.

Grid positioning can have much wider implications. For instance: should management aim to have as many customers as possible in the passive sector or simply aim not to have 'aggressive' customers? It is also interesting to contemplate if one customer can be positioned in more than one position on the grid when examining a particular time period even though this is not directly displayed in the examples studied. Studying these grid positions can have important consequences for marketing and this customer classification matrix can be a very useful tool for industrial marketing managers when they are formulating their strategies.

Profit dispersion

Project profitability

Table 1 gives the individual project profitabilities using the profit margins calculated via the Shapiro et al. cost to serve method. Graphical representation of net price against cost to serve is shown in Figure 3. It is interesting to note that a wide range in project profit margin (from –52% to 33%) is observed across the whole range of projects and that there is some indication that customers could also be classified as having a wide range of profitability. This observation confirms Shapiro et al.'s supposition about the variability of profitability and is also interesting from a management point of view, as the managers stated aim is to make about 5 per cent net profit on all projects and this is clearly not the case.

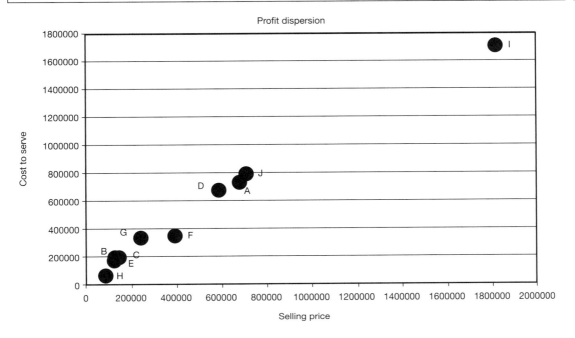

Figure 3 Profit dispersion.

Customer profitability

The average profitability of each customer has been calculated:

Customer 1   16.1%
Customer 2   −11.1%
Customer 3   19.3%
Customer 4   −51.7%

This illustrates that a wide range of customer profitability has been observed in this study.

The results give a customer profitability ranking of 3, 1, 2 and 4. Using this ranking suggests that the relationships with customers 2 and (especially) 4 should be reviewed. However, the data sample used is only part of the overall picture, for example it does not cover all the work done for the customers being studied and does not, therefore, give a good overview of the real situation.

It is also interesting to note the change in profitability over time by customer. For customer 3 it increases from 11.02 per cent to 27.47 per cent while for customer 1 the fluctuations are not quite so straightforward and are illustrated in Figure 4. This also seems to reflect the situation noted by Shapiro et al. in one capital equipment company where "the big national accounts ... were generating losses that were large enough to offset the rise in volume and the profitability of smaller, allegedly less attractive accounts" (page 101). This finding gives an indication of the complex nature of the customer/supplier relationship and shows that it would be simplistic to expect a constantly upward increase in the profits made from a single customer (see Turnbull and Turku, 1994).

A NEW WAY FORWARD

Three-dimensional customer classification matrix

As a result of the empirical work described above, we propose a three-dimensional basis for customer portfolio analysis, as illustrated in Figure 5. This proposal resulted from a consideration

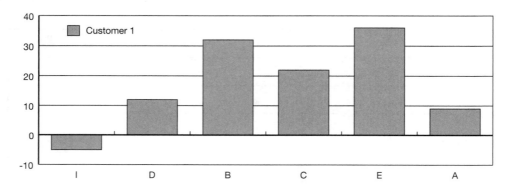

Figure 4 Change in profitability over time of customer 1.

of the differences in the nature of the matrix axes (i.e. the variables being used), with the Shapiro et al. (1987) axes being relatively easy to measure while the Krapfel, Salmond and Spekman (1991) axes are much more subjective. They argue that three-dimensional analysis based upon cost to serve, net price and relationship value is appropriate when segmenting the customers of any firm. simply because such an analysis provides a more comprehensive overview than can be gained from using two variables. The approach is also not beset by the complex mix of subjective and quantitative data calculations that are required in many of the other models.

Using three-dimensional analysis allows a more refined customer classification in terms of dimensions of analysis and number of classifications. It provides a mechanism for combining hard

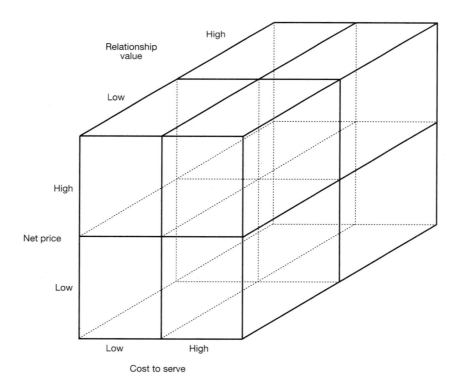

Figure 5 Three-dimensional customer classification matrix (Turnbull and Zolkiewski, 1997, p. 320).

data (profitability of customers) with more judgemental data (relationship value). Managers can then assess customers in light of these findings and determine which relationships need developing and/or maintaining and which, if any, need to be broken. Initial analysis would suggest that customers/relationships which have a high value and net price combined with a low cost to serve are the most attractive and, those with low relationship values and net prices combined with a high cost to serve are least attractive.

It is imperative, however, that such analyses of relationships are not a unique process. The most informative data will be that which monitors the positions of customers/relationships over time, for instance can high net price be maintained over time (Shapiro et al., 1987 and Turnbull and Zolkiewski, 1997 both observe such migrations). The manager will then need to consider the investments in relationships that are needed to maintain the status quo.

It is unfortunate that the case study used by Turnbull and Zolkiewski (1997) was not extended to cover all the proposed customer matrices. Such an analysis would probably have provided much stronger evidence for their choice of axes. However, it is clear from Turnbull and Topcu's (1994) and Yorke and Droussiotis's (1994) analysis of the Fiocca (1982) model, that his axes are much more difficult to use in terms of provision of replicable and comprehensive data (they are almost too subjective). This lends support to the choice of axes made by Turnbull and Zolkiewski (1997), where net price is obviously an extremely important factor; cost to serve calculations – presale, production, distribution and postsale costs – ensure that due consideration is given to all aspects of the product development and selling process; and, relationship value allows judgemental data (management intuition) to be included in the analysis. Additionally, the complex pseudo calculation of relationship value they used (derived from Krapfel, Salmond and Spekman, 1991) could also be calculated in other ways. For example, the mechanism suggested by Wilson and Jantrania (1994) could be used. Other proxy measures of relationship value such as whether the relationship is valuable because it provides access to technical or commercial information, or the customer acts as a reference site could also be used.

Portfolios and network model

Our work on portfolios can be developed by considering the relationship between networks and portfolios. This is because we believe that relationship management should be explicitly placed within the context of all the relationships in the network. It can be suggested that networks can be visualized by viewing them in terms of their constituent portfolios. This would usually be:

- Customer portfolio
- Supplier portfolio
- Indirect portfolio

See the example in Figure 6 for an illustration of this. Various alternatives to this can be proposed, according to the situation of the focal firm. For instance, public sector organizations may view their network in terms of supplier, funder, influencer and user portfolios. This perspective stresses the importance of modelling the set of indirect relationships[5] that surround a firm. The identification and analysis of important indirect relationships is difficult and can only be determined by extensive analysis of the micro-environment of the organization in question. However, by identifying indirect relationships as well as critical customer and supplier relationships, managers can gain additional strategic insight into the network in which they operate.

By viewing portfolios in a network context the problem of portfolios not depicting the interdependencies between customers and suppliers (Olsen and Ellram, 1997) is ameliorated. We would suggest that strategic management involves the identification and management of the different sets

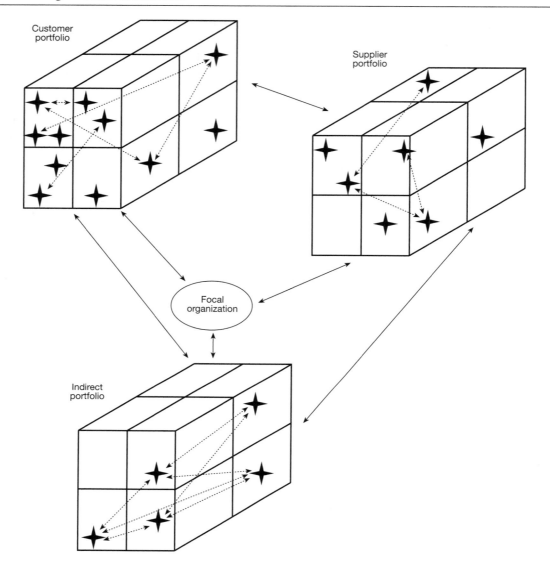

Figure 6 A network perspective of portfolio analysis.

(or portfolios) of relationships that surround an organization, whilst at an operational level, the challenge is to manage each portfolio optimally.

The discussion above illustrates that the concept of relationship portfolios is interesting and varied. It provides both scope for academic investigation and managerial prescription, especially as an aid to strategic decision making. The empirical evidence derived from tests of the models also demonstrates that the concept of portfolio management is of relevance to management. Not withstanding the usual criticisms of portfolio modelling, this area should provide an exciting area for strategic management support.

The concept of the indirect portfolio needs further development. Within its context it is possible to propose the development of competitor portfolios. These, when incorporated into the overall set of portfolios, should allow a strategist to map the links from competitors to an organization's customers and suppliers. This should facilitate wider thinking by, for example, introducing a consideration of possible competitor actions. In a similar vein potential supplier or potential customer portfolios could be introduced and they could be used in decisions about targeting new customers or selecting new suppliers.

Advances in technology mean that modelling such data should be easily accomplished. Computer databases should mean that financial data can be easily assimilated and managers should be able to record qualitative data alongside this to allow their decision-making processes to be audited and available for future comparison.

MANAGERIAL IMPLICATIONS

One of the most important questions associated with the use of relationship portfolio analysis is: under what circumstances can it be most effectively used? Figure 7 illustrates a hierarchical approach to understanding customer needs (and therefore provides a key to managing those needs). This process begins by segmenting industrial customers into anonymous, homogenous groups. Following this it recognizes that in a business-to-business context it is often advantageous (from a strategic perspective) to identify clusters of customers within segments. Finally, at the micro level, portfolio analysis (analysis of individual relationships) can take place; this forms the basis of relationship management schemes. The process illustrates how, as the level of analysis increases, companies can increase their knowledge and understanding of the value of groups of (and individual) customers.

The discussion above illustrates how relationship portfolios can provide a valuable mechanism for developing a coherent relationship management strategy and also shows that all relationships do not necessarily need to be strong. However, choice of models or dimensions is not simple; it will partly depend on the nature of the firm itself and partly how it perceives its micro-environment – which factors are most important for its current strategy and operational management; relationship management; competitors' share; emergence of new markets etc. However, we firmly believe that two-dimensional matrices do not provide enough depth of analysis. The answer may be in step-wise analysis (Fiocca, 1982; Campbell and Cunningham, 1983) or in multidimensional analysis (Turnbull and Zolkiewski, 1997). Indeed, by taking a network perspective and considering all the constituent portfolios that surround an organization (both direct and indirect) a manager can begin to analyze the micro-environment of the firm.

Choice of model must also be made with a full consideration of the limitations of using portfolio modelling. Each model has its own limitations, many of which have been highlighted in earlier

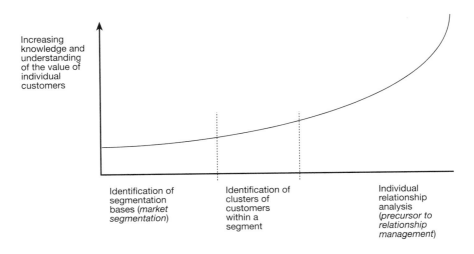

Figure 7 Levels of analysis.

discussions (see Zolkiewski and Turnbull (1999) for a summary of the criticisms of portfolio analysis).

It is also apparent from the various practical attempts to use portfolio models that although these models are inherently appealing as a means for analysis, in practical terms they are extremely difficult to define and operationalize. The models are largely based upon variables that are difficult to define and measure quantitatively; for example, many organizations do not have mechanisms that allow them to calculate the real cost-to-serve of individual customers or even market segments.

The question of customer profitability and relationship value again has an inherent appeal. All firms want profitable customers and valuable relationships. The difficulty comes with the associated calculations. Not many companies have accounting systems that can provide relationship costs and profits. This is changing though, as more and more companies are recognizing the need for this data and technological capabilities are developing. However, it is imperative that Shapiro et al.'s (1987) suggestion that the real costs of supporting various customers should not be considered in isolation by managers and that they should be aware that high variations in these costs do often exist. Changes need to be monitored periodically, not simply as a 'one-off' action. It is also crucial that the data used to calculate customer profitability takes into account adaptation/development costs for new products/services as well as the more 'tangible' indirect costs such as sales expenses. Yorke (1984) notes how infrequently management attention is paid to the effects on profit of applying resources to a particular segment or even a particular customer.

It must be remembered that there may be good reasons why a particular relationship or market segment is not financially profitable and there may be good reasons to 'invest' in such relationships. For example, the relationship may be an integral part of competitive strategy, it may be needed for R&D purposes or the 'unprofitability' may be temporary, e.g. because of unstable exchange rates. Managers must therefore take care to ensure that unprofitable relationships are not as a result of poor management within a firm. Nonetheless, it is important that the concept of customer (or account) profitability is understood by management.

On a tactical level, managers need to consider what is the optimum spread of customers on a matrix. This needs careful attention and the application of managerial judgement and experience. It cannot be prescribed by a text. They should also be prepared to vary their management style in response to the outcome of the analysis. For example a different style may well be needed to deal with customers who do not yield much profit and present high costs to serve. In other words, it may be necessary to "sack" customers in order to utilize the released resources more effectively.

CONCLUSION

Relationship portfolio modelling can play an important role in strategic marketing management. On a simple level, analysis of either customer or supplier relationships can provide important inputs into the management process. However, by moving to a view of the network as a set, or series, of portfolios, a much wider strategic perspective can be gained.

All the models that have been discussed can provide valuable inputs to management decision-making. However, consideration needs to be given as to which are the most pertinent variables and how subjective data can be included in a way which will allow consistency of comparison in future years. Additionally, other appropriate quantitative measures of customer/portfolio management may need to be determined.

The notion of the network as a set of portfolios (customer, supplier, indirect, competitor, potential customer and/or supplier) provides an exciting opportunity for academic research and managerial practice. It offers a mechanism which allows managers to map the complexity of the network concept in a relatively simple manner, without needing to understand and critically evaluate the multitude of associated theory. By taking the perspective of a firm as being embedded in three types of relationship portfolio we can infer that that portfolio analysis provides the key to successful relationship management and important inputs to strategic management.

There is great potential for further empirical testing and for conceptualization. In particular, rigorous comparisons of the various axes proposed in the different models need undertaking along with the provision of definitive descriptions of the components, especially when qualitative issues are at hand. The standardization of such definitions is essential if the models are to be effectively and efficiently used as a strategic decision-making tool.

Whether or not this type of modelling can be successfully transferred into the wider arena of relationship marketing is a more unpredictable situation. Despite advances in technology, the ability to precisely record the necessary data and then to model it may prove to be a far too onerous task. It may be that relationship management moves more to a scenario where segments rather than individual customers are subjected to portfolio analysis.

NOTES

1. This paper is developed from the ideas presented by the authors in *Understanding Business Markets*, 2nd edition, David Ford, ed. (1997).
2. See Håkansson and Snehota (1989, 1995), Håkansson and Johanson, (1992), Axelsson and Easton (1992) and Möller and Wilson (1995) for a wider discussion of business networks.
3. Influential authors in this area include: Cunningham and Homse (1982), Fiocca (1982), Campbell and Cunningham (1983), Dickson (1983), Dubinsky and Ingram (1984), Shapiro et al. (1987), Krapfel, Salmond and Spekman (1991), Rangan et al. (1992), Salle and Rost (1993), Yorke and Droussiotis (1994), Turnbull and Zolkiewski (1997) and Olsen and Ellram (1997).
4. Shapiro et al. do not define what values represent low and high costs to serve, hence for this research it was decided, somewhat arbitrarily, to define projects sold for less than £250,000 as having a low net price and a low cost to serve as being one which was less than 75 per cent of selling price.
5. Indirect relationships can be seen as relationships with actors who influence the operation of the organization; examples include government (national and local), institutions such as universities and lobby groups.

REFERENCES

Axelsson, Bjorn and Geoff Easton (eds) (1992) *Industrial Networks: A New View of Reality*. London: Routledge.

Campbell, Nigel C. G. and Malcolm T. Cunningham (1983) 'Customer Analysis for Strategy Development in Industrial Markets', *Strategic Management Journal*, 4, pp. 369–380.

Cunningham, Malcolm T. and Elling Homse (1982) 'An Interaction Approach to Marketing Strategy' in *International Marketing and Purchasing of Industrial Goods*. Håkansson, Håkan (ed.) New York: John Wiley & Sons.

Dickson, Peter R. (1983) 'Distributor Portfolio Analysis And The Channel Dependence Matrix: New Techniques For Understanding And Managing The Channel', *Journal of Marketing*, 47 (Summer), pp. 35–44.

Dubinsky, Alan J. and Thomas N. Ingram (1984) 'A Portfolio Approach To Account Profitability', *Industrial Marketing Management*, 13, pp. 33–41.

Fiocca, Renato (1982) 'Account Portfolio Analysis for Strategy Development', *Industrial Marketing Management*, 11, pp. 53–62.

Ford, David (ed.) (1990) *Understanding Business Markets*. San Diego, California: Academic Press.

Ford, David (ed.) (1997) *Understanding Business Markets, 2nd Edition*. London: The Dryden Press.

Ford, David, Lars-Erik Gadde, Håkan Håkansson, Anders Lundgren, Ivan Snehota, Peter Turnbull and David Wilson (1998) *Managing Business Relationships*. Chichester, England: John Wiley & Sons Ltd.

Håkansson, Håkan (ed.) (1982) *International Marketing and Purchasing of Industrial Goods*. New York: John Wiley & Sons.

Håkansson, Håkan and J. Johanson (1992) 'A Model Of Industrial Networks', in *A New View Of Reality*. Axelsson, Bjørn and Geoffrey Easton (eds) London, UK: Routledge.

Håkansson, Håkan and Ivan Snehota (eds) (1995) *Developing Relationships in Business Networks*. London: Routledge.

Iacobucci, Dawn (ed.) (1996) *Networks in Marketing*. Thousand Oaks, California, USA: Sage Publications Inc.

Krapfel, Robert E. Jr., Deborah Salmond and Robert Spekman (1991) 'A Strategic Approach to Managing Buyer–Seller Relationships', *European Journal of Marketing*, 25,9, pp. 22–37.

Möller, Kristian and David T. Wilson (eds) (1995) *Business Marketing: An Interaction and Network Perspective*. Massachusetts, USA: Kluwer Academic Publishers.

O'Connell, William A. and William Keenan Jr. (1990) 'The Shape of Things to Come', reprinted in Hartley, Bob and Michael W. Starkey (eds) (1996) *The Management of Sales and Customer Relations*. London, UK: International Thomson Business Press.

Olsen, Rasmus Friss and Lisa M. Ellram (1997) 'A Portfolio Approach to Supplier Relationships', *Industrial Marketing Management*, 26, pp. 101–113.

Rangan, Kasturi V., Rowland T. Moriarty and Gordon S. Swartz (1992), 'Segmenting Customers in Mature Industrial Markets' *Journal of Marketing*, 56 (October), pp. 72–82.

Salle, R. and Rost, C. (1993) Une Methodé de Gestion des Portefeuilles de Clients en Milieu Industriel', *Gestion 2000*, 2, pp. 69–87.

Shapiro, Benson P., V. Kasturi Rangan, Rowland T. Moriarty and Elliot B. Ross (1987) 'Manage Customers for Profits (not Just Sales)', *Harvard Business Review*, September-October 1987, pp. 101–108.

Turnbull, Peter, David Ford and Malcolm Cunningham (1996) 'Interaction, Relationships and Networks In Business Markets: An Evolving Perspective', *Journal of Business & Industrial Marketing*, 11, 3/4, pp. 44–62.

Turnbull, Peter W. and Jean-Paul Valla (eds) (1986), *Strategies for International Industrial Marketing*. London: Croom Helm.

Turnbull, Peter W. and Sule Topcu (1994) 'Customer Profitability in Relationship Life Cycles', *Proceedings of the 10th IMP Conference,* Groningen, Netherlands

Turnbull, Peter W. and David T. Wilson (1989) 'Developing and Protecting Profitable Customer Relationships', *Industrial Marketing Management*, 18.1, pp 1–6.

Turnbull, Peter W. and Judy M. Zolkiewski (1997) 'Profitability in Customer Portfolio Planning' in Ford, David (ed.) *Understanding Business Markets, 2nd Edition*. London: The Dryden Press.

Wilson, David T. and Swati Jantrania (1994) 'Understanding The Value Of A Relationship', *Asia-Australia Marketing Journal*, Vol. 2, No. 1, pp. 55–67.

Yorke, David (1984) 'Market Profit Centres: Fiction Or An Emerging Reality?', *Management Accounting*, February 1984, pp. 21-27.

Yorke, David A. and George Droussiotis (1994) 'The Use of Customer Portfolio Theory: An Empirical Survey', *Journal of Business & Industrial Marketing*, 9,3, pp. 6–18.

Zolkiewski, Judith M. (1994) *Marketing of Large Contracts: Selling Costs and Profitability*. MSc Dissertation, UMIST, UK.

Zolkiewski, Judy and Peter Turnbull (1999) *A Review of Customer Relationships Planning: Does Customer Profitability and Portfolio Analysis Provide the Key to Successful Relationship Management?* Manchester, UK: MSM Working Paper Series.

Zolkiewski, Judy M. and Peter W. Turnbull (2000) 'Relationship Portfolios – Past, Present and Future', in proceedings of the 16th Annual IMP Conference at the University of Bath, September 2000.

Zolkiewski, Judy and Peter W. Turnbull (forthcoming) 'Do Relationship Portfolios and Networks Provide the Key to Successful Relationship Management?' *Journal of Business & Industrial Marketing*.

4.4

Organizing marketing in industrial high-tech firms: the role of internal marketing relationships

Kristian Möller and Arto Rajala

INTRODUCTION

Relationship marketing, characterized by reciprocal, long-term relationships between producers and customers, dominated much of the managerial and academic discussion in business marketing during the 1990s. Following changing company practices, a considerable amount of research has been carried out on the management of customer relationships, the application of portfolio management practices in handling a firm's customer and supplier base, and lately also on developing and managing suppliers and customers from a network perspective (Möller and Wilson, 1995; Iacobucci, 1996; Special Issue on Relationship Marketing, 1997; Ford et al., 1998). Much less attention has been paid to an issue that, we contend, has equal importance for successful business marketing: the development and management of efficient intra-organizational solutions for carrying out marketing activities. This theme is especially relevant in high-technology companies, the focus of our article.

Marketing is an increasingly demanding function in industrial high-technology companies due to the expanding complexity and uncertainty faced by the management. Several factors are behind this trend. Intensifying technological complexity, high knowledge intensity, and systemic quality characterize the products of high-tech industries such as biotechnics, industrial electronics, and telecommunication systems. These characteristics encompass a high level of both technological and market uncertainty (Moriarty and Kosnik, 1989). Because of the inherent complexity, marketing tasks in high-technology companies are becoming very knowledge intensive (Nonaka and Taceuchi, 1995). They demand highly differentiated professional skills and capabilities. This development in knowledge intensity means that both supplier and customer companies are increasingly taking on the role of professional organizations, staffed by highly qualified personnel at all levels of functioning (Achrol, 1991). In terms of the customer–supplier interface, intensive personal interaction is needed for carrying out business. This involves organizing cooperation between groups of functional experts within both the supplier and customer organizations and between these organizations.

This specialization, together with the establishment of business process-based organizational solutions, has led to the rapid dismantling of traditional marketing departments. Marketing activities are increasingly being spread out among several organizational units forming intricate nets of marketing activities. Complex matrix organizations, multifunctional teams, account management systems, and forms of business process management are replacing functional departments. Only scant research is available on this development in a high-tech context (Achrol, 1991; Cespedes, 1994, 1995; Piercy and Cravens, 1995).

Another trend fragmenting marketing activities and personnel even further is the rapid globalization of most high-tech industries. Companies are increasingly operating globally; this involves the primary decision on which activities and operations to centralize and which to localize. This tension creates another organizational problem for international high-technology corporations (Hedlund, 1994).

Finally, the organization of the interface between technology and marketing is relevant for understanding how high-tech firms operate and compete. This aspect has also attracted limited attention from the traditional marketing perspective (Capon and Glazer, 1987), although it is much more prominent in industrial network studies (Håkansson, 1987, 1989; Ford et al., 1990, 1998).

Thus, in spite of their managerial significance, organizational issues have received only scant attention in marketing with the exceptions of the seminal general works of Weitz and Anderson (1981), Piercy (1985), Cespedes (1995), and recently Workman et al. (1998), studies related to organizational buying behavior, relationship marketing, and, more recently, marketing networks have only made passing reference to organizing marketing activities Hutt and Speh, 1984; Cunningham and Homse, 1986; (Piercy and Cravens, 1995; Cravens et al., 1996). The discussion concerning key account management (KAM) was one positive exception, but this only covers one limited aspect of the organization of marketing activities (Pardo et al., 1995).

This article addresses the knowledge gap concerning the organization of marketing activities in high-tech industrial companies. We contend that the interaction and relationships between intra-organizational corporate units and the actors involved in marketing activities form a critical element in implementing the marketing concept in a high-technology context. We believe that the management of internal, corporation-wide marketing networks and relationships is a prerequisite for the efficient management of customer relationships. Our purpose is to describe how successful industrial high-technology companies, operating in a global context, are organizing their marketing activities. Special attention is paid to the question of how they manage the interfaces between the different internal marketing units and actors. In this sense we are interested in the management of internal marketing relationships and in emerging network solutions.

We pursue our aim by first briefly reviewing existing knowledge of organizing industrial marketing. Next we describe the case study approach employed in the process automation industry which provided the empirical material for the study. We then present the results, based on an analysis of business units of ABB, Honeywell, Measurex, and Valmet Automation, and conclude by discussing the managerial and theoretical implications of our study and suggesting directions for future research.

MARKETING ORGANIZATION IN INDUSTRIAL HIGH-TECH COMPANIES

Marketing organization in industrial companies often differs from that in consumer goods companies. Due to the complexity of industrial products, a larger number of people representing different types of special expertise is involved in development and marketing activities. Because the number of customers is smaller, most companies have to operate on a global level. In order for them to cope with these problems, marketing activities are generally assigned to independent organizational groups or units.

Current views on marketing organization

Cespedes has labeled these marketing groups product management, sales, and customer service units. His studies (Cespedes, 1990, 1994, 1995) summarize much of the extant knowledge of the organization of industrial marketing.

The product management unit employs one or several product managers who are in charge of the marketing activities related to the products assigned to them. They are often involved in product development activities as well. These managers form the critical interface between R&D and sales, and between R&D, production, and the customers (Lysonski, 1985). Product managers tend to experience role conflicts because they face requirements from several internal units and from customers.

Field sales organizations were originally established to integrate mass production with mass distribution. The sales function in industrial companies is often organized as an autonomous department or a subsidiary abroad. Sales jobs vary greatly depending on the kind of product or service sold. In spite of the rapid development of electronic channels, sales remain an essential part of marketing activities, and the salesperson prevails at the heart of the company's encounters with customers. Therefore, s/he also plays a key boundary role in organizations (Cespedes, 1990).

To support with field sales, industrial companies often have separate units for customer service and maintenance purposes. These units are mainly responsible for the so-called post-sale service by giving customers the necessary support in installation and maintenance. Cespedes (1995) argues that customer service often also provides presale support by helping customers with their purchasing – in favor of closing the sale. Although the role of service has been a supporting one in most industrial organizations, it is becoming more critical as many high-technology companies are generating a major proportion of their revenues by providing different types of services to customers – beginning from installation and training, and ending with long-term maintenance contracts.

Internal relationships in the marketing of high-technology products

Cespedes has no doubt captured the dominant characteristics of industrial marketing organizations. However, there are several trends, discussed in the introduction, that bring new challenges and changes to the management of high-tech marketing activities. These are recapitulated in Figure 1.

According to current research, marketing activities are carried out primarily by the three units (product management, field sales, and customer service) depicted in the center of Figure 1. We contend that the coordination of the interfaces between these units, between them and R&D and production, and between them and the corresponding organizational units of customers, constitutes the key challenge for marketing management in today's and tomorrow's high-tech companies.

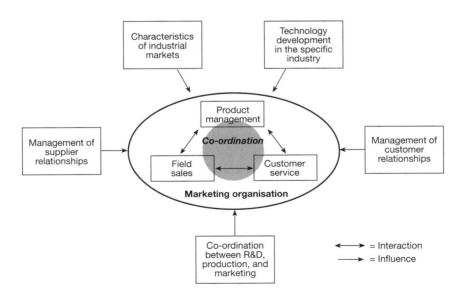

Figure 1 Factors affecting the role and status of marketing in industrial high-technology companies.

A number of speculative propositions, based primarily on our current knowledge (Cunningham and Homse, 1986; Snow, 1992; Cespedes, 1994, Möller and Wilson, 1994; Cespedes, 1995; Håkansson and Snehota, 1995; Cravens et al., 1996) and on the emerging anecdotal evidence, provided the focus of the empirical study.

The more complex the product or system to be exchanged, in terms of the number of technologies involved, the more it is essential to find personnel with a variety of skills and competencies to ensure the development of the system, and in its selling and implementation. This tends to increase the number of organizational units involved within both the producer and the buyer companies.

The greater the technological complexity and knowledge intensity the higher the level of tacit knowledge involved in product development, marketing, and the implementation of the system. This tends to impede communication between actors having a different knowledge basis or logic. Communication barriers exist both within organizations and between suppliers and buyers.

Taken together, the above propositions imply that intra-organizational integration of the actors carrying out specific activities is both important and difficult. Because of the knowledge intensity involved we expect to find non-hierarchical groups such as project teams, key communicators, and teams within a business process setting.

As far as the supplier–buyer interface is concerned, the supplier must have the capability of implementing the product/system in accordance with the customer's technology. This involves mastering the technology, understanding the customer's business, and having the competence to market the product and to implement it. Because different actors carry the necessary capabilities, we can expect teams to be the primary mode of conveying the supplier–customer relationship.

It follows from the last point that if there is only a limited number of customers, each one can generally be handled by a team containing a "complete set of actors," meaning all the actors whose special competencies are needed in carrying out the business transaction and then maintaining the relationship. However, in industries where the number of customers is large, we expect the competencies which are rare and expensive to be centralized and provided for the customer teams only as temporary supportive services. This need for expertise on the one hand, and its scarcity and high value on the other, forms a crucial balancing problem in high-technology marketing.

METHODOLOGY: A CASE STUDY IN THE PROCESS CONTROL AND AUTOMATION INDUSTRY

Choice of research approach and case companies

The multiple-case method was selected as the basic research approach because relatively little a priori information existed about the focal phenomenon, the organizing of marketing activities in high-tech companies. Further, it became evident, through interviewing a few industry experts, that the complexity of the organizational solutions could not be captured without direct interviews and access to company documents. According to Yin (1994), multiple cases can be employed in various ways. Often the underlying idea behind selecting more than one case is to increase understanding of the phenomenon under study by comparing the individual cases. A researcher can also use multiple cases to provide an experimental research setting. We used multiple cases in a replicative way because of the lack of prior knowledge (Miles and Huberman, 1994). Replication is used by the researcher to increase understanding of the phenomenon by focusing more deeply on issues emerging from the earlier cases.

Industrial electronics was chosen as the high-tech organizational and marketing context due to its prominence and rapid development in many countries. In Finland the industry's annual growth rate varied between 25%–30% during the 1990s. Within the field of industrial electronics we selected our case companies from the industrial automation sector. The process control and automation suppliers in this specific sector form their own sub-industry, characterized by a multidimensional technology base (instrument and measurement technology, process technology, information-processing technology), and complex systemic products involving high knowledge intensity. The main customer sector for the process control and automation suppliers operating in Finland is the chemical forest industry (pulp and paper mills), and energy production (power plants).

By excluding all small firms (they do not face the complex organizational problems we are interested in), we reduced the number of suppliers available in Finland to five: ABB, Honeywell, Measurex, Siemens, and Valmet Automation. All these companies, except Siemens, have product development and production units in Finland. Because product responsibility is a crucial aspect of our study, we decided to select all the companies as case units except Siemens. ABB's operative process automation company in Finland is called ABB Industry, and we selected the Paper and Pulp Division's Automation unit. Honeywell was represented by its Varkaus Automation Center, and Measurex by its Roibox unit.[1] Valmet Automation is a subsidiary of its Finnish parent company (Valmet Corporation), and takes care of all automation and instrumentation-related business. It should be noted that, although we only had four case units, they covered close to 50% of the global sales of process control and automation systems for the paper and pulp sector (Fadum, 1992).

Data collection process and analytical heuristic

The data was collected through personal interviews and with the help of archival industry data. A total of 20 interviews were made. The managing directors, or the division heads of the case companies were contacted in order to get permission for carrying out intensive interviews. These managers suggested the key informants, in most cases communication managers, who then provided additional informants when necessary. Also, three industry experts were interviewed before the primary data collection in order to increase the understanding of industry characteristics, technical terminology, and to enhance the overall validity of the themes and topics. Two to three rounds of interviews, tape recorded with permission, were carried out using the technique of drafting the interim case descriptions that formed the bases of the next round. This procedure, and the cross-checking between the multiple respondents and the archival data, were used to enhance the validity of the data (Yin, 1994). The interviews were carried out during late 1994, 1995, and the first half of 1996.

The following issues and "working heuristic" were used in both the data collection and the analysis. First, we needed to see the overall organizational structure of the companies in order to understand the context in which the marketing activities were carried out. Second, we identified all the units and actors carrying out marketing or marketing-related activities. Cespedes' (1995) listing of marketing activities formed the basic classification device. Third, we needed to identify all the internal units and external organizations with which these marketing units interacted. Fourth, we tried to examine the character of the interaction and the type of skills required in effecting satisfactory interaction. The charting of the organizational arrangements and the reasons given for these by the company representatives concluded the analysis. This heuristic enabled us to highlight the specific role and status of each marketing unit.

ORGANIZING MARKETING IN THE PROCESS CONTROL AND AUTOMATION INDUSTRY: MARKETING DOMAINS AND INTERNAL MARKETING RELATIONSHIPS

Overall organizational structure

The case companies, and their parent corporations, have established world-wide matrix structures involving several business (industrial systems, building control, power generation, etc.) and market areas (Europe, the Americas, and Asia-Pacific). This multi-level matrix structure, illustrated in Figure 2, seemed to be quite similar in the four case companies.

These global, corporate-wide matrices determine the general structural arrangements used to organize marketing activities at the company and business unit levels. Typically, each of the

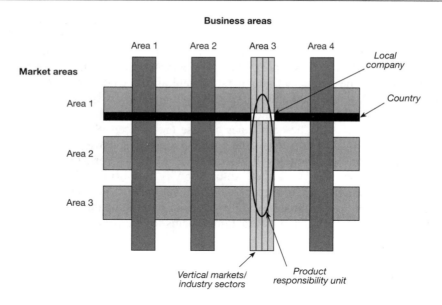

Figure 2   Matrix structure used by the case companies.

business areas comprises a number of different industry sectors which, in turn, are assigned to the so-called product responsibility units (PRU). The market areas consist of local sales and service affiliates in different countries.

The product responsibility units operate on a global basis in their particular industry sectors. These sectors form separate so-called vertical markets. A particular PRU may also serve different vertical markets by modifying the basic platform product according to the specific customer application needs in each market. For example, a supplier's process control and automation systems could be used in the production processes of the pulp, paper, energy, and graphics sectors.

Because of the key position of the PRU (the oval in Figure 2) we analyzed the inter-organizational relationships from that perspective. Figure 3 illustrates the pivotal role of the PRU as a nexus of the matrix formed by vertical and horizontal markets. Vertical markets describe the different industry sectors, or customer groups, to which the unit is selling its products and systems.

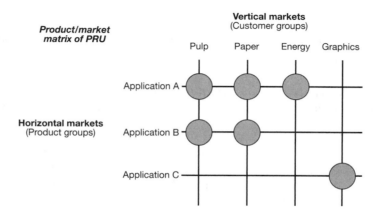

Figure 3   Example of a product/market matrix in a product responsibility unit (PRU).

Horizontal markets, on the other hand, consist of the different product and system applications the unit is developing for the different customer groups. As the figure shows, some of the systems can be used in several vertical markets, whereas one application (C) is only targeted to a specific market.

As the term indicates, the PRU or platform product management is in charge of the basic products and systems, such as Alcont in Honeywell and Damatic in Valmet. Because these product managers focus on products across different markets, concentrating on technical development aspects, there is also an evident need to manage them at the business level which involves, for example, traditional product-market decisions. In order to do this, case companies have established application product management systems which approach markets across the different products that the PRU develops and sells. The application product managers form a direct link to the field sales units and end customers by providing technical help and expertise, for example. The vertical marketing function forms the global dimension of the PRU's business.

Identification of the internal marketing domains

We will not describe the different marketing units and actors in each company in detail. Instead, we attempt to synthesize the common characteristics of the marketing organizations in the four case companies. These findings are summarized in Figures 4 and 5. Figure 4 portrays the three identified basic marketing domains, and the actors forming the internal marketing network. We have purposely used the term "domain," instead of "unit," to indicate that these do not necessarily represent any formal organizational units, but rather refer to an interconnected set of marketing activities, organizational groups, units, and persons. Figure 5 illustrates the interaction between the different marketing domains and their actors.

As Figure 4 shows, the sales and service domain of marketing comprises sales personnel, account managers, project managers, and customer service and maintenance personnel. Most of the case companies have also established project manager positions. These managers are responsible for carrying out customer projects after the sales personnel have negotiated a project contract. The sales and customer services in all the case companies are localized into market area-based units,

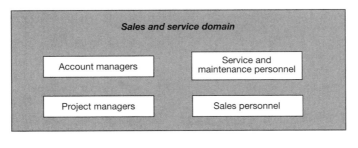

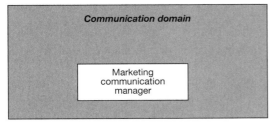
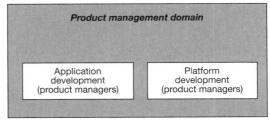

Figure 4 Marketing domains in an industrial high-technology context.

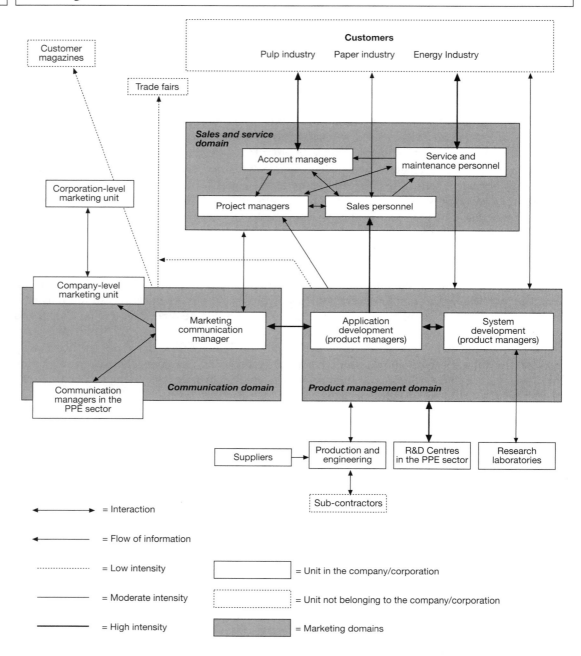

Figure 5 Interaction between marketing domains in the process control and automation industry.

which form extensive networks of sales and service subsidiaries or affiliates located in 30–50 countries throughout the world.

An interesting dualistic differentiation is taking place in the product management domain. Separate units are emerging to take responsibility for customer application development and basic technology or platform development, as we indicated earlier. Platform development is organized according to the different product groups. The main ones include distributed control systems (DCS), which comprise a basic process control system in which the functions are distributed to different stations which, in turn, are connected to each other through a bus interface (DCS offer complete process control tools); quality control systems (QCS offer tools for controlling specific parts of the process); and production management and information systems.

Application development consists of product lines that are based on the different customer segments such as pulp, paper, and energy (PPE), also called vertical markets. Efficient information exchange between these two product management groups is essential for effective product development. The application developers provide the customer point of view, whereas the platform developers are in charge of following the developments in basic technologies. It can be argued that combining these two capabilities is one of the basic requirements for successful high-tech product marketing.

Global corporations such as ABB, Honeywell, and Measurex have also established their own customer sector-related research centers. This centralization, although regarded as essential for product development, was also perceived by some of the interviewees to distance the development engineers from the customers. Many applications need cooperative development with specific pilot customers. Maintaining these direct customer contacts, in spite of the centralized "centers of excellence," may prove to be an essential issue in the future.

The marketing communication domain often comprised a small unit, the key person being the marketing communication manager. However, marketing communication seems to have been playing an increasingly strategic role because it has formed links from the business units up to the company, and even up to the corporation level of marketing. In the global context, the communication manager also interacted with the other communication managers representing the same business area (industry automation), but in charge of other market areas such as North America or Asia-Pacific.

Identification of internal marketing-based relationships

The complex matrix structures utilized in the case corporations created a need for effective coordination and information exchange between the different internal domains and their units and actors. Figure 5 gives a summary of our empirical results on the interaction between the three identified marketing domains and between the different units and actors in each domain.

All the actors in the sales and service domain – sales representatives, account managers, project managers, and service and maintenance personnel – have, naturally, intensive interaction with customers. The internal contacts between these persons were also of great importance. The need for domain-specific coordination is intensified by the project selling character of high-technology systems where correctly timed involvement of all the actors in the sales and service domain is needed. The key account manager positions, established fairly recently, are specifically targeted at establishing this coordination of customer contact.

The account manager system attempts to make the interaction as easy as possible for the customer. As one marketing manager suggested: "Account managers are, in a sense, customer representatives in the company." These positions were perceived to be even more important when the company had several products or product lines. Before the account management system, each product line had direct contacts with its customers, which had led to situations where several supplier representatives contacted a specific customer in an uncoordinated fashion.

The service personnel also play an important role in the sales and service domain. Besides carrying out their main service or system maintenance-related tasks, they are often in charge of providing feedback information concerning customer satisfaction, customer needs, and competitor action. In order to fully carry out this information activity, service personnel must have close contacts not only with the other actors in the sales and service domain (project and account managers and sales engineers), but also with the product management domain. It seems that the customer service and maintenance personnel are also taking a greater role in the pre-sales phase, keeping the other parts of the marketing organization informed about what is happening in the field, such as when customers are planning to buy a new paper machine or are rebuilding an old one.

The product management domain consists of two types of actors: system or platform product managers and application product managers. The distinction between these types was explained in the previous section. The application product managers reported intensive interaction with sales personnel and project managers. Persons from the application development side provide sales support and technical expertise to the sales subsidiaries throughout the world. These product managers are usually involved in different customer projects in order to bring in the specific technical expertise and know-how of customers' processes (e.g., paper or pulp production) to the project.

External supplier relationships were also found to be important in maintaining the developmental capability of the two product management units. Because of the way process control and automation business is set up, subcontractors and other suppliers carry out most of the hardware and component production. This dependence on external resources is also increasing in core areas such as systems programming, and even in traditional research and development activities. Close contacts with research laboratories and universities, and with information technology and systems suppliers, and a network of component suppliers, are crucial for the management of these developments.

Because the different marketing domains are managed quite independently in the case companies, coordination was needed in order to disseminate marketing-related information between the different product lines (or product responsibility units), the market areas, and between the three marketing domains. Interestingly, the marketing communication domain seems to have been given partial responsibility for this internal communication, to add to more traditional marketing communication tasks such as advertising, sales support material production, organizing seminars and trade fair participation, and managing general publicity. The major automation sector trade fairs are especially important, as new products or versions are often released through them. The communication manager cooperates with the product managers from the different PRUs on product release occasions. The establishment and maintenance of a corporate or a company-wide image for all the products and product line units was regarded as essential. This can be understood, because many case corporations had built up their process automation companies through acquisitions which had resulted in a number of different business cultures inside the company, and in some uncertainty about the lines of responsibility among the customer industries.

DISCUSSION

We have examined the organizational arrangements for carrying out marketing activities in high-technology companies. Our basic perception is of the complexity of the internal interfaces between and within the three marketing domains identified. The sales and service domain, the product management domain, and the communication domain together made about a dozen internal connections between various marketing units, in addition to their external interfaces. The solutions identified are more complex than the organizational structures previously reported in industrial companies. (Cespedes, 1990, 1994, 1995).

Another striking finding was the emerging enhanced role of marketing communications.

Organizational solutions for managing complexity

Marketing and its organization turned out to be a multi-faceted phenomenon in the high-tech companies we examined. We suggest that this is primarily related to the functional specialization driven by technological complexity, and to the necessity to be close to the customers in order to understand their application needs. The global character of the case industry also contributed to the organizational complexity; all the companies operated through customer sector and market area matrices.

As our findings show, functionally focused departments have vanished during the early 1990s. This has resulted in a numerous collection of marketing-oriented cross-functional teams and projects. Due to the rather temporary nature of these organizational arrangements, a large number of actors such as account managers, project managers, product managers, and marketing communication managers are involved in customer relationships. The organization of good communication between these actors, as well as the coordination of their activities, presented a major challenge to all the case firms.

The dismantling of marketing departments is also a result of adopting a process-based view of arranging tasks and activities, which makes a department-based line organization inefficient. Process organizations require more flexible and lean structures than the traditional ones. According to our results, this reorganization has resulted in the assignment of more responsibility and power down to the product lines and product managers. However, it needs to be borne in mind, that although the formal boundaries (i.e., departments) between the units have been removed, the basic business functions (such as marketing, R&D, and production) still exist in the companies as activity flows. However, the new organizations are better suited to supporting the diverse professionals needed in high-tech marketing than the traditional centralized marketing departments.

The marketing activities were mainly organized in three marketing domains, identified as sales and service, product management, and marketing communication. These domains comprise several sub-units employing personnel with specialized expertise and responsibilities.

Emergence and consequences of customer value orientation

Although we have emphasized the importance of coping with technological complexity and change, it became evident that technological competence no longer guarantees competitive advantage in the process automation sector because most suppliers can offer the latest technology. Suppliers are therefore starting to emphasize the value that the customer receives from process automation systems. This change in orientation is reflected in the relatively recent establishment of account manager positions. These managers are boundary spanners and they coordinate the interaction between the company and its customers. This emphasis on customer interface is also related to the finding that the role of service personnel is becoming stronger. Besides being responsible for post-project implementation activities such as maintenance, they are also involved in the pre-sales phase (consulting the sales personnel about customer needs) and in the implementation phase supporting the project managers.

Product management as core business competence

It can be argued that the product responsibility units (PRU) in the product management domain form the core of business competence in this high-tech branch because they take care of product management. One significant aspect is the emergence of the dualistic product development system comprising a basic platform development unit and an application development unit. This complicates the traditional product management organization, but it seems to be an important vehicle for keeping abreast of developments and utilizing the advancement of both basic and customer-sector technologies. Product management interacts intensively with sales and project personnel, thus providing customer-specific technical support.

Coordination of a customer relationship

Figure 6 portrays a supplier–customer relationship as a combination of the basic activity "groups" of project marketing: sales, implementation, and maintenance. This simplistic framework illustrates the boundary-spanning role of both the account managers and the project managers. In the case of

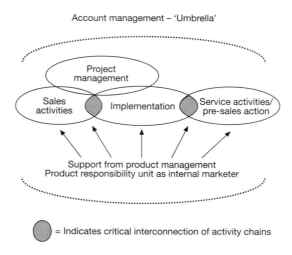

Figure 6 Supplier's activity chain in a high-technology supplier–customer relationship.

developing a new customer relationship, sales supported by product management, initiates the negotiations. If a contract is achieved, a project manager takes over the responsibility of coordinating the actors needed in installing and starting up the product or system. This involves technical personnel, the customer's personnel who need to be trained, and often also information systems personnel. The service and maintenance personnel take over the post-implementation relationship. If the customer is important enough, an account manager is nominated who is in charge of both mediating customer needs concerning the present system and other product lines of the supplier.

The account manager is expected to act as the key integrator of the supplier's and the customer's personnel. The supplier's performance, as perceived by the customer, is very much dependent on the smooth management of the interconnections in the activity chain – presuming obviously that the individual activities can be managed competently.

New product generations: product responsibility units as internal marketers

The above comments focused on managing an individual customer relationship. On a more aggregate level, and on a longer-term basis, the issue of bringing technology (new product generations or new designs) to the market is crucial. This requires collaboration between systems and application development, account and project managers, and marketing communications. A specific feature in our international case companies was that the PRUs have first to sell their products to the corporation's international sales organization, and later to offer support. Sales organizations, and especially account managers, act as gatekeepers, and PRUs are competing for their interest and time in introducing their products to the customers. This means that PRUs need internal marketing skills in their relations to the sales organizations. In a more abstract sense, all internal marketing units and actors can be shown to have internal customers. It seems that internal marketing (Piercy and Morgan, 1991) will play an increasingly important part in implementing the marketing concept in high-technology companies.

Can marketing communications coordinate the marketing organization?

We have repeatedly emphasized the need for internal coordination and integration among marketing actors. This demands efficient support systems and internal communications for orchestrating marketing-related activities. In the case companies, marketing communication was, quite unexpectedly, given the task of interacting with and coordinating the different marketing units. It plays an internal boundary-spanner role. The problems the case companies reported in coordinating marketing activities between different product lines (or product responsibility units), between customer sectors, between account and project managers, and between project managers and product application managers, gave us serious doubts about the capability of current marketing communication units to master the demanding coordination task. The communication units did not have enough resources or competence, nor were they given adequate decision-making authority.

GENERAL THEORETICAL AND MANAGERIAL CONCLUSIONS

What conclusions can be drawn on a general level? We argue that current research into business relationships and networks has overlooked the importance of the organizational arrangement of marketing activities. Our findings support the argument that, in a high-technology context, the competent management of the internal marketing network is a prerequisite for the successful management of the portfolio of customer relationships. Obviously this proposal has to be validated with future studies in other high-tech industries. In order to derive a deeper understanding of effective organizational arrangements, we suggest that the marketing and organizational perspectives should be combined with the resource and capability-based theory of the firm (Day, 1994; Grant, 1995; Barney, 1997). The capability view is relevant for analyzing the interrelatedness of the specialized skills and competencies needed in the successful linking of internal marketing domains with customer organizations. Another recommendation is to go more deeply into customers' organizational arrangements, although this would make the research setting very complex.

From a managerial perspective, our findings indicate that, by dispensing with their marketing departments, companies have created highly specialized and flexible, and as such necessary and successful, marketing sub-units. The number of these units and their decentralized character puts great pressure on inter-unit coordination and communication. Paradoxically, this has created a need for new centralized coordination systems. Established marketing communication units do not have the capability, resources, or authority to meet this challenge properly. We contend that new marketing centers, comprising representatives from all the relevant units, should be formed. These centers should have responsibility for interfunctional coordination and the integration of the diversified marketing units. There are signs that this kind of "marketing excellence center" seems to be emerging.

Another important aspect, which needs further examination, is the impact of the managing part of marketing and sales activities through external relationships. Typically, manufacturing and logistics-related functions have been outsourced in this manner but there are also signs that certain key marketing and R&D activities are carried out by outside vendors, especially in small and medium-sized companies. This development involves organizational challenges, such as how to integrate outside vendors under the companies' account management umbrella and how to ensure the total quality of the offered products, systems, and customer service.

As the external outsourcing of marketing activities was not explicitly addressed in the current study, only a few, speculative, comments are offered. Employing an external sales force is obviously a potential solution, especially for small and medium-sized companies with a limited product range. In high-tech fields this involves a tricky incentive problem. How can the firm get an external sales network committed to its products and customers with an affordable compensation? One solution is to develop partnerships with equally small companies devoted to the specific high-tech area in question, and assign them the direct responsibility of managing the customer relationships in their geographical area. Following a kind of modified franchising format these value-added distributor partners would be supported by a centralized product excellence center. They would also need to feed essential customer knowledge back to the product development centers. Another important theme concerns the involvement of extra-organizational members in cross-functional teams of a marketing firm. Besides the commitment problem, this issue involves the question of sharing vital company and customer information with these new team members. Because of this, a partnership type of relationship seems again like a viable solution. The external marketing/sales partners have to be committed to the parent company and its customers, which means that they are not able to serve competing companies. The limited availability of this kind of specialized sales and customer service organizations in high-tech fields restrains the pace of outsourcing marketing and sales activities.

The above comments are very simplistic. With the increasing trend of outsourcing activities we need more research in order to identify efficient organizational solutions for the high-tech companies of the new millennium.

NOTE

1. Honeywell and Measurex merged in 1997 and the new company is called Honeywell-Measurex.

REFERENCES

Achrol, R. S.: Evolution of the Marketing Organization: New Forms for Turbulent Environments. *Journal of Marketing* **55(4)**, 77–93 (1991).

Barney, J. B.: *Gaining and Sustaining Competitive Advantage.* Addison Wesley Publishing Company, Reading, MA, 1997.

Capon, N., and Glazer, R.: Marketing and Technology: A Strategic Coalignment. *Journal of Marketing* **51(3)**, 1–14 (1987).

Cespedes, F. V.: Agendas, Incubators, and Marketing Organization. *California Management Review* **33(1)**, 27–53 (1990).

Cespedes, F. V.: Industrial Marketing: Managing New Requirements. *Sloan Management Review* **35(3)**, 45–60 (1994).

Cespedes, F. V.: *Concurrent Marketing: Integrating Product, Sales and Service.* Harvard Business School Press, Boston, MA, 1995.

Cravens, D. W., Piercy, N. F.. and Shipp, S. H.: New Organizational Forms for Competing in Highly Dynamic Environments: The Network Paradigm. *British Journal of Management* **7(3)**, 203–218 (1996).

Cunningham, M. T., and Homse, E.: Controlling the Marketing-Purchasing Interface: Resource Development and Organizational Implications, *Industrial Marketing and Purchasing* **1(2)**, 3–25 (1986).

Day, G. S.: The Capabilities of Market-Driven Organizations. *Journal of Marketing* **58(4)**, 37–52 (1994).

Fadum, O.: *Millwide Information and Process Control Systems in the Pulp and Paper Industry: A Worldwide Technology Assessment and Market Report.* Fadum Enterprises, Boulder, CO, 1992.

Ford, D. ed.: *Understanding Business Markets: Interaction, Relationships, Networks.* Academic Press, Inc., San Diego, CA, 1990.

Ford, D., Gadde, L-E., Håkansson, H., Lundgren, A., Snenota, I., Turnbull, P., and Wilson, D.: *Managing Business Relationships.* John Wiley & Sons, Chichester, UK, 1998.

Grant, R. M.: *Contemporary Strategy Analysis: Concepts, Techniques, Applications, 2nd Edition,* Blackwell Publishers, Cambridge, MA, 1995.

Håkansson, H.: *Industrial Technological Development. A Network Approach.* Croom Helm, London, 1987.

Håkansson, H.: *Corporate Technological Behavior: Co-operation and Networks.* Routledge, London, 1989.

Håkansson, H., and Snehota, I., eds.: *Developing Relationships in Business Networks.* Routledge, New York, 1995.

Hedlund, G.: A Model of Knowledge Management and the N-Form Corporation. *Strategic Management Journal* **15(special issue, Summer)**, 73–90 (1994).

Hutt, M. D., and Speh, T. W.: The Marketing Strategy Center: Diagnosing the Industrial Marketer's Interdisciplinary Role. *Journal of Marketing* **48(4)**, 53–61 (1984).

Iacobucci, D., ed.: *Networks in Marketing.* Sage Publications, Inc., Thousand Oaks, CA, 1996.

Lysonski, S.: A Boundary Theory Investigation of the Product Manager's Role. *Journal of Marketing* **49(1)**, 26–40 (1985).

Miles, M. B., and Huberman, A. M.: *Qualitative Data Analysis, 2nd Edition.* Sage Publications, Inc., Thousand Oaks, CA, 1994.

Möller, K., and Wilson, D.: Die Interakstionsperspektive im Investtitionsguler-Marketing: Ein explorativer Bezugsrahmen', in *Netzwerkansatze im Business-to-Business Marketing*, M. Kleinaltenkampand and K. Schubert eds., Gabler, Wiesbaden, 1994, pp. 51–92.

Möller, K., and Wilson, D., eds.: *Business Marketing: An Interaction and Network Perspective*. Kluwer Academic Publishers, Boston, MA, 1995.

Moriarty, R. T., and Kosnik, Th. J.: High-Tech Marketing: Concepts, Continuity, and Change. *Sloan Management Review* **30(4)**, 7–17 (1989).

Nonaka, I., and Taceuchi, H.: *The Knowledge-creating Company: How Japanese Companies Create the Dynamics of Innovation*. Oxford University Press, New York, 1995.

Pardo, C., Salle, R., and Spencer, R.: The Key Accountization of the Firm: A Case Study. *Industrial Marketing Management* **22(2)**, 123–134 (1995).

Piercy, N.: *Marketing Organization: An Analysis of Information Processing, Power and Politics*. George Allen & Unwin, London, 1985.

Piercy, N. F., and Cravens, D. W.: The Network Paradigm and the Marketing Organization: Developing a New Management Agenda. *European Journal of Marketing* **29(3)**, 7–34 (1995).

Piercy, N., and Morgan, N.: Internal Marketing: The Missing Half of the Marketing Programme. *Long Range Planning* **24(2)**, 82–93 (1991).

Snow, C. C.: Managing 21st Century Network Organizations. *Organizational Dynamics* **20(3)**, 5–20 (1992).

Special Issue on Relationship Marketing, *International Marketing Management*, **26(2)**, 82–222 (1997).

Weitz, B., and Anderson, E.: Organizing and Controlling the Marketing Function, in *Review of Marketing*, B. M. Enis and K. J. Roering, eds., American Marketing Association, Chicago, IL, 1981, pp 134–142.

Workman, J. P. Jr., Homburg. Ch.. and Gruner, K.: Marketing Organization: An Integrative Framework of Dimensions and Determinants. *Journal of Marketing* **62(3)**, 21–41 (1998).

Yin. R.: *Case Study Research: Design and Methods, 2nd Edition*. Sage Publications, Inc., Beverly Hills, CA, 1994.

4.5 Managing business relationships by analyzing the effects and value of different actions

David Ford and Raymond McDowell

INTRODUCTION

Many of a company's customer or supplier relationships are vital for its continuing competitive survival, and each may involve a substantial commitment of resources that cannot be easily used elsewhere. A company's decisions on what actions to take in each relationship are of great importance to the development of its overall portfolio of relationships and its competitive success.

This article considers how companies make sense of the possible effects of their own and other companies' actions and how they value what happens in their relationships. To do this, we first need to explore the complexities and difficulties that arise when we think about value in business relationships. We also need to develop a structure to examine the multiple effects of a company's actions in a relationship. Managers are unlikely to be able to foresee all of the effects of their actions, and they may not intend some of them to happen. This article examines how managers behave in a relationship when seeking to achieve specific effects and how they describe the value of these effects. This provides insights for those trying to understand business relationships and for managers who need to examine both their own plans and those of the companies with which they deal.

The article examines several real relationship cases, and we map out the outcomes that managers seek; the effects that they expect to occur through their actions, and how they value those effects.

VALUE IN BUSINESS RELATIONSHIPS

It is important to be clear about what we mean when we use the term value in business relationships, since there are a variety of ways in which it can be used:

It is possible to consider the value-in-use of the product offering that is exchanged (Wind, 1990). This is a customer's assessment of value and will be related to the perceived value of alternative offerings. It is the "economic value to the customer" (Forbis and Mehta, 1981). However, this use of the value concept is restricted to narrowly defined product related variables that may not be of major importance in the context of many relationships.

The narrowness of this view was recognized by Wilson and Jantrania (1994). They present a view of relationships between companies involving economic, behavioral, and strategic elements and argue that the value of a relationship is an aggregation of these elements. Their analysis does not provide for the detailed assessment of this value except in the narrow terms of product usage.

They conclude that, "Value is a problematic concept" (p. 63) and that the ". . . perception of value even in a relatively straight forward economic example illustrates the difficulty in estimating value in a more complex relationship" (p. 63).

Krapfel et al. (1991) provide a definition of relationship value that embodies the factors from which dependence upon a trading partner flows. These are criticality and quantity of the goods exchanged, replaceability of the counterpart, and the cost savings resulting from the practices and procedures of the counterpart. But the authors admit that little is known of the relative importance of these factors and it is for this reason that this article focuses on the value that companies attach to outcomes in specific relationship situations so as to get a view of the factors that are most important to them.

It is important for a manager to distinguish between the value to him of a relationship as a whole and his views of the value of specific outcomes in that relationship. But the value of a relationship as a whole is inherently difficult to gauge in precise terms because it is a composite concept and is "perceptual in nature" (p. 5) (Anderson et al., 1993). This complexity is made worse because a participant's perception of the value of a relationship owes much to the "personal values" or belief system of the person making the valuation (see below). Also, perceptions of overall value of a relationship owe much to the specific outcomes that the individual anticipates in the relationship.

For the manager, all relationships are valuable in that they generate sales or product/service supplies, but some are more valuable than others. It is common to find that a relatively small number of counterparts account for a large proportion of sales or purchases. But financial dependence alone may not mean that the company values a relationship more highly than others. Relationships of low financial significance may be highly valued for their knowledge transfer, reputational, or network-access characteristics. The important consideration for companies is to know what elements of a relationship confer its value and the extent of that value.

Personal values in a relationship

Value expressions say as much about the personal values of the individual making the expressions as they do about the object of their valuation. At their most general, personal values concern an individual's feelings about his role in society. In a relationship they show up in the views and behaviour of the individual. For example, in our research in a ladies' fashion retailer, buyers' beliefs about their role were expressed largely in terms of fashion. They were overwhelmingly concerned in their work with demonstrating their "handwriting" or their fashion statement, both as individuals and as part of that of the store. This handwriting and the supplier relationships with which it was associated was transferred with them when they changed jobs between different fashion retailers. The primacy of fashion meant that buyers often took decisions in their relationships that meant that they had to accept inadequate product quality and delivery scheduling that would have been unthinkable in most manufacturing companies. Because of the primacy of fashion in their self-image, the buyers had little commitment to their suppliers. If a supplier failed, either because a design sold badly or there were quality or delivery problems, then buyers would be more likely to drop them rather than work together to make improvements.

In contrast, many of the buyers in the auto industry that we interviewed saw their primary role as providers of relatively standardized material to ensure continuity of production. The effects they sought in their relationship decision making were expressed in terms of production reliability and consistency. This contrasted with project buyers in the aerospace industry whose belief systems centered on their role in developing and integrating the various technologies of their suppliers.

Valuing the effect of relationship actions

Relationship actions have effects, some of which are intended and foreseen and others that are neither foreseen, nor intended. Some of these effects may be valued positively by the participants

Table 1 Relationship effects and nature of value to the participants

	Level 1	Level 2	Level 3	Level 4
Level of effect	In the relationship	On the relationship	On the relationship portfolio	Within the network
Nature of value	Immediate	Value in terms of change to the state of the relationship	Value in terms of change in the total relationship portfolio	Value in terms of change in the network

and others valued negatively. A manager's view of the current state of the relationship and his experience of previous interactions both in the relationship and elsewhere will influence his predictions of the likely effects of different relationship actions, the responses to them of others in the relationship or the wider network and his valuation of those effects. We can usefully structure these effects by examining them on four levels (Ford et al., 1996). These four levels of effect are illustrated in Table 1 from the perspective of a single participant.

Level 1: Effects in the relationship

Any action by a relationship participant will have a number of direct effects in that relationship. For example, a decision by a customer to source a particular component from only a single supplier will reduce the number of orders it places and reduce the workload of its purchasing staff. It may also reduce the need for inward inspection and simplify the company's assembly processes and hence reduce its costs. Buying more units from a preferred supplier may produce changes in the supplier's organization. These effects in the relationship are likely to be apparent relatively quickly and are easily identified and attributable to the company's decision.

The perceived value to the participants of these effects relate to the transactions that will unfold as a consequence of the decision. For example, it may be that the customer's main motivation in the single-sourcing decision was to streamline its production, and so if this effect occurs then it will be valued highly. Conversely, the effect of reducing the workload on its buyers may not be valued as it may not be able to dispense with any of them. The preferred supplier that has also been subject to the effects of the decision may value the reduced logistics costs of supplying a larger volume to a single customer but may not value the higher levels of contacts, questions, and checking that immediately ensue.

Level 2: Effects on the relationship

The initial decision to sole-source a product will also have effects on the relationship between the companies and the value of that relationship. These effects may be less easily identifiable at the time of the initial decision than its LEVEL 1 effects. For example, the decision to sole-source may have the direct effect of increasing the mutual dependence of the two companies and paradoxically, this increased dependence may reduce the trust that previously existed. The initial decision may also lead less directly to an increase in the resources required in one or other of them. For example, the supplier company's increased attention to this important relationship may lead it to change its production methods and so to enhance its process technology resources. The trade-off between effects in a relationship and effects on that relationship is a classic issue in buyer–seller relationships. A supplier may have the opportunity to achieve a short-term gain by increasing price to a customer in a time of product shortage. However, it may well decide to forego the positive effects of the price increase in the relationship because of its concerns about the possible negative effects on the relationship of a lessening of trust between the companies.

Of course, many situations are less straightforward than that of a simple price decision. For example, a company may seek to achieve more subtle changes to a relationship over time by a series of decisions over relatively detailed issues. It may be concerned that a long-term supplier is taking it for granted, and so it will seek to make the relationship less "close" by being less predictable in both its ordering pattern and its more personal interactions (Ford et al., 1986). More generally, a company may take a decision narrowly to achieve an effect in a relationship and may be oblivious to, or uncaring about any longer term effects of that decision on the relationship. Alternatively, it may take a decision on the basis of some explicit or implicit view of the current state of a relationship and of the state it would like to achieve at some stage in the future. Thus, it may seek to achieve a LEVEL 2 effect that changes the state of that relationship.

Level 3: Effects on a portfolio

As well as a decision having a future effect on a relationship, it may also have effects on other relationships in the company's portfolio. Just as in the case of LEVEL 2 effects, these wider effects can be both direct and indirect, conscious and unconscious. For example, when a customer engages in a single-sourcing deal for a particular product with a supplier, this will have the direct and conscious effect that it will not buy that product from other suppliers in its portfolio. The decision may also have the indirect effect that other suppliers of other products to that customer believe that this is part of a more general policy. Sending this "message" could have been the conscious intent of the original decision with one supplier. Some of these other suppliers may seek similar sole-supply arrangements, while others may believe that they are unlikely to be considered as single suppliers and so will reduce their commitment to this customer.

Level 4: Effects on a network

A decision within a relationship may also have effects on the wider network. Some of these effects may take a considerable time to become apparent. For example, if a supplier takes the decision to develop a new technology for application in a particular relationship, this may subsequently become the standard throughout the network. Such standardization could generate positive value to the initiator in terms of royalty revenue or may indeed be a prerequisite for the success of its own products in a market. Similarly, a decision by a major customer to buy a large supplier could be emulated by others in the industry and hence radically alter the pattern of supply and competitive activity within a network. Other network effects are more immediate, such as when a relationship decision by one party can affect the other parties' relationships with companies elsewhere in the network. For example, in UK retail circles, when a company becomes a supplier to Marks & Spencer, it is tacitly accepted that the supplier's customer portfolio will revolve around this single customer relationship. This is likely to lead to a major change in that supplier's relations with its own suppliers and with other customers elsewhere in the network.

We do not suggest that participant managers do take all of the potential levels of effects into account in all their decision making, although it would often help if they did. Rather, we see the "LEVELS of EFFECTS" as a device to enable both managers and researchers to better understand the effects of relationship actions. A strong indication of the value of a specific relationship to a company and how it fits in the company's overall portfolio is given by the effects that they seek to achieve in it, the outcomes that they predict from different actions and the value that they place on those outcomes.

EXPLORING VALUE IN REAL RELATIONSHIP CASES

Perhaps the simplest way of finding out why managers behave as they do in relationships is simply to ask them. However, this approach would be based on three assumptions. First, it assumes they think about what they do. But this is unlikely always to be the case. Many decisions within relationships seem to be taken on the basis of habit (Robinson et al., 1967; Cunningham and White, 1973). Second, it assumes that they do what they say. But there are many occasions when action does not precisely follow intention and where circumstances deflect action. For example, inadequate skills or resources may prevent achievement of an intention. Equally, there are occasions in relationships when a manager will say one thing and do the opposite, or where different managers in the same company will behave inconsistently with each other or over time (Ford et al., 1986). Finally, it assumes that they are free to act. But there are a variety of elements that constrain an organization's freedom of action. Resource dependence (Pfeffer and Salancik, 1978) imposes a direct constraint upon a firm and its network embeddedness (Håkansson and Snehota, 1995) means that the actions of other organizations in the network impact upon a company. At the personal level, resource dependencies between departments within the firm means that relationship participants' freedom to act is limited (Ford and McDowell, 1998).

Nevertheless, managers do act and they do take decisions in relationships, and we can gain an understanding of how they value the outcomes of their actions by recording their beliefs, attitudes, and expectations and by observing what they actually do. The complexity of business-to-business relationships and the depth of understanding required meant that a case-study approach was used in the research. Interviews were conducted first with senior managers in the case companies. These provided an introduction to the operations of the company and its history, markets, and competitive/network position. The senior managers also nominated one or more supplier or customer relationships that they considered important to their company. In most cases the choice was based on the proportion of sales or purchases that each represented. Other factors were the lack of available alternatives to a counterpart, the importance of relationship-specific investments, or the difficulty of justifying to superiors if an important sales or supplier relationship had been lost.

Interviews with nominated participants covered a range of topics:

(a) "The current state of the focal relationship" (Ford et al., 1998). This required examination of its history and development pattern, the volume of trade, its importance to the parties, the transaction process, along with any adaptations by either company, the contact pattern between them, and the width (complexity), depth (extent of mutuality), and closeness (understanding of each other) of the relationship (Ford, 1989). The state of the relationship was further analyzed by reference to the counterpart company, from which at least one individual was interviewed.

(b) "The core beliefs of the individual (and the company)" was the next area in which questions revolved around how the individual defines himself and how the company sees itself, the role that he sees for himself in the relationship with the counterpart company and the company's approach to relationships in general, along with the direction in which the individual sees the company going and how it sees the network of companies surrounding it.

(c) "The effects of one or more recent relationship actions and the value that the individual attaches to them" were analyzed using the four-level approach discussed above.

DISCUSSION

Because of considerations of space, only four of the cases in the study are reported here. The first two cases deal with a single focal company's relationships with its suppliers. The second two deal with a single focal company's relationships with its customers. This enables comparisons and contrasts to be made between how the focal companies behave in one relationship compared to another. The cases are described in Table 2.

Focal company 1: UK National Feeds and its raw materials suppliers

The focal company in case A and case B is a buyer of traded commodity goods, food ingredients, such as grains and meals, which are important constituents of its own products that are themselves bound for the UK domestic market. For this focal company we will be examining its relationships with two suppliers.

Table 2 Profile of two focal companies and four relationship cases

	Focal company 1	Focal company 2
Size and scale	Large, national	Large, national subsidiary of large global
Type	Food producer	Materials manufacturer, construction industry
Role	Customer	Supplier
Industry information:		
Industry maturity	Very mature	Very mature
Industry concentration	High concentration	High concentration
Market trends	Slowly declining market	Slowly growing market

	Case A	Case B	Case C	Case D
Counterpart:				
Size and scale	Large, global	Small, European	Small, regional	Medium, National
Type	Food commodities grower, shipper and trader	Food commodities shipper and trader	Building components manufacturer	Building components manufacturer
Role	Supplier	Supplier	Customer	Customer
Relationship information:				
Relationship age	Long established	Long established	< 10 years old	Long established
Relationship trend	Growing sales	Growing sales	Growing sales	Growing sales
Cost of switching	Low	Low	Low	Low
Ease of switching	Low	Low	Low	Low
Number of alternatives	Very few	Very few	Several	Several
Exchange arrangments	Parallel sources	Parallel sources	Preferred source	Single source

Core beliefs of those in focal company 1

The views about themselves were different between a manager at the company's headquarters and one at the business unit level. The headquarters respondent sees himself as a part of a team rethinking relationships with the few major available suppliers and developing alliances to ensure high-volume, low-cost throughput for its plants. He sees himself as being above operational concerns. The headquarters manager takes a national market-oriented view. He sees himself as the major player in the country in an industry that has consolidated heavily and is in long-term decline. He is concerned to retain share at a particularly difficult time for the group.

The business unit respondent sees himself as someone who should be kept informed by suppliers. He believes that the company's network position gives him the right to know what his counterpart is thinking. He is not concerned with the increasing closeness of the headquarters-supplier relationship but is more concerned with short-run service, efficiency, and pricing questions. He expects to be "treasured" by suppliers who should do what he wants them to do.

Company's role in its relationships

The headquarters manager sees his role as a smoothing activity, raising customer issues while at the same time believing that the company's future lies in its relationships with the major suppliers (in cases A and B, below), thus he does not want to harm these relationships for short-term gain. This contrasts with the business unit manager whose concerns are to achieve immediate efficiency improvements in his operations without compromising plant throughput rates or quality. His approach is to use any source that will give it the best deal at any particular time.

Company's network view

The company's view of the surrounding network is expressed almost exclusively in terms of the current trading difficulties that it is experiencing. A major public health concern, the BSE crisis, meant that the most profitable sector of its market dried up within a few days. It is undergoing a period of introspection and self-analysis rather than trying to look outwardly.

Value of outcomes in relationships for focal company 1: Case A

The counterpart company in this case is a global provider of the commodity goods required by the focal buyer. The supplier's operations are integrated from the farm, through storage and transport to the sale of finished products to end users. It is thus both a supplier and a competitor to the focal company. The focal company is a small customer for the seller overall and accounts for only about 1% of its world sales but is a major account in the UK. The seller accounts for about 50% of the buyer's need for the goods. There is no product or process adaptation by either party, and the relationship is low width, low depth, and low closeness.

The relationship action. The seller is considering withdrawing from direct sales to final customers, which is an area in which it is less successful and in which it directly competes with the focal company, to a position where it uses the focal company as its sole channel to the end market. The seller would then concentrate on its upstream activities, in which its main skills lie. In return for this move, the seller would expect the focal company to rationalize its buying operations by reducing the number of contact points and increasing the role of central purchasing.

Level of effects

Level 1: Effects in the relationship

Expected effects: The focal company expects the seller's action to lead directly to increased market share for it as it becomes the seller's preferred channel to market. The seller expects to improve its cost basis as a result of the action.

Perceived value of effects: There is obvious financial value of the action to the focal company. But the company's headquarters sees the greatest value of the action to be on the relationship itself (level 2). In contrast, the seller seems to value the effects at this level more than any other and seeks to reduce further its cost-to-serve by the focal company concentrating its buying and operations.

Level 2: Effects on the relationship

The expected effects are that the action will have the effect of increasing the interdependence between the companies and would be seen by the focal company as evidence of a strong commitment by the seller to a closer long-term relationship. The buyer is likely to increase its purchasing centralization as a way of showing its commitment.

The perceived value of effects is that it is at this level that the focal company anticipates the greatest effects of the seller's action, and it is these effects that appear to be valued most. The seller seems less concerned with the effects of its actions on the relationship itself, though it would not wish to damage the relationship to attain short-term cost advantages. Instead, it aims to achieve cost advantages in the relationship in the longer term.

Level 3: Effects on the relationship portfolio

The expected effects are that the seller's action will extend the focal company's customer portfolio and correspondingly reduce that of the supplier. The focal company has no intentions to reduce its supplier portfolio by, for example, using the seller company as a single source. It has been concerned with explaining to its other suppliers the extent and limitations of its relationship with the seller.

The perceived value of effects is that the focal company is clearly happy with the prospect of an enlarged customer base and foresees no problems with assimilating new customers into its existing sales structure or meeting their requirements. It has reservations about the effects of the action upon its other suppliers but sees these concerns as something to be coped with after the fact, rather than precluding the action from taking place.

Level 4: Effects within the network

The expected effects are that the focal company has strong concerns about the current network of relationships in this industry. Two major suppliers account for more than 60% of its input raw materials, and the company is one of three large players of similar size that account for 60% of their market. The focal company sees the network as heavily constrained, with little scope for large-scale action by any of the three large players. It feels that any attempts to increase market share would invariably lead to counter competitive action by the others and could have antitrust implications. The focal company does not believe that the seller's action will be seen as large scale enough to cause such effects in the network.

The perceived value of effects is that the focal company sees the main value of the relationship effects to be at level two and seems prepared to cope with any other effects at other levels, including network effects.

Case B

The counterpart company in this case is a European subsidiary of a global U.S. company that originates traded commodity goods. The subsidiary's principal business is shipping, buying the goods from its parent, and selling in Europe. Unlike the seller in CASE A, this company does not compete at all with the focal company. The focal company is a major UK account for this seller and comes closest to what it regards as a "preferred customer". The seller accounts for about 50% of the focal company's requirements for the traded goods, which are important constituents of its own products. There is no product adaptation by the seller, but it frequently provides a level of advice that it does not extend to other customers. This advice has even extended to recommendations that the focal company should not buy from it on occasions when the seller believes that it cannot offer a competitive price at that time, in what is a very volatile market. The seller has also adapted its logistics to suit the focal company and this has led to increased purchases. Despite the approach of the focal company business unit manager appearing to be unrealistic when the company is heavily dependent on a seller, this seller seems willing to tolerate that approach while working to build the relationship with a preferred customer. Despite these efforts, the relationship can be described as low width, but with medium levels of depth and closeness (Ford, 1989).

The relationship action. The relationship between seller and the focal company has come under a threat recently from the parent company of the seller, which has started to trade a commodity item from the parent directly to end users, bypassing the seller. This focal company has bought small amounts of the product from the seller's parent, something of which the seller is aware. We examine the actions of the buyer in this situation where it is faced with an alternative supplier to the seller and where it appears to be happy to buy.

Level of effects

Level 1: Effects in the relationship

Expected effects: Having an extra supplier means that the focal company is more able to switch between suppliers to achieve lower prices for this product. This has slightly reduced the volumes that it buys from the seller.

The perceived value of effects is that the business unit manager in the focal company takes a short-term view of relationships and particularly values the benefit of lower prices at the expense of a longer-term view of the value of the relationship with the seller.

Level 2: Effects on the relationship

The expected effects are that the focal company has anticipated that its action would be seen as showing less commitment to the relationship with the seller.

The perceived value of effects is that the manager at the focal company's business unit believes that it has a "good" relationship with the seller. It feels comfortable with the seller, likes the way of working that has developed between them, and it appears to trust the seller. This comfortable view of the relationship is shared by the seller. The business unit manager recognizes that switching to the seller's parent shows a lack of commitment to the existing relationship but is prepared to cope with any negative consequences of the switch, believing that these will not be great. He is sure that because of the interdependence between them the seller will not stop supplying and that punitive future pricing is unlikely. He justifies its lack of loyalty in the short term by saying that he is confused by the two faces of the company in the marketplace, that the problem is of the seller's own making and that he can't possibly know how to behave until the confusion is resolved.

Level 3: Effects on the relationship portfolio

The expected effects are that the focal company doesn't believe that this action will have any real effects upon its portfolio of relationships. It is regarded as a little local difficulty with no repercussions elsewhere. The company claims not to feel as comfortable working with the supplier's parent company as it does with the supplier itself. It sees its current purchases as transient and not likely to be of sufficient volume to have a portfolio effect.

The perceived value of effects is that the focal company sees no outcomes at this level so there is no value (positive or negative) to perceive.

Level 4: Effects within the network

The expected effects are that the focal company does not consider there to be any effects of this action at a broader network level. The perceived value of effects is none.

Discussion of the relationship evaluations of focal company 1

These cases illustrate inconsistency in approach to relationships between headquarters and operating companies and between different relationships. The focal company considers the suppliers in cases A and B to be parallel, but despite its overall approach to its relationships it behaves differently towards them. The focal company sees its future in terms of close relationships with major suppliers, and its headquarters, in contrast to the business unit, is seeking to build such a relationship with seller A. In contrast, it is prepared to act against seller B by going over its head. In doing this it is counting on the interdependence between it and the company, seller B's feelings towards it and the unlikelihood of immediate negative consequences. It does not seem concerned that the relationship with seller B might suffer.

The inconsistency between headquarters and operating company is a common problem in the development of purchasing strategy and is a major concern for marketing management in trying to build a relationship strategy. In these cases, the approach of all of the companies also appears to be affected by its view of the network position of the different suppliers when compared with itself. The focal company can be described as a big fish in a national pond, seller B as a small fish in a slightly larger pond, compared with seller A, which is a very large fish in a global pond. Seller A is very critical of the focal company's approach based on its experience elsewhere in the network. In contrast, seller B is much more positive in its approach, based on its own narrow network perspective. Finally, the cases illustrate the important difference between the development of a relationship strategy and its implementation. The focal company's strategy is to develop close relationships with important suppliers, but once the basis to that closeness is forged, it doesn't appear to believe that it has to work to maintain them. By operating in the belief that suppliers can be easily replaced, it is discounting the cost of developing a relationship and the value of that relationship.

Focal company 2: UK national building product and its regional customers

The focal company in case C and case D is a UK national subsidiary of a global manufacturer and provider of a basic building product with sales of over 400M pounds. The company employs 36,000 people, over 4,000 of whom are located in the UK. The cases will describe the focal company's relationships with its customers.

Core beliefs of those in focal company 2

The focal company's staff see themselves as facilitators, matching buying company's needs with what the seller can provide, while at the same time ensuring that the seller's new products are pushed, and the seller's downstream businesses are used to add value to sales within the network. For this reason, the focal company's staff believe that it is imperative that they know as much about the buying company's customers as the buyer itself.

The focal company sees itself as a leader in the industry. It has a massive share of UK market, and it is responsible for almost all of the R&D investment and technological advances. It has always been seen as an innovator and takes a strong view about the future of the industry as a whole and sees its competitors as followers. The production costs of the company's main products are very volume sensitive and this imposes sales pressures to shift products, "whatever it takes."

Company's role in its relationships

The seller sees its role as marshalling or helping its smaller customers to make better use of its product so that everyone in the chain can add value and get "a piece of the action." Current company policy reinforces this: it wants to see more value-adding customers, wants to spend more time working with them, and wants to differentiate a product that is essentially a commodity. At the same time, the company wants to make good use of its own downstream businesses, by competing with its independent customers on the one hand and channeling product to them via its downstream businesses on the other.

Company's network view

The seller does not appear to have a clear view of the industry in network terms. It worries about the industry, but its worries translate into considerations about itself. In its field of view it only sees "itself" and "the rest," and its concern is to maintain share in a mature industry, particularly in the face of foreign competition. Many of its relationship actions seem to be reactions to the actions of competitors. For example, it acquired a number of its own customers to prevent a competitor from increasing its tied customer base. Much of its strategy since then seems to have been driven by that defensive acquisition, at the expense of its relationships with its customers.

Despite this, the focal company acknowledges that without a value-adding customer base it would have to compete head-on with competitors who have a lower cost base. This drives its search for product differentiation by using new added-value products and for service differentiation, which cannot be replicated by its competitors.

Value of outcomes in relationships for focal company 2: Case C

The counterpart company in this relationship is a small regional customer (100 staff, sales volume 5M pounds). This customer accounts for a very small proportion of the seller's national sales but is a major account in its own geographic region. The seller provides 75% of the customer's needs for the product, which is effectively a commodity item. Consequently, there is no product adaptation. However, the seller has adapted payment terms for the customer and provides it with specific market information. The relationship can be characterized as having slow width, medium depth, and high closeness (at least, until the relationship action of the seller described below).

The relationship actions. Two separate actions are currently important in this relationship – one taken by the seller and one by the customer. Examination of these will provide insights into how each values its relationship with the other.

Action 1: Seller's redefinition of its sales/marketing regions. The seller has increased the number of its marketing regions from four to six. This is intended to reduce the number of accounts per region and so enable sales/marketing personnel to spend more time working on key regional accounts, particularly those that are considered to be value-adders. However, as a result of the change the counterpart in this case is now served by a new sales/marketing office and new staff.

Level of effects

Level 1: Effects in the relationship

Expected effects: The seller expects the action to increase the amount of sales force time per customer and to increase and retain sales in existing and new relationships.

The perceived value of effects is that the seller values the growth in sales achieved through increased sales effort and so is prepared to commit the resources to provide two sets of new regional office staff. The customer does not perceive value in the relationship as a result of this action by the seller. It doesn't believe that there is a need for more sales representation and hasn't actually noticed an increase in contact time. It takes the view that if the seller wants to increase sales, it should reduce prices.

Level 2: Effects on the relationship

The expected effects are that the seller expects level 2 effects in closer, deeper, and wider individual relationships.

The perceived value of effects is that the seller values the effect of its action in increasing customers' dependency on it for technical expertise as well as products. The current action is perceived as being a way of achieving these sorts of effects on relationships. However, this value may not be achieved on this particular relationship. The action has had the effect of reducing the closeness in the relationship by unilaterally switching to a new office with new contact points. The customer has reduced its purchases from the seller in favor of a competing supplier by way of alerting the seller to the customer's unhappiness at the way that the action has been handled. Whilst this is a level 1 effect, it has its origins in level 2 issues. For the seller, the negative value of this action in this relationship is unavoidable if it wants to achieve level 3 and 4 effects.

Level 3: Effects on the relationship portfolio

The expected effects are that the seller expects that the action will give its sales and marketing teams more time with all customers, particularly its key accounts.

The perceived value of effects is that the seller sees the value of its action in terms of improving its relationships with its current high-value customers. But it also believes that the action will change a number of its low-value customers into the high-value category.

Level 4: Effects within the network

The expected effects are that the seller does not have a coherent view of the effects of its action on the network. It views it simply as a device for increasing sales and hence improving its position against current competition.

The perceived value of effects is that the seller's view of the value of its action is strongly influenced by its concern with retaining manufacturing volume, which it implicitly sees as the key to its strength in the wider network.

Action 2: Customer's plans for expansion. This action by the customer is currently only at the planning stage. It currently sources three-quarters of its raw material from the seller but also sells some of its own products to one of the seller's downstream businesses. The customer wishes to increase these sales and is currently seeking a display of interest from the seller, without any firm commitment at this stage.

Level of effects

Level 1: Effects in the relationship

Expected effects: If the customer's proposals come to fruition, they would have the immediate effect of doubling the customer's requirement for material from the seller and its capacity to meet the requirements of the seller's downstream business.

The perceived value of effects is that the customer would value these level 1 effects. However, its primary aim is to enhance its relationship with the seller (level 2) by appealing to the seller's wish for more business (level 1).

Level 2: Effects on the relationship

The expected effects are that the customer has told the seller of its proposals to demonstrate its commitment to their relationship. It expects its standing with the seller to be enhanced by this action with the effect that the relationship will become more predictable as a consequence.

The perceived value of effects is that the customer company came into existence as the result of a management buyout after a forced receivership, and it feels that it is treated by the seller in a dismissive way. It appears to see the value of its action as an opportunity to boast to the seller and as a form of approval seeking, designed to show that it is around to stay and that it is the sort of firm with which the seller prefers to do business. Also, alongside the drop in its purchases after the seller's reorganization, it sees its action as a valuable way of showing its relationship partner that it is now a "bigger fish" and doesn't want to be pushed around. The seller has made no response to the proposals of the buyer, indicating that it does not consider the action to have any significance for the relationship between them.

Level 3: Effects on the relationship portfolio

Expected effects and perceived value of relationship are both none.

Level 4: Effects within the network

The expected effects are that this action could have significant network effects if, for example, it is emulated by others and leads to changes in the relative importance of different types of companies. But, neither company appears to have considered the wider potential effects of the action. The perceived value of effects is none.

Case D

The customer company in this relationship is a regional customer of the seller. The customer is part of a national group and it sources and manufactures products that are then sold by a number of its sister companies. The customer only accounts for a tiny proportion of the seller's national sales but is a major account in its own region. The seller provides all of the customer's needs for one commodity-type product. Consequently, the seller makes no product adaptation for this customer. However, the seller provides marketing assistance to the buyer to increase product pull-through for its products. The relationship can be characterized as having low width and depth but high closeness.

The relationship action. The seller is about to bid for the contract with the buyer for another related product. This will increase the seller's share of the customer's purchases of all raw materials from 40 to 80%. The seller used to have this contract but lost it as a result of service deficiencies. The contract is currently held by a competitor of the seller who is also one of its customers. This competitor has been having problems supplying product to the quality and reliability required by the buyer.

Level of effects

Level 1: Effects in the relationship

Expected effects: A successful bid would have clear level 1 effects as it would more than double sales volume to this buyer in one move.

   The perceived value of effects is that a successful bid for the related contract has direct sales value to the seller. For the customer, there would be obvious cost savings associated with a better performing supplier. However, the customer regards supplier nonperformance as inevitable for this type of product and is not yet convinced that awarding the contract to the seller will resolve its current supply problems.

Level 2: Effects on the relationship

The expected effects are that this action will have strong consequences for the relationship. It will increase the customer's overall dependence on the seller. It will also place demands upon the seller to improve its service provision compared to the last time it held the contract. It will increase the range of contacts and contact time to ensure that the exchange process runs smoothly. Hence it will increase the width, depth, and closeness of the relationship.

   The perceived value of effects is that the seller values the increased dependence of the buyer that a successful bid would lead to, especially because switching costs are high. The customer is aware that it will become more dependent on the seller. However, it is also clear about its performance requirements, and it will hold the seller to them regardless of the degree of dependence. The customer is aware of the potential effects upon the relationship, but the value that it seeks does not appear to be at this level.

Level 3: Effects on the relationship portfolio

The expected effects are that the seller does not expect its increased commitment to the customer as a result of winning the additional contract will have any effects on its customer portfolio. It takes the view that it can provide as much product as anyone wants to buy. The seller's downstream business would undertake the additional contract and the seller does not believe that it would have any problems in adding this customer to its portfolio. The seller does not believe that the action of taking away the contract from the other supplier which is also its customer will have any effects on its relationship with that customer. The perceived value of effects is none.

Level 4: Effects within the network

The expected effects are that a successful bid would give extra business to the seller's downstream business rather than its competitor. It would increase the requirement for material from itself, and reduce the amount of product sourced from a French competitor – the seller sees cheaper imports as a major long-term threat.

The perceived value of effects is that the seller does not appear to consider this action in network terms; it is merely a device for increasing its own sales and those of its downstream company.

Discussion of the relationship evaluations of company 2

This company is anxious to maintain its margins and to hold off the competitive attacks of cheap importers with lower cost bases. It is seeking to forge closer relationships with those customers that it sees as value-adders ("key processors" in its own language). The customers in cases C and D are examples of these. The seller's action to redefine the number and size of its marketing regions was designed specifically to support the strategy and seems to have been universally regarded by the seller's staff as the right thing to do (both counterparts also say that this strategy makes sense to them, even if it has posed problems for one relationship).

The seller has developed this strategy at an overall level, but there are clear issues that surround its implementation at the level of single relationships. Specifically, the seller does not seem to have a clear view of the potential of each relationship or the managerial or other resources that are required to achieve that potential. Instead, its approach is based on achieving short-term gain in each relationship within the context of its overall strategy that is expressed almost solely in terms of its own requirements. This leads it to "damage" any one relationship as in case C. The seller's view of each relationship, its portfolio, and the network is egocentric, and it does not appear to take into account the fact that intercompany relationships are two sided, with both companies having a separate strategy and a view of the potential and portfolio position of that relationship. This may be due in part to the traditional asymmetric nature of relationships in this industry, with high customer dependence on the seller and low seller dependence on individual customers.

MANAGERIAL IMPLICATIONS

This article is part of a continuing program of research aimed at helping managers to take a strategic approach to the management of intercompany relationships in the complex networks that comprise business markets.

The complexity of these networks adds to the difficulties of both marketing and purchasing management. But, if a manager takes a network view then this can highlight the multiple influences on a company from others in the network, the multiple potential effects of any action by companies in the network. A network view also highlights the importance of widespread scanning of the network in addition to narrower customer and competitive analysis.

A network view and the cases in this article show that the task facing a business marketer or purchaser is not to develop an individual strategy working against those around it. Instead, both marketing and purchasing managers need to see themselves as enmeshed in a network of relationships with companies, each with their own motivations, strategies, problems, and technological resources. These relationships are both major resources and a source of problems for a company. The cases in this article and our other work show that marketing and purchasing success comes through the development of a long-term approach to relationships. This approach needs to be based on the reality of individual self-interest, rather than some naïve view of loyalty or trust.

It is important for managers to have a clear view of the nature of the value in their interactions with others. In this article, we have distinguished between the value of a relationship and the value of the specific effects of action taken in that relationship. A manager's view of the value of a relationship should form the basis of his strategy for that relationship. Our research has shown the difficulty of expressing this value in simple financial terms. Instead, it is important for that value to be expressed in a disaggregated form, such as its value as a source of new process technology or as a way of gaining access to new relationships, etc. The value of any one relationship must also be considered as part of an overall portfolio of relationships each of which contributes in different ways to some total value (Ford, 1998).

This article examined the effects of the actions of managers on four levels. This type of analysis helps the manager to take a more strategic view of his actions. It assists the manager in integrating a longer term, a portfolio, and a network view as well as the straightforward examination of the likely immediate effects of his own and his counterparts actions in a relationship. The cases illustrate the situation where companies do not carry out an analysis at the different levels. The case companies were not able to relate individual actions in a relationship to a strategic view of that relationship and their portfolio. Perhaps more importantly, the cases illustrate a situation that we have found to be common in our research – a difficulty in understanding that overall strategy cannot be developed in an individualized manner and that business marketing strategy needs to be developed both in a relationship and network context and can only be implemented through those relationships.

Our research has shown that there is often a clear difference between what managers think they are doing in their relationships, what they say they are doing, and what they actually do. There is of course also a difference between what they think will happen and what actually does happen. Equally problematic is that there is often a difference between what they say they value in their relationships and what their actions show that they really seek.

Success in business relationships depends on a thorough analysis of the value of a company's relationships. It also requires an ability to think through the effects of a company's actions on different levels. It requires clarity in establishing aims for a relationship in the context of that company's portfolio and that of its counterpart. Finally, it requires a realization that relationship management is a task for both of the companies involved and each must proceed on the basis of realistic assumptions about the position of their counterpart.

REFERENCES

Anderson, J. C., Jain, D. C., Chintagunta, P. K.: Customer Value Assessment in Business Markets: A State-of-Practice Study. *Journal of Business-to-Business Marketing*, **1**, 3–29 (1993).

Cunningham, M. T., White, J. G.: The Determinants of Choice of Supplier. *European Journal of Marketing*, **7**, 189–202 (1973).

Forbis, J. L., and Mehta, N. T.: Value-Based Strategies for Industrial Products. *Business Horizons*, **24**, 32–42 (1981).

Ford, D., Gadde, L.-E., Håkansson, H., Lundgren, A., Snehota, I., Turnbull, P., Wilson, D.: *Managing Business Relationships*, John Wiley, New York, 1998.

Ford, D., McDowell, R.: Intra-firm Diversity and Relationship Strategy, in *Relationships and Networks in International Markets*, H-G. Gemünden, T. Ritter, A. Walter, eds., Pergamon, London, 1998.

Ford, D., McDowell, R., Tomkins, C.: Relationship Strategy, Investments and Decision Making, in *Networks in Marketing*, D. Iacobucci, ed., Sage Publications, Thousand Oaks, CA, 1996.

Ford, D., McDowell, R., Tomkins, C.: Relationship Strategy: Decisions on Valuing and Managing Network Options, in *Networks in Marketing*, P. Naude and P. Turnbull, eds., Pergamon Press, London, 1998.

Ford, I. D., Håkansson, H., Johanson, J.: How Do Companies Interact? *Industrial Marketing and Purchasing*, **1**, 26–41 (1986).

Ford, I. D.: One More Time, What Buyer–Seller Relationships Are All About, IMP Conference, Penn State University, September, 1989.

Håkansson, H., and Snehota, I., eds.: *Developing Relationships in Business Networks*, Routledge, London, 1995.

Krapfel, R. E., Salmond, D., Spekman, R.: A Strategic Approach to Managing Buyer–Seller Relationships. *European Journal of Marketing*, **25**, 22–37 (1991).

Pfeffer, J., Salancik, G.: *The External Control of Organizations: A Resource-Dependence Perspective*, Harper and Row, New York, 1978.

Robinson, P. J., Faris, C. W., Wind, Y.: *Industrial Buying and Creative Marketing*, Allyn & Bacon, Boston, 1967.

Wilson, D. T., Jantrania, S.: Understanding the Value of a Relationship. *Asia – Australia Marketing Journal*, **2**, 55–66 (1994).

Wind, Y.: Getting a Read on Market-Defined Value. *Journal of Pricing Management*, **1**, 5–14 (1990).

4.6 The networking company: antecedents for coping with relationships and networks effectively

Thomas Ritter

INTRODUCTION

It has been noted that interorganizational relationships fulfil a whole variety of functions; with regard to customer relationships, functions such as increasing sales volume in the relationship, technology development through the existing relationship or opening market access were discussed (Gemünden et al., 1996). But it is not only the customer or customer relationships that are contributing to a company's performance (Sharma and Sheth, 1997). Especially within the new-product development process, a range of different types of external partners (e.g., supplier, universities, research institutions, consultants, and competitors) can play an important role (Gemünden et al., 1996) as cooperation was identified to contribute significantly to a company's innovation success.

This variety of potential companies for interorganizational relationships leads us from single relationships to networks of relationships in which a company is embedded. The notion of networks also takes into consideration that, in addition to the variety of different types of partners, a company has several relationships within one type of external partner (e.g., a company has more than one customer).

Furthermore, most of a company's relationships are interconnected with each other. Any one relationship can affect other relationships both positively (support or even force) or negatively (hinder or even forbid), Blankenburg and Johanson (1992).

Given this interconnectedness, we cannot isolate a single relationship out of the context of a company's network. This means that choices regarding the set of cooperation partners have to be made and interdependencies between relationships have to be considered while a company is developing and using its network.

It also has been noted that close relationships are not always a good thing and that relationships may have advantages as well as disadvantages (Ford, 1997). For example, dependencies and mistrust can occur and the establishment of access to external resources is a lengthy and costly process that should be seen as an investment (Mattsson, 1988).

Given desirable functions, interconnectedness and accompanied risks of relationships, there is a need for companies to consider its whole network and to cope with the situation. Also a company is dependent on other companies in developing and using relationships and, thus, is not a master on its own (Ford and Saren, 1996); it is both sensible and useful to discuss a company's ability to manage its network. Due to the fact that resources possessed by different companies will not lead to exchange relationships on their own, this article also seeks to increase the understanding of how companies make their resources accessible to each other.

Previously it has been discussed and empirically shown that a company's degree of network competence has a positive impact on its degree of technology oriented interactions with other organizations, including customers, suppliers, competitors, and research institutions (Ritter, 1998). In this analysis, network competence also has been identified as an important input factor for a company's innovation success. Furthermore, the impact of network competence remains its significantly positive impact when technological competence is included in the analysis.

Given the importance of network competence for a company's performance, two important issues will be addressed in this article. First, organizational preconditions of network competence are analyzed: How will organizational characteristics of the company affect its network competence? Second, based on the empirical results presented in this article, managerial implications for managing the networking company are presented: How can companies positively stimulate the development of network competence?

Before I address the two questions, the concept of network competence is introduced.

THE CONCEPT OF NETWORK COMPETENCE

To measure competence, the terms qualification and task need to be distinguished. Qualifications are personal characteristics that enable a person to do something. In the context of network management, those qualifications will be discussed that allow a person to develop, to maintain, and to use relationships. Tasks refer to different bundles of activities that need to be performed to achieve something. Through task execution individuals (or groups of individuals) demonstrate their qualifications. Also, task execution observation allows assessment of qualifications. To understand a company's ability to manage its network, it is important to analyze network management qualifications on a personal level (how qualified are those people who are involved) and the aligned action of those who are involved in coping with a company's network on a company level (what are those people doing together). Referring to empirical results about the management of relationships, it is already known that several people are performing the tasks of managing a single relationship (Walter, 1998). Therefore, it can be assumed that there would be several people involved in the management of a set of relationships. Those elements will be discussed in more detail below (see Figure 1 for an overview).

Network management qualifications

Looking at qualifications needed from the people dealing with relationships, we can distinguish between specialist and social qualifications (Helfert, 1998). Specialist qualifications include technical skills, which are important to understand the partners, their needs, and their requirements. Economic skills are required to define inputs and set prices. Skills in legal matters are mainly relevant to set up contracts but can be even more important in areas where partners did not agree on a formal contract. Network knowledge includes information about other companies, their personnel and resources, which is important to understand the development of the network. Of particular importance is experiential knowledge received through interactions with external partners that can be used to anticipate and evaluate critical situations and to select appropriate action.

Social qualification is the extent to which a person is able to exhibit autonomous, prudent, and useful behavior in social settings. It contains communication ability, extraversion, conflict management skills, empathy, emotional stability, self-reflectiveness, sense of justice, and cooperativeness. Social qualifications are of special interest because individuals are interacting with one another within a relationship.

Both specialist and social qualifications are needed because interorganizational relationships are built around interpersonal exchanges (social qualifications) but are based on economic and technological objectives (specialist qualifications). It is important to note that relationships may differ quite significantly from each other, and thus those qualifications need to be applied in specific contexts. But a high degree of the discussed qualifications serves as a basis of but is also affected by the execution of network management tasks that are described below.

Network management tasks

As mentioned earlier, a company's network consists of several relationships, which are interconnected. Therefore we distinguish between tasks that are necessary in managing a single relationship (a dyad) and tasks that are necessary to manage the network as a whole (Mattsson, 1985).

Relationship-specific tasks. The literature on relationship management suggests three different relationship-specific tasks.

Initiation can be seen as starting activities of a relationship. Hereby, it is important to identify potential partners and to convince them by showing one's own technological strength and possible outcomes of the collaboration. Even if we can assume that most companies have already established relationships, changing requirements may necessitate the initiation of new relationships.

Exchange activities (Bagozzi, 1975) refer to all sorts of transfers between the two companies, for example, transfer of products, services, money, information, know-how, and personnel. Focussing on technology-oriented relationships, we distinguish between technology-related, person-related, and company-related exchange activities. Technology-related exchange activities include the transfer of technological information, needs, and requirements of both parties, as well as further technological development trends within or even outside the industry. Person-related exchange activities build the basis for the development of personal relationships between members of the two companies to know personal needs, requirements, and preferences and to establish social bonds. Company-related exchange activities are important to understand the partner's strategic aims and the decision-making process within the partner's company.

Coordination activities are needed to be in tune with the other company – to synchronize the activities of both companies (Mohr and Nevin, 1990). Coordination includes the establishment and use of formal roles and procedures and the utilization of constructive conflict resolution mechanisms (Ruekert and Walker, 1987).

Adaptation is often discussed in relationship management (Hallén et al., 1991). From our point of view, adaptation has to be seen in a broader network perspective, particularly if an adaptation in one relationship may imply deadaptation or additional adaptation in another. Thus, adaptation may involve relationship-specific and cross-relational tasks. Strategic decisions, concerning amount of investment and bonding risk, concerning the policy of how to deal with "preferred" customers, and those concerning essential implications to other partners in the value chain or even in the whole web, have to be made at a higher hierarchical level from a network perspective. Minor and more relationship-specific decisions should be made at the relationship level. However, even strategic adaptations also have to be prepared, implemented, and controlled at the relationship level.

Cross-relational tasks. Drawing on literature about general management, I identified four different cross-relational tasks (Koontz and O'Donnell, 1984).

Planning activities refer to the definition of a desirable state in the future. In terms of networking, they comprise internal analysis (resources, strength, and weaknesses within the company), network analysis (quality of external contributions, fit to internal resources, and strategic and resource fit within the network), and environmental analysis (general technological and market developments and analyses of competitors).

Organizing activities enable the realization of the plans developed. External management contributions must be specified and agreed on among partners. Resources must be allocated to specific relationships within the company. Internal ways of communication between the people dealing with relationships must be defined and implemented.

Staffing activities deal with the allocation of personnel to specific relationships and allocate responsibilities to those persons. This includes guidance and coordination from the people involved to prevent or solve conflicts between different individuals. Conflicts can occur when several relationships compete for the same resources within the company.

Controlling activities are seen as the last management activity but also must be seen as the beginning of repeating the management process. As a network management task, controlling refers to the control of the output of the network, including the quality of the partners (e.g., through portfolio approaches (Olsen and Ellram, 1997)), and the employees involved in network management.

Degree of network competence

The term "core competence" was introduced into business administration and economics by Prahalad and Hamel (1990). Since then, increasing attention was paid to a company's competencies by both academia and managers. Whereas the focus has traditionally been on "technological" competencies and their impact on corporate success, more recent studies have taken a broader point of view into consideration by including also "managerial" competencies (Malerba and Marango, 1995). Of particular interest is the ability to apply a company's technologies, which is done within and through interorganizational relationships. From this perspective the importance of network competence for a company's corporate success can be derived.

The term competence stands not only for "being qualified", that is, having knowledge or possessing skills (i.e., network qualifications), but it also denotes using those qualifications (i.e., network management task execution). Only possessing qualifications and not taking behavioral consequences or performing tasks without having qualifications is regarded as incompetent (Gemünden and Ritter, 1997).

Therefore, a company's degree of network competence is defined as the degree of network management task execution and the degree of network management qualification possessed by the people handling a company's relationships.

Thus, a company's network competence can be measured as a twofolded construct as shown in Figure 1. On one hand, personal qualifications can be measured that enable the group of people in the company to act properly. On the other hand, the intensity of task execution on behalf of the company can be observed. Network competence offers a company the potential to effectively use interorganizational relationships. The effects of a company's network competence may be measured in terms of degree of interaction with other organizations, position in its network or innovation, and corporate success.

However, in this article I am concerned about the organizational antecedents of a company's network competence that will be discussed in the next section.

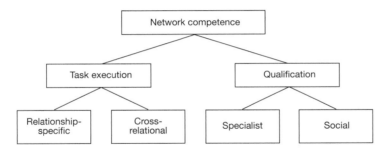

Figure 1 Elements of a company's network competence.

ANTECEDENTS OF NETWORK COMPETENCE

To offer managerial implications, our discussion needs to be extended to find out what kind of antecedents affect a company's degree of network competence. The following discussion is drawn from experiences within companies and from the literature on market and customer orientation (Jaworski and Kohli, 1993).

The "availability of internal resources" stands for internal management sources that are necessary for handling interactions with external partners. Internal resources can be distinguished in Hoffer and Schendel (1978) financial resources, which are needed for obtaining information, for communicating via telephone or fax, for traveling to partners' companies, and for performing adaptations to special needs and requirements of partners; physical resources that represent computers, telecommunication facilities, and meeting rooms; personnel resources, which means that a certain amount of personnel is needed to perform the network management tasks and to provide the necessary qualifications; and informational resources within the company to support personnel handling relationships and to avoid double work and information lags within the company. Through a sufficient availability to resources, intensive and goal-oriented execution of network management tasks will be enabled and the development of qualifications can be ensured.

> *H1*: The better the access to resources, the higher a company's degree of network competence will be.

With regard to human resource management, selection, development, and assessment of personnel will be discussed. The process of personnel selection can be network-oriented in the sense that networking abilities and networking experiences will be explicitly a part of the job announcement, the job description, and the selection process itself. As there are also a great number of network management qualifications, there are many possibilities for personnel development activities, for example, technical training, communication seminars, and conflict management workshops. Furthermore, network orientation of the human resource management can be seen in the implementation of relational aspects into the assessment of personnel, for example, through connecting the salary with the relationship success and including partners' statements into personnel evaluations (Lambert et al., 1997). Network orientation in the described sense would lead to a higher network competence as qualified personnel will be found and attracted to work for the company within the career selection process. Personnel will be promoted and developed to be even better qualified and to perform the network management tasks effectively and will be bound to the company.

> *H2*: The extent of network orientation taken by a company's human resource management is positively associated with its degree of network competence.

The communication structure of a company represents the information exchange between different departments within the company. The degree of interaction is called integration of communication structure. A high degree of integration would mean that there is an intensive exchange between all departments within a company. Regarding the communication structure of a given company, we have to distinguish between formal (defined by the management and laid down in the organization chart) and informal (as people interact in reality) structure (Schreyögg, 1996).

A high integration of the communication structure makes information available to the people dealing with relationships. It also ensures that cross-departmental communication is not a rare exception and that other members of staff will not hinder this transfer. This will again lead to a higher level of task execution and a higher level of qualifications.

> *H3*: The higher the integration of a company's communication structure, the higher its network competence will be.

Corporate culture is defined as "the pattern of basic assumptions that a given group has invented, discovered, or developed in learning to cope with its problems of external adaptation and internal integration, and that have worked well enough to be considered valid and therefore to be taught to new members as the correct way to perceive, think, and feel in relation to those problems" (Schein, 1992). We define openness of corporate culture in terms of emphasizing flexibility, spontaneity, and individuality (as typical characteristics of the adhocracy culture) in contrast to control, regulation, and stability (as typical characteristics of a hierarchy culture). In addition, openness is seen in emphasizing competition and differentiation rather than to focus on smooth processes within the company (for a typology of corporate culture and its measurement cf. Deshpandé et al. (1993)).

An open culture will ensure entrepreneurial spirit within the company. This will motivate employees to take over decision making and responsibility, and they will become accustomed to always doing so. This is of special importance for relationship and network management as relationships are dynamic and thus all people involved need entrepreneurial spirit. External orientation is also a driving force to analyze a company's environment and will likewise lead to higher task execution. Furthermore, it can be assumed that companies with an adhocracy culture will be more innovation oriented, and therefore employees will be better qualified and more used to performing network management tasks. We conclude:

H4: The degree of a company's network competence is positively associated with the openness of its corporate culture.

EMPIRICAL RESULTS

Data collection and sample

After the construction of a questionnaire and a pretest with 14 companies, 741 German companies operating in the fields of mechanical and electrical engineering, measurement technology, and control engineering were contacted and asked for participation in the study. Data were collected between August and December 1997 in standardized personal interviews. We obtained data from 308 companies, which equals a response rate of 43.3%.

To use the key informant approach (John and Reve, 1982), and to obtain data not used in the analysis presented here, we asked for respondents with an overview of the company, the technological network, and the innovation success. Half of our respondents were CEOs in their companies. Another quarter of our interviews was made with the head of the R&D department. In all other cases, we had spoken to the head of the sales, production, or controlling department when innovation and networking responsibilities were attached to these positions. Given the above-described approach, we can assume the high quality of the answers.

Measurement

First-order constructs were measured by seven-point multi-item rating scales. The only exception from this approach is the measurement of corporate culture where the respondent had to distribute 100 points between four different descriptions. In terms of measuring network competence, items of first-order constructs were measured by seven-point multi-item rating scales (overall 96 variables were used to measure nine first-order constructs).

Items were summarized by building the scale mean of each first-order construct. Reliability of the first- and second-order constructs was checked by computing Cronbach's Alpha coefficients and item-to-total correlations. Convergent validity of the second-order constructs was conventionally checked by performing exploratory factor analyses with the first-order constructs as input variables. In all cases, only one factor was extracted by the Kaiser criterion (eigenvalue above 1).

Table 1 provides an overview of the Cronbach's Alphas for any first- and second-order construct and of the explained variance of the exploratory factor analyses on second-order construct level.

Table 1 Reliability and validity of measurement

First-order construct* (n of items/dimensions)	Cronbach's Alpha	Scond-order construct† (n of first-order constructs)	Cronbach's Alpha	Explained variance by one factor (%)
Financial resources (9)	0.86	Availability of internal resources (4)	0.73	55.5
Physical resources (5)	0.81			
Personnel resources (4)	0.77			
Informational resources (6)	0.82			
Personnel selection (3)	0.74	Network orientation of human resource management (3)	0.69	62.3
Personnel development (5)	0.72			
Personnel assessment (4)	0.77			
Formal communication structure (3)	0.80	Integration of communication structure (2)	0.67	76.0
Informal communication structure (4)	0.80			
Adhocracy culture (4)	0.70	Openness of corporate culture (2)	0.68	77.1
Hierarchy culture (4)	0.79			
Task execution (7)	0.89	Degree of network competence (2)	0.72	79.7
Qualifications (2)	0.74			

* Number of items/dimensions is in parentheses.
† Number of first-order constructs is in parentheses.

The results are very good on both levels: On first-order level, all Cronbach's Alphas are above 0.70, and on second order level four Cronbach's Alphas are above 0.70, whereas three Cronbach's Alphas are only slightly under 0.70 and still far above the limit of 0.60 (McAllister, 1995). In all cases, the explained variance by one factor is more than 50%. Therefore, sufficient reliability and convergent validity of the measures are given.

Data analysis

To examine the relationships between organizational antecedents of a company's network competence and network competence itself, antecedents (second-order constructs) were divided into three groups (low, medium, high) by using mean plus/minus standard deviation criteria. Means of the depended variable (network competence) for those three groups were computed. The results of these analyses are shown in Figure 2. As one can see, all four antecedents have a positive impact on a company's network competence as with increasing the quality of each organizational characteristic network competence increases as well.

In a second step, the impact of all four antecedents is analyzed simultaneously by using regression analysis. The result given in Figure 3 suggests that all four antecedents affect a company's network competence simultaneously. Furthermore, no antecedent seems to have a greater impact as all regression coefficients are very much the same. Thus, a company's network

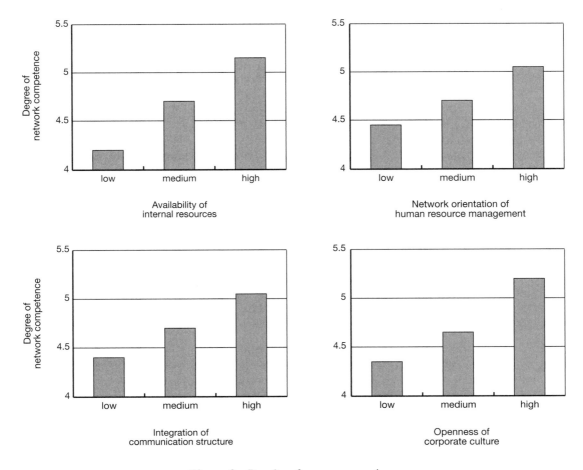

Figure 2   Results of group comparison.

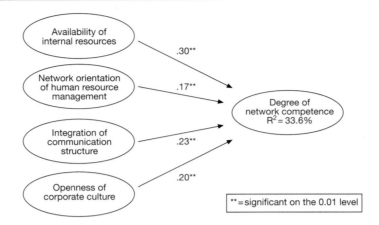

Figure 3 The impact of organizational antecedents on network competence.

competence is a function of all company characteristics. Networking cannot be separated within the company because it is affected by the whole company.

MANAGERIAL IMPLICATIONS

A company's network competence was identified to consist of the two dimensions qualifications and execution. Qualifications were split into specialist and social skills. Regarding network management tasks relation-specific and cross-relational tasks were distinguished that led to seven different task bundles. With that, a powerful concept had been developed to describe a company's ability to handle its network effectively. The purpose of this article is to identify organizational preconditions of a company's network competence. Our theoretical discussion and the empirical study suggest the following conclusions and managerial implications.

The empirical results show that a company's network competence is embedded within the whole company. All our antecedents have a significant impact on network competence on nearly the same level. Therefore, organisational improvements can be made in various ways but at the same time can only be successful if all areas are taken into account. It is important to note that all factors influence a company's network competence, and thus networking is integrated into the company as a whole and cannot be isolated out of this context – the whole company is networking. The following managerial implications can be derived.

Allocate resources

The results made clear that resource availability is a precondition for the development of network competence. Those companies that strive for a free-of-cost strategy while trying to interact cannot expect gains. Networking activities depend on resources such as the following.

- *Physical resources.* To facilitate internal communication, meeting facilities are needed. If only inappropriate facilities are available, personnel is likely to restrict the exchange of information with negative impacts on a company's transparency towards employees. Information flow can be facilitated through boardrooms and common rooms as well as through information technology for internal and external communication.
- *Financial resources.* A lack of financial resources (e.g., for travel expenses) will hinder network management task execution. If members of staff need to fight for resources they obviously won't have time to manage their relationships. It is important to note that availability of resources does not mean to hide funds behind a bureaucratic wall where no one can find them.

- *Personnel resources.* In many of our cases, we have seen network management done as a minor part-time job – whenever there was time for doing so. This is a disregard for the importance of network management that leads to a low degree of network competence. Network management task execution should be part of the daily routine. Situations in which collaborating partners only disturb are to be avoided.
- *Informational resources.* Network management involves information exchange to a large extent both inside the company and between different companies. The more information available the better the quality of decisions can be. Of course, there is a limit to the extent to which a person can process information but not without reason do we live in a so-called information age. Practical solutions to improve the flow of information inside the company include regular meetings and unified documentation rules for information.

Motivate qualified personnel

The impact of network orientation of human resource management has shown that several areas may attract attention at this stage. Searching for qualified personnel involves the active search for persons with network qualifications through advertising for and analyzing those skills. A way of increasing qualifications of personnel is offering attractive development programs that are frequently used and not seen as punishments. Also evaluating personnel according to relationship execution will guide members of staff to develop desired and necessary skills for networking.

Communicate across functions

By increasing the interdepartmental communication, network competence can be improved. Interfunctional borders may be broken down through cross-functional seminars and workshops, through limited personnel exchange between departments or (again) through implementing communication means (e.g., company newspaper or a new web page). Such efforts do not only provide important insight into information but also allow a better understanding of others' positions. In addition there is nothing wrong with going through the official channels for information. But given the dynamic nature of network management, it also might be advisable to implement some unofficial shortcuts that allow a more flexible way of doing things.

Open the corporate culture

The external orientation has been empirically proven to be vital for the development of network competence. Therefore, companies need to understand other organizations (at least sometimes) as partners as opposed to enemies. This also needs to be shown within and outside the company to make this a part of the corporate culture. Corporate culture is probably the most difficult precondition to improve because it can be done only in the long run, if at all. However, means to improve are slogans such as "together we are strong" and CEOs' commitment to external relations and awarding prizes, such as "networking person of the month."

The first step of improvement probably is to realize that there is a problem. Therefore, managers in companies should analyze the company's network competence and the company's organizational characteristics to find out potential areas for improvements if necessary. To allow self-assessment two checklists are given in Figures 4 and 5. The questions reflect on problems we have seen in companies during the empirical stage in our research. Those lists should not be answered in a yes or no format nor do they represent the measurement tool used. They should facilitate discussions within a given company on how to improve a particular company's ability to cope with networks.

The first list may point to strengths and weaknesses in network management qualifications and/or network management task execution, whereas the latter allows one to evaluate company characteristics that increase or decrease the degree of network competence a company has. It would be advisable to ask different groups within the company in question to discuss those issues because

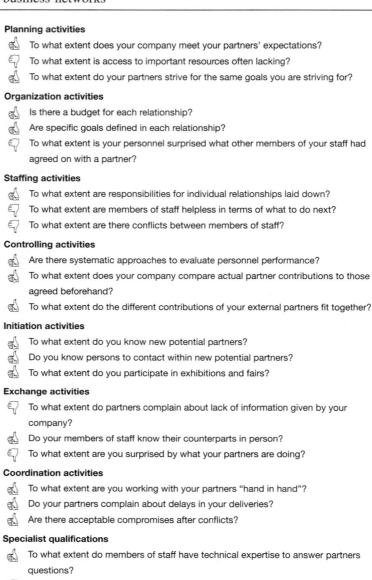

Planning activities

To what extent does your company meet your partners' expectations?

To what extent is access to important resources often lacking?

To what extent do your partners strive for the same goals you are striving for?

Organization activities

Is there a budget for each relationship?

Are specific goals defined in each relationship?

To what extent is your personnel surprised what other members of your staff had agreed on with a partner?

Staffing activities

To what extent are responsibilities for individual relationships laid down?

To what extent are members of staff helpless in terms of what to do next?

To what extent are there conflicts between members of staff?

Controlling activities

Are there systematic approaches to evaluate personnel performance?

To what extent does your company compare actual partner contributions to those agreed beforehand?

To what extent do the different contributions of your external partners fit together?

Initiation activities

To what extent do you know new potential partners?

Do you know persons to contact within new potential partners?

To what extent do you participate in exhibitions and fairs?

Exchange activities

To what extent do partners complain about lack of information given by your company?

Do your members of staff know their counterparts in person?

To what extent are you surprised by what your partners are doing?

Coordination activities

To what extent are you working with your partners "hand in hand"?

Do your partners complain about delays in your deliveries?

Are there acceptable compromises after conflicts?

Specialist qualifications

To what extent do members of staff have technical expertise to answer partners questions?

To what extent is handling relationships too much for members of staff?

To what extent are members of staff experienced in handling relationships?

Social qualification

To what extent are members of staff and partners getting along with each other?

To what extent are members of staff reliable and predictable?

To what extent are members of staff dealing with relationships well?

Figure 4 Questions regarding a company's network competence.

points of view and opinions may vary between different departments and different hierarchical levels.

Despite the powerful support of the hypothesized relationships between the constructs, there are several further questions to be addressed in later studies. In our study, we focused on task execution

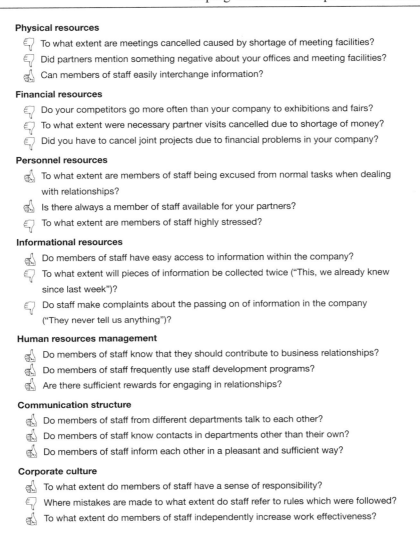

Physical resources

- To what extent are meetings cancelled caused by shortage of meeting facilities?
- Did partners mention something negative about your offices and meeting facilities?
- Can members of staff easily interchange information?

Financial resources

- Do your competitors go more often than your company to exhibitions and fairs?
- To what extent were necessary partner visits cancelled due to shortage of money?
- Did you have to cancel joint projects due to financial problems in your company?

Personnel resources

- To what extent are members of staff being excused from normal tasks when dealing with relationships?
- Is there always a member of staff available for your partners?
- To what extent are members of staff highly stressed?

Informational resources

- Do members of staff have easy access to information within the company?
- To what extent will pieces of information be collected twice ("This, we already knew since last week")?
- Do staff make complaints about the passing on of information in the company ("They never tell us anything")?

Human resources management

- Do members of staff know that they should contribute to business relationships?
- Do members of staff frequently use staff development programs?
- Are there sufficient rewards for engaging in relationships?

Communication structure

- Do members of staff from different departments talk to each other?
- Do members of staff know contacts in departments other than their own?
- Do members of staff inform each other in a pleasant and sufficient way?

Corporate culture

- To what extent do members of staff have a sense of responsibility?
- Where mistakes are made to what extent do staff refer to rules which were followed?
- To what extent do members of staff independently increase work effectiveness?

Figure 5 Questions regarding organizational antecedents of network competence.

and qualifications and thus have paid little attention to the question: Who is doing what? Therefore, we need to develop an organizational implementation for network management. In addition, we have to challenge the issue of dynamics of network competence over time. This will be of particular interest for the understanding of newly founded, technology-based firms. Last, the concept of network competence can be used to understand collaboration and competition within and between different networks.

REFERENCES

Bagozzi, R. P.: Marketing as Exchange. *Journal of Marketing* **39 (4)**, 32–39 (1975).

Blankenburg, D., and Johanson, J.: Managing Network Connections in International Business. *Scandinavian International Business Review*, **1 (1)**, 5–19 (1992).

Deshpandé, R., Farley, J. U., and Webster, F. E.: Corporate Culture, Customer Orientation and Innovativeness in Japanese Firms – A Quadrad Analyses. *Journal of Marketing*, **57 (1)**, 23–37 (1993).

Ford, D.: *Understanding Business Markets*. Second edition. The Dryden Press, London, 1997.

Ford, D., and Saren, M.: *Technology Strategy for Business.* International Thomson Business Press, London, 1996.

Gemünden, H. G., Helfert, G., and Walter, A.: Geschäftsbeziehungen in Europa. *Absatzwirtschaft,* **39 (10),** 104–114 (1996).

Gemünden, H. G., Ritter, T., and Heydebreck, P.: Network Configuration and Innovation Success: An Empirical Analysis in German High-Tech Industries. *International Journal of Research in Marketing,* **13 (5),** 449–462 (1996).

Gemünden, H. G., and Ritter, T.: Managing Technological Networks: The Concept of Network Competence, in *Relationships and Networks in International Markets.* H. G. Gemünden, T. Ritter, and A. Walter, eds., Elsevier Science, Oxford, (1997), pp 294–304.

Hallén, L., Johanson, J. and Seyed-Mohamed, N.: Interfirm Adaptation in Business Relationships. *Journal of Marketing* **55 (4),** 29–37 (1991).

Helfert, G.: *Teams in Relationship Marketing: Design effektiver Kundenbeziehungsteams.* Gabler, Wiesbaden, 1998.

Hofer, C. W., and Schendel, D.: *Strategy Formulation: Analytical Concepts.* West Publishing Co., St. Paul, MN, 1978.

Jaworski, B. J. and Kohli, A. K.: Market Orientation: Antecedents and Consequences. *Journal of Marketing* **57 (7),** 53–70 (1993).

John, G., and Reve, T.: The Reliability and Validity of Key Informant Data from Dyadic Relationships in Marketing Channels. *Journal of Marketing Research,* **19 (11),** 517–524 (1982).

Koontz, H., and O'Donnell, C.: *Principles of Management: An Analysis of Managerial Functions.* McGraw-Hill, New York, 1984.

Lambert, D. M., Sharma, A., and Levy, M.: What Information Can Relationship Marketiers Obtain from Customer Evaluations of Salespeople? *Industrial Marketing Management,* **26,** 177–187 (1997).

Malerba, F., and Marango, L.: Competence, Innovative Activities and Economic Performance in Italian High-Technology Firms. *International Journal of Technology Management,* **10,** 461–477 (1995).

Mattsson, L.-G.: An Application of a Network Approach to Marketing-Defending and Changing Market Positions. In *Changing the Course of Marketing: Alternative Paradigms for Widening Marketing Theory,* N. Dholakia and J. Arndt, eds., JAI Press, Greenwich, CT, 1985, 263–288.

Mattsson, L.-G.: Management of Strategic Change in a "Markets-as-Networks" Perspective, in *The Management of Strategic Change,* A. M. Pettigrew, ed., Basil Blackwell, Oxford, 1988, 234–256.

McAllister, D. J.: Affect and Cognition-Based Trust as Foundation for Interpersonal Cooperation in Organizations. *Academy of Management Journal,* **38 (1),** 24–59 (1995).

Mohr, J., and Nevin, J. R.: Communication Strategies in Marketing Channels: A Theoretical Perspective. *Journal of Marketing,* **54 (10),** 36–51 (1990).

Olsen, R. F., and Ellram, L. M.: A Portfolio Approach to Supplier Relationships. *Industrial Marketing Management,* **26,** 101–113 (1997).

Prahalad, C. K., and Hamel, G.: The Core Competences of the Corporation. *Harvard Business Review,* **6 (3),** 79–91 (1990).

Ritter, T.: *Innovationserfolg durch Netzwerk-Kompetenz: Management von Unternehmensnetzwerken.* Gabler, Wiesbaden, 1998.

Ruekert, R. W., and Walker, O. C.: Marketing's Interaction with Other Functional Units: A Conceptual Framework and Empirical Evidence. *Journal of Marketing,* **58 (1),** 1–19 (1987).

Schein, E. H.: *Organizational Culture and Leadership.* Jossey-Bass, San Francisco, 1992.

Schreyögg, G.: *Organisation: Grundlagen moderner Organisationsgestaltung.* Gabler, Wiesbaden, 1996.

Sharma, A., and Sheth, J. N.: Relationship Marketing: An Agenda for Inquiry. *Industrial Marketing Management,* **26,** 87–89 (1997).

Walter, A.: *Der Beziehungspromotor. Ein personaler Gestaltungsansatz für erfolgreiches Relationship Marketing.* Gabler, Wiesbaden, 1998.

4.7

Assessing relationship quality

Pete Naudé and Francis Buttle

INTRODUCTION AND LITERATURE REVIEW

Within the rapidly expanding literature of business-to-business marketing, supply-chain management, relationship marketing and customer relationship management there is relatively little attention paid to the issue of relationship quality. Important issues remain poorly addressed: What are the features that distinguish successful relationships from unsuccessful ones? What is it that makes a relationship highly valued by those within it? Why do actors in a relationship wish and act to pursue and protect that relationship?

Our focus in this paper is on developing more clearly our understanding of what counts as a "good" or "poor" quality relationship. This is integrally linked to the issue of customer and relationship value, currently one of the most pressing and important managerial issues (Gale and Wood, 1994). Our key research question in this paper focuses on the benefit rather than the cost element of value, and develops our understanding of what the characteristic attributes of a good relationship are, and how they might vary in importance.

Despite the general shortage of empirical investigation, there have been some useful contributions from a number of authors. However, these authors employ a variety of different constructs that are not always clearly defined or distinguished from each other. Some write of relationship quality, others of relationship value or of partnership success. There is some face validity about the use of these terms, but their construct validity remains unproven. It seems probable that a high quality relationship will create value and be regarded as successful by at least one of the parties. Broadly, however, they are all seeking answers to the same question: what counts as good relationship? These different contributions are reviewed briefly below.

Gummesson (1987) identified relationship quality as one of four forms of quality encountered by customers. He regarded it as the quality of the interaction with the customer, arguing that ". . . high relational quality contributes to customer-perceived quality and thus enhances the chances for a long-term relationship." This construal of quality has been absorbed into the Nordic School's overall conceptualization of service quality (see for example, Grönroos, 1984, 1990). In later work, Ravald and Grönroos (1996) distinguish between episodic and relationship value, noting (as do Gale and Wood, 1994) that value in relationships can come either from increasing the benefit or decreasing the sacrifice.

Crosby et al. (1990) studied relationship quality within the context of selling services. They examined the nature, consequences and antecedents of relationship quality. Relationship quality was defined from the customer's perspective as being achieved through the salesperson's ability to reduce perceived uncertainty, leading to an environment where ". . . the customer is able to rely on the salesperson's integrity and has confidence in the salesperson's future performance because the level of past performance has been consistently satisfactory." Relationship quality is accordingly a bivariate construct comprised of trust and satisfaction. Trust was operationalized as the confident belief that a salesperson can be relied upon to behave in such a manner that the long-term interest of the customer will be served. The authors found that relationship quality had a significant influence on the customer's anticipation of future commitment, arguing that ". . . relationship quality contributes to a lasting bond by offering assurance that the salesperson will continue to meet the customer's expectations (satisfaction) and not knowingly distort information or otherwise subvert the customer's interests (trust)."

Despite these insights, the need for more work to be done in this area is argued by Mohr and Spekman (1994) who stated that, ". . . an understanding of the characteristics associated with partnership success is lacking." On the basis of empirical research, they suggest that the primary characteristics of any successful partnership are commitment, coordination and trust; communication quality and participation; and conflict resolution through joint problem solving. The focus of their research, partnership, was defined as ". . . purposive strategic relationships between independent firms who share compatible goals, strive for mutual benefit, and acknowledge a high level of mutual interdependence." Their analysis was based on over 120 questionnaires from partners in computer manufacturer–dealer relationships. In their model they used two indicators of partnership success: an objective indicator (sales volume flowing between the dyadic partners) and an affective measure (satisfaction of one party with the other).

Storbacka et al. (1994) built on some of these ideas by developing a conceptual model of the dynamics of relationship quality. Their core thesis is based on the following relationships between the variables: service quality → customer satisfaction → relationship strength → relationship longevity → customer relationship profitability.

Relationship strength is their indicator of relationship quality, and they comment that, ". . . there are obviously aspects of relationship strength other than customer satisfaction. These include, for example, the existence of bonds between the customer and provider. These bonds function as switching barriers beside customer satisfaction. Another dimension relates to the customer's (and the provider's) commitment to the relationship. Commitment might be based on customers' intentions and plans for the future."

Relationship strength, they observe, is reflected in both purchase behavior and communication behavior (e.g., word of mouth, complaints, etc.). Repeat purchase behavior based on positive commitment by the customer indicates a stronger relationship. Relationships in turn are strengthened by the presence of bonds between the customer and the provider.

Arguing from a conceptual basis, Wilson and Jantrania (1996) propose that successful business-to-business relationships are characterized by seven attributes: goal compatibility; trust; satisfaction; investments; structural bonds; social bonds; and the relative level of investment in alternative relationships. These are the ". . . glue which holds it [the relationship] together and allows it to develop." If goals are compatible, the companies will view joint action as mutually beneficial. Carruthers (1996) also claims that for a ". . . relationship to be an effective collaborative effort, or partnership, there should be a high degree of goal congruence concerning the major issues between the parties."

Trust, a construct common to this body of research on relationship quality, is widely thought to be associated with successful relationship development. Morgan and Hunt (1994) argue that trust is the cornerstone of relationship commitment. Without it commitment flounders. Geyskens and Steenkamp (1995) conclude that there is a consensus emerging that trust encompasses two essential elements: trust in the partner's honesty and trust in the partner's benevolence. Trust brings about a feeling of security, reduces uncertainty and creates a supportive environment. Morgan and Hunt's research (1994) suggests that functional conflict and uncertainty arise from a lack of trust and conversely that cooperation between partners arises directly from relationship commitment and trust. Trust also enhances the willingness to collaborate further (Pruitt, 1991).

It seems logical to agree with the obvious premise that any dissatisfaction with the outcomes of an exchange process, whatever the underlying constructs of quality or value, will tend to precipitate dissolution of that relationship (Wilson and Jantrania, 1996). Based on this, it has long been thought that customer satisfaction was sufficient to promote customer retention. Other research, however, indicates two apparent paradoxes: satisfied customers may defect, and dissatisfied customers may remain loyal (Buttle, 1999). There has been recent evidence that a significant percentage of satisfied customers are not retained, taking their business elsewhere despite reporting their satisfaction with product, service and process. Reichheld (1993) points out that 65–85% of recently defected customers claimed they were satisfied or very satisfied with their previous suppliers. Jones and Sasser (1995) report that customers indicating 4 on a customer satisfaction scale (out of a possible maximum of 5) were six times more likely to defect than those scoring 5. Reichheld (1996) reported that the repeat purchase rates of cars in the U.S. market remains in the 30–40% range though satisfaction has reached 90%. More recently, a financial services firm found that 10% of those customers giving it the highest possible score in a satisfaction survey (rating it 10 out of 10) defected to a rival the following year (Mitchell, 1998). There do appear to be a number of product and service categories (such as restaurants, vacations, wine, and some financial services) in which the impetus to try something new, driven by strong variety-seeking consumer motivation, is a more powerful force than the urge to stay loyal, driven by customer satisfaction. These special circumstances aside, it can still be argued that customer satisfaction is not a sufficient condition to bond customers to suppliers long-term.

This position was endorsed in the context of supply-chain relationships by Wilson and Mummaleneni (1986) when they described the developmental process of customer–supplier relationships. They suggested that commitment to a supplier came only when investments were made in the relationship, subsequent to satisfaction with the outcomes of their transactions. As they argue, ". . . investments in general, of course, are made into those relationships which are considered satisfactory. These investments might take the form of several adaptations in product and process areas . . . In addition to satisfaction, the quality of available alternatives as well as the level of investment determine the level of an organisation's commitment to that relationship."

This perspective, of commitment versus satisfaction, was reinforced by Ulrich (1989) who urged companies to strive to develop committed rather than just satisfied customers. He argues that ". . . satisfied customers are pleased, humoured and fulfilled; committed customers are dedicated and faithful . . . the totally committed customer says, 'we have developed interdependencies, shared values and strategies to the extent that our separate needs can best be met through long-term devotion and loyalty to each other'."

When trust exists between partners, both are motivated to make investments in the relationship. These investments, which serve as exit barriers, may be either tangible (e.g., property) or intangible (e.g., knowledge). Such investments may or may not be retrievable when the relationship dissolves (Wilson and Mummalaneni, 1986).

Wilson and Jantrania (1996) also comment on the significance of strong social and structural bonds to successful relationship development. Social bonds are close personal relationships that exist between actors in partner organizations. Where these bonds are highly valued, they enhance the probability that the relationship between the actors will endure (Mummalaneni and Wilson, 1991). Structural bonds, such as mutual asset specific investments in product development, property and technology, make relationship dissolution both costly and difficult. Where structural bonds exist, they indicate that the parties are or have been committed to relationship maintenance, effectively serving as exit barriers. Companies that form weak structural bonds to their supply-chain neighbors may be indicating that an alternative relationship is equally, or perhaps more, attractive.

Buttle (1997) conducted observational research and interviews in a dozen supplier–customer contexts with a view to better understanding the nature of relationship quality. Examining the communication between these dyads, he addressed two questions relevant to this paper: Does it make sense to talk of relationship quality? What counts as a relationship of high or low quality? All the dyads studied were able to identify qualitative differences within their customer–supplier relationships. Having observed a number of episodes between supplier and customer, these were categorized as task-centered (e.g., paying invoices, placing an order, raising a query) and process-centered (e.g., joking, story-telling). He noted that the more asymmetric the relationship (unequal power/knowledge distribution), and/or the more mediated the relationship (communication by

Table 1 Major constructs of relationship quality identified in the literature

Construct	Cosby et al., 1990	Mohr and Spekman, 1994	Storbacka et al., 1994	Wilson and Jantrania, 1996	This research
Trust	✔	✔		✔	✔
Satisfaction	✔		✔	✔	✔
Commitment		✔	✔		
Coordination		✔			✔
Communication		✔	✔		
Joint problem solving		✔			
Bonds			✔	✔	
Goal congruence				✔	
Investments				✔	
Power					✔
Profit					✔

phone, fax), the more task-centered were the communication episodes. Communication episodes indicative of high quality in one context were construed as low quality in another. For example, rapid completion of an episode was highly valued by both parties in an Information Technology (IT) help desk context; but slow completion was highly valued, again by both parties, in a financial advisor context. It did appear that customers and suppliers were able to discriminate between relationship types and adjust their communication accordingly.

The different constructs underlying relationship quality that have been identified in the literature above are summarized in Table 1, in which we also indicate the constructs that we have used. Trust is included by almost all authors. We have categorized "needs fulfilment" as being similar to satisfaction and "supply chain integration" as being coordination, although we accept that it also overlaps with many of the other constructs in the table. The aspects of power and profit are more problematical as they do not easily relate to other constructs. We are especially cognisant of the fact that relationships may be profitable for both parties in a financial sense, and yet not offer less tangible or personal quality. Indeed, the opposite is also possible: dyadic relationships that both parties consider to offer quality in terms of being enjoyable, fulfilling or rewarding, and yet which do not yield financial profit. The same conclusion is drawn by Geyskens et al. (1999) in their meta-analysis of satisfaction within channels, arguing that a distinction needs to be drawn between economic and non-economic satisfaction, both of which can lead independently to trust and commitment.

RESEARCH METHODOLOGY

Our sample consisted of a group of 40 middle to senior executives attending a management development course. The average age across the sample was 33 years, and they had been with their current companies for an average of six years. The respondents were asked to indicate what they thought to be the most important attributes of a good supply chain relationship of which they had experience. We did not specify the nature of the relationship, and they were encouraged to look either backward to their own suppliers, or forward to their customers. They were asked simply to write down these attributes, without any constraints as to structure or order. These responses were then collated, and five attributes were found to dominate the lists: trust; power; integration; mutual understanding of needs; and profit. We can see from Table 1 that two of the most commonly found attributes from the literature review (trust and satisfaction) were reflected in our sample. The third, coordination, was reported only by Mohr and Spekman (1994). However, there is clearly a lot of overlap between constructs such as commitment, coordination, communication, bonds, and goal congruence, and this remains an area for future clarification. As mentioned above, the two remaining constructs that we found to be present, power and profit, have not been explicitly reported in the literature reviewed.

Each of the five attributes was then specified at three different levels (essentially better than, the same, or worse than the current relationship). By using the process of factorial designs (Addleman, 1962), 15 different combinations of these five different attributes and levels were used to draw up a questionnaire based on conjoint analysis (Green and Wind, 1975). This is an approach well suited to understanding how buyers trade off different features, and has been much used in industrial marketing (see, for example, Auty, 1995). Our interest in using this approach was to develop our understanding of how the various constructs would be traded off against each other in different relationship settings and/or types. While other quantification techniques do exist that measure attribute or construct importance (Naudé, 1995), conjoint analysis remains the best approach to understand how such trade-offs are made. A common problem with the approach is to ensure that the appropriate attributes are selected (Auty, 1995), which was overcome by getting the respondents to generate the initial attributes themselves, and then selecting only the most common among them. However, problems such as how the different attribute levels are anchored and the number of attribute levels to use remain problematical (see, for example, Green and Wind, 1975; Wittink and Cattin, 1989). The latter problem was largely dispensed with by the relatively low numbers of both attributes and levels that were used, while the former was effectively negated by anchoring each person's response in the middle of the scale (i.e., the same level of the attribute as currently experienced).

These questionnaires were then distributed to the same group of respondents as before. They were now asked to consider the same relationship that they had in mind before, and to rank order the 15 different alternatives from that which described the best possible way for the particular relationship to develop, through to the worst.

Analysis of the collected demographics indicated that respondents typically worked for Industrial Services, Raw Materials, or Manufacturing companies (nine, six, and five cases, accounting for 40% of the sample). Most considered supply chain relationships with similar kinds of companies (Financial Services Providers, Manufacturing, and Industrial Services accounted for 70% of the customers/suppliers considered). The average length of the relationship under consideration was 14 years (with a range of two to 110 years!), and it typically involved an annual revenue of $90 million per annum.

RESULTS

The overall results of the study are shown in Table 2. As can be seen, the two most important attributes to the respondents were that there should be high trust in the relationship (29.64%), and yet also that the relationship should yield a profit (25.46%). The overall results can be seen as being rational in that higher utilities are achieved by the "better" level of each attribute, apart from the case of power. However, this is the least important attribute to the whole sample, and we would interpret the fact that higher levels of power achieved a lower utility than lower levels as being the result of insufficient attention having been paid to the least important attribute when filling out the questionnaire. The results indicate, therefore, that the most valuable relationship is seen as one in

Table 2 The overall conjoint analysis results showing attribute scores and part-worths

	Trust	Needs	Integration	Power	Profit
Importance (%)	29.64	20.14	12.79	11.97	25.46
Utilities:					
better	2.37	1.67	0.72	−0.03	2.30
the same	0.78	0.45	0.23	0.02	−0.15
worse	−3.15	−2.11	−0.95	0.01	−2.16

which trust, needs, integration and profit are all somewhat better than they currently are, but that power does not have a strong influence on perceived relationship quality.

The question that needs to be addressed next is the extent to which there is meaningful variation in the data. Are the results in Table 2 indicative of a general consensus among the managers concerned, or are there, in fact, different perspectives on what constitutes a good quality relationship? In order to answer this question, the data were subjected to two different forms of clustering. Figure 1 shows the output of a standard cluster analysis based on each individual's original rank ordering of the 15 alternatives. We can see, for example, that respondents 23 and 40, as well as 29 and 32, are very similar in their perspective. Respondent 30 (at the bottom of the figure), however, is very dissimilar to all the other respondents. Figure 2 shows the results of submitting the same data set to correspondence analysis, a perceptual mapping procedure (Greenacre, 1984, 1985; Hoffman and Franke, 1986). We can see here that respondents 40 and 23 are plotted fairly close together, as are 29 and 32, as we would expect from Figure 1. In this case, the two axes account for 48% of the variation in the data, suggesting that there are more complicating underlying dimensions to the data, and hence the clusters shown in Figure 2 should be interpreted with some care. Respondent 30, for example, is closer to both 5 and 25 that Figure 1 would suggest.

The output from these two approaches suggests that the data could be grouped into four different clusters. The first, shown at the top of Figure 1, would consist of all the respondents numbered from 23 through to 28. This group forms the largest sub-cluster, accounting for 23 of the 40 respondents. The second group lies largely to the left in Figure 2, and would consist of the 11 respondents labelled as 8 through to 26 in Figure 1. The final multiple-respondent cluster would be the four individuals (5, 39, 25, and 36) shown at the bottom of Figure 1/lower right of Figure 2. Finally, although interpretation of Figure 2 does not readily lead one to suggest this, interpretation of Figure 1 would suggest that individual 30 is treated as a cluster of one, with his/her profile being somewhat different to the rest. The overall results for each of these four segments is shown in Table 3.

The results from Table 3 suggest that there are indeed fundamentally different perceptions concerning just what determines quality in a supply chain relationship. Cluster 1 is the largest and hence has most influence on the overall figures in Table 2. These respondents regard trust and needs issues to be the most important, with profit being third. Integration and power are less important to them than to any of the other four clusters. Cluster 2, on the other hand, is clearly profit oriented, with the remaining attributes all clearly of less importance. Cluster 3 is concerned with integration in the supply chain, and hence is logically also interested in issues surrounding trust. To the manager making up cluster 4, how power is handled in the relationship was the dominant issue – far more so than to any of the other clusters, and justifying the inclusion of this manager as a cluster of just one. These conclusions are shown more clearly in Figure 3 which again uses Correspondence Analysis, this time to plot the data from Table 3. The extent to which the four clusters are associated with different criteria is now clear.

Of course, the analysis above falls short on one important dimension. Although conjoint analysis does yield insights into overall attribute importance, it also indicates the part-worths of the different levels of the attribute, as was shown in Table 2. The point was made there that the full set of results were indicative of some overall rationality, in the sense that "better" levels of each attribute tended to be associated with higher utility levels. Given that it has been ascertained that there are indeed different clusters within the data set, it needs to be determined whether or not this is still the case across all segments.

This data is shown in Table 4, which indicates both the importance of the different attributes to each cluster, as well as the part-worths for the different levels of each attribute. It is clear from these figures that both clusters 1 and 2 behave in the expected fashion, in that more of each attribute has greater utility (This is not true in the case of power to Cluster 1, but the attribute is of such low importance that we would disregard this result).

Dendogram using Average Linkage (Between Groups)

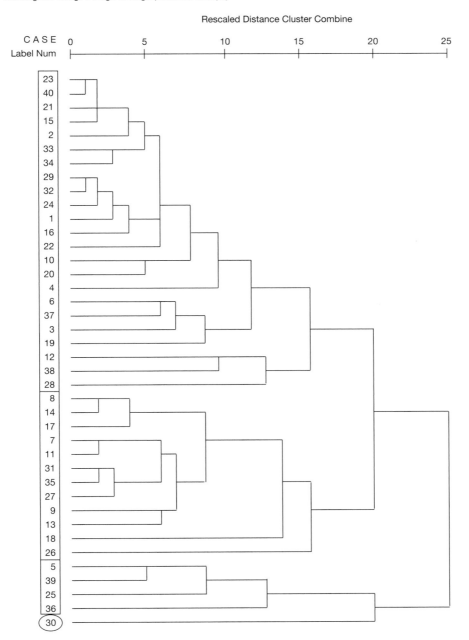

Figure 1   The different relationship types, based on cluster analysis.

For clusters 3 and 4, some apparent anomalies arise. In the case of cluster 3, we can see that less power is preferred to more. We interpret this as being a corollary of the importance placed on both integration (36%) and trust (23%). If both of these are above average, there should be little need for power to play a part in the relationship. The results of the one individual in cluster 4 also requires closer inspection. Although Table 3 shows the importance of power to this person, it is only by

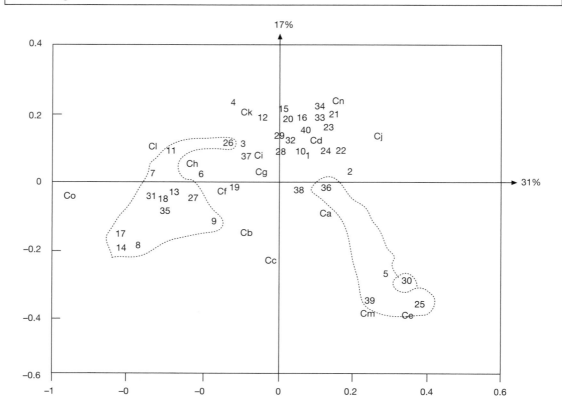

Figure 2 The different relationship types based on correspondence analysis.

Table 3 The conjoint analysis results for each cluster, showing attribute importance scores

	Trust	Needs	Integration	Power	Profit
Overall (n = 40)	29.64	20.14	12.79	11.97	25.46
Cluster 1 (23)	38.00	25.25	9.98	8.89	17.88
Cluster 2 (11)	17.28	12.31	10.51	13.91	46.00
Cluster 3 (4)	22.75	15.79	35.99	15.76	9.70
Cluster 4 (1)	13.33	14.07	11.85	44.44	16.30

looking at Table 4 that it becomes clear that in fact higher levels of the attribute are more negatively evaluated, i.e., more power is worse. Our interpretation of this, backed up by discussion with the individual concerned, is that this is indicative of a close and mature relationship. In this case the relationship was between two very large multinationals in the telecommunications and IT industries, involved a turnover of over about $40 million a year, and had been in existence for many years. A core requirement, from both sides, was to be seen to not be exerting excessive influence over the counterpart.

CONCLUSIONS AND MANAGERIAL IMPLICATIONS

The core contribution of many researchers over the past two decades has been to identify the importance of relationships in business-to-business markets. However, defining just what managers regard as a good relationship is not an issue that has been studied in any depth. We believe this paper to be a start in developing our understanding of this important issue.

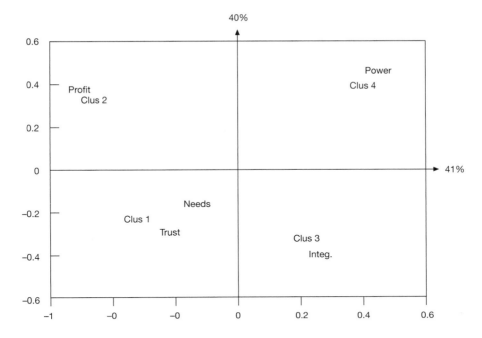

Figure 3 The four clusters indicating different views of relationship quality.

Table 4 Conjoint analysis per cluster, showing attribute scores and part-worths

Cluster 1	Trust	Needs	Integration	Power	Profit
Importance (%)	38.00	25.25	9.98	8.89	17.88
Utilities:					
better	3.03	1.98	0.58	−0.08	1.77
the same	1.08	0.83	0.16	−0.01	−0.41
worse	−4.11	−2.80	−0.74	0.09	−1.36
Cluster 2	Trust	Needs	Integration	Power	Profit
Importance (%)	17.28	12.31	10.51	13.91	46.00
Utilities:					
better	1.20	1.18	0.17	0.74	4.27
the same	0.63	−0.12	0.23	0.08	−0.08
worse	−1.83	−1.06	−0.40	−0.82	−4.19
Cluster 3	Trust	Needs	Integration	Power	Profit
Importance (%)	22.75	15.79	35.99	15.76	9.70
Utilities:					
better	2.54	1.33	3.25	−1.05	0.12
the same	−0.49	0.28	0.50	−0.07	0.78
worse	−2.05	−1.60	−3.75	1.12	−0.90
Cluster 4	Trust	Needs	Integration	Power	Profit
Importance (%)	13.33	14.07	11.85	44.44	16.30
Utilities:					
better	0.75	1.58	0.58	−3.92	−0.25
the same	0.75	−0.79	0.71	0.33	1.50
worse	−1.50	−0.79	−1.29	3.58	−1.25

As our results show, there is not one explanation of this construct: rather, there are different views of what determines a good relationship, and managers need to take this into account in planning the operationalization of their supply chain relationships. Although based on a relatively small sample, it does appear that just what determines the quality of a relationship is contingent upon wider contextual factors. In our case, levels of trust and the mutual integration of needs seemed to be the most common attributes of relationship quality, but certainly not the only ones. Other groups of managers are more profit oriented, or perhaps motivated by needs concerned with integration and power.

Further research is needed to shed light on how different independent variables might influence just what is required from a relationship. Based on our informal discussions with the managers involved, we would suggest that there are a number of factors that may act to influence the way in which relationships vary in terms of what constitutes quality, and managers need to identify these. Macro variables, such as the industries involved and the broader economic climate are obvious candidates, since they are likely to influence the levels of investment and of asset specificity dedicated to the particular relationship. However, we would suggest that there are also, possibly, potentially more subtle relationship-specific variables concerning both the companies involved, and also the relationship itself that determine the quality of the relationship. Managers need, for example, to consider the influence of the relationship age, whereby "mature" or "young" relationships within the same industry might well vary in what determines quality. In addition, the key players or decision makers involved in the relationship have an influence in determining the overall relationship quality. Future research therefore needs to focus not only on identifying the obvious demographic factors that influence how managers need to vary their approach to relationship management, but also the more subtle and variable ones.

REFERENCES

Addleman, S.: Orthogonal Main-Effect Plans for Asymmetrical Factorial Experiments. *Technometrics* **4, February**, 21–46 (1962).

Auty, S.: Using Conjoint Analysis in Industrial Marketing. *Industrial Marketing Management* **24**, 191–206 (1995).

Buttle, F.: Exploring Relationship Quality, in *Marketing Without Borders*. Proceedings of the 31st Annual Conference of the Academy of Marketing, R. Ashford, et al., eds., Manchester Metropolitan University 143–156, (1997).

Buttle, F.: The S.C.O.P.E. of Customer Relationship Management. *International Journal of Customer Relationship Management* **1(4)**, 327–336 (1999).

Carruthers, N.: Principal–Agent Relationships, in *Relationship Marketing: Theory and Practice*, F. Buttle, ed., Paul Chapman Publishing, London, 29–39, 1996.

Crosby, L. A., Evans, K. R., and Cowles, D.: Relationship Quality in Services Selling: An Interpersonal Influence Perspective. *Journal of Marketing* **54, July**, 68–81 (1990).

Gale, B. T., and Wood, R. C.: *Managing Customer Value: Creating Quality and Service That Customers Can See*. Free Press, New York, 1994.

Geyskens, I., and Steenkamp, J.-B.: An Investigation Into the Joint Effects of Trust and Interdependence on Relationship Commitment, in Proceedings of the 24th EMAC Conference, M. Bergadaa, ed., ESSEC, Cergy-Pontoise, 1995.

Geyskens, I., Steenkamp, J.-B., and Kumar, N.: A Meta-Analysis of Satisfaction in Marketing Channel Relationships. *Journal of Marketing Research* **36, May** 223–238 (1999).

Green, P. E., and Wind, Y.: New Way to Measure Consumers' Judgments. *Harvard Business Review*, **53, July/August**, 107–117 (1975).

Greenacre, M. J.: *Theory and Applications of Correspondence Analysis*. Academic Press, London, 1984.

Greenacre, M. J.: *Correspondence Analysis: Programme SIMCA* (Version 1.0). University of South Africa, South Africa, 1985.

Grönroos, C.: A Service Quality Model and Its Implications. *European Journal of Marketing* **18(4)**, 36–44 (1984).

Grönroos, C.: *Service Management and Marketing*. Lexington Books, Lexington, MA., 1990.

Gummesson, E.: The New Marketing; Developing Long-Term Interactive Relationships. *Long Range Planning* **20(4)**, 10–20 (1987).

Hoffman, D. L., and Franke, G. R.: Correspondence Analysis: Graphical Representation of Categorical Data in Marketing Research. *Journal of Marketing Research* **23, August**, 213–227 (1986).

Jones, T. O., and Sasser, W. E., Jr.: Why Satisfied Customers Defect. *Harvard Business Review*, **November–December**, 88–99 (1995).

Mitchell, A.: Loyal Yes, Staying No. *Management Today* **May**, 104–105 (1998).

Mohr, J., and Spekman, R.: Characteristics of Partnership Success: Partnership Attributes, Communication Behavior and Conflict Resolution Techniques. *Strategic Management Journal* **15**, 135–152 (1994).

Morgan, R. M., and Hunt, S. D.: The Commitment-Trust Theory of Relationship Marketing. *Journal of Marketing* **58**, 20–38 (1994).

Mummalaneni, V., and Wilson, D. T.: *The Influence of a Close Personal Relationship Between a Buyer and Seller on the Continued Stability of Their Role Relationship*. Institute for the Study of Business Markets, Penn State University, University Park, PA **working paper** (1991).

Naudé, P.: Judgmental Modeling as a Tool for Analysing Market Structure: An Application in the Plastics Industry. *Industrial Marketing Management* **24(3)**, 227–238 (1995).

Pruitt, D. G.: *Negotiation Behavior*. Academic Press, New York, 1991.

Ravald A., and Grönroos, C.: The Value Concept and Relationship Marketing. *European Journal of Marketing* **30(2)**, 19–30 (1996).

Reichheld, F. F.: Loyalty-Based Management. *Harvard Business Review*, **March–April**, 64–73 (1993).

Reichheld, F. F.: *The Loyalty Effect*. Harvard Business School Press, Boston, 1996.

Storbacka, K., Strandvik, T., and Grönroos, C.: Managing Customer Relationships for Profit: the Dynamics of Relationship Quality. *International Journal of Service Industry Management* **5(5)**, 21–38 (1994).

Ulrich, D.: Tie the Corporate Knot: Gaining Complete Customer Commitment. *Sloan Management Review* **Summer**, 19–27 (1989).

Wilson, D., and Jantrania, S.: Understanding the Value of a Relationship. *Asia-Australia Marketing Journal* **2(1)**, 55–66 (1996).

Wilson, D. T., and Mummalaneni, V.: Bonding and Commitment in Supplier Relationships: A Preliminary Conceptualization. *Industrial Marketing and Purchasing* **1(3)**, 44–58 (1986).

Wittink, D. R., and Cattin, P.: Commercial Use of Conjoint Analysis: An Update. *Journal of Marketing* **53(3)**, 91–96 (1989).

4.8 Adaptive behavior in buyer–supplier relationships

Ross Brennan and Peter W. Turnbull

INTRODUCTION

There is growing recognition that successful business-to-business marketing, in an era of globalization, outsourcing, right sizing, and intensifying competitive pressure, involves the positive management of individual buyer–supplier relationships. Sheth (1996) and Sheth and Sharma (1997) have reviewed the evolution of our understanding of organizational buying behavior over three decades, and concluded that as a result of the environmental and competitive pressures which buying firms face, it is to be expected that there will be a continuing trend in procurement practices from transactional approaches toward relationship approaches. Lewin and Johnston (1996) reinforced Sheth's argument, and emphasized that such trends in organizational buying behavior have serious consequences for the conduct of business-to-business marketing. It is at the individual level that interactions between buyers and suppliers take place, and it is at this level that the well-being of buyer–supplier relationships is affected. However, those individuals responsible for developing and managing buyer–supplier relationships need to work within a strategic framework, so that the "right" relationships are developed in the "right" ways.

Developing buyer–supplier relationships in the right ways requires an understanding of the adaptations which two firms engaged in a long-term relationship implement for each other. The purposes of this article are to report the results of a study of adaptive behavior in the telecommunications and automotive industries, to draw conclusions about the forces which drive adaptive behavior in buyer–supplier relationships, and to reflect on the meaning of these findings for managers responsible for business relationship management.

Prior studies have confirmed that specific adaptations by both buying and selling firms in the context of a single business relationship are not unusual. Hakansson (1982) reported examples of adaptations, and concluded that they could be classified as adaptations of the product specification, product design, manufacturing processes, planning, delivery procedures, stockholding, administrative procedures or financial procedures. Hallen et al. (1991, 1993) found that adaptations were associated with the power balance in the relationship, and with the level of commitment and trust between the partners. They suggested that there might be a systematic relationship between the extent of adaptive behavior within a relationship and the development stage of the relationship. Han et al. (1993) emphasized that close buyer–supplier relationships can have a downside, because the specific investments which the parties make in adaptations for each other reduce their freedom of choice in developing alternative relationships. Adaptive behavior for a single partner often creates sunk costs within the relationship, and the opportunity cost of adapting for one partner may be foregoing another good partnering opportunity. Adaptations, and the adaptive behavior which brings them about, are, therefore, conceptually similar to the idea of transaction-specific investments (Williamson, 1985; Nielson, 1996). However, the concept of inter-firm, buyer–seller adaptations is rather broader than that of transaction-specific investments, and more compatible with what Möller and Wilson (1995) have described as the interaction and network perspective on business marketing, since the unit of analysis is the dyadic relationship rather than the transaction.

Adaptive behavior in buyer–supplier relationships can be usefully, and simply, conceptualized in terms of the motivation causing one or other party to adapt, the process by which the adaptation is brought about, and the outcomes of the behavioral process (Brennan, 1998). In this article the outcomes of adaptive behavior and the processes of adaptation are addressed only briefly. On the basis of case study data, confirmatory evidence is described supporting earlier arguments that the concepts of power and social exchange in relationships are important drivers of adaptive behavior. It is argued that, although important, these factors are not exhaustive, and that the strategic marketing (purchasing) orientation of the partners to a relationship is also relevant. A question of considerable interest to marketing practitioners emerges from this discussion, namely, to what extent is the rhetoric of partnership sourcing (and relationship marketing) reflected in the reality of genuine adaptive behavior for relationship partners?

METHODOLOGY

Case study design

Wilson (1996) has urged researchers investigating buyer–supplier relationships in business-to-business markets to adopt methods which involve data collection at both ends of the dyad. She argued that the collection of richer data, incorporating the perspectives of respondents from both ends of the dyad, would compensate for the necessarily smaller sample sizes involved. That is the approach which has been adopted here. The results are based on the analysis of only 13 case studies of buyer–supplier relationships, but each of those case studies involved at least two in-depth interviews with managers directly involved in the management of the business relationship, one each from the buying and the selling organization.

The case study approach adopted employed what Yin (1994) has described as a multiple case, embedded design. Case studies were developed in the automotive and telecommunications sectors.[1] In each sector the process of case study development began with an investigation of the purchasing and supplier management strategies of three major purchasing organizations. Contacts within the purchasing organizations were asked to suggest two supply companies which could be used for the development of dyadic case studies. Respondents in the purchasing and the selling organizations were interviewed regarding the nature of the relationship. In both the purchasing and selling organizations respondents were identified who had direct involvement in the management of the focal relationship. Semi-structured interviews were used as the primary method of data collection, with a topic guide indicating the following broad areas to be investigated:

- background information on the respondent and the company
- the marketing (purchasing) strategy of the company
- trends in the business environment and market
- identification of key actors within the broader industry network
- history of the focal relationship
- adaptations within the focal relationship.

In all, 36 qualitative interviews were conducted with a total of 37 managers, representing 15 companies. The fieldwork was conducted in the United Kingdom, with firms headquartered in Europe and North America. A total of 13 buyer–supplier relationships were investigated, between six purchasing organizations and nine supply companies (see Table 1 (see Appendix 1)). Interview length varied from 1 hour to 4 hours, with a mean length of 2 hours. In addition to the face-to-face interviews, a variety of methods (fax, mail, phone, e-mail) were used to clarify or expand upon the data gathered. A number of characteristics of the fieldwork are noteworthy:

Table 1 Summary data on the case studies

Code	Customer/supplier	Custr adaptation	Custr orientation	Supplier adaptations	Supplier orientation	Age (yrs)	Power Balance
T1	UKTelco/ABC	3	(P)	3	T	30	Customer
T2	UKTelco/Softco	3	(P)	3	(P)	10	Symmetrical
T3	Intelco/ABC	2	(P)	2	T	30	Symmetrical
T4	Intelco/Canatel	2	(P)	3	P	10	Symmetrical
T5	Newco/ABC	1	P	1	T	3	Supplier
T6	Newco/Canatel	5	P	5	P	3	Supplier
A1	USAuto/Intl Exhausts	1	T	3	P	19	Customer
A2	USAuto/UK Metal	1	T	5	(P)	43	Customer
A3	Detroit Inc/Intl Exhausts	2	(P)	5	P	19	Customer
A4	Detroit Inc/Nippon Components	3	(P)	3	P	2	Customer
A5	Detroit Inc/Deutsch Components	2	(P)	2	T	30	Symmetrical
A6	UKAuto/UK Exhausts	2	P	4	P	20	Customer
A7	UKAuto/US Components	2	P	2	P	2	Symmetrical

- while it was anticipated that interviews would be on a one-to-one basis, a number of respondents chose to invite an interested colleague to the meeting, someone whom they believed could provide complementary information
- a number of respondents were interviewed more than once
- in the telecommunications sector, where the industrial concentration of the supply industry is high, a number of "purchasing" respondents selected the same supplier.

This last point had not been anticipated in the original research design, but proved fortuitous as it enabled direct comparisons to be made of the interactions between a single supply company and two or three purchasing organizations. This echoes Yin's (1994) comparison of the case study method with the experimental method. In the original research design it was intended to hold the "purchaser" variable constant, and to alter the "supplier" variable. Fortuitously, the case studies created instances where the "supplier" variable was held constant while the "purchaser" variable was altered. This made it possible to explore the impact of one supplier's marketing strategy in the context of two or more customer relationships.

As a means of validating the information gathered, notes of each qualitative interview were sent to the respondent for comment shortly after the meeting. A number of respondents provided feedback on the interview notes, usually where a point of fact regarding the industry or the relationship needed to be clarified. Subsequently, respondents were sent a report summarizing the results from the complete series of interviews, and again invited to comment. At this stage, presumably because it was by now some time since the interviews had been conducted, the number of responses received was low. This kind of process, sending interview notes and findings to respondents, is advocated by Miles and Huberman (1994) as one method of validating qualitative research data. In this study, some useful responses were received, and the process of engaging respondents in a dialogue improved the researcher/respondent relationship, facilitating subsequent access.

Measurement and analysis

For purposes of research convenience it is easier to concentrate on the perceptions of one party to the relationship concerning inter-firm adaptations (single-end research). Where the research objectives clearly pertain to single-end perceptions of adaptation behavior, this approach is valid. However, where the research objectives are to establish the "truth" of inter-firm adaptation behavior, this approach can only be valid if the perceptions of the parties do not differ substantially.

One of the findings from this study is that differences of perception regarding adaptive behavior do exist between buying and selling organizations. To summarize:

1. In general, respondents tended to emphasize adaptations made by their organization, and place less emphasis on adaptations made by the counterpart. Self-adaptation tends to be more visible than partner adaptation. Undoubtedly, there is a tendency to classify what the other party does as "no more than should be expected" (not an adaptation), and what one's own company does as "over and above normal expectations" (an adaptation).
2. More particularly, where a large customer interacts with a small supplier, the customer tends to underestimate the effort required within the supplier organization to respond to routine requests. For example, the large car OEMs expect their suppliers to adopt the current fashion in quality standards (e.g., ISO9000, QS9000 and customer-specific systems), and appear not to realize the administrative burden which this places on a small firm. The scale of an adaptation is normally judged against the resources available to your own organization.
3. The interpretation placed on a specific adaptation by the supplier and the customer can be different. For example, an adaptation perceived by Intelco respondents as a "breakthrough" in developing their relationship with ABC (where ABC were persuaded to release proprietary source code) was regarded by ABC respondents as a crude exploitation of power by Intelco, if anything damaging rather than strengthening the relationship.

It follows that all the other aspects of measurement of adaptation are colored by the perspective of the respondent. A relationship in which the customer (let us say, an automobile OEM) believes that the supplier has adapted infrequently, and on only a small scale, could be the same one in which the supplier (say, a small-scale automotive component manufacturer) believes that he has adapted often, and has devoted substantial resources to specific investment for the customer. Therefore, straightforward measurement techniques based on the reporting of the frequency and magnitude of adaptations by a respondent from one or other party to a relationship are fundamentally flawed. To reinforce Wilson's (1996) argument concerning the desirability of dyadic methods, the measurement of adaptation frequency and magnitude must be based, at least, on reports from respondents in both organizations.

The preliminary analysis of the data was conducted using the qualitative data analysis software QSR NUD.IST (version 3 for Windows). The use of specialist software for the analysis of qualitative data has been discussed by Weitzman and Miles (1995). Such software only facilitates the traditional qualitative analytical processes of developing an appropriate coding structure and applying the codes to the data; it cannot do the analysis. Once the data had been coded, the procedures recommended by Miles and Huberman (1994, pp. 197–200) for the development of qualitative scatterplot displays were followed. The basis for the scatterplots is presented in Appendix 2, where the definitions of the variables constructed from the case study data are also provided. Clearly this kind of display is not intended to serve the same purpose as a scatterplot derived from a representative, large-scale sample, employing quantitative analytical procedures. In an intrinsically quantitative study the data points in a scatterplot are largely decontextualised (although, even here, the analyst is likely to return to the original data to try to explain outliers). In an intrinsically qualitative study, such as this, the purpose of the analysis is to identify patterns in the data, which can then be further explored by returning to the original, rich case descriptions – the displays cannot be interpreted on their own, but only in the context of the case analyses. Therefore, throughout the following sections of this article, in which the results are discussed, there is a constant interplay between the convenient, but highly simplified scatterplot displays, and the original qualitative data. Figures 3, 5, 7, and 8 present scatterplots of the association between supplier adaptations and relationship age, power balance, customer and supplier managerial orientation. Figures 4, 6, 9, and 10 present the same analyses for customer adaptations.

PROCESSES OF DECISION MAKING IN BUYER–SELLER ADAPTATIONS

In this section the findings from the study concerning managerial decision-making processes involved in adaptive behavior are discussed. The field research revealed an enormous variety of adaptive behavior, ranging from minor adaptations involving some additional inter-organizational contact and exchange of non-confidential information, to major adaptations such as investment in large-scale customer-specific manufacturing equipment. Not surprisingly, there was an equally wide range of decision-making processes. In some cases adaptations took place without any conscious decision having been taken, while in other cases adaptations occurred only after extensive and formal data gathering, analysis, and decision-making processes. In the former case, adaptation is an unplanned process that "just happens," and there is no explicit evaluation of the net gain from adaptation either propter hoc or post hoc. In the latter case, adaptation is an extensively planned process, based explicitly on the formal evaluation of net gain, with post hoc evaluation of whether the anticipated return has been achieved.

Given this diversity in the decision-making process, an attempt is made here to categorize the different decision processes, and to identify the circumstances under which different decision-making processes are applicable. The theoretical framework suggested by Brennan and Turnbull (1997) is used to structure the analysis.

In Figure 1 adaptive behavior in buyer–supplier relationships is evaluated using the dimensions scale and formality. Relatively minor adaptations which are also planned are designated "tactical adaptations," because they can be thought of as political bargaining chips within the relationship. Major, planned adaptations, such as investment in large-scale manufacturing plant for a single customer, are designated "strategic adaptations," and involve formalized decision-making processes such as discounted cash-flow analysis. Minor, unplanned adaptations are regarded as a kind of organizational socialization process, by which two organizations learn how best to do business with each other. However, the accumulation of relatively small-scale adaptations over time can cause one firm to become substantially adapted to meet the needs of another, by a process rather like Mintzberg's (1994) idea that strategy can emerge as a pattern in a stream of decisions. Another way of thinking about this is that one or both firms in a buyer–supplier relationship can evolve in such a way that, over time, they become highly adapted for that single relationship. In this way, without any explicit decision being taken, extensive relationship-specific adaptation can take place.

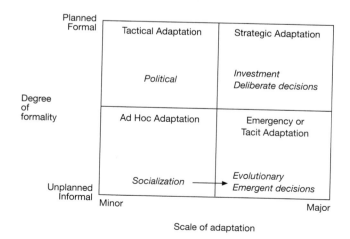

Figure 1   Adaptation process: Scale and formality.

Table 2 Decision-making in adaptation processes

Tactical adaptations: Political process
    Decision-making level: Typically at senior level of functional management (e.g., Purchasing Director to sign-off amended terms of contract) or at Board level
    Departments involved: Limited number of departments, nature of which depends upon the area in which the decision lies (e.g., purchasing and legal affairs where terms of contract are involved)
Ad hoc adaptations: Socialization process
    Decision-making level: Various, but generally at operating manager level in a large company. Decisions may be made at a senior level within a small company (within which (a) there are fewer decision-making levels and (b) a given adaptation is comparatively more important than in a large company).
    Departments involved: Normally only the department actually implementing the adaptation.
Strategic adaptations: Formal decision-making or investment process
    Decision-making level: Top management
    Departments involved: Wide range of departments for purposes of data gathering and analysis including marketing/purchasing, engineering, quality, production/operations, finance, legal affairs
Tacit adaptations: Emergent decision or evolutionary process
    Decision-making level: Undefined, since such decisions are 'emergent' rather than planned.
    Departments involved: Also undefined. Multiple departments will have been involved in the decisions which have created a situation of 'tacit adaptation'.

The involvement and influence of different managerial levels and departments in the adaptation process is associated with the nature of the adaptation and of the decision-making process. This association is illustrated in Table 2. Broadly, where planned adaptation decisions are involved the decision-making level, and the number of departments involved in the decision-making process vary with the magnitude of the prospective adaptation. Where the adaptations are unplanned, it is not possible to specify either a decision-making level or the range of departments involved in the process.

EXPLAINING ADAPTIVE BEHAVIOR

Trust and commitment

It is to be expected that the levels of trust and commitment will affect adaptive behavior, and that adaptations, in turn, will "feed back" into increased trust and commitment. A number of specific examples from the case studies illustrate this process:

- Newco/Canatel: in a very short time, the parties to the relationship have succeeded in bringing about a relationship atmosphere which is so close and trusting that some of Canatel's competitors have withdrawn from bidding for Newco contracts – adaptations on both sides have been extensive, bringing about a rapid growth of trust.
- Detroit Inc./International Exhausts: International Exhausts' investment in specific manufacturing capacity for Detroit Inc. was a demonstration of both trust and commitment within the relationship, and the atmosphere of the Detroit Inc./International Exhausts relationship is characterized by notably higher levels of cooperation and trust than the comparable International Exhausts/USAuto relationship.

Equally, it is to be expected that the absence of trust in a relationship will discourage important adaptive behavior. For example:

- USAuto/UK Metal: UK Metal reported that they withhold important cost information from USAuto because they are convinced that it would be used against them (i.e., that USAuto would use their considerable power advantage to appropriate any efficiency gains achieved by UK Metal, in this case an atmosphere of mistrust prevents adaptations from taking place which could be of mutual benefit).

- UKTelco/ABC: despite partnering overtures from senior management levels within UKTelco, operational managers within ABC have grown used to being treated harshly by this powerful customer in negotiations, and this inhibits adaptation; again, a low-trust/high-antagonism atmosphere prevents potentially beneficial adaptations from taking place.
- Intelco/Canatel: there is a similar pattern in this relationship, with the difference that power is more symmetrical, but again the problem was observed that entrenched mistrust and antagonism at operational levels was inhibiting a planned partnering initiative from bringing about beneficial adaptations. This relationship can be fruitfully compared with the Newco/Canatel relationship (the supplier is a constant, the purchasing organization is different), where substantial mutual adaptation was observed, alongside the rapid development of trust. In the Newco/Canatel relationship there was no entrenched mistrust to oppose the partnership development process, since Newco is a relatively young company, formed only a few years ago to exploit the deregulation of the British telecommunications market.

It seems to follow, therefore, that absent adaptations can be regarded as the opportunity cost of a low trust, antagonistic relationship.

The evidence from the case studies, therefore, supports the following assertions:

1. That a relationship characterized by high levels of trust and low antagonism is associated with high levels of adaptation.
2. That high levels of adaptation feed back into the relationship, increasing levels of trust and cooperation.
3. That a relationship characterized by low levels of trust and high antagonism, is associated with the withholding of potential adaptations.

Given these assertions, reciprocal adaptation would be expected from the parties to high-trust/high-commitment relationships, and an association would be expected between levels of supplier and customer adaptation. Figure 2 provides limited evidence in support of this idea. There is a broadly positive association between supplier and customer adaptations. However, there is a discrepancy between the telecommunications case studies (prefix T) and the automotive case studies (prefix A). An explanation may lie in the generally asymmetrical balance of power in automotive industry relationships. The role of power in adaptive behavior is discussed below.

Figure 2 Supplier and customer adaptations.

Adaptations and relationship age

Ford (1980) has suggested a link between adaptive behaviour and relationship life cycle stage, and Hallen et al. (1991) proposed a systematic relationship between adaptations and the stage of relationship development. However, Figures 3 and 4 suggest that there is little association between adaptations and relationship age. There was some evidence from the automotive sector that OEMs expect certain adaptations (such as JIT delivery and implementation of recognized quality systems) as a matter of course from their new suppliers, implying a clustering of adaptations in the early years of the relationship. On the other hand, in the case of the longest-lived relationships in the telecommunications sector (UKTelco/ABC, Intelco/ABC), it was the relative scarcity of adaptations which was a cause for surprise. In such cases, where two firms have done business together for so long, then it is possible that most of the necessary inter-firm adaptations have already been implemented, so that little recent activity is reported. This is akin to Ford's idea that adaptations would become less noticeable during the long-term phase of the relationship life-cycle (Ford, 1980).

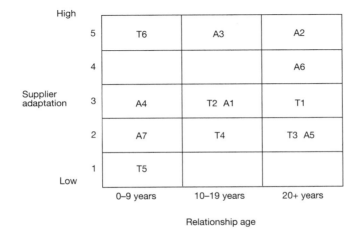

Figure 3 Supplier adaptations and relationship age.

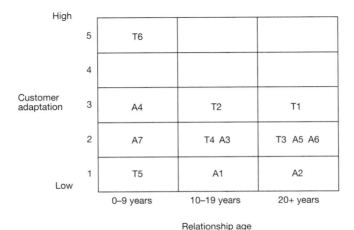

Figure 4 Customer adaptations and relationship age.

There is little evidence of any regular pattern in the timing of adaptations within buyer–seller relationships. In some cases there may be an early cluster of adaptations, primarily of the socialization type, in order to facilitate business between the two firms. In other cases there are long periods of relative inactivity, followed by bursts of new adaptation (for example, UKTelco/Softco [T2]). Major investment-type adaptations have been observed both at an early stage of the relationship (Newco/Canatel [T6]) and in a well-established, mature relationship (Detroit Inc/ International Exhausts [A3]). Naturally, adaptations which fall into the "tacit" or "emergent" category, and which follow from a long sequence of decisions which eventually bind a company very tightly to a partner, will only be seen in mature relationships (e.g., USAuto/UK Metal [A2]).

Adaptations and relationship power balance

Hallen et al. (1991) found that adaptations in buyer–supplier relationships were associated with relative power. Figure 5 indicates the existence of an association between supplier adaptations and the relationship power balance, while Figure 6 indicates little association between customer adaptations and power balance.

The association between supplier adaptations and the relationship power balance is expected, based on the resource-dependence theory of Pfeffer and Salancik (1978). The presumed causal mechanism linking adaptations to power is based upon the high degree of dependence of the supplier on the customer, and therefore the ability of the customer organization either through the coercive or the implicit exploitation of this power balance to enforce adaptations. Underlying this process is the knowledge that "you need us more than we need you," and the threat (usually implicit, sometimes explicit) that "if you don't do what we want, then we will take our business elsewhere." Such a causal mechanism is highly plausible in the USAuto/UK Metal case (A2), but less plausible in the Detroit Inc/International Exhausts case (A3). In the former case, managers at UK Metal are very conscious of the company's dependence on USAuto, and clearly feel coerced into substantial organizational adaptations. Where UK Metal resisted this coercion (and refused a specific adaptation for a USAuto division), they are convinced that this caused a loss of goodwill and of subsequent business. However, in the latter case the impression of the relationship is different. The Detroit Inc./International Exhausts case is characterized by apparently high levels of trust, and there is no evidence that International Exhausts was coerced into the major adaptations which it has undertaken for Detroit Inc. The managerial orientations of the two parties were at least as important as the relationship power balance in bringing about supplier adaptations. International

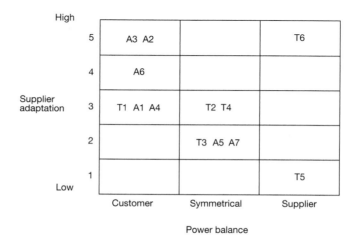

Figure 5 Supplier adaptations and power balance.

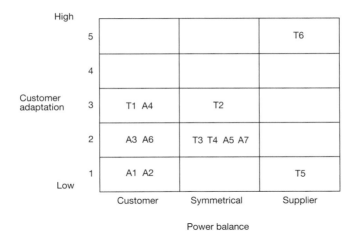

Figure 6 Customer adaptations and power balance.

Exhausts were determined to foster long-term relationships with key customers, while Detroit Inc. is in the process of developing a supplier partnering strategy.

There is little evidence in Figure 6 of an association between customer adaptations and the relationship power balance. However, important instances of customer adaptation were identified during the field research which did seem to be associated with power. For example, Detroit Inc. has adapted their standard terms of contract for Deutsch Components – this is not a major adaptation in resource terms, but is significant from the Detroit Inc. perspective. In another case (from the pilot study), a Detroit Inc. manager described how Detroit Inc. had tamely acceded to an 8% price increase from an American supplier, when price reductions were being demanded from other suppliers. In both of these cases, the explanation from Detroit Inc. is that the supplier is acknowledged to have a world-wide technological lead in an important product area, so that Detroit Inc.'s buying power is effectively canceled out. It may be that the contradiction between such examples and the absence of any association in Figure 8 may simply be attributed to the limitations of the data. The study was designed to understand adaptation behavior in context, and therefore uses comparatively few, in-depth case studies, which were selected non-randomly.

The outlier relationships in Figures 5 and 6 revolve around the telecommunications organization Newco. In the Newco/Canatel relationship (T6), there has been substantial supplier adaptation, despite a power balance clearly favoring the supplier. In the Newco/ABC relationship (T5), there has been negligible customer adaptation, again despite a power balance which favors the supplier. These examples demonstrate that power alone is insufficient as an explanation of adaptation behavior. Another striking example is that between the USAuto/International Exhausts relationship (A1) and the Detroit Inc./International Exhausts relationship (A3). Despite a similar power balance in each case, International Exhausts has adapted markedly less for USAuto than for Detroit Inc.

Adaptations and managerial orientation

The role of managerial orientation in explaining adaptive behavior has not been explored in prior research, but emerged from the preliminary analysis of the qualitative data. Each of the firms investigated has a unique orientation toward partnership development. However, these can be classified into three dominant categories.

Table 3 Buying and selling firms managerial orientation

Transactional	Transitional	Partnering
Buying	Buying	Buying
USAuto	UKTelco	Newco
Selling	Intelco	UKAuto
ABC	Detroit Inc	Selling
Deutsch Components	Selling	Canatel
	Softco	International Exhausts
	UK Metal	Nippon Components
		UK Exhausts
		US Components

1. Transactional. Inter-firm relationships are managed predominantly on a transactional basis: if a buying organization, then there is no policy to develop long-term partnership sources, if a selling organization, there is no (explicit or implicit) policy of relationship marketing.
2. Transitional. Historically, inter-firm relationships have been managed on a transactional basis. However, the organization is now committed, at the top management level, to develop a relational approach. If a buying organization, a policy of partnership sourcing has been developed, if a selling organization, efforts are being made to develop long-term customer relationships.
3. Partnering. Partnership sourcing, or relationship marketing, are now firmly embedded in organizational practice (i.e., the problems of implementation have been successfully addressed).

Each organization has been classified according to this framework in Table 3.

Figures 7 and 8 examine the following associations:

- between supplier adaptations and customer orientation: does a partnership sourcing policy tend to promote adaptations on the part of supply firms?
- between supplier adaptations and supplier orientation: does an orientation toward relationship marketing tend to promote adaptations within the supply firm?

Only the direct association between supplier adaptations and supplier managerial orientation emerges clearly from the diagrams. In five relationships, supplier adaptations were judged to be

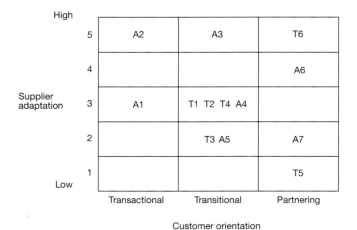

Figure 7 Supplier adaptations and customer orientation.

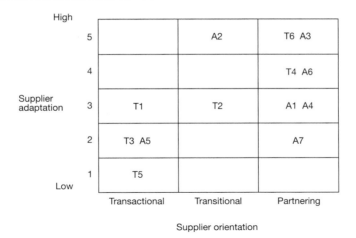

Figure 8 Supplier adaptations and supplier orientation.

substantial (level 4 or 5), and in four of these relationships the supplier has successfully implemented relationship marketing. In four relationships, supplier adaptations were judged to be relatively minor (level 1 or 2), and in three of these relationships the supplier pursues a transactional approach to marketing.

Figures 9 and 10 examine the following associations:

- between customer adaptations and supplier orientation: does a relationship marketing approach tend to promote adaptations on the part of customer firms?
- between customer adaptations and customer orientation: does an orientation toward partnership sourcing tend to promote adaptations within the customer firm?

There is no real support for these associations from the figures, nor from the detailed information which was gathered in the case studies. There is an outlier relationship (Newco/Canatel, T6) which, if excluded, would remove any discernible pattern from the scatter. This was, indeed, a rather

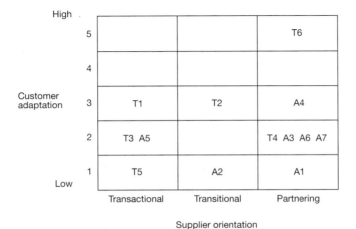

Figure 9 Customer adaptations and supplier orientation.

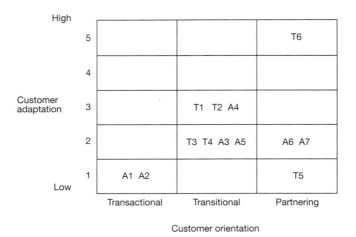

Figure 10 Customer adaptations and customer orientation.

unusual buyer–seller relationship, in which the relatively young buying organization (Newco) has made an explicit strategic management decision to out-source the bulk of its systems operations. The substantial adaptation of Newco for Canatel is best explained in terms of concrete managerial decision making, not in terms of resource dependence (power) or pre-existing trust/commitment.

MANAGERIAL IMPLICATIONS

Adaptive behavior in buyer–supplier relationships is both planned and unplanned. Where adaptation is planned it appears that the relationships between the magnitude of the adaptation decision, the seniority of the decision-making level, and the complexity of the data gathering and decision-making processes are fairly direct, as might be expected. However, substantial adaptations can emerge incrementally over time as a result of a sequence of decisions, each of which was individually relatively unimportant. This conclusion has immediate managerial significance. Managers must be aware that, as a result of a series of incremental decisions none of which is in itself substantial, their firm can become substantially adapted to the needs of one other firm. Han et al. (1993) have pointed out that close relationships have disadvantages as well as advantages and, consequently, that the acquisition of such relationships should be handled with care. In the absence of some process of strategic relationship management, there is a danger that a firm could, through an unplanned process of adaptation, become deeply involved in a disadvantageous relationship. In the process of strategic relationship management, the actual and desired balance of adaptive behavior in the relationship is a matter which should receive attention.

This study has provided further evidence to support the finding reported by Hallen et al. (1991) that adaptations within a buyer–supplier relationship tend to increase levels of trust and enhance commitment to the relationship. In turn, as trust and commitment grow, so there is a greater likelihood of mutually advantageous adaptive behavior. However, in one of the case study relationships there was evidence that this kind of virtuous cycle had gone too far, and the perception of both parties was that some reduction in intimacy would be desirable – sharing just a little less confidential information, being involved less in each other's strategic planning processes, taking it less as a given that the supplier would always be first choice for certain types of equipment purchase. Managers should be aware that there is a healthy limit to the relationship development process, beyond which the costs begin to outweigh the benefits.

The age of a relationship appears to be a poor predictor of the extent of current adaptation activity. If age is used as a proxy for the stage of relationship development, then there is no evidence of a link between relationship stage and adaptive behavior. Certainly there are cases where the early phase of a relationship is characterized by a burst of adaptation activity. Equally, there are relationships in which, after a "quiet period," there is a further burst of adaptations – perhaps in response to some external change (e.g., in technology), perhaps in response to a change of managerial policy in one of the parties to the relationship (e.g., a customer implements "supplier partnering"). However, there seems to be no general relationship between adaptation intensity and relationship age. It might be possible to establish some link between adaptive behavior and the stage of development of a relationship measured using something other than relationship age. However, in recent years academic opinion has turned against the notion that buyer–supplier relationships pass through neat stages of development (Halinen, 1994; Turnbull et al., 1996). On balance, these findings are probably good news for managers. What is implied is that the age of a relationship is not intrinsically a barrier to adaptive behavior. Relationships which appear to have settled into a long-term pattern of behavior, perhaps of only marginal value to the parties, can be revitalized by positive management action (for example, the UK Telco/Softco relationship).

An unsurprising conclusion is that adaptive behavior is influenced by the power balance within the relationship. This confirms earlier findings (Håkansson, 1982), and corresponds with common sense. From a managerial perspective, perhaps the key finding is that adaptations are driven by other factors in addition to power. Admittedly, to the small supplier, dwarfed and dominated by a major OEM customer which accounts for a very large proportion of its sales, this finding may not be very comforting. Certainly, there are circumstances in which an imbalance of power is the primary factor driving adaptive behavior (for example, UK Metal/USAuto).

Managerial orientation emerges as an important factor driving adaptations in the case of suppliers which adopt a relational approach to marketing. Other associations between managerial orientation and adaptations were less clear. In particular, examples have been found of buying firms which explicitly espouse a partnership sourcing philosophy, but whose suppliers perceive no enhanced support. No general relationship between a commitment to partnership sourcing and concrete actions to support suppliers emerged from the data. Managers marketing to firms which are in the process of implementing such programs are, therefore, advised to exercise all of their natural caution, and to look for tangible outcomes from the program before investing further in the relationship. Additional investment creates additional dependency, which enhances buyer power. In the absence of compensating relationship investments by the buying organization, all that has happened is that the supplier has reduced its bargaining power in the relationship.

NOTE

1. Company pseudonyms are used throughout to preserve respondent confidentiality. A summary of the case study companies and relationships is provided in Appendix 1.

REFERENCES

Brennan, D. R.: *Adaptations in Inter-Firm, Buyer–Seller Relationships*, unpublished PhD thesis, University of Manchester Institute of Science and Technology (1998).

Brennan, R., and Turnbull, P. W.: The Process of Adaptation in Inter-Firm Relationships, in *Relationships and Networks in International Markets*, H-G. Gemunden, T. Ritter, A. Walter, eds., Elsevier, Oxford, 1997.

Ford, D.: The Development of Buyer–Seller Relationships in Industrial Markets. *European Journal of Marketing* **14(5/6)**, 339–354 (1980).

Håkansson, H. (ed): *International Marketing and Purchasing of Industrial Goods*. John Wiley and Son, Chichester, 1982.

Halinen, A.: *Exchange Relationships in Professional Services: A Study of Relationship Development in the Advertising Sector*. Publications of the Turku School of Economics and Business Administration, Turku, 1994.

Hallen, L., Johanson, J., and Seyed-Mohamed, N.: Interfirm Adaptation in Business Relationships. *Journal of Marketing* **55**, **April**, 29–37 (1991).

Hallen, L., Johanson, J., and Seyed-Mohamed, N.: Dyadic Business Relationships and Customer Technologies. *Journal of Business-to-Business Marketing* **1**(**4**), 63–90 (1993).

Han, S.-L., Wilson, D. T., and Dant, S. P.: Buyer–Supplier Relationships Today. *Industrial Marketing Management* **22**, 331–338 (1993).

Lewin, J. E., and Johnston, W. J.: The Effects of Organizational Restructuring on Industrial Buying Behavior: 1990 and Beyond. *Journal of Business and Industrial Marketing* **11**, 93–111 (1996).

Miles, M. B., and Huberman, A. M.: *An Expanded Sourcebook: Qualitative Data Analysis*, 2nd edition. Sage, Thousand Oaks, CA, 1994.

Mintzberg, H.: *The Rise and Fall of Strategic Planning*. Prentice Hall, New York, 1994.

Möller, K., and Wilson, D. T. (eds): *Business Marketing: An Interaction and Network Perspective*. Kluwer Academic Publishers, Dordrecht, 1995.

Nielson, C. C.: An Empirical Examination of Switching Cost Investments in Business-to-Business Marketing Relationships. *Journal of Business and Industrial Marketing* **11**(**6**), 38–60 (1996).

Pfeffer, J., and Salancik, G. R.: *The External Control of Organizations: A Resource Dependence Perspective*. Harper and Row, New York, 1978.

Sheth, J.: Organizational Buying Behavior: Past Performance and Future Expectations. *Journal of Business and Industrial Marketing* **11**, 7–24 (1996).

Sheth, J., and Sharma, A.: Relationship Marketing: An Agenda for Inquiry. *Industrial Marketing Management* **26**, 91–100 (1997).

Turnbull, P. W., Ford, D., and Cunningham, M.: Interaction, Relationships and Networks in Business Markets: An Evolving Perspective. *Journal of Business and Industrial Marketing* **11**, (3/4), 44–62 (1996).

Weitzman, E. B., and Miles, M. B.: *A Software Sourcebook: Computer Programs for Qualitative Data Analysis*. Sage, Thousand Oaks, CA, 1995.

Williamson, O. E.: *The Economic Institutions of Capitalism*. Free Press, New York, 1985.

Wilson, E. J.: Theory Transitions in Organizational Buying Behavior Research. *Journal of Business and Industrial Marketing* **11**(**6**), 7–19 (1996).

Yin, R. K.: *Case Study Research: Design and Methods*, 2nd edition. Sage, Thousand Oaks, CA, 1994.

Appendix 1   Case study companies

PURCHASING ORGANIZATIONS

UKTelco	UK and international telecommunications provider
Intelco	UK based international telecommunications provider
Newco	UK telecommunications provider
USAuto	US based global automobile manufacturer
Detroit Inc	US based global automobile manufacturer
UKAuto	German owned, UK based automobile manufacturer

SELLING ORGANIZATIONS

ABC	UK/German owned, UK based telecommunications manufacturer
Softco	Major American software company
Canatel	Canadian owned global telecommunications manufacturer
International Exhausts	UK exhaust manufacturer, subsidiary of a US conglomerate
UK Metal	Small UK metal component manufacturer
Nippon Components	Joint UK/Japanese owned automotive component manufacturer
Deutsch Components	Large family-owned German automotive component manufacturer
UK Exhausts	UK exhaust manufacturer, subsidiary of a UK automotive group
US Components	UK components subsidiary of USAuto

RELATIONSHIPS INVESTIGATED

Purchasing organization		*Selling organization*
UKTelco	with	ABC
UKTelco	with	Softco
Intelco	with	ABC
Intelco	with	Canatel
Newco	with	ABC
Newco	with	Canatel
USAuto	with	International Exhausts
USAuto	with	UK Metal
Detroit Inc	with	International Exhausts
Detroit Inc	with	Nippon Components
Detroit Inc	with	Deutsch Components
UKAuto	with	UK Exhausts
UKAuto	with	US Components

Appendix 2   Basis for the cross-case matrix analysis

Definitions of terms

Adaptations scale
  I. Negligible adaptations of any kind
  II. Some adaptations, relatively minor (socialization)
  III. Considerable socialization adaptation or small-scale strategic adaptation
  IV. Substantial strategic adaptation has taken place
  V. The organization is substantially adapted to the partner, several strategic adaptations, or evidence of extensive tacit adaptation

Orientation scale
  • *T = Transactional*: buying and selling processes are managed on a predominantly transactional, arm's length basis
  • *(P) = Transitional*: the organization is in the process of implementing a partnership sourcing or relationship marketing strategy (policy)
  • *P = Partnering*: evidence that the organization has successfully implemented a partnership sourcing or relationship marketing strategy (policy)

Power scale
  • *Customer*: the supplier is relatively more dependent than the customer on the relationship
  • *Symmetrical*: there is an approximate equivalence between the parties in terms of dependence
  • *Supplier*: the customer is relatively more dependent than the supplier on the relationship

4.9

First steps in technology strategy

David Ford and Mike Saren

INTRODUCTION

In this chapter we first examine three different views of the relationship between technology and strategy. This leads to a definition of technology strategy. We examine the technological interdependence that exists between companies and provides a categorisation of three generic types of technology. We believe that a strategic approach to technology is as much about attitude as about plans, and as much about ideas as about structure. A strategic view of technology is more likely to emerge slowly through careful thought and self-analysis, rather than be produced by a conscious, deliberate strategy development programme. This means that we should not start our discussion with a view that "strategy" means the same as "plan". Instead, we see company strategy more as the formation of perspective (Quinn and Mintzberg, 1991) and this book is about the development of that perspective.

THREE VIEWS OF TECHNOLOGY AND STRATEGY

It is important to make clear the exact relationship between technology strategy and the more general concept of corporate strategy and hence the precise area of our attention in this book. We can think of three aspects of this relationship. First, there is a technological dimension to overall corporate strategy in the same way that there is a financial, production or marketing dimension to it. Each dimension is an area to which attention must be devoted, each provides ingredients for the strategy development process and each is a way in which strategy is implemented and through which the effects of strategy become apparent. Thus, a corporate strategy to achieve a low-cost position can be implemented through process technology improvements to achieve lower production costs. This strategy also has a product technology element as design improvements can lead both to product cost reductions and a smoother production flow. Further, a low-cost strategy will affect the brief given to the purchasing department on the types of components which should be bought and the product technology on which they are to be based.

Second, technology can be used as a unit of analysis in evaluating a company's behaviour and performance as a basis for strategy development. This is similar to the way in which we could evaluate a company in terms of its financial or market performance. Thus, if we have the tools of analysis we could consider such factors as technological leadership, exploitation performance, technology share, etc. In this book we are involved with questions of evaluation of a company's overall technological position and performance. We argue strongly for the value of an analysis in technological terms as a basis for strategy building and suggest that this is particularly important in today's conditions of rapid technological change and uncertainty.

Third, we can consider the development of strategy for the acquisition, management and exploitation of the company's technology. This is the view of technology strategy with which we are mainly concerned in this book. The elements of technology strategy are illustrated in Figure 1.

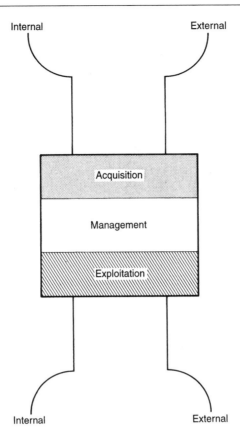

Figure 1 The elements of technology strategy.

The acquisition of technology includes far more than conventional R&D. Technology can be acquired internally, through the company's own R&D, or externally, by licensing from other companies, or from contract research houses, or via joint ventures with others or from suppliers of products, etc.

Similarly, technology can be exploited internally, by incorporating it in the company's own products, processes or market offerings or externally, by licensing it to others, by turnkey deals, by contract manufacturing for others, by designing or marketing products for them, or by joining in joint ventures with them.

Finally, technology management includes a variety of activities:

- the development of long-term strategy for technology;
- the co-ordination of different means of acquisition and exploitation of technology;
- effectively transferring technologies between different operating units within the company;
- efficiently inserting new technologies where they are needed;
- integrating the different technologies which are held by the company and those around it to meet the requirements of any chosen customer.

Our approach to technology strategy is not confined to the issue of technological innovation, because introducing innovative technology may be irrelevant to a company at any one time. Instead, it may be vital for that company to concentrate on strategy for the fullest exploitation of its existing technology. This exploitation may involve difficult choices between a variety of different means such as new product introduction, licensing or joint ventures, all of which can have both short- and long-term consequences for the company. Perhaps even more importantly, we would argue that a strategic approach to technology is vital even for companies that may see themselves as being low-tech or would never think of being involved in innovation. These companies also need a clear understanding of the technologies on which their companies are based, their respective positions in these technologies and their performance in exploiting their technological assets.

TECHNOLOGY STRATEGY

We use the following working definition of technology strategy: Technology strategy is the tasks of building, maintaining and exploiting a company's technological assets, no matter what their level or newness when compared to other companies in the same or other industries.

This definition emphasises that technology strategy is central to a company, whether it is a "high" or "low" technology company, a product or service provider, a technological "innovator" or a "follower". This means that in order to make sense of technology strategy we cannot simply concentrate on what is to be the content of that strategy. Instead, we must look at technology strategy in its wider organisational and corporate strategical contexts, both of which have such an impact on the outcome and success of strategy. For example, collaboration between different functions in the company is vital for success in the technological innovation process (Ford, 1990; Nonaka, 1990).

A company's technology is the sum total of its abilities – including that which exists inside the heads of all its staff. Technology strategy is not something which can be separated out as the responsibility of a single department. It cannot be relegated to a terse request from marketing or elsewhere for R&D to produce "something new and quick". Nor is technology a question of detailed implementation and hence beneath the dignity of those with strategic responsibilities. On the contrary technology is a thread which runs through *all* aspects of a company and hence it can only be understood within the context of the whole company and its culture.

BASIS OF ANALYSIS: TECHNOLOGY AS ASSETS

A prerequisite for the development of strategy is a process of self-analysis to establish current position. This analysis must be expressed in a language which is appropriate to the subject of the strategy. Thus our language must be about technology and not about products or markets. Technology is embodied in products or services and these are the final outputs from technology strategy, not its ingredients. Technology strategy is not just about managing R&D, or the process of introducing new technology into the company. Nor is it just about new ventures or new products. An approach to technology strategy must start with the following questions:

1. What are the technological assets on which the past, present and future success of the company depend?
2. Can these assets be divided into those which are core and those which are more peripheral?
3. How can we assess the strength of our assets, relative to those of our competitors, how can we maintain them and how can we grow them?
4. How can we ensure that we achieve the best possible return on the investment we have made in these assets?

Our view of technology strategy looks at least one level behind a conventional listing of strengths in terms of products and markets. Instead of taking these products and markets as the units of analysis, we believe that we must examine and evaluate the underlying technologies which form the basis of its products and processes: "The core of a company is not its products or its markets, but what it knows and what it can do" (Ford, 1988).

Internal and external technologies

The distinction between internal and external technologies is important in the development of technology strategy. Internal technologies are those which the company owns or controls, possibly because they were developed by the company itself. External technologies are those from which the company benefits but does not own, such as those that have been developed by companies which supply it with products or services. The management task in developing technology strategy includes decisions on which areas of technology the company wishes to develop internally. It also includes decisions on which technologies it should not develop for itself, but on which it will continue to depend. These external technologies are increasingly vital as the cost and range of technologies needed to operate in any market escalate. Therefore, relationships with product or service suppliers must increasingly be seen in technological terms, rather than as routine, cost-reducing, fail-safe activities which are labelled as "purchasing".

Ideas such as those concerning partnership purchasing, if properly conceived, can tie together the existing and potential technologies of both buyer and seller companies. But a failure by a company to effectively use and develop the technologies of its suppliers means that the sum total of the technology which the buying company has available is restricted to its own internal "stock", or that which it is able to develop internally. The value of external technologies was illustrated by Kenichi Ohmae when he spoke of "the heart of IBM's accomplishment with the PC is its decision – and its ability – to approach the development effort as a process of managing multiple external vendors" (Ohmae, 1982).

Example
Externalising technology. The interrelationship between distinctive and external technologies over time
This example shows how the technologies controlled by the firm can change in value and lose their distinctiveness as technical change elsewhere impacts upon them. In this case the development of microprocessor technologies for applications in other industries made redundant some of the central skills of the company.

This datacommunications firm manufactured and sold a range of products, services and systems to business users. One of its core product groups, modems, was traditionally supported by substantial R&D expenditure, particularly on system software. The ability to use standard circuitry, adapted to differing product and customer needs by varying software configurations, was considered a key distinctive skill.

Within the microprocessor industry, however, major investments were being made in the development of integrated circuits aimed at specific applications. In this way, manufacturers sought to counter the growing "commoditisation" of chips. In due course the communications industry was targeted with the development of the "modem on a chip". Much of the functionality of earlier combined hardware and software could now be integrated on to a single microprocessor.

The result for the company was that many of its product technologies based on its own design skills in this area became obsolete. In response it elected to rely on external sources of product and process technology rather than invest heavily in updating its own. The company concentrated on maintaining its market skills and developing new skills in managing critical supplier relationships (marketing technology). It accepts that a key technology is now external to the firm and gains access to this technology through a purchasing relationship.

Example
Externalising technology: Massey Ferguson
Snowballing development costs have led to rationalisation in the tractor market. Survivors have had to reduce development resources and activities, and learn to rely more on specialist suppliers.

Massey Ferguson, a long-established tractor maker has, along with its competitors, faced hard commercial times over the last ten years. It used to make a full range of tractor models and related equipment such as combine harvesters.

Now, under the same sustained competitive pressures which led Ford and Fiat to merge their tractor operations in 1992, it makes two middle-market tractor ranges in the UK and France respectively, and fills in its product range by selling badged models sourced mainly from Japan. More fundamentally, it is re-examining its engineering and development activities and deciding which areas of tractor design should remain inhouse and which should be left to suppliers. In future Massey Ferguson aim to compete by "maintaining a core tractor knowledge and utilising outside resources as and when appropriate for specific design tasks".

To this end a major reorganisation has taken place at the two manufacturing locations. At the UK factory in Coventry, tractor assembly and marketing is now separate from the manufacture of components and subassemblies. Internally manufactured parts consist of gears and driveshafts, major chassis castings and the linkages to towed implements such as ploughs. Towed implements are to be outsourced, in line with a strategy to produce only transmission and associated castings internally. While the logic underlying this simplification of business philosophy is clear, it creates new management tasks and changes priorities both within and between functional areas.

For engineering, a major task now is the overseeing and co-ordination of design activity within suppliers and contracted design houses. In general, a more modular overall product design philosophy has had to be adopted to allow components and subsystems to be effectively integrated.

More specifically, intense design collaboration is needed. For example, in developing a new range of tractors to replace its current basic models (which derive from a 1950's design), Massey Ferguson decided that even in the core area of transmissions, specialist design input was desirable for four-wheel drive models. A four-wheel drive firm was contracted to provide leading edge knowledge in this area. Because the bulk of this firm's experience was in road and rally cars, considerable joint activity was needed to link these skills to Massey Ferguson's knowledge of tractor performance, reliability, operating conditions, etc. As a result a team of Massey Ferguson engineers has been sited with the supplier for the duration of the project. In a similar example for engines, the need to trim external designs to specific requirements has led Massey Ferguson to "do more engine design in the last 12 months than in the last 20 years".

For the purchasing function, a routine order management role has been transformed by the need to manage these critical supplier relationships. For bought components such as fuel injection systems, tractor firms represent a small niche market in comparison to mass-production car makers. A major challenge for Massey Ferguson will therefore be persuading suppliers to meet its particular technical requirements. Skill in choosing co-operative suppliers, and in carefully managing relationships with them, will be a key to its future competitive success.

TECHNOLOGIES AND INTERCOMPANY NETWORKS

We have already emphasised that an understanding of technology and its management needs to take place within the context of the network of competing and co-operating companies within which all firms are enmeshed. A technology in itself has no value. It is simply a passive resource which is only activated when its owner interacts with another company which places some value on it –

either because the other company wishes to acquire the technology for its own use, or because it wishes to buy products or services based on the technology, or plans to combine this technology with its own skills to provide something of value to others in the network. The value of a technology is specific to the other company and will be related to that company's own technologies and to its view of the technologies of other companies in the surrounding network.

A company which seeks to meet the requirements of its customers will use its own technologies and those which are embodied in the products and services of other companies which supply it. In order to meet customer requirements it may also seek to acquire other technologies directly, from licensors, contract research houses or those with which it has a joint venture. In this way it builds a "bundle" of technologies suitable for its own customer (Figure 2). It may also use the services of other companies that provide the means by which the bundle of technologies can reach the customer, such as distribution companies or subcontract manufacturers, etc. Of course the company will not control this bundling process entirely. Other companies will have their own ideas of the importance of the company and its customer, and their own role in the network. Thus for example,

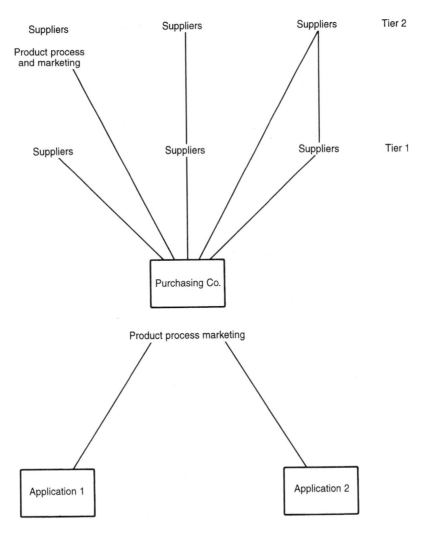

Figure 2 Technologies and networks.

a component maker may seek to influence how its components are used and who the final products are sold to.

The interaction between a company and those that surround it is not simply to acquire the use of their technologies. This interaction is not a zero-sum gain; both sides benefit by the exchange which takes place and by the learning which occurs from each other through the interaction, perhaps over many years. In this way the technological resources of both parties can grow through that interaction.

Interaction and product development

This brings us to a second reason for emphasising the interdependence between companies. A large proportion of new products are not developed by suppliers alone or by buyers, but interactively between them. Because of this, our ideas of the nature of the product development task in industrial firms may need to be revised and the question of intellectual property rights becomes much more complicated. Additionally, companies will need to think very carefully about how the product development task carried out with any one partner will affect its dealings with others. Even more importantly, interdependence between companies means that a nationally independent company is not surrounded by a solid boundary, but by one which is permeable. In fact, when we look at many companies which buy and sell from each other or develop products together, it is rather difficult to identify the boundary between them or where the areas of each company's responsibility, ownership or even culture start and finish. The extent to which a company will allow others to influence its nominally internal activities and will seek to involve itself within others is an important issue of managerial decision-making and control. For example, when a company is developing a new product it will often be influenced in that activity by the product development departments of a customer or its own suppliers. Similarly, the production plans for a new product will often be largely determined by the quality specifications of a main customer. Lake and Trayes (1990) describe this interaction as occurring across "discretionary boundaries" and this is illustrated in Figure 3.

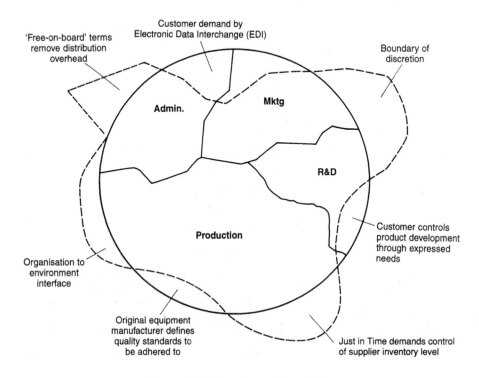

Figure 3 Discretionary boundaries.

TECHNOLOGY STRATEGY, PRODUCTS AND PROCESSES

A technological perspective on analysing a company may give a different view of the activity of buying products or services. For example, a customer may appear to choose a supplier because it wishes to buy its particular products. However, that supplier's products may be absolutely standard and unremarkable. Instead the buyer may have chosen the supplier because of the distinctive way in which it produces these standard products, which provides greater consistency of quality. In this way the purchase is actually determined by the process technology of the product supplier. The customer values these skills of the supplier, either because of its own lack of production capacity or because it does not have the necessary process technology itself. This may mean that if it produced the product itself its costs of production would be higher or its quality lower. In this way the company is treating these process technologies as "external".

In some cases the importance of the supplier's process technology is reinforced because the customer may be buying to its own product design. Even when this is not the case and the product is designed by the seller (based on their product technology), the customer may not be prepared to pay a premium for those technologies and will decide between suppliers on the basis of competing process strengths.

On the other hand, a buying company may not be primarily interested in either the product or process technologies of a supplier. It may seek to take advantage of the supplier's Marketing technology. Marketing technology includes the skill of market analysis, the ability to tailor product and process technologies to the particular requirements which have been analysed and skills in logistics, advertising and selling. These skills are necessary in order to transfer a package of product and process technologies to a particular application. In many cases it is the marketing technologies of the seller which are critical in meeting the buyers' requirements. For example, the functionality may be very similar between many proprietary software packages used in such areas as business logistics. In these circumstances, success comes to the software company which is best at tailoring its offering and its sales presentations to the requirements of its potential clients. Similarly in many consumer markets it is often the distinctive marketing technology of a manufacturer which enables it to build the appeal of its product for a particular group of customers, even though its product is functionally identical to others in the market.

Marketing technology requires similar investments to develop as product and process technologies. It is also exploitable in a number of different ways, such as when a company uses its skills to market the complementary products of another company on an agency basis. More importantly, a bundle of product, process and marketing technologies is needed to meet any set of customer requirements. For example, many companies have the product technology suitable for a particular group of customers, they may also be able to develop the process skills to manufacture for that application. But, they also need the appropriate marketing technology to determine those customers' requirements precisely, tailor, package and communicate their offering, and transfer it to the customer at an appropriate price. Without this marketing technology they will fail, or have to use the services of someone else who has these skills or form a joint venture with another company to assemble a package of the requisite technologies. For example, when Arm and Hammer decided to introduce their baking-powder toothpaste internationally they obviously had the necessary product and process technologies. However, they did not have the skills or marketing resources to support the launch of the product in unfamiliar markets. For this reason, in the UK, they used the resources of the marketing agency Food Brokers to provide the necessary marketing technologies.

Definitions of the three types of technologies are given below:

1. Product technology is *knowledge* of the physical properties and characteristics of materials and the *ability* to incorporate these into the design of products or services which could be of value to another company or individual.
2. Process technology is *knowledge* of ways of producing products or services and the *ability* to produce these so that they have value to others.

3. Marketing technology is *knowledge* of ways of bringing these product and process technologies to a particular application and the *ability* to carry this out. This involves the skills of market analysis, branding, packaging, pricing, communications and logistics.

THE INTERDEPENDENCE OF COMPANIES

The second major issue of technology and interaction centres on the interdependence of companies. It is a false picture to see a company as the master of its own destiny, building its independent strategy and trying to get a favourable reaction from the market – such a view is more appropriate to the rather colourful newspaper accounts of the lives of famous industrial "barons" than it is to an understanding of industrial reality.

There are a number of reasons for this. It is difficult to imagine a company which is able to meet any application in a modern market solely on the basis of its own technologies. A hundred years ago, railway companies brought-in raw timber and billets of iron and created locomotives, carriages and wagons using their own skills and abilities. Nowadays, the products of most companies depend to a great extent on the technologies of others, whether they are supplying technology in its "pure" form via licence etc., or whether the technology is incorporated in the products or services which the company buys. Increasingly, both the pace of technology change and the escalating up-front cost of R&D mean that it becomes more and more difficult for a company to maintain a position in even a relatively narrow technological area, much less in a wide range of technologies. A company is faced with the difficult question of which technologies it should continue to devote its resources to maintaining and developing internally and which it should regard as external technologies it has the benefit of, such as when the company buys products based on external technologies but does not own them.

CONCLUSIONS

This chapter has introduced the idea of technology strategy as three interrelated tasks of acquiring, managing and exploiting technology. The tasks are interrelated because the process of technology acquisition takes place with the specific purpose of, and frequently in parallel with, the exploitation of that technology. The task of managing technology has both short-term and longer-term strategic aspects. It involves managing a set of resources, only some of which are tangible, and many of which exist in the form of the knowledge and abilities of the company's employees and, indeed, in the culture and collective experience of the company. A good analogy for this management task is that of the farmer who seeks to exploit the assets of his land, but at the same time seeks to replenish those assets and leave the land "in good heart" for his successors.

Although some technologies are individually important, a bundle of product, process and marketing technologies are needed to meet the requirements of a company's markets. In some cases it is prowess in only one or a subset of these technologies which makes for competitive advantage. In other cases none of the company's technologies will be distinctive when compared to other companies. But it is the company's skill in assembling the appropriate bundle of technologies to deliver the requirements of its customers which is distinctive. No company has all of the technologies which are needed to satisfy the requirements of a market. A company must work with others around it and use their skills as external technologies so as to assemble the required bundle of technologies. This bundling will involve many companies; the process of bundling may be more or less controlled by all the companies in a wide network ranging from component manufacturers to retailers. The management of a company's position and interactions in that network is a major issue of strategy. Through those network interactions its technological resources acquire their value to other members of the network and to final customers.

REFERENCES

Ford, D. Develop your technology strategy. *Long Range Planning*, **21** (5): 85 (1988).

Ford, D. (ed.) *Understanding Business Markets*, Academic Press, London (1990).

Lake, K. and Trayes, A. Technology and networks, unpublished MBA project report, University of Bath (1990).

Nonaka, I. Redundant, overlapping organization: a Japanese approach to managing the innovation process, *California Management Review*, Spring: 27–38 (1990).

Ohmae, K. *The Mind of the Strategist – the Art of Japanese Business*, McGraw-Hill, New York (1982).

Quinn, J. B. and Mintzberg, H. *The Strategy Process: Concepts, Contexts and Cases*, Prentice-Hall, Englewood Cliffs, New Jersey (1991).

Part 5
Purchasing in
Business Networks

Business marketers and business purchasers face similar tasks. Both need to understand the network of companies that surrounds them and each must plan, develop and manage relationships with a portfolio of companies, whether they are customers or suppliers. This means that purchasers as well as marketers need to understand the nature and dynamics of interaction, relationships and networks. Also, if business marketers are to be effective they must understand the problems and approaches to relationships of their purchasing counterparts. Similarly, business buyers must not only address their own problems, but be aware of the problems and approaches of the companies that seek to supply them.

The first reading in this section of the book by Nigel Campbell is chosen for two reasons. Firstly, it provides a useful link between the more "traditional" analyses of business buyer-behaviour and an approach that emphasises the *interaction* between buying and selling firms as a basis for analysis. Secondly, the reading provides a valuable framework for discussing the *choices* that face purchasing managers under different circumstances. In this way the reading highlights our view of business buyers as being strategically *active* in their markets.

The second reading is taken from the most comprehensive of the works on purchasing by IMP group members and develops these ideas further. Håkansson and Gadde use a major study of purchasing activity to describe, categorise and analyse buyer–seller relationships from the perspective of the purchasing company. Also included in this reading are a number of illustrative case studies which deal with the relationship tasks facing the buying organisation in respectively: the purchase of MRO (Maintenance, repair and operating supplies); new-product development, supplier-development programmes and subcontracting. The next reading by the same authors highlights three key issues facing buying companies; the question of make-or-buy, the structure of the company's supply-base and the nature of its supplier relationships.

Reading number four, by Lars Erik Gadde and Ivan Snehota, discusses the ways in which a customer company can have different degrees of involvement with its suppliers. It concludes that a company can be highly involved with only a limited number of suppliers and needs a variety of relationships, each of which provides it with different benefits. This reading is an important counter to some of the more simplistic ideas on purchasing that over-emphasise the value of "purchasing partnerships".

This theme of the need for diversity in supplier relationships is expanded on in reading number five, by Luis Araujo, Anna Dubois and Lars-Erik Gadde. They suggest four different interfaces with suppliers, each serving different purposes and having their own costs and benefits. Finally, after looking at different theoretical approaches to managing relationships, the reading by Paul Cousins and Euan Stanwix provides a fascinating examination of why Japanese companies appear to be better than Western companies at managing their long-term supplier relationships.

CONTENTS

5.1 An interaction approach to organizational buying behavior

Nigel Campbell

Although interest in and research on organizational buying have increased over the past two decades, few empirical generalizations have emerged to provide specific guidelines for management action. This conclusion by Wind and Thomas (1981) reinforces the view expressed by Wind (1978) in the first edition of *Review of Marketing*. This paper attempts to fill this gap by developing the interaction approach associated with the International Marketing and Purchasing (IMP) Group.

The lack of empirical generalizations may be due to the complexity of available models (Sheth, 1973; Webster and Wind, 1973; Möller, 1981). The popular Webster and Wind model placed great emphasis on analysis of the buying center, the buying decision process, and the buying situation. In practice, this tripartite analysis has proved difficult to perform because the interpersonal process at work in a buying center are hard to unravel, the stages of the buying decision process are hard to distinguish, and even the distinction between "new buy" and "modified rebuy" is not always clear. Industrial marketing managers are well aware that their jobs are complex.

In order to guide marketing managers and resolve the research problems, attention has focused on discrete buying decisions. In consequence, research has concentrated on new buy situations in which discrete decisions are easy to identify. Routine response behavior, which Möller (1981) claims is more common, has been neglected. In other words, the emphasis has been on the process of discrete purchase decisions rather than on the development of strategies for the management of a pattern of relationships over long periods of time.

In contrast, this paper stems from research in areas where long-term stable relationships are important, as attested to by many authorities (Wind, 1970; Bubb and Van Rest, 1973; Cunningham and Kettlewood, 1976; Ford, 1982). In such situations, the study of discrete purchase decisions is less relevant than the study of the patterns of interaction between buyers and their supply markets.

This paper results from an intensive two-year research study designed to complement previous work carried out by the IMP Group. The original IMP research project (Håkansson, 1982) was an international, cross-sectional study aimed at understanding the nature of buyer–seller relationships. Some 300 companies covering 15 different industries in five countries were involved. The IMP researchers placed great emphasis on a comparative analysis of how suppliers and customers in various product technologies and end-use industries handled their relationships with counterpart companies in domestic and foreign markets. In contrast, the research study on which this paper is based focused on 167 trading relationships in the packaging industry in Europe. Both sides of the buyer–seller relationships were researched, and by examining one industry, the product technology variable in the relationships was held constant.

To understand the trading relationships, this paper classifies buyer–seller relationships and

he common strategies which buyers and sellers use in their interactions. This classifica-
attention to focus on the critical variables which give rise to the different strategies. In
ful managerial guidelines are developed which assist sellers in choosing a strategy in
the strategy being used by their counterpart.

CLASSIFICATION OF BUYER–SELLER RELATIONSHIPS

The classification adopted is based on the three types of governance structure proposed by Williamson (1979) for commercial transactions. Campbell and Cunningham (1985) provide an extensive review of other approaches to the classification of buyer–seller relationships. Williamson's approach arises from his work on markets and hierarchies (Williamson, 1975) and is linked to Ouchi's (1979, 1980) concern with ensuring equity in relationships.

Equity is assured in many exchanges by the market mechanism. A fair price is established by competitive market forces, and the price itself contains most of the information needed by the parties. Such relationships are independent. However, where the exchange is contingent on uncertain future events, assessment of price is very difficult. Nevertheless, the requirement for equity remains and, for this reason, a bureaucratic, or hierarchical, relationship is preferred. The perception of equity depends on a social agreement that the bureaucratic system has the legitimate authority to decide what is fair. In these relationships, one party is dependent on the other.

Intermediate between the market and bureaucratic mechanisms is the clan mechanism, which Ouchi claims can also ensure equity. Equity based on clan control involves a long process of socialization, which develops common value and beliefs. The evidence for long-term relationships and source loyalty suggests that the clan form, an interdependent relationship, is common in buyer–seller relationships.

Independent, dependent, and interdependent relationships arise in different situations. For example, independence arises when the buyer plays the market and the seller has plenty of potential customers. Marketing and purchasing strategies in these commodity-type markets are competitive. Independence also arises in a buyer's market, in which there are many competitive sellers, and in a seller's market, where there are many buyers. On the other hand, interdependence arises when both parties approach the relationship with a strategy of cooperation. They are both willing to establish a long-term relationship, to exchange information openly, and to trust each other. Finally, a dependent relationship results from the dominance one party exerts over the other.

Marketing or purchasing strategies which result when one party has a dominant position of strength are called *command* strategies. Thus, the independent, interdependent, and dependent types of relationships result from the interplay of interaction strategies, classified here as competitive, cooperative, and command. Campbell and Cunningham have described similar classifications developed by other researchers (Blois, 1972; Corey, 1978; Farmer, 1978; Cunningham, 1982; Håkansson, 1982). The interplay of these strategies leads directly to the nine-cell matrix in Figure 1.

In Figure 1 there are three cells with independent relationships, one with interdependent relationships, two with dependent relationships, and three labelled "Mismatch". The typical strategies and responses which apply to these different situations are discussed in the final section of this paper.

Thus, in place of the Webster and Wind classification of buying situations into new buy, modified rebuy, and straight rebuy, Figure 1 proposes a new typology of buyer–seller relationships. In this typology, the buying situation is determined by the interplay or marketing and purchasing strategies, which are themselves determined by a variety of other factors. Therefore, a model is required which incorporates the interplay of marketing and purchasing strategies and identifies the conditions which determine their choice.

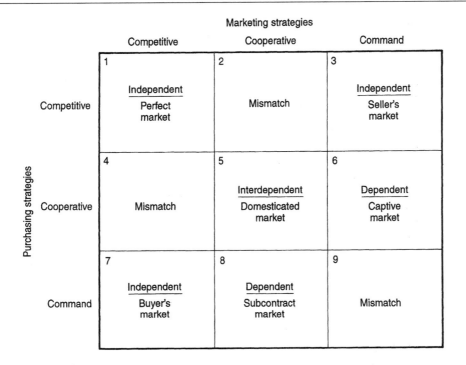

Figure 1 Classification of buyer–seller relationships.

INTERACTION MODEL

Neither the Sheth (1973) model nor the Webster and Wind (1972) model fulfils the above-stated need to incorporate the interplay of marketing and purchasing strategies and their determinants. The Sheth model is mainly concerned with the psychological aspects of individual buyer behavior. However, in addition to individual factors, Sheth introduces product-specific and company-specific factors, as well as the outcome of previous decisions and situational factors, which he says are too varied and broad to analyze in detail. These factors converge in a "black box" called the *industrial buying process*.

Although it is more comprehensive and considers four sets of variables – environmental, organizational, interpersonal, and individual – the Webster and Wind model also poses problems. The desire for comprehensiveness leads to the inclusion of every possible influence, which makes the model difficult to use. Laczniak and Murphy (1982) have cautioned against a "laundry list of possible influences."

Another disadvantage of both models is that they concentrate on the buyer's side. Scant attention is paid to the seller's influence on buyer behavior. By contrast, the interaction model developed by the IMP Group (1982) stresses the interaction between two active parties, and the model proposed here (see Figure 2) gives equal weight to buyer and seller characteristics.

This model goes beyond the work of the IMP Group by introducing the concepts of *interaction strategies*, whose interplay affects the interaction mechanisms and interaction atmosphere in a two-way exchange. Figure 2 also emphasizes a different set of variables from those in the IMP model.

Three groups of variables are shown – the characteristics of the buyer, the supplier, and the product. The characteristics of the buyer and the supplier are divided into three sets representing

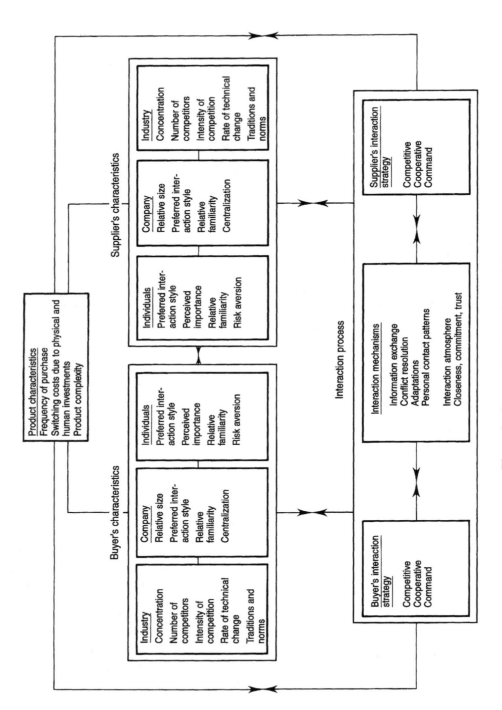

Figure 2 Buyer–seller interaction model.

Table 1 Interaction variables

Buyer's side	Interaction variables	Supplier's side
Product	Frequency of purchase Switching costs due to physical and human investments Product complexity	Product
Industry characteristics	Concentration Number of alternative partners Intensity of competition Rate of technical change Traditions and norms	Industry characteristics
Company characteristics	Relative size Preferred interaction style Relative familiarity Centralization of purchasing	Company characteristics
Individual characteristics	Relative familiarity Preferred interaction style Perceived importance of the purchase (sale) Risk aversion	Individual characteristics

the industry, the company, and the individuals or buying center members. One could argue that the characteristics of the two industries should be separated from those of the two companies and the two groups of individuals. However, the strong inter-connection between company strategy and industry structure suggests the need to keep them together (Porter, 1980). The impact of general environmental factors is presumed to take place through changes in the characteristics of the buyer's and/or supplier's industry. This has the advantage that the environment of both buyer and seller are explicitly considered, and it avoids the weakness of the IMP model, which includes only an aggregated environment.

A full list of the variables considered in the model is given in Table 1. There is no attempt to be comprehensive. Rather, variables are included which research indicates cause a particular buyer or seller to choose a strategy.

Product characteristics

Different writers have used different attributes in their attempts to classify products. Robinson, Faris, and Wind (1967) proposed the three buy classes. Cardozo (1981) suggests a classification by product use, degree of standardization, and the product's importance to the buyer. Other writers have also used characteristics of the product's importance to the buyer (Porter, 1980; Möller, 1981). Homse (1981) classifies products according to their complexity, and Williamson (1979) concentrates on the three key dimensions of frequency of transaction, switching costs, and uncertainty.

Frequency of transaction distinguishes between the purchase of capital goods required infrequently and components and raw materials delivered more regularly. Where the transaction occurs frequently, the relationships are likely to be more interdependent. At the other extreme, the infrequent purchase of standard capital equipment is often dealt with by competitive tenders.

Switching costs are the costs incurred in changing suppliers. This dimension incorporates the ideal of standardization because standard products will normally have lower switching costs than customized products. The higher the switching costs, the greater the specific investments which each party has made in the relationship. Switching costs can result from human as well as physical

Table 2 Source of switching costs in buyer–seller relationships

Activity	*Source of switching costs*	
	Supplier	*Customer*
Product introduction	Supplying prototype and test data Training customer's staff	Testing a new product Training own staff
Production	Changing materials, design, processing, or production equipment to meet customer's needs	Changing product, design, or production methods to accommodate the supplier
	Special quality control Especially rapid production	Special quality control
Logistics	Special stock-holding and delivery requirements	Special warehousing and handling
Product development and technical service	Time needed to get to know customer's problems and technical staff	Time needed to understand supplier's technical resources and staff
Buying, selling and administration	Time required to get to know the customer, his or her staff, and ways of doing business; special documentation and procedures	Time required to get to know supplier, his or her staff, and ways of doing business; special documentation and procedures

investments. Salesmen and buyers invest in getting to know each other's business. Table 2 summarizes the main sources of switching costs between industrial buyers and marketers.

While switching costs are a function of the product in the sense that some products must be more closely adapted to the customer's needs than others, they also reflect the type of relationship that exists. In an independent relationship, a buyer pursuing a competitive strategy in a particular supply market will try to minimize switching costs to avoid being tied to one supplier. The aim is to standardize purchasers, and the buyer tends to have a technical staff to solve problems. On the other hand, a buyer pursuing a cooperative strategy is more ready to pay switching costs in return for joint efforts to find the best solution to his or her problem. Such a buyer has a relatively smaller technical staff, and is willing to cooperate on development work and to accept special products. In general, the higher the switching costs, the greater the tendency for cooperative or command strategies to be used.

The third dimension, product complexity, is preferred by Williamson's uncertainty. Homse (1981) has identified six types of product complexity. A product has *functional complexity* when it consists of numerous parts and subassemblies. *Manufacturing complexity* is straightforward, but *specification complexity* refers to products which require extensive trial periods (Homse, 1981). Products have a high *application complexity* due either to the extensive training required before the buyer knows how to use them or to the uncertainty inherent in the customer's pattern of demand. *Commercial complexity* refers to transactions involving complicated commercial arrangements, such as stage payments, penalty clauses, and performance bonds. Finally, *political complexity* applies to purchases which Lehmann and O'Shaughnessey (1974) call "political problem products" – purchases for which different factions will be for and against. In general, the more complex the product, the more interdependent the buyer–seller relationships.

Industry characteristics

The variables proposed in Figure 2 are concentration, number of competitors, intensity of competition, rate of technical change, and traditions and norms. These variables are similar to those proposed by Robinson, Faris and Wind (1967) in their discussion of the key characteristics of the supplying industry which influence buyer behavior. Their variables are the number of potential suppliers, the type of competition (whether price or nonprice), the threat of material or parts shortages, the traditional ways of doing business, social–political–economic conditions, and significant events such as technological breakthroughs.

The importance of concentration and the number of alternative partners was recognized by the IMP Group in their original formulation of the interaction model. They also included "dynamism" as a variable, referring to the heterogeneity of the supply market. Buyers in dynamic markets or buyers purchasing from dynamic markets, in which there is a high rate of technical change, tend to use competitive buying strategies to protect themselves from being tied to a partner who cannot keep pace. Most writers recognize that the traditions and norms of each industry have an important influence on buyer behavior, and these represent the final variable. Some industries, such as automobile manufacturing, have a reputation for using competitive buying approaches, which they are only now beginning to change (*Business Week*, 1982).

Company Characteristics

The interplay of marketing and purchasing strategies and the mechanisms and atmosphere of the relationship depend on the characteristics of the parties involved. The IMP researchers proposed that the technology, size, structure, and strategy of the company be considered (Håkansson, 1982). Some of these variables are included in Figure 2.

The relative size of the two companies is obviously important; command buying is more likely to occur when the buyer is larger than the supplier. *Relative familiarity* refers to how well the two companies know each other relative to their knowledge of other partners. Familiarity resulting from many years of trading together, as found in mature markets, favors cooperative purchasing.

Familiarity is also important with respect to technology and the costs and ways of doing business. The buyer who is familiar with the technology of the supplier and knows the supplier's costs is in a powerful position. This buyer can either use a command strategy or, where several alternatives exist, adopt a competitive purchasing approach.

The interviews on which this paper is based also revealed that companies tend to have a preferred interaction style. One well-known US consumer company opening in Europe invariably uses a competitive purchasing strategy. In contrast, another US company has a policy of preferring interdependent relationships with one or two key suppliers for each class of purchase.

The last interaction variable covers organization. Möller (1981) distinguishes between departmental and company organization, recognizing that the structure, managerial style, and organizational climate of individual departments, as well as those of the company as a whole, must be taken into account. Möller identifies many variables but does not indicate which ones he considers most important. Research in the packing industry suggests that the extent of centralization in the buying department is a key variable. For simplicity, this is the only variable included in the model.

Individual characteristics

A relationship must ultimately depend on the interaction of the individuals who participate. In complex interactions, several members of a buying center interact with their opposite numbers in the supplying company.

Understanding of the patterns of behavior between members of a buying center is still rudimentary (Johnston and Spekman, 1982) and only recently has work been done on the interaction between the buying center and the sales team (Cunningham and Turnbull, 1982; Homse, 1981). Cunningham and Turnbull (1982) point out that interpersonal contacts fulfil different roles in different circumstances and that they vary widely in intensity and style. Indeed, individuals in some companies have preferred interaction styles. An individual's preference depends on his or her

Table 3 Conditions favoring different buying strategies

	Competitive buying	Cooperative buying	Command buying
Product characteristics	Low or high frequency of purchase Low switching costs (standardized product) Product performance can be precisely specified	High frequency of purchase High switching costs (customized product) Product performance difficult to specify	High frequency of purchase High switching costs Products can be specified but is customized
Industry characteristics	Supplier's industry fragmented Intense price competition among suppliers High rate of technical change Tradition of competitive buying	Both industries are concentrated Stable competitive situation in each industry Low rate of technical change Tradition of cooperative buying	Buyer's industry concentrated but supplier's industry fragmented Average level of competition Low rate of technical change Tradition of command buying
Company characteristics	Buying company is larger than supplier Buying company prefers competitive buying Buying company lacks familiarity with the product (new buy) Centralized buying organization	Both companies are similar in size Both companies seek a cooperative relationship Both companies are familiar with each other and respect each other's technical knowledge Organizational structures are similar	Buying company much larger than supplier Buying company prefers to dominate supplier's costs and technology Buying company is familiar with suppliers Buyer has more professional organization than supplier
Individual characteristics	Product perceived as important by buyer Buyer is not risk averse for this purchase Individuals who interact do not know each other well Buyer prefers competitive buying approach	Product is perceived as important by both parties Buyer is risk averse for this purchase Individuals who interact know each other Both buyer and seller prefer a cooperative relationship	Product is important to buyer Buyer is risk averse for this purchase Individuals know each other personally Buyer prefers a command strategy and supplier accepts cooperative role

psychology. The IMP Group emphasizes motivation and experience. Möller includes all of these factors. In addition, he includes buying-related knowledge and interindividual behavior. Again, there are too many variables. In the interests of simplicity, only four variables are included in Figure 2: preferred interaction style, perceived importance of the sale or purchase, relative familiarity, and risk aversion.

If the buyer has a number of alternatives and the product is perceived as important, then a competitive buying approach is more likely to prevail. High relative familiarity indicates the close, cooperative relationship of the buying center members with suppliers' sale teams.

Summary

Figure 2 develops the IMP Group's interaction model by introducing the interaction strategies of the buyer and seller. It identifies the main variables which determine the choice of strategy of the buyer or seller. Three groups of variables are discussed: the product and, for both buyer and seller, the characteristics of their industry, their company, and the individuals involved in the interaction. Table 1 identifies 16 variables of prime importance. Table 3 summarizes the above discussion and identifies the conditions favoring competitive, cooperative, and command purchasing strategies.

MANAGEMENT IMPLICATIONS

Figure 1 identified six common types of relationship. Marketing and purchasing managers can readily identify the type of situation they are facing. Table 4 indicates the typical strategies and responses used in these situations. In a buyer's market, there are normally many suppliers and only a few powerful buyers. The buyers request quotations or put out competitive tenders; their approach is to "play the market." Suppliers must submit quotes and try to gain a competitive advantage by obtaining cost leadership or buy differentiating.

In a seller's market, there are a few large suppliers and many small buyers. The sellers may see the advantage of forming a cartel to maintain prices. In this event, buyers may collaborate with other buyers and try to break the cartel, or at least exchange information to improve their

Table 4 Marketing and purchasing strategies and responses in different types of markets

Type of market	Typical strategies and responses	
	Marketing	Purchasing
Perfect market	Take it or leave it Try to obtain lower cost Try to differentiate	Play the market Standardize requirements
Seller's market	Take it or leave it Form a cartel Legitimize, placate Standardize the product	Accept gracefully Buy jointly Exchange information with other buyers Complain, agitate Encourage competitors
Buyer's market	Competitive bidding Try to obtain lowest cost	Put out tenders Play the market
Domesticated market	Customize, specialize, differentiate, innovate	Adapt, cooperate, work together
Captive market	Educate the buyer	Learn from the supplier
Subcontract market	Learn from the buyer	Educate the supplier

bargaining position. Monopoly suppliers have different problems. Their marketing strategies are frequently directed at legitimizing their position and placating customers with elaborate complaint procedures and information campaigns. Thus, at this general level, some management insights are possible. More specific guidelines for marketing and purchasing management now follow.

Marketing management

First, the marketer must remember that buyers use more than one approach in a given supply market. Nevertheless, one approach usually predominates, and the marketer's own sales force can help to collect some simple data, such as those in Table 5, which will help to distinguish between competitive and cooperative buying strategies. Once the buying approach or strategy has been identified, clear guidelines for marketing strategies are available, as detailed in Table 6.

Table 5 Buying characteristics and buying strategies

	Buying strategy	
Buying characterstic	Competitive	Cooperative
Number of suppliers	Many	Few
Proportion of purchases held by main suppliers	Low	High
Number of new suppliers taken on recently	Several	Few
Proportion of business given to new suppliers	Moderate	Low
Willingness to accept special adaptations	Unwilling	Willing
Desire for standardization of the product	High	Average
Technical dependence on suppliers	Low	High
Emphasis in buying	Price	Service, quality

Table 6 Marketing strategies to match different buying approaches

	Cooperative	Competitive	Command
Existing customers			
Pricing	Don't overcharge	Match market price	Negotiate prices
Customer service	Nothing is too much trouble	Competitive but no frills	At your service
Personal contacts	Frequent, including courtesy visits from senior managers	Regular visits	Ensure that personal relationships are maintained
Product development	Grasp all opportunities to work with the customer Stay ahead technically	Do what is required Beware of stealing of ideas	Work as required by the customer
New customers	Where competition is established, offer a major advantage, e.g. by innovation, or wait until there is a lapse by current competitors Beware of being exploited by a customer who has no intention of changing	Offer comparable price, service, and quality, and stress benefits of multiple sourcing	Offer facilities to make whatever is required; propose trial order

Marketing strategies for cooperative customers

Cooperative customers require a lot of attention. They need reassurance that their decision to concentrate their purchases and put their faith in one or two suppliers is correct. To give this reassurance, senior management from the supplying company must visit these customers and take every opportunity to develop social changes. The service which cooperative customers receive needs to be excellent, and the supplier must stay ahead technically to justify this privileged position. Pricing is one of the most difficult areas with cooperative customers, since the marketer must recover operating costs but avoid overcharging lest this provide an opportunity for competitors to penetrate the account. The objective should be to use customers' cooperation to find ways to meet their needs, preferably over time. This could lead to reduced costs, and enable a marketer to supply at a competitive price and make a good margin. Marketers who take advantage of a cooperative customer's loyalty and charge an elevated price run the risk of permanently ruining the relationship if the customer realizes that he or she has been overcharged. Such an occurrence breaks the feeling of mutual dependence and shared objectives on which this type of relationship depends. Derived of reassurance of equity in the relationship, the customer is likely to react sharply.

Knowledge of a customer's purchasing approach is very helpful when deciding which companies are the best prospects for future business. In mature markets, customers with cooperative purchasing strategies have, by definition, developed long-term relationships. These are difficult to penetrate unless the marketers can offer a significant price reduction or innovation which the existing supplier cannot match.

Marketers should be cautious about spending large sums in an effort to obtain business from such customers, who normally favor existing suppliers and are likely to give them an opportunity to match any new offers they receive. If the marketer has no significant advantage to offer, the only option is to wait until the customer is dissatisfied with the existing supplier or until there is a structural change such as a merger or takeover, which may sever existing links between personnel. The bonds with existing customers are also broken when there is a change in the customer's own market position. Such events provide good opportunities for the astute marketer.

Marketing strategies for competitive customers

Customers with competitive purchasing strategies require different handling. Marketing costs and contracts with competitive customers must be kept to a minimum because their prime concern is price. Many suppliers know the frustration of losing an order to a lower-priced competitor. A careful balance has to be struck between the advantages of differentiating the product by providing additional services and the disadvantage of a price which is out of step with the market price. Resources may be better deployed in searching for production economies which will lower the price.

Companies with competitive purchasing strategies may be the easiest to obtain as new customers. Their interest can often be gained by offering a comparable, or preferably better, price, quality, and service. The marketer should stress the benefits of multiple sourcing.

Marketing strategies for companies with command purchasing

The company subject to a command purchasing strategy should also keep its marketing costs to a minimum. The supplier's role is to do the buyer's bidding, and the keys to success are flexibility, personal attention to the buying company's needs, and efficient production facilities. These are the points to stress in the search for new customers.

CONCLUSIONS

This paper sets out to overcome the problem that research on organizational buying behavior has yielded few guidelines for management action.

Marketing and purchasing behaviors are classified into three interaction strategies. The buying decision process is modeled as resulting from the interplay of these strategies, which in turn are influenced by the characteristics of the product, the buyer, and the seller. A multitude of variables influence buyer and seller behavior. Sixteen variables relevant to both buyers and sellers are incorporated in the model because they seem to be the most important in influencing the choice of interaction strategy. Although useful guidelines have been developed, research has been conducted only in the packaging industry, and additional research in other industries is now required.

REFERENCES

Blois, K. J. Vertical quasi-integration. *Journal of Industrial Economics*, **20**, 253–72 (1972).

Bubb, P. L. and Van Rest, D. J. Loyalty as a component of the industrial buying decision. *Industrial Marketing Management*, **3**, 25–32 (1973).

Business Week, pp. 62–3 (1982).

Campbell, N. C. G. and Cunningham, M. T. Interaction strategies for the management of buyer/seller relationships. *Journal of Marketing*, (1985).

Cardozo, R. N. Situational segmentation of industrial markets. *European Journal of Marketing*, April/May, 222–38 (1981).

Corey, E. R. *Procurement Management: Strategy, Organization and Decision Making.* CBI Publishing, Boston (1978).

Cunningham, M. T. An interaction approach to purchasing strategy. In Håkansson, H. (ed.), *International Marketing and Purchasing of Industrial Goods: An Interaction Approach.* Wiley, Chichester (1982).

Cunningham, M. T. and Turnbull, P. W. Inter-organizational personal contact patterns. In Håkansson, H. (ed.), *International Marketing and Purchasing of Industrial Goods: An Interaction Approach.* Wiley, Chichester (1982).

Cunningham, M. T. and Kettlewood, K. Source loyalty in the freight transport market. *European Journal of Marketing*, **10**, January, 66–79 (1976).

Farmer, D. H. Developing purchasing strategies. *Journal of Purchasing and Materials Management*, Fall, 6–11 (1978).

Ford, D. The development of buyer–seller relationships in industrial markets. In Håkansson, H. (ed.) *International Marketing and Purchasing of Industrial Goods: An Interaction Approach.* Wiley, Chichester (1982).

Håkansson, H. (ed.) *International Marketing and Purchasing of Industrial Goods: An Interaction Approach.* Wiley, Chichester (1982).

Homse, E. An interaction approach to marketing and purchasing strategy. Unpublished Ph.D. dissertation. University of Manchester. Institute of Science and Technology (1981), p. 150.

Johnston, W. J. and Spekman, R. E. Industrial buying behavior: a need for an integrative approach. *Journal of Business Research*, **10**, June, 135–46 (1982).

Laczniak, G. R. and Murphy, P. E. Fine tuning organizational buying models. In Lamb, C. W. and Dunne, P. M. (eds) *Theoretical Development in Marketing.* American Marketing Association, Chicago (1982).

Lehmann, D. R. and O'Shaughnessy, J. Difference in attribute importance for different industrial products. *Journal of Marketing*, **38**, April, 36–42 (1974).

Möller, K. *Industrial Buying Behaviour of Production Materials: A Conceptual Model and Analysis.* School of Economics Publications, Series B-54, Helsinki (1981).

Ouchi, W. G. A conceptual framework for the design of organizational control mechanisms. *Management Science*, **25**, 833–48 (1979).

Ouchi, W. G. Markets, bureaucracies and clans. *Administrative Science Quarterly*, **25**, March, 129–39 (1980).

Porter, M. E. *Competitive Strategy.* Free Press, New York (1980).

Robinson, P. J., Faris, C. W. and Wind, Y. *Industrial Buying and Creative Marketing.* Allyn and Bacon, Boston (1967), pp. 119–212.

Sheth, J. N. A model of industrial buyer behavior. *Journal of Marketing*, **37**, 50–6 (1973).

Webster, F. E. and Wind, Y. *Organizational Buying Behavior*. Prentice-Hall, Englewood Cliffs, NJ (1972).

Williamson, Oliver E. *Markets and Hierarchies*. Free Press, New York (1975).

Williamson, O. E. Transaction cost economics: the governance of contractual relations. *Journal of Law and Economics*, **22**, October, 223–61 (1979).

Wind, Y. Industrial source loyalty. *Journal of Marketing Research*, **7**, November, 450–57 (1970).

Wind, Y. Organizational buying behaviour. In Zaltman, G. and Bonoma, T. (eds), *Review of Marketing*, American Marketing Association, Chicago (1978).

Wind, Y. and Thomas, R. J. Conceptual and methodological issues in organizational buying behavior. *European Journal of Marketing*, **14**, May–June, 239–61 (1981).

5.2

Supplier relations

Håkan Håkansson and Lars-Erik Gadde

Our starting point is that there is a relationship, or connection, between a buyer and each of the individual suppliers. Also, a fundamental change is occurring, in which purchasing companies have gradually been making a transition from "looser" to "more solid" connections with suppliers. Because the concept of "solid" connections is far from simple or homogeneous, we devote this chapter to a discussion and analysis of some of its central elements. This chapter is divided into eight sections. The first section characterizes supplier relationships, and identifies six of their specific features, to each of which a subsequent section is devoted. The first of these features is the complexity of these relationships in terms of the multifaceted contacts between the companies. The second is the long-term nature of the relationship, which often stretches over decades, and the third is the scope of adaptation of individual relationships required, from both the technological and organizational points of view. A fourth main characteristic, because it emphasizes the informal nature of the relationship, is the low degree of formalization, indicating that the firms do their best to safeguard themselves against unpleasant surprises through reciprocal trust rather than through formal agreements. The fifth characteristic is the power–dependence balance in the relationship, and the sixth and final one is the simultaneous presence of conflict and co-operation, with one conclusion being that effective relationships must contain elements of both.

GENERAL CHARACTERISTICS OF BUYER–SELLER RELATIONSHIPS

Business transactions between buyers and sellers may differ greatly from one another. At one end of the spectrum there are simple deals in which a person from the buying firm has a limited number of contacts with a person from the selling firm, and in which the products and conditions of their discussion are virtually standardized. At the other, a large number of officials representing several functions at the buying firm have contacts with officials in corresponding positions at the selling firm. In this case a large number of technical, administrative, and economic problems are ventilated.

Every business transaction is an interesting phenomenon in itself. We use the term "episode" to define this type of event, limited in time. Many things which can happen between a buyer and seller such as a joint development project, testing a new product, or re-negotiating a long-term contract, can comprise an episode. How each episode is handled will depend first on how complex the episode is in itself, and second on the history of the previous relationship between the parties. They may already have met in many past episodes, and have developed an existing relationship.

The way the current episode is handled will depend largely on the past history. If the parties have come to trust one another, the situation will be handled differently from the way it will if the opposite applies. In other words, actions in given situations must not be seen in isolation, but must be viewed and understood in the light of previous occurrences.

For these reasons, it is important to base an analysis of upcoming actions on the complexity of past episodes, and the degree to which the relationship has already developed. Table 1 may be seen as a point of departure for discussing what happens when these two dimensions are combined. If

Table 1 Business transactions: four cases

	No previous relationship	*Well-developed relationship*
Simple episode	Case 1	Case 2
Complex episode	Case 3	Case 4

there is no previous relationship, behaviour within the episode will be complete unto itself, and thus has to be judged and optimized as if it were to remain an isolated episode. If, as in case 1, the episode is a simple one, a typical market situation arises in which both parties are truly independent and may even be previously unknown to one another. Taking such an episode to its extreme, it may even be mediated via an exchange market. There is no past history and no likelihood that the transaction will lead to the initiation of a relationship.

Every company has purchases which fall under case 1. These may be highly standardized raw materials, or very simple products purchased in small amounts.

If the episode is a complex one in itself, a different situation arises (case 3). Complexity generates uncertainty. For this kind of business transaction to be completed, for example when a company is going to buy a non-standard product from a new supplier, the episode must be handled in such a way as to build up sufficient trust between the parties. The experience gained when a complex episode is carried out may lead to the creation of some kind of special interest, as a typical first episode which may lead to an established relationship, and which gives both parties a good opportunity to get to know one another.

Case 3 may also be a one-off purchase, for instance, when a firm buys a piece of equipment which is not normally part of its plant. Large investments also have these characteristics, even when the parties have been in contact previously. Such episodes are so large and unique that the past relationship becomes relatively less significant. However, there are still rules applying to technical relationships which make it better for the purchasing firm to work with suppliers from whom they have bought in the past.

When there is an established relationship (cases 2 and 4), each individual transaction always has to be seen in relation to it. As a rule, the relationship facilitates individual episodes, which should be formulated so as to strengthen the relationship. In other words, how each episode is structured in relation to previous and anticipated episodes is more important than the fact that it is well formulated in itself. This is particularly important in relation to complex episodes. This connection between individual episodes and the long-term relationship means both considerable simplification of day-to-day work and the establishment of a dependency relation. One way in which the complexity becomes visible is that a number of officials at each firm are in contact with one another over time. In other words, the relationship consists of a number of intertwined, interdependent connections at the individual level, which require special efforts to handle.

A second important trait of relationships, as pointed out above, is that they are of long-term nature. A relationship comprises a number of episodes and, in some cases, has a protective, strengthening function, for instance when there are tensions among the parties involved. At the same time, in other situations, the existence of a relationship may impose limitations, for example when one of the firms wants to implement rapid changes. The very fact that a relationship is, by nature, a long-term undertaking, means that it has pros and cons. One way of elucidating this long-term characteristic is to see a relationship as an investment which, in terms of resources, makes it comparable to machinery or equipment used over a long period of time.

One vital aspect of the relationship being long term is that both parties adapt. Many adaptations are conscious and considered, while others happen more automatically, as a result of the complexity in the course of events described above. Handling of adaptations is important in several respects, as it can either give rise to blocks or enable skill and development potential to be used to advantage. Moreover, adaptations can be made in different dimensions: product and/or production technology, administration, knowledge, or economic aspects.

Furthermore, relationships are social processes in which different types of confidence-building activities are extremely important. It is impossible to cover all conceivable issues in agreements and contracts. There must be space in which informal, personal one-to-one contact takes over.

There are stages in the process of a relationship in which each party – the buyer and the seller – plays the key role in relation to the other, and in which situations of more or less strong dependence take over. Dependence carries power in its wake, and thus it is very important, and often extremely difficult, to handle a relationship in terms of power and dependence. The power–dependence relationship is often an asymmetrical one, and also shifts with time owing, *inter alia*, to the general state of the economy.

Finally, it is important to see that a relationship has other aspects to it besides co-operation. There will always be conflicting interests, which give rise to tension. One important attribute of effective relationships is that such conflicts are not suppressed, but allowed to surface and then to be handled constructively.

In the coming sections, the attributes identified above, the complexity, long-term nature, adaptability, informal social processes and power-dependence, as well as the existence of conflict and co-operation in relationships, will be discussed one by one. When we do this, it is important to keep in mind that relationships are entities, and their holistic nature implies that they do not easily succumb to being classified into different dimensions. We consider these classifications useful primarily from a pedagogical point of view.

COMPLEXITY

In one of our studies, there was a supplier relationship in which roughly 600 people in the purchasing firm were in regular, significant contact with no fewer than 200 people in the selling firm. This extreme case gives some indication of the complexity of relationships in terms of sheer numbers of people involved. At another large mechanical engineering company, the purchasing manager admitted that he had held his position for a whole year before learning that two large meetings were held annually at which the technicians at his firm met with the technicians from one of their main suppliers and discussed technical issues. Apparently, since the technicians thought that "no commercial issues were discussed" at these meetings, they did not see any reason to involve the purchasing department. These examples indicate that, in many cases, there are extensive contacts with many officials from various departments on both sides meeting to discuss and solve more or less advanced problems. Even if these problems are solved independently of one another, though, this does not mean that they are independent. Rather, they are interconnected in many ways, and improved contacts between the firms would undoubtedly be very important. Figure 1 depicts the complexity that may be found in an extensive relationship.

Thus it can be seen that a particular extensive relationship may be highly complex, and require substantial co-ordination of operations at the purchasing firm. One interesting solution, seldom applied today, is appointing a specific person to manage co-ordination of a given supplier relationship. At many firms the purchaser fulfils this function indirectly, but as he is concurrently responsible both for many suppliers and other tasks as well, it is often not possible for him to be an effective co-ordinator in practice.

The complexity of personal contacts and patterns of communication discussed above is, of course, attributable to complexity at a deeper level, relating to dependence with regard to each individual supplier relationship, and the interdependence among them. First, there is dependence in relation to the way the production technology, logistics and administration of the purchasing firm work. All supplier relationships have to be co-ordinated with regard to the technical and organizational resources of the purchasing firm. The solution found in relation to one supplier also

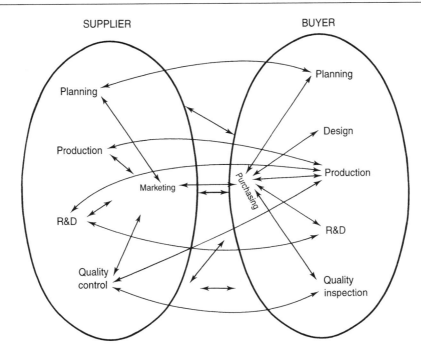

Figure 1 Pattern of contacts in an advanced supplier relationship.

affects this function in other relationships as well, which means that solving a problem with regard to one relationship may give rise to consequent problems in others.

Second, the relationship of the purchasing firm with supplier A may be contingent on how well relations with supplier B or customer C work, and vice versa, i.e. the purchasing firm may use its relationship with A to affect a third party. This means, for example, that the purchasing firm may discuss a technical development project with one supplier in order to get that supplier to behave in a certain way in relation to another party the buying firm wishes to affect. The more concentrated the network the individual firm works within, the more elaborate this type of behaviour has to be.

The type of complexity related to co-ordination of an individual relationship with others is considerably more difficult to handle than the type of complexity which arises with regard to co-ordination within one relationship. This is because there is an infinite number of ways of implementing the former type of co-ordination, and a conspicuous absence of simple solutions. It should be an appropriate first step to have the executives in the purchasing department identify the main connections and then, in systematic discussions with other executives, raise the awareness both of the current and the potential connections, so that they will both respect and take advantage of the opportunities arising from various situations.

Generally, we find that the complexity of the supplier relation can be explained by the fact that the "coupling" in the relationship is complex in itself from a technical, organizational and social point of view, i.e. a large number of officials are involved. This in turn creates a large number of problems of communication and co-ordination. Secondly, the complexity is attributable to the fact that there is dependence on other relations.

RELATIONSHIPS AS INVESTMENTS – THEIR LONG-TERM NATURE

One very important element of relationships is that they are of a long-term nature. Deep relationships are often decades old. In other words, there is always a history which affects and is

Table 2 Duration of supplier relationships for technical development

Duration	Proportion of relationships (%)
0–4 years	28
5–14 years	41
> 15 years	29
Weighted average	13 years

Source: Håkansson (1989), p. 112.

affected by the current interplay. Furthermore, there are often more or less overtly expressed expectations. Every action in a relationship must, therefore, be seen in a time perspective. Table 2 illustrates the relevant kind of time dimension by recapitulating the duration pattern of a number of supplier relationships for technical development (Håkansson, 1989).

One of the classic ways of accounting for the time dimension in economics is to examine activities with long-term effects as if they were investments. The difference between an investment and a cost, in principle, is that the revenue accruing from them is expected to take different courses in time. An investment is made on one occasion (in one period of time), and is expected to provide return over several periods, while a cost is associated with an activity the return on which is expected to come during the same period.

If we begin by examining the costs in a supplier relationship, we find that there are many items, and that they can mainly be divided into two groups: contact/information costs and adaptation costs. The contact/information costs of a relationship are high in the initial stages, when the buyer is getting to know the suppliers and their abilities and expertise, and these costs fall later. During certain later episodes contacts may need to be supplemented, which is associated with short-term additional costs, but generally the lower cost level may be maintained. Adaptation costs are all of a one-off nature, but as they arise successively, there is some natural adaptation over time, although there is a tendency for them to crop up early in a relationship. All the elementary adaptations necessary for the buyer to use the supplier must be made initially, which means that neither of the two main categories of costs is evenly distributed over time, and that the introductory period is liable to be a costly one.

We have discussed revenues which result from relationships above. Such revenues may include rationalization benefits or contributions to technical development. Some benefits (such as price benefits) may occur from the very first day, while many others, such as development benefits, take time. Studies made to date indicate that for two parties to venture to take the step of initiating joint development work, they need to have a long shared history. In other words, the return on a relationship also changes over time, but in the other direction, compared with costs.

If we examine the cost and revenue aspects in overview, we find that relationships very clearly have some of the same characteristics as investments. The costs arise in an early stage (the investment), while the revenues are accrued over a longer period of time. Figure 2 illustrates this relationship from the perspective of a selling firm. The figure shows changes in customer profitability over time. In the first few years, costs are slightly in excess of revenues, which do not exceed costs until the fourth year. If the figures are accumulated, it can be seen that the relationship is not profitable until year seven. According to this report, from an Italian consultancy firm, it appears to be more effective to retain and maintain old customer relationships than to seek out new ones. The cost/revenue distribution is probably similar for a purchasing firm.

Another way of seeing relationships with regard to investments is to ask whether a relationship is a resource which can be taken over. The answer is not completely clear. It is difficult to transfer a relationship to some other unit. If a firm acquires another firm, and somehow takes over operations, relationships may come along as part of the package. This is not necessarily simply an advantage, as it may pose an obstacle to implementing changes. If, however, the purchasing firm

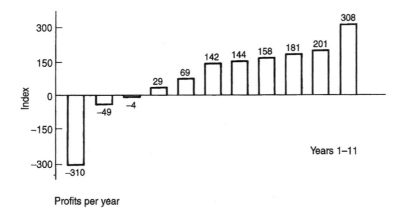

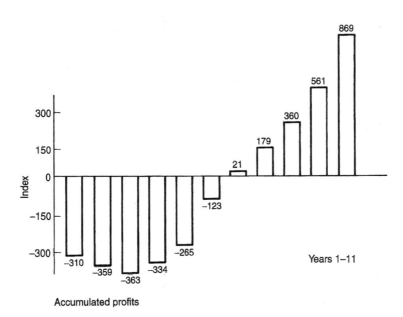

Figure 2   Cost/revenue structure in customer–supplier relationships.

wants to take advantage of the established relationship it can easily do so, and this may be a cheaper way of getting into a new network than trying successively to build up new relationships.

One important corollary is how to maintain these relationships, and how much exploitation they can withstand. Maintenance is obviously important, and there are infinite examples showing how quickly a relationship is undermined when it ceases to develop. This means that day-to-day activities must remain at a relatively high level. This places demands in terms of creativity and continuity in day-to-day work with suppliers. With regard to exploitation, there are two possibilities. If, during a given period, a firm does not maintain its connections, it may still keep much of its position, thanks to inertia. If, on the other hand, a firm is experienced as systematically attempting to over-exploit its connections, the effect may be both very rapid and painful. In other words, having some problems and difficulties is acceptable, but consciously abusing one's established connections is not.

ADAPTATIONS

Adaptation is one of the characteristic phenomena associated with relationships. In principle, adaptation in a relationship means that a certain supplier is handled in a unique way, either to give lower total costs or to give that supplier priority in relation to others. If all the parties involved – suppliers or customers – looked identical, purchased the same volumes and quantities, and had the same technological structure, adaptation would be irrelevant. Thus the degree of adaptation stands in direct proportion to the differences between the parties: the greater the differences the greater reason to make specific adaptations, and these may be seen as the means available to a firm to take advantage of the unique attributes of its supplier. By discovering and making use of these unique attributes, the purchasing firm may achieve a number of positive effects.

For instance, some specific attributes may be associated with the technology used by the supplier. Various suppliers may use the same technology and thus have some of the same attributes. Consequently, some adaptations may mean that a firm adapts not to a single supplier but to a certain category of supplier, with interchangeable members.

We now go on to discuss three particular aspects of adaptation. First we describe and exemplify various types of adaptation: technical, knowledge-based, administrative, economic and legal. Second, we analyse the way adaptations take place by distinguishing major adaptations occurring on isolated occasions from gradual, incremental adaptations over time. Third, we discuss some of the factors affecting the demand for and content of adaptations, primarily those relating to the technological structure of the firms and products concerned.

There are many types of adaptations. This has been shown in our previous discussions of effectiveness measures and elsewhere. One very important type is the technical ones. Buyers and sellers on industrial markets have plants and equipment with specific technical attributes, and their relationships are intended to bind them to one another effectively. Naturally, this places demands on and opens potential for technological adaptations, both in terms of the product sold by the supplier and the product manufactured by the buyer, as well as in terms of the production processes of each. In one large study we found that the purchasing firms primarily had technological co-operation with materials suppliers (Håkansson, 1989). In other words, materials adaptations appeared to be the most common type of adaptations, and we found this somewhat surprising. It may be explained by the fact that, from a production point of view, input goods are often the main cost factor. Of course we also found a number of adaptations regarding components and equipment.

Knowledge-based adaptations gain in importance the more development issues are emphasized in supplier relationships. In this respect as well, one may easily speak in terms of the necessity for a purchasing firm to market its needs. Buyers who encourage their suppliers to increase their knowledge of the buyer's application of technology, give themselves an important developmental boost. But in doing so the purchasing firm also commits itself, as it becomes better and better at using the technology of the supplier in question. Thus two bases of knowledge, that of the buyer and that of the supplier, proceed to approach one another, with reciprocal adaptation. Probably they should not be allowed to become too similar. There is some advantage in retaining a modicum of "friction", as the differences between them become a point of departure for future developments. This potential may be more positive if the two units remain separate. There may also be adaptations of administrative routines. Planning, supply and communications systems may need to be adapted so the firms can work together effectively.

Such adaptations take the form both of major one-off measures and small, successive steps over time. As a rule, major adaptations are highly visible ones which the parties involved consider strategic, while smaller adaptations are handled "locally" in the organization, and are considered natural measures necessary to facilitate collaboration. Frequently, such adaptations are substantial, although this may not be evident until one of the parties wants to implement a major change. The size and value of these successive adaptations are thus often difficult to overview, and there is a general tendency to underestimate their significance.

The need for adaptation will clearly depend on the attributes of the two parties. First, the need may arise because of specific characteristics of the seller, for example if the seller is a foreign company the buyer may demand local warehousing or some kind of local service. Second, the need may arise because of unique demands made by the purchasing firm. These may come up because the buyer is, in turn, subjected to unique demands from his customers or is working under special conditions for some other reason. Thirdly, the combination of seller and buyer and their interaction may create both demands and potential for specific adaptations.

The nature of these adaptations also depends on the type of product involved. Some products (such as some equipment) are routinely adapted, while others (such as material and standard components) tend to appear in standardized versions. Some customers purchase in such volumes that supply and inventory adaptations are important, while others (such as materials supplies) may be marked by considerable variation in both content and volume, making administrative adaptation of interest. This implies that product type and adaptation type are closely interrelated.

RECIPROCAL TRUST RATHER THAN FORMALITY

One of the things that characterizes business deals is that they always contain uncertainty. Some of this is about the future, and is genuine, i.e. it can never be reduced, only handled with more or less sophisticated assessments. Other aspects of insecurity are directly related to the other party in the transaction. For example, there is often a time lag between the transaction itself and the delivery. In addition, it is impossible to specify or measure all the functions or characteristics of a product, even at a specific delivery. Instead, they become visible gradually. Unexpected events may also mean that the content of the business deal must be adjusted, and the technology may be both complex and difficult to assess in advance. Thus there are a number of factors which are difficult to overview at the point when the deal is made. These difficulties are so great that it is often pointless – or far too costly – to try to formulate agreements to cover all conceivable situations. Instead, the relationship has to provide the security. Table 3 demonstrates that the degree of formalization in a relationship is generally low and, even when the relationship has developed to include substantial technical development, this is only established to a limited extent through formal agreements.

Security in a relationship cannot be created on a single occasion, but must develop over time. The connection must be built up through a process of interaction in which reciprocal trust can successively be deepened. Interaction may lead to the development of a learning process in which

Table 3   Use of formal contracts in supplier–customer relationships involving technical development

Type of relationship	Customer relationships	Supplier relationships
Formal	%	%
Annual contracts	20	11
Long-term contracts	13	8
Joint corporation	2	22
	35	41
Informal		
Ongoing relationship	51	67
Other informal pattern	14	12
	65	79
Totals	100	100

Source: Håkansson (1989), p. 113.

both sides gradually get a better idea of the situations in which it is suitable to do business. The typical process follows a course in which the two parties first test one another through small business deals, and then move along to more complete deliveries. In addition to its being important to get to know one's counterpart well, it is also important to facilitate that party's learning about one's own operations. In other words, it is important to create different types of social situations in which the personnel in the functions needing contact with one another get to know their counterparts and their problems. There is even an example in which these contacts have been extended to comprise all personnel at a given unit. In one particular case, a supplier brought his whole staff to see a major customer so that all those involved would gain understanding of the consequences of delays, and failure to meet quality standards.

The benefits of and the need for personal contacts in building up confidence cannot be too much stressed. This is often recommended from a marketing point of view, but it is certainly equally important for purchasing. We might even claim that the personal-contact network is one of the most important personnel resources, and that it should therefore be taken into consideration in recruitment of purchasers.

What happens, then, in situations in which one of the parties implements a measure which has a negative effect on the other? The answer will depend on how the other side sees that measure. If there are persuasive arguments for it, the dissatisfaction may be short-lived, but if the measure is interpreted as a long-term change of attitude, even a small shift may have grave consequences. This is where personal contacts between individuals at both firms become most important, as these may serve to give the other party a far more complete picture of why a certain measure is necessary. With such a personal network, a relationship can withstand substantial strain occasionally if the underlying policy remains the same. However, even small changes may impact greatly on the relationship if they are interpreted as shifting this underlying position.

POWER AND DEPENDENCE

Power and dependence are important aspects of supplier relationships. At least for large firms, the most important supplier relationships always involve large volumes, and are thus the principal ones for both parties from an economic point of view. They also affect both parties in a number of indirect ways, which further increases their significance. Significance creates dependence, and the way in which the power–dependence issue is handled thus becomes an important aspect of purchasing work. In the past, it was recommended that purchasers should try to behave in such a way that dependence did not arise. Independence was a key objective. As purchasing has begun to work more systematically with long-term relationships, dependence is now more accepted, and the question has become how to handle the various dependence situations.

One of the problems associated with power–dependence relations is that they are seldom symmetrical. As a rule, they are unbalanced with regard to individual dimensions. For example, the relationship may be more important to the seller than to the buyer from a volume point of view, or vice versa. However, a certain amount of imbalance in one dimension may be set off against the equivalent but opposite imbalance in another dimension. If this is not the case, it is important for the buyer to attempt to create such imbalances. If a purchasing firm wishes to try to get priority from one supplier despite the fact that it is not one of that firm's major buyers, it must begin by trying to make itself interesting in some other way, for instance from a technical point of view. The firm must try to set off its volume disadvantage with some other advantage. This type of "balancing act" is an important aspect of handling suppliers.

Another characteristic attribute of the power–dependence relationship is that it usually varies with the general state of the economy. The seller may have more power during a boom, as may the buyer when supply exceeds demand. It may be tempting to exploit this variation for short-term gain, and there are examples from the Swedish steel industry of such behaviour between manufacturers and wholesalers (Gadde, 1978). But a firm which tries to take advantage of such opportunities runs the risk of reprisals. If a buyer abuses his position during a recession, his firm may very well suffer when an economic upswing ensues. Handling of pricing issues is very important in this respect. Klint (1985) describes how buyers and sellers of paper pulp built up reciprocal trust through their behaviour in different business cycles.

There are no simple solutions to recommend to the problem of imbalance in the power–dependence relationship arising, for instance, as a result of changes in the economy. It is not easy to say what the best strategy is in any individual case. Certainly, though, awareness of the problems and regular, systematic discussions are a first step towards learning to handle these questions better.

CONFLICT AND CO-OPERATION

The parties in a business relationship have both contradictory interests and shared ones. If they do not learn to deal with the contradictory ones, conflicts arise. In the classic model of purchasing, relationships have been fraught with conflict. One typical example is this subcontractor, who characterizes his customers in the automotive industry as follows:

> They are nasty, abusive and ugly. They would take a dime from a starving grandmother. They steal our innovations, they make uneconomic demands, like "follow us around the globe and build plants near ours. We need good suppliers like you but if you can't do it we'll find somebody else." (Helper, 1986, p. 17).

There are an endless number of such examples, and both sellers and buyers have plenty of examples of dirty tricks they have played on one another, and they tend to blow their own trumpets about them. Needless to say, this type of behaviour does nothing to promote close relationships.

Reciprocal trust is a prerequisite for long-term relationships, adaptations, and joint investments. Realization of this fact led one representative of the automotive industry to make the following statement with regard to an essential change in existing relations:

> We need new relationships with what we have to think of as a family of suppliers. We need to throw off the old shackles of adversarial confrontation and work together in an enlightened era of mutual trust and confidence. (Berry, 1982, p. 26).

The description and aspiration is so heavenly that it almost makes one want to close with an "amen". At the same time, it is probably an erroneous appraisal of the ideal content of collaboration and conflict in a relationship. Unfortunately, there are altogether too many people who believe that elimination of all conflict in a relationship is a prerequisite for developing new supplier relations. It is important to point out that this is a misunderstanding. Of course effective relationships require some collaboration, but they require an equal measure of conflict. Figure 3 depicts the ideal relationship.

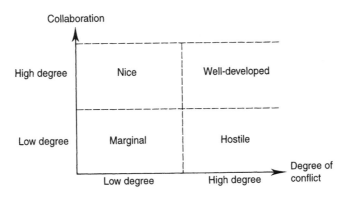

Figure 3 Relationships with different combinations of collaboration and conflict.

The Figure describes one dimension of collaboration and one of conflict. If the degree of both are low, the relationship will not be especially meaningful to either party – such relationships are characterized as marginal. If there is a high degree of conflict and a low degree of collaboration, the relationship will not work very well. Significant relationships come into being with a high degree of collaboration. A relationship with a low degree of conflict tends to be somewhat too "nice". The parties place too few demands on one another. Provided that it can be handled well, raising the degree of conflict in such a situation enables a better climate for innovation and development.

It seems that the desirable type of relationship is one in which conflict is handled constructively. In this, we agree with Gemünden (1985, p. 405) who says that "buyer and seller should neither smooth over existing conflicts nor let them escalate". There will be conflict as long as both parties remain independent, because they will never have identical goals. There will always be conflicts of interest between buyers and sellers, because there will always be the distribution problem: the profits generated by their joint work will have to be shared. This problem of distributing profits is mainly accentuated when their shared processing value falls. For these reasons, collaboration must continually develop so as to keep shared revenues at least at a constant level. Continuous development of collaboration to achieve "mutual profits" or "mutual success" (Hay, 1988) is thus an effective way of preventing the escalation of conflict. Increased openness appears to be a prerequisite for this, particularly in relation to strategic issues. Expressions of this openness should include involving the supplier in the product-development process from an earlier stage than has previously been the case.

In conclusion, there is good reason to believe that there are many measures for improvement of the fundamental working climate between buyers and suppliers which can contribute substantially to future development of purchasing work. As indicated in the discussion above, this does not mean that a firm must neglect its own aims or interests. On the contrary, the only possibility for establishing long-term working relations is for all the parties involved to have the courage to work on the basis of their own ambitions at the same time as they accept the fact that their collaborators have different ones, and that these must also be taken into account.

SUPPLIER RELATIONS – A CRITICAL RESOURCE

The main characteristics of a firm's supplier relations are summarized below. Our first conclusion is that relationships with suppliers are very important. They have considerable economic impact, because such a large proportion of the firm's activities are channelled through them. As a rule, more than half of the total turnover of the firm (sometimes up to 70 per cent) is handled within these relationships. They are important from a technical point of view, as they integrate the technology of the purchasing company with that of the supplier. Consequently, they also become central from an innovative point of view. They are one of the most important interfaces at which the knowledge possessed by the firm encounters other large bodies of knowledge.

Secondly, supplier relations comprise major investments. It requires a great deal of work both to establish a relation and to adapt the firm to it internally. Consequently, well-established supplier relations is one of the most important resources any firm has.

Supplier relations are built up through human effort and human contacts. Thus, their third characteristic is that they are "dynamic" in a number of respects. In order for them to survive, they must be under continual development. If they are not, there is a clear risk that one of the firms will develop the opinion that the other firm no longer considers the relationship important. The dynamic feature means both that all relations can be affected and that, in the long run, they are difficult to manipulate. Honesty is probably the word which recurs most frequently in our discussions with sellers and buyers of what characterizes good relations. Any sign of dishonesty has an immediately harmful effect on the relationship.

A fourth characteristic, to which we have thus far only alluded, is the fact that all the relationships a company has are interrelated and interdependent, and actually need to be seen as a network.

THE CASE STUDIES

Case 1: Procurement of MRO supplies for Volvo

The first case study deals with mundane, everyday supplies – the customer is Volvo. The type of large-scale, mass production that characterizes the automotive industry made car companies aware from an early stage of the need to link their activities with those of their suppliers. In order to achieve more substantial rationalization benefits, they have to extend their analysis and involvement several steps backward into the supplier network.

The "change project"

Roos (1988) reports on a change project carried out at Volvo, the aim of which was to make operations more effective by closer co-operation with suppliers. The project was carried out at the procurement and purchasing department of the Volvo Car Corporation between 1984 and 1987. In emulation of the Japanese experience, efforts were being made to increase delivery frequency and decrease lot sizes purchased. To achieve this, a number of substantial changes were required. One was that purchasing decisions of a routine nature were taken directly by the operational units. In these cases, they made their requisitions directly to the supplier, via computerized communication, instead of via the purchasing department, as had previously been the case. This made it possible to decrease lead times from two weeks to twenty-four hours. A new purchasing strategy was also adapted. The previous strategy had been to have at least two suppliers of each individual product. In order to work with JIT deliveries and total quality control, the intended modification was to purchase all that was needed of a given product group from a single supplier, which was meant to lead to a tangible reduction in the number of suppliers. However, it proved to be difficult to reduce the number of suppliers in this way. Many articles had unique properties and were not interchangeable. Therefore, the new principle gradually became that of asking one firm to supply the entire volume of a given article. In a few cases it became possible to further reduce the number of suppliers by having others increase their product range.

Effects at Volvo

Three inventory units were affected by this project for change: tools and MRO supplies, uniforms and work boots. The change project went on for three years, with the following effects (see Table 4).

Stock reduction was particularly notable in warehouses 2 and 3, where it was cut back by substantially more than half, despite volume increases of 33 to 51 per cent. The number of articles kept in stock remained unchanged in one case, but increased considerably in warehouse 2 and decreased slightly in warehouse 3.

It was also found that the stock reduction could be combined with improvements in service level. There are no statistics from warehouse 1, but both the others indicate shortened delivery times and increased delivery reliability (a sharp decrease in the number of back orders).

Thus it can be seen that it was possible for the Volvo warehouses to increase their degree of service in spite of substantial reductions of the goods in stock, with a consequent reduction in capital costs. It is interesting to find that even greater savings could be made in relation to other costs in materials administration. The primary effects here were a result of it becoming possible to eliminate one warehouse, which meant a need for fewer facilities, less administration and handling, and shorter process times. Another considerable rationalization benefit was that, once the goods

Table 4 Effects of changes in purchasing behaviour

	Warehouse		
	1	*2*	*3*
Purchased volume (index)			
Before	100	100	100
After	137	151	133
Number of articles (index)			
Before	100	100	100
After	100	540	81
Inventory volume (index)			
Before	100	100	100
After	65	30	44
Delivery times (days)			
Before		21	12
After		2	5
Delivery reliability (no. of back orders/time unit)			
Before		1500	1800
After		100	160

reception centre was moved, less quality-control work was necessary, and previous repetition of work was eliminated. The total effect of these cost reductions was nearly twice as great as the reduction of capital costs *per se*.

In the process of obtaining these effects, other costs increased. Improvement of in-house handling necessitated renovation of a warehouse, and investment in equipment for effective, flexible stock handling. The warehouses were also brightened up to increase personnel satisfaction and motivation.

The estimates made of the total effect indicated that these changes resulted in annual savings corresponding to 25 per cent of the tied-up capital of the warehouse.

Effects on the suppliers

Roos also describes how the suppliers were involved in this process of change. One of his examples relates to deliveries of uniforms. The supplier (Tvättman) is situated in the immediate vicinity of Gothenburg, and supplies Volvo with new uniforms as well as laundering the ones already in use. This amounts to 85000 articles per year, of which one-third are replaced annually. This clothing is manufactured by the Bergis company, which has three plants in western Sweden, which deliver 55 per cent of their production to Tvättman. One of Bergis' most important suppliers is an Italian cloth manufacturer (Klopman) (see Figure 4).

In the introductory section of this case study we primarily analysed in-house-effects at Volvo warehousing, and what happened in relationship A. Let us go on to examine effects on other relationships.

Volvo is one of Tvättman's main customers. For this reason, the changes initiated by Volvo had substantial effects when they were passed along via relationship B. The increased demand thus also

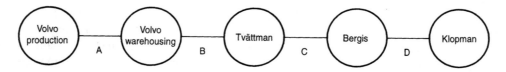

Figure 4 The supply chain.

meant that Tvättman had to change its purchasing behaviour. First, there had to be in-house changes with regard to its view of customer and supplier relations. Secondly, there had to be changes in actual working methods. To prevent Tvättman's stock from increasing owing to measures implemented at Volvo, it was necessary for Tvättman, in turn, to become more effective with regard to frequency of deliveries and lot sizes in relationship C. Ordering routines were changed so that Tvättman in Gothenburg submitted its orders directly to Bergis via telex. Previously, it had ordered by writing to its own head office in Malmö which then placed the order with Bergis. This made it possible to shorten the lead time from two weeks to twenty-four hours.

For Tvättman, the effect was that stock volumes decreased by more than one third, despite the fact that the volume of uniforms handled increased by over one third during the three-year period. Service – in terms of delivery reliability – also improved from 85 to 97.3 per cent, in spite of the substantial increase in the number of items.

Tvättman's demands shifted down to the next link in the chain (Bergis). Bergis has not decreased its total stock of finished garments, because in conjunction with these changes Bergis began to serve as a central warehouse for special garments for all 24 Tvättman plants. The result was that both volume and number of articles increased for Bergis. Relatively, therefore, its stock of the garments it previously supplied has dropped considerably, in part thanks to changes in its work organization.

Production workers previously performed only specialized parts of the process. In principle, this meant that twelve people contributed to every finished garment. Personnel received training to raise their competence, and today only one to three people are needed to sew each whole garment. The effects of this were that the production pipeline was shortened from nine to three weeks, and an estimated productivity improvement of 5 to 10 per cent. To make it possible to live up to the demands of JIT delivery and handling of the increased number of articles, the firm computerized its production, inventory and delivery follow-up and monitoring.

Bergis' orders, in turn (relationship D), also changed in the direction of increased frequency and smaller lots. The result of this has been a 60 per cent decrease in the stock of cloth on hand, and a drop in lead time from eight to three weeks. The firm itself claims that these changes in suborder routines have had no effect at all on the Italian cloth supplier, in whose total production volume Bergis is a marginal customer.

Case comments

The benefits of analysing the interface between the suppliers and the purchasing company's in-house activities is well illustrated by this case. Volvo is systematically trying to develop its supplier network for MRO supplies. The aim of these activities is not just to decrease costs, but also to improve the service level. The lesson to be learned is that the purchasing company must develop its own planning work and improve its execution of administrative and physical tasks to find out better ways of using its suppliers. Activities must be analysed step by step, through several links of companies, stretching from the buying firm, through the supplier, the subcontractor and eventually even the sub-subcontractor. For other products, such as components, this analysis should also be expanded forward to customers and their customers. This systematic analysis and co-ordination of the activity chain may show substantial potential for rationalization improvements whenever large quantities are handled. So when a company buys large quantities of any product (materials, components or MRO supplies) attempts should always be made to analyse the chain at least a few steps back.

The need to adapt resources to facilitate the close linking of activities can also be found in this case study. Volvo had to invest in order to implement its new way of using its suppliers, and so did the suppliers. This mutual investment process facilitates the interaction, but it also increases the mutual dependence of the counterparts.

The investments made in this case are small compared to what is needed when cooperation concerns the development of new products. Such a project is the theme of the next case study.

Case 2: Biopharm's use of suppliers in developing a new product

Our second case study is an illustration of using suppliers in an active way in terms of technical development. The case deals with the development of a new system and the role the suppliers can play in developing different components of that system. The case illustrates the need for an actor analysis, in order to find suppliers who are both willing to be and are capable of being development partners. Other important issues are financial compensation for the suppliers and the need to involve the right personnel in the relationships. The data for this case study have been collected through interviews and from written documents, project documentation, etc. The interviews were made with four members of the project team, including the project leader and the product manager, and with two of the suppliers involved (Eriksson, 1989).

Biopharm and its product

Biopharm (disguised name) is a company which designs, manufactures and markets systems for the production of pharmaceuticals. It is a relatively large company, operating on a global basis.

In the early 1980s, Biopharm began manufacturing "The System". This system was used for the purification of pharmaceutical raw materials. It was produced in units or small lots, mainly for special orders, and the number produced and sold was about 30 units a year. Customer needs regarding quality and design were different, so the systems were often tailored to the buyer's requirements.

The production of the system was highly specialized, i.e. it was built mainly from components purchased from external suppliers. Purchased components made up about 85 per cent of the total production cost of the system.

Another characteristic of the original system was that only about 20 per cent of its components were technically adapted to the system, while 80 per cent were purely standard. This fact made supplier contacts easy to handle, not least from a technical point of view.

The development project

In 1987, Biopharm decided to update and redesign the system to develop one single version. Biopharm wanted the system to be of high quality, as the buyers with high-quality requirements were growing in number. One important means of enhancing the quality was to obtain components that were well adapted to their functions in this particular system. In the original version, the large proportion of standard components led to a number of technical compromises in the system, or as one technician from Biopharm expressed the problem: "The system was a mish-mash of more or less well suited components, and badly documented."

Biopharm assigned a project group to redesign the system. The group started out by determining the functional standards of the system as a whole. Then every part was gone through carefully, and detailed specifications for individual components set. At this stage, some discussions and inquiries were carried out with component suppliers. It was not, however, until the specifications were ready and set, that a more systematic call for tenders was issued.

The companies that already supplied Biopharm with standard components for the original system then received inquiries concerning the new technical specifications. The majority of the old suppliers, however, turned out to be either unable or unwilling to meet the new requirements. Some of them were large companies and quite uninterested in adapting their standardized products just to satisfy a relatively small customer such as Biopharm. Actually, only two out of the approximately thirty former suppliers of major components (minor details excluded) turned out to be potential suppliers.

Table 5 Supplier structure of "The System"

Total number of suppliers	60
Suppliers of major components	30
Old suppliers of major components	2
New suppliers of major components	28
Suppliers with close collaboration during the project	12–15

In effect, most of the components needed could not be obtained from the existing suppliers. This meant that much of the project work had to be devoted to contacts and discussions with a large number of potential new suppliers. Some 30–40 major components had to be purchased and throughout the project Biopharm was in touch with various suppliers of each one.

A number of suppliers presented samples and prototypes. An important task for Biopharm was to run tests on these in their own laboratory. These tests required competence within fields of knowledge related to the use of the system. Therefore the tests could not be performed by the component suppliers. This testing was time consuming, and progress in the collaboration with individual suppliers was often delayed, pending test results.

Many of the suppliers under consideration by Biopharm during the project, were either dropped or accepted but backed out after only a few contacts. During the process, however, a core of 12–15 especially interesting partners crystallized. An intensive discussion with these suppliers then evolved. Many people from each side were involved and engaged in frequent contacts, technical discussions, visits, etc. Among these innovative relationships, the two remaining old suppliers were found. Not surprisingly, they both had 20–25 year connections with Biopharm, and each of them supplied components that constituted a large proportion of the total system value.

The technical specifications demanded by Biopharm were sometimes perceived by the suppliers as being nearly impossible to fulfil. One example was a valve manufacturer who was asked to make a new type of valve, cast in one piece. To begin with, the supplier found the whole idea absurd and rejected the proposition. However, after a lot of involvement on the part of their own technicians, Biopharm eventually made the supplier see the point of the proposed design. The supplier began to see the idea more as a "new way of thinking" and decided to give it a try. The new type of valve was not completed by the time of the launching of the new system in the fall 1989, but the first delivery was expected by the end of the year.

Biopharm's persistence – and sometimes "absurd" requirements – made the company quite a fussy customer to deal with. Nevertheless, their demands and ideas also made them an interesting and stimulating partner. Some of the suppliers perceived their interaction with Biopharm as an opportunity to develop their own field of competence.

Biopharm's relationships with its two former suppliers developed even more during this project, and assumed a somewhat different character. Both suppliers were foreign companies, whose sales to Biopharm had previously been handled entirely through local agents. During this project, however, technical matters became too complex to handle via intermediaries. Therefore a direct dialogue between Biopharm and the manufacturers was established. In other words, the earlier standardized, routine ways of handling these relationships were not adequate when the product was no longer standardized. Both the social and technical exchange between the companies was extended, as was the number of people involved in the relationship.

The financial side of the collaboration was managed in different ways in different relationships. Some of the suppliers were very small firms, not able to finance development costs themselves. Such firms also saw very little possibility of benefiting from the outcome in other areas. In some of these cases Biopharm either paid for the whole or part of the cost and thereby obtained exclusive rights to the product. In other cases, however, the supplier was large enough to bear the expense and also saw possibilities in other areas. Some of these companies were offered financial support by Biopharm, but refused it, since Biopharm required exclusive rights in return.

Not all collaborative attempts in this project were successful. One of the 12–15 promising relationships mentioned earlier was with a domestic manufacturer of electronic instruments. This was a very small company, specialized in a narrow niche. The instrument Biopharm wanted them to design was unique. The supplier seemed receptive to Biopharm's technical instructions, and at the beginning of the collaboration both parties were quite optimistic. The supplier began working on the product, and over the next 4–5 months the firms had frequent contact. The supplier behaved as if everything was working out as planned. When the first delivery arrived, however, the product was not at all satisfactory. Technical discussions continued. The supplier still wanted to proceed with the project. One year later, Biopharm had major doubts about the outcome of this collaboration, and was seriously considering dropping the supplier. It was discovered that the supplier had considerable problems connected with the establishment of a production unit in Southeast Asia. According to Biopharm, the supplier had not been frank about the scope or impact of its internal problems.

In the successful cases of collaboration, i.e. where a satisfactory component was obtained, Biopharm's efforts and active participation in the suppliers' development work seems to have been of great importance. First, especially in the completely new relationships, Biopharm's commitment was necessary to reinforce the suppliers' faith in the project. In this way resources could more easily be mobilized. Second, the input of Biopharm's knowledge about the function of a supplier's component in this particular application was important to the supplier. Third, because Biopharm's expertise was mainly in a different field than that of the suppliers, "absurd" – but also innovative – solutions were suggested and new ways of thinking could sometimes be found.

Results

When the project was completed, the outcome was a system that fulfilled Biopharm's expectations with regard to quality and design. Proper documentation had also been accomplished. The original version of the system had consisted of 20 per cent specially designed or adapted components and 80 per cent standard components. In the new version these proportions were reversed. These results could to a large extent be considered as products of the close collaborations between Biopharm and the suppliers.

The outcome of the project could, however, be seen in other respects besides the quality of the system developed. First, because of the technical adaptations in the new components and also because of the documentation produced for the components, Biopharm's new supplier relationships are much tighter than were the old ones. For most of the components there is now only one supplier, which would be rather difficult to replace quickly.

Second, the social bonds with suppliers have become rather strong since a lot of people got to know each other during the development process.

Third, indirect technical dependencies between different suppliers have been created as their components are all adapted to fit the system. In effect, one supplier cannot change his component without affecting the functioning of other components.

Fourth, new ways of thinking and developed knowledge within supplier companies could open new possibilities for them in other networks.

Case comments

It is interesting to compare Biopharm's supplier network for its earlier system with its new one. In producing the first system, Biopharm was in contact with a group of suppliers with no connections between them. The relationships were not especially developed, i.e. Biopharm simply bought products, standardized items, that had been developed for other applications. It was easy for Biopharm to change suppliers, because there were always other suppliers who could offer them the same products. All units were relatively independent.

The new structure moves Biopharm to the other end of the spectrum, with all the relationships, and thus also the companies, much more dependent on one another. The products are much more specialized and they fit together in a much more integrated way than before. There are even dependencies among suppliers. Today, it is quite difficult for Biopharm to change a single supplier. Such a process takes time and means a loss of investments. On the other hand, all the suppliers are under pressure. If the final system becomes too expensive there will be no sales, which will affect them all, independently and as a whole. They could, of course, use extortion upon one another, but only for a short time because there is still the opportunity to exchange any part of the system. If a supplier has to be changed, it will never be given a second chance. The new network thus contains much more tension than the first. As long as this tension can be used constructively, however, it will be beneficial to most of them. But there may always be a loser. If the costs of making the adaptations are larger than the revenues accrued from Biopharm or some other complementary relationships, the supplier will operate at a loss. As is shown in this case study, a number of the previous suppliers decided that this might be the case for them when they chose not to participate.

The necessity of interplay between the competence of the purchasing company and that of its suppliers for development of an effective network is thus brought into focus. This is further elaborated on in the next case, where a purchasing firm works systematically to educate its suppliers in order to make them better partners.

Case 3: Motorola and a supplier–development programme

Our first case dealt with purchasing problems in terms of how to develop individual relationships or how to develop a supplier network for a certain type of purchased products. The second case extended the problems into the development of products and knowledge. In the last two cases, we extend the analysis one step further and look at the whole company's supplier network. The first case study shows how Motorola has developed a general training programme in an attempt to develop more or less all of its suppliers. This case provides us with a good illustration of the need to make long-term purchasing strategy very clear, in order to communicate it effectively to suppliers. Even then, however, complementary activities must be undertaken to stress the importance of this issue.

Supplier involvement

Motorola, Inc. is one of the world's leading manufacturers of electronic-equipment systems and components. During the 1980s, the company has become a well-known example of a promoter of total quality. Our case description is based on Cayer (1988).

Of every Motorola sales dollar, between 30 and 60 per cent (depending on the business group) goes to suppliers. This alone makes it quite clear that suppliers have a heavy impact on the quality of Motorola products. Company representatives think that suppliers "affect quality more than any other factor in the equation" except for design. Owing to increasing foreign competition, Motorola is committed to accelerating its quality-improvement programme. For this process to be successful, considerable supplier improvement is vital.

Supplier involvement is known to be a major source of potential for improving competitiveness. One company representative states that all the Motorola factories have made tremendous efforts and gains in product quality, reduction of cycle times, and cost reductions. Although some suppliers have played important roles in these improvements, the majority of the supplier base is considered not to have kept up with the pace of Motorola.

Four demands on suppliers that are part of the Motorola improvement process are stated. Motorola needs suppliers who:

- keep pace in attaining perfect quality
- are on the leading edge of technology

- use JIT manufacturing
- offer cost-competitive service.

According to the company, stating the requirements is the easy part – the difficult thing is implementing them. Motorola has worked with supplier development for a number of years. The major problem has been to change the culture associated with the relationships – from the old adversarial type to "win-win" partnerships. After observing good examples at other companies (such as Rank Xerox and Ford) Motorola has been able to improve supplier relations through a series of programmes carried out with their suppliers.

Training and education of suppliers

Training and education were very important factors in the internal quality programme at Motorola. They estimate that they invested 40 million dollars annually in training in more sophisticated manufacturing, design and management techniques. In the beginning, the programmes were open only to the employees of Motorola. Then, through an analysis of best-practice firms Motorola found that one significant difference between itself and Ford and Rank Xerox was that these companies had extended their training to suppliers as well. Motorola considered that fact to be an important key to its subsequent success.

This was the starting point for the supplier-training programme established in 1988, with the aim of training suppliers to keep up to par in efficiency and productivity. The reason Motorola provided this programme was that its training courses had already been proved to work internally, and it had gained a great deal of hard-earned experience when developing them. Another reason was that only a small part of the supplier base would have had the resources necessary to develop the kind of training needed.

The benefits of the partnership training programmes are mutual. Motorola, of course, has a vested interest in improving supplier performance as they are a part of the assembly line. But suppliers also stand to gain, as the training provided by Motorola will strengthen their overall competitive power. They will be able to broaden their customer base to include other companies striving for zero defects.

The Motorola training programme provides us with an illustration of the structural role of purchasing. By increasing their strength and capabilities, suppliers become more competitive. In the US a trend has developed in that many domestic suppliers have encountered difficulties because foreign competitors are more efficient. According to one Motorola representative, there are several component categories for which there are no longer any domestic suppliers. An increasing dependency on foreign suppliers is not considered a desirable future by Motorola. Therefore it is in its own interest to help develop and promote the capabilities of domestic suppliers so that they will be able to make significant quality improvements.

The programme

Motorola began by establishing a "partnerships for growth advisory board", which initiated a programme with three courses. These training courses covered SPC (statistical process control), design for manufacturability and short-cycle management (where the JIT concept is introduced).

Suppliers were made aware of the courses in a letter signed by the general managers of the Motorola divisions concerned, with a brochure enclosed describing the Partnership for Growth Training Series. Response was limited and suppliers were encouraged again, and were also reminded of the fact that the completion of the three courses was a condition for ongoing business. Even then reactions were slow in coming. Many suppliers felt they didn't need the training. Others were so established that SPC appeared to them to be a basic technique. After almost one year Motorola increased the pressure on suppliers and insisted that suppliers had to take all three courses if they were interested in doing business in the future. The reason for this increasing pressure was the findings presented in a five-year study conducted by the Automotive Industry Action Group, which indicated that suppliers implemented technology, JIT and other viable programmes only to the extent enforced by their customers, and that they did not take opportunities to improve their own productivity.

Motorola considered this a serious drawback to the future competitiveness of suppliers, and intensified its pressure on them. After five months, 167 of the 500 suppliers intended for the programme had completed courses. The results achieved were considered very substantial by Motorola representatives. Within some weeks of basic SPC training, suppliers had made dramatic leaps towards better quality.

The supplier-training programme is only one of a number of activities undertaken to encourage partnership in relationships. Another is promotion of early supplier involvement in new product development. In a number of commodity-product areas, the suppliers' technicians are considered to be the true experts. Therefore, a growing interest has been shown in many of the divisions of the company in facilitating participation of supplier technicians in new product development from a very early stage.

The Communication Sector, Motorola's largest business, encourages supplier participation by focusing on four formalized functions – the supplier advisory board, annual conferences, annual technical symposia and the supplier show. The supplier advisory board was formed to improve two-way communication between Motorola and a core of selected suppliers. The annual supplier conferences provide an exchange of information and insights into various business activities. Conference speakers are always top managers at Motorola. This is an indication to the suppliers of the importance the corporation attaches to the conference and to the development of supplier partnerships. The technical symposia and supplier shows provide Motorola's engineering, manufacturing and purchasing people with an awareness of a broad range of products and technologies available from suppliers. The symposia take the form of in-depth technical seminars on topics presented by technical experts from supplier companies.

Case comments

It might appear relatively uncomplicated to change a purchasing strategy. However, doing so requires a complete change in the way relationships with suppliers are handled. Only when there are no previous relationships to have an influence, might it be easy to change one's own strategy, but in all other cases a change has a substantial effect on how the suppliers should work. Making this type of change takes a long time and is extremely demanding on resources, as can be seen in the case of Motorola. Even for such a very large buyer, it proved difficult to get the suppliers to take an active part in development work.

There is some resistance to change in all networks. This makes it necessary to work with systematic mobilization strategies. Nothing will be accomplished without the support of the counterparts, and all changes must, accordingly, be seen from the other actors' point of view. Neither purchasing nor marketing strategies can be formulated only from the point of view of one's own company. For changes to be accepted by other actors, therefore, both purchasing and marketing must be analysed and structured so as to create business opportunities for other parts of the network as well.

This type of network strategy can be seen in the last case study, of Nike.

Case 4: Nike's network strategies for subcontracting

One of the keys to a successful network strategy for purchasing is making the different suppliers systematically interrelated. One of the aims is to mobilize the suppliers for development and production in what the buying company considers the right way. In this last case study, Nike's purchasing strategy stands as an illustration of how this can be done.

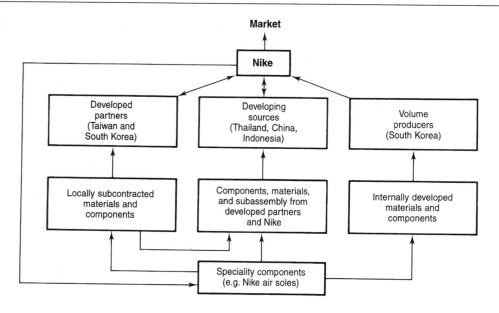

Figure 5 Nike's system of first- and second-tier subcontracting (Donaghu and Barff, 1990, p. 545).

Nike's supplier network

Nike is a major US athletic footwear producer. The case study deals with their supplier network structure and strategy. It is based on information in an article written by Donaghu and Barff (1990).

Nike's supplier network is structured in two layers (Figure 5). The first thing to observe is that Nike's current production system is almost entirely based on out-sourcing to independent suppliers. First-tier suppliers are considered "production partners", rather than subcontractors. Many of their supplier relations are of a long-term nature (eight to ten years) and suppliers are given various kinds of responsibilities within the Nike production system.

The subcontracting system

Three groups of first-tier suppliers can be identified. One is "developed partners". These firms are responsible for the production of Nike's latest and most expensive products. Their factories are located in Taiwan and South Korea. In these countries, production costs have risen substantially during the late 1980s, and so production of price-sensitive products has been moved to factories elsewhere. The shoes produced by developed partners are characterized by rather low price elasticity, however, which means that they can absorb increasing production costs. Nearly all the developed partners manufacture Nike shoes on an exclusive basis. These relations are therefore characterized by strong mutual dependence, making it important for both parties that stability and trust are promoted. These firms are typically characterized by a lack of vertical integration. Their factories are usually supplied by local subcontractors.

"Volume producers" are suppliers of more standardized footwear. They generally manufacture a specific type of footwear (e.g. football boots, athletics shoes, etc.). They tend to be more vertically integrated than developed partners. They often own leather tanneries, rubber factories and assembly plants. Volume producers have a production capacity four or five times that of developed partners. Their customer relations are not exclusive. Instead, they have ten or more separate buyers purchasing shoes from them. Therefore, Nike does not develop or manufacture any of its up-market and innovative products in these plants. Nor do the competitors manufacture their newest footwear in these volume factories, where other brands are produced at the same time. Rather, volume producers are used to balancing demand and supply in various phases of the business cycle. The cyclical variations in demand can only be marginally absorbed by developed partners, owing to their limited capacity.

Consequently, variations in demand can be considerable. Monthly orders to individual volume producers may fluctuate by 50 per cent or more. Therefore Nike makes only limited efforts to stabilize and deepen its relationships with the volume producers as the strategy is to utilize them for cyclical subcontracting.

The third supplier group is represented by "developing sources". Producers in this group are attractive owing to their low costs (especially labour) and their potential to diversify assembly location. Presently, these firms are located in Thailand, Indonesia and China. Almost all of the development sources are exclusive Nike manufacturers. Due to their limited expertise, Nike is very active in assisting these firms in their development. At the beginning of the collaboration, the product and production standard of these firms can be compared to the situation forty years ago in the United States. One important thing for Nike, therefore, is to increase the production capability of these factories to meet the global production standard of Nike. The long-term goal is that a significant proportion of the developing sources over time will become developed partners.

The management of supplier relations

We can see that Nike's supplier network is a mixture of different kinds of relations. Some are long-term while others change from year to year. Some are characterized by deep commitment while others are of an arm's-length nature.

Long-term, intimate partnerships with suppliers must somehow be promoted by customers. Nike uses three main strategies to do this:

1. Nike operates what it calls an "expatriate programme" wherein Nike expatriate technicians become permanent personnel in the factory producing Nike footwear. While at the factory, they function as liaison between Beaverton's headquarters and R&D to help insure a smooth product development process and maintain quality control.
2. Nike encourages its partners (particularly the older ones) to participate in joint product development activities. Most basic research is performed at Nike's Beaverton facilities, but the responsibility for the development of new footwear is shared with its production partners. The partners are especially important in the search for new material inputs and the implementation of improved production processes, but these close ties also serve to keep the production partners abreast of the directions Nike intends to take in the marketplace.
3. With those factories that manufacture only Nike products (over half of all the partners), Nike places a monthly order, preventing production from varying more than 20 per cent per month. These efforts to stabilize the production of Nike shoes take place with those factories that have been with Nike for many years as well as with newer producers (Donaghu and Barff, 1991, p. 542).

It is interesting to observe the activities undertaken by Nike to increase the capability of their developing sources, but the developed partners also participate in this process. The establishment of developing sources often takes the form of joint ventures between local factories in China or Indonesia and a Nike exclusive developed partner in South Korea or Taiwan, which means that the developed partners have a financial interest in the development of the new sources, and will be interested in transferring their sharing capabilities with these partners.

In this way all three actor groups benefit from deeper co-operation. Developed partners are able to move production of the price-sensitive part of the product programme to locations where cost is lower. They concentrate their own manufacturing activities on the more expensive, image-creating products, where price is less important. Developed partners will also be able to supply developing sources with both components and materials.

Developing sources will clearly be able to benefit from the joint venture. The transfer of various capabilities (from Nike and the developed partner) will accelerate the development of these firms as compared with a situation without these links with the larger network. Advantages will be obtained in terms of manufacturing techniques, owing to the demands from competent customers and the availability of important input resources.

Finally, Nike also stands to benefit from the new structure of the production system. The diversified structure of production hedges against currency fluctuations, tariffs and duties. The joint venture arrangements seem to be an efficient way for a natural transfer of capabilities which must be efficient for the entire network. But the system also keeps the pressure on the developed partners at the first tier. They need to keep production costs low as developing sources might otherwise mature into full-blown developed partners.

Case comments

Nike's way of organizing the production system is an excellent example of a network strategy. It is an extreme case, as the whole production process is out-sourced, but similar tendencies can be found in almost all types of production. Suppliers are becoming more important from a volume point of view, and efficiency is more and more determined by how different production units – internally and externally – are systematically interrelated. In this kind of co-ordination, the activities as well as the resources of the different units must be co-ordinated, and a key issue is to find and develop points of complementarity. For the same reasons, the selection of companies to include in the network is very critical. Nike seems to do this in an excellent way. Their ability to do so is probably attributable to their marketing position in relation to the end market, and to two important knowledge bases. Their position in relation to the end market – the image and the distribution network – is their major asset. In the long run it might not be sufficient, however, and should be supplemented with at least two knowledge bases. The first base is the product knowledge and a need for continuous development regarding individual components, as well as the interaction between different components. This knowledge of how to create good footwear must be kept centrally, in order to keep up the central position within the network. There is always a risk, otherwise, that the developed partners, or the volume producers, might be able to take over. The second base is knowledge of potential suppliers. The development of the production network will never be finalized. There will always be both possibilities of and needs to increase efficiency in terms of finding better activity structures as well as better resources constellations. Every network can, and must, be developed in order to be sustainable.

CONCLUSIONS

Our four case studies have clearly illustrated the potential for increasing efficiency and effectiveness in purchasing activities. With systematic development of individual supplier relations and supplier networks, significant improvements can be made.

It has also been shown, however, that the potential benefits can be quite difficult to attain. Companies have to change their internal activities, as well as change the suppliers in various ways. Such a process means that a number of critical issues are raised. The major one is that companies need to facilitate co-operation, as their own activities will be increasingly dependent on other actors. For such a division of work to be efficient, two major issues must be dealt with. One is the organization of the companies. Certain types of organizational structures might increase the opportunities for an efficient linking of the actors, activities and resources. The other issue is communication. A critical aspect of supplier relations and supplier networks is the exchange of information. As activities undertaken by suppliers are dependent on (and affect) the activities of the customer, there is a strong need for information exchange.

REFERENCES

Berry, B. Is Detroit prompting a shake-out in the supplier network. *Iron Age*, 14 July, 25–8 (1982)

Cayer, S. World class suppliers don't grow on trees. *Purchasing*, 25 August, 45–9 (1988).

Donaghu, M. and Barff, R. Nike just did it: international subcontracting and flexibility in athletic footwear production, *Regional Studies*, **24** (6), 537–52 (1990).

Gadde, L. -E. *Efterfrågevariationer i vertikala marknadssystem*, Business Administration Studies, Gothenburg, (1978).

Gemünden, H. G. Coping with Inter-Organizational Conflicts. Efficient Interaction Strategies for Buyer and Seller Organizations, *Journal of Business Research*, **13**, 405–20 (1985).

Håkansson, H. *Corporate Technological Behaviour – Co-operation and Networks*. Routledge, London (1989).

Hay, E. It takes more than low bid to be world class, *Purchasing*, 10 November, 50–80 (1988).

Helper, S. Supplier relations and technical progress: theory and application to the auto industry. Department of Economics, Harvard University (1986).

Klint, M. *Mot en konjunkturanpassad kundstrategi*. Department of Business Administration, University of Uppsala.

Roos, L. -U. *Kapitalrationalisering i varulager – kan japansk management och japansk syn på inköp untnyttjas?* Handelshögskolan i Göteborg, Företagsekonomiska institutionen.

5.3 The changing role of purchasing: reconsidering three strategic issues

Lars-Erik Gadde and Håkan Håkansson

During the last 20 years a new view of purchasing has gradually emerged. From being considered a clerical function – with the ultimate purpose of buying as cheaply as possible – it is today regarded in many companies as a major strategic function. This new attitude towards purchasing is responsible for more than half the total costs in many companies. Nevertheless, the scale of the recent change is so considerable that an analysis of its development is of interest. This paper draws on our own research and that of many others. Our focus is manufacturing and assembly industry.

Let us begin with a quotation that gives a representative statement on the traditional view of efficiency in purchasing:

> Price has been the principal yardstick by which manufacturers have traditionally selected their suppliers. By spreading their purchases among several suppliers, it is argued, manufacturers can achieve the cheapest price and the greatest assurance of a secure flow of material (Dillforce, 1986, p. 3).

Such purchasing behaviour does not allow for making direct use of the total resources of the suppliers. This can be a considerable drawback, according to the analysis provided by, for example, Axelsson and Håkansson (1984) and Spekman (1985). During the last decade, however, many companies have changed their behaviour in the directions proposed (see for example Carlisle and Parker, 1989; Gadde and Håkansson, 1993; Lamming, 1993).

In 1987, Morgan observed a tendency among customers to move from an arm's-length relationship (a number of competing suppliers) towards single sourcing and even to "alliances". The last type of relationship involves a deepened cooperation between the customer and a specific supplier. Similar frameworks have been presented by Frazier *et al.* (1988) and Lamming (1993). Frazier *et al.* have developed a conceptual model where the traditional view is called *market exchange*. The deeper relationships are then characterized as *relational exchange* and *just-in-time exchange*. Lamming's discussion is based on empirical observations from the automobile industry. This model takes a dynamic view and identifies a four-phase development process from the traditional model (prior to 1975) to the partnership model (after 1990).

The strategic purchasing context for the partnership model is very different from that of the traditional model, and similarly for just-in-time exchange versus market exchange. The aim of our contribution, therefore, is to analyse the changing role of purchasing in terms of purchasing strategy and purchasing behaviour. We shall discuss the impact of the new view in three dimensions of purchasing strategy.

The major strategic decision is always whether to buy or to rely on in-house production. Consequently, the first strategic issue is related to the question of *make or buy*. If the role of the purchasing is changing, the nature of the make-or-buy decision might be affected.

The second strategic choice is to decide on the *supply-base structure*. This issue regards the number of suppliers to use, as well as how the suppliers should relate to one another. The third strategic aspect deals with the nature of the *customer–supplier relationship*. When buyer–seller relationships turn into alliances, partnerships or just-in-time exchanges, the suppliers become more or less parts of the customer's production system. We discuss the benefits that can be obtained from this kind of close relationship.

MAKE OR BUY

The first strategic issue deals with the decision of whether to make or to buy. This question has been a major topic ever since industrial activities were established but it does not seem to have been considered as a strategic problem by manufacturing firms. Culliton (1942) concluded that most managers, when they were asked about their make-or-buy problem, said they had none. According to Culliton, however, that answer should be considered as representing a lack of insight into strategic issues, rather than the absence of the problem. The relevance of this aspect seems to have been neglected even in more recent times: see for example Janch and Wilson (1979), Leenders and Nollet (1984), and Ford *et al.* (1993). These authors conclude that make-or-buy problems have generally been ignored by top management. Where they have been considered, they seem to have been handled by purchasing departments and based on short-term cost criteria, rather than on strategic analysis.

In spite of the perceived absence of strategic decisions, it is possible to identify a clear trend over time towards the increasing importance of "buy". In 1942 Culliton argued that, in general, it seemed that "buying is preferable to making". The reasons for his conclusion, however, appear to be the disadvantages associated with a "make" strategy, owing to rapid changes in the market, and the lack of flexibility that characterizes in-house production. Hayes and Abernathy (1980) agree with Culliton in advocating a "buy" strategy. Their main reason is the risks associated with being locked into a specific technology, which might be challenged by new developments. A company with asset-specific investments, they argue, may have problems in maintaining its innovativeness. The authors therefore warn companies against too high a degree of vertical integration. Dirrheimer and Hübner (1983) analysed the vertical integration in the automobile industry and discovered a considerable variation between different companies and different countries. For all manufacturers analysed, however, vertical integration had decreased during the previous five-year period.

In total, therefore, as the levels of vertical integration have increased, suppliers appear to have become more and more important as sources of resources. This is illustrated by examples in Gadde and Håkansson (1993). In a study of four large multinationals in the Swedish engineering industry, it was shown that components and systems purchased from outside suppliers accounted for about two-thirds of the turnover. In the construction industry, it was found, the proportion is even higher. The situation also seems to be familiar for small and medium-sized firms. In a study of 123 Swedish companies, purchasing accounted for more than 40% of the turnover for 70% of the companies. For almost every fifth firm, the proportion extended to 70% (Håkansson, 1989).

The figures also seem to be representative for a general trend in other countries (Ford *et al.* 1993) and other industries (Kumpe and Bolwijn, 1988). These findings show that many manufacturing companies are increasingly relying on competent suppliers, which have been able to contribute to the customer's efficiency in production as well as in R&D.

It is possible, therefore, to identify a decreasing rate of vertical integration. A strategic shift of this kind can lead both to advantages and to disadvantages. One interesting question is whether this trend will continue. Miles and Snow (1986) predict that it will. In their opinion, the changing environmental conditions and new competitive forms will result in industries being characterized by completely new organizational forms in the future. They suggest that the functions necessary in an industrial system (such as design, production and marketing) will be performed by specialized companies, each one undertaking separate functions. Such dynamic networks are supposed to be fairly loose coalitions intertwined by "brokers" responsible for the integration of the functions. In this integration, exchange of information will be a crucial determinant of efficiency and effectiveness, as the network governance is based on market mechanisms. Such an industrial system is characterized by a lack of vertical integration.

Kumpe and Bolwijn (1988), in contrast, argue that the degree of vertical integration will increase in the future, because value chains today are characterized by an imbalance in the distribution of profits. Enterprises in the final stages of the production chain (assembly and marketing/distribution) usually tend to be profitable, while profits in the earlier stages (such as component production) are generally substantially less profit-making. For the value chain as a whole to be competitive, however, there is a great need for investments in these stages as well. There is an obvious risk, then, that the investments necessary for long-term competitiveness (in design, product development and component production) will never be undertaken, because suppliers might be unable to raise the necessary financial resources. Therefore, Kumpe and Bolwijn argue, firms in the final stages of the value chain will be forced to integrate backwards and provide these resources; otherwise suppliers might be driven out of business, implying severe problems for the customer. A strategy aiming at an even lower degree of vertical integration, which might be efficient in the short term, is therefore considered to be a disaster in the long run.

We have thus been able to identify two contradictory views of the future of vertical integration. The divergent opinions can partly be explained by their focus on the formal degree of integration: that is, on ownership ties. As we have seen, vertical integration in this respect has decreased over time. It has been replaced, however, by informal arrangements that keep the industrial networks together. This is what is usually called "quasi-integration" (Blois, 1972). Quasi-integration can take various forms and include, among other things, customer investments in production tools, joint product development and various forms of financial support. It is apparent that these informal mechanisms are increases in importance over time. Therefore, the divergent opinions held by Kumpe and Bolwijn and Miles and Snow need not be as conflicting as they appear at first sight. Through quasi-integration arrangements customers can provide suppliers with support, without moving back to ownership relations. However, buying firms will not be free to change suppliers as easily as indicated by Miles and Snow. Investments undertaken on either side of the dyad will restrict the opportunities to change supplier.

We do not foresee any major strategic shift in the view of make-or-buy decisions. Our opinion is that the observed tendency – towards buying more from outside suppliers – will continue. The driving forces towards increasing specialization will still be strong in the future, and will favour outsourcing not only of components but also, at an increasing rate, of systems of components, design and product development. One important implication following from our discussion, however, is that make-or-buy decisions should be given more strategic attention than in the past. When most of the resources of a company are provided by outside suppliers it is necessary for these decisions to be given top priority. This need is heightened because make-or-buy decisions are increasingly characterized by technical complexity. Venkatesan (1992) has found that the aim of preserving jobs has been one important determinant of make-or-buy decisions. The effect, in many cases, has been insourcing of parts that are easy to manufacture and outsourcing of components and systems that are more complicated. In the long run, such a strategy might erode the capability of the firm. According to Venkatesan, therefore, the management challenge is to identify the really strategic components among the thousands of parts that they know mostly in terms of cost, rather than function or importance to the product.

DESIGN OF THE SUPPLY-BASE STRUCTURE

The issues regarding the supply-base structure can be divided into two strategic aspects. One has to do with the *number of suppliers*, the other with the *way suppliers are organized*. The number of suppliers has always been an important aspect of purchasing strategy. As mentioned above, the traditional view of purchasing meant that there was a group of suppliers eagerly competing with one another – mainly in terms of price: thus the more suppliers a company had in its supply base the better. We know that this view of efficiency has been increasingly questioned and we discuss the implications below. One of the reasons for the changing view is the insight into the advantages that can be obtained from more cooperative relationships with a reduced supply base. Activities that deepen individual relationships will also have an effect on the supply-base structure as a whole. In fact, many companies today have clear strategic aims for the shape of the supply-base structure. This is a growing dimension of purchasing strategy.

Number of suppliers

The choice between single sourcing and multiple sourcing is a classical issue in purchasing strategy. The established criterion of efficiency has often resulted in multiple sourcing, as supplier competition has been given priority. By promoting competition among suppliers, customers are expected to be given better control of price levels as well as more reliable supply through diversification of risks.

It is obvious that purchasing strategies have undergone considerable changes in this respect during the 1980s. Newman (1988) has identified a clear trend towards single sourcing. The significance of the changes differ between industries. It seems to be most obvious in the automotive industry. The North American motor manufacturer Chrysler decreased its number of suppliers of wiring harnesses from fourteen to three and its paint suppliers from five to two: one for the US plants and one for the Canadian plants (Raia, 1988). General Motors reduced its supplier base for its Quad-four from 140 to 69 through single sourcing (Offdile and Arrington, 1992). A US survey of more than 1000 suppliers showed that the average number of firms competing with the average supplier to produce the same product for a given customer decreased from 2.0 to 1.5 in five years (Helper, 1991).

Such changes for specific components and firms have substantial effects on the supplier structure as a whole. Considerable changes in the total number of suppliers have been reported for Ford US, from 3200 in 1981 to 2100 in 1987 (Burt, 1989), and Chrysler, from 3000 suppliers on the roll only a few years ago to just over 1000 today (Raia, 1993). Similar changes are evident in other industries and companies: in 1981 Rank Xerox had almost 5000 suppliers, but six years later the number had been reduced to just over 300 (Morgan, 1987).

These observations contrast sharply with the traditional view of purchasing efficiency. Newman (1988) states that only a decade ago a purchasing strategy relying on single sourcing would have been characterized as an "invitation to disaster". At that time customers implementing single sourcing were expected to lose opportunities for price control, as well as diversification of risks. The reason for looking at this trade-off through other glasses is the changing role of purchasing. Today it is possible, in fact, to argue that single sourcing leads to an increase in the reliability of supply. Purchasing firms that reduce the number of suppliers and try to strengthen their relationships with the remaining ones might be able to establish very efficient logistical systems together with their suppliers. We discuss this below when dealing with the quality of supplier relations. Regarding price control, Newman (1988) argues that the price competition perceived when dealing with multiple sourcing can often be illusory. Price is only one of the costs affected and changed, when purchasing activities are handled differently. A number of indirect costs are also affected, as discussed below.

Organization of the supply-base structure

The second dimension of the supply-base structure has to do with organization of suppliers. The effects of various organizational forms are illustrated in a study of supplier relationships in the automobile industry (Gadde and Grant, 1984). The number of suppliers dealing directly with automobile manufacturers showed substantial variability. General Motors, in their US operations, used around 3500 suppliers, while Volvo Car Corporation relied on 800 suppliers. The difference between GM and Volvo can be explained by scale factors such as number of plants and number of cars produced. The corresponding figures for manufacturers from Japan, however, did not fit into this pattern. Only around 200 suppliers delivered directly to Toyota and Nissan in spite of the fact that the production output of these companies was closer to that of GM than that of Volvo.

The main reason for these deviations was shown to be the different ways that companies organized the supply-base structure. GM and Volvo, in fact, had no organization at all. The strategy of supporting competition among suppliers through multiple sourcing had resulted in fairly "wild" structures. Toyota and Nissan had organized their suppliers in hierarchies. Only the suppliers on the first level delivered directly to the customer. These first-tier suppliers were made responsible for just-in-time deliveries. They had also become more "system" than "component" suppliers over time, and were to an increasing extent responsible for product development. Furthermore, they were responsible for the activities of the suppliers on the other levels in the structure. Nishiguchi (1987, 1993) provides a detailed discussion of these systems and their characteristics.

The first analysis of the Japanese supplier structures concluded that customers were relying on single sourcing. More recent research, however, has shown that this is true for large complex systems that require massive investments in tools. In other supply situations, however, two or more vendors can be used (Womack *et al.*, 1990). The same observation is further elaborated by Richardson (1993) who characterized the purchasing strategy used by Japanese auto-manufacturers as *parallel sourcing*. This system is observed when the car manufacturer produces a number of models at different plants using a sole source for a component of one model at one assembly plant, while another source is used at another plant. A second aspect of parallel sourcing is that some components can be common to various models and may have multiple sources, while they may still be sole sourced for a particular model.

When the number of suppliers is reduced, the customer becomes more dependent on individual suppliers. The traditional view of efficiency recommends that customers avoid such dependencies. In spite of this we have seen firms turning in this direction. The underlying reason is that reducing the number of counterparts is a prerequisite for improved and deepened supplier relationships.

THE NATURE OF CUSTOMER–SUPPLIER RELATIONSHIPS

The main reason for reducing the number of suppliers has been to provide opportunities for deeper cooperation with selected individual firms. Two driving forces can be identified in this process. One is reduction of costs: the potential for rationalization through a close relationship. The other is the possible exploitation of supplier resources in order to improve technical development: that is, development through a close relationship. We shall now discuss these two dimensions of increasing quality in supplier relations.

Cost rationalization effects can be obtained in several ways. A number of indirect costs can be affected through a deeper cooperation with suppliers. We shall discuss these effects in terms of administrative costs, production costs and costs related to the material flow. Costs of R&D and product developments can also be affected. These are discussed in the section on development cooperation.

Rationalization of administrative costs

The flow of administrative information between customer and supplier provides substantial potential for rationalization. In Gadde and Håkansson (1993) a number of examples are presented. One of the them deals with a customer whose ambition was to decrease the paper flow in one of the supplier relationships. By eliminating purchase orders and introducing daily deliveries with monthly invoicing, it was possible to decrease the number of documents per transaction from seventeen to three. Another illustration of the substantial administrative costs is a big Swedish company in the construction industry that receives around 1.2 million invoices a year. Internal calculations indicate that the cost for handling one invoice is more than 300 SEK (about US$40). Clearly, the administrative costs represent an enormous potential for rationalization.

A powerful tool for attacking these costs has been obtained through the development of information technology. Enquiries, orders and invoices can be transmitted today, very quickly and accurately. In addition to reducing administrative costs, such arrangements provide purchasing officers with more time for working with strategic questions. An analysis of the impact of information technology on purchasing is presented in Dubois *et al.* (1989).

Rationalization of production costs

One way of affecting production costs is to combine in-house production capacity and capability with the corresponding supplier resources. This is the general make-or-buy problem as already discussed. By moving production activities from one firm to another it is possible to increase efficiency. It is clear, however, that such changes in the division of labour can be handled in a more sophisticated way within more intimate customer–supplier relationships. In long-term relationships successive adaptations will enhance performance. Another effectiveness measure may be coordination amongst suppliers: for example, by increasing the cooperation between them. Marler (1989) exemplifies this by illustrating how Ford told all their suppliers of door components that they were no longer interested in purchasing individual components. The suppliers were encouraged to do what they could to form alliances and then tender for complete door systems.

The Ford example illustrates the increasing interests of many automotive firms in purchasing complete systems rather than separate components. One implication of this general trend is a development towards networks of highly specialized production units. As shown by Dubois and Håkansson (1993) the activity structures of such networks can be combined in a number of different ways. This is another reason why the make-or-buy decisions must be given increasing strategic attention.

Rationalization of material flow costs

Costs related to material flow include the costs of handling goods, costs of keeping inventories, and costs of capital. A reduction in these costs is probably the most significant advantage that can be obtained through closer supplier relationships. Many firms have achieved substantial improvements in efficiency by reducing stocks of input goods and work in process. Activities of this kind were originally inspired by observations from Japan:

> It only takes 10 minutes inside an assembly plant in Japan to realize that relationships with suppliers are very different. The visitor accustomed to the loading docks, the large storage areas and the large incoming inspection area, typical of US plants, is likely to be taken aback by the stocking of Japanese assembly lines. Trucks from suppliers back up through large bay doors right to the assembly line; supplier personnel unload a few hours of parts, clean up the area and depart. There is no incoming inspection, no staging area, not expediting of material, just a seemingly continuous flow of material (Hervey, 1982, p. 6).

This just-in-time philosophy is generally considered to be one of the major factors underlying the competitive power of the Japanese auto industry over the past three decades. It is natural, therefore, that competitors in other parts of the world have tried to neutralize this competitive edge. Raia (1988) claims that Chrysler's early extensive JIT initiatives were one of the main factors contributing to the recovery in the mid-1980s. The tied-up capital could be reduced by one billion dollars by improving material flow efficiency.

The major changes when adopting JIT deliveries are a decrease in lot sizes and an increase in delivery frequency. In the Honda plant in Ohio there is no tyre inventory at the assembly plant. A local tyre supplier makes 136 deliveries each day by truck. The supplier is responsible for ensuring that the tyre specified is loaded on the conveyor belt connected to the assembly line, according to the schedule decided by the purchaser. This system then works in the same way as the Japanese system discussed above: no storage, no inspection, and no extra handling (Offodile and Arrington, 1992).

Development through supplier relations

Purchasing companies can benefit in a number of ways from cooperation with suppliers in technical development regarding their products and processes. Two of the most frequently mentioned issues deal with increasing and activating the resource base and shortening lead times in technical development projects.

In close relationships, it is possible to identify and activate complementary resource bases. Many products are characterized by the need for deep knowledge in several areas of technology. Owing to increasing specialization, it is not possible for one company to cover all these areas. It is necessary, therefore, to find suppliers who are willing and able to contribute to technical development. One positive effect will be an extension of the total resource base. Another is that interactive effects might emerge. In the active confrontation of two resource bodies innovative sparks can arise (Håkansson, 1987).

It is not surprising, therefore, that suppliers have, over time, been increasingly used as a resource in product development. Eriksson and Håkansson (1993) describe two interesting examples of supplier involvement. They deal with development of a robotized system and a piece of medical process equipment. A large number of suppliers are activated in the development processes. In both cases suppliers are responsible for the most innovative parts of the new system.

The other main reason for activating suppliers in development processes is to shorten lead times (see for example Takeuchi and Nonaka, 1986; Burt, 1989; Raia, 1991). Raia presents a number of interesting examples. One is that of Xerox, which has managed to reduce lead times for new products by more than half as a result of increasing supplier involvement. Ingersoll-Rand introduced several suppliers to a project when the new product was only "a gleam in the eye of the marketing manager". In this way it is possible to shift certain development activities to suppliers, making it possible to reduce lead times substantially. One important prerequisite for successful implementation of programmes with such aims is that suppliers are involved in the development processes much earlier than they have previously been allowed to be.

IMPLEMENTATION OF CHANGES

New forms of supplier relations provide customers with opportunities for rationalization as well as development activities. It is important to observe, however, that such effects do not follow automatically from a concentration to fewer suppliers and policy declarations. On the contrary, a lot of hard work is needed to attain the potential benefits. A number of problems can arise when changes are implemented.

The advantages associated with JIT deliveries can be substantial, but the transition to JIT is far from simple. This is shown by an observation from a purchasing company that could demonstrate that supplies arrive precisely on schedule. On the shopfloor, however, the impression was entirely different.

> But when I walked through the plant I saw weeks of stampings, acres of work-in-process, and subassemblies strewn around the body-shop. Boxes of parts were stacked so high on the chassis and trim lines, that it was difficult to see what was going on in these areas. In fact, the inventory took up so much room that they could have put five major press lines in the same space. This is JIT, I wondered? (Harbour, 1986, p. 14).

It is interesting to compare this observation with the attitudes of the American whilst visiting the Japanese company, described earlier. It is very clear that JIT must not be regarded only as a purchasing strategy affecting lot sizes and delivery frequencies. In fact, JIT is a basic determinant of the efficiency of an integrated production system. Activities and requirements directed towards suppliers therefore have few positive effects if they are not followed – or rather preceded – by changes at the buying firms. If this is not done, subdeliveries of the JIT type might increase problems when delivery frequencies are increased.

When JIT was first introduced into the West, the effect seems to have been that inventories were moved to an earlier stage in the production chain. This was found in a comparative study of JIT in Europe, Japan and the USA (Nishiguchi, 1989). In the US automotive industry it was observed that suppliers increased their delivery frequencies. However, these deliveries often came from newly established warehouses. The inventory business in Detroit was booming; one company even picked the name "JIT Warehousing" (Raia, 1988).

In a major survey of US automotive suppliers, Helper (1991) concluded that suppliers implemented JIT mainly because customers demanded it, but that no major effects were attained in the production processes of suppliers. The prevailing attitude to JIT was that it only transferred responsibility for inventories. Less than one-third of the respondents were of the opinion that JIT decreased the inventory levels for the chain as a whole. The major reason stated for the shortcomings was that customers did not provide suppliers with stable delivery schedules.

The conclusion to be drawn is that efforts to increase efficiency in material flow are major undertakings requiring a number of changes both from suppliers and from the purchasing companies. Therefore it should not be surprising that progress takes time. To establish the links of a total JIT system is a highly demanding process. Toyota began experimenting with its system in 1948. Not until 1965 was a fully synchronized system between Toyota and its first-tier suppliers completed (Nishiguchi, 1987, 1994).

Regarding development cooperation with suppliers, several problems can be identified. One is related to the knowledge of the potential in such collaboration. Burt and Sukoup (1985) concluded that suppliers, at that time, were rather neglected as resources relating to product development. Most customers did not seem to understand the potential available, which the authors considered a major strategic defect. A study of a large number of small and medium-sized firms in Sweden showed that more than one quarter of them had had no cooperative development projects with any supplier during the preceding three-year period (Håkansson, 1989).

What is the explanation for this reluctance towards using supplier resources? One important reason could be a lack of insight into the actual potential. Another reason can be identified as a reluctance on the supplier side. Increasing cooperation should also be of interest to suppliers: through such activities they might be able to strengthen their ties to customers. In spite of this potential advantage, suppliers often appear to hesitate to enter into deeper relations with customers. The reason is that market investments of this type have a cost side that must be compared with the benefits. Suppliers have to invest in specific resources in order to be attractive partners. These resources may be difficult to obtain, as the costs associated with them may be substantial. Furthermore, they sometimes create a very strong dependence, as they might have no alternative use if they are very specialized solutions.

It is also clear that suppliers who are used to customer behaviour such as playing suppliers off against one another will think twice before entering into a close relationship. One prerequisite for increased involvement is some kind of confidence in a long-term business relation. The usual adversarial relationship must be changed to a more symbiotic one. Before this can be achieved, customers themselves have to change their attitudes. Communications of long-term strategic ambitions must be undertaken at the buying company as well as towards the supplier company. It is obvious that changing attitudes is a very time-consuming activity in a large company, especially if the new attitudes deviate substantially from the old ones. Only after these changes within the companies is it possible to change the relationship between them.

IMPLICATIONS

Our analysis of the changing role of purchasing indicates the following tendencies regarding the three strategic issues identified:

1. An increasing importance of "buy" as compared with "make" – i.e. reducing the degree of vertical integration and because the make-or-buy problems are becoming increasingly complex, they deserve more strategic attention;
2. Systematic attempts to structure the suppliers, including a reduction of the supply base, and improvement of coordination among suppliers;
3. Deeper cooperation with individual suppliers to achieve benefits regarding rationalization and technical development.

These changes have naturally brought with them related changes in purchasing and marketing activities. The most dramatic ones have certainly taken place on the purchasing side. The most significant changes have to do with the relationships with individual suppliers, but this has also had important implications for the way purchasing strategies have been formulated and the ways in which purchasing activities have been organized. The marketing function within selling companies has also had to make substantial adaptations but these changes have been easier to integrate into already existing strategies and organizational forms. These changes have also affected the general industry level in terms of production structures and degree of innovativeness. Our final section, therefore, deals with implications for marketing, purchasing and the aggregate industry level.

Purchasing implications

The first and most important implication is that purchasing strategy has become an issue for top management. Never before have so many companies discussed, analysed and formulated offensive strategies for purchasing. The analyses are directed towards finding efficient supplier structures, forming alliances with key suppliers, developing training programmes together with suppliers and activating suppliers in technical development projects. This is a considerable change from the earlier concentration on formulating procedures for efficient purchasing, such as the number of bids that had to be asked for. These changes reflect a new view of purchasing efficiency, which is further analysed in Gadde and Håkansson (1993).

A second implication is related to the organization of purchasing. The major shift has been towards a decentralization of purchasing activities away from the centralized purchasing departments that used to characterize large manufacturing firms. There are two main reasons for this change. The first is that the purchasing decisions must be made by people who are close to the problems to be solved. They must have a good knowledge of the use of the products and about the problems regarding logistical and administrative routines, to be able to capture the potential for rationalization and development. The second reason is that decentralization of purchasing has been well in accord with general organizational trends towards independent profit centres with decentralized responsibility. If purchasing costs account for more than half of the total costs, then each profit centre must be given the right to make its own decisions regarding purchasing and suppliers. Decentralization makes it generally easier to develop close relationships, while also making it more difficult to coordinate the relationships of the whole company.

A third implication, following the organizational change, is a trend away from functional specialization. The changing role of purchasing will call for a shift towards more integrated problem-solving. Purchasing today is much more focused on technical and logistical matters than before, when strictly commercial issues dominated. Developing supplier relationships means finding efficient solutions, considering the trade-offs between direct costs (mainly price), various indirect costs (in production, administration, material flow, for example) and other strategic benefits from the relationships. This aspect will also affect the role of individual purchasers. Highly specialized purchasers will be replaced by more general problem-solvers. Before, a purchasing officer was often regarded as a rather isolated person responsible only for the commercial aspect of procurement and sometimes considered only as an executor of decisions taken by others. Today, a purchaser must be a member of a team, working closely together with, and coordinating, specialists from other functions. In some companies this change has been so considerable that the purchaser as a functional specialist no longer exists.

Marketing implications

The changes described from the purchasing perspective have, of course, also affected and involved the selling companies. Some suppliers have been very actively involved and have even been change agents, while others have taken part more reluctantly or have even tried to counteract the changes. Those who have considered the transition of purchasing as an opportunity have had to learn a new way of dealing with customers. One characteristic of this new role is the development of mutual relationships, which have two consequences, both contradictory to established marketing traditions. The first is that reaction is as important as action. This means that strategic marketing decisions should increasingly be based on adaptations to the changing purchasing strategies of customers.

The second consequence is that departments other than sales and marketing have to be much more involved in developing the relationships. Direct contacts have to be established between technicians in the two companies, as well as between departments taking care of material and information flows. Furthermore, issues regarding technical development must be discussed between R&D people on both sides. Sometimes even the purchasing department of the selling company needs to be involved in the process, as the customer might have requirements regarding which subsuppliers to use, especially for critical components and materials.

Owing to these conditions, marketing will be much more of an organizational problem than has been previously recognized. The main issue will be to handle the development of individual customer relationships. Developing these relationships will call for coordinating activities from the selling company. The first is that the internal activities of the supplier must be coordinated with those of the customer. The second is that the various customer relationships have to be considered in several dimensions. The third, finally, is that the customer relationships have to be coordinated with the selling companies' other external relationships, such as suppliers and technical consultants.

Implications on an aggregate level

The new purchasing philosophy also has effects at a more aggregate level. The development of relationships and networks increases the potential for further specialization. Consequently, companies become increasingly specialized production units, within a network structure. In the future, various production activities will be undertaken by highly specialized companies, which are bound together through close relationships into efficient production structures. As pointed out by Richardson (1993), the combination of a high level of relationship-specific investments and single sourcing might lead to problems with supplier performance, but it is also possible to say that close relationships will increase the pressure on supplier performance. Deepened customer–supplier relationships will be characterized by clear, directed, individually based pressure, as the counterparts are mutually dependent. This also means that the pressure can be expressed in much more detailed and specific terms than is possible in market-mediated pressure. Our conclusion is thus that production structures based on deepened relationships need not be less flexible *per se*.

The transitions in purchasing and buyer–seller relationships also influence the nature of innovation and innovativeness. At an increasing rate, innovations will be developed in the interactions between users and suppliers. In general, this will shorten lead times in product development, which is considered to be an important strategic issue in most industries today.

Another consequence is that innovations will be more in accordance with the needs of the established network structure. It is reasonable to believe that such a change will have positive effects on the failure rate in product innovation. Conversely, a potential negative outcome might be a decrease in the number of revolutionary innovations.

Purchasing's concern for innovativeness is a far cry from its former role. The strategic role of purchasing will emerge naturally as the competitive pressures on businesses increase.

REFERENCES

Axelsson, B. and Håkansson, H. *Inköp för konkurrenskraft*. Liber, Stockholm (1984).

Blois, K. Vertical quasi-integration. *Journal of Industrial Economics*, **20** (3), 33–41 (1972).

Burt, D. Managing suppliers up to speed. *Harvard Business Review*, July–August, 127–35 (1989).

Burt, D. and Sukoup, W. Purchasing's role in new product development. *Harvard Business Review*, September–October, 90–7 (1989).

Carlisle, J. and Parker, R. *Beyond Negotiation, Redeeming Customer–Supplier Relationships*. John Wiley and Sons (1989).

Culliton, J. *Make-or-buy*. Harvard University Graduate School of Business Administration, Boston (1942).

Dillforce, W. Purchasing – a singular way to increase competitiveness. *Financial Times*, 24 October (1986).

Dirrheimer, M. and Hübner, T. Vertical integration and performance in the automotive industry; paper presented at the Future of Automobile Forum, Boston, MIT (1983).

Dubois, A. and Håkansson, H. Relationships as activity links. *Proceedings of the conference: Forms of Interorganizational Networks: Structures and Processes*. European Science Foundation, Berlin (1993).

Dubois, A., Gadde, L.-E. and Håkansson, H. The impact of information technology on purchasing behaviour and supplier markets. Working Paper No. 1989:11, Gothenburg, Institute for Management for Innovation and Technology (1989).

Eriksson, A.-K. and Håkansson, H. Getting innovations out of supplier networks. *Journal of Business-to-Business Marketing*, **1** (3), 3–34 (1993).

Ford, D., Cotton, B., Farmer, D., Gross, A. and Wilkinson, I. Make-or-buy decisions and their implications. *Industrial Marketing Management*, **22**, 207–14 (1993).

Frazier, G., Spekman, R. and O'Neal, C. Just-in-time exchange relationships in industrial markets. *Journal of Marketing*, **52** (October), 52–67 (1988).

Gadde, L.-E. and Grant, B. Quasi-integration, supplier networks and technological cooperation in the automotive industry. *Proceedings of the International Research Seminar on Industrial Marketing*. Stockholm School of Economics, Stockholm (1984).

Gadde, L.-E. and Håkansson, H. *Professional Purchasing*. Routledge, London (1993).

Håkansson, H. *Corporate Technological Behaviour – Cooperation and Networks*. Routledge, London (1989).

Harbour, J. What is just-in-time manufacturing? *Automotive Industries*, January, 14 (1986).

Hayes, R. and Abernathy, W. Managing our way to economic decline. *Harvard Business Review*, July–August, 67–77 (1980)

Helper, S. How much has really changed between US automakers and their suppliers? *Sloan Management Review*, Summer, 15–28 (1991).

Hervey, R. Preliminary observation on manufacturer–supplier relations in the Japanese automotive industry. The Joint US–Japan Automotive Study, Working Paper series No. 5, University of Michigan, Ann Arbor (1982).

Janch, L. and Wilson, H. A strategic perspective for make or buy decisions. *Long Range Planning*, **12** (December), 56–61 (1979).

Kumpe, T. and Bolwijn, P. Manufacturing: the new case for vertical integration. *Harvard Business Review*, March–April, 75–81 (1988).

Lamming, R. *Beyond Partnership. Strategies for Innovation and Lean Supply*. Prentice Hall, Hemel Hempstead, UK (1993).

Leenders, M. and Nollet, J. The grey zone in make or buy. *Journal of Purchasing and Materials Management*, Fall, 10–15 (1984).

Marler, D. The post Japanese model of automotive component supply: selective North American case studies. IMVP International Policy Forum, MIT, Boston (1989).

Miles, R. and Snow, C. Organizations: new concepts for new forms. *California Management Review*, **18** (3), 62–73 (1986).

Morgan, I. The purchasing revolution. *The McKinsey Quarterly*, Spring, 49–55 (1987).

Newman, R. Single source qualification. *Journal of Purchasing and Materials Management*, Summer, 10–17 (1988).

Nishiguchi, T. Competing systems of automotive components supply: an examination of the Japanese "clustered control" model and the "Alps" structure. First Policy Forum, International Motor Vehicle Program, MIT, Boston (1984).

Nishiguchi, T. Is JIT really JIT? Third Policy Forum, International Motor Vehicle Program, MIT, Boston (1989).

Nishiguchi, T. *Strategic Industrial Sourcing: The Japanese Advantage*. Oxford University Press, New York (1993).

Offodile, F. and Arrington, D. Support of successful just-in-time implementation: the changing role of purchasing. *International Journal of Physical Distribution and Logistics Management*, **22** (5), 38–46 (1992).

Raia, E. JIT in Detroit. *Purchasing*, 15 September, 68–77 (1988).

Raia, E. Taking time out of product design. *Purchasing*, **4** (April 4), 36–9 (1991).

Raia, E. The extended enterprise. *Purchasing*, 4 March, 48–51 (1993).

Richardson, J. Parallel sourcing and supplier performance in the Japanese automobile industry. *Strategic Management Journal*, **14**, 339–50 (1993).

Spekman, R. Strategic supplier selection: understanding long-term buyer relationships. *Business Horizons*, July–August, 75–81 (1985).

Takeuchi, H. and Nonaka, I. The new new-product development game. *Harvard Business Review*, January–February, 137–46 (1986).

Venkatesan, R. Strategic sourcing: to make or not to make. *Harvard Business Review*, November–December, 98–108 (1992).

Womack, J., Jones, D. and Roos, D. *The Machine that Changed the World*. Rawson Associates, New York (1990).

5.4 Making the most of supplier relationships

Lars-Erik Gadde and Ivan Snehota

THE CHANGING SUPPLY SIDE IN BUSINESS

The strategic importance of the supply side in companies increased considerably during the two last decades of the 1900s. These changes are commonly referred to as a shift from purchasing to supply management (Davis, 1993). According to this perspective, competitive advantage no longer resides with a company's own innate capabilities, but rather with the relationships and linkages the firm can forge with external organizations (Lewis, 1995). Forging these linkages required a revision of the prevailing perspectives regarding purchasing efficiency and the role of suppliers (Gadde and Håkansson, 1994). It has been particularly emphasized that buying companies tend more and more:

- to outsource non-critical activities;
- to establish close "partnership" relationships with suppliers;
- to reduce and trim their supplier bases.

Our impression is that these changes in supply strategy reflect a growing awareness of the role supplier relationships can play in a company's strategy and are an attempt to better exploit this potential. This evolving perspective on purchasing efficiency has been beneficial to many companies and has been generally received by researchers and consultants with acclaim (Lewis, 1995).

Outsourcing to suppliers is linked to business strategies aiming at enhanced specialization and at a focus on core competence. Increasing technical complexity and diversity make it more and more difficult for a company to stay at the cutting edge in several different areas of technology at the same time (Quinn, 1999). Earlier recommendations of arm's length relationships to suppliers to avoid dependency and keep prices down have been replaced by an emphasis on the benefits that can be reaped from close relationships (Carlisle and Parker, 1989). Today, it is argued, companies ". . . both large and small are making partnerships with suppliers a foundation of their supply strategies" (Minahan, 1998). Furthermore, many companies have reduced their number of suppliers considerably (Cousins, 1999) because partnering is resource-intensive and can be managed only with a limited number of suppliers.

The problem is that, in many cases, these changes have been presented as transitions from something old and obsolete to something new and up-to-date. In particular, there has been a tendency to portray close relationships to suppliers as the superior solution for making the most of supplier relationships. We believe that such a view is often based on blurry assumptions, oversimplifies the issues involved and may be bad for practice. Outsourcing, partnering with suppliers and reduction of the supplier base can be effective options in a supply strategy, but they are not always the only means that companies have to make good use of suppliers. A more nuanced and balanced view is required.

In this paper, we argue that a more differentiated approach is needed to make the best use of supplier relationships. A framework is developed for analysis of the dimensions in supplier relationships that are important for choices of supply strategy. The main argument presented is that the most critical element of supply strategy is a company's capacity to handle various types of supplier relationships.

COPING WITH SUPPLIER RELATIONSHIPS

Making good use of suppliers is a complex task for at least two reasons. The first is that the economic consequences are difficult to assess. The critical supplier relationships of a company are often complex in terms of the range of products and services supplied and people involved. The second is that companies can exercise only limited control over a vendor. Suppliers pursue their own business logic in relationships to customers. Buyer–seller relationships are interactive and solutions applied are continuously changing – the resulting uncertainty and ambiguity cannot be escaped. Problems that arise between the supplier and the customer are solved in interaction. Any substantial intervention in a supplier relationship is likely to have a number of rather complicated consequences.

There is a common illusion that choices that add up to the profile of a company's supply strategy are an outcome of distinct "strategic decisions," taken periodically by top management. This is, at best, a rationalization in hindsight. Even if, and when, such decisions are taken they are almost always immediately amended, modified, and changed as managers involved discover that something either does not work or could be done better. Impulses for these changes come to large extent from interacting with suppliers and the solutions adopted add up to changes in supply strategy. However, this does not mean that strategizing (i.e., reviewing the way in which the supply side is handled in a broader perspective) is pointless. On the contrary, it is important to take a wider look at the complex set of operational activities on the supply side as guidance to the decisions and choices. So strategizing makes sense when it is based on realistic pictures of how the supply side in companies works.

Companies make different use of supplier relationships, depending on the nature of their business, the kind of technology used and the context in which they operate. The supply side is characterized by continuous changes in these relationships. Over time, companies modify the *scope of supplies*. They rely on external suppliers to varying extents. For some companies the added values are high and the incidence of purchasing in relation to the total cost is only limited; for others, purchasing is the dominant portion of the total costs. Further, buying firms change the *configuration of the supplier base*. Some companies have thousands of suppliers as their operations make use of many different items. Typically, however, few materials or components dominate, account for the major portion of purchasing costs and are concentrated to only a limited number of suppliers. Finally, companies develop different *postures of supplier relationships*, i.e., ways of handling and dealing with individual suppliers. In some relationships there are close interpersonal contacts, in others vendors are kept at arm's length distance. Joint product development projects are undertaken with some suppliers, while others are typical subcontractors relying on customer specifications. Certain suppliers deliver just in time, while buffers and inventories characterize the material flow in other relationships.

On the whole, it appears to be justified to have different types of supplier relationships coexisting within one and the same company. This fact makes generalized solutions problematic to apply and implies a need for a set of criteria to provide guidance for effective supply strategy development. Such criteria have to be based on the business logic and insight into the cost-benefit consequences of supplier relationships.

Economy of supplier relationships

No business can do without suppliers and, as a rule, there is a notable continuity in relationships to suppliers (Håkansson and Snehota, 1999). The set of suppliers a company uses reflects the nature of its operations. The actual supplier relationships represent one of the most important assets the company can make use of. As with all other assets, the value is not absolute but context dependent.

Some supplier relationships are important because of the volume of business they represent, others because they affect the future of the company in that they are sources of technical development and important for product quality and performance. The impact of a specific supplier relationship depends on how it fits into the operations and the strategy of the buying company and how other supplier and customer relationships are affected. This means that the role and value of a particular relationship cannot be assessed from its product/service content only.

Various technical, commercial and organizational solutions in a supplier relationship, and any change in the actual arrangement, ultimately affect costs and benefits of both companies. Some consequences are quite easy to expose, measure and quantify; others are less obvious, more indirect and more difficult to measure, but no less important. Our impression is that the recent changes on the supply side of companies have been spurred by the fact that some of the important but less obvious and immediate economic consequences have been revealed.

In order to develop effective supply strategy, companies need to understand the multiple economic consequences of changes in relationships. This approach makes it necessary to consider the costs they entail and the benefits to which they can give rise. The broad categories of costs and benefits of supplier relationships are illustrated in Figure 1.

The most obvious item on the cost side is what shows up on the invoice from the supplier, i.e., the "direct procurement costs." These costs are generally easy to identify and measure. The direct procurement costs have always been the focus of purchasing attention. But there are other costs that originate in supplier relationships as well. Every purchasing transaction is associated with other expenses such as costs of transportation, goods handling, ordering, etc. These costs, "direct transaction costs," may be more difficult to measure, but as a rule they can be traced. Other costs cannot be directly related to specific transactions but to an individual supplier. Some relationships require lots of continuous interaction – and thus costs – for maintaining the relationship and sometimes for investments in terms of adaptations among the counterparts. These costs depend on the extent of involvement with individual suppliers and are identified as "relationship handling costs." Finally, the customer sustains costs that cannot be attributed directly to particular suppliers or specific transactions. "Supply handling costs" are structural and common costs for the purchasing organization as a whole, including communication and administrative systems, warehousing operations, process adaptations, etc.

Assessing the benefits of supplier relationships is a more difficult task than assessing the costs, because the benefits show up less clearly in company accounts. Two categories of relationship benefits can be distinguished – cost benefits and revenue benefits. "Cost benefits" are savings in various costs of operations that can be related to collaboration with suppliers. Numerous examples have illustrated supplier contributions to efficiency improvements through, for example, joint efforts in product development and integrated logistic operations. Cost benefits are tricky to measure – and even to identify – owing to interdependencies between various types of costs and benefits.

Relationship costs	Relationship benefits
– Direct procurement costs	– Cost benefits
– Direct transaction costs	– Revenue benefits
– Relationship handling costs	
– Supply handling costs	

Figure 1   Economic consequences of supplier relationships.

The second type of relationship benefits are the "revenue benefits" which represent the economic consequences of supplier relationships that are related to the income side of the financial statement. Revenue benefits arise when a solution in a relationship increases the revenues of the buying company. They are extremely difficult to assess, as they are usually indirect and linked to improvements in product quality or performance that affect the competitiveness of the customer. While there is no systematic evidence of these benefits, there are many examples of companies that have achieved substantial product innovation and quality improvements by making better use of suppliers (Carlisle and Parker, 1989; Davis, 1993; Gadde and Håkansson, 1994; Lewis, 1995; Quinn, 1999).

We have shown that not all the various costs and benefits related to a supplier relationship can be calculated. In spite of this a management assessment of potential consequences is imperative when any major intervention in a relationship is being considered. Trying to balance all the various cost and benefit consequences of a potential change in strategy can lead to radically different decisions than those based on a partial evaluation.

One major point that becomes apparent is that the economic consequences cannot be evaluated only from the content of the relationship. The value of a supplier relationship stems to large extent from how it fits into the operations of the customer and its other relationships. The economic consequences of one and the same solution will be different in different companies and are likely to change over time as the company operations and its other relationships change. The critical aspect of supply strategy in this respect is the posture of each individual relationship.

The posture of supplier relationships

A review of the current literature reveals a general consensus on the importance and merits of "partnership posture" in supplier relationships. It has even been remarked that the type of relationships firms develop to suppliers will be the main source of future competitive advantage (Sheth and Sharma, 1997). At the same time, feelings of confusion have been voiced about what exactly a partnership is (Minahan, 1998) and in a recent review of the purchasing field (Macbeth, 1998), we found a warning for overselling "partnership" as a buzzword:

> . . . used by all which read something about management or had attended some seminar or conference and then applied the new label to existing practice in an attempt to look trendy and aware as well as to demonstrate that they had really always behaved in the newly desired way.

There is no easy answer to the question about what makes a relationship a partnership. Common suggestions that partnership is a "close" relationship are vague and do not offer much help. Ford et al. (1998) argue that in order to give meaning to "closeness" one has to consider the degree of integration between the buying and the selling company. A recent study (Bensaou, 1999) shows that the extent of integration between customer and supplier, expressed in terms of the specific investments made by either partner, has a clear impact on the performance of the relationship. A distinction is made between tangible assets (buildings, tools, equipment, and processes), and intangibles (time and effort spent on learning the business partner's practices and routines). There is significant evidence that the size of investments dedicated to a specific counterpart ". . . significantly correlates with practices commonly associated with strategic partnerships, such as long-term relationship, mutual trust, cooperation, and wide-scope relationships" (Bensaou, 1999).

Focusing on integration is an important step toward a better understanding of the critical dimensions of supplier relationships. It requires consideration of the actual behavior in relationships, rather than relying on a notion of partnerships as a matter of vaguely defined positive attitudes. We need to elaborate further on the extent of integration in relationships, and so we propose "involvement" as a relevant concept. We have found it useful to distinguish three dimensions of involvement that affect outcomes in supplier relationships: coordination of activities; adaptations of resources; and interaction among individuals. We refer to the degree of involvement in the three dimensions as activity links, resource ties and actor bonds (Håkansson and Snehota, 1995). First, the activities carried out at the supplier and customer companies can be more or less tightly coordinated. Examples of tight activity coordination are integrated delivery systems developed to reduce the costs of capital equipment investments and of the material flow. Second, the resources of the companies can be more or less specifically adapted to the requirements of the counterpart. Joint development of customer specific products and dedicated processes, common in many supplier relationships, exemplify the case of extensive resource adaptations. Third, the individuals in the companies may interact more or less intensely. Close interaction among individuals in the two organizations make their choices more interdependent and affect both commitment and trust in the relationship, which in turn impacts on coordination and adaptations.

Some supplier relationships score high on all three of the relationship dimensions and others only on one or two. Let us take an example of supply of a high-volume commodity, such as cement, where intense interaction takes place between many individuals at different production plants and sites, particularly about deliveries, wastage and returns. The production scheduling of the two companies is tightly coordinated, but there are few, if any, adaptations in the products supplied. Another example is delivery of specialized components, where we find extensive mutual product and equipment adaptations, but only limited contacts and interaction between individuals and a moderate degree of activity coordination. A third example is a supplier relationship that involves "just in time" deliveries and entails very tight coordination of the activities of the two companies, while the products and processes of both companies are standardized and there is only limited interaction with other functional areas in the companies. The actual variation in terms of links, ties and bonds is, in practice, very large.

High and low involvement relationships

The existence of strong links, ties and bonds describes the degree of involvement of the companies in a relationship. We prefer the concept of involvement rather than integration, because it makes possible a distinction between supplier involvement and customer involvement. In the analysis we refer to relationships characterized by extensive activity links, resource ties or actor bonds as high-involvement relationships and to those that score low on all three as low-involvement.

Focusing on the degree of involvement brings us back to the economic consequences of supplier relationship postures. High-involvement relationships are costly because coordination, adaptation and interaction entail costs. Increasing involvement usually means a substantial increase in relationship and supply handling costs, but may, under certain circumstances, lead to lower direct procurement and transaction costs. However, the main rationale for high involvement is either to achieve cost benefits in terms of reduced costs in production and materials flow, improved flexibility and service levels, or revenue benefits, for instance, through taking advantage of supplier skills and capability to improve the quality of the customer's end product. Increased involvement makes sense only when the consequently increased relationship costs are more than offset by relationship benefits. Reaping these benefits most often requires non-standardized solutions and customer specific adaptations. High-involvement relationships are associated with investment logic.

Low-involvement relationships have their rationales as well. They can be handled with limited coordination, adaptation and interaction costs. Generally this is the case when the context is stable and the content of the relationship can be standardized. In these situations the requirements of the customer can be satisfied by use of existing solutions. This means that no specific product or service adaptations are needed, implying that resource ties are minimized. When activity coordination can be limited to standardized shipments and order processing, the activity links are weak. Finally, when interaction among individuals in the two companies involved can be contained to sales and purchasing administration, the actor bonds will also be limited. The low-involvement relationships are potentially cost effective and require lower relationship handling costs. In practice, however, there may be hidden costs in these relationships. Low-involvement relationships may lead to higher direct procurement costs and transaction costs. On the buyer side, there may be costs for adapting internal resources to fit with what suppliers have to offer. In the absence of tight coordination, the buyer might be obliged to build up inventories to buffer against possible risks. Furthermore, in order to assure availability of supplies, the customer might tend to use many suppliers, resulting in increased supply handling costs.

THE VARIETY OF RELATIONSHIP POSTURES

Most companies make use of a variety of supplier relationships characterized by different degrees of involvement. In a recent study Bensaou (1999) found that firms ". . . balance a portfolio of different types of relationships rather than rely on one type". Companies need both high- and low-involvement relationships, in part because differing degrees of involvement lead to different costs and benefits, in part because the resources that can be dedicated to management of supplier relationships are limited. Accordingly, Spekman et al. (1999) have observed that ". . . not all suppliers are created equally, nor should they be".

There is thus an increasing awareness of the need to differentiate the approach to supplier relationships, which is in contrast with generalized recommendations to pursue the partnership posture. Dyer et al. (1998) advise firms to avoid a "one-size-fits-all" strategy for procurement and argue for supplier segmentation, mainly because the best utilization of suppliers requires that resources be allocated to relationships in proportion to expected potential outcomes.

Following the line proposed by Kraljic (1983), various criteria have been suggested to establish supplier segments and relationship portfolios. Recent examples include product, market and supplier characteristics (Bensaou, 1999), and product complexity and commercial complexity (Spekman et al., 1999). These criteria tend to link differentiation to market or product variables rather than to relationship features. Therefore, they provide only limited guidance for increasing or decreasing the level of involvement in a specific supplier relationship. Our stance is that in order to settle the issue of the degree to which involvement is appropriate, we have to turn the attention to relationship specific features in the actual context of the buying company.

The particular issue of whether and when high-involvement in a supplier relationship is appropriate is often only implied. There are three relationship characteristics that tend to be considered relevant in this respect. The first is the monetary volume of business in the relationship. The second is the continuity of the relationship over time. The third is whether or not the supplier in the relationship is used as a single source. It has been argued that partnership, i.e., a high-involvement approach, is appropriate in supplier relationships with significant business volumes, characterized by stable, long-term relationships, and coinciding with single sourcing. It is further implied that relationships with small volumes of business are best handled with a low-involvement approach and possibly by adopting short-term based multiple sourcing. Below we show that such recommendations tend to oversimplify the issue and do not lead to the best use of supplier relationships.

Involvement and the volume of business in the relationship

In order to explore the relationship between the degree of involvement and the importance of a supplier relationship in monetary terms, we consider the options illustrated in Figure 2. It is generally suggested that high involvement is desirable in supplier relationships that represent major volumes of business for the buying company (A). It is further recommended that low involvement can be practiced in relationships with minor volume of business (D). It is also hinted that (B) and (C) are less appropriate combinations of posture and volume of business.

We argue that both (B) and (C) are viable alternatives in a company's supply strategy. A buying company can only handle a limited number of high-involvement relationships because they are

Posture of relationship	Volume of business with the supplier	
	Major	Minor
High involvement	A	B
Low involvement	C	D

Figure 2 Relationship posture and volume of business with the supplier.

resource intensive. Therefore the customer faces the choice of which of its major relationships should be of type (A) and which must be handled in other ways. Low involvement with a major supplier (C) is appropriate when the potential gains from further involvement are limited, which is often the case where standardized product and solutions are concerned and when the supplier lacks the motivation for a high-involvement relationship. The latter imbalance of interests has been shown to be quite common (Krause and Ellram, 1997). Savings from reducing the degree of involvement in a large volume relationship can be substantial.

Increasing involvement in relationships with minor volumes of business (B) is an effective approach when the supplier has particular skills and capabilities that are critical to the buying company's own offerings or that represent great development potential. This situation is well illustrated by the example of large pharmaceutical companies that establish high involvement relationships with small innovative companies in biotechnology (Ford et al., 1998).

The core of our argument is that for decisions regarding the degree of involvement, the current volume of business is an insufficient criterion. The balance of interests and economic consequences owing to changes in involvement has to be explored and assessed. Such assessments may indicate both low-involvement relationships to major suppliers and high-involvement relationships to minor suppliers as viable and effective strategies.

Involvement and relationship continuity.   Several studies have shown that many high-involvement relationships are of a long-term nature (Gadde and Mattsson, 1987; Håkansson and Snehota, 1995). This is mainly because it takes time to develop strong resource ties, activity links and actor bonds and once they have been established they represent investments of major value which makes it worthwhile to continue the relationship. These characteristics provide the rationale for relationships of type (E) in Figure 3.

However, it does not follow automatically that the long lasting supplier relationships of a company are always the obvious candidates for increased involvement, nor does it necessarily mean that short-term supplier relationships are to be handled with a low-involvement approach. Nevertheless, short-term relationships with low involvement characteristics of type (H) are common in many companies because they make it possible to easily switch from one vendor to another. Bensaou's study (1999) identified a further type of what was classified as "market exchange." Some buying firms used short-term contracts with suppliers where the relationships ". . . had actually lasted for thirty years with intermittent periods of no business together." This means that even long-lasting relationships can be effectively managed with limited involvement (G). Dyer et al. (1998) also observed the existence of "durable arm's length relationships,"

Posture of relationship	Continuity of relationship	
	Long term	Short term
High involvement	E	F
Low involvement	G	H

Figure 3 Relationship posture and continuity of relationship.

characterized by ". . . less face to face communication, less assistance, fewer relation specific investments and frequent price benchmarking". Furthermore, under certain circumstances (F) represents a rational alternative. High involvement in short-term relationships is common, and apparently effective, for example, concerning procurement of equipment and investment goods.

Summarizing the argument with respect to posture and continuity of a supplier relationship we find that high involvement often coincides with long-term relationships. However, not all long-term relationships do require high involvement and in some short-term supplier relationships high involvement may be an effective approach.

Involvement and sourcing policy. High involvement is commonly associated with single sourcing policy and low involvement with multiple or parallel sourcing, i.e., alternatives (J) and (M) in Figure 4. Single sourcing tends to be regarded as a prerequisite for extended integration, as it can be motivated in terms of reduced supply handling costs. Yet, buying firms seem to stick to multiple sourcing for several reasons and argue that by using parallel suppliers they can avoid dependency on individual vendors and limit the risk of discontinuity of supply. Furthermore, multiple sourcing is supposed to promote healthy competition among suppliers as the customer can easily shift orders between different suppliers, which may reduce the direct costs of procurement. However, multiple sourcing can increase hidden costs. By splitting orders between two or more suppliers, a customer will increase its relationship handling costs and be unable to take advantage of any one supplier's economies of scale. This may also prevent the buying company from deriving potential benefits from high involvement. Furthermore, as pointed out by Hahn et al. (1986) competition is always associated with certain costs.

On closer examination, however, the issues involved appear more complex. There is no straightforward association between the actual posture and the sourcing policy, even if most texts on management of supplier relationships today recommend that companies move toward high involvement with a single supplier. There are good reasons for both high involvement and single sourcing, but the other alternatives in Figure 4 also represent viable and perfectly sound options. Some companies still rely on low involvement and multiple sourcing (M) because it is efficient for them. It has been shown that many purchasing professionals ". . . continue to manage the procurement process with a tactical price-based mentality" (*Purchasing*, 1998). There are documented cases of movement from single sourcing to multiple sourcing and reduced involvement. For instance, a recent survey indicates that 43% of purchasing managers say they have been, at times, forced to change back from single- to multiple-source supply arrangements (*Purchasing*, 1999).

The other combinations in Figure 4 are not only possible but also common and desirable. A buying firm may develop high-involvement relationships with two or more suppliers of the same product or service (K) because its customers prescribe which supplier to use. Low-involvement relationship with a single source (L) is another representation of the durable arm's length relationships identified by Dyer et al. (1998). They argue that the traditional notion of arm's length relationships – buyers that frequently rotate purchases across multiple sources – is no longer an economically sensible approach. First, the administrative costs associated with managing a large number of vendors outweigh the benefits and by using single sourcing the supply handling costs can be reduced. Second, dividing purchasing across multiple sources reduces both the ability of

Posture of relationship	Sourcing policy	
	Single	Multiple
High involvement	J	K
Low involvement	L	M

Figure 4 Relationship posture and sourcing policy.

suppliers to achieve significant economies of scale and the bargaining power of the customer. This means that low involvement and single sourcing (L) may be preferred when direct procurement costs account for most of the total costs. If the buying firm is small it may try to be perceived as a more interesting business partner by allocating the whole of its business to one supplier. However, if concerned about the vulnerability, it may avoid high involvement to retain the option of changing to another supplier.

MANAGING IN RELATIONSHIPS

Any company uses a set of supplier relationships as part of its business system, which impacts on its performance in different ways. The core of our argument is that the economic consequences of supplier relationships depend on the postures developed and, in particular, on the degree of involvement in each specific relationship. The capacity to cope with various types of relationships in differentiated ways has a profound impact on performance. Bensaou's portfolio analysis of supply management principles found no major performance differentials among the four types of relationships (Bensaou, 1999). These findings support the argument that there is no such thing as a generally best type of relationship. Both high- and low-involvement approaches have their pros and cons. However, Bensaou's study also showed that each of the four postures contained both low- and high-performing relationships depending on the way they were handled. Obviously, management principles matter.

Effective managing in relationships requires careful assessment of the economic consequences of prevailing postures and possible changes in the degree of involvement. While different models for assessing relationships have been presented (Lamming et al., 1996), it remains a fact that, all too often, effects of relationships are only loosely assessed. For example, Cousins (1999) found that firms ". . . appear to be pursuing supplier reductions without a clear assessment of the costs and benefits involved." Kapour and Gupta (1997) observed a relationship where the customer ". . . had been overpaying for services in the name of partnerships, the terms and the benefits of which could not be identified, let alone quantified". A balanced assessment requires a wide-angle perspective on the costs and benefits of the relationship along the lines of the framework outlined in this paper.

There is huge potential in better exploiting the opportunities offered by coping with suppliers. However, potential benefits are not reaped automatically. The success stories presented point out the necessity of reconsidering many of the existing purchasing practices and show the risks of overly generalized, undifferentiated solutions. Our discussion on managing in supplier relationships highlights three issues: the need for monitoring and changing postures; the interactive nature of managing within relationships; and the impact of the relationship atmosphere.

The prevailing degree of involvement characterizing a relationship must never be considered a permanent solution. Modifying the posture in the light of changing conditions is the critical issue in supply management. Changes in the contexts of relationships must be continuously monitored and analyzed in relation to the question of what is an economically justified degree of involvement in a specific relationship. If this is not done properly, buying firms may end up in either over- or under-designed relationships, both of which have been shown to be paths to failure (Bensaou, 1999). Over-designed relationships evolve when more resources than necessary are put into a relationships. Over-designed relationships are not only costly, but also tend to be risky because of the specific investments. High-involvement relationships are liabilities. There are times when it becomes necessary to reduce the degree of involvement. Sometimes substantial economic gains may be achieved by relying on standardized low-involvement relationships. At the other end of the spectrum – under-designed relationships – the movement needs to go in the opposite direction, because potential benefits may be achieved through higher involvement. Both increases and decreases in involvement are thus always options when considering changes of posture and neither applies generally, but only within the specific context of the ongoing relationship.

When changes in the degree of involvement are considered, it has to be kept in mind that supplier relationships are two-sided, implying that the input and output of both customer and supplier determine performance. Interests and resources of both parties must be considered. In many cases, however, the role of the supplier tends to be decided only from the perspective of the buying firm. We agree with Quinn who argues that one of the most crucial issues in effective supplier management is to shift the buyer outlook toward managing the desired output rather than the operations of the suppliers. If the buyer imposes overly detailed requirements about how the job should be done ". . . it will kill innovation and vitiate the supplier's real advantage" (Quinn, 1999). Similar arguments are presented by Araujo et al. (1999) regarding how relationship productivity and innovativeness are affected by the way customers choose to access supplier resources. Effective managing within relationships requires a perspective that takes both customer and supplier into consideration, rather than the one-sided perspective often reflected in supplier development programs.

Our final element is the relationship atmosphere. Even in this case, we believe generally held attitudes need reconsideration. There are special risks in viewing arm's length relationships as conflictual and portraying the partnership type of supplier relationships as friendly. All relationships – whether of the high- or low-involvement type – are characterized by a mixture of conflict and cooperation. It may be of interest to observe that high-involvement relationships tend to involve more conflict than arm's length relationships. It is true that in low-involvement relationships there are frequent and heated discussions about prices, delivery terms and quality levels, but on the whole there is not so much else to argue about. The higher the level of involvement between companies the greater the interdependence, and the more pronounced becomes the potential for conflicting interests. In high-involvement relationships the decisions concerning joint investments and product adaptations usually call for compromises on both sides. However, the presence of conflict is not only negative. On the contrary, diversity of goals and convictions are often mentioned as prerequisites for innovation and creative development. Strong conflicting interests and heavy commitment sharpen the focus of the parties and tend to guarantee that only solutions effective and acceptable to both parties are adopted.

Managerial implications – making the most of supplier relationships

Making good use of suppliers is different from buying well. Suppliers can do much more than delivering reasonably priced items on request. The supplier relationships represent some of the most important assets of a company and should thus be considered and treated with a similar logic to other types of investments. Exploiting some of the potential of a supplier requires that the operations of the two companies become more closely integrated in the various facets of the relationship. This involves extensive and intense interpersonal interaction, coordination of various activities, and mutual adaptations of resources, which entail costs for both companies.

It would be a mistake, however, to apply the investment logic across the board. Heavy involvement with a supplier is not always feasible or desirable. First, it takes two to effectively integrate operations and the supplier may lack the necessary motivation and interest. Second, in some situations potential relationship benefits are exceeded by the investment costs that are incurred. Third, there are always limits to the investments a company can afford and every investment competes with other opportunities. In practice, it means that companies are confronted with a variety of situations in relation to suppliers and have to deal with them through different postures. Furthermore, the buying company will have to reconsider the degree of involvement in each relationship in the light of changing conditions.

We have argued that the ability to handle the relationships requires understanding, monitoring, and assessment of their economic consequences, as well as an insight into their interactive nature and in the forces driving the change. It is important to recognize that both the origins of changes and their implementation are always at least partly out of the company's control.

Even when the analysis is focused on only two parties, it is clear that coping with a relationship is a complex task. Yet, if we are to understand the interactive nature of customer–supplier relationships in business markets and their dynamics, the scope of analysis needs to be broadened. Each relationship is interdependent with a number of other relationships, together forming a network. Studies of business networks have documented the impact of customer–supplier relationships on the development of companies and have shed some light on the interdependencies management has to cope with. Håkansson and Ford (2000) have discussed the changing reality facing managers today pointing to three paradoxes in business networks that we find effective also when managing the supplier relationships.

The first paradox regards the need to balance the involvement in the relationships a company has to suppliers and customers. Applied to the supply side of the company, the first paradox is:

> Well-developed, high-involvement supplier relationships are at the heart of a company's survival and the basis of its growth and development. But the high-involvement relationships also tie the company into its current ways of operating and restrict its capacity to change. Supplier relationships are, for a company, both the impulse to development and the cage that imprisons it.

The second paradox relates to the interactive nature of relationships. We have emphasized the need to take the supplier's situation into account when considering appropriate postures for the buying company in order to reap the desired benefits. Applied to supplier relationships, the second paradox is:

> The supplier relationships of a company are the outcome of its strategy and its actions. But at the same time, the company is itself the outcome of the relationships and what has happened in them. It is, therefore, necessary to consider the position of the buying company from the premise that it forms its supplier relationships but also that it is itself formed by these. Both premises are equally valid.

Finally, the third paradox refers to the aspirations to control what is going on in the relationship. We have argued that the buying company should avoid imposing restrictions and specifications on suppliers because this may limit their creativity and innovation. In particular, it may prevent them from making use of solutions emanating from their other relationships. The third paradox in managing supplier relationships is:

> Both the supplier and the customer try to control and manage the relationship so as to achieve their own aims. This ambition is one of the key forces in development of the relationship and of the entire network. But the more that one of the companies is successful in its ambition to achieve control, the less effective and innovative will be the specific relationship and the whole supplier network over time.

Once the logic shifts from buying well to making the most of supplier relationships, the focus of "management" has to be modified toward managing within relationships. Managing within relationships is about coping with interdependencies. More complex and subtle issues than normally associated with purchasing management will face the management when the ambition becomes to make the most of supplier relationships. That is the consequence of recognizing the link there is between the supply management and the overall business strategy of the company.

REFERENCES

Araujo, L., Dubois, A., and Gadde, L.-E.: Managing Interfaces with Suppliers. *Industrial Marketing Management* **28**, 497–506 (1999).

Bensaou, M.: Portfolios of Buyer–Supplier Relationships. *Sloan Management Review* **Summer**, 35–44 (1999).

Carlisle, J., and Parker, R.: *Beyond Negotiation. Redeeming Customer–Supplier Relationships*. John Wiley and Sons, Chichester, 1989.

Cousins, P.: Supplier Base Rationalization – Myth or Reality? *European Journal of Purchasing and Supply Management* **5**, 143–155 (1999).

Davis, T.: Effective Supply Chain Management. *Sloan Management Review* **Summer**, 35–46 (1993).

Dyer, J., Cho, D., and Chu, W.: Strategic Supplier Segmentation: The Next 'Best Practice' in Supply Chain Management. *California Management Review* **40**(2), 57–76 (1998).

Ford, D., Gadde, L.-E., Håkansson, H., Lundgren, A., Snehota, I., Turnbull, P., and Wilson, D.: *Managing Business Relationships*. John Wiley and Sons, Chichester, 1998.

Gadde, L.-E., and Håkansson, H.: The Changing Role of Purchasing – Reconsidering Three Strategic Issues. *European Journal of Purchasing and Supply Management* **1**(1), 27–36 (1994).

Gadde, L.-E. and Mattsson, L.-G.: Stability and Change in Network Relationships. *International Journal of Research in Marketing* **4**, 29–41 (1987).

Hahn, C., Kim, K., and Kim, J.: Costs of Competition: Implications for Purchasing Strategy. *Journal of Purchasing and Materials Management* **22**(4), 2–7 (1986).

Håkansson, H., and Ford, D.: How Should Companies Interact in Business Networks. *Journal of Business Research* (2000 forthcoming).

Håkansson, H., and Snehota, I.: *Developing Relationships in Business Networks*. Routledge, London, (1995).

Kapour, V., and Gupta, A.: Aggressive Sourcing: A Free Market Approach. *Sloan Management Review* **Fall**, 21–31 (1997).

Kraljic, P.: Purchasing Must Become Supply Management. *Harvard Business Review* **61**, September–October, 109–117 (1983).

Krause, D., and Ellram, L.: Critical Elements of Supplier Development. The Buying Firm Perspective. *European Journal of Purchasing and Supply Management* **3**(1), 21–31 (1997).

Lamming, R., Cousins, P., and Notman, D.: Beyond Vendor Assessment. Relationship Assessment Programmes. *European Journal of Purchasing and Supply Management* **2**(4), 173–181 (1996).

Lewis, J.: *The Connected Corporation*. The Free Press, New York, 1995.

Macbeth, D.: Partnering – Why not? Proceedings of the 2nd Worldwide Research Symposium on Purchasing and Supply Management. London, 1998.

Minahan, T.: Is Partnering a Shame? *Purchasing* **June 4**, 68–69 (1998).

OEM-Buyers Are Up to the Same Tricks. *Purchasing* **June 4**, 68–69 (1998).

Quinn, J.: Strategic Outsourcing: Leveraging Knowledge Capabilities. *Sloan Management Review* **Summer**, 10–21 (1999).

Sheth, J., and Sharma, A.: Supplier Relationships. Emerging Issues and Challenges. *Industrial Marketing Management* **26**, 91–100 (1997).

Single Sourcing – Some Love It, Some Fear It. *Purchasing* **June 3**, 22–24 (1999).

Spekman, R., Kamauff, J., and Spear, J.: Towards More Effective Sourcing and Supplier Management. *European Journal of Purchasing and Supply Management* **5**(2), 103–116 (1999).

5.5

Managing interfaces with suppliers

Luis Araujo, Anna Dubois and Lars-Erik Gadde

INTRODUCTION

The 1997 *Industrial Marketing Management* special issue on relationship marketing included a review of the state-of-the-art of supplier relationships (Sheth and Sharma, 1997). One of its conclusions is that the purchasing focus is "dramatically shifting" from a transaction to a relational oriented approach. A number of earlier publications came up with similar accounts of the changing nature of buyer–seller relationships (Carlisle and Parker, 1989; Gadd and Håkansson, 1993; Van Weele and Roszemeijer, 1996). According to these findings, earlier recommendations for "arm's-length" relationships have been abandoned today. Instead, the emphasis has moved to the benefits that can be attained from collaborative relationships. "Partnering" with suppliers has been put on top of the agenda. Yet, many seem to share a feeling of uncertainty concerning the conditions for and the benefits to be reaped from collaborative relationships. According to one source, there is "a pervasive confusion over what exactly a partnership is" (Minahan, 1998). Sheth and Sharma (1997) speculate that the source of future competitive advantage will be the "type of relationship" that firms will have with their suppliers.

To continue in the same vein, it is important to clarify the nature and benefits that supply relationships can bring to customers. Suppliers differ widely in their capabilities and in what benefits they can bring to a customer. Some suppliers can provide benefits in terms of cost rationalization whilst others can act as sources of new ideas and practices. The contributions from suppliers will be dependent on how "close" the relations are, for example, in terms of the degree of involvement (Gadde and Snehota, 1998). On the other hand, the higher the involvement between the parties in terms of coordination of activities and interaction among people, the more resource demanding the relationship will be. Thus, the benefits from closer involvement with suppliers must offset the investments to set up and maintain the relationship.

PURPOSE

The objective of this article is to analyze the character and consequences of different types of relationships via the notion of customer–supplier interfaces. We are in particular concerned with resource interfaces. The focus of our approach is on the way buyers and sellers relate their resources to each other. It is a well-established finding that a company can substantially expand its resource base through access to supplier resources (Carlisle and Parker, 1989; Gadde and Håkansson, 1993; Sheth and Sharma, 1997; Gadde and Snehota, 1998). Even companies that historically have not been noted for collaborative supply relationships, today recognize the potential benefits stemming from close involvement with suppliers. One example is General Motors whose corporate supply strategy "looks at competitiveness in terms of how well the company uses the resources of suppliers" (Minaham, 1996).

Our basic point-of-departure is that a firm's competitive advantage resides not simply within the boundaries of what it owns and controls, but also on idiosyncratic interfaces it develops with other firms, e.g. its suppliers (Dyer and Singh, 1998). In short, control of resources as well as access to resources controlled by other parties defines a firm's competitive position (Håkansson and Snehota, 1995).

An investigation of the benefits and costs associated with relationships requires an understanding of the interface types that firms establish with their suppliers. Relationship consequences have been analyzed in a number of dimensions (Gadde and Snehota, 1998). Our intention in this paper is to focus on resource interfaces as a key component of buyer–supplier relationships. We subscribe to the conclusion in a recent study that the quality of a relationship is strongly influenced by its interface structure (Christopher and Juttner, 1998).

We argue that access to supplier resources is a function of the type of interface developed in the buyer–supplier relationship. We will identify a typology of interfaces defined from the perspective of the customer. The typology distinguishes between different ways of relating resources. We will analyze the consequences arising from each type of interface and derive some managerial implications for the buying firm.

RESOURCE INTERFACES

To manufacture products, to provide services, to assemble systems, etc., firms make use of a variety resources. No company controls all the resources they require. Both internally controlled and externally accessed resources are important to a firm. Resources have two sides since their value is determined by the way they fit the producers and user contexts (Loasby, 1998). Usually the user and the producer are two different firms. Resources and the ways they are developed and used set the static and the dynamic efficiency of firms. The productivity of firms is determined by the efficiency in the utilization of a given resource combination at any one time, whereas innovativity is related to the development of new resource combinations over time.

Two important issues can be singled out, based on the resource characteristics described above: (1) What resources should be controlled internally and what resources should be accessed externally from suppliers?; and (2) How should the buyer access suppliers' resources?

The first issue relates to the efficient boundaries of the firm, the make or buy decision (Barney, 1999). The second issue addresses in detail the question of how to access the resources that the firm has decided not to bring within its boundaries. Our argument in this article is that the resources the buyer controls internally are influenced by how the interfaces between the focal customer and its suppliers evolve. Therefore, the two issues highlighted above become interdependent over time, that is, the forms of access to suppliers' resources affects make or buy decisions and vice versa. Although these two issues are intimately related in practice, we will focus the following discussion on the second issue.

Resource interfaces are primarily concerned with the technical interdependencies that arise when the resource bases of buyer and supplier are connected through exchange activities. In some cases, as we will show later, these interdependencies are handled by simple routines. In other cases, these interdependencies will require mutual investments and complex procedures. We will focus on the customer's perspective and thus on the different ways customers access their suppliers' resources.

Other authors have identified different types of exchanges between buyers and suppliers (Asanuma, 1989; Clarke and Fujimoto, 1991). One of these classifications categorizes products exchanged into (1) parts manufactured according to the drawings provided by the customer, (2) parts manufactured according to the drawings provided by the supplier, or (3) parts bought through catalogues or "marketed goods" (Asanuma, 1989). Another scheme is based on the different types of parts bought by car manufacturers: "supplier proprietary parts," "detailed controlled parts," and "black-box parts" (Clarke and Fujimoto, 1991).

These classifications are based on the division of labor, in particular design and manufacturing, between supplier and customer rather than by how each firm relates their internally controlled resources to those externally accessed. Hence, the categorization of parts provided by these authors are descriptions of the outcomes of resource interfaces. The consequence of making a distinction between the interfaces, and the outcomes that flow from them, namely, the products being exchanged, is that a focus on interfaces provides a different way of understanding the dynamics of exchange relationships. In particular, it shifts the managerial emphasis from the evaluation of suppliers' current offers to the evaluation of supplier capabilities and the value they add to the customer's business (Anderson and Narus, 1999).

The starting point of our approach is how customer and supplier relate their resources. Thus, we need to take the producer and user contexts into consideration. The most important distinction between different resource interfaces is to what extent the customer and the supplier are aware of each other's contexts. The first type of interface that can be identified is when the knowledge of use and the knowledge of produce are unrelated to each other. In these situations the supplier does not need to know about the user context nor does the customer need to understand the producer context. In these cases the interfaces, as well as the products exchanged, are standardized (Demsetz, 1991).

In other situations the buying firm might prefer a customized product. This in turn will require an interface where the resources of buyer and seller to some extent are adapted to each other. The supplier then needs certain directions from the customer. One type of direction is prescriptions regarding the characteristics of the product and/or how it is to be manufactured. This will be referred to as a specified interface. A third type of interface appears when the buyer's direction is based on the function of the product in its user context. This interface is labeled "translation" because the supplier has to translate the functional characteristics supplied by the customer into a product.

A fourth interface type is based on open-ended dialogue based on how the buyer and supplier can join their knowledge of user and producer contexts and develop the specifications together. This process has been described as joint learning: "Two resource holders will in an interaction process develop the knowledge and skills to utilize each other's resources. Joint learning is a double (or mutual) specialization which includes adaptation." (Håkansson, 1993).

These four interfaces can now be described in detail. The supplier providing a standardized range of products from which the customers choose characterize standardized interfaces. This interface represents the classical arm's length market relationship. There are no relevant technical or organizational interdependencies between the two parties and the two organizations only require a simple sales-to-purchasing functional interface to conduct exchanges.

For the buyer, there is an assortment to choose from, and prices act as the main coordinating device between buyer and seller. Moreover, the cost of using standardized interfaces is low for both parties, since transaction costs are low and no dedicated investments are required. For the customer this is due to the absence of a need for investments in knowledge about how the products bought are designed or manufactured. And for the supplier the low cost of setting up and maintaining these interfaces derives from economies of scale in production and marketing since the same product is sold to many customers through identical interfaces. However, indirect costs may arise for the customer since other resources may need adaptation for the standardized products to fit in (e.g., other components in a system). In addition, the lack of direct contact with customers may pose problems for the development of new products.

Specified interfaces are characterized by the buyer specifying the object of the exchange. Traditional subcontracting or outsourcing are good examples of this interface. In these cases, the buyer uses the supplier as an extension of its own production structure. These arrangements can work very efficiently; for example, a subcontractor is able to pool orders together and reaps economies of scale and scope beyond the reach of any of its customers. Contrary to standardized interfaces, the supplier requires specifications and production schedules from the customer. Hence, specified interfaces entail a degree of interdependence between the parties since production schedules need ex ante coordination.

The buyer specifying the required functionality from a product rather than the actual product characterizes translation interfaces. The specification is thus based on how the product will have to perform in the user context. The supplier takes on the translation from the user's functional description into product design and manufacturing specifications. Although the division of labor between supplier and buyer may be similar to the one used in specified interfaces, the supplier takes on a greater responsibility in the relationship. As in the case of specified interfaces, translation interfaces are based on directions given by the buyer. However, in translation interfaces, these directions leave important degrees of freedom for the supplier in deciding how best to meet the buyer's specifications based on user context.

The buyer and supplier jointly developing product specifications characterize interactive interfaces. Buyer and supplier may, based on considerations on their joint set of resources, discuss different solutions and the various trade-offs between them. Hence, this interface enables the firms to consider productivity consequences for both parties as well as the benefits that can be jointly developed vis-à-vis specific third parties, for example, the buyer's customers. The direct costs associated with establishing interactive interfaces have to be carefully considered. In addition, the returns on investing in interactive interfaces may be difficult to predict ex ante. However, because interactive interfaces open up the possibility of both high productivity and innovativity gains, these investments have to be considered as multiperiod to estimate the costs and benefits they yield over time.

The four interface categories differ in terms of (1) the costs associated with the use of the respective interface; and (2) the benefits provided by them differ in terms of (a) productivity and (b) innovativity. The consequences of the different interfaces is discussed in the next section and illustrated by an example of a supplier whose customers require different types of interfaces. By focusing on one supplier, we are able to explore the consequences and trade-offs involved in different types of interfaces.

SB STEEL WORKS

SB Steel Works is a Swedish company founded 300 years ago. The main production activity is steel forging. Today, the firm employs 250 people and has an annual turnover of 300 million SEK (US $38.7 million). The company is involved in steel production, forging, heat treatment, and rough machining. It produces mainly shafts and rotors to customers who use them as components for large electrical engines, propeller systems, generators, etc.

Except for some standardized ingots (in terms of size and material composition) sold to some customers (forgers) who do not have their own steel mills, all products are customer specific and customized for every end use. The company has approximately 100 customers working in such diverse fields as energy, offshore, paper, marine, and mechanical tools. The demands of these different customer groups are, due to the different end-use applications, reflected in different product specifications, such as length, materials specification, and geometrical shape.

The first activity is steel production. The steel mill produces ingots of set sizes determined by mould capacities. Thereafter the steel is forged and heat-treated. To profit from the heat content of the milling operation, forging is undertaken immediately after milling. Finally, rough and final machining takes place before delivery. The lead time for production is between 10 and 20 weeks. The product specifications encompass two dimensions: the geometrical shape and material composition of the shaft or rotor.

The way product specifications are set differs. Some customers have their own metallurgists and develop product specifications independently. These customers place orders specifying the physical shapes of the shaft together with material composition. Other customers specify strength requirements instead of steel specifications. In these cases, SB uses its own metallurgists to translate mechanical properties into specifications for material composition and manufacturing. Still, other customers want to develop the product specifications jointly with SB. In these instances, customer and supplier discuss trade-offs between forms and materials to develop the best solution for a specific end use. We will now illustrate our four interfaces by using the SB example.

STANDARDIZED INTERFACES

As mentioned earlier, SB has few customers who require standardized products. These customers tend to be forgers who source ingots from any steel mill. The specifications for these ingots are standardized and forgers tend to source them on price and availability. Prices are largely determined by the prevailing supply–demand relationship in the global steel market. From the supplier's perspective, ingots can be milled to fill spare capacity based on expectations of supply–demand relationships and mills can also set their prices to take advantage of temporary supply–demand imbalances. There are few or no switching costs for customers even though they face search costs to find the right product at the right price, for when they need it.

Investments in this type of interface are minimal for both supplier and customer and are of a generic nature. Customers need to know who produces regularly the ingots they require, and suppliers need to know what product variations are required by whom and when it is worth filling spare capacity in this way.

SPECIFIED INTERFACES

In the SB case, this interface applies where customers place an order specifying both physical shapes and materials to be used. The joint specification of shape and material composition constitutes a complete blueprint for production. SB simply follows a set activity pattern to achieve the desired output.

The benefits of this type of interface for SB reside in its simplicity and expediency. Well-honed routines ensure that the end product matches the specification supplied by the customer. From SB's perspective, however, there are also costs associated with this type of interface. Having the material specified by the customer means that the processing of ingots resulting from the milling process is usually inefficient. Ingots can only be produced in set sizes determined by mold dimensions. If there are no similar orders at the same time, the excess ingots will be melted as scrap. The probability of matching orders is low, and thus the ability of SB to utilize its resources efficiently is also low. In these situations, customer specifications effectively "lock in" SB's resource base and opportunities for increasing productivity rest on attempts to find customers with similar requirements and match the timing of their orders.

TRANSLATION INTERFACES

This interface occurs when the customer specifies the physical shape and mechanical strength requirements of the shaft or rotor. In these situations, SB uses its own team of metallurgists to translate strength requirements into material specifications. The utilization of ingots can be more efficient in this case, since mechanical strength requirements do not fully determine material composition. SB thus has some leeway on how to achieve the required mechanical strength. Flexibility results from being able to achieve the required strength specification either through material specifications before melting or by resorting to heat treatment after melting.

SB can achieve important economies in production by, for example, matching different orders for melting and use downstream operations to adjust the mechanical properties of the shafts or rotors. By allowing for some resource sharing amongst different customer orders, translation interfaces allow the supplier to achieve some productivity and innovativity gains. The improvements in productivity result, for example, in the noticing of opportunities to spread overheads over a larger numbers of units. Opportunities for learning may emerge from the fine-tuning of routines in areas, such as product specification, production scheduling, material flow control, etc.

As in specified interfaces, the supplier does not require detailed knowledge of the user context, to either design or manufacture the product. But, unlike interactive interfaces, the parameters set by the customer constrain to an important degree product specifications and manufacturing operations.

INTERACTIVE INTERFACES

In SB's case the development of an interactive interface with a customer means the increase in the number of open-ended parameters for design and manufacturing. The customer will simply inform SB about the setting of the component in terms of connected components, working temperature, rotation speeds, corrosion characteristics of the working environment, etc. These parameters will, instead of forming platforms for translation into SB's production activities, become the subject of negotiations before any decisions on specifications and production activities can be made. SB and the customer are then in a position to discuss trade-offs between forms and materials to develop the best solutions for a particular end use.

When the specifications are worked out jointly with the customer, there are also possibilities to deal with the cost consequences of, for example, using different materials. However, in these cases the impact of changes in the specification of the shaft or rotor may be felt elsewhere in the system where this component fits. Furthermore, the consequences usually are not limited to the customer–supplier dyad but also affect third parties, for example, other suppliers to the same customer, since form adjustments may impact on other components in the system where the shaft or rotor will operate.

Interactive interfaces from SB's perspective pose rather different challenges to either specified or translation interfaces. Keeping many parameters open ended increases the possibility of spotting opportunities to increase productivity by reusing existing knowledge in materials specification, reaping economies of scale in melting operations, increasing the batch size of downstream operations, etc.

On the other hand, interactive interfaces require important investments in learning about customer's operations and the end uses to which shafts or rotors are put. The benefits of learning about end uses play a key part in the accumulation of technological capabilities within SB but also represent a significant cost that may never be recouped if opportunities to exercise these capabilities never materialize. In short, the development of interactive interfaces present SB with significant opportunities and risks as far as productivity and innovativity are concerned.

CONSEQUENCES OF THE USE OF DIFFERENT INTERFACES: A CUSTOMER PERSPECTIVE

The main question raised at the beginning of this article was "How can the buyer access the supplier's resources?" The SB case has shown the effects for the supplier depending on what type of interface is used by the customer. For the customer, these effects determine what benefits flow from the use of the respective interfaces. These benefits must be balanced against the investments required to establish and maintain each interface. On the benefit side, the interfaces differ in terms of how they contribute to the productivity and innovativity of the buying firm. The resources required to handle the interfaces will be discussed in terms of the capability needed in-house, the resources needed to set up and maintain the interface and the need for coordinating the total set of interfaces.

PRODUCTIVITY

The SB case illustrates the economic consequences of accessing supplier resources through different interfaces. The costs of developing and maintaining different interfaces for the supplier will be reflected partly in the prices charged to customers. Standardized interfaces provide customers with the best option to make use of large-scale supplier operations. Often, the most appropriate route for a customer is to rely on arm's length market relationships and adapt to generic market standards even if it means incurring indirect costs elsewhere. Specified interfaces provide limited opportunities to attain productivity gains since they place important constraints on the supplier's operations. Translation interfaces allow room for economies of scale and scope that can be translated into lower prices for customers. Interactive interfaces involve joint efforts with the potential to affect cost structures on both sides of the interface. This also means increased opportunities to reduce indirect costs.

INNOVATIVITY

We will deal with innovativity in terms of the learning effects that can originate from use of each type of interface. There are two types of learning effects to consider. One is the direct, situated, and joint learning that takes place between the customer and the supplier. The other is to which extent the customer can benefit from what the supplier learns from interacting with other counterparts.

Standardized interfaces provide no opportunity for direct learning. However, the indirect effects can be substantial as the typical "learning curve" effects, focusing on cost reductions over time, exemplify. Cumulative output and repetition of tasks and raising awareness of these effects induces further learning (Argote and Epple, 1990).

Similarly, specified interfaces do not foster direct learning from suppliers except in situations where the customer will deliberately set in train procedures to teach suppliers new routines and skills (MacDufie and Helper, 1997). Indirect learning effects also may be limited in this case because the dominant role of the customer can make it difficult for suppliers to reuse knowledge gained from other counterparts. Translation interfaces also represent limited potential for direct learning. On the other hand, the degrees of freedom involved in complying with functional requirements rather than detailed product specifications may enable suppliers to reuse knowledge gained from other interfaces. Indirect learning effects depend on the nature of the functional specifications, which may be characterized by different degrees of technical challenge and variety. A recent study by Von Hippel (1998) illustrates these indirect learning effects. Suppliers of customized and technically complex products found ways to transfer the responsibility of the product design process to customers based on the development of design tools that do not require expert knowledge of the underlying technologies. Instead of relying on complex processes of translating customer specifications into product designs, the supplier develops a general-purpose design tool that can then be used by a customer to specify a uniquely customized product.

Last, interactive interfaces provide significant direct and indirect learning opportunities. Joint development is the cornerstone of direct learning and at the same time increases the potential for making use of what the supplier learns in activities with other customers as well as with its own suppliers. The open-ended nature of the exchange provides room for an overview of resource utilization and the pooling of "best practice" experience across all interfaces.

RESOURCE REQUIREMENTS ON THE CUSTOMER SIDE

Standardized interfaces require minimal investments by a buying firm. Customers need to know who the suppliers are and the most convenient way to get hold of the product. Normally this requires simple administrative routines in purchasing departments, where the information on sources of supply is usually held.

In a specified interface the customer makes only limited investments in the relationship. However, the customer will need easy access to the resources necessary to specify the design and manufacture of a product, such as in-house metallurgists in the SB case. Suppliers and subcontractors can be used as flexible capacity reservoirs. The need to coordinate the inputs among

Table 1 Consequences of different types of supply interfaces from a customer-based perspective

Interface category	Characteristics	Customer benefits productivity	Customer costs productivity	Customer benefits innovativity	Customer costs innovativity
Standardized	No directions. No specific connection between user and producer contexts.	Cost benefits from supplier economies of scale and scope, as well as learning curve effects.	Adaptation to standardized solutions may create indirect costs elsewhere.	None	No direct costs. Allows only indirect feedback to suppliers based on sales figures.
Specified	Precise directions given by customer on how to produce.	Supplier can pool together similar orders; economies of scale and scope can be attained.	Supplier's resource base "locked in." Limited possibilities to influence specifications.	Minimal (supplier can propose changes to blueprints).	Suppliers used as capacity reservoir. Development of supplier resources may suffer.
Translation	Directions given by customer based on user context and functionality required.	Supplier can propose efficient solutions that improve its own as well as the customer's productivity.	Supplier may reap benefits that are not shared with customer.	Supplier has some leeway to propose innovative solutions.	Supplier may not know enough about customer context to innovate radically.
Interactive	Joint development based on combined knowledge of use and production.	Open-ended exchange allows full consideration of direct and indirect costs for both parties.	Investments in knowledge of how best to make use of existing resources.	Supplier learning about user context opens up the gamut of solutions offered.	Requires investments in joint development and learning.

different suppliers is limited since the translation from "context-of-use" into "product design and manufacturing" is made in-house.

In translation interfaces, the customer is able to make better use of the suppliers' resources. Through accessing external resources the amount of internally controlled resources can be reduced. For example, in the SB case the customer does not need an in-house metallurgist. The resource input into the relationship is not much different from a specified interface – there are few or no dedicated investments. Switching costs are low in this type of interface. However, the coordination among different translation interfaces might be substantial due to their open-ended nature.

Hence, the flexibility given to each supplier might require extensive integration efforts on the customer side. The case of integrated production systems in the aerospace and car industries illustrate this point (Table 1) (Paliwoda and Bonaccorsi, 1993).

CONCLUSIONS

The type of interface used in a relationship will have direct consequences for the way the resources of the supplier are activated. Accordingly, interfaces affect the way a customer accesses the resources of a supplier. We have illustrated how the four interfaces differ in terms of the benefits provided as well as the costs of establishing and maintaining them for a focal customer. Clearly each interface has its pros and cons. None of them performs better in any absolute sense. The advantages and disadvantages are determined by the context in which they are applied. Benefits and costs need to be weighed against each other.

On the resource side, the main dimensions to consider for a customer are related to internal control versus access to resources controlled by existing or potential suppliers. And, of course, a firm's relational capabilities and objectives in how to relate these two internally controlled to externally accessed resources.

The first conclusion we offer is that a buyer needs a variety of interfaces. For example, interactive interfaces provide major opportunities for productivity and innovativity gains through joint learning. On the other hand, they are complex to handle and represent substantial investments. Therefore, a buying company can be involved only in a limited number of interactive interfaces at the same time. This will require that the resources of other suppliers be accessed through less resource demanding interfaces. On the other hand, accessing resources through standardized interfaces may provide a customer with cost benefits that can only be attained when suppliers rely on large numbers of customers to achieve economies of scale and learning effects derived from cumulative output. Often, access to these benefits means foregoing other benefits that may emerge from direct interaction with suppliers and the specification of customized solutions.

Other reasons supporting the need for variety are to be found on the supply side. The capabilities of suppliers are diverse. For example, some suppliers, who are used to receiving design and manufacturing blueprints from their customers, may lack the capabilities needed to translate required functionality into product specifications. In short, they are unable to sustain a move from specified to translation interfaces. Other suppliers might have these capabilities but for various reasons will not be interested in developing either translation or interactive interfaces with a specific customer. In such cases, the buyer might have little option but to rely on specified interfaces.

The second conclusion we offer is that interfaces are interdependent. A major task for every customer is to coordinate and combine the solutions developed by suppliers with the in-house developed solutions. Above, we argued that this was an important reason for limiting the number of interactive interfaces. One way to bypass this limitation is to form supplier hierarchies, as found in the automotive industry. These structures are characterized by interactive interfaces between the customer and a limited number of first-tier suppliers, whereas specified and standardized interfaces are used further down the supply chain (Fruin and Nishiguchi, 1993).

The third conclusion is that the choice of interfaces must take dynamic features into account. The need for, as well as modes of access to external resources, changes over time. There are internal and external factors that need continuous reassessment. It appears as though buying firms often adopt a sequence of interface development. Returning to the automotive industry example, car manufacturers historically have tended to use specified interfaces. With the changing view of the benefits that suppliers can provide, these interfaces have in many cases been replaced by translation and interactive interfaces (Helper, 1991).

Because of changing internal and external conditions, it is important that interfaces with suppliers are continuously monitored and purposefully managed. A resource demanding relationship must yield substantive benefits. It is important to emphasize that resource-demanding interfaces do not automatically result in benefits for both parties as the common "win-win" notion implies. That is, a customer must avoid situations described in the following way: "[The customer] had been overpaying for services in the name of partnerships, the terms and commitments of which were entirely unclear and the benefits of which could not be identified, let alone quantified" (Kapour and Gupta, 1997). Direct benefits and costs often are difficult to apportion between two interacting parties. Often, they must be considered jointly and the indirect effects of benefits and costs also must be assessed.

MANAGERIAL IMPLICATIONS

We began this article questioning the wisdom of simple maxims, such as "move from arm's length relationships to partnering with your suppliers." Our focus on interfaces and the investments necessary to set up and maintain different interfaces highlights the need for managers to question these simple prescriptions. There are different sets of costs and benefits to be derived from each of the interfaces described here. Three managerial implications flow from our analysis: (1) preserve variety amongst your set of supplier or customer interfaces; (2) understand the interdependence amongst interfaces, and (3) avoid the dangers of focusing too narrowly on core competencies.

Variety amongst interfaces is crucial to achieve a balance between productivity and innovativity objectives. Productivity and innovativity are not internally determined but a product of how companies activate their resources in relation to suppliers and customers. A narrow range of interfaces or too much emphasis on one type of interface is likely to steer firms either towards stagnant, short-term efficiency or overambitious accumulation of unrelated capabilities. Learning too much, too fast through the pursuit of too many interactive interfaces is ultimately as likely to lead to poor performance as an unremitting concern with productivity gains.

Designing interfaces is never a one-sided affair, no matter how powerful the focal customer or supplier is. An interface is always the outcome of decisions made on both sides of a dyad and always related to the other interfaces that each of the parties develops with third parties. The ability of a supplier to accede to the request of a customer to, for instance, take responsibility for "black-box" parts is contingent on what resources that supplier has developed over time and how these resources are currently being deployed. And often, to accommodate this request would imply changes to other interfaces both on the demand and supply side. In short, there are often intended and unintended effects of changes to one interface.

The problem is that often this cascade of interdependencies is poorly understood and addressed by different people within a company. Different managerial agendas, functional balkanization, and different reward and control systems compound the problem. The challenge of recognizing interdependence amongst interfaces is to develop an integrated view of the company's resource base and how it is activated across a range of interfaces with both customers and suppliers.

Last, our discussion of interfaces highlights the danger of focusing too narrowly on core competencies. The ability to develop complex interfaces with suppliers and customers requires the development of competencies that relate two different but complementary specialisms. By definition, these competencies cannot be described as "core" but are nonetheless crucial for the successful operation and development of core competencies. Thus the notion of "retreating to the core" and disposing of all competencies regarded as peripheral is as harmful as believing that firms can handle all their customers or suppliers with the same type of interface.

REFERENCES

Anderson, J. C., and Narus, J. A.: *Business Market Management. Understanding, Creating, and Delivering Value.* Prentice-Hall, Upper Saddle River, NJ, 1999.

Argote, L., and Epple, D.: Learning Curves in Manufacturing. *Science* **247**, 920–924 (1990).

Asanuma, B.: Manufacturer-Supplier Relationships in Japan and the Concept of Relation-Specific Skill. *Journal of the Japanese and International Economies*, **3**, 1–30 (1989).

Barney, J.: How a Firm's Capabilities Affect Boundary Decisions. *Sloan Management Review*, **40**, 137–145 (1999).

Carlisle, J., and Parker, R.: *Beyond Negotiation. Redeeming Customer-Supplier Relationships.* John Wiley and Sons, Chichester, 1989.

Christopher, M., and Juttner, U.: Developing Strategic Partnerships in the Supply Chain. Proceedings of the 2nd Worldwide Research Symposium on Purchasing and Supply Management, April 1–3, 1998. IPSERA and CRISPS, London, pp. 88–107.

Clarke, K., and Fujimoto, T.: *Product Development Performance. Strategy, Organization and Management in the World Auto Industry.* Harvard Business School Press, Cambridge, MA, 1991.

Demsetz, H.: The Theory of the Firm Revisited, in *The Nature of the Firm. Origins, Evolution and Development.* O. E. Williamson and S. G. Winter, eds, Oxford University Press, New York, 1991.

Dyer, J. H., and Singh, I.: The Relational View: Cooperative Strategy and Sources of Interorganizational Competitive Advantage. *Academy of Management Review*, **23**, 660–679 (1998).

Fruin, W. M., and Nishiguchi, T.: Supplying the Toyota Production System: Intercorporate Organizational Evolution and Supplier Subsystems, in *Country Competitiveness: Technology and the Organizing of Work*, B. Kogut, ed., Oxford University Press, New York, 1993.

Gadde, L.-E., and Håkansson, H.: *Professional Purchasing*. Routledge, London, 1993.

Gadde, L.-E., and Snehota, I.: Making the Most of Supplier Relationships. Proceedings of the 2nd Worldwide Research Symposium on Purchasing and Supply Management, April 1–3, 1998. IPSERA and CRISPS, London, pp. 191–213.

Håkansson, H.: Networks as a Mechanism to Develop Resources, in *Networking in Dutch Industries*, P. Beije, Håkansson, H., and Snehota, I.: *Developing Relationships in Business Networks*. Routledge, London, 1995.

J. Groenewegen, and O. Nuys, eds., Leuven-Apeldoorn, Garant, 1993.

Helper, S.: Strategy and Irreversibility in Supplier Relations – the Case of the United-States Automobile Industry. *Business History Review*, **65**, 781–824 (1991).

Kapour, V., and Gupta, A.: Aggressive Sourcing: A Free Market Approach. *Sloan Management Review*, **39**, 21–31 (1997).

Loasby, B.: The Organization of Capabilities. *Journal of Economic Behavior and Organization* **35**, 139–160 (1998).

MacDuffie, J. P., and Helper, S.: Creating Lean Suppliers: Diffusing Lean Production throughout the Supply Chain. *California Management Review* **39**, 118–151 (1997).

Minahan, T.: Is Harold Kutner GM's Comeback Kid? *Purchasing*, **121**, 40–44 (1996).

Minahan, T.: Is Partnering a Sham? *Purchasing* **124**, 61–64 (1998).

Paliwoda, S. J., and Bonaccorsi, A. J.: Systems Selling in the Aircraft Industry. *Industrial Marketing Management*, **22**, 155–160 (1993).

Sheth, J., and Sharma, A.: Supplier Relationships. Emerging Issues and Challenges. *Industrial Marketing Management*, **26**, 91–100 (1997).

Van Weele, A., and Roszemeijer, F.: Revolution in Purchasing. Building Competitive Power through Proactive Purchasing. *European Journal of Purchasing and Supply Management*, **2**, 153–160, 1996.

Von Hippel, E.: Economics of Product Development by Users: The Impact of "Sticky" Local Information. *Management Science*, **44**, 629–644 (1998).

5.6

It's only a matter of confidence! A comparison of relationship management between Japanese and UK non-Japanese owned vehicle manufacturers

Paul D. Cousins and Euan Stanwix

INTRODUCTION

There is a wide and varied range of literature on the subject of buyer–supplier relationships, the key focus appears to be how good Japanese firms are at managing these relationships, and how poor Western firms are at implementing and benefiting from them. This begs the question: why are Japanese firms better than Western ones at managing long-term supplier relationships? Are these differences just because of Japanese management style, culture and/or structural or strategic issues?

To understand these differences, we studied Japanese and non-Japanese owned manufacturers in the UK vehicle manufacturing industry. This also allowed us to investigate how Japanese transplants worked with their UK non-Japanese owned suppliers, and to compare them with their non-Japanese owned counterparts.

Some authors argue (Lamming, 1993; Hines, 1994; Nishiguchi, 1994) that fundamental historical differences have created different industry structures in Japan, with respect to financial systems, geographical co-location of suppliers and manufacturers, joint ownership, etc. They propose that these cultural and structural aspects combined to enable Japanese firms to be more successful at managing long-term relationships. In fact, some have stated that Japanese firms in all sectors naturally view buyer–supplier relationships as long-term, which creates benefits from mutual investment reduced cycle times and improved innovation acquisition (Syson, 1992; Morris and Imrie, 1993; Nishiguchi, 1994; Womack and Jones, 1994). On the other hand, there is also a view that Western firms tend to view all relationships as a series of short-term relationships, some of which just happen to last a long time!

Other authors (Dore, 1987; Contractor and Lorange, 1988; Sako, 1992; Sako and Helper, 1998) have proposed that buyer–supplier relationships in Japanese and Western firms differ because they are based on different kinds of contracts which are placed on a spectrum ranging from Obligational Contractual Approaches (OCR) to Arms-Length Contractual Approaches (ACR) (Dore's J-Type and A-Type contracts respectively). It is argued by these authors that Japanese manufacturers would see themselves as working at the OCR end of the spectrum, whereas Western firms are operating at the ACR end of the continuum. It is proposed that this could be due to cultural rather than structural differences in the manner in which the firm views relationship management.

A central concept in the OCR approach is trust (Luhmann, 1979; Hurst, 1984; Bernstein, 1988; Bhide and Stevenson, 1990; Thorne, 1991; Pascarella, 1993; Lane and Bachmann, 1995; Sako and Helper, 1998). The concept of trust is seen as fundamentally important for the effective development of a long-term successful business relationship. However, few authors actually clearly define what they mean by trust (Sako, 1992). Table 1 summarises the major findings of the trust literature, which spans a wide range of disciplines. As a concept in business relationships, trust makes intuitive sense, but trust is so intangible and nebulous that it is impossible to define and measure. As a framework for relationship management, it becomes impossible to implement. This is reflected in the lack of consensus on a definition of trust in the literature.

The concept of trust within relationship management appears to be very important, however it is also difficult to define. It is clear from the literature that there are many types of trust. Ranging from personal (individual) to organisational trust. Sako (1992) attempted to create a workable framework for trust for business relationships. She distinguished between contractual, competence, and goodwill trust, which are influenced by the varying levels of asset specificity between the customer and supplier. Other forms of trust have been identified, such as Seligman's (1997) inter-personal and inter-organisational trust. Trust has also been referred to as a mechanism by which firms reduce uncertainty; as Gambetta (Gambetta, 1988) says, "trust is seen as a precursor to building effective relations, not as an *ex post* condition".

This paper addresses the central concept of trust in buyer–supplier relationships. It begins by developing a conceptual framework that focuses on how trust enhances inter-organisational

Table 1 Summary of the trust literature

Trust categories	Type of study/main points	Authors
Trust as an isolated concept	Trust in a social context.	Luhmann (1977)
		Gabetta (1968)
	Trust and power.	Lane (1997)
	Risk modeling with trust in relationships.	Ring and Van de Venn (1992)
		Simon (1957)
		Williamson (1985)
		Kanter (1989)
		Bernstein (1988)
		Fukeyama (1996)
Trust within an Interaction model	Conceptual, focus on the relationship.	Ford (1990)
	Philosophical ideas focussing on relationship development.	Handy (1994)
		Carlisle and Parker (1989)
		Ketelhohn (1993)
		Lorenz (1988)
		Sullivan and Peterson (1982)
Trust within an Industrial Context	Economic perspectives.	Ford (1990; 1997)
	Empirical Research.	Farmer and MacMillian (1976)
		Lamming (1993)
		Sako (1992)
		Aoki (1989)
		Hines (1994)

relationships. It then presents the results of an empirical study that compares buyer–supplier relationships between Japanese and UK non-Japanese owned vehicle manufacturers (VMs). The purpose of the study was to develop a working definition of trust in business relationships and then to demonstrate how trust can be used to create and sustain effective business relationships.

THE DEVELOPMENT OF "TRUST" IN INTER-ORGANISATIONAL RELATIONSHIPS

Some strategists (Ring, 1992) view trust as emerging in two ways: the first way is reciprocity, i.e. the way the other party judges each other. This is also formalized in Game Theory (Abernathy, Clark et al., 1983; Axelrod, 1984; Axelrod, 1997) as the number of interactions or pattern building. Lorenz states that, "*if transactions costs are thought of as the friction in the economy, then trust can be seen as an extremely efficient lubricant.*" A second way is trust is based on "norms of equality". This can be thought of as the way that one party will judge the other with regard to fulfilling its commitments.

It is also important to consider trust on several levels. Intra-organisational trust is just as important, if not more so, than the inter-organisational trust. Hurst emphasises this point, viewing trust as a 'soft' intuitive model of organisational design. Other authors argue that within a firm trust can be thought of as a social system (Desgupta, 1995). Desgupta argues that individuals belonging to different organisational factors need to speak with 'one voice', a style of working which reflects the organisation's strategy. As trust develops at both the personal and systems level, expectations about behaviour are generated.

Seligman (1997) points out that trust can be viewed as a means of increasing the tolerance of future uncertainty, as creating 'confidence'. This use of trust concept becomes very pertinent in areas of rapid technological achievement, e.g. telecommunications, I.T. and vehicle manufacturing. Luhmann (1979:16) states, ". . . *One should expect trust to be increasingly in demand as a means of ensuring the complexity of the future which technology will generate . . .*". Gambetta (1988) also views trust as particularly relevant in conditions of ignorance or uncertainty. Trust is seen, in this context as a way of coping with the limits of foresight.

DOES TRUST HAVE A ROLE TO PLAY IN INTER-ORGANISATIONAL RELATIONSHIPS?

It is clear from the variety of research undertaken (see Table 1) that trust does have a role to play within and between inter- and intra-organisational relationships. The problem appears to be defining trust. Perhaps authors are using the concept of trust to explain the unexplainable, i.e they know that there is something else that makes business-to-business relationships work, but are not sure what it is – therefore they call it 'trust'. This misunderstanding tends to create confusion between trust, risk, power and dependency, which tend to get used interchangeably.

To understand how trust impact relationships we conducted an in-depth study of key buyer/ supplier relationships within an industry. Our research examined five major Vehicle Manufacturers (VMs) and their suppliers. Its main focus was to compare the "best practice" Japanese manufacturers, who are constantly cited as being 'trust' driven (OCR) with their suppliers and non-Japanese owned Vehicle Manufacturers, who have earned a reputation for being much more Arms Length or adversarial. The research will produce a model that can help firms think about what they need to do in order to create mutually advantageous business relationships, i.e. trust based relationships. The definition of trust as a concept would appear to be very difficult. Therefore, our research focused on identifying a range of characteristics of trust that appear to be important in developing inter firm relationships. These characteristics add depth as opposed to replacing existing work such as Sako's contractual spectrum model.

Table 2 A comparison of the number of suppliers of VMs globally

Vehicle manufacturer	No. of non-Japanese owned plants	No. of suppliers	No. of suppliers per plant
Ford	67	7,800	116
Chrysler	36	4,000	111
General Motors	147	12,500	85
Mazda	2	110	55
Honda	6	150	25
Toyota	11	250	22
Nissan	9	170	18

The research approach

The research focused on the characteristics of trust used in relationships between first tier suppliers and non-Japanese owned and Japanese vehicle manufacturers. A detailed analysis of several relationships was undertaken using both qualitative and quantitative techniques. The data were collated and analysed using a range of methodologies: interviews, cause and effect analysis, questionnaires, impact diagrams and statistical hypotheses testing.

A sample frame was developed in conjunction with the Vehicle Manufacturers (VMs). They were asked to provide details of their first-tier suppliers; a selection of suppliers was then randomly selected for each VM. Table 2 shows the major vehicle manufacturers within the population and their dispersal of plants (globally). It is interesting to note the distribution of suppliers to manufacturers.

Therefore, the sample was organized so that the same supplier would not be selected twice. The purpose of the study was to examine as many relationships as possible and not to explain why relationships differed with the same supplier over a range of OEMs (although, with time, this would have been very interesting).

Interviewees were asked to identify factors that they believed could affect high-trust 'partnership-type' relationships between VMs and first-tier suppliers. These factors were expressly linked to the interface between the two organisations. The presence, or absence, of these factors could therefore have a tangible beneficial or detrimental impact upon the VM's relationship with its first-tier suppliers. Root cause diagrams were used to visually represent the data; a total of seventeen root-cause factors were identified.

Interview data

These factors are listed in Table 3. They map very closely to the main categories identified from the literature. Once these data were collected, we wanted to understand the relative importance of each of these categories for both the buyer and supplier. We also wanted to see if there was a difference between how Japanese VMs and non-Japanese owned VMs managed the relationships (specifically trust or non trust focused). To do this we used a survey instrument, as follows.

Questionnaire data: impact diagrams

In the second stage of the research questionnaires were sent to all interviewees. This was to allow comparison of the VMs and first-tier suppliers based on the seventeen common characteristics identified through root-cause analysis of the interviews. Twenty-one questionnaires were sent and fourteen returned, yielding a response rate of 67%.

Table 3 Summary of high-trust effecting factors

Factor	Characteristic
1	Full and Open Communication
2	Consistent View from all personnel
3	Long-term commitment
4	Material/Currency Payments
5	Dedicated Supplier Development Teams (DSTs)
6	Full Cost Transparency
7	Price note the Over-riding factor
8	Honesty and Openness
9	Early input in project design
10	Mutual Advantage
11	Words backed up by actions
12	Receptive to Supplier Ideas
13	Attitude and Loyalty
14	No 'Market Testing' on current products
15	Confidence in customer Personnel
16	Honoring Price commitments
17	Help providing to the supplier with no 'strings' attached

The survey instrument was designed using the seventeen root cause factors and sent to the interviewees, they were asked to rank the factors relative to each other. This process allowed the construction of a cause and effect diagram (see Figure 1) which was used to identify potential root causes of problems and solutions; an 'inventory' of trust. The recipients were asked to rank the list of factors against two criteria:

1. The favorable impact on the relationship if successfully implemented (Ranked 1 to 10 where 10 is the cause which would effect the most favorable Impact).
2. The ease of implementation within the relationship (Ranked 1 to 10 where 10 is the cause that would be the easiest to implement)

The total set of responses to the survey is listed in Table 4.

To obtain an average score each factor was divided by the number of responses. Two comparisons using impact diagrams were made using the questionnaire data: the Japanese transplants VMs view of themselves compared with the first-tier supplier's view of them; the non-Japanese owned VMs view of themselves compared with the first-tier supplier's view of them.

From the results listed in Table 4, we constructed a cause and effect chart, which showed six clear clusters around which trust was either built or lost, as shown in Figure 1. This clearly shows that trust does not just come from Communication or consistency or mutuality, etc., it comes from a combination of all of these categories. The next question was to identify how and why these various categories varied between the different VMs.

To answer this question, we plotted an Impact Diagram (ref.) based upon the results from the survey data in Table 4. We made several plots examining the differing relationships and used the range of categories listed in Table 3.

Each of the Impact Diagrams will now be discussed. The main point of this exercise was to identify where the clusters and characteristics fell. Due to the sample size it is difficult to infer any statistical significance of the positioning of the individual characteristics. However, these have been identified within the impact diagrams for interest.

Table 4 Table of questionnaire data

Question/factor	Japanese transplant VMs				Suppliers view				Domestic VMs				Supplier's view			
	R	C	I	E	R	C	I	E	R	C	I	E	R	C	I	E
1. Communication	3	8.7 (10,8)	7.3 (10,3)	7.0 (7,7)	9	7.8 (10,5)	9.2 (10,8)	6.9 (10,3)	2	7.5 (8,7)	9.5 (10,9)	4.5 (6,3)	10	6.2 (10,2)	9.3 (10,8)	5.9 (10,2)
2. Consistent View	3	8.3 (8,7)	8.3 (10,7)	5.3 (6,5)	9	7.2 (9,3)	8.6 (10,7)	7.0 (10,5)	2	7.0	8.0	4.0	10	4.3 (7,2)	8.6 (10,7)	5.1 (10,2)
3. Long-term Contracts	3	10 (10,10)	10	9.7 (10,9)	9	9.4 (10,5)	9.6 (10,8)	7.3 (10,1)	2	9.5 (10,9)	10.0 (10,10)	8.0 (8,8)	10	7.9 (10,4)	9.2 (10,7)	7.4 (10,1)
4. Mat/Currency Payments	3	5.0 (5,5)	6.3 (7,5)	5.7 (8,4)	9	7.4 (10,1)	7.6 (10,2)	5.2 (10,1)	2	2.5 (4,1)	9.0 (10,8)	3.0 (5,1)	10	3.3 (10,1)	6.8 (10,1)	4.9 (10,1)
5. Dedicated SDT's	3	10.0 (10,10)	10.0 (10,10)	8.0 (10,5)	9	5.9 (10,1)	7.8 (10,2)	5.8 (10,3)	2	5.5	9.0 (10,8)	4.0 (7,1)	10	4.4 (10,1)	7.8 (10,3)	5.6 (10,3)
6. Cost Transparency	3	7.3 (9,6)	9.3 (10,8)	4.3 (6,3)	9	7.2 (10,1)	7.6 (10,5)	3.9 (8,1)	2	7.5 (7,4)	9.5 (10,8)	5.5 (7,1)	10	6.4 (10,1)	7.9 (10,3)	4.0 (8,1)
7. Price not Overriding Factor	3	10.0 (10,10)	10.0 (10,10)	9.7 (10,9)	9	7.3 (10,3)	7.9 (10,5)	5.8 (10,1)	2	10.0	10.0 (10,10)	10.0 (10,10)	10	6.1 (10,2)	8.0 (10,4)	6.0 (10,1)
8. Honesty/Openness	3	8.3 (10,7)	8.0 (10,5)	6.3 (9,3)	9	6.0 (8,1)	9.1 (10,8)	6.0 (10,1)	2	8.0 (8,8)	8.5 (9,8)	2.0 (2,2)	10	4.9 (9,2)	9.2 (10,8)	5.3 (10,2)
9. Early Input into Design	3	8.0 (10,6)	8.0 (10,7)	5.3 (7,3)	9	6.7 (10,3)	9.4 (10,6)	5.7 (10,1)	2	8.5 (8,5)	10.0 (10,10)	8.5 (9,8)	10	7.2 (9,2)	9.2 (10,8)	5.5 (10,2)
10. Mutual Advantage	3	5.3 (10,8)	9.3 (10,8)	6.7 (9,4)	9	5.6 (10,3)	9.0 (10,6)	4.9 (10,1)	2	7.5 (8,7)	8.5 (10,10)	5.5 (9,8)	10	4.0 (8,2)	8.8 (10,5)	3.9 (10,1)
11. Words to Actions	3	8.0 (10,8)	9.3 (10,8)	5.7 (9,5)	9	5.8 (10,3)	8.9 (10,6)	5.2 (10,1)	2	7.0	9.0 (9,8)	3.5 (7,4)	10	4.0 (8,2)	9.1 (10,5)	3.9 (10,1)
12. Receptive to Supplier Ideas	3	8.3 (9,7)	8.7 (9,8)	5.0 (9,5)	9	6.0 (8,1)	8.6 (10,5)	6.0 (10,2)	2	8.6 (8,6)	10.0 (10,8)	7.0 (10,4)	10	6.5 (8,1)	8.7 (10,5)	7.0 (10,2)
13. Attitude and Loyalty	3	9.3 (9,8)	10.0 (10,10)	7.3 (8,6)	9	6.9 (10,2)	9.0 (10,7)	6.3 (10,2)	2	9.0 (10,8)	9.5 (10,9)	5.0 (9,1)	10	4.5 (7,1)	9.6 (10,7)	4.8 (10,1)
14. No Market Testing	3	4.0 (9,1)	9.0 (10,8)	8.3 (8,6)	9	5.8 (10,1)	7.1 (10,4)	6.3 (10,3)	2	9.5 (10,9)	9.5 (10,9)	7.0 (10,4)	10	5.5 (7,1)	7.3 (10,3)	5.7 (10,1)
15. Confidence in Customers	3	7.7 (9,7)	9.0 (10,8)	6.0 (8,4)	9	6.8 (10,3)	8.4 (10,6)	5.4 (10,3)	2	6.5 (7,6)	8.5 (10,5)	4.0 (7,1)	10	5.2 (8,2)	8.9 (10,5)	4.8 (10,1)
16. Honour Commitments	3	8.3 (10,7)	9.0 (10,8)	6.0 (9,4)	9	6.7 (10,3)	9.3 (10,7)	4.6 (10,3)	2	8.5 (9,8)	8.0 (8,8)	5.0 (8,2)	10	5.0 (10,2)	9.3 (10,5)	3.9 (10,1)
17. Help with No Strings	3	9.0 (10,7)	9.0 (10,7)	7.3 (8,7)	9	5.1 (10,1)	7.7 (10,6)	5.3 (10,3)	2	5.5 (8,3)	8.0 (8,6)	5.0 (6,4)	10	5.0 (8,1)	9.3 (10,3)	3.9 (10,2)

Notes:
1. R = No. of responses received
2. C = Average response as to current implementation status of each factor
3. I = Average response as to impact of each factor upon the relationship if fully implemented
4. E = Average response as to ease of implementing each factor within the relationship
5. Figures in brackets indicate the highest and lowest individual response against each factor

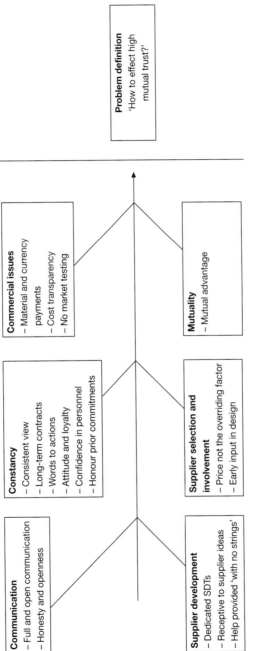

Figure 1   Cause and effect diagram.

JAPANESE TRANSPLANT VMS AND FIRST-TIER SUPPLIERS

The Japanese transplant VMs view of their relationships with first-tier suppliers is illustrated in Figure 2. It is clear from this plot that the majority of data are clustered in the high impact, reasonable ease cluster, indicating that Japanese VMs see relationship management as an essential element of their supply strategy.

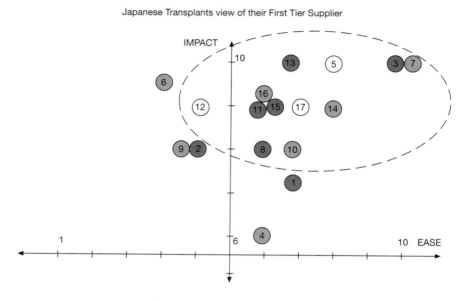

Figure 2 Impact diagram for the Japanese transplant VMs view of their relationship with first-tier suppliers

The first-tier supplier's view of their relationship with the Japanese transplant VMs is illustrated in Figure 3. A comparison of Figures 2 and 3 highlights some differences of viewpoint between the Japanese transplant VMs and first-tier suppliers although some correlation exists. The first-tier suppliers have a slightly more pessimistic view; the individual relationship factors will have a lesser impact, if fully implemented, than is believed by the Japanese transplant VMs. To illustrate this, the first-tier suppliers believe that only one factor, long-term contracts, will have the maximum impact if fully implemented. The Japanese transplants believe that four factors will have the maximum impact. The first-tier suppliers also believe it to be generally more difficult to implement these relationship factors than is believed by the Japanese transplant VMs. No factor was scored higher than seven by the first-tier suppliers in terms of ease of implementation. The Japanese transplant VMs scored two factors as eight and two as ten in terms of ease of implementation. There also appears to be little consistency of view across individual relationship factors. First-tier suppliers and Japanese transplant VMs appear to share the most common view with factor three, long-term contracts.

NON-JAPANESE OWNED VMS AND FIRST-TIER SUPPLIERS

The non-Japanese owned VMs view of their relationships with first-tier suppliers is illustrated in Figure 4. The first-tier supplier's view of their relationship with the non-Japanese owned VMs is illustrated in Figure 5.

A comparison of Figures 4 and 5 indicates some similarities with the previous analysis. The first-tier suppliers generally have a more pessimistic view; the individual relationship factors will have

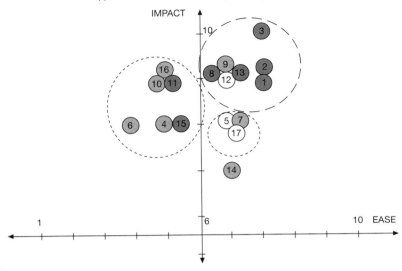

Figure 3 Impact diagram for first-tier supplier's view of their relationship with the Japanese transplant VMs.

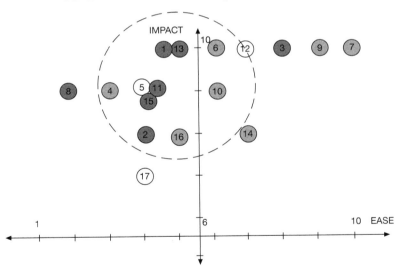

Figure 4 Impact diagram for the non-Japanese owned VMs view of their relationship with first-tier suppliers.

a lesser impact, if fully implemented, than is believed by the non-Japanese owned VMs. Figure 6 provides overviews of the main clusters.

Comparing all of the relationships, it is clear that two relatively distinct groups emerge. The non-Japanese owned VMs and non-Japanese owned First Tier Suppliers are clearly to the left of the model, indicating a view that relationship characteristics are difficult to manage and implement, although accepting the fact that they can have an important effect. The Japanese transplants and

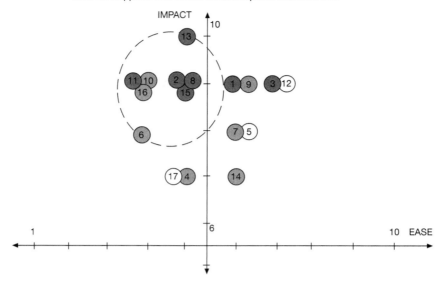

Figure 5 Impact diagram for first-tier supplier's view of their relationship with the non-Japanese owned VMs.

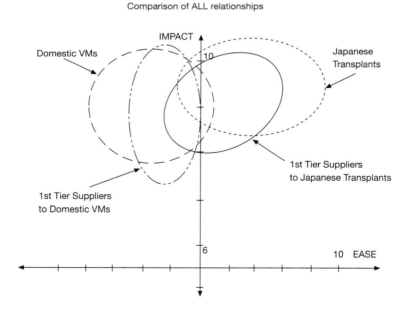

Figure 6 Comparison of ALL Relationships.

their first tier suppliers (although non-Japanese owned) view the relationship characteristics as easier to implement, and again accept, if not more so, the importance of their impact on the business.

From the interviews it was clear that a major difference in relationship management between Japanese and non-Japanese owned firms was that non-Japanese owned manufacturers viewed

Table 5 Summary table of comparison between Japanese and non-Japanese owned vehicle manufacturers

Approach	Japanese Transplants	Non-Japanese owned OEMs
Sourcing strategy	• Single sourcing • Long Term contracts • Little active search for new supply sources • Suppliers chosen for vehicle life time • Focus – quality, cost and delivery • Emphasis on supplier development and management	• Parallel sourcing strategy • Maintain tension in the relationship • Constant 'new' supplier search • Cross-quoting policy • Focus on price for a delivery run not life of vehicle
Cost analysis & control	• Open book costing • Perception of cost reduction not margin reduction • No use of escalation formula • Supplier has to justify price increases. These costs are offset over the medium to long-term • Focus on cost transparency	• Fear of hidden costs • One-sided open book – Stress model • Short-term contracts do not allow for long term cost reduction
Contract life	• Move towards vehicle life contracts • Contracts becoming less formalised – move towards agreements • Some differentiation between long term contracts & long term relationships	• Generally short term • Formalised contracts • No differentiation between long term relationships and long term contracts
Partnership and loyalty	• Supplier integration as the way forward • Loyal suppliers are seen as a strength • Investment in sustaining & creating supply sources • Level of pressure to perform in the relationship, i.e. cost reduction is a key focus	• Price rather than cost focus. Aggressive price reduction targets. Focus on ZBP • Minimal/no investment in suppliers – suppliers seen as a cost not an investment • Level of pressure seen as high, but view is that it is the supplier's problem
Working methods and culture	• Long range and accurate planning systems • Good inter and intra communication processes • Seen as aggressive but fair culture. Inclusive in nature – feel as though you are part of a family	• Perceived as having poor planning systems. Full sales information rarely disclosed to 1st tier suppliers • Supplier generally does not have forward view of the order book • Aggressive culture seen as mainly exclusive
Team working and supplier investment	• Very high degree of team working & supplier involvement • High structural approach to supplier involvement • Value Analysis and Value Engineering seen as key drivers	• Move towards higher involvement (G.M. seen as the exception to the rule) • Focus on 'stress' relationships, buyers seen as powerful and prepared to use it, in the market place
Purchasing expertise	• Highly aggressive recruitment campaign Recruitment from outside of the purchasing function • Buyers are highly sought after by other firms (particularly 1st tier suppliers) • Aim for a multiple skill set	• General recruitment drive • Looking to rebuild existing workers • Focus on buying new graduate level personnel
Supplier development	• NMUK perceived to be the 'best in class'. Supplier Development Teams (SDT) deployed to help with initiative • Holistic approach to entire supplier's business	• Self centered focus • Focus on manufacturers own product lines as opposed to the supplier's entire business
Supplier associations	• Key focus on Japanese approach to establish incentive demands and supplier networks • Appear to be successful although modified format	• Some evidence of supplier associations forming. Little to no expertise on how to implement

supplier development (as they called it) as something in addition to their normal jobs. Whereas their Japanese counterparts saw relationship management as part of their normal daily work. This attitude is further evidenced in the type of contracting witnessed by authors and substantiated from this research, that non-Japanese owned VMs are much more ACR focused than Japanese Transplants.

Finally, there is also a cultural difference evident. Japanese firms have a much more 'can do' philosophy to working with their suppliers. Indeed they are aggressive and want to maintain constant pressure for cost reduction, however they are prepared to do this by working together and utilizing their shared knowledge. This does indeed involve "trusting" the supplier, or having confidence in them. It appears that it is the combination of cost focus, contractual terms and cultural attitude that creates the confidence to allow the relationships to work effectively. Table 5 summarises the major differences in approach identified in our research in Japanese Transplants and non-Japanese owned Vehicle Manufacturers.

To increase the 'inventory' of trust, VMs and first-tier suppliers need to concentrate on the relationship factors that are high-impact, high-ease. These factors are illustrated in the impact diagrams. It is proposed that relationships between the VMs and first-tier suppliers can improve as a result of this exercise.

A MODEL OF MUTUALLY ADVANTAGEOUS BUSINESS RELATIONSHIPS (MABR)

The research clearly illustrates a range of characteristics or as we have called it an 'inventory' or trust that need to be present in order to facilitate inter firm relationships. We have combined these in a conceptual model that suppliers can use to assess their current and possible future relationships with VMs. The model includes structural factors (size, infrastructure, etc.), strategic planning (technology and market strategy) and operational policies (project management, *kaizen*, etc.).

The MABR model is not meant to be exhaustive or indeed mutually exclusive. Some suppliers may not be able to exactly relate their current situation to the four areas proposed. However, it should be used to promote discussion on areas that need to be developed in order to make existing and future relationships operate more effectively. The MABR model is presented in Table 6. Suppliers are firstly categorised as either 'core' or 'peripheral'. This distinction is taken from the VMs viewpoint. The 'core' suppliers are generally those who manufacture and supply high-value, complex-function components to the VMs. These companies tend to be global concerns capable of proactively supporting the VMs demands. The distinction between 'core' and 'peripheral' may vary across the UK VMs. Some of this variance could be due to in-house technologies; Nissan and Toyota manufacture their own fuel tanks whereas Rover, who does not, would view the supplier of this product as core to their business.

The second factor refers to the customer-supplier relationship itself, viewed from both sides. The relationship is considered to be either one of dependence or interdependence (Campbell and Cunningham, 1983; in Ford, 1997). This leads to four types of supplier relationships; these are explored below.

CORE INTERDEPENDENT SUPPLIERS

The demands being placed upon first-tier suppliers are becoming increasingly more complex, particularly in the vehicle development process. The VMs are seeking core component suppliers who can provide world class levels of quality, JIT supply, continuous cost reduction, project management capability, technological advance, etc. These criteria require a global, technically expert organisation – one that can develop high-risk technologies for specific automotive applications and be flexible enough to cope with local demands.

Such companies are termed core interdependent suppliers and provide the focus for the VMs activities. This is because 30% of the number of components on a vehicle can represent 80% of the

Table 6   A model of mutually advantageous business relationships

	Level of dependence	
	Interdependent ←——————————————→	**Dependent**
Core ↑	• System developer of critical Components • Mutually advantageous • Supplier-led innovation and vehicle-specific technologies • Supplier views automotive as strategic area of the business • Competence, contractual and goodwill trust • Probably first-tier supply • Recognition of 'shared destiny' by both parties • Global supply capability, use of alliances • Supplier manages individual vehicle projects • VM uses single or parallel sourcing • Long-term, certain relationship • Both parties invest in infrastructure	• Critical components • Suppliers with very high or very low turnover with one VM • Supplier views automotive as sole area of business or one of many areas • Raw material or proprietary technology suppliers • Competence and contractual trust only • First or second tier supplier • Supplier is reactive to technology innovations and project management • VM uses parallel or multiple sourcing • Medium-term, uncertain relationship • One party can exploit the other party
↓ **Peripheral**	• Low-value or non-critical components but with a technological edge • Non-integrated components • Supplier views automotive as strategic area of the business • First or second tier supplier • Competence, contractual and goodwill trust • Supplier involved in vehicle development but does not project manage • VM uses single or parallel sourcing • Medium, long-term, relatively certain relationship • Similar to Stress/Resolved model (Lamming, 1993: 152)	• Low value, non-critical components • Low technology areas • Non-integrated components • Neither supplier nor VM views components as critical • Supplier views VM as critical customer • First, second or third tier supplier • Competence and contractual trust only • Supplier is reactive to VM demands • VM uses parallel or multiple sourcing • Short, medium-term, uncertain relationship • Similar to Stress model (Lamming, 1993: 152)

*(Left axis label: **Competence**)*

vehicle bought-out spending by a VM. The core interdependent suppliers will be the major source for these high value components.

Suppliers in this area will need to demonstrate a technological edge over both their competitors and customers: to maintain competitive leadership in the first case and contribute to lean supply in the second. This lead would involve significant patenting activity as a result of 'shelf' R&D projects. Current products also require continuous improvement in terms of their quality and cost performance. This is necessary to retain the VMs confidence because, as one VM stated:

> [Suppliers] need to stay in the forefront and they will need to be able to display [world class performance], moving forwards little by little each year as well as periodically making a technological leap. I think those who sit back and rest on laurels, and pass through business costs incurred at their site automatically to the customer are probably numbered.

Organisations in this area are likely to be engaged in mergers and acquisitions (M&A) activity to meet the demands of a global customer and maintain a competitive lead. Two examples would be Valeo and Robert Bosch, companies that are among the largest automotive suppliers in Europe. Valeo is a French company with a global presence, some of which has been gained through acquisition,[1] and is technologically strong. It develops 'black box' solutions for the VMs, managing vehicle-specific projects for them. Robert Bosch is a German company that has maintained a lead in the field of antilock braking systems (ABS) among other technologies. It has expanded its customer base for its ABS product partly through a license agreement with Denso and a joint venture with Nabco.

Core interdependent suppliers require a global presence to locally support the VMs in the three main regions; Asia-Pacific, America, Europe. The supplier needs to be financially strong enough to support infrastructure investment at this local level. Joint ventures with local firms may be used to secure an initial foothold in new markets such as China. At this local level, the supplier needs to demonstrate an aptitude for effective project management: translating 'shelf' R&D projects into vehicle-specific applications.

Core interdependent suppliers will tend to view automotives as a critical area of their business portfolio. Of the eight largest suppliers in the European automotive industry, seven (Bosch, Valeo, Magnetti Marelli, ZF, GKN, TRW and Delphi) have over 50% of their sales turnover within the automotive industry.

For a situation of true interdependency, the supplier and VM must recognise their shared destiny; each party is reliant upon the other for products and services required achieving valued goals. It is recognised that this situation is difficult to achieve in practice; the UK market represents a small proportion of total European sales volume.[2] Buyers at the UK VMs can feel uncomfortable with 'powerful' European and global suppliers dictating terms and conditions. The crux of the issue appears to be one of mutual advantage; both parties need to genuinely believe that the greatest mutual benefit will result from long-term cooperation, as opposed to another strategy. One supplier stated that the same degree of attention should be paid to the supplier by the VM and *vice versa*. Unconditional help should be provided by the VM in resolving difficulties. It would appear that the UK VMs have a policy of parallel sourcing with their core interdependent suppliers. This policy appears to be one of competitive tension, whilst providing a relatively certain outlook for the supplier.

CORE DEPENDENT SUPPLIERS

In the case of the dominant supplier, the company will supply components deemed critical by the VM. The supplier would therefore need to have a proven track record in specific technologies. The supplier would exhibit a level of R&D activity but this is unlikely to be in support of a single customer. The supplier will probably be reactive to vehicle-specific requests from the VM, who will conduct the necessary project management. In this instance, the supplier provides a professional service up to a point; the supplier fulfils the agreed contractual obligations in a competent manner. The supplier will probably not, however, provide a level of service over and above the VMs expectations. As such, relationship improvements are driven by the VM.

An example of suppliers in this area would be Corus or polymer suppliers such as BASF and DuPont. They can dictate terms to the VMs because automotive is a small area of their overall business. The VMs are relatively dependent upon these sources of supply due to the absence of competition and the lengthy approval process required by changing suppliers.

All interviewees expressing an opinion stated that their raw materials suppliers were a problem; prices were provided on a 'bottom line' basis and increases imposed without negotiation. Products were supplied in line with terms and conditions but the absence of 'goodwill trust' (Sako, 1992) is evident. In these situations, companies tried to parallel (Richardson, 1993) or multiple sources to reduce this dependence. Where this is not possible, the dominant supplier can exploit the relationship to the detriment of the other party. A situation of mutual advantage would not exist in this scenario. An interesting example of a dominant supplier would be Honda, as a supplier to Rover. Even though the Rover-Honda alliance has dissolved, Rover is still dependent upon Honda for some components. Honda could exploit this relationship if it overcame its dependency upon Rover for body pressings.

In the case of responsive suppliers, a situation of dependency could exist through the supplier's small customer base. This situation is however discouraged by the VMs who were interviewed; most stated that they would feel uneasy controlling more than 30% of a supplier's turnover. The situation could also exist at a local, rather than global, level. The seating manufacturer, Johnson

Controls, is not particularly dependent, globally, on one VM. In fact, only 35% of its business is within the automotive industry. The Johnson Controls factory at Telford is, however, almost completely dependent upon Toyota for its current business. A situation could therefore exist of core dependence at a micro level that is not reflected at a global level.

PERIPHERAL INTERDEPENDENT SUPPLIERS

Organisations in this area supply low value or non-critical components that are nevertheless technologically complex. In safety critical areas, the supplier must be able to demonstrate a technological edge and provide vehicle-specific solutions in advance of any legislation taking effect. This is required to take account of the VMs lengthy testing and validation programs for each vehicle. Suppliers in this area have a relatively close liaison with the VMs engineers but tend to be more reactive.

Either the VM or another first-tier supplier supplying a larger system manages the project management for individual components. As such, products supplied in this area tend to be 'build-to-print' rather than supplier-driven 'black box' designs. The supplier will tend to drive the generic product technology whilst the VM drives the application technology. Suppliers will tend to do more than is required, certainly in the technological field, but not necessarily in support of any particular customer. In some instances, the ongoing technological development of the product can be sufficient to maintain a competitive edge. Examples of suppliers in this area would be companies manufacturing braking and fuelling lines. The materials used are generally proprietary in nature and technologically complex due to their safety critical nature. The components are relatively inexpensive but the VMs would incur substantial revalidation costs by changing suppliers. This would tend to result in a medium to long-term, relatively certain relationship.

PERIPHERAL DEPENDENT SUPPLIERS

Organisations in this area may receive the least attention from the VMs but, paradoxically, may supply a large number of components. This low level of focus is a result of the components being of a low value, non-critical nature. The components tend not to be integrated as part of a larger supply module and have a low technological input. The supplier can nevertheless be vulnerable if a single VM accounts for a large proportion of its turnover; the VM can change the source of supply relatively easily without incurring substantial switching costs. This can lead to a short or medium term, uncertain relationship. This is particularly evident whilst the non-Japanese owned VMs are reducing their first-tier supply base.

Examples of suppliers in this area would be metal fastenings or small moldings companies. The VM can dictate the terms of the relationship due to the number of supplier options that are available.

COLLABORATIVE TENSION AMONG SUPPLIERS

A major dilemma for the core interdependent supplier is coming to terms with the VMs Parallel sourcing strategy. As one supplier stated:

> No supplier wants competitive tension, someone else continually sniping at them. Everyone wants to be a single source. There's a practical and real answer to that. That's going to be life. That's the way industry is.

The main concern for suppliers appears to be whether a sustainable level of business will be enjoyed in the future. This uncertainty is reflected in the investment decisions that suppliers make. As one supplier stated:

> If I'm sitting here thinking 'am I going to be in business or out of business with [a VM] in a years time', am I going to go away and invest a million pounds in new plant? I'm not. If I'm sitting here knowing,

because we've worked together and we've got a good understanding, that unless I make a serious screw up, I'm going to be in business, then we'll make the associated investment at this end.

The VMs need to make clear their component strategy in key areas. This could be a 'come clean' of their current strategy; the VMs currently appear to parallel source to avoid a situation of dependence that may result from single sourcing. As one VM stated:

> [We are] trying to build up a nucleus of strong suppliers who would then compete from generation to generation of vehicles so that a level of business enjoyment was sustained but they were never completely certain as to what level they would enjoy. It's a balance between the longevity of the trading relationship with a degree of uncertainty as to just how big that may be.

If the VMs declare a parallel sourcing strategy, suppliers may feel more inclined to invest in the relationship infrastructure. Correct investments should help preserve their competitive advantage and that of their VM customers. This would avoid the costly exercise of introducing new sources of supply required to maintain or regain the VMs market advantages.

In this scenario of parallel sourcing, competitive tension is maintained. Core interdependent suppliers keep secret any source of competitive advantage over their competitor. It can be argued that another change is required for the VMs to fully harness the expertise of their suppliers. The Mazda sourcing strategy for seating illustrates the change required. Competitors can learn from each other, within a semi-guaranteed business environment. Suppliers and VM alike benefit as a result of this process. The adoption of supplier networks can facilitate greater supply chain benefits than currently exhibited in the UK. The research indicates that a system of *kyoryoku kai* is in its infancy in the UK. Much further work is required before a Japanese-style structure is replicated.

Creating a culture whereby competing first-tier suppliers co-operate may be more problematic but it would appear that Mazda, Delta Kogyo and Toyo Seat all benefit from such cooperation. This 'collaborative tension' strategy may well achieve more mutually beneficial outcomes than a strategy of competitive tension?

CONCLUSION

It is clear from our research that there are significant differences in the way that Japanese and non-Japanese owned vehicle manufacturers treat their suppliers and visa versa. The key question is whether this can be attributed to 'trust' or something else?

Our findings clearly showed that Japanese vehicle manufacturers have a substantially different attitude to their suppliers, viewing relationships as long-term and therefore taking the mutual exchange of knowledge and cost reduction as a mutually beneficial strategy. They view relationship development as what they do and not as an addition. Whereas their non-Japanese owned counter parts have an almost diametrically opposed viewpoint. They tend to view relationships as short-term and do not think of relationship development, but rather "supplier development" as an additional task that might get done if the resources are available.

This paper presents an empirical model designed to help VMs and their suppliers focus on some of the keys issues that sit within relationship development. The model is designed to enhance existing work in this field and to persuade companies to focus on the key issue of 'trust' generation, however it is defined.

The issues then are perhaps not about trust but about creating mutual business advantage. The key to this advantage is to create business success by using the relationships to deliver tangible business outputs. We conclude by suggesting that perhaps this is really a matter of confidence in the ability of both customer and supplier to work well together as opposed to an indistinguishable concept known as 'trust'?

NOTES

1. Valeo gained a UK manufacturing capability through acquisitions of Nieman (Security Systems), Tudor (Wash/Wipe Systems) and Delanair (Climate Control). Valeo recently acquired the climate control division of Siemens to strengthen it's position within Europe.
2. Rover sales, for example, account for less than 4% of the total European market (excluding BMW).

REFERENCES

Abernathy, W. J., K. B. Clark, et al. (1983). *Innovation in the US Automobile Industry from 1893–1981.* New York, Basic Books Inc.

Axelrod, R. (1984). *The Evolution of Co-operation.* New York, U.S.A., Penguin Business Books.

Axelrod, R. (1997). *The Complexity of Co-operation.* Chichester, U.K., Princeton University Press.

Bernstein, P. (1988). "The Trust Culture." *SAM Advanced Management Journal* (Summer): 4–8.

Bhide, A. and H. H. Stevenson (1990). "Why be Honest if Honesty Doesn't Pay?" *Harvard Business Review* November–December: 127–135.

Contractor, F. J. and P. Lorange (1988). *Cooperative Strategies in International Business.* New York, D. C. Heath and Company.

Dore, R. (1987). *Taking Japan Seriously.* Stamford, U.S.A., Stamford University Press.

Ford, D., Ed. (1997). *Understanding Business Markets.* London, Academic Press.

Gambetta, D. (1988). *Trust: Making and Breaking Co-operative Relations.* New York, U.S.A., Basil Blackwell Publications.

Hines, P. (1994). *Creating World Class Suppliers: Unlocking Mutual Competitive Advantage.* London, Pitman.

Hurst, D. (1984). "Of Boxes, Bubbles and Effective Management." *Harvard Business Review* May–June: 78–88.

Lamming, R. C. (1993). *Beyond Partnership: Strategies for Innovation and Lean Supply.* London, Prentice-Hall.

Lane, C. and R. Bachmann (1995). *Risk, Trust and Power: The Social Constitution of Supplier Relations in Britain and Germany.* Cambridge, University of Cambridge: 51.

Luhmann, N. (1979). *Trust and Power.* Chichester, U.K., John Wiley and Sons.

Morris, J. and R. Imrie (1993). "Japanese Style Sub-Contracting – Its Impact on European Industries." *Long Range Planning* 26(2): 53–58.

Nishiguchi, T. (1994). *Strategic Industrial Sourcing: The Japanese Advantage.* Oxford, U.K., Oxford University Press.

Pascarella, P. (1993). Fifteen Ways to Win People's Trust. *Industry Week.*

Ring, P. S. V. d. V., A.H. (1992). "Structuring Co-operative Relationships between Organisations'." *Strategic Management Journal* 11(1): 483–498.

Sako, M. (1992). *Prices, Quality and Trust: Buyer Supplier Relationships in Britain and Japan.* Cambridge, U.K., Cambridge University Press.

Sako, M. and S. Helper (1998). "Determinants of trust in supplier relations: Evidence from the automotive industry in Japan and the United States." *Journal of Economic Behaviour and Organisation* 34: 387–417.

Syson, R. (1992). *Improving Purchase Performance.* London, U.K., Pitman Publishing.

Thorne, P. (1991). "Taken on Trust." *International Management*: 96–98.

Womack, J. and D. Jones (1994). "From Lean Production to the Lean Enterprise." *Harvard Business Review* (March–April).

Conclusions: Managing in business markets

The third edition of this book demonstrates how ideas on business marketing and purchasing have evolved since the first edition, published in 1990. Over this period, there has been a considerable refinement of our understanding of what does and what should happen in business relationships. More importantly, the group has devoted considerable efforts to an understanding of the networks that surround, constrain and provide opportunities for managers to change their relationships and their overall position.

The readings in this edition of the book are perhaps more managerial in approach than in those in previous editions and they illustrate the *use* of some concepts in addition to simply explaining the concepts themselves. This orientation stems from a continuing concern that many marketers still fail to address the issues involved in taking a long-term view of their relationship investments. Many buyers fail to develop a clear idea of how to effectively use the resources of their suppliers and integrate them with their own. Both sets of managers frequently find it difficult to structure and make sense of the surrounding network. Perhaps in part, this is because much of the management literature implies that companies are able to *design* their supply and distribution "chains". It also implies that companies can analyse their general "environment" and then develop and implement an *independent* strategy to achieve their own objectives.

In contrast, the interaction approach to business networks argues that these companies are not simply part of a linear "chain", nor do they have a one-dimensional view up or down the line to a particular customer or supplier. Instead, they are part of a complex network of companies. Each of them has a wide portfolio of direct and indirect relationships and each has a view of the relative value and importance of each one *to them*. Each tries to act on the basis of that individual view. From this, the IMP Group emphasises that the outcome of each companies' actions in a network depends on the actions of others. This means that strategy is not a process of independent analysis, formulation and implementation. Instead it is one of anticipation, accommodation, action, re-action and re-re-action. The IMP approach also highlights that companies are increasingly dependent on the abilities and technologies of others. These abilities are not only exploited in relationships, but are also developed interactively in them. Managers have to face up to the situation that many of the abilities on which they depend are not in their own company or even in a counterpart, but instead occupy a place in the relationship *between* them.

The interdependence of companies in business networks has profound implications for the task of understanding business marketing and purchasing. All of us in the Group are still trying to achieve some of this understanding. We hope that this book will in a small way help others to do the same.

Index

Page numbers in *italics* refer to illustrations and tables; page numbers in **bold** refer to main discussion.